Systemic Liquidity Risk and Bipolar Markets

For other titles in the Wiley Finance series
please see www.wiley.com/finance

Systemic Liquidity Risk and Bipolar Markets

Wealth Management in Today's Macro Risk On/Risk Off Financial Environment

Clive Corcoran

WILEY
A John Wiley & Sons, Ltd., Publication

Cover image reproduced by permission of Shutterstock.com

Registered Office
John Wiley & Sons Ltd, The Atrium, Southern Gate, Chichester, West Sussex, PO19 8SQ, United Kingdom

For details of our global editorial offices, for customer services and for information about how to apply for permission to reuse the copyright material in this book please see our website at www.wiley.com.

Library of Congress Cataloging-in-Publication Data

Corcoran, Clive M.
Systemic liquidity risk and bipolar markets : wealth management in todays macro risk on/risk off financial environment / Clive Corcoran.
pages cm
Includes index.
ISBN 978-1-118-40933-6 (hbk.) – ISBN 978-1-118-41075-2 (ebk.) – ISBN 978-1-118-41076-9 (ebk.) – ISBN 978-1-118-41080-6 (ebk.) 1. Finance, Personal. 2. Investments. 3. Portfolio management. I. Title.
HG179.C68197 2013
332.024–dc23 2012039741

A catalogue record for this book is available from the British Library.

ISBN 978-1-118-40933-6 (hbk) ISBN 978-1-118-41075-2 (ebk)
ISBN 978-1-118-41076-9 (ebk) ISBN 978-1-118-41080-6 (ebk)

Set in 10/12pt Times by Aptara, Inc., New Delhi, India
Printed in Great Britain by CPI Group (UK) Ltd, Croydon, CR0 4YY

Contents

Foreword

In today's tightly coupled financial system asset class returns are so highly correlated, that investors and asset managers are, to a much larger degree than previously, and very often much more than they realize, essentially undiversified and subject to the risk of abrupt and severe wealth destruction. The ultimate risk, which far exceeds the widely touted notion of tail risk, is the systemic risk which arises when liquidity in capital markets evaporates as it did in 2008 and episodically has done since – most notably in May 2010, in an incident known as the Flash Crash, and in the fall of 2011 when correlations were at historically elevated levels.

Conventional asset allocation tools and techniques have failed to keep apace with the changing financial landscape which has emerged since the 2008 global financial crisis. In addition to a decline in the *quality* of market liquidity, in part epitomized by the prevalence of algorithmic churn, a new paradigm of *risk on/risk off* asset allocation has emerged. Risk on/Risk off, sometimes abbreviated to RoRo, is a style of trading and macro allocation strategy, adopted by a broad cross section of participants in the financial markets, where positions are taken in several closely aligned asset classes depending on the prevailing sentiment or appetite for risk.

The following table shows, in summary form, a delineation between a set of asset classes which can be categorized as *risk on* and those which may be designated as *risk off.* Not all asset classes can be fitted into this twofold division and a more detailed examination of the nuances between different constituents of each of the main RoRo camps will be explored in what follows.

When markets are optimistic about such matters as economic growth, the resolution of difficult financial issues such as those facing the Eurozone, then there will be a greater propensity to acquire riskier assets. Since several classes of assets are deemed to be more suited to a portfolio when there is a greater appetite to take on risk there will be a coordinated movement of buying interest in that group of assets indicated in the left hand side of the table. Alternatively, when tactical asset allocators are more risk averse there will be a notable switch in the market into avoidance of the risk on assets and a retreat into the risk off assets as reflected on the right side of the table. For aggressive traders there will even be a tendency to short the risk on assets when risk appetite is subdued and short the risk off assets when the *animal spirits* are running high.

RISK ON ASSETS		RISK OFF ASSETS	
Primary Motivating Factors	Positive GDP surprises	Primary Motivating Factors	Negative GDP surprises
	More accommodative monetary policy		Geo-political tension
	Enhanced China growth		Eurozone concerns
	Eurozone progress		Weaker Chinese prospects
TYPE	SPECIFIC EXAMPLES	TYPE	SPECIFIC EXAMPLES
EQUITIES	Long S&P 500, DAX, FTSE, Shanghai, Hang Seng	MONEY MARKET INSTRUMENTS	US T Bills & Notes, UK Short Term Gilts, Bobl & Schatz, Swiss government notes
EMERGING MARKET EQUITIES (EM)	Long Brazil, India, Chile, Turkey, Indonesia	LONG TERM SOVEREIGN ISSUES	Long US 10 YR, Gilts, Bunds, Short Spanish, Italian government bonds
HIGH YIELD BONDS	Long HYG*, Long EM Fixed Income	INVESTMENT GRADE BONDS	AA rated corporates
RESOURCE ECONOMIES	Long Russia, Canada, Australia, South Africa	SAFE HAVEN ECONOMIES	Long USA, Switzerland, Singapore
COMMODITIES	Long Copper, Crude Oil, Corn, XME*, DBB*	COMMODITIES	Short Copper, Crude Oil, Natural Gas, XME*, DBB*
FAVORED CURRENCY POSITIONS	Long AUD/JPY, AUD/USD, NZD/USD, Short USD/CAD	FAVORED CURRENCY POSITIONS	Short EUR/USD, AUD/JPY, AUD/USD, NZD /USD
MARGINALLY FAVORED CURRENCIES	Long EUR/USD, USD/JPY	MARGINALLY FAVORED CURRENCIES	Long GBP/USD, Long Yen, Swiss Franc, Singapore Dollar
VOLATILITY	Short/Neutral VIX	VOLATILITY	Long VIX
OPTIONS	Long Calls on equities, metals, EM	OPTIONS	Long Puts on equities, metals, EM
N.B. Aggressive traders may take inverse positions to those identified for each risk mode as well			
* Refers to widely followed exchange traded funds (ETF's) which are good proxies for the assets indicated			

The much greater extent to which these broad movements of the different asset classes shown in the table have produced increased correlations across multiple asset classes is one of the central themes of *Systemic Liquidity Risk and Bipolar Markets.* The consequences of the day-to-day (and intraday) switching between either a risk on or risk off tactical strategy poses significant new challenges to investors who are still making allocation decisions with outmoded notions from the Capital Asset Pricing Model (CAPM) and Modern Portfolio Theory (MPT). Moreover, since the 2008 financial crisis, markets are now more susceptible to sporadic volatility, temporary bouts of illiquidity, and heightened left tail dependencies – in more straightforward terms, the tendency, when markets are under stress, for most asset prices to plunge together as correlations move towards unity.

How can one cushion the impact of systemically threatening events when the ability to exit financial instruments becomes almost non-existent? How can one trust the integrity of financial models and orthodox macro financial theory when they have become increasingly discredited? Can central bankers be relied upon to become the counter-parties of last resort and provide a safety net under the financial system? These vital questions, and many others, need to be addressed by everyone who has a stake in modern financial markets, and they are addressed in this book.

For many investors still traumatized by the watershed events of 2008 there has been a growing interest in tail risk protection strategies and products. But such products often provide a spurious degree of risk mitigation and can dramatically understate the extent of damage done to one's portfolio when bouts of illiquidity arise. Increasingly one needs to go to next generation concepts and tools to manage risk and this will entail using unorthodox strategies to minimize drawdowns. In general terms, investors need to undertake more diligent research into how asset class correlations perform under stress, and recognize that markets are far more likely to seriously misbehave than conventional risk management tools suggest. Insights from such stress analysis enable one to determine how to combine assets which are more capable of absorbing shocks in a crisis, while at the same time still providing one with an attractive upside when markets are not under stress.

Apart from the practical risk management tools and tactics that are recommended in what follows there is the strong belief that anxious and perplexed investors need a more cogent narrative to explain the post GFC financial environment, and assist them to navigate through the choppy waters ahead. New macro modeling tools may, on the surface, appear counter intuitive but in order to adequately account for the bubble and bust dynamics which are endemic to human nature and, in turn, the financial system, it will be necessary, at times, to embrace the inscrutable and ambiguous.

Proper functioning markets require fractiousness or divided opinion, and this needs to be lubricated by communications from central bankers, economic forecasters, corporate executives and so on; these then become open to adversarial interpretations. As long as such messages and market conditions remain ambiguous, providing asymmetric information to different market players, then the conditions are present to enable systemic liquidity to be preserved. Seen in this context the prevailing paradigm of bipolar *risk on/risk off* asset allocations is both a prerequisite to liquid markets, and also paradoxically, when one side of the polarity becomes too extreme, a major source of systemic instability. Should such polarities become critically unbalanced, and should the signals received by market players become symmetrically disadvantageous as they were in the fall of 2008, then an even more substantial systemic liquidity crisis than that seen in those troubled times is a dangerous possibility.

The principal objective in what lies ahead is to provide both a better understanding of the new characteristics and risks that are in evidence in today's financial markets, and to offer practical steps to avoid the kind of value destruction experienced when markets crash.

ACKNOWLEDGEMENTS

I am indebted to the following people who have provided invaluable assistance in the preparation of this book: John Lounsbury, Steve Keen, Marcos Lopez de Prado, Michael Hewson, Craig Ellis, and David Tuckett. In addition for the support given by my publisher, I would like to thank Werner Coetzee, Jennie Kitchin, Tessa Allen, and, in particular, Caroline Quinnell who conscientiously edited the final draft of the manuscript. Needless to say any remaining errors remain my sole responsibility.

1 Introduction

The events of 2007/8 pulled back the magician's curtains and revealed a rather shocking truth about the global financial system – markets can seize up and become completely illiquid. Although previous generations may have experienced similar episodes of systemic illiquidity, in the fall of 2008 the magnitude of the near meltdown came as a traumatic shock to most working in the financial world as well as those beyond. Even for assets such as short-term commercial paper and money market instruments, the liquidity which had been taken for granted completely evaporated. During Q4, 2008 the only asset class for which there was real liquidity was short-term government securities of very highly rated sovereigns. Banks did not want to deal with each other and most asset managers refused to purchase assets, where the risk of not knowing when they might be able to sell them again reflected a profound crisis in confidence regarding the efficacy of markets and the liquidity of market instruments.

At the limit there is ultimately a fundamental paradox regarding liquidity which is that when it is most required it is likely to be non-existent. John Maynard Keynes had a keen eye for noting paradoxes at the root of economic behavior, and made the following observation regarding what today would be called systemic liquidity. [1]

> Of the maxims of orthodox finance none, surely, is more anti-social than the fetish of liquidity, the doctrine that it is a positive virtue on the part of investment institutions to concentrate their resources upon the holding of 'liquid' securities. *It forgets that there is no such thing as liquidity of investment for the community as a whole.*

To slightly paraphrase another of Keynes's classic observations about markets, one could sum up the worst case scenario for the demand for liquidity in the following aphorism "When average opinion comes to believe that average opinion will decide to turn assets into cash, then liquidity may be confidently expected to go to zero."

One of the central tasks of this book will be to explain [2] in as comprehensive and precise a fashion as possible the threat posed by critical financial episodes which can best be described as periods when there is a *disappearance of systemic liquidity*. As will become clearer, the notion of liquidity is one of the more elusive and poorly addressed concepts in the macro-economic and finance literature. Rather than assuming liquidity of markets as a given [3] a full blown account of systemic liquidity and the risks of its disappearance should be an indispensable component of any macro theory of financial economics. It is also imperative that there is recognition that we need to move beyond a view of the kind of liquidity crisis that may face an individual firm and realize that the much greater systemic threat is the kind of crisis – as seen in the second half of 2008 – where many if not most financial firms were, *at the same time*, confronting a liquidity crisis. One useful starting out definition for the risks posed by a systemic liquidity crisis is one proposed by the IMF in some useful analysis of the events of that troubled period. [4] "Systemic liquidity risk is the risk that multiple institutions may face simultaneous difficulties in rolling over their short-term debts or in obtaining new short-term funding through widespread dislocations of money and capital markets." We shall return to the IMF study on systemic liquidity risk and other related analysis in later chapters and in particular in regard to the vital function of the money markets which is one of enabling maturity transformation. [5] If this ongoing facility is interrupted or breaks down there is a real risk of systemic meltdown and it will be suggested that rather than being complacent that the worst has already been seen with regard to the global financial crisis, there just might be an even bigger crisis on the horizon.

Although much of the focus in the literature on the global financial crisis is on the tumultuous events which took place in the second half of 2008 and especially in the wake of the collapse and bankruptcy of Lehman Brothers on September 15, 2008, the foreshocks of the crisis were being felt in 2007 especially during August of that year. August as a month has had a habit of producing nasty financial surprises – the LTCM crisis broke in August 1998 and it was a crisis in August 1971 that saw the US abandon gold convertibility for the US dollar [6] – and during August of 2007 there were some severe shocks to the financial system, the full implications of which would not be fully absorbed by the markets until one year later.

During August 2007, as the press release seen below indicates [7] even Goldman Sachs, which rarely acknowledges its own misfortunes, had to come to the rescue of one of its in-house hedge funds as a result of abnormal market conditions within the US markets during that time frame:

> NEW YORK, August 13, 2007 – The Goldman Sachs Group, Inc. (NYSE: GS) today made the following statement: Many funds employing quantitative strategies are currently under pressure as recent conditions have resulted in significant market dislocation. **Across most sectors, there has been an increase in overlapping trades, a surge in volatility and an increase in correlations. These factors have combined to challenge many of the trading algorithms used in quantitative strategies.** We believe the current values that the market is assigning to the assets underlying various funds represent a discount that is not supported by the fundamentals.

The CFO of Goldman also made the comment that "Liquidity conditions were most extraordinary during early August (2007)," and then went on with the simple minded observation: "We were seeing things that were 25-standard deviation moves, several days in a row." We shall return to this quotation again in what follows, but at this point we can just register the fact that invoking statistical assumptions based on a normal distribution to measure such disorderly behavior was to use a model that is not fit for purpose. [8]

Across the Atlantic during the same month another debacle was unfolding in what was yet another early warning of what was to come one year later. Although it was a relatively small mortgage lender the collapse of Northern Rock in the UK, with news footage of anxious depositors lined up outside the high street branches, is most definitely not the kind of image that bankers and policy makers like to see. The bank had to be taken over by the UK government due to its inability to fund itself in the money market. In a disingenuous comment, that would come to be echoed quite often since, the head of the British Bankers Association remarked to the media, while people were lining up outside the branches: [9]

> "This isn't about solvency, this is about a short-term problem that the Northern Rock has in getting liquidity – that is, getting some cash from the normal interbank lending market," said Angela Knight, chief executive of the British Bankers' Association.
>
> "I think that anybody who is waking up this morning who is either a saver with Northern Rock or has got a mortgage ... can be absolutely confident that they have got their money with or they have borrowed from a very sound financial institution," she told the BBC.

Only the part in that statement that the depositors would be safe was accurate – the British government saw to that – but the institution was far from being sound or solvent as it soon transpired. Although the spokeswoman for the BBA had her own reasons for downplaying the magnitude of the Northern Rock episode, it is also worth recalling that in the summer of 2007 there was still a large degree of complacency on the part of central bankers and many policy makers with respect to the seriousness of the unfolding crisis in the financial system. By way of illustration the Deputy Governor of the Bank of England is on record in an interview with the Financial Times expressing the view that many key policy makers failed to recognize the gravity of the situation at the onset of the crisis: [10]

> "I think it's fair to say that in the early stages of the financial crisis most of us expected this to be a relatively short-lived seize-up in the financial markets; it would be over by Christmas, if you like. Whereas it was only gradually, over time, that we appreciated the full severity of what was occurring."

The effort to explain the existence of abnormal market conditions which can give rise to bouts of extreme illiquidity will be a central theme of this book. Some other signposts to guide the reader as to the way things will proceed are that we will also need to examine such issues as the increasing sovereign debt risk, the possibility of a disintegration (even partial) of the Eurozone and the single currency, severe stresses in the European banking system, and numerous other wild cards that can contribute to a general discomforting sense that uncertainty and potential systemic risk, which have been very much in evidence since 2007, are not going to be ameliorated any time soon. Further themes which will be examined are the notions that *price discovery,* the primary function of markets, is being increasingly hampered, even distorted, by central bankers' efforts with QE, in Europe by LTRO and the Outright Monetary Transactions (OMT) program announced by the ECB in September 2012, in FX markets by the very large footprint of the People's Bank of China (PBOC) with more than $3 trillion of liquid reserves, and also by the aberrations which can and have arisen following the proliferation of algorithmic trading practices now omnipresent in many markets.

As the discussion proceeds it should become more apparent what the factors are, at the micro level of individual trades within a financial market, which are the principal determinants of liquidity and "price discovery." In turn the dynamics and interplay of these various factors can then be used as heuristics for scaling up to a better understanding of the nature of systemic illiquidity events which are at the centre of the kinds of crisis episodes that have become more apparent since 2007/8.

Macro-economic theory is notoriously deficient in providing any real understanding of market liquidity, rather, as with so many other fundamental features of the contemporary financial economy, we are essentially told to take "liquidity" as a given. So one of the most crucial characteristics of the manner in which prices are determined, and the quality of trading activity which takes places in markets, as well as the nature of extreme price behavior which can arise from "an evaporation of liquidity" [11] remains as an unexplained article of faith. Surely one has grounds to be seriously troubled by the intellectual foundations for orthodox macro-economic theory which fails to account for liquidity, fails to explain how credit creation is a major dynamo for financial capitalism – a dynamo which has a proclivity for creating bubbles, and an absence of any tools which can anticipate when bubbles have gone too far and are about to burst.

What is the evidence of increasing abnormality in market prices over the past few years?

Figure 1.1, which comes from a presentation by the Bank of England's Andrew Haldane who will appear again in this book, [12] is useful in illustrating the interdependency of market

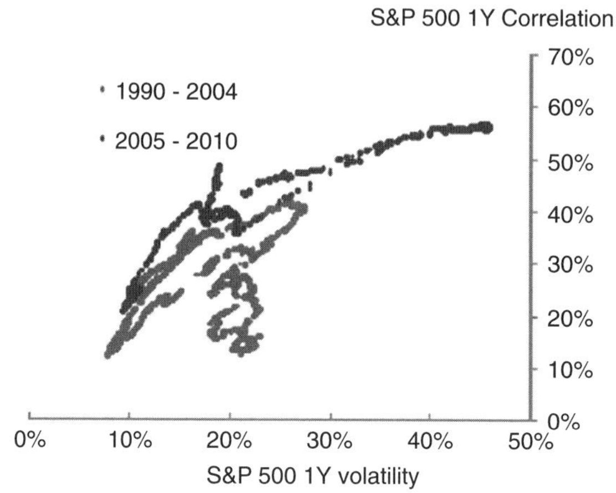

Figure 1.1 Volatility and correlation of S&P 500 1990–2010
Source: Haldane, A G (2011), "The Race to Zero".

volatility and correlation, which are two good measures that can throw light on the observed increase in the propensity towards abnormal episodes in the financial markets in recent years. The chart plots the volatility of, and correlation between, the individual constituents of the S&P 500 from 1990 to 2010. In general terms, as shown over the 20-year period the relationship between volatility and correlation is positive which could suggest that higher volatility increases the degree of co-movement between stocks. But as Haldane points out, have we got the cause and effect the wrong way round?

That there is some circularity which needs explanation will be one of the tasks undertaken in what follows. It will also be shown that there is overwhelming evidence of increased cross correlations, not just within the major US equity indices, but across many asset classes in the wake of the global financial crisis. Examination of the inter-relationships between the correlations of asset returns, market volatility, and macro liquidity provides scope for a fascinating exercise in forensic analysis of markets. To the extent that it is possible to disentangle the underlying dynamics which account for these inter-connections it will be argued that this will enable one to be better equipped to navigate the choppy waters which are a feature of contemporary financial markets.

Figure 1.1 shows how the interconnection between volatility and correlation has changed over the 20-year period from 1990–2010. Two things are clearly noticeable in the latter period since 2005. First, both volatility, as indicated on the horizontal axis, and correlation, seen on the vertical axis, have been higher than during the earlier period. Volatility is more than 10 percentage points higher than in the earlier sample, while correlation is about 8 percentage points higher. Secondly, as Haldane observes "the slope of the volatility/correlation curve is steeper. Any rise in volatility now has a more pronounced cross-market effect than in the past." It would be worth adding, once again, the comment that it may well be appropriate to think of the direction of influence as the other way around. In other words, it is just as feasible that it is the adoption of a more binary approach towards asset allocation – where the degree of cross-sectional correlations between both *risk on* assets and another set of *risk off* assets – is ultimately the determining factor in heightened volatility and the propensity for markets to experience bouts of illiquidity.

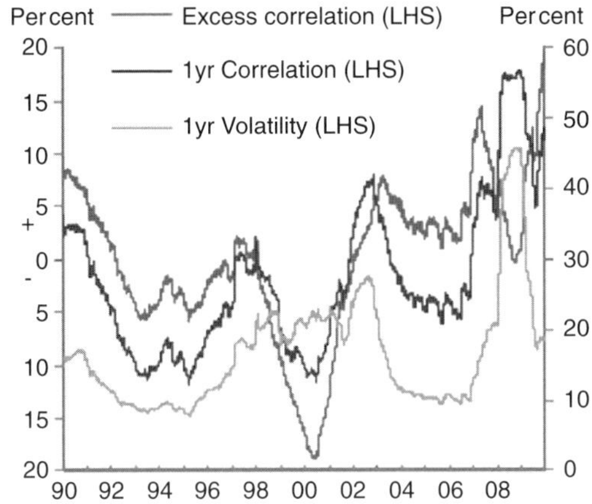

Figure 1.2 Excess volatility for S&P 500 1990–2010
Source: Haldane, A G (2011), "The Race to Zero".

A simple way to demonstrate the trend towards increased cross-sectional correlations is to subtract the one-year volatility measures from the correlation values as displayed in Figure 1.1. The result of this can be seen in Figure 1.2 which is also taken from the BOE presentation. The measure of "excess correlation," as used by Haldane, is simply the observed correlation minus the observed volatility. By referring to the right-hand axis, it can be seen that "excess correlation" in 2010 was at its highest level in the 20-year period under consideration. Further evidence which will be reviewed in Chapter 2 extends the historical back testing for comparison back even further and reveals that there is no comparable period of excess correlation in the post World War 2 period. [13] In summarizing the evidence from the two charts Haldane suggests that market volatility in the years since 2005 is both higher and propagates further than in the past. "Intraday evidence on volatilities and correlations appears to tell a broadly similar tale. Overnight and intraday correlations have risen in tandem."

Financial markets are clearly reflecting a greater propensity for many asset returns to be more highly correlated and more volatile, and when pursuing a more in-depth analysis of market internals it becomes abundantly clear that a new kind of behavior on the part of traders and investors has emerged in the wake of the global financial crisis (which sometimes will be referred to simply by the convenient acronym of GFC), and this new binary mode of market behavior has come to be known as the "risk on/risk off" paradigm. I will argue quite tenaciously that this new binary pattern of trading is both a symptom of, and dominant contributory factor to, much increased cross asset correlations and that this results in a broad range of asset prices rising or falling in lockstep. These asset classes can almost be divided into two quite distinct camps and instruments within these classes will move with little regard for idiosyncratic fundamentals, generating further volatility and closer alignments along the frontier of the risk on/risk off demarcation. On the one hand the risk on assets will include, broadly, equities, emerging market instruments including their bonds and currencies, commodities, high yielding corporate bonds, and certain currency pairs especially those involving the Australian dollar. Within the other camp of risk off assets can be found US Treasuries, German bunds, the Japanese yen, previously the Swiss Franc (although this has lost some of its former status in this class since being pegged to the euro) [14] and in more general terms a tendency towards taking short positions in the other camp of risk on assets.

One of the many consequences of the global financial crisis has been that many traditionally active market participants have taken to the sidelines. There is mounting evidence of substantial declines in real institutional trading volume in US equity markets, [15] and despite the much increased presence of HFT and other algorithmic trading activity, which has boosted trading volumes without adding to the quality of liquidity in markets, [16] there have been momentary bouts of illiquidity, some of which have been severe. One of the most notorious occurred on May 6, 2010 and has come to be known as the Flash Crash (the term "flash" comes from the manner in which HFT algorithms can send rapid fire signals into electronic platforms and which customarily have mischievous motives). [17] The events of May 6, 2010 – which included the largest intraday points move ever seen in the trading of the Dow Jones Industrials – will be the focus of an entire chapter of this book and a forensic like examination of the trading patterns seen that day reveal some remarkable features of modern markets and their capability of producing extreme and highly abnormal conditions for traders and investors.

What evidence is there that contemporary markets are exhibiting more fat tail behavior?

In recent years, perhaps as a result of the proselytizing by financial pundits such as Nicholas Taleb, [18] there has been a widespread, but not ubiquitous, realization that financial asset prices exhibit an unconventional distribution pattern. By that is meant that the shape of the "bell curve" (actually it is not bell-like at all), and the lengths and size of the tails of the distribution for returns of financial instruments do not "fit" within a normal distribution model. There have been several attempts to find more applicable distributions but it will be argued later that this is most likely to prove fruitless. The peculiar shape of the distribution of asset returns can be quite convincingly illustrated by reference to Figure 1.3 which traces the distribution around the mean returns for the S&P 500 during the period from January 1985 until mid-May of 2012.

The period covered in Figure 1.3 includes almost 7000 separate data points which correspond to the daily percentage changes in the S&P 500. As can be seen if the shape could be described as bell-like at all, it is a very narrow bell. Also discernible is the fact that the tails are very elongated stretching to both ± ten standard deviations on either side of the mean. This kind of pattern is called leptokurtic, and, in essence, reflects the fact that on a day to day basis there will be relatively small changes in the S&P 500, and therefore there will be a concentration of the distribution around the central tendency. More pertinent to the concerns of this book,

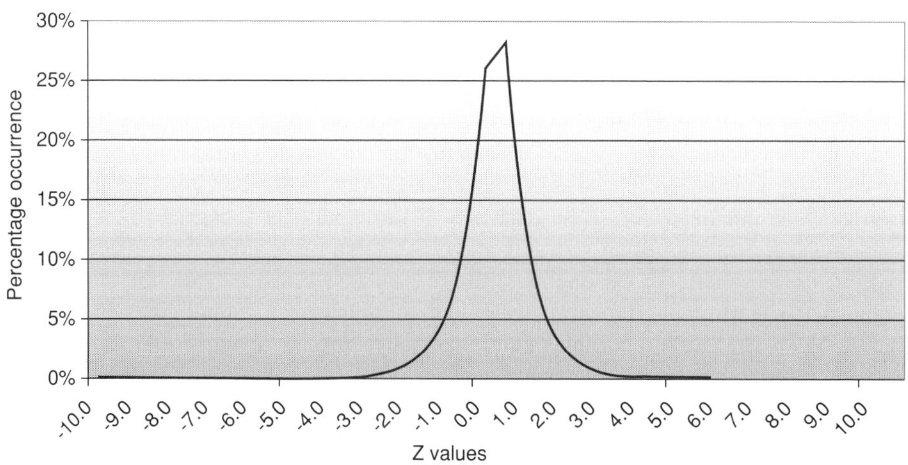

Figure 1.3 Normalized distribution of daily changes to S&P 500 1985–mid-2012

Table 1.1 Table of outlier values for daily changes to S&P 500 1985–mid-2012

TOTAL DATA POINTS	6899
LEFT TAIL OUTLIERS <−3 SD	51
RIGHT TAIL OUTLIERS > 3 SD	77
TOTAL OUTLIERS	128
PERCENTAGE OF OUTLIERS	**1.9%**
LEFT HAND CENTRAL TENDENCY WITHIN – 2SD	3170
RIGHT HAND CENTRAL TENDENCY WITHIN +2 SD	3410
TOTAL WITHIN ± 2 SIGMAS	6580
CENTRAL TENDENCY PERCENTAGE >−2 SD and < 2 SD	**95.4%**

the outliers of the distribution are far more severe and frequent than would be expected from the type of normal distribution which, for example, is a good representation of the distribution of heights of human beings (at least a specific category such as adult males). With respect to a normally distributed data series – such as heights – the likelihood of someone exceeding (or being less than) a height which is more than 3 sigmas from the mean is very small – approximately 0.15%.

During the 27-year period covered in Table 1.1 there were almost 7000 data points and 4.6% of those that exceeded the threshold of ± 2 sigmas. That this frequency of 4.6% also concurs with the expectation from statistical theory that ± 2 sigma events should occur with approximately 5% probability may be seen as validation of the theory that asset returns are normally distributed, *but* the problems arise when considering the frequency of the outliers and their distribution or tendency to cluster. There is a pronounced tendency for abnormal moves to cluster, and not be distributed haphazardly across the time line, as will be demonstrated in Chapter 4. This should not be surprising of course as prices are determined by human beings who have memories, fears, and emotions and, when they are stressed and anxious, their reactions to events are going to be more extreme and erratic.

Also evident from Table 1.1 is the fact that 1.9% of the daily returns for the S&P 500 lie outside the six sigma window which is often used as a simple metric for characterizing this fact about financial returns as having "fat tails." According to a Gaussian model [19] the probability of an event falling outside the six sigma window is just shy of 0.3%. So the US benchmark index distribution has six times more outliers than would be expected by this model. Not shown on the table is the fact that since July 2007 the number events that lie outside the six sigma window is 58, which is almost one half of the total outlier events in the full 27-year period. The prevalence of these outliers, both during the GFC and in its aftermath, clearly demonstrates that there is a greater likelihood of "tail" events in recent financial history.

The following graphic, Figure 1.4, and the excerpted commentary, which comes from a Credit Suisse research note cited again in the discussion below, are also helpful in answering the question which began this section regarding evidence for increased "tail risk" events. [20]

> ... fat-tail events have occurred more frequently, and have been exacerbated by the 2008 credit crisis. For example, [Figure 1.4] shows that, for US equities and global fixed income, the number of three-sigma days per year has increased, reaching a peak of 46 and 15 days in 2008, respectively. As such, the probability of a fat-tail event occurring under a normal distribution is actually much higher—at 4.7%—just during the last decade.

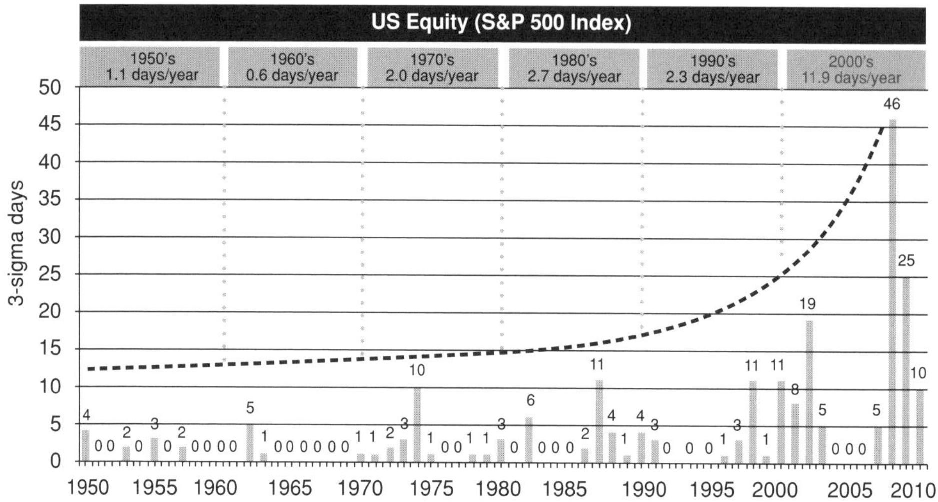

Figure 1.4 Extreme events for S&P 500 1950–2011
Source: Credit Suisse: Is the (Fat) Tail Wagging your Portfolio?

For the reader that notices a discrepancy between the incidence of three sigma days in my own table and that shown in the research note just cited, the simple explanation is that Figure 1.4 covers a different period back to 1950 but terminating in 2010, and this will affect the calculations of the mean and standard deviation and therefore the counting of six sigma events.

In the analysis which will follow it is suggested that, while looking at some of the extreme price activity which has been seen in markets since 2007, the nomenclature of fat tails and outlier events which exceed the six sigma boundaries, really doesn't do justice to the extraordinary severity and magnitude of drawdowns which can be inflicted on an investor. Furthermore by using the terminology of standard deviations (sigmas) and couching the analysis in terms of normal distributions, there can be a spurious sense of the reliability and accuracy of the methodology. *Markets are more badly behaved than statistically obsessed risk managers would like to believe!*

There is another potential danger when just focusing on statistical data such as increased volatility and the presence of fatter tails, of ignoring some facts about the financial environment which may be considered as part of the "new normal" but which are nonetheless quite extraordinary. For example, at the time of writing, the yields on both the 10-year US Treasury note and the 10-year German bund are hovering around 1.5%, short dated Swiss, German, and Finnish government securities have negative yields, the UK 10-year gilt is below 2%, and the Bank of England base rate has been at 0.5% for three years – its lowest level in the Bank's three-hundred-year history. Moreover the balance sheets of the ECB, the US Federal Reserve, and the Bank of Japan have expanded by several trillions of their respective currencies in just the last two years since 2010.

The remarkable paths taken by government bond yields in each of the US, UK, Germany, and Japan since 1990 are very well illustrated in Figure 1.5. [21]

What is perhaps even more remarkable about the steady decline in yields and their convergence towards levels seen in Japan for several years, [22] that is around 1% for a ten-year

Figure 1.5 10-year government bond yields

maturity bond, is that these yields have been coming down steadily, especially in the period since the GFC, despite the fact that gross government debt in each sovereign has been climbing at an accelerating rate as can be seen in Figure 1.6.

The most notable feature of Figure 1.6 is the disproportionately large share that Japanese government debt has to its GDP, and if the IMF forecasts prove accurate this will have risen above 250% by 2017. Just how sustainable that level of public debt is remains to be seen, but there are a growing number of pessimists (realists) who believe that with adverse demographics

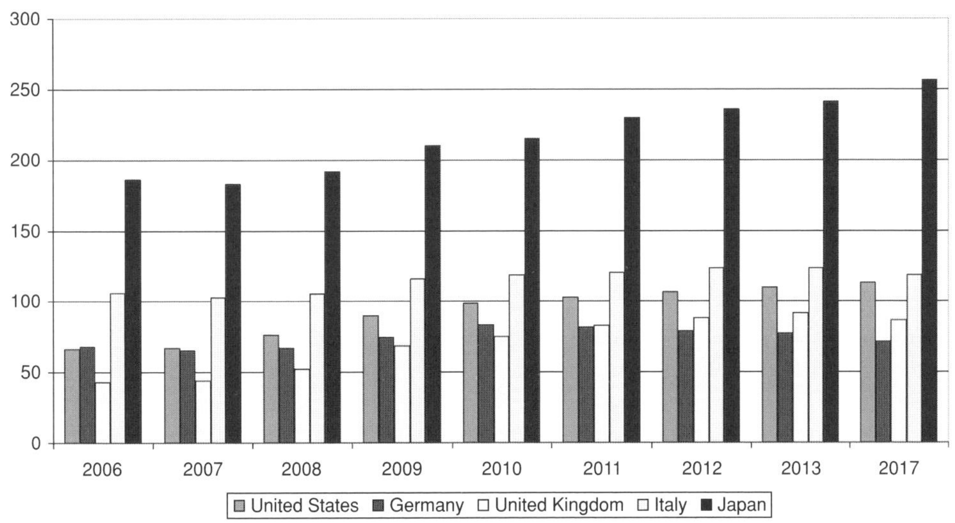

Figure 1.6 Government Gross Debt as percentage of GDP: data source IMF WEO April 2012

and increased competition from other Asian exporters the Japanese debt situation resembles a "fly looking for a windscreen." By comparison the situation for the other territories looks less foreboding but to seek comfort from this would be a dangerous complacency. As can be seen the debt to GDP ratios for both the US and Italy are already above 100% and are expected to continue rising over the forecast period. Germany is the exception in that while there was a jump in 2009 and 2010 the projections going forward in the IMF data suggest that the rate will flatten out in the next several years. However IMF projections have often proved too optimistic in the past. Another wild card for Germany is the extent to which its public balance sheet will become burdened by efforts to keep the Eurozone afloat, a subject discussed further in Chapter 11.

So we are faced with an enigma which defies any straightforward explanation from classical demand/supply theory. If the supply of sovereign debt by these G10 states is increasing why, with the exception of Italy, are the yields on their sovereign bonds declining? (The prices of sovereign issues would have to be going up and/or bonds would have to be issued with lower coupons for this to happen.) The answer to this is both easy and hard. The easy answer is that there has been strong risk aversion on the part of many institutional investors since the GFC and the demand for safe sovereign issues (which can be claimed for four of the five countries shown in Figure 1.5) has replaced the "cult of equity" which prevailed through much of the 1990s and early years of the new millennium. If one couples risk aversion to equity with the fact that issues from many lesser rated sovereigns are definitely not on a buy list for most pension funds and insurance companies, and there is a satisfactory explanation for the paradox of increased supply but increased demand and therefore price. The harder explanation relates to a fuller analysis of risk on/risk off dynamics, the nature of a *balance sheet recession*, and the phenomenon of *vendor financing*, and discussions of each of those is still to come. [23]

There are two charts on the adjacent page which will be discussed in more detail later as we proceed, but both in their way are worthy of attention at this early stage in the discussion. The 20-year chart of the yield on the US 10-year note, Figure 1.7, shows a quite remarkable steady descent from a yield above 8% in 1991 to well below 2% in the late spring of 2012. The other long-term chart, Figure 1.8, shows the inexorable rise in the Japanese yen against the US dollar since 2007. It will turn out that there are some interesting dynamics connected with safe haven and risk off dynamics that need to be considered with regard to the cross-asset correlation of such apparently different instruments. These risk off dynamics need to be counterbalanced by considering the exceptional performance of other risk on assets such as equities where US equities almost doubled between 2009 and 2011 and Germany's DAX to mention just another example, more than doubled from its low of 3588 in March 2009 up to a peak above 7600 in May of 2011.

1.1 HOW HELPFUL IS THE NOTION OF TAIL RISK?

The notion of tail risk has become *de rigueur* amongst financial analysts and is itself at risk of becoming overused. Although this was already touched on in the earlier part of this chapter, the key idea is to consider it in relation to the related notion of "fat tails" – a phenomenon which everyone in the financial world should be familiar with, if for no other reason than the meme planted by Nicholas Taleb in his best-selling book *The Black Swan: The Impact of the Highly Improbable*. [24] Based upon the normal distribution, an assumption which is highly questionable when trying to understand probability and risk in regard to financial markets, an event which falls outside ± 3 sigmas from the mean return could be said to be an outlier or

Figure 1.7 Yield on 10-year US Treasury note monthly 1990–mid-2012

tail event. It would then follow that such an event – such as a drop in an asset price of more than three standard deviations – has exposed the holder of such an asset to "tail risk." But how relevant is that to an estimation of how probable such an event is?

According to a Gaussian normal distribution the likelihood of a data point that falls outside the six sigma window should only arise about 15 times in a series of 10 000 observations. Now this may be true with respect to the chances of meeting an adult male who is more than three standard deviations above the mean height for adult males – which is about 6ft 6inches or, for those more familiar with the metric system, approximately 199 cm. [25] However the data on S&P 500 returns, as illustrated earlier, shows that financial data does not fit a normal distribution, and that there is a chance of almost 100 observations out of 10 000 exceeding the six sigma window. So the frequency of outliers is much higher, and critically so too is the magnitude of the difference from the mean. Just for amusement if we consider the remark made by the CFO of Goldman Sachs, and noted earlier, regarding 25 standard deviation moves "that happened several days in a row," we would have to subtract 25 times 8 centimeters (the sigma for heights of adult males) from the mean height of 176 cm and that would give us an individual with a height of about minus 20 cm.

When we talk about tail risk the thesis developed here is that we might be misleading ourselves into thinking that this is just an extreme form of lesser risk. The implication when using terms like *extreme* is that there is a scale of reference, but the question that really needs to be addressed is – what is the proper scale for comparison of different degrees of risk? In finance there are many kinds of risk – credit/default risk, inflation risk, counter-party risk

Figure 1.8 Japanese yen/US dollar monthly 1990–mid-2012

and so on – but in much of the theoretical side of financial economics, risk is taken as being synonymous with volatility. The tendency of prices or asset values to fluctuate is something that can be measured, and, from this simple method of calculating the degree of fluctuation and the application of statistical and probability axioms, many kinds of extrapolations and forecasts can be made. But just how valid are such extrapolations and forecasts? This is a crucial question for wealth protection and risk management.

So does it follow that since we can measure degrees of volatility, and therefore risk in the narrow sense favored by financial economists, and make sense of them in relation to textbook statistics, that we can simply scale this understanding up to provide a theoretical framework for comprehending financial crashes or episodes of extreme volatility? I take this to be a hard question to answer, and also one that is both fascinating and extremely pertinent to a better understanding of today's financial markets. Moving away from statistics for a moment, the question might be framed along slightly different lines as follows – is the difference, from a psychological and emotional point of view, between anxiety and outright panic just a matter of degree or is there such a difference in the order of magnitude of each that categorically different explanations are required?

Not to confuse the reader too much at the beginning of this journey, there are echoes from the question just posed to a similar one which can be posed in what may seem to be the totally unrelated field of geophysics. This question can be framed along the following lines: Are extreme earthquakes, which are mercifully quite rare, simply to be understood as smaller earthquakes that didn't stop or failed to attenuate? The reason for asking this question will become clearer when examining the concept of power laws for which there is evidence certainly in the case of earthquakes and also in terms of the magnitude of movements in financial markets. In simple terms, an event is said to behave in accordance with a power law if the frequency of the event is inversely proportional to its magnitude. The dimension of the magnitude or scaling variable could be the amount of energy released (or ground motion) in the case of an earthquake or, in the case of the financial markets, it could be the magnitude of price discontinuities. [26] Even if we are able to discern a power law relationship in regard to financial dynamics (which we can) does this enrich our understanding of these dynamics, and more pertinently does it provide us with any means of anticipating when financial crashes may occur? Or are we in the same position as geo-scientists in having no real means of predicting when and where (exactly) a mega quake is likely to occur?

The reason for posing these questions in an introductory chapter is to alert the reader to the possibility that for those who have a fetish for quantification of all things in the realm of finance, they may end up being frustrated by our inability to arrive at the proper scalar for understanding risk. In turn it may be that the notion of tail risk – which has a pseudo scientific flavor to the term, suggesting that there is some robust theoretical framework which can be referenced – is actually not a quantitatively determinable concept. Instead it may turn out that by thinking about financial crashes, market panics, and extreme risk in a fresh manner we will be better armed to understand the origins of such phenomena and from an investment management perspective better able to deal with them.

Although we shall return in Chapter 13 to the manner in which an investor can alleviate the dramatic drawdowns [27] that arose during the 2008 crisis, and which will arise again during future bouts of systemic illiquidity, it is very useful to make reference to a key limitation of some of the tail risk protection strategies that are now being offered by various providers such as PIMCO and large investment banks. [28] Many of the world's leading hedge fund managers attend the GAIM conferences each year, and at the June 2012 meeting in Monaco a number of managers made the excellent point that some of these tail risk protection products may not perform as required (and promised by the providers) when markets experience systemic illiquidity. An article from Reuters entitled "Investors Cast Doubt on 'End of World' Hedge Strategies" [29] reports on doubts expressed at the GAIM conference "whether such funds can perform as they are expected to, leaving investors dangerously exposed to a deepening global debt crisis."

> Pension funds and family offices, still smarting from the huge losses they suffered in the 2008–2009 financial crisis and fearing another blow-up is just around the corner, are handing over billions of dollars to bank and fund providers promising protection – many without really knowing if the funds will pay out when they need them to.

The fallacy inherent in the design of some of the products on offer is that *they assume market liquidity* in the instruments that will purportedly be providing the protection. This is a dangerous assumption as will become more evident in what follows but it was also brought out at the conference by one of the delegates who is quoted as follows:

> "You guys better figure out how, while hedging tail risk, you're not letting liquidity risk sneak in the back door ... you don't know how to get out and we've just had a liquidity event not so long ago," one investor told a panel of managers discussing their funds on Wednesday.

He accused firms who offer the strategies of not knowing how to exit their positions, particularly if markets seize up and liquidity in the derivatives markets these funds trade evaporates.

Normal functioning of markets depends upon adversarial views on the appropriateness of the current valuation of assets. Depending on one's economic circumstances, orientation, and cognitive frames of reference, some will want to be buyers at current prices and others would prefer to sell to the former. The fractious dimension to market participants is the driver towards *price discovery* which is the primary purpose of markets. (The more cynical view is that markets have become the playground for hedge funds and HFT algorithms, but we shall not go down that path at this juncture.) The adversarial or fractious quality of market dynamics will be enhanced by asymmetry of information and knowledge (or ignorance), enabling those with insight into "real" or "true" information to exploit those with "mistaken" knowledge. It is also true that, as a result of many within markets wearing several hats as both principals and agents, the asymmetry of information can in a real sense be one that crosses the borderline between information that is in the public domain and that which is not.

If a vital prerequisite for the existence and functioning of proper markets is information asymmetry, in light of the events of 2007/8, a strong argument could be made that markets will be more dangerous when there is essentially symmetry of ignorance, i.e. where no one knows what is going on. That is where no one has an information advantage. In such a case markets lose their liquidity, disagreement over the appropriateness of valuations is suspended, and a lot of wealth destruction can and will take place.

1.2 DICHOTOMIES AND AMBIGUITIES

Epistemologists, concerned with the theory of knowledge, have sometimes pointed to the role of metaphor in our language and underlying cognitive framework. We know about many abstractions by being able to use analogy and metaphors to translate a complex idea into simpler and more intuitive notions. Such metaphorical devices could be as simple as the difference between being inside a container of some sort or outside it, being above or below some reference point and in general terms being able to imagine a simple schema which then allows us to add on further layers of abstraction – themselves aided by metaphorical heuristics. Another key strand of thought is that some of our knowledge derives from the mind's facility with contemplating opposites or being able to polarize qualities. Good and bad, tall and short, volatile and calm are just a few of thousands of dichotomies that the mind is capable of laying out at each end of a spectrum of dichotomies.

Most dichotomies are susceptible to what can be called *semantic shading*, in other words they can be thought of as black and white extremes at the end of a spectrum, but with many shades of gray in between.

Most dichotomies are tolerant of ambiguity . . . they are susceptible to semantic shading without posing truly uncomfortable choices and cognitive dissonance. The capacity of human beings to entertain a disparate variety of dichotomies as foundations to a set of beliefs is testimony to this tolerance. But there are certain kinds of dichotomies which cannot be nuanced and where cognitive anxieties will demand disambiguation.

1.3 TRUST AND SOLVENCY ARE ALL OR NOTHING DICHOTOMIES

In the realm of finance and economics two such dichotomies, which are not so readily susceptible to shading, are solvency and trust. This is not to suggest that for many people they cannot be smudged at times – as attested to by the saying that you can fool some of the people all of the time. Under normal circumstances we are not faced with having to make a vital decision on whether or not it is wise to place trust in another or whether a prospective counter-party may be solvent.

When circumstances become critical there is no longer a continuum for trust -> distrust or solvency -> insolvency. After a certain tipping point there is a dramatic discontinuity in the willingness to consider mitigating factors or compromises in the judgments we make. We may start out, if transactions are small and inconsequential, in overriding any discomfort that we may be experiencing about having to make a critical decision as to whether to trust the solvency or ability of counter-parties to honor their obligations. However once we move beyond a certain threshold of inconsequentiality, when more critical circumstances (perhaps life threatening) present themselves to us there is absolutely no propensity to tolerate doubts or mistrust. To the extent that we have a choice we will refuse to engage with that counter-party. The discontinuity is not just a jump from a linear to a nonlinear method of weighing up the risks/benefits, but rather our decision about the uncertainty of the outcomes is best thought of as totally unacceptable. Beyond a certain threshold the decision making and willingness to accept a certain degree of "fuzziness" and to fudge the issue becomes an *all or nothing proposition*.

As an example, in September 2008 counter-parties that were dealing with Lehman Brothers *completely lost trust* in the company, refused to fund it in the money markets, and quite rapidly the overall market realized that the company was insolvent. Traders and investors were no longer prepared to tolerate self-serving statements from the company's CEO and its management team that its balance sheet was sound and that it could fund itself. There was a total breakdown in trust of the company's declarations regarding its financial position. In such circumstances, there are no degrees of solvency – a company, especially a bank, either is solvent or it is not – there is no halfway house. It is this unwillingness to tolerate any ambiguity regarding solvency that explains why companies can be full of employees in opulent offices one day and then bankrupt the next, with the employees walking out of those same opulent offices with cardboard boxes containing their hastily packed personal possessions.

The switch from all or nothing in decision making with respect to whom we can trust, or what kinds of intermediation (also intervals) we can have faith in, is precisely the explanation for the dramatic and non-quantifiable element of systemic risk. As human agents with survival instincts (to call these emotions is to understate their visceral quality) there is no longer a calculus of probabilistic reasoning but rather a gut level response to danger. Failure to account for this very abrupt switching rather than a gradualist change of mind, it will be suggested, is one of the principal shortcomings of the theoretical framework which underpins financial economics. It will be argued that the bias in our theories of economics and finance towards gradualism and uniformitarianism – which have occupied a powerful position in the history of ideas including the vital work of Charles Darwin [30] – has inhibited us from confronting true dichotomies in a robust manner, and thus to fudge a lot of hard questions. Just one further thought in this regard is the fallacy of believing that all large effects – such as the collapse of a bank for example – has to have a large cause. But there are several insights from complexity theory which suggests that this is not the case. [31]

One influential insight which is related to the gradualist fallacy is found in the work of Per Bak, a physicist and computer scientist, and this was developed in a fascinating book entitled *How Nature Works*. [32] It will not be necessary to go into depth on this work but in essence Bak showed that under controlled experimental conditions very large effects, specifically massively disruptive avalanches in sand piles, could result from just adding one more grain of sand to the pile. Over time the sand piles have taken on the condition of *self-organized criticality* [33] in which, although they have preserved their state of being in the form of a heap or pile, they are also highly unstable; the incremental addition of just one more grain causes a collapse. Bak found that there is no linear relationship between the cause (the addition of one tiny grain of sand) and the disproportionately large effects, i.e. a massive avalanche.

With regard to our understanding of extreme events in markets, such as have been seen since 2007, there is a parallel in that they had by 2007 reached a position of criticality and the ensuing collapse does not require a single big cause as the explanation. It may also help to account for why not many macro economists had an answer to the question famously asked by Queen Elizabeth II on a visit to the London School of Economics soon after the events of late 2008 – "Why didn't anybody see this coming?"

Just as the grains incrementally falling on to the sand-piles which haphazardly will produce avalanches, or small earthquakes that just don't stop, the rupturing or abrupt discontinuity which takes place with regard to systemic risk is not susceptible to easy quantification. How else can one account for the manner in which assets are disgorged with no regard to price or favorable arbitrage opportunities. To have confidence to conduct arbitrage one needs to have confidence in spanning a time interval and that will be lacking when the total aversion to trusting counter-parties prevails.

Imagining circumstances at the individual or microcosmic level which could cause an individual to suddenly lose trust or faith in another is not too difficult to contrive. Most of us will have had experiences with others where the desire to rid oneself of any engagement with that other person is total and uncompromising.

It is also possible to reflect that this is scalable and can be extended to circumstances where there is a sudden collective suspension of belief in the value of intermediation, i.e. relying on another person to perform. To the extent that most market participants become unwilling to rely upon the promises and solvency of others there is a systemic breakdown.

How could the value of one of the world's largest banks – Citigroup – be marked down by 95% within a little more than a year? Or to put in a slightly different fashion: What rationalization could be made for an investor suffering a 95% drawdown in one of the world's most highly capitalized companies, to want to continue to own that asset? Even more acutely, after the fact when surely trust in that institution's solvency must be at rock bottom, how can someone be enticed to invest in that same company? Later in the book, the suggestion will be made that it is necessary to radically amend our framework for understanding and evaluating financial risk in order to understand why such "abnormal" events have occurred, will occur again, and what strategies one can adopt to assist in alleviating the wealth destruction that can arise in their wake.

Bubbles will keep inflating until they don't – is that the best that can be said? To express the same question in terms of the analogy with the difficulty in knowing when the avalanches in Bak's sand-piles will occur, or when a large earthquake might happen, it may be that we can have a good sense that the financial system has reached a point of critical instability, but, much more pointedly, what is the triggering event – the extra grain of sand or the additional foreshock – which will cause the system or financial markets to crash? The difficulty in identifying the exact triggers – especially at the time – captures the difficulty which prevents the "rationalizing" mind from having great specificity about outcomes in the highly uncertain world of economics and finance. Notwithstanding our inability to understand the precise interplay of the highly complex dynamics that are present in a sophisticated financial economy, there is quite a bit more that could be done to avoid crashes. Most pertinently central bankers should expand their mandates from monitoring inflation at the level of the price of bananas and haircuts to monitoring asset inflation.

Although this is a contentious issue it would seem to be self-evident in the aftermath of the GFC that central bankers should have the macro-prudential task of ensuring that bubbles do not become as crisis prone as they were in 2006/7. The chairman of the Federal Reserve Ben Bernanke has famously said that it is not desirable for central banks to become "bubble poppers," and his predecessor, Alan Greenspan, has often been accused of allowing the US real estate market to become overly frothy by keeping interest rates at extremely low levels for too long after the Nasdaq crash and the events of 9/11. [34]

> I think for the Fed to be an "arbiter of security speculation or values" is neither desirable nor feasible ... Aggressive bubble-poppers would like to see the Fed raise interest rates vigorously and proactively to eliminate potential bubbles in asset prices. To be frank, this recommendation concerns me greatly, and I hope to persuade you that it is antithetical to time-tested principles and sound practices of central banking.

In macro-economics the problem goes even deeper than that expressed in the comments above by Bernanke. It is not only that central bankers may not think it feasible to become "bubble poppers" but more alarmingly they seem not to have an adequate framework for understanding the dynamics behind the creation of bubbles, much less how to arrest their development.

As the discussion proceeds it will be useful to look at good and bad theories in macro-economics which either have, or do not have, any explanatory force as to why bubbles and booms arise and also why they will inevitably, to mix metaphors, crash and burn. The main-stream economic orthodoxy as taught within many universities and business schools which is often referred to as neoclassical economics, really suffers from an inadequate framework for explaining bubbles because it fails to account for, even acknowledge, the manner in which the banking system via its ability to create credit, fuels bubbles and provides the lubrication to the dynamo which helps to motivate investments – the Keynesian "animal spirits" – to excess and over-exuberance. The superior theories of the modern monetarist school (inspired in large part by the work of Hyman Minsky) provide a much better explanatory framework for understanding bubbles in terms of Minsky's notion of ponzi financing and other insights about the role of credit and money within a sophisticated economy. [35] Even with this better framework there is still a deficiency in that we are not adequately prepared to know when bubbles have been inflated to their maximum extent, and when financial crashes and instability will emerge.

Attempts at specificity with respect to "tail risk," when they become preoccupied with trying to measure it precisely, are spurious as they will fail to reflect the astounding magnitudes of total asset price collapses that are evident in recent economic history. These collapses range from outright bankruptcies of companies ranging in recent times from corporate giants such as Enron, Worldcom, General Motors, Lehman Brothers and many others, to the reorganizations/rescues of others such as AIG, Citigroup, Merrill Lynch, Fannie Mae, Freddie Mac, Bear Stearns, Royal Bank of Scotland and too many others to mention.

When a bubble bursts, all confidence in the immediate basis for normal financial intermediation disappears. Admittedly over time some semblance of trust can be restored but only after some form of re-structuring. No one is going to lend money to a person who is on the verge of bankruptcy. After a bankruptcy re-organization, when the slate has been wiped clean, there will be a different perspective on the riskiness of making such a loan. But what if there is a cultural taboo about wiping the slate clean for certain kinds of debt?

1.4 THE ASYMMETRY OF PRIVATE GAIN AND PUBLIC LOSSES

At present central bankers and policy makers do not have to make a choice between preserving or abandoning the asymmetry of the private gain/public pain dichotomy. Although there has been growing hostility to continuing bailouts, until there is a radical change in the political climate (which just might come within struggling European states), there is still acquiescence in the status quo whereby institutions that are deemed Too Big To Fail *have to be rescued by taxpayers*. Even when assisted back to robust health there is often no gratitude from some institutions for the public assistance that was provided during the GFC.

In fact it has become part of the revisionist rhetoric since 2008 that certain financial institutions, particularly in the US, were actually forced into accepting TARP assistance and could have withstood the systemic liquidity crisis without such aid. It is always difficult to adjudicate on a counter-factual but there is understandably some public distaste with the bold assertion that these reluctant recipients of taxpayer assistance received no benefit from the massive government programs that were put in place to counter the tumultuous conditions in financial markets in the second half of 2008. When bubbles burst and crashes occur there are very substantial external costs involved in cleaning up the messes. It will be argued later that for an individual bank to turn a blind eye to these externalities is akin to a chemical company failing to pay for the environmental damage caused by dumping pollutants into its nearby rivers.

Preservation of the private gain/socialized losses asymmetry ultimately hinges on the notion of protecting creditors – the *stickiness of debt*. The entire financial system revolves around the notion that while all other variables, especially equity, should be encouraged to vary – with or without the efficacy of price discovery and market clearing forces – there should be constancy and certainty with respect to most debt financing – including mortgage debt and, to a large extent, sovereign and corporate IOUs. In a financial system where uncertainty is omnipresent it is remarkable that there is almost total deference to creditors and bond-holders in preserving the fixed value of their claims, and an unwillingness to allow it to fluctuate as does the value of almost all other financial instruments.

The calculation seems to be that whereas the public may well be very critical and opposed to transferring private liabilities to the public balance sheet, the financial establishment would be even more hostile to a collapse in the banking system and the interlocking contractual claims that underlie indentures, loan agreements (mortgages), and swap arrangements. The reasoning seems to proceed along the following lines. It might be argued that there is no obvious sense in which bailouts violate statutory cornerstones – raising the debt ceiling has resulted in Congressional gridlock in the US but there is no constitutional transgression *per se* in expanding the balance sheet of the public authorities – however to unpick indentures, swaps, mortgage agreements etc. would undermine the very fabric which binds a society/economy together by undermining the rule of law.

Why did the US government pay out 100% on AIG's contractual promises? The answer is probably not one for which it would be easy to find a consensus view. The argument has been made that it was important for the US government to honor the promises and commitments made by AIG to its counter-parties in order that the integrity of the legal and contractual framework at the heart of financial transactions is fully maintained.

An alternative, and some might say, more cynical viewpoint is that Henry Paulson, the Treasury Secretary at the time when a negotiated settlement reducing the payout by the government that had taken over AIG could have been reached, had a conflict of interest with respect to his former employer Goldman Sachs who was one of the main beneficiaries of the 100% payout. [36]

The main thrust of this book is not polemical but sometimes it is good to give an airing to alternative and radical viewpoints as they help in clarifying what is often seen as beyond discussion. Following the calamities of 2008 it would seem that the "official" view and the revisionist rhetoric alluded to just now, should be subjected to very critical scrutiny so that we might learn worthwhile lessons from mistakes made in the past. When one is increasingly required to think the unthinkable with regard to the way that the rolling financial crisis has evolved since 2008, the foundations of financial capitalism should be open to honest debate.

One of the deeply held foundations that has been challenged, but still by a small minority of economists, relates to the almost sacrosanct manner in which providers of debt financing must have their financial claims protected at almost any cost. Apart from the manner in which the AIG payout was conducted as exemplifying this predilection, there is the more general point that unlike most players in the financial markets who win sometimes and lose sometimes, it seems to be accepted that debt holders should never be on the losing side.

Another way of expressing this asymmetry between providers of equity financing and those investors that buy bonds or banks that lend money so that people can buy houses or companies can buy capital assets, is to consider what can be called the "stickiness" of debt.

Macro-economic theory is quite preoccupied with the stickiness of wages and other rigidities which inhibit the ability of markets to *clear*, but the rigid and unbending liabilities of the borrower (or the assets for the debt holder) are an all pervasive stickiness to the macro economy and financial system. Some would argue that this stickiness is the single most important obstacle to a clearing, in the market sense of that term, of the detritus left over from the GFC.

As an example of the attempt to put the issue of the stickiness of debt into the realm of economic discourse the following comes from one of the more outspoken and articulate critics of economic orthodoxy. [37] Steve Waldman raises the following question in regard to this issue:

> Here's my question. Looking forward to the next thirty years, after we have decisively defeated wage rigidity by ensuring that the unemployed are numerous and miserable, don't you think we should devote just a bit of our attention to tackling that other sticky price?... perhaps we should think about the bargaining power of creditors as well, so that if we get ourselves into a pickle where the "cost structure" of honoring debts is high, we have technocratic and politically acceptable means of managing the burden of loan contracts just as we've developed mechanisms to control wages.
>
> To "unstick" the price of debt really means to resolve a mismatch between the asset and liability side of the swap. If assets values have depreciated, you can do that two ways:
>
> 1. you can write down the debt;
> 2. you can somehow cause the asset values to reflate.

Waldman makes the point that bailouts are often intended to reflate asset values and rejuvenate the "animal spirits." At least at the time of writing they seem not to have been too successful in regard to the latter. Moreover, "bailouts tend to unstick some peoples' debt and not others: the government picks winners and losers. Bailouts destroy incentives to choose assets well and maintain or improve their value. This raises the classical question posed by Walter Bagehot, Keynes and others regarding moral hazard – why should one be financially prudent, as long as one holds assets that will be bailed out?" Once again the matter of the external costs of financial crashes raises its head. As Waldman also observes this is particularly pointed as "focused bailouts are often targeted towards those 'in the most pain' — exactly the people who were the worst choosers and stewards of assets *ex ante*."

Waldman's questions are well put, and there are echoes of exactly the same desire to encourage an open dialogue about the stickiness of debt in the writing of Steve Keen, professor of Economics at the University of Western Sydney, who engaged in a lively war of words in the blogosphere with Nobel prize winner Paul Krugman in the spring of 2012 and who has made a personal campaign of calling for a "debt jubilee." [38]

However the calls for debt write-downs and the "unsticking" of debt values have fallen on deaf ears amongst policy makers. Rather the tacit assumption by central bankers and policy makers is that there is a systemically vital need to prolong the Minskyesque ponzi financing of the debt overhang from the GFC, via continuing enlargement of the public sector balance sheet. The unspoken and somewhat hidden agenda (it is getting much harder to keep agendas hidden in the age of ubiquitous blogs and Twitter) behind ongoing bailouts and rescue programs is that if the can is kicked down the road for long enough then reflation will ultimately kick in and the animal spirits will be rejuvenated. For now, at least in mid-2012, policy makers have to hope that we are still in the convalescence phase of a burst debt bubble, and programs such as QE, LTRO, and ZIRP for as far as the eye can see should ultimately mitigate deflation and restore asset valuations towards their former elevated values. One of the critical questions remains: Even when (if) such valuations are restored will these values have been restored on a nominal or a real basis? In other words might real estate prices return to their previously lofty values but homeowners are confronted with $10 per gallon for gasoline and £10 for a bar of chocolate?

The real systemic risk to the ponzi financing programs being undertaken by all G10 economies is what might happen with the apparently endless saga of Eurozone bailouts. At present the ECB remains transparent about the nature of its financing of Member States, but such transparency could ultimately become the weak link in the global daisy chain. The reason to presume that this weak link could eventually snap is that the underlying framework of the EZ is one of *several but not joint responsibility*. This characteristic of the legal framework of the EZ will be the subject of Chapter 11 so will not be elaborated further at this stage.

In a truly federal system such as that in the USA or for an economy which is autonomous (i.e. it can print its own currency) such as the non EZ European economies and Japan, there will, during critical episodes, when the economy is highly stressed and in risk of systemic crisis, be a "circling of the wagons" to obfuscate the fact that the emperor might not have a full set of clothes. However in the case of a looser structure such as that of the EZ where the separate members of the currency union want to preserve *pro rata* obligations towards the liabilities incurred by other members, the audit trails for a disentanglement of collective liabilities will have to be preserved. In such circumstances the wagons won't be able to complete a full circle and the emperor's humble wardrobe is in danger of coming into full view. Without joint responsibility for all EZ liabilities, which Germany seems desperately keen to preserve, the Bundesbank and Bundestag will also be very keen to ensure that all of the financing operations conducted on behalf of the EZ Member States remain fully transparent – how else would it be possible to continue to insist that they are only liable for their pro-rated share? Full transparency is often to be admired, but as the opening sentence to this chapter suggested there are reasons why diversionary tactics have been employed to keep unsettling and untidy facts from public attention.

So the really crucial question becomes who might be willing to carry out a full blown bail-out of the EZ, one that could see Spain and Italy needing to be rescued? Will it be Germany?

If not then who else will be the counter-party of last resort? Would not a cascading of debt dominoes as numerous contractual claims burst asunder wreak systemic breakdown? The risks of the Eurozone disintegrating are likely to remain long-lived and the system threatening risks are likely to see a prolongation of the kind of post-GFC investor demeanor which is well characterized as the *bipolar switching between behavior which is either risk on or risk off.* In a nutshell the thesis of this book is that the post-traumatic stress of the GFC, and the ongoing threats of an even larger systemic liquidity breakdown looming on the horizon, are the background conditions which have led to a mode of investor behavior which can be characterized, at one level, as risk on/risk off, and at another level, in a theme which is to be developed, as bipolar.

At the time of writing the deteriorating situation with regard to Spain's financial position prompted a remarkably candid outburst from Spain's finance minister in which he likened Europe to the Titanic and Spain to a seriously ill patient undergoing critical surgery. [39] Although events are moving fast in the Eurozone crisis, and there is a risk in dwelling too much on the day-to-day news flow, that quotations could easily be outmoded by the time this book is published and read, the following comments from the Spanish finance minster are well worth repeating for their poignancy:

> "This is like the Titanic," he told state radio. "If there's a sinking here, even the first-class passengers drown."
>
> "If the banks are loaded down with doubtful assets on their balance sheets, and if the only safe thing they can do is buy sovereign bonds, then there is virtually no new credit for the private sector. Then the economy's seized up and that strangles the banks again, because the people becoming unemployed don't pay their debts."

Financial contagion brings with it nonlinear dynamics which is why, beyond a certain tipping point, the deterioration in the Spanish economy (and other countries not yet acknowledged to be distressed), coupled with accelerating increases in Spanish bond yields could quickly start to resemble those of previously distressed borrowers ranging from Lehman Bros to Argentina. The above remarks underscore the increasing fragility of the great European project, and, prompt the statement that – to provide the flavor to another major theme of what lies ahead, dilemmas which pessimists claim are irresolvable and I believe are going to be quite threatening – *if one wants to save the single currency and the Eurozone one wouldn't start from where we are now.*

ENDNOTES

1. J. M. Keynes, *The General Theory of Employment, Interest and Money* (BN Publishing 2008) ch 12.
2. *Risk versus Uncertainty: Frank Knight's 'Brute' Facts of Economic Life*, by William Janeway. Social Science Research Council (19 October 2005).
3. An example of the assumption that low-cost liquidity can be considered as a "given" in financial markets can be found in Standard & Poor's, *The Leveraging Of America: Corporate Financial Policies Evolve Toward The More Aggressive Standard & Poor's*, October 2007. The report is available at: http://mountainmentorsassociates.com/files/Aggressive_Corporate_Finance_Polices_S_P_Nov07.pdf.

4. International Monetary Fund, *Global Financial Stability Report: Durable Financial Stability: Getting There from Here*, April 2011, http://www.imf.org/external/pubs/ft/gfsr/2011/01/index.htm.
5. Maturity transformation is discussed at length in Chapter 14. *Leverage, maturity transformation and financial stability: challenges beyond Basel III, a* presentation at the London Cass Business School by Adair Turner, March 16, 2011:

> Maturity transformation is a key function of the financial system, enabling non-financial agents – corporates and households – to hold longer-term financial liabilities than assets.

   http://www.fsa.gov.uk/pubs/speeches/031611_at.pdf.
6. The following extracts are from Lewis E. Lehrman, *The Nixon Shock Heard 'Round the World, Wall Street Journal*, August 15, 2011:

> On the afternoon of Friday, Aug. 13, 1971, high-ranking White House and Treasury Department officials gathered secretly in President Richard Nixon's lodge at Camp David ... Nixon and Safire put together a speech to be televised Sunday night. It had taken only a few hours during that August 1971 weekend for Nixon to decide to sever the nation's last tenuous link to the historic American gold standard, a monetary standard that had been the constitutional bedrock (Article I, Sections 8 and 10) of the American dollar and of America's economic prosperity for much of the previous two centuries.

> At least one Camp David participant, Paul Volcker, regretted what transpired that weekend. The "Nixon Shock" was followed by a decade of one of the worst inflations of American history and the most stagnant economy since the Great Depression. The price of gold rose to $800 from $35.

   http://online.wsj.com/article/SB10001424053111904007304576494073418802358.html.
7. Press release from Goldman Sachs, August 13, 2007, http://www.goldmansachs.com/media-relations/press-releases/archived/2007/2007-08-13.html
8. More scathing criticism of the mistaken use of the normal distribution in the analysis of asset returns is found in many places and especially in the work of Nicholas Taleb. See for example the following: Nassim Nicholas Taleb, *The Black Swan: Second Edition: The Impact of the Highly Improbable*: With a new section "On Robustness and Fragility" (Random House Paperbacks, 2nd edn, May 2010); *Fooled by Randomness: The Hidden Role of Chance in Life and in the Markets* (Random House; 2nd updated edn, October, 2008).
9. Bank of England tries to stop a run on mortgage bank, ABC News, http://abcnews.go.com/Business/story?id=3609705&page=2.
10. The court of King Mervyn, *Financial Times*, May 5, 2012, http://www.ft.com/cms/s/2/f853d068-94b7-11e1-bb0d-00144feab49a.html#axzz1udaalwlu.
11. Findings regarding the market events of May 6, 2010
    Report of the staffs of the CFTC and SEC to the Joint Advisory Committee on Emerging Regulatory issues, September 30, 2010. Available at: http://www.cftc.gov/ucm/groups/public/@otherif/documents/ifdocs/staff-findings050610.pdf.
12. Andrew G. Haldane, *Financial arms races*, April 14, 2012. Speech by Mr Andrew G. Haldane, Executive Director, Financial Stability, Bank of England, at the Institute for New Economic Thinking, Berlin, 14 April 2012, http://www.bis.org/review/r120426a.pdf.
13. Barclays Capital Equity Research, *U.S. Equity Quantitative Strategies*, August 4, 2010. This report is no longer available online.
14. Grahame Wearden, Swiss bid to peg "safe haven" franc to the euro stuns currency traders, *The Guardian*, September 6, 2011:

> The Swiss National Bank in effect devalued the franc, pledging to buy "unlimited quantities" of foreign currencies to force down its value. The SNB warned that it would no longer allow one Swiss franc to be

worth more than €0.83 – equivalent to SFr1.20 to the euro – having watched the two currencies move closer to parity as Switzerland became a "safe haven" from the ravages of the eurozone crisis.

15. *Dark Pools Win Record Stock Volume As NYSE Trading Slows To 1990s Levels*, Bloomberg, March 1, 2012:

    Dark pools got a larger piece of a shrinking pie. Trading at the New York Stock Exchange has declined to the lowest level since 1999, with the average volume over the 50 days ended Feb. 28 slowing to 789.5 million shares, according to data compiled by Bloomberg. The 50-day average for all exchange-listed securities, including transactions on dark pools, fell to 6.62 billion shares on Feb. 28, the lowest in Bloomberg data going back to June 2008.

    http://www.bloomberg.com/news/2012-03-01/dark-pools-capture-record-share-of-declining-u-s-equity-volume.html.
16. The following reference to comments from CFTC Commissioner on the contribution to liquidity appears at the website for Themis Trading:

    CFTC commissioner Bart Chilton is not usually shy about telling the investment world his opinions about high frequency trading. He has coined the term "cheetah" traders when referring to HFT. In this must watch Bloomberg television interview , Chilton holds nothing back:

    "Technology in markets isn't always what it's cracked up to be. As regulators, we need to take a step back and say "Is there more that we need to be doing?"

    "There are 160 million financial transactions per day around the globe. And its these traders, that I call "cheetah traders", that are just trying to scoop up dollars in milliseconds. I'm not saying they're bad, but they're new to the market and there are bound to be problems. They are not even required to be registered at the SEC and CFTC."

    "The claim from these cheetah traders, the high frequency traders, is they add liquidity and of course, they do because somebody is on the other side of those trades. But it is fleeting liquidity."

    "Are they adding long term liquidity, deep liquidity, that helps markets? I question it."

    http://blog.themistrading.com/page/3/.
17. An interesting and readable account regarding the nature of HFT activity and also its contributions to the Flash Crash can be found in Michael Pelz, Inside the Machine: A Journey into the World of High-Frequency Trading, *Institutional Investor*, May 5, 2012:

    Under Reg NMS, exchanges were given the ability to "flash" marketable orders electronically for a split second to some professional traders before they are displayed to the broad public.

    http://www.institutionalinvestor.com/Popups/PrintArticle.aspx?ArticleID=2593339.

    Themis Trading have been frequent critics of HFT algorithms and have the following quotation at their website from Berkshire Hathaway's Charlie Munger:

    Take the rapid fire trading by the computer geniuses ... those people have all the social utility of a bunch of rats admitted to the granary. I never would have allowed the rats to get in the granary. I don't want the brilliant young men of America being rats in someone else's granary. That's not the right way to run the Republic, and if you let me write the law, that wouldn't happen. If we changed the incentives, a lot of this regrettable behavior would go away.

    There would be less gambling and productive investment and more long term thinking and less of short-term trading frenzy. We do a lot of things that are literally insane. Once you allow this wrong culture to be entrenched and be remunerative, you create political power that protects activities that are regrettable. *What good is it doing civilization to have people "clipping" money through computer algorithms that work a lot like legalized front-running of orders? Why has the situation gone on as long as it has? Both parties are getting a lot of donations from these people.*

    http://blog.themistrading.com/munger-strong-leadership/.

18. See endnote 8 above for references to the work of Nicholas Taleb.
19. The Gaussian distribution model, named after the German mathematician, Friedrich Gauss, is just another term for the normal distribution which is typified by the bell shaped curve which represents a probability density function. Many variables in the natural world can be modeled using the normal distribution but asset returns are not normally distributed. Also see endnote 8.
20. *New Normal Investing: Is the (Fat) Tail Wagging Your Portfolio?* Credit Suisse Asset Management White Paper, April 2012, https://www.credit-suisse.com/asset_management/downloads/marketing/new_normal_investing_white_paper_042012.pdf.
21. Martin Wolf, The journey towards becoming Japan, *Financial Times*, May 12, 2012, http://blogs.ft.com/martin-wolf-exchange/2012/05/12/the-journey-towards-becoming-japan/.
22. The following chart showing Debt Issuance by the Japanese government and JGB yields comes from a JP Morgan report entitled *Japan's Debt Trap: Who's in the Trap?*

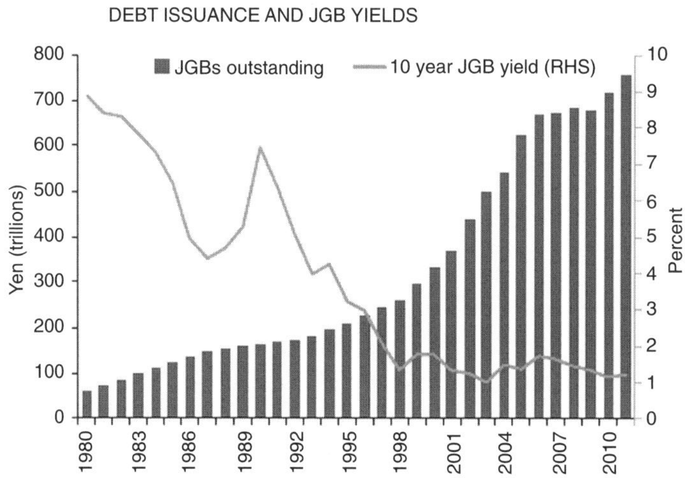

Japanese government debt issuance and JGB yields
Source: JP Morgan Research Report – Japan's Debt Trap: Who's in the Trap?
Notes: The data for JGBs outstanding is as of March (i.e. the fiscal year-end) while that for JGB yield is the yearly average of each month-end value except the figure for the year 2011, which uses the average through April.

http://www.jpmorgan.com/cm/BlobServer?blobkey=id&blobwhere=1158636672388&blobheader=application%2Fpdf&blobcol=urldata&blobtable=MungoBlobs.

23. See the discussion of vendor financing in Chapter 10.
24. See endnote 8.
25. According to Wikipedia "the average height for adult men in the United States is about 70", with a standard deviation of around 3". This means that most men (about 68%, assuming a normal distribution) have a height within 3" of the mean (67"–73") – one standard deviation – and almost all men (about 95%) have a height within 6" of the mean (64"–76") – two standard deviations." http://en.wikipedia.org/wiki/Standard_deviation.
26. Price discontinuities or gaps are discussed in Clive Corcoran, *Long/Short Market Dynamics* (John Wiley & Sons, 2007) ch 7.

27. Portfolio drawdowns are a far better reflection of the investment risks encountered during a systemic liquidity crisis than the notion of a tail risk loss. A drawdown measures the extent to which the portfolio has declined from a previous "high water mark" for the portfolio, i.e. when the account equity had reached a maximum. The maximum drawdown is a measure of the largest drop from the highest water mark to the deepest trough experienced by an investor.
28. PIMCO offers a variety of "off the shelf" products to provide tail risk protection. An insight into these products and the rationale behind them is provided in the following article from the *Economist*: Fat-tail Attraction: Investors' interest in hedging tail risk is growing, March 24, 2011, http://www.economist.com/node/18443412.
29. Investors cast doubt on "end of world" hedge strategies, Reuters, June 22, 2012, http://uk.reuters.com/article/2012/06/22/uk-hedgefunds-gaim-tail-idUKLNE85L00920120622.
30. The influence of uniformitarianism in intellectual history is discussed in *Long/Short Market Dynamics* – see endnote 26:

    > There have been several advocates of gradualism amongst the more prominent are two seminal writers and thinkers of the 19th century, Darwin and Lyell. The views of Charles Darwin are too widely known for there to be much discussion except to note the very general point that, in his view, the evolution of life forms took place gradually in conjunction with the logic of ecological adaptation. Less well known is the influence that the principal work of Charles Lyell, *The Principles of Geology*, had on his friend Charles Darwin.

    The proposal that a giant asteroid impact in the Yucatan peninsula was responsible for the extinction of the dinosaurs, and Wegener's theories regarding continental drift and tectonic plates were initially shunned, as they conflicted with the broad prejudice of gradual uniformitarianism.
31. Per Bak, *How Nature Works: The science of self-organized criticality* (Copernicus Books, Springer, 1999). Also a popularized treatment of the issue that large effects do not require large causes can be found in Malcolm Gladwell, *The Tipping Point* (Little, Brown and Co, 1st edn, March 2000).
32. See Bak's book in endnote 31.
33. Bak's book (cited in endnote 31) has a good discussion of this concept but in general terms the following brief definition is taken from a clearly written article in Wikipedia: "In physics, self-organized criticality is a property of dynamical systems which have a critical point as an attractor." http://en.wikipedia.org/wiki/Self-organized_criticality.
34. Remarks by Governor Ben S. Bernanke before the New York Chapter of the National Association for Business Economics, New York, October 15, 2002, http://www.federalreserve.gov/boarddocs/speeches/2002/20021015/default.htm.
35. The key work of Minsky and many of his disciples is Hyman Minsky, *Stabilizing an Unstable Economy* (McGraw-Hill, 2008).
36. Goldman Sachs defends $13-billion payment from AIG, *Los Angeles Times*, March 21, 2009.

    > The Wall Street powerhouse says money it received from the bailed-out insurer was fully justified. Critics say Goldman should have agreed to take less than it was owed.
    >
    > WASHINGTON — Beleaguered Wall Street powerhouse Goldman Sachs Group switched to offense Friday, contending that the $13 billion the firm received from bailed-out American International Group Inc. was fully justified and in fact was good for taxpayers.
    >
    > But that did little to quell the criticism that Goldman and other financial institutions should have taken less than they were owed on insurance for their risky bets on the subprime housing market.

37. *The stickiest price* from the Interfluidity blog of Steve Randy Waldman:

    > "Sticky prices" are the foundation of "Great Moderation" monetary policy, the core justification for why we have inflation stabilizing central banks. As the bedtime story (or DSGE model) goes, if *only* prices

> were perfectly flexible, markets would always clear and the great equilibrium in the sky would prevail and all would be right and well in the world. Hooray!

http://www.interfluidity.com/v2/910.html.

38. The Keen/Krugman Debate: A Summary, *Unlearning Economics*, April 3, 2012, http://unlearningeconomics.wordpress.com/2012/04/03/the-keenkrugman-debate-a-summary/.
39. Vulnerable banks under the spotlight, *Financial Times*, April 27, 2012, http://www.ft.com/cms/s/0/1a10b2ac-9080-11e1-9e2e-00144feab49a.html.

2

Cross-Sectional Asset Correlations

There is an abundance of research, compiled by investment bank research departments among others, which support the generalized statement that asset returns have become more highly correlated since the 2007/8 global financial crisis than at any other time in recent financial history. [1] As will be shown by reference to several studies the degree to which constituents of global equity indices moved in tandem with each other – one example of cross-sectional correlation – reached extraordinary levels in the summer of 2010 and also again, even more so, starting in August of 2011 and in evidence throughout much of the remainder of that year.

The nature of the increased co-movement of returns is seen not just in relation to equities but across multiple asset classes. For example the degree to which certain foreign currency pairs have become highly correlated with different global indices, commodities, and other asset sectors will be demonstrated in Chapter 5. Insights into heightened correlations can be ascertained by using various statistical and other quantitative techniques, across the full spectrum of asset markets, to observe a surprisingly large degree of inter-dependence and intriguing patterns of co-movement. Contrary to the approach taken by many research analysts who tend to confine their focus to individual securities or specific asset markets, part of the silo mindset which Gillian Tett has described in her book *Fool's Gold: The Inside Story of J.P. Morgan and How Wall St. Greed Corrupted Its Bold Dream and Created a Financial Catastrophe*, [2] there has been a noticeable trend since the global financial crisis for more analysts to use an holistic and macro market approach. The decision to adopt a macro or systemic approach can partly be explained by a realization, following the lessons learned from the collapse of such institutions as Lehman Brothers and AIG, that the global financial system is far more inter-connected and vulnerable to crises than had been fully appreciated prior to 2007.

As in many instances it becomes hard to separate cause and effect, but it will be argued that the recognition of the need for a system-wide vantage point has assisted in both providing an understanding of, and also a driving force behind, the dynamics, observable in contemporary financial markets, that result from a preponderance of global macro/top down strategies. [3] Adoption of global macro strategies, which are employed by many asset managers and hedge funds, have resulted in an increased pre-occupation with risk on/risk off asset allocations, which can sometimes be very abrupt. The motivating forces behind this increased global macro focus are one of the central themes of this book and underline the fact that the silo approach to investment management is becoming increasingly outmoded and less rewarding than it was prior to 2007/8. [4]

In this chapter it will be valuable to link up the observable fact that since 2008 asset markets have become increasingly correlated with other important phenomena of the post-GFC financial landscape. Numerous regulatory and legislative initiatives are continuing to impact the financial services industry. Increased capital adequacy standards, required under Basel III, and a greater focus on macro-prudential issues, often instigated by central banks and encouraged by the Bank for International Settlements (BIS), can be directly attributed to the concerns which linger about the possibility of further systemic crises. [5] There have been ongoing changes to the micro-structure of markets, which although they were under way before the crisis, have seen a massive transfer of business away from traditional securities exchanges to a variety of trading platforms. Algorithmic trading activity is now dominant in the trading of equities, futures, and even foreign exchange. [6] Despite concerns about new risks associated with HFT algorithms there appears to have been an implicit trade-off by the owners of the major exchanges and their regulators, which is that these risks may have to be tolerated in order to maintain healthy market liquidity following the 2008 crisis. The rationale for this trade-off is further enhanced by the fact that, at the time of writing, "animal spirits" remain subdued, retail trading and investment activity is almost non-existent, and institutional trading volumes are diminishing as will be illustrated further in Chapter 3.

The need for liquidity provisioning, which HFT operations can supply to markets, even if it is sometimes disparagingly referred to as algorithmic churn, is a paramount concern for market regulators when there is a deficiency in real market depth provided by robust institutional participation. I would suggest that it is the recollection of the complete breakdown in liquidity which arose in 2008, and the need to avoid those conditions again, which has been a tenaciously held counterpoint in the positioning of regulators to those criticisms, expressed by many, that markets are no longer a level playing field for all participants.

Andrew Haldane, Executive Director of Financial Stability at the Bank of England, is one of the more astute observers of the financial landscape, and he has suggested [7] that there is an *arms race* being conducted by large hedge funds and investment banks in regard to their day-to-day trading activities. The Cold War-like arms race is being waged in terms of access to ever more powerful computing platforms with super fast processors and lightning speed executions. A graphic from Haldane's presentation to the INET Conference in Berlin in April 2012, and which is shown in Figure 2.1, illustrates not only the dramatic increases in execution speeds but also highlights the much increased incidence of order cancellations, another consequence of the proliferation of HFT trading (about which much more later), and which can contribute to occasional market mayhem, which is the much greater percentage of orders that are "flashed" on trading platforms and then rapidly cancelled. There will be a detailed examination of HFT trading and the event which came to be known as the Flash Crash in Chapter 8.

The race to zero

Year	Estimated trade execution speed
1970s	Around 10 minutes
1990s	Around 2 minutes
Today	Around 250 microseconds

Order cancellations

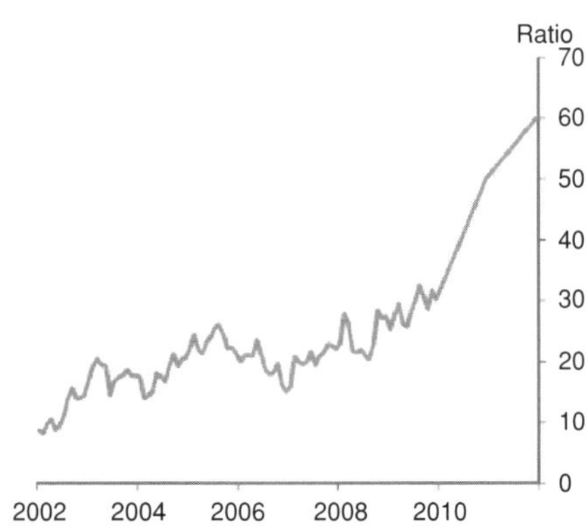

Figure 2.1 Speed races – algorithmic execution times
Source: Haldane, A G (2012), "Financial Arms Races".

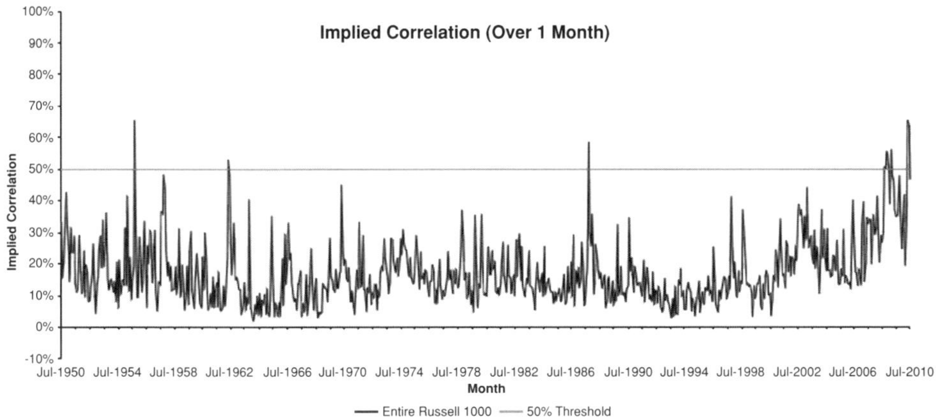

Figure 2.2 Cross-sectional correlation analysis of Russell 1000 July 2010
Source: Barclays Capital U.S. Equity Quantitative Strategies, August 4, 2010.
Note: Past performance is no guarantee of future performance.

A by-product of the perception that there is no longer a level playing field and that HFT activity contributes to increased systemic liquidity risk from events like the Flash Crash of May 6, 2010, has undoubtedly contributed to the observable fact that retail investors are largely missing in today's markets. It is also contended that smaller and medium-sized institutional trading firms as well as some large pension funds and insurance companies, unable to keep up with the technological might of very streamlined trading operations of investment banks and hedge funds, have become wary of playing alongside them in today's markets.

Substantiating the claim that there is a higher degree of cross asset correlations than has been previously observed can begin with an initial focus on equity markets, and specifically a broad cross-section of US equities. Figure 2.2 takes a long-term view on the degree to which the components of a well-known US index, the Russell 1000, have exhibited a tendency to move either in close alignment with each other or independently of each other. The Russell 1000 Index measures the performance of the large-cap segment of the US equity universe. It is a subset of the Russell 3000 Index and includes 1000 of the largest securities based on a combination of their market cap and current index membership. The index represents approximately 92% of the US market capitalization.

On the vertical scale of Figure 2.2 low readings would suggest that most of the Russell 1000 constituents are moving in a largely independent fashion, whereas higher readings would suggest that all of the one thousand stocks were moving in a much more coordinated and correlated fashion. Theoretically a reading of 100% would suggest that all stocks are moving uniformly. Limiting cases such as this are not going to be found in the real world, but rather it is the tendency of the correlation values to move above the 50% line on the chart that highlights those occasions when there are untypically strong alignments in the movements of the constituents of the index.

Barclays Capital, who published the findings from which the diagram in Figure 2.2 is taken, made the observation in August 2010 [8] that "cross-sectional correlation across all stocks in the market was at its highest level in July 2010 – measured all the way back to July 1950." Furthermore at the time when the survey was published they were able to make the claim that "[i]n June/July 2010 there have never been two months back-to-back with anything approaching these levels." Later research conducted by others, including this author, will show that in the second half of 2011 when the sovereign debt concerns within the Eurozone were reaching quite critical levels, the cross-sectional correlations exceeded even the elevated levels from the summer of 2010, shown on the right hand side of Figure 2.2.

Figure 2.2 illustrates that there have, since 1950, been sizable spikes upwards on a number of occasions. These spikes are indicative of the tendency for stock returns to become more highly correlated when the capital markets in general are undergoing stressful or critical episodes. In relatively "normal" times – as reflected in the long periods on the chart when the cross-sectional correlation is between about 10–20% – the degree to which different individual companies' shares will move together is far looser and more reflective of the idiosyncratic features of the individual stocks rather than the macro or systematic influences which cause the spikes.

Just for clarification the jump upwards in cross-sectional correlations – across the whole spectrum of equities which are included in the Russell 1000 index – can be characterized as a systematic increase in the positive correlations present in the market. A high degree of positive systematic correlation, somewhat counter-intuitively, arises because of the tendency for all of the stocks to be moving much more in alignment with each other *and the movements will predominantly be to the downside*. Increased positive correlation is a measure of the closer alignment or co-movement of two assets – it does not semantically suggest that the direction of the co-movement will be "positive" in the sense of being to the upside. Echoing back to earlier discussions, in the aftermath of the breakdown in liquidity during the GFC and the emotional scarring left in the minds of many asset managers and investors since, there has emerged a new kind of *modus operandi* in market behavior characterized by the upward slope to cross-sectional correlations shown clearly on the right hand side of Figure 2.2.

Additional research from Forward Management in San Francisco has also provided indubitable evidence that the observations just considered with respect to the Russell 1000 index can equally (as expected) be found in regard to the S&P 500. The excellent research note entitled "Managing Correlation Risk with Alternative Investments: Breaking The Back of High Correlations" by Nathan Rowader [9] contains a couple of graphics which not only illustrate the increased correlation between individual US equities and the benchmark indices, but also the evidence that international equities are becoming increasingly correlated with US equities. Heightened equity correlation is indeed a global phenomenon.

Figure 2.3 covers the period from 1995 until the end of 2011 and there is a clearly discernible trend line through the correlation trajectory which illustrates that the individual constituents of the S&P 500 are becoming less distinguishable from each other on a correlation or dispersion basis as we move from left to right of the time-line.

As the graphical display of Figure 2.3 should suggest the greater the correlation between individual components of the S&P 500 the more difficult it becomes for stock picking and attention to the idiosyncratic features in security selection to be worthwhile. The point is made in the Forward Management white paper as follows: [10]

> Unfortunately, the assumption that a diverse group of U.S. stocks will be uncorrelated with each other is no longer valid. Due to the increased use of index funds and the ease of accessing company information online, the correlations among stocks have increased dramatically. In fact, in October 2011 the median correlation between the S&P 500 Index and its constituents hit an all-time high of 0.86 (Figure 2). As a result, investors who have selected a group of S&P 500 stocks will likely match the risk and return of the index itself, without enjoying any specific diversification benefit.

The diminishing benefit of seeking out diversification opportunities (a subject which will occupy us in what follows) from stock selection becomes even more pronounced as one

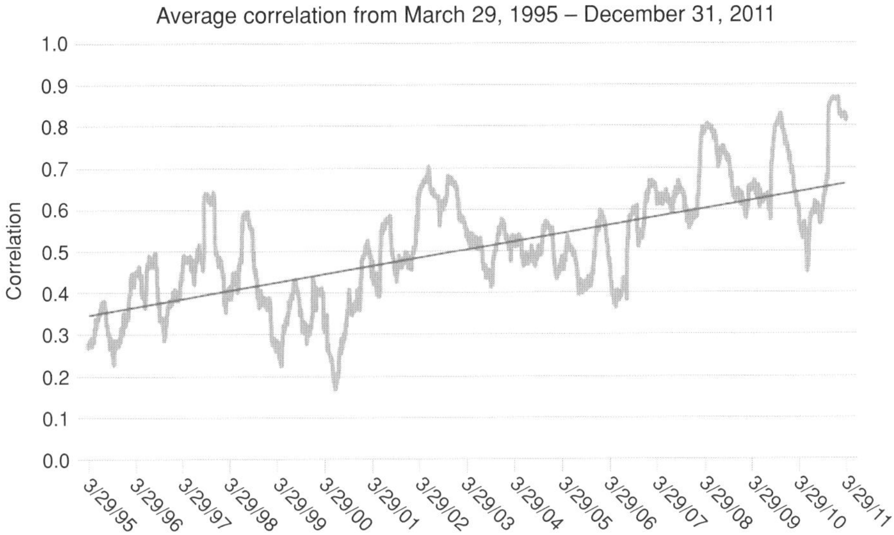

Figure 2.3 Individual S&P 500 stocks are increasingly correlated to the Index
Reprinted with permission from Forward, "Managing Correlation Risk with Alternative Investments", 2012. Copyright © 2012, Forward Management, LLC.

contemplates that coincidentally with increased correlation within US equities, there has been a greater correlation of international and US equities. This is very well illustrated in Figure 2.4.

Returning to the narrative from the Forward Management white paper, the corollary to the much enhanced difficulty of finding diversification benefits from security selection within US

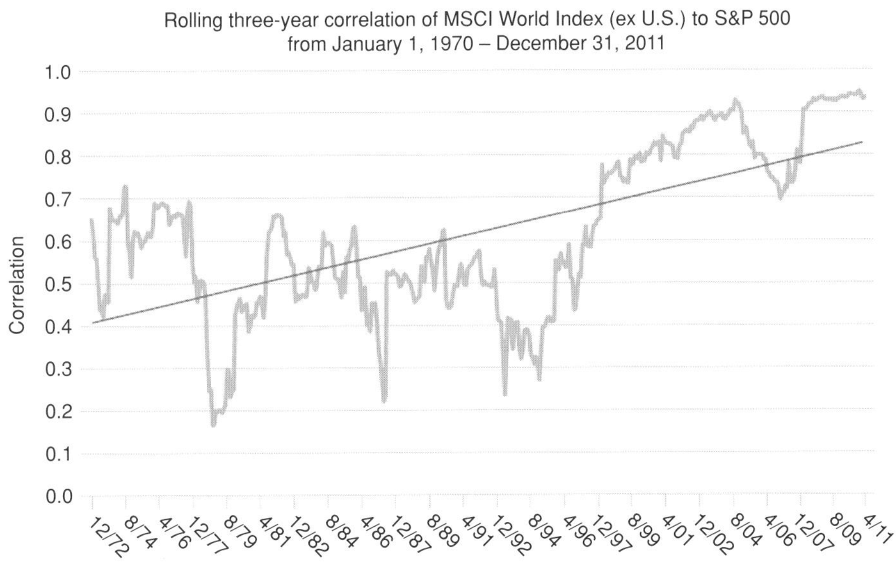

Figure 2.4 International and US stock correlations are rising
Reprinted with permission from Forward, "Managing Correlation Risk with Alternative Investments", 2012. Copyright © 2012, Forward Management, LLC.

markets is that global investing offers much less diversification than is often thought (see endnote 11):

> The benefits of [global] diversification appear to be diminishing. Due to the effects of economic globalization and the increased popularity of international investment options, in the 12-month period ending December 31, 2011, the realized correlation between U.S. and international stocks was 0.93. Moreover, this rise in correlations appears to be structural, as correlation between the two indexes has been rising steadily, and has been persistently high in the past 15 years.

Entirely in accordance with the conclusions that have been touched on in relation to increased correlations across the full spectrum of global equities, when the Barclays Capital report, discussed previously, says that stock return dispersions have been at all time lows this reflects the fact that the *risk* of holding even a large number of stocks should be primarily attributed to systematic or market-wide factors. The risks of holding individual equities within a portfolio therefore has relatively little to do with the specific or idiosyncratic factors that, under more "normal" conditions, would differentiate one stock from one another. As the Barclays Capital report emphasized "[t]he reason this matters to all stock pickers – fundamental or quantitative – is because with stock return dispersions at all-time lows, it is extraordinarily difficult to be picking stocks."

The extraordinarily low dispersion in returns or, looked at from the other side of the coin, the high degree of correlation, raises a rather pointed and awkward issue for advocates of the Capital Asset Pricing Model (CAPM) and Modern Portfolio Theory (MPT). [11] The notion expounded in those two doctrines is that a well diversified portfolio can be constructed from a sufficient number of securities (research has suggested that this should be approximately 15–20) and also securities which have relatively uncorrelated returns. The benefit to this kind of diversification is that the idiosyncratic risk of the individual components of the portfolio will be compensated for, or counter-balanced, by the fact that while some may be experiencing adverse conditions, others will be enjoying upside surprises. As a result of these benign characteristics of diversification with weakly correlated assets there will be a substantial decline in the variability of returns, or investment risk in the specific sense that it has within the CAPM.

There is an opportunity to demonstrate a core idea of this book diagrammatically, by reference to the theoretical tenets of CAPM, by comparing the relationships between systematic risk, idiosyncratic risk and the returns typically available to an investor under both normal market conditions and those available during critical market episodes. Figures 2.5 and 2.6 enable us to contrast the diversification possibilities and likely returns under these two scenarios. Additionally, and in accordance with the evidence from the cross-sectional analysis of the Russell 1000, the two scenarios depicted will throw light on the phenomenon of increased tail dependencies outlined in Chapter 1.

In Figure 2.5, which is the normal market scenario, the convex line (with the boxes) represents the idiosyncratic or unsystematic risk of a portfolio while the horizontal line (with diamonds) represents the risk which is systematic, i.e. the risk associated with being in the market and having exposure to equities in general. The left hand vertical axis of risk is typically understood to be the variability of the returns and can be thought of in percentage terms as the degree to which the returns will deviate from the mean or, in other words, disperse around an average return. The right hand vertical axis represents the scale for reading the returns trajectory on the graphic which is the line with the triangles.

As can be seen from Figure 2.5, CAPM theory suggests that as one moves along the horizontal axis adding more securities to the portfolio, at the point where one has added

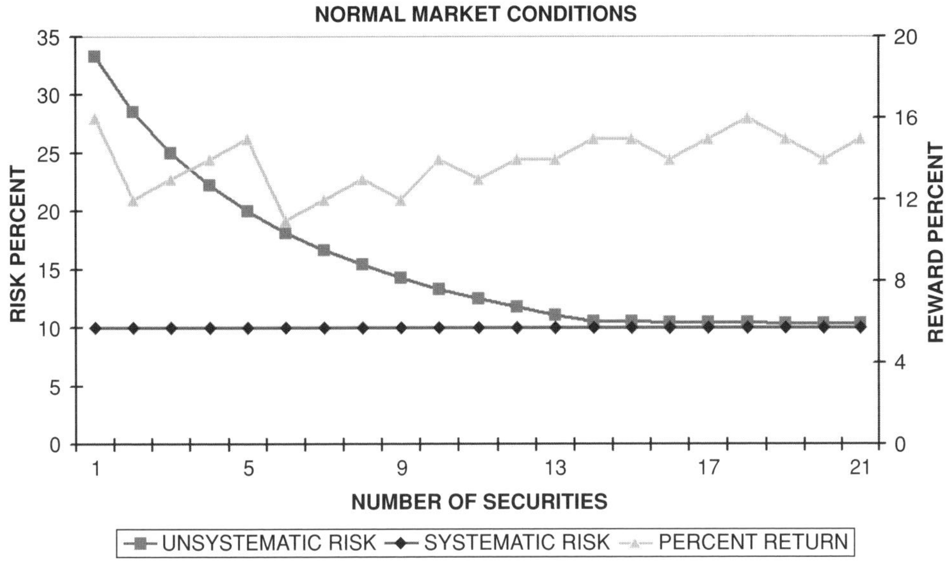

Figure 2.5 CAPM simulation for normal market conditions

around 15 securities the idiosyncratic risk will have been essentially removed and all that is left is the market or systematic risk. With 20 securities in the portfolio and when markets are behaving normally, under the hypothetical scenario depicted in Figure 2.5 the risk to the portfolio will have leveled off at 10% which is essentially the benchmark or macro risk and cannot be reduced any further by adding more securities; the portfolio has taken on the same risk as the market as a whole. The returns to the portfolio will depend upon the skills of the fund manager in selecting securities, and from further elements of the CAPM theory the fund manager will be rewarded for identifying positive alpha securities (although under the theory in the long run these positive alpha attributes should eventually disappear [12]). The hypothetical returns will also vary depending on the increments in the number of securities and in the graphic these have been assumed, under fairly benign assumptions, to have attained a level of 16% per annum when there are 20 securities.

It has already been illustrated from the previous discussion of heightened cross-sectional correlation within the Russell 1000 index that in a more highly correlated world of asset returns there will be a tendency for all assets to be moving in much closer alignment. When the great majority of stocks are moving more closely in tandem with each other it necessarily follows that the typical performance of individual equities will be such that they will also have a tendency to be "tracking" the overall market returns.

Figure 2.6 is a modification of what was seen in Figure 2.5 and is another hypothetical scenario, this time of abnormal market conditions. What is seen on the graphic, although hypothetical, is now much more in accordance with the kinds of behavior which are observable under stress scenarios. This scenario is not addressed in the exegesis of the CAPM in the finance literature and raises serious issues for that theory. The key issue is not that the correlations of asset returns are highly unstable, although that certainly is true and also not factored into the CAPM assumptions, but that they will tend to move closer towards unity when markets are stressed.

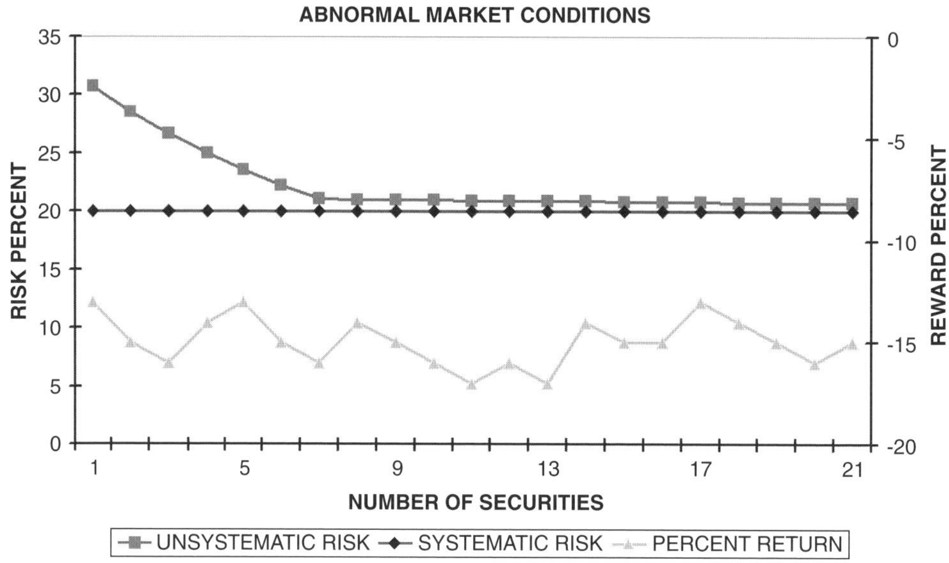

Figure 2.6 CAPM similation for extreme market conditions

The empirical evidence for much tighter correlations under stress has been previously noted [13] and is also revealed in the research on the Russell 1000 cross-sectional correlations above. Figure 2.6 illustrates that, under stress, when correlations have risen to very elevated levels the line with boxes representing unsystematic risk will have two notable differences from that seen under the more "normal" circumstances shown previously. Firstly the overall amount of risk – as indeed for the overall level of systematic risk (the line with diamonds) will be at a more elevated level; the systematic risk is here assumed to have risen to 20%. Secondly, and this is a vital difference, there will be much reduced convexity to the shape of the line for the unsystematic risk. Heightened stress will cause each security to be far more correlated with others than under normal conditions and therefore the addition of more securities to the portfolio will achieve far less benefit in terms of risk reduction through diversification. The unsystematic line will drop away quickly and begin to more or less flat line with the systematic risk even after relatively few securities have been added to the portfolio. In addition if we consider the right hand vertical axis the returns achieved at times of market stress would typically be considerably below zero. Figure 2.6 is clearly depicting that, under market stress, there is a tendency of asset correlations to move towards much higher levels and also there is a likelihood of substantial drawdowns for a portfolio – the extreme version of this was seen during the second half of 2008.

It is possible to draw together all of the characteristics displayed under the different market scenarios and summarize them as follows:

- Asset returns have fat tails.
- Correlations between asset returns are unstable and will increase during critical market episodes.
- Under normal market conditions it may be that left tail dependency across different securities itself is not seriously mis-represented by thinking of that as following an approximate

normal distribution. This is the assumption made in financial modeling as exemplified by the Gaussian copula approach in determining joint probabilities. [14]
- Left tails of a collection of assets reveal much greater dependency when markets are stressed and at these times the use of a Gaussian copula methodology will dramatically misrepresent joint outcomes.
- In essence the schematic for a vicious feedback loop from a quasi-statistical point of view is that as stress levels rise, left tail behavior becomes more prevalent, correlations tighten, this will cause left tail dependencies to rise, this in turn creates systemic liquidity concerns which will exaggerate the likelihood of extreme left tail events and increased left tail dependencies etc.

2.1 LESSONS FOR RISK MANAGEMENT

The articulation of the above schematic poses severe problems for risk management techniques which have been derived from the CAPM doctrine. In subsequent discussion it will become clearer that the elements of the vicious feedback loop outlined above fit rather well onto a much broader boom-bust dialectic or model and help us to better understand the ever present risks to systemic liquidity. More controversially they will provide a good background for a robust explanation of the risk on/risk off dynamics which have been characterized as the new paradigm of contemporary financial markets. [15]

Heightened cross-sectional correlations are, at once, both a symptom of and also a contributory factor to, increased left tail dependency, increased volatility and risk and also significantly increase the likelihood of negative returns. One consequence of this realization is that "as the movements of individual stocks increasingly coincide, the unique individual components of a stock's story tend to shrink in importance and the common and systemic (macro) factors gain in importance." Expressed in slightly different language there is a further reminder that there are rapidly diminishing returns or benefits from the study of the idiosyncratic features of individual securities. As macro-financial or systemic factors dominate a market, how a stock is exposed to those factors will become the principal determinant of that stock's return. The value of CAPM and MPT is undermined and individual security selection becomes redundant as a passive tracker fund (based on a benchmark index – such as the S&P 500, the FTSE 100 or the DAX 30) will very closely resemble the portfolio which had, under misguided assumptions, been diligently constructed on the basis of careful differentiation of the individual security's idiosyncrasies.

Figure 2.4 makes a convincing case that wealth managers need to reconsider some of the foundation stones upon which portfolio construction techniques are based. If return dispersion amongst most equities is so low and therefore diversification is becoming much harder to achieve, then trying to outperform the overall market becomes even harder to achieve for an active fund management approach. But the problems cut even deeper as further analysis will show. The schematic outlined above, instigated with respect to the work on the Russell 1000 and with reference to the CAPM which is primarily focused on equities, can also be applied when widening the scope to take in asset classes as well as equities. Evidence will be presented which shows that the tendency when markets become stressed for heightened left tail risk, increased correlations extending across multiple asset classes, and therefore heightened left tail dependency on a system-wide basis, will have profound implications for individual fund managers trying to manage risk in a portfolio. More alarmingly these profound implications extend to the global economy and culture in general, as a feral feedback loop in systemic liquidity risks has the scary limiting case of a systemic meltdown.

These topics will be discussed in greater detail throughout this book, but to set the tone for the remainder of this chapter the following points, which address the issue of why mounting asset correlations are of vital concern to individual fund managers attempting to implement sound risk management practices, were made in a report to investors by HSBC bank in January 2012. [16]

- "The rise in cross asset correlations has important implications for active, absolute return focused fund managers."
- "Crucially, the similarity in asset class behavior makes it harder to profit from relative value opportunities, as both longs and shorts are more likely to move in tandem."
- "Attempts to analyse the idiosyncrasies of specific assets may prove fruitless, as broad ranging risk on/risk off moves can overwhelm fundamental drivers of value."
- "Portfolios may easily become less diversified and more susceptible to sharp risk reversals."

2.2 CORRELATIONS AND VOLATILITY

In Chapter 1 there was an initial reference to the inter-dependence between heightened correlations and the increased volatility characteristics of financial markets in recent years, and the following section is designed to give a more substantial understanding of this pivotal inter-dependence.

Figure 2.7 is designed to demonstrate the linkage between heightened correlations amongst equity sectors – or indeed the equity market in general – and bouts of volatility. It will be worthwhile to fully explain the method followed and the meaning of the different components of this diagram as there will be a similar analytical approach taken elsewhere in this book.

The period covered in Figure 2.7 is from January 2006 until June 2008 and reflects the transition from the relatively calm equity market conditions that prevailed during the "Great

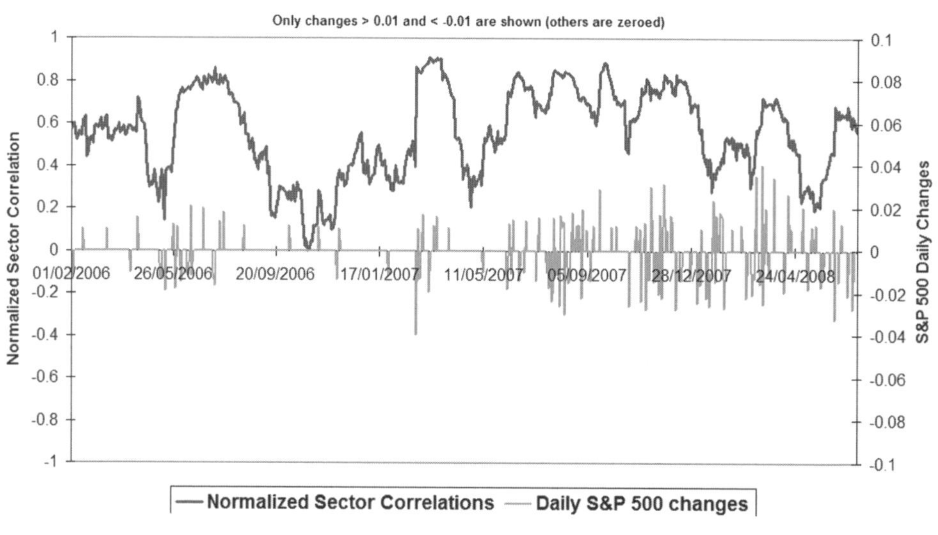

Figure 2.7 Normalized market sector correlations and daily changes in the S&P 500 2006–8

Moderation" through the initial rumblings of the sub-prime crisis in Q2/Q3 of 2007 until the period when, finally, most market participants began to get a really good view of the iceberg known as the "global financial crisis" which had been accumulating just below the surface for the previous two years (or more).

It is worth spending some time discussing the method of construction for the chart above, and the two more in a series which follow. The line on the chart in Figure 2.7 described as Normalized Sector Correlations is constructed by using a number of sector indices that "ordinarily" should not be highly correlated. The actual selection of sector indices is not critical, nor is the number of different sectors which have been used; rather the purpose is to take a broad cross-sectional look at the extent of correlations within the equity market. This differs from the earlier discussion on the Russell 1000 which are individual equities, but by examining diverse sector funds – each of which contains tens of individual securities – one gains access to a similar insight into the extent of correlation in the returns of a substantial part of the overall market. The following sectors were included in preparation for this analysis:

- SPY – S&P 500
- XLF – ETF for Financial Sector
- XLI – ETF for the Industrials
- XLY – ETF for the Consumer Discretionary
- XLP – ETF for Consumer Staples
- XLV – ETF for Health Care Sector
- XLB – ETF for Industrial Materials.

The daily returns (i.e. the percentage change from day to day) are calculated for each one of the sectors. Then the correlation between each of the sectors is calculated using a rolling 20-day lookback period. For example starting from the earliest date sampled for both XLF (call this the x variable) and XLI (and call this the y variable) the correlation cannot be calculated until there are 20 pairs of x-y returns. For that period the correlation coefficient is calculated and registered. The sampling then advances to the 21st data points and the first x-y data pair is then dropped from the calculation. Once again the correlation is registered and the process moves on to the 22nd data point dropping of the second x-y values, and so on ... this is what constitutes a rolling 20-day lookback period.

Once all cross correlations have been collected a simple aggregation or summing of the values takes place for each session; more complex methods could be used including using a square of the correlation coefficient to ensure that each value is positive. However the focus is on a simple methodology since the next step involves the normalization of all of these correlation sums for the entire period. The purpose of normalization is to cram all of the correlation sums into the interval between 0 and 1 where 0 would be the lowest sum found in the entire series and 1 the highest; intervening values are scaled according to the range between the highest and lowest observed correlation sums. A more detailed explanation of the technique for creating a normalized chart can be found here. [17]

The darker line which is positioned nearer to the top of Figure 2.7 tracks the normalized amount and the actual values can be calibrated from the left hand scale. It will be seen that there is no point on this chart where the value goes to 1 as the highest values were seen on the next time segment after the end of June 2008 which is the end point on the horizontal/time axis for Figure 2.7. The lowest point for the darker line is found in Figure 2.7 at 0 on the left hand scale and this occurs in the last quarter of 2006.

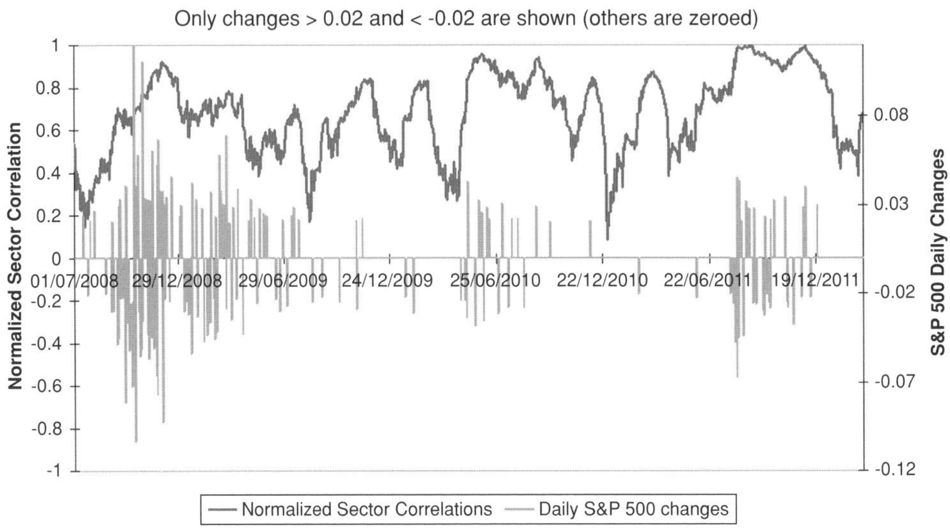

Figure 2.8 Normalized market sector correlations and daily changes in the S&P 500 2008–12

The lighter toned bars on the chart are coincidental with the dates for the darker line and show those occasions when the daily change for the S&P500 exceeded either a 1% upward move or more than a 1% downward move. All of the lesser moves have been filtered out in order to make the diagram less "noisy."

The key relationship which is revealed in this chart is the extent to which the onset of heightened sector correlations anticipates heightened volatility for the benchmark equity index. A corollary is that those periods when the degree of sector correlation is diminishing or in a declining trend also coincide with the periods when the S&P 500 is less volatile... indeed there are extended periods with no absolute moves of more than 1%.

Figure 2.8 continues from where the prior chart finished and covers the period from July 2008 until the end of March 2012. On this time segment it is possible to find the highest correlation sum values for the entire six-year period, and, somewhat surprisingly, these were not found in the second half of 2008 as might be expected, or even in the summer of 2010 as was discussed in the Barclays Capital research in relation to the Russell 1000 discussed above, but two peaks were found in the second half of 2011. The lighter colored bars have this time been filtered to exclude any daily moves in the S&P 500 which were below the higher absolute threshold amount of 2% – as the overall level of volatility prevailing during the period covered in Figure 2.8 for July 2008–March 2012 is of a higher order of magnitude than that seen in the period for January 2006–June 2008 which is reflected in Figure 2.7.

Reviewing the 2008/12 period, as depicted in Figure 2.8, there is a clearly visible and severe bout of volatility in the second half of 2008 and extending into the first quarter of 2009. Reading the lighter colored bars from the right hand vertical scale shows back to back daily moves of plus and minus 5–10% in notable clusters during much of the second half of 2008. (Volatility clustering will be discussed further in Chapter 3.)

The second highest cross-sectional sector correlations can be observed in Q2/Q3 of 2010 and are a substantial contributory part of the explanation for the Flash Crash of May 6, 2010 as will be discussed in Chapters 4 and 5. Also notable during this period was heightened intraday volatility which is not captured in Figures 2.7 and 2.8. By way of illustrating how the measure of intraday volatility in contrast to inter-day volatility can be a key financial risk indicator it is worth considering an example as follows. The S&P 500 covered an 8% intraday range on May 6, 2010, but ended up the session only 3% from the closing price of the previous session. Based just on the inter-day volatility metric there would be inadequate recognition of the enhanced intraday volatility which has also been a characteristic of many trading sessions during the period between 2008 and 2012.

Whereas some commentators might be tempted to conclude that the summer of 2010 saw a peaking of cross-sectional correlation – which was noted in the Barclays Capital research (which was published in 2010) – Figure 2.8 shows that the broad equity market became even more highly correlated in the second half of 2011. This period coincided with major stresses within the Eurozone and heightened concerns about the linkage of problems for major European banks with high exposure to the sovereign debt of the peripheral territories within the EU. [18]

Figure 2.9 takes a different perspective on the correlation and volatility connection that is displayed in the two time segments displayed in Figures 2.7 and 2.8. The data has been consolidated into a single view of the period from 2006 to spring of 2012 and the normalized correlation sum of the sectors is displayed as the darker line on the graphic, and can be scaled according to the right hand vertical axis. The columns on the chart represent a numerical count of the number of trading sessions within a ten-day moving window that there was an absolute move of more than 1%. Counts below three sessions within the ten-day window are excluded from the display.

The most notable feature of Figure 2.9 is the very close relationship between the more elevated periods of cross-sectional correlation within the sectors and the coincidental occurrences of back to back sessions where the S&P 500 is revealing greater inter-day volatility. This is also reflected in the low readings for the cross-sectional correlation which coincide with those periods where there are no columns visible on the diagram. Also the two periods where the columns are most densely packed are the extended period covering the second half of 2008

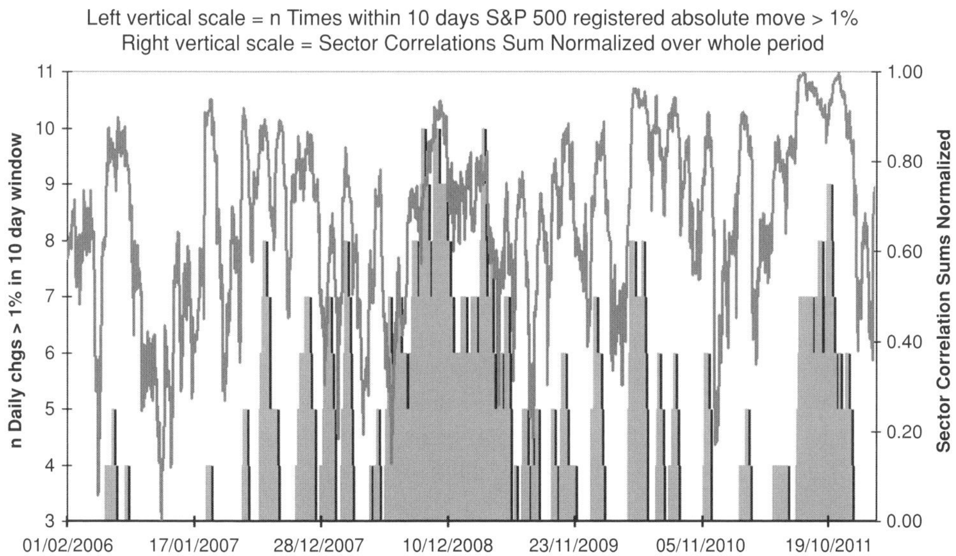

Figure 2.9 Normalized market sector correlations and volatility 2006–12

through to the third quarter of 2009 and also, as pointed out in the preceding discussion, the third and fourth quarters of 2011 where the cross-sectional correlations were at the most elevated levels for the period covered.

At the time of writing and preparation of Figure 2.9 it is possible to discern a rather notable decline in the degree of correlation and associated volatility at the end of 2011 and early part of 2012 which could be attributed to the perceived alleviation of EZ sovereign funding problems resulting from the two LTRO operations conducted by the ECB in November 2011 and February 2012. However, as the large degree of fluctuations in the darker line suggest it would seem highly likely that any subsidence of the correlations is likely to prove temporary. The crucial question which many asset managers would like answered is in the form of "how long lived is this tendency of persistent and bouts of extreme heightened cross-sectional correlation likely to be?" Alternatively one could ask: Have we entered a period where the "new normal" is going to be one where the back and forth rotation between risk on assets all moving together on some occasions followed by all risk off assets moving together at other times is to be expected?

In attempting to answer this quite crucial question it will be necessary to understand more of the motivation between what has been christened as the new risk on/risk off paradigm in financial markets. It will be useful to examine from a macro-economic perspective the nature of the 2008 crash, the dynamics of bubbles and their inevitable collapses, and other reasons to believe that we may have entered a period of rolling crises. In addition to exploring the nature of a balance sheet recession to use the appropriate terminology of Richard Koo, [19] other factors to consider (but not in great depth) will be to dig deeper into the possibility of systemically threatening consequences from a disintegration of the Eurozone, the risks associated with a hard landing for the Chinese economy, and the ongoing risks of over indebtedness not only by the household sectors in many of the "developed" nations but also by sovereigns across the globe. Tangentially we also need to consider some demographic issues and also in particular there will be a focus on the disappearance of income for a sizable constituency in the economies of the developed world. The relative impoverishment of middle class consumers throughout Europe and North America will, in the foreseeable future, until replaced by more energetic consumption patterns from the emerging middle classes in the developing nations, act as a major drag on global economic growth.

From the point of view of investment management a lot hinges on whether the 2008 crisis was a watershed event following which new rules apply and a new normal is to be expected. It is dangerous to say that this time is different as there are plenty of instances where this has turned out to be a myopic error which seems so clearly a mistaken and naïve assumption in the fullness of time. The voluminous study by Kenneth Rogoff and Carmen Reinhart in a book which bears that motif of *This Time is Different: Eight Centuries of Financial Folly* [20] as its title, reminds us that public and private debt problems have been recurrent themes throughout financial history, and that there is often a fallacy in thinking that the current situation is so fraught with problems that an entirely new mode of thinking about solutions is required.

An equally misguided fallacy can be identified relating to the emergence of economic "booms" where they have been launched from erroneous assumptions that the world has been so transformed – for example by the internet, or in earlier history by the railways or the development of computers – that new rules apply and this time is different. The evidence suggests that the bust of the Nasdaq and dot com stocks which took place in 2000/1 and which will be discussed further in what follows, was the result of exactly the "this time is different" thinking based on euphoria about the internet. When one is immersed in them, economic boom periods have a tendency to be so overpowering that one cannot see that they have limited lifetimes, and that inevitably more realistic expectations will return and frothy valuations will deflate as they move back towards more normal levels. The same could be said of the difficulty in stepping outside the gloominess and negative feedback loops which become prevalent during periods following the bursting of major bubbles. Just think how hard it is to remember what it feels like to be uncomfortably hot on a sweltering day when one is freezing on a windswept day in the midst of a bitter winter. It is also worth making the point that after the culmination of a boom, things will usually return to normal not in a gradual fashion but in the busts and crashes which echo the collapsing of other bubbles and manias which have punctuated our economic history. [21]

Having said all of that, and thereby providing myself with some cover from the charge of intellectual naivety, it will be a contention of this book that there are some reasons to believe that, even if it is not the case that the current economic environment is unprecedented, it certainly does seem to be the case that it has some extraordinarily daunting challenges. Even if one does not want to go so far as claiming that in many respects the contemporary financial system presents a smorgasbord of no-win scenarios – although some gloomy commentators have reached such conclusions [22] – it surely is the case that we are confronted with a series of very hard choices. These extremely difficult policy choices apply not only in the realms of finance, but also at the interface of economics and politics where it does not require a febrile imagination to conjure up some potentially very disruptive and alarming scenarios on the horizon.

The very challenging dilemmas, some of which appear on the surface to be irresolvable, are exemplified also by the difficulties in getting a sustained recovery started in much of the world, the endless kicking of cans (full of wriggly worms no doubt) down the road by politicians, the fact that unorthodox monetary policy seems to have reached its limits and that many thoughtful people are complaining that mainstream economics and financial theory seems to be fundamentally lacking in providing explanations or prescriptive policy solutions to current concerns. Some of the most striking criticisms that are made by many center on the fact that, for the senior financial executives, economic advisors, and technocrats who held sway over policy makers in the years leading up to the 2008 crisis and who still occupy similar positions of influence in its aftermath, there has been an almost complete absence of accountability or culpability. The associated critique of "crony capitalism," the mounting evidence of corruption and criminality in such cornerstone financial activities as the setting of the LIBOR interest rates, and the disproportionately large rewards enjoyed by those often perceived as least deserving, is contributing to a growing dissent and deep disaffection with the practice of modern finance.

The belief that a modern and complex economy and the financial institutions within it are manageable, and can be steered in a socially optimal fashion by clever technocrats, is now more and more appearing, to the disaffected, as nothing but an illusion at best and a malign conspiracy at worst. Lest it be thought that such criticisms amount to a sorry tale about the impending doom of modern civilization I should state my intentions quite clearly. It will be contended that many of the frustrations, anger, and concerns about the state of the world in the aftermath of the 2008 crisis have arisen as a result of the misconceived notions from mainstream finance and macro-economics about how the global economy really works. It will also be suggested that it was a fundamental error to have removed the word "political" from the study and practice of what is today called economics but which traditionally was called political economy. The concerns of finance and economics are deeply rooted in matters requiring value judgments and should be guided by reference to principles of morality. To pretend otherwise can be seen as both a side stepping of the need for an ethical perspective and an excuse to engage in the pursuit of ingenious complexity and disingenuous mystification. This book will have achieved its goal if it assists even a little in the process of demystification.

2.3 INCREASED ASSET CORRELATIONS

Amongst the most important by-products of the extreme market activity which was seen in 2008, and which has resurfaced on occasion since, are the insights that have been provided into the manner whereby the covariance of different assets converge towards unity when market conditions are especially stressful, as they were in the second half of 2008. That they do this highlights the need for precautions when extracting the statistical values – correlation coefficient, beta, alpha, variance etc. – from studying price series data. For example, to say that two assets may have a correlation coefficient of 0.6 is rather meaningless in that this value is likely to be unstable even under "normal" market conditions, and when markets begin to behave "abnormally" as they did in the latter part of 2008 and again in the second half of 2011, this value could rise dramatically. In fact, under extreme stress, there is a tendency for many instruments, even from different asset classes, to see their correlations head towards the limiting case of unity. Translating this into rather plain English, and this is well depicted in Figure 2.10, there is the documented observation that at the height of the global financial

Figure 2.10 Correlations head towards unity in October 2008

crisis of 2008 most financial instruments did all plunge together. When the direction of travel is the same for most assets – downwards – the nuanced approach to specifying correlation coefficients to five significant figures goes out of the window!

In the second half of 2008 most global equity indices plummeted in unison as is illustrated in Figure 2.10. Using a base of August 2007 the equity indices for Canada, China, Emerging Markets, and Germany had all dropped by around 50% by late October 2008. The Russian market had moved down even more dramatically registering a collapse of more than 70%. Similar charts for other regions and sectors could be shown to make the case that any notion of de-coupled markets and supposed diversification benefits from holding geographically disparate equities were rebuked by the crisis as it unfolded. The fact that asset correlations head towards unity in times of crisis needs to be more widely acknowledged by financial theorists and, more pragmatically, by asset managers relying on articles of faith derived from orthodox portfolio construction and risk management practices.

What is required is much greater attention to what happens to asset correlations at the extremes. Even more pointedly this is an exercise which involves analyzing the empirical data and measuring the extreme values from the observed data, it is not something that can be divined from theorizing about the nature of statistical distributions and probability theory. When it is observed that two previously weakly correlated variables will, under stress, exhibit a correlation coefficient close to one that should be a very strong reminder that precisely at those times when risk management should be of value it will fail to perform because of misguided and complacent reasoning from data sampling during periods when the markets are not stressed.

Fortunately, owing to the manner in which a linear regression analysis is conducted it is possible to drill down on outlier values and determine just how the variables perform within the outliers or tails of a distribution. It will be beneficial to consider an explanation of how this is possible.

Figure 2.11 shows, in a normalized fashion, the co-movement of the S&P 500 and the MSCI Emerging Markets Index for the period from late June of 2009 until mid-July of 2012. The pathways taken by each are remarkably closely aligned across the time interval until Q3, 2011 when the US index begins to noticeably outperform the EM index. However even in the second half of 2011 – a troublesome period for risk on assets arising from deepening problems within the Eurozone – both indices tracked each other directionally but the magnitude of the moves was less for the S&P 500 than for the Emerging Markets Index.

In preparing a linear regression for the S&P 500 and the MSCI Emerging Markets Index during the period shown in Figure 2.9 there are 800 pairs of data points to consider. Each one of these pairs of data points, which correspond to the daily change in the US index and the index for the emerging markets, has been plotted on a scatter graph as shown in Figure 2.12. Each of the data points is registered as a tiny diamond and its position on the graph is determined by locating exactly the coordinates on the X and Y axis which correspond to the observed returns (daily changes) of each of the two variables, i.e. the X variable, in this case the S&P 500, and the Y variable, the EM Index.

In creating this scatter graph there is no longer a temporal dimension to the series of data points – as the term suggests the separate observations will now be *scattered* across the graph solely in relation to where they occur with respect to the values on the vertical and horizontal axes. This is unlike the display of most price development data in that the horizontal axis for a scatter graph does *not* act as a timeline in any sense. The linear regression technique is not bounded by the need to preserve the historical sequencing of data points.

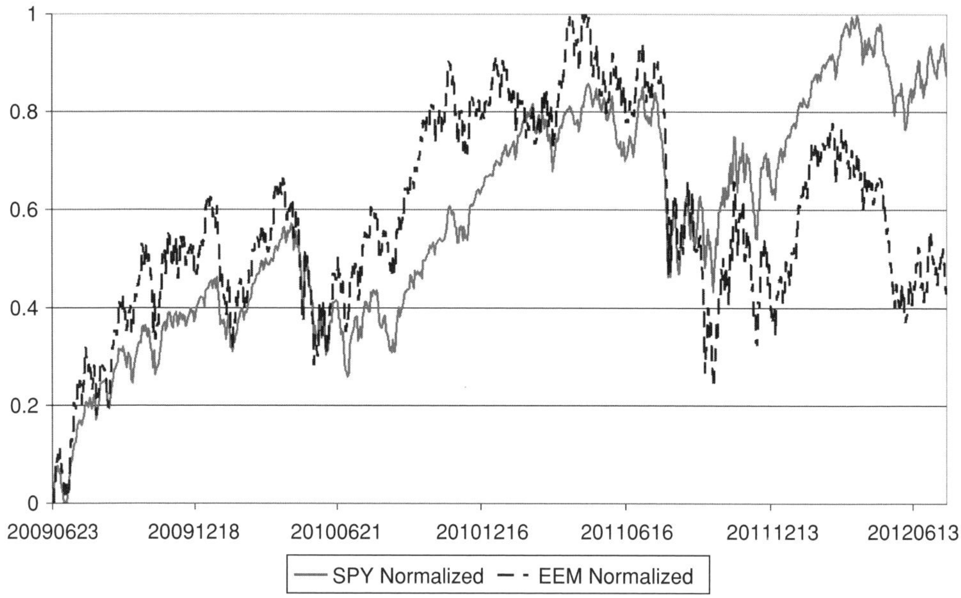

Figure 2.11 S&P 500 (SPY) and MSCI Emerging Markets (EEM) normalized mid-2009-mid 2012

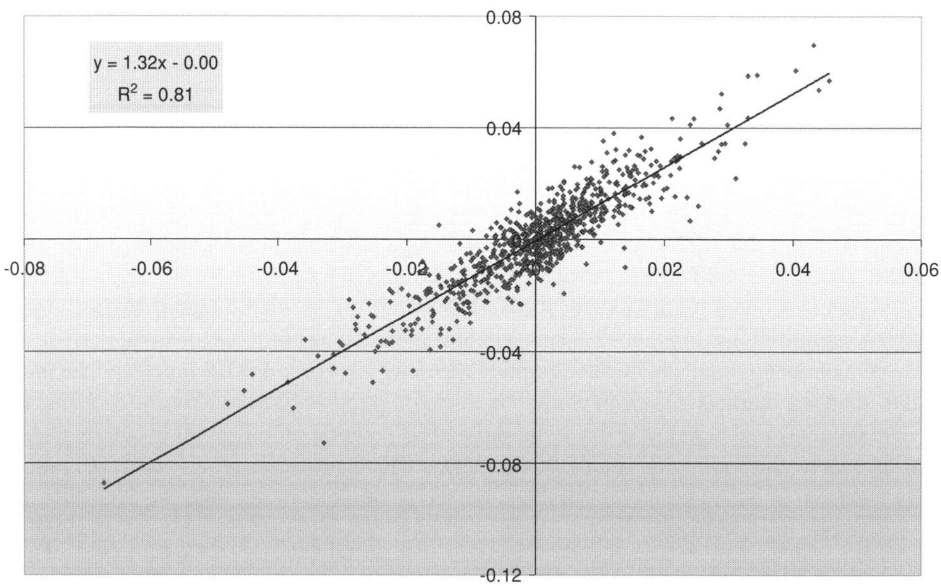

Figure 2.12 Linear regression of daily changes of SPY and EEM mid-2009–mid-2012

Once all of the 800 XY values or diamonds have been plotted, a line of best fit can be calculated and this line (shown on Figure 2.12) itself will have theoretical coordinates (i.e. it has its own notional XY values) and in essence this is the line whereby the distances from the diamonds or actual data points to the nearest coordinates of the line of best fit are at their minimal value. Where the line fits the data very well, as it does in Figure 2.12, the correlation coefficient or R value – which is calculated separately – will have a high value, and if the fit is not so good then the R value will be lower. As can be seen from the figure the R^2 value is 0.81 which means that the square root or R value is 0.9 which indicates a very strong correlation between the two indices.

Also visible on Figure 2.12 is the equation for the line of best fit which has a value of $y = 1.32x - 0.00$. This equation provides us, via the gradient of the slope of that line, which is 1.32, with the beta value for the relationship. What the beta value really conveys is the sensitivity of the dependent variable to a change in the independent variable. In the current context, the S&P 500 is considered to be the independent variable and the MSCI Emerging Markets Index is the dependent variable. So the value of 1.32 informs us that, across the whole period, the Emerging Markets index is 1.32 times more sensitive than the S&P 500. If the US index were to rise by 10% then the EM index would be expected to rise by 13% and likewise a drop of 10% for the S&P 500 would be accompanied by a drop of 13% for the MSCI Emerging Markets Index. If the linear regression were to yield a value of one for the gradient of the slope this would inform us that the two variables moved exactly in harmony with each other, with equal percentage moves being applicable to both.

The higher the R^2 value the more confident that we can be that *under normal conditions* this relationship will be useful. It also follows from the equation that if we are provided with any X value (or Y value) that we can plug that into the equation to determine the appropriate value for the other variable. Once again the degree of confidence one can have about the reliability of that prediction will depend directly on the size of the R^2 value. The very small constant value in the equation of 0.0004 (to four decimal places) can act as a guide to the alpha value for the relationship but will not be considered further in this context, although it has other applications in portfolio theory. [23]

The vital qualification of *under normal market conditions* was inserted into the previous paragraph to underscore the fact that all of the values calculated are based on taking into account all of the data points and accordingly extreme values that will have been experienced will have got lost in the mix or smoothed away. Since preserving the historical dimension is not a requirement for the linear regression technique it is possible to screen out the "normal" data and just focus on the subset of data points which will be those which occupy the tails of the distribution. Using as a simple rule of thumb the subset of 5% of data points which will have arisen in the 2 $^1/_2$% of data points in the left tail and right tail, it is possible then to recalculate new values for the correlation coefficient and beta values from a new regression based on outliers only.

2.4 STRESS REGRESSION ANALYSIS

At this point I shall introduce a technique into the discussion which will be returned to a number of times in what follows. It could either be called outlier regression analysis or stress regression analysis and it is the latter term which is the preferred one. Figure 2.13 illustrates the technique and follows on from the discussion of the preceding section. As mentioned,

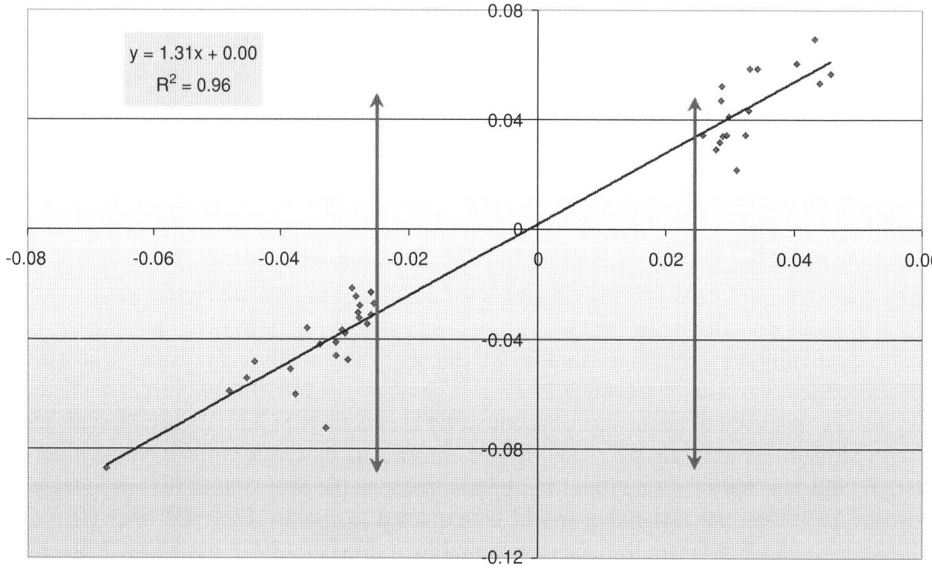

Figure 2.13 Stress regression showing only outliers for daily changes of SPY and EEM mid-2009–mid-2012

since there is no historical dimension to a linear regression, removing the bulk of the data and confining attention to the outlier values enables an inspection of how two assets are correlated only in "abnormal conditions." Of the 800 paired values displayed in Figure 2.11, 95% of them have now been removed and just the 40 outlier paired values (i.e. the 5% tail values) are displayed and used in the calculation of the appropriate R^2 and linear equation values. Within the interval on the horizontal axis between ± 2 sigmas or 2.55% in either direction, all of the values (within the two arrows) have been screened out and only the outlier values on each tail have been displayed. The benefit of this technique is that the chart, and the output which accompanies it, is now ignoring the "noisier" data in the central tendency of the distribution, and presents an opportunity to illuminate the correlation between assets when conditions are untypical and experiencing abnormal conditions.

The table below summarizes the various statistical values which arise in connection with the stress regression analysis shown in Figure 2.13. Those values which are now included in the outlier subset represent those occasions when the absolute moves by the independent variable, in this case the S&P 500 proxy SPY, exceeded a threshold amount of 2.55%.

Independent Variable: SPY Dependent Variable: EEM
Period covered from 20090623 to 20120724

Independent Variable Performance 58.50% Dependent Variable Performance 29.39%
****
OUTLIER CORRELATIONS, BETA AND RSQ VALUES
****
Outlier absolute change threshold: 2.55%
n Extreme Moves 40 percentage of data points 5.0%

Extreme Correlation Coefficient: 0.98
Correlation coefficient for whole period: 0.90

Extreme Beta: 1.31
Average Beta (based on rolling window period of size 21): 1.39
Beta for whole period: 1.32

Extreme RSQ: 0.96
Average RSQ (based on rolling window period of size 21): 0.78
RSQ for whole period: 0.81

The output from the stress regression analysis, which is outlined above, is quite revealing. Principally, it shows that the correlation coefficient for this subset of extreme values is about as close to unity as it is possible to get with an observed value of 0.98. This is higher than the 0.9 value which arose as the correlation coefficient from consideration of the whole period. The R^2 or RSQ values at the bottom of the table reflect this jump in the outliers as the RSQ for the whole period was 0.81 as shown on the Figure 2.11, whereas for the subset of outliers the RSQ value jumps to 0.96. The average RSQ for the whole period based upon calculating the R value sequentially for a rolling lookback period of 21 observations is 0.78 which is not dissimilar, in this instance, to the single observation for the whole period. An examination of the beta values indicates that this value remains fairly constant on both the normal case analysis and the extreme case analysis.

What can be learned from this approach? Firstly, the analysis demonstrates the fact that the correlation coefficient is not only unstable when measured across different time spans, but more importantly, that when confining examination to how asset correlations will perform under stress the value will exhibit a tendency of jumping towards unity. It should be emphasized that this is not the case with all pairs of assets. This brings up the second and most relevant application of the stress analysis methodology which is to address the task of anticipating and mitigating tail risk in the management of portfolios. I would suggest that the most useful consequences of this framework for analysis – from the point of view of seeking out relative diversification even under market stress – is to look for pairs of assets where there is far less tendency for there to be a significant jump in correlation under stress. For example, there is very little difference between the observed correlation between the S&P 500 and spot gold prices whether the market is or is not stressed. Other interesting results will be discussed in later sections of the book.

By undertaking a stress regression analysis, in the manner just outlined, for a wide variety of pairs of assets it becomes possible to identify components of a portfolio which are not just weakly correlated under normal market conditions but remain relatively weakly correlated even during times of stress. This task becomes even more necessary when contemporary markets, inherently, have stronger co-movement characteristics. Not only are the co-movements more tightly coupled but there are strongly associated moves in one group of assets which are categorized as "risk on" and similarly strongly associated moves within a separate group of assets which can be categorized as "risk off." This characteristic is very well illustrated in a useful report published by HSBC Global Research in August 2010. [24] The theme of their analysis is summarized in the following headline to the report "Risk on – risk off – how a paradigm is born." Their key recommendation, which seems just as applicable at the time of writing in mid-2012 as it did in August 2010, is that "Risk on – risk off must be the foremost consideration in any trading activity today." Some of the other radical implications of this new paradigm are outlined below.

From this it is imperative for those involved in wealth management – which ultimately must extend to anyone who is a stakeholder directly or indirectly in financial assets – to take on board the radical nature of the changes in the way that markets behave. In particular, and this should resonate with the benefits of the kind of stress regression analysis which was advocated in the previous section, it is worth contemplating the statement from the HSBC report that *"There are no longer easily identifiable, uncorrelated trades, which should be borne in mind when developing new trading strategies."*

As financial markets moved from the moderate and quiescent conditions of late 2005 and 2006 further into the global financial crisis the degree of cross asset correlations underwent a remarkable transition. The heat maps featured later in this section are a subset of those which appeared in the HSBC Research study just cited. The comprehensive treatment of multi-asset class correlations by the HSBC team greatly extends the scope of the findings of the Barclays Capital research group which were examined earlier in this chapter. In essence it reinforces and solidifies the overall thesis that very closely aligned asset class movements are the driving force behind trading strategies in today's markets. Spelling this out as starkly as they could the HSBC team make the observation that "[w]ithin this risk on – risk off framework, the nuances between different assets have disappeared, which makes diversification extremely difficult. Risk takers may be holding more risk in their portfolios than they realize." The lack of diversification which inevitably arises from much strong cross-sectional correlation has reduced the value of MPT and poses much greater challenges to risk management techniques such as VaR, and the consequences of this have still not been as widely appreciated as they should have been.

A corollary of the binary, macro driven strategies so widely adopted by many participants in today's markets, especially numerous hedge funds, is that the classic distinction between investing based on fundamental analysis versus technical analysis has now tipped rather decisively in favor of the latter. It may not be so much that the traditional tools from technical analysis have become uppermost in asset allocation decision making, as the fact that these tools have been superseded by more sophisticated "quant" and statistically oriented methodologies, but certainly there has been far less focus on investing based on "fundamentals." While many research departments continue to issue detailed analysis of corporate performance, analysis of balance sheets, forecasts of earnings, and ponder whether to make buy or sell recommendations based on fundamental valuation metrics, there would appear to be diminishing returns for this type of analysis. The more quantitatively focused strategists within trading firms and hedge funds are now in the ascendancy and coupled with the proliferation of algorithmic trading routines there is much greater attention to meta-market information – trends, the quality of the order book, the ebb and flow of cross asset correlations – than on the micro analysis of individual firms.

In concluding this section it will be worth citing, once again, from the HSBC report a couple of comments which reflect the demotion of bottom up allocation strategies and the promotion of top down strategies: "In current market conditions, there is little point trying to understand the nuances between different asset classes, or the relative value within asset classes ... Within this (risk on/risk off) ... paradigm, one either believes that risk is on or risk is off, and that this single factor drives all markets. Relative value is out the window for now and finding non correlated assets is extremely difficult."

2.5 HEAT MAPS ILLUSTRATE THE BINARY NATURE OF RISK ON/RISK OFF

The previous section focused on increased alignments of diverse asset classes which have become more prevalent following the GFC, as I attempt to give more clarity and more substance to the new risk on/risk off paradigm. For present purposes let us accept the premise that "we have moved from sophisticated and diverse markets to the simple and binary risk on – risk off mantra that dominates today." [25] If this is so what kinds of analytical tools and methods will enable us to understand these new market dynamics? How can we get a better handle on the sub-surface currents of cross-sectional correlations that are now dominant in the way that markets behave?

A method and framework which can be very useful in this regard involves the construction of "heat maps." Heat maps are very helpful as information can be communicated to the reader in a very easily digestible fashion. Trends can be seen much more readily if information is displayed using colors than if it was conveyed in a numerical form. This is especially useful when one is analyzing a multi variable matrix showing, for example, cross correlations amongst a diverse set of assets. It will also be the preferred method for illustrating the manner in which certain FX pairs are unusually correlated with other asset classes which will be the focus of Chapter 5.

The concluding heat maps for this chapter provide a remarkably good perspective on the degree to which the correlations across a wide variety of financial instruments tightened during the period prior to the GFC, during the critical period of 2008 itself, and in the aftermath.

Table 2.1 shows the constituents of what will be rendered as a correlations matrix covering 50 separately traded financial instruments in global asset markets. The instruments range from

Table 2.1 Assets used in creating heat maps for HSBC Research Report on risk on/risk off

Details of the assets used in the heat maps					
	Asset		Asset		Asset
1	US 10yr bonds	18	DAX	35	AAA corp bonds
2	UK 10yr bonds	19	Hang Seng	36	AA corp bonds
3	Japan 10yr bonds	20	Sao paolo SX	37	USD
4	EU 10yr bonds	21	Singapore SX	38	GBP
5	Norway 10yr bonds	22	Johannesburg SX	39	JPY
6	Sweden 10yr bonds	23	EM Asia equities	40	EUR
7	Autralia 10yr bonds	24	EM LatAm equities	41	NOK
8	Canada 10yr bonds	25	VIX	42	SEK
9	Brazil 2yr bonds	26	Corp credit – main	43	AUD
10	Singapore 10yr bonds	27	Corp credit – high vol	44	CAD
11	SA 10yr bonds	28	Corp credit – snr fin	45	BRL
12	Hong Kong 10yr bonds	29	Copper	46	ZAR
13	S&P	30	Gold	47	CHF
14	Russell 2000	31	Oil	48	3m eurodollar
15	FTSE 100	32	Natural gas	49	3m euribor
16	Nikkei	33	Soybean	50	3m euroyen
17	Eurostoxx 50	34	Wheat		

Source: HSBC FX Quantitative Strategy Team, Oxford Centre for Industrial and Applied Mathematics, Mathematical Institute, University of Oxford.

the total returns from a variety of sovereign bonds, other fixed income instruments, global equity indices, several different commodities, certain currencies and short-term interest rates. From this list of instruments it is possible to create a 50 by 50 matrix which then shows the correlations of the returns of each asset to each of the others. Due to the layout of the matrix, the diagonal line from top right to bottom left on the matrix will always show a value of unity since at that point of intersection each asset is being correlated with itself. In each of the other cells of the matrix there will be the numerical expression of the observed correlation. These numerical values can take on any value between −1 and +1. However, rather than this being expressed in numerical form in each cell of a matrix presentation, which would be mind bogglingly unfriendly to the human eye, the cell is presented in the form of a colored heat map. As this book will be printed in grayscale it will not be possible to witness such coloring so the task of differentiating the different "heat" tones will be left to the good sense of the reader.

Each cell will be rendered with a color ranging from a dark blue which represents extreme negative correlations – the cold values in the heat map corresponding to values close to −1 for the correlation coefficient – through greens, yellows, oranges which correspond to weaker correlations, and eventually to different hues of red as the correlations get hotter. The limiting value of plus one which would represent perfect positive correlation would be expressed in color terms as a very dark red. The first heat map which is shown in Figure 2.14 covers the "normal" period from September 2005 to September 2006 which is before the onset of the various foreshocks which culminated in the events of H2, 2008. The right hand side of each

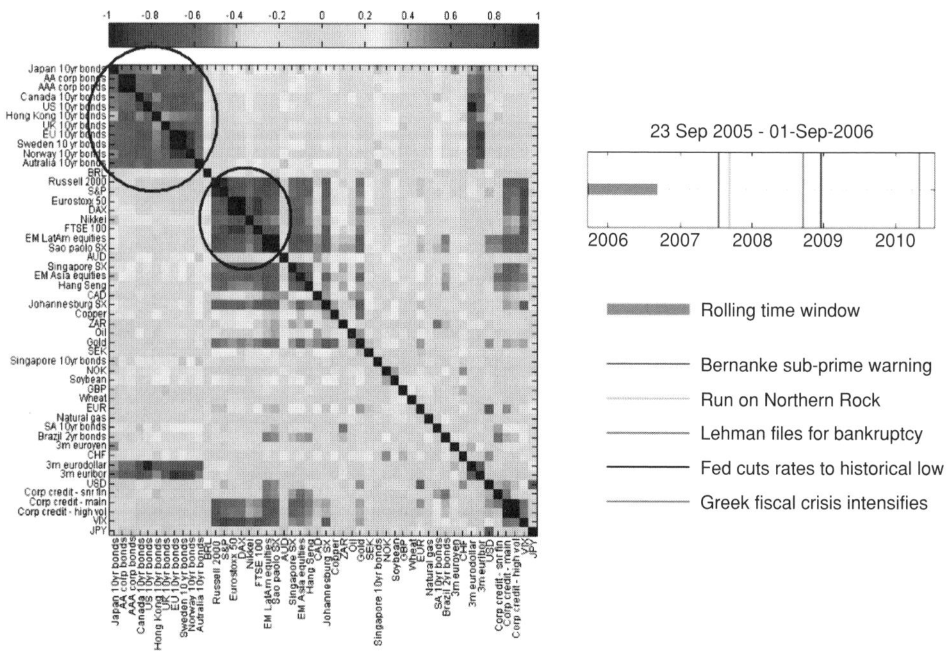

Figure 2.14 Heat map for "normal" market conditions 2005–mid-2006
Source: HSBC FX Quantitative Strategy Team, Oxford Centre for Industrial and Applied Mathematics, Mathematical Institute, University of Oxford.

graphic situates the time frame within a window covering both the 2008 crash and subsequent stressful events up to the rapid deterioration of the Greek public finances in spring of 2010 and other Eurozone woes as 2010 progressed.

Some points to consider about Figure 2.14 which can be considered as the baseline scenario are as follows:

- The diagonal line from top left to bottom right in very dark red represents the case where each of the asset returns is being correlated with itself which, as noted, must be equal to one.
- At the top of the diagram there is a color key which shows how the colors displayed in each cell map on to the possible values of the correlation coefficient.
- In the top left hand corner where the co-movement of the returns on a variety of highly rated sovereign bonds is being measured there is an island of red cells which is not too surprising as the yield and price returns of this sector of the capital markets will typically be well correlated even when markets are not experiencing stressful trading conditions.
- There are a few islands of very dark blue and again these are to be expected since they tend to coincide with relative performance of fixed income securities and commodities and equities which will tend to move inversely with respect to each other.

From an overall perspective the key characteristic of this base case is that a very large number of the cells are yellows, greens and light orange which correspond to the more weakly correlated observations. Under "normal market conditions" – which is one of the assumptions made by the CAPM as discussed earlier in this chapter – there will be many financial instruments which are loosely correlated with others and which then permit a satisfactory degree of diversification when combining them together in a portfolio.

Figure 2.15, which is entitled *Crisis and correlations intensify – collapse of Lehman,* covers the period from November 2007 through to October 2008 and takes in some of the most turbulent and stressful market conditions seen at the height of the global financial crisis.

The large circle on Figure 2.15 reveals, in contrast to the previous baseline heat map, that there is much greater positive correlation in the returns for all of the global equity indices in the matrix. In comparing the heat map from 2007/8 to that of 2005/6 shown in Figure 2.14, the area of reds in the circle is larger, the degree of correlations involving different geographical regions for the equity indices has increased, and by inspecting the two axes it can be seen that some of the commodities and the commodity currencies are now correlating positively with these equity indices. It should be remembered that an increase in positive correlation can arise because two financial instruments are showing a tendency to go down in tandem. The term positive correlation only requires that the directionality of co-movement is the same and is not related to the actual direction of travel.

One of the more noticeable qualities of the 2007/8 heat map shown as Figure 2.15 is that in addition to the much greater correlation between equity indices and the commodity currencies – Australian dollar, Brazilian real, Canadian dollar, and South African rand – it can also be seen that some commodities such as oil and copper are now much more highly correlated with the equity indices than in the 2005/6 heat map.

In the 2007/8 heat map displayed as Figure 2.15, there is also more evidence of dark blue cells than for the earlier period which indicates that the extent of negative correlations is also becoming more widespread. Just to take a further feature of the later heat map the correlations between two "safe haven" currencies – the Swiss Franc and the Japanese Yen – shown on the heat map as CHF as JPY – have become increasingly negative respectively in

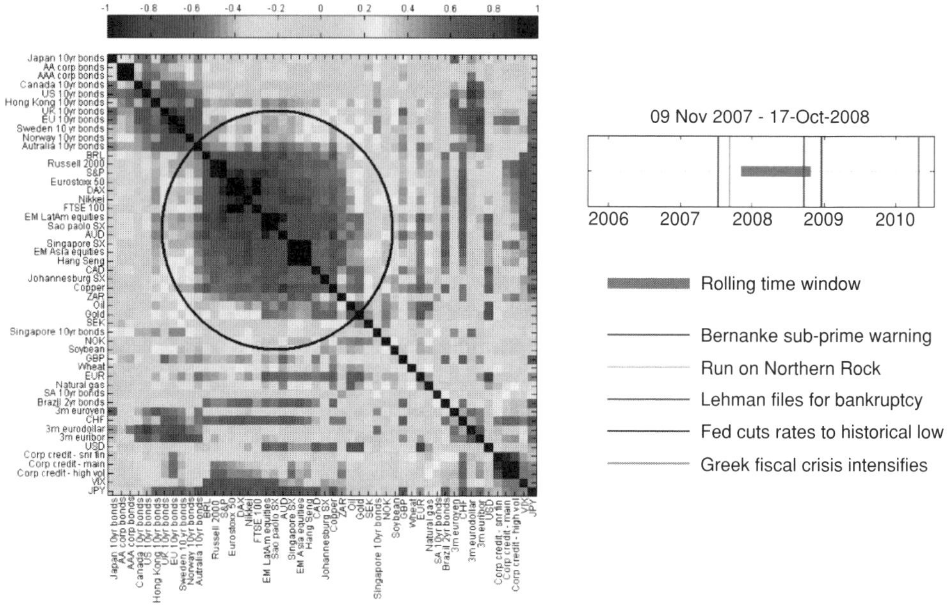

Figure 2.15 Heat map for "crisis" market conditions November 2007–October 2008
Source: HSBC FX Quantitative Strategy Team, Oxford Centre for Industrial and Applied Mathematics, Mathematical Institute, University of Oxford.

their relation to global equity indices. Each of these safe haven currencies is moving inversely to a greater extent with global equity indices as the flight from risk assets to safe harbor assets is gathering pace.

Figure 2.16, covers the period following the extreme market movements of 2008 and extends from March 2009 to late February of 2010. This coincides with the major recovery in global equity indices and other risk assets. During the time interval shown in Figure 2.16 the S&P 500, for example, moved from a level of 768 on March 20, 2009 to 1104 on February 26, 2010, a 44% increase. However as the heat map for this later period reveals, the degree of correlation between markets has actually increased from the 2007/8 heat map. There are even larger areas of the heat map which are colored as deep red and deep blue regions indicating strong positive and negative correlations and there has been a further reduction in the green and yellow regions which shows that the number of weakly correlated instruments had declined.

The HSBC team, which is affiliated with the Oxford University's Centre for Industrial and Applied Mathematics, has produced a revised and smaller group of assets in their April 2012 report which is entitled *Risk on-Risk Off: Fixing a broken investment process.* [26]

Using the smaller set of instruments there is an opportunity to contrast the profound difference in the degree of cross asset return correlations between the 2005 period and that which is observed in markets in April 2012. The complexion of Figure 2.17, which covers the period from June through October 19, 2005, is primarily one of weak correlations – as revealed by the large presence of yellows and greens – with small boxes of higher correlations. The relatively small boxes of hotter red colours in the top left hand corner tracks the not surprisingly stronger degree of correlations between various global equity indices, and the box at the bottom right hand corner registers similarly elevated correlations for various and comparable fixed income

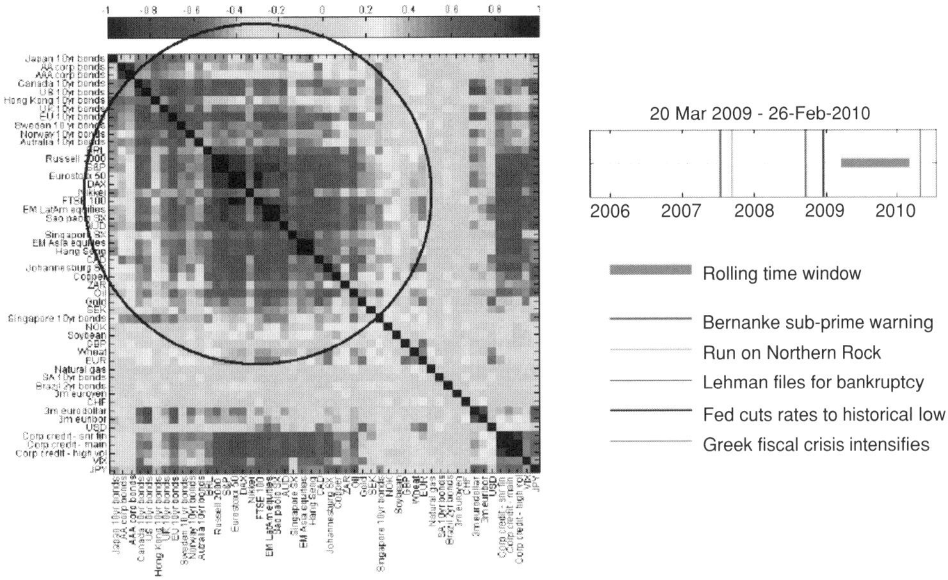

Figure 2.16 Heat map for "crisis aftermath" market conditions March 2009–February 2010
Source: HSBC FX Quantitative Strategy Team, Oxford Centre for Industrial and Applied Mathematics, Mathematical Institute, University of Oxford.

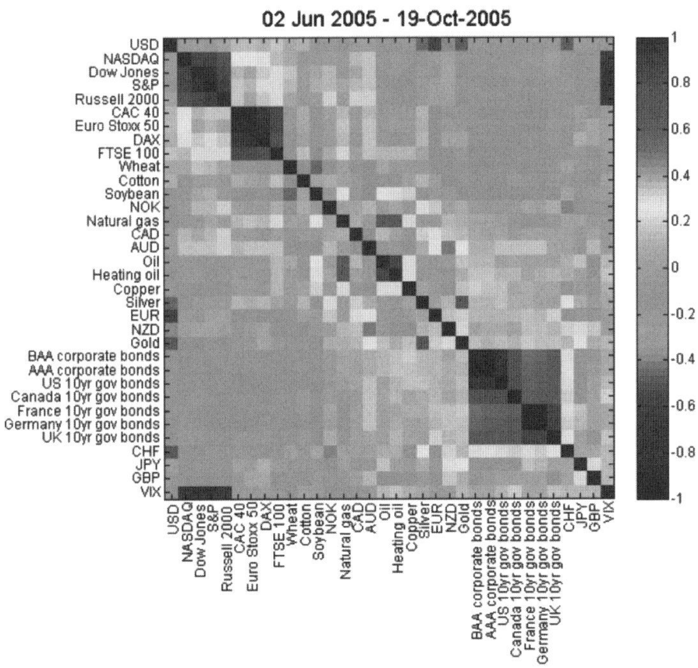

Figure 2.17 Heat map for pre-crisis June 2005–October 2005
Source: HSBC FX Quantitative Strategy Team, Oxford Centre for Industrial and Applied Mathematics, Mathematical Institute, University of Oxford.

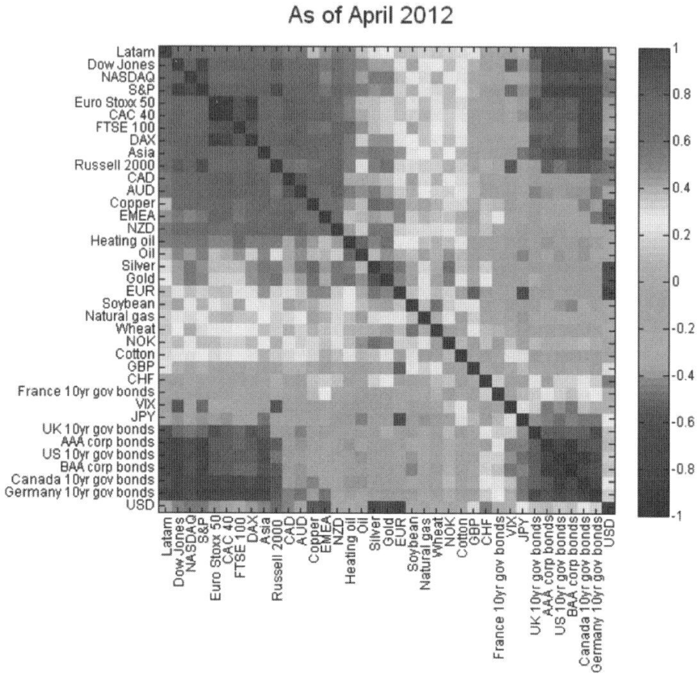

Figure 2.18 Heat map as of April 2012
Source: HSBC FX Quantitative Strategy Team, Oxford Centre for Industrial and Applied Mathematics, Mathematical Institute, University of Oxford.

instruments. There are small areas of strong negative correlation such as in the very last row at the left of the matrix which relate to the covariance of the VIX with US equity indices – again as would be expected.

The heat map depicted in Figure 2.18, and which was rendered from correlations data in April 2012, stands in marked contrast to that for the 2005 period which is shown in the previous matrix of Figure 2.17. There are very few yellow and green cells in evidence and instead there is a preponderance of dark red and dark blue regions. As will be seen in the following chapters the evidence from HSBC's data in 2012 is confirming that the more strongly correlated nature of asset class movements far from dissipating as we move further away from the GFC is actually showing signs of becoming even more acute. There is good reason to believe from this that rather than the binary risk on/risk off paradigm fading it would appear to be entrenched as a feature of the contemporary investment landscape.

Another useful technique which can be derived from the cross asset return correlation analysis is to monitor the extent to which certain assets can change their risk profile over time. Figure 2.19 is a snapshot for the 34 assets which the HSBC track in their 2012 research and the assets are placed on a spectrum of "risky" to "safe haven" depending on their observed correlation characteristics. On the left hand side of Figure 2.19 the riskiest assets are global equities and on the right hand side those assets deemed to have safe haven characteristics are bonds of highly rated corporations and sovereigns. By monitoring these profiles across time it can be seen that certain assets will shift their position within the spectrum. For example, in the snapshot shown in Figure 2.19, French government bonds have been observed to have

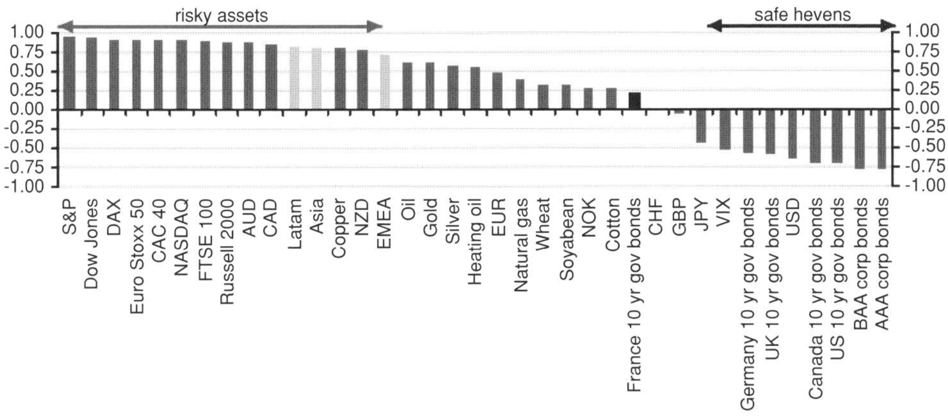

Figure 2.19 Profile of risky assets and safe haven assets March 2012
Source: HSBC FX Quantitative Strategy Team, Oxford Centre for Industrial and Applied Mathematics, Mathematical Institute, University of Oxford.

decoupled with other safe haven assets and moved further to the left of the spectrum from previous profiles. This transition indicates that the market perceptions had shifted in March 2012 towards considering these bonds as more risky than they had been perceived in earlier time frames. Monitoring these shifts in risk perception can obviously be of considerable value to fund managers operating within a more binary asset allocation framework.

The concluding diagram for this chapter, Figure 2.20, also comes from the 2012 HSBC research and introduces an innovative extension of the heat map techniques. Arising from their extensive and historical examination of cross-sectional correlations the quantitative team at HSBC and the Oxford Institute of Applied Mathematics have produced a risk on/risk off or RORO index. The precise method of calculating this index is covered in the research note referenced as endnote 26 but in essence increases in the RORO index are driven by the increased correlatedness of different asset classes, heightened beta characteristics across assets and, in more general terms, a predominance in the influence of macro or systemic factors influencing market direction.

I shall leave the concluding remarks for this chapter to a comment from the HSBC team on how best to interpret all of the illustrations in the latter part of this chapter: [27]

> The consequences of RORO for asset managers and the investment process are profound. In a world where most asset classes are synchronised, it becomes very difficult to achieve diversification. It also means that since most individual assets are dominated by a common price component, it becomes increasingly futile to invest in them based on their usual fundamentals . . . Stock picking is harder in a RORO environment when prices move together so closely.

The overwhelming evidence of the much greater extremes in the coloring of the heat maps since financial markets became preoccupied with the 2007/8 crisis and its aftermath "is consistent with a shift in markets to the 'risk on – risk off' paradigm and a binary world." [28]

The use of the term *binary* has some intriguing semantic overtones, with implications and insights from investor psychology, which will be explored further in subsequent chapters.

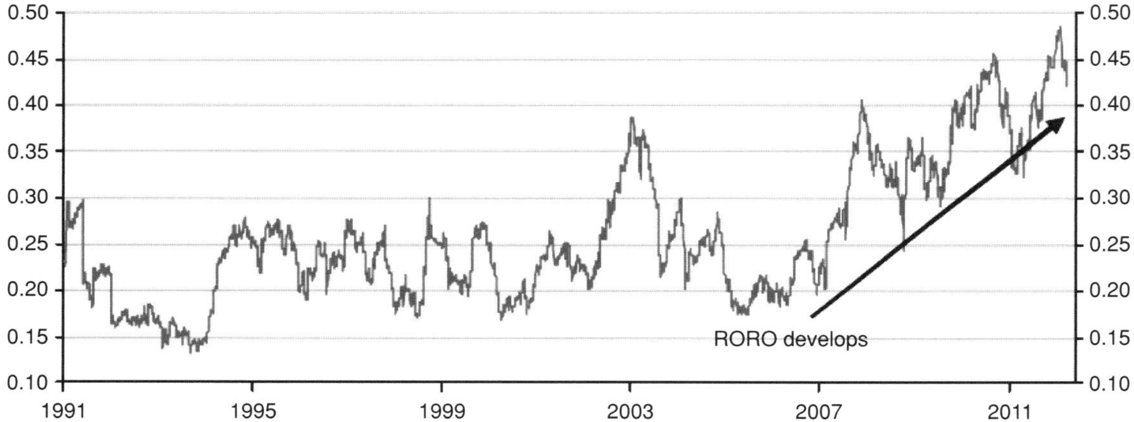

Figure 2.20 HSBC Research: Risk on/Risk Off Index
Source: HSBC FX Quantitative Strategy Team, Oxford Centre for Industrial and Applied Mathematics, Mathematical Institute, University of Oxford.

ENDNOTES

1. Research from HSBC and Barclays Capital on asset correlations: Strategies Barclays Capital Equity Research, *U.S. Equity Quantitative*, August 4, 2010; HSBC Global Research Macro Currency Strategy, *Risk on – risk off – how a paradigm is born*, August 2010
   http://www.research.hsbc.com/midas/Res/RDV?ao=20&key=CjLQyHQJjB&n=274256.PDF.
2. Gillian Tett, *Fool's Gold: The Inside Story of J.P. Morgan and How Wall St. Greed Corrupted Its Bold Dream and Created a Financial Catastrophe* (Free Press; Reprint edition, 2010).
3. The table below shows the performance of different hedge fund strategies during 2011

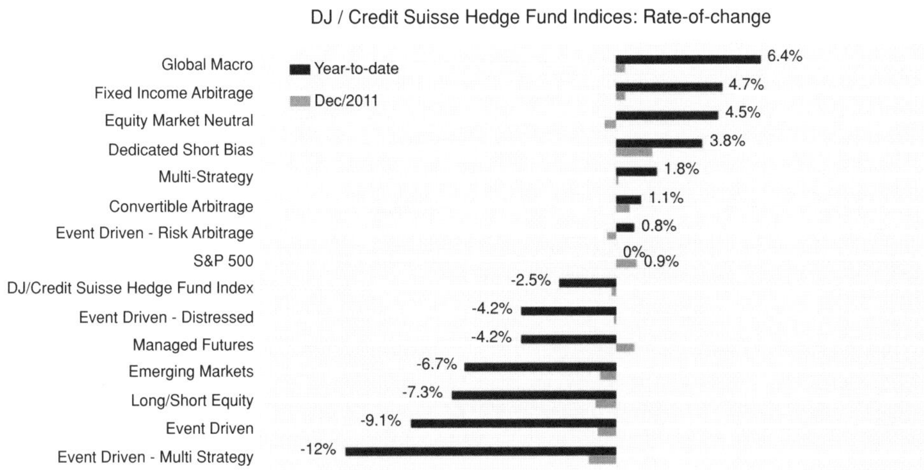

Hedge fund returns 2011
Source: DJ Credit Suisse Hedge Fund Returns 2011.

4. See above.
5. Bank for International Settlements:

> The mission of the Bank for International Settlements (BIS) is to serve central banks in their pursuit of monetary and financial stability, to foster international cooperation in those areas and to act as a bank for central banks.
>
> In broad outline, the BIS pursues its mission by:
>
> promoting discussion and facilitating collaboration among central banks;
> supporting dialogue with other authorities that are responsible for promoting financial stability;
> conducting research on policy issues confronting central banks and financial supervisory authorities;
> acting as a prime counterparty for central banks in their financial transactions; and
> serving as an agent or trustee in connection with international financial operations.
>
> The head office is in Basel, Switzerland, www.bis.org.

6. Greenwich Associates, *FX algo trading to take off*, April 2012, http://www.finextra.com/news/fullstory.aspx?newsitemid=23592:

> Last year electronic trading accounted for more than 60% of global FX volumes for the first time, says the Greenwich study, based on tracking of volumes at 1632 end-user corporate and institutional customers.

Despite the prevalence of e-trading, only eight per cent of global market participants use algorithmic trading strategies for foreign exchange, up from six per cent in 2010, leaving "little doubt that these strategies have yet to gain much traction market-wide".

However, there are signs of life in certain segments; with use of algo trading strategies among the market's biggest and most active traders increasing in 2011 to 16%, from 12% the previous year.

Algo strategies are now used by 12% of participants in the UK and 10% in the US. Hedge funds are also ahead of the curve, with 20% using algorithmic trading, up from just 14% the previous year.

Peter D'Amario, consultant, Greenwich Associates, says: "As FX evolves into a mainly electronic marketplace, competition is taking place in milliseconds as opposed to minutes or hours. In such an environment, algorithmic trading strategies will play a much bigger role for both investors and banks."

More generally, from 2010 to 2011 electronic trading volumes increased 47% in the Americas, 20% in Europe and 22% in Asia Pacific. As a result of those increases, the share of total foreign exchange trading volume executed electronically in the Americas increased to 60% in 2011 from 51% in 2010 and the share of overall volume executed electronically expanded to 62% from 58% in Europe.

7. The Race to Zero speech given by Andrew G. Haldane, Executive Director, Financial Stability and member of the interim Financial Policy Committee, International Economic Association Sixteenth World Congress, Beijing, China, 8 July 2011:

   As recently as 2005, HFT accounted for less than a fifth of US equity market turnover by volume. Today, it accounts for between two-thirds and three-quarters.

   http://www.bankofengland.co.uk/publications/Documents/speeches/2011/speech509.pdf.
8. Barclays Capital Equity Research, *U.S. Equity Quantitative Strategies*, August 4, 2010.
9. *Managing Correlation Risk with Alternative Investments Breaking The Back of High Correlations* by Nathan Rowader of Forward Management, LLC, 2012.

   Available online at http://www.forwardinvesting.com/wp-content/uploads/managing-correlation-risk.pdf.
10. From the above report.
11. The Capital Asset Pricing Model or CAPM is the tool which enables us to create portfolios where we have determined the degree of risk that the client is willing to face.

    An individual seeking a high return would need to take on high risk in order to have the chance of a higher return. To achieve a higher return we would need to construct a portfolio with a high β. A portfolio with a β greater than 1 could be expected to give a return greater than that of the market, but at a correspondingly enhanced level of risk. A young investor, who is not overly risk-averse, might seek out adventurous investments and be willing to take additional risks in the promise of higher returns. A more risk averse individual, such as someone reaching retirement, is liable to be seeking a more secure and less risky portfolio and would, therefore, prefer a portfolio with a β less than 1.

    Modern Portfolio Theory (MPT) originated with an article entitled 'Portfolio Selection' by Harry Markowitz which appeared in 1952 in the *Journal of Finance*. MPT stresses that a trader or investor should allocate assets based on the characteristics of a portfolio rather than the individual characteristics of the constituent securities considered separately.

    Prior to the MPT, the received wisdom on the manner of combining securities in a portfolio was to screen securities that offered the most attractive opportunities for gain with the least risk and then add these together in a portfolio. Bringing individual securities together in such a fashion would often lead to exposing the portfolio to too many securities from the same sector, where the correlations between the returns amongst the securities selected would be imprudently high. In other words, the portfolio would lack the benefits of diversification.

    The procedures advocated by Markowitz enable a fund manager to calculate the correlated portfolio volatility and the expected returns for numerous combination scenarios. From the space of possible portfolio combinations there are a series of combinations that will optimally balance the risk and reward. The optimal combinations that maximize the reward for the different possible levels of risk lie on what Markowitz termed the *efficient frontier*. The fund manager can settle on the level of risk that is acceptable and then select the particular combination of securities that optimize the reward for this level of risk.

12. According to the CAPM alpha is an abnormal return which will eventually be arbitraged away. If the asset's returns are above the Securities Market Line then demand for it will reduce its yield and if the returns are below then supply of the asset will cause its yield to rise.
13. Richard Bookstaber, The Myth of Non Correlation, *Institutional Investor*, September 2007, http://bookstaber.com/rick/RickBookstaber_TheMythOfNonCorrelation.pdf.
14. In essence the fallacy of using the Gaussian copula uncritically is that it substantially under-estimates the probability of adverse outcomes developing for *all* of a set of related financial instruments when confronted with macro crises. For example, in regard to the use of the copula for assessing the likelihood that a variety of mortgages might all default together the risk modelers, principally the credit ratings agencies, failed to take into account the possibility of a system-wide decline in real estate prices.

    A well written account of the Gaussian copula is to be found in *Recipe for Disaster: The Formula That Killed Wall Street*, by Felix Salmon, Wired, February 23, 2009. This can be found online at http://www.wired.com/techbiz/it/magazine/17-03/wp_quant.
15. HSBC Global Research Macro Currency Strategy, *Risk on – risk off – how a paradigm is born*, August 2010, http://www.research.hsbc.com/midas/Res/RDV?ao=20&key=CjLQyHQJjB&n=274256.PDF.
16. HSBC Research Hedge Fund Review, January 2012.
17. The following is a discussion of the normalization technique:

    Co-movement between two different financial instruments can be illustrated and measured in a number of ways. Both of the assets can be shown on the same graph with different scales – on the left and right hand vertical axes for each, and another useful technique is to display the paths taken in two time series by normalizing the data. This technique has the benefit of showing the extent to which the peaks and trough values for the respective variables either coincide or deviate. Visual inspection will also provide an easy clue as to how closely the pair may be correlated, which can then be subject to more rigorous testing by applying statistical techniques such as linear regression.

    Here is a brief description of the method for normalizing time series data:

    - Establish the period of analysis for displaying the relationship between the two variables.
    - Find the highest and lowest values for each variable over the entire period.
    - Determine the range for each variable, i.e. the difference between the highest and lowest value observed over the entire period.
    - Each value is then normalized, i.e. take each separate value and subtract the lowest observed value for that variable over the entire period.
    - Divide that value by the range.
    - Provides a value between 0 and 1 which can then be plotted on a two-dimensional graph with time along the horizontal axis and the normalized value on the vertical axis.
    - Zero is the lowest value observed during the entire period.
    - One is the highest value observed during the period.
18. Louise Armitstead, Eurozone crisis fears continue as Italy forced to pay higher rates to borrow, *Daily Telegraph*, July 28, 2011:

> The Italian government was forced to pay the highest borrowing costs for 11 years in a bond auction that underscored market fears that a new phase of the European debt crisis is set to be unleashed.

The concerns about the possible disintegration of the euro currency came to the fore in late July/early August of 2011 and remained the focus of attention until they were temporarily ameliorated by the first LTRO program from the ECB in December 2011.

19. Richard Koo, *Balance Sheet Recession: Japan's Struggle with Uncharted Economics and its Global Implications* (John Wiley & Sons, 1st edn, October 2003). See also by the same author *The Holy Grail of Macroeconomics: Lessons from Japan's Great Recession* (John Wiley & Sons, August 2009).
20. Kenneth Rogoff and Carmen M. Reinhart, *This Time Is Different: Eight Centuries of Financial Folly* (Princeton University Press, 2009).
21. Charles MacKay, *Extraordinary Popular Delusions and the Madness of Crowds* (Wordsworth Editions Ltd, June 1995); Charles P. Kindleberger, *Manias, Panics and Crashes: A History of Financial Crises* (Palgrave Macmillan, 6th edn, August 2011).
22. For a longer discussion on the notion that certain scenarios have characteristics of impossible dilemmas or "no-win" outcomes see Chapter 15.
23. The alpha value can be determined through a linear regression and is equal to the y intercept value. The y-intercept is the value which is shown on the y-axis when the x value is zero.
24. HSBC Global Research Macro Currency Strategy, *Risk on – risk off – how a paradigm is born*, August 2010, http://www.research.hsbc.com/midas/Res/RDV?ao=20&key=CjLQyHQJjB&n=274256.PDF.
25. From the above report.
26. HSBC Global Research Macro Currency Strategy, *Risk on-Risk Off: Fixing a broken investment process, April 2012*. HSBC FX Quantitative Strategy Team, Oxford Centre for Industrial and Applied Mathematics, Mathematical Institute, University of Oxford.
27. From the above report.
28. This comment is taken from the HSBC 2010 research report which is referenced in endnote 24.

3

The Changing Character of Financial Markets

In this chapter, and in preparation for future discussions of critical events such as the Flash Crash, it will be helpful to outline some of the more significant changes which have occurred in the topology of markets, newer execution platforms and the changing micro-structure of markets which has resulted from the development of new technologies on new platforms as well as a result of high frequency trading algorithms (HFT).

In the US and Europe, but to a lesser extent in Asia, at least in mid-2012, there has been a fragmentation of what used to be more centralized platforms of trading activity. The public securities exchanges such as the New York Stock Exchange (NYSE) in the US, and the London Stock Exchange (LSE) and Deutsche Boerse, for example, in Europe were until around the turn of the millennium the dominant "locations" where most trading in equities and often fixed income instruments took place. By 2012 this has been completely transformed and, as will be seen, a variety of alternative trading venues and platforms have largely usurped the dominant position previously enjoyed by the traditional exchanges. There were some key developments in this fragmentation and these can be outlined in a brief historical sketch.

In 1998 the Securities and Exchange Commission (SEC), the regulator of the US securities markets, authorized the introduction of electronic communication networks (ECNs), which are also often referred to as Alternative Trading Systems (ATSs) or venues. The primary motivation for the SEC to authorize ECNs was its desire to increase competition among trading firms by lowering transaction costs, giving clients full access to their order books, and offering order matching outside of traditional exchange hours. [1] As the number of ECNs has increased, and the capabilities of these alternative trading venues have become increasingly sophisticated, there has been a migration away from traditional exchanges resulting in the fragmentation in the locus and composition of daily trading activity.

Another key development, with far reaching implications, resulted from the SEC revisions to the National Market System in 2005 which mandated that trades should always automatically be executed at the best quote possible. This customer friendly mandate created the perfect environment for the proliferation of high speed transactions that would be automatically executed and not sit in a queue waiting for approval by a market maker or exchange rules. The rapid expansion in ECNs and alternative trading venue business created huge competition for exchanges causing traditional exchanges to merge, for example, the amalgamation of the NYSE and Euronext, and some traditional exchanges to merge with large ECNs, for example the merger of the NYSE and Archipelago. In Europe, the Markets in Financial Instruments Directive, known under its acronym of MiFID, which was authorized in 2004 but not fully implemented until 2007/8, was an EU-wide regulatory initiative, similar to that ushered in by the SEC with its revised NMS Rule 611, and designed to boost competition and choice in financial market trading by attracting new entrants.

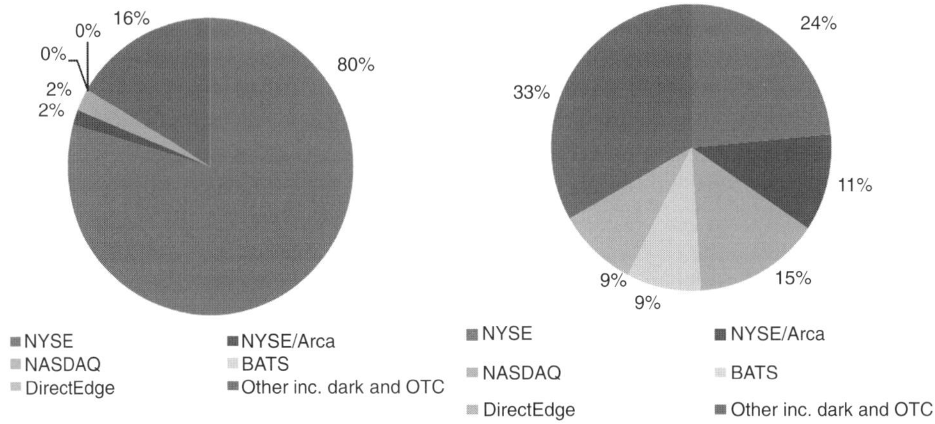

Figure 3.1 NYSE trading volume breakdown for 2005 and 2011
Source: Haldane, A G (2011), "The Race to Zero".

Since these two developments have gathered momentum, and with an increased emphasis on the desire to execute transactions not only more cheaply but at ever increasing speeds, the "landscape" of financial markets has been radically transformed. Figure 3.1 shows just how radically different the topology of trading has become in the US market since 2005. Trading is now split across more than half a dozen exchanges, multilateral trading platforms, and "dark pools" of anonymous trading. [2] Having accounted for around 80% of trading volume in NYSE-listed securities in 2005, the trading share of the NYSE had fallen to around 24% by February 2011. A similar pattern is evident across Europe. In the UK, the market share of the London Stock Exchange has fallen from two-thirds in June 2008 to less than one third in 2012 and similar patterns can be seen in Germany. [3]

In addition to fragmentation, and facilitated by the technological innovations of the more sophisticated ECNs, the type of trading has become largely automated with algorithmic activity now predominant. In 2005, HFT accounted for less than a fifth of US equity market turnover by volume. In 2012 it accounts for between two-thirds and three-quarters. [4]

Asset management has also become increasingly institutionalized with very little participation by retail investors. Individuals have deserted financial markets and handed their wealth management to institutions, such as mutual funds, pension funds, insurance companies, and investment managers. In turn, institutional asset managers in recent years have shown an increasing propensity to invest in managed products such as funds of funds, exchange traded funds (ETFs), and other collective investment vehicles. [5] The net result of this is that the vast majority of investable assets are held through institutionally managed vehicles. Figure 3.2, which comes from a Morgan Stanley research report published in April 2012, [6] shows the dramatic changes in the ownership of corporate equity in the USA from 1950 to the end of 2010.

In 1950, the category shown on the legend as "households and non-profit" owned more than 90% of US equities directly. By 2000 that figure had fallen to around 50% and in the next ten-year period it lost more than another 10%. Mutual funds and pension companies have substantially increased their share of ownership of US equities, foreign participation has

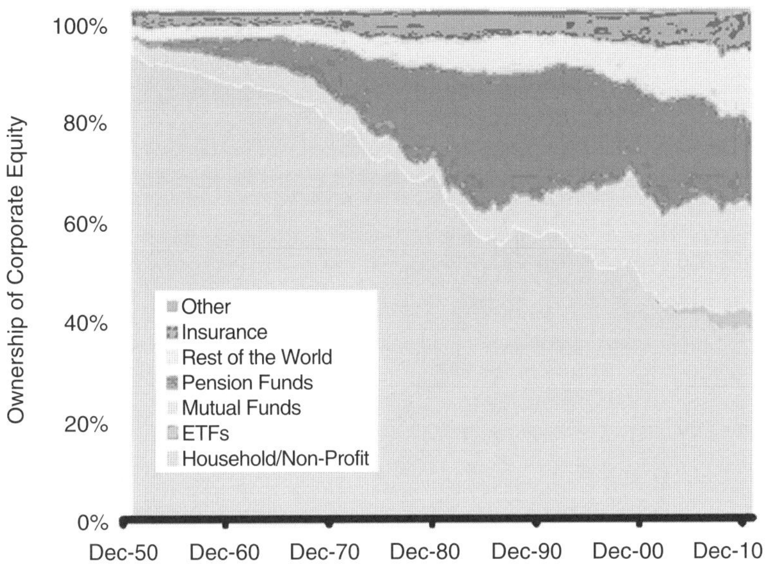

Figure 3.2 Ownership of equity in US
Source: Federal Reserve Bank, Morgan Stanley QDS.

expanded to more than 10%, and in the most recent period exchange traded funds (ETFs) are becoming more important.

Perhaps the most important change that has taken place during the last ten years, initially more focused in the US market but now almost omnipresent (except in Asia), has been the proliferation of automated trading and most recently the predominant role of HFT activity. HFT trading will be examined in more detail in Chapter 5 and for present purposes the focus will be on the more "traditional" kinds of algorithmic trading activity. Algorithmic trading was originally conceived to alleviate the concerns that large institutions had about exposing their substantial sized orders to the market, and algorithmic routines were developed to disguise the true intent of these large fund managers. The process not only facilitates the more efficient execution of large orders, but can even introduce subtle false signals into the procedure which are designed to confuse the markets about the underlying transaction objectives. For example if a fund wants to buy a large quantity of a particular stock, the parent order is "sliced and diced" into a series of much smaller child orders and then executed over a period of time where the objective is to achieve actual price executions at an optimal cost. The most common type of algorithm, called Volume Weighted Average Price (VWAP), slices the parent order into a series of child orders over a certain time frame, attempting to conceal the true size of the parent order. As part of the procedure the algorithms can also throw off contrarian trades that will from time to time reverse the original motivation by, for example, creating a selling phase within a large buy order.

An inevitable consequence of this type of algorithmic activity is that the typical order size which is now executed on the various platforms has shrunk considerably. Figure 3.3 reveals that in 2003 the average trade size executed on the NYSE platform was more than 1000 shares and that by late 2011 this had diminished to around 250 shares.

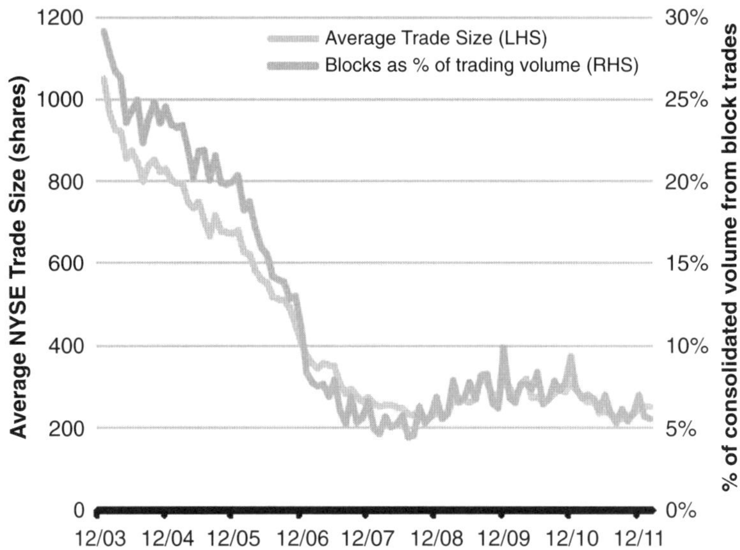

Figure 3.3 NYSE average trade size and % volume from block trades 2003–2012
Source: NYSE.
Block trades are defined as single trades of greater than 10,000 shares.

The following quotation comes from the Morgan Stanley research report previously cited: [7]

> One of the responses to ... concentration in assets under management ... has been automation in execution strategies. The algorithms used tend to split parent orders into smaller child orders. As a result, we find that block trades, which made up around 30% of trading volume in 2003, accounted for just over 5% of trading volume in 2011. At the same time, the average trade size has fallen to around 250, from more than 1,000 back in 2003. Both data series are based on NYSE listed stocks.

There is an interesting asymmetry at work in this regard. On the one hand, the fact that the retail investor has gone missing from financial markets and that institutional asset management now predominates would suggest that the typical order size should actually have risen. On the other hand, as the comments from Morgan Stanley quoted above suggest, parent orders by institutions have increased, but, also the percentage of block size orders has declined to only 5% of trades, so the role of algorithmic trading to break these orders into smaller sizes has led to the somewhat counter-intuitive result that the typical trade size is for about 250 shares.

Having established that small trade size is a key characteristic of contemporary markets it is now possible to examine some fascinating research which has revealed a change in the statistical qualities of trading activity. In a moment we will introduce some statistical theory that will enable this change to be properly appreciated, but, in essence, the empirical evidence shows that there is greater trend persistence in the flow of orders and trades executed, and also that trading patterns are exhibiting greater self-similarity. As will become clearer in the discussion of the next section, the quality of self similarity, brilliantly developed by the polymath Benoit Mandelbrot, [8] is best expressed in the fractal quality of a natural object such as a cauliflower or a snowflake, and the beautiful objects that have been created by computer programs based on fractal image generators. [9] From a statistical perspective the evidence of recurring patterns at different scales, which are the essential qualities of a fractal, runs counter to long-held views that time series data for financial assets are essentially random.

At this point it will be useful to refer to a recent piece of research entitled "Is high-frequency trading inducing changes in market microstructure and dynamics?" [10] The author of this article has conducted back testing against a very large database of high frequency trading data and has determined that, in recent time frames since 2006, there has been a very noticeable increase in a statistical metric known as the Hurst coefficient. This coefficient (which will be explained below) can be used to measure trend persistence and the presence of self similarity or fractal quality in the patterns of how trading orders are executed on contemporary trading platforms. The article's conclusion is worth stating at this point, and then it will be necessary to examine the nature of the Hurst coefficient and why its implications for market micro-structure and liquidity are significant: [11]

> HFT is having an increasingly large impact on the microstructure of equity trading dynamics. We can determine this through several main pieces of evidence. First, the Hurst exponent H of traded value in short time scales (15 minutes or less) is increasing over time from its previous Gaussian white noise values of 0.5. Second, this increase becomes most marked, especially in the NYSE stocks, following the implementation of Reg NMS by the SEC which led to the boom in HFT. *Finally, $H > 0.5$ traded value activity is clearly linked with small share trades which are the trades dominated by HFT traffic.*

The last sentence is highlighted because the assertion is that the smaller size of trades, and the fact that these are being conducted by algorithms, which are essentially rule governed and deterministic, [12] has transformed the statistically observable properties of trading. To state things provocatively if there were any doubts about how nonsensical it is to claim that markets follow a random walk, the changes in the micro-structure of markets and the advent of HFTs which have in just a few short years become the dominant mode of market activity, should finally put to rest the premises upon which the Efficient Markets Hypothesis is based.

The author of the article just cited provides explanations for this transformation towards greater evidence of trend persistence and self similarity, and while they are intriguing and attribute the self similarity and higher Hurst values to algorithmic processes, the exact details are not required for our present purposes:

> . . . the breaking down of large orders to smaller ones approximates a multiplicative cascade which can generate self-similar behavior over time as outlined by Mandelbrot. Second, the queuing of chunks of larger orders . . . could also generate correlations in the trade flow.

The following discussion of the Hurst coefficient and trend persistence will be somewhat technically abstruse and if the reader wishes it can be stepped over without too much loss of continuity in our narrative. However, with the kind of evidence uncovered in the preceding discussion it should hopefully be more intuitively apparent why this is a worthwhile excursion. Once it has been substantiated that asset price behavior exhibits trend persistence and self similarity we will be redressing the often unchallenged but clearly false allegation that asset prices move in an essentially haphazard and random manner. Displacing this cornerstone assumption of much finance theory has wide-reaching implications.

3.1 MARKET RETURNS DO EXHIBIT MEMORY

Just one of the many difficulties involved in the application of Gaussian statistical theory to the understanding of price behavior in asset markets relates to the somewhat abstract concept of stationarity. [13] Stationarity is a statistical property of a set of data points and, in essence, means that time series data should *not* reveal evidence of memory or clustering. This will be seen to be patently false from analysis of the empirical data, and this conclusion has been reached in several important studies, [14] but let us at least examine the theoretical assumptions regarding stationarity and why it is integral to the Gaussian distribution before examining real world data.

Stationarity is a property that may or may not be present in time series data. In its more general sense it provides an answer to the question of whether the time series preserves a constant mean and standard deviation over the entire series of data points, and equally for any randomly chosen subset of such data points. If the time series is stationary then it should reveal a constant mean and standard deviation. With regard specifically to financial time series, it becomes quickly clear that they do not preserve constancy of either value and therefore do not exhibit stationarity. Expressed in other words asset price movements do exhibit "memory" which far from being heretical, as some financial analysts would like to believe, seems to be a statement of the obvious when one considers that asset prices move up and down because traders have different viewpoints, changing perceptions, and emotions about pricing. Traders and investors have memories so surely this should be reflected in the empirical data!

Let us begin though by looking at an example of a time series that does have the property of stationarity. The classic example is white noise which can be seen from the image presented in Figure 3.4. White noise or Brownian motion fluctuates in a random fashion but which

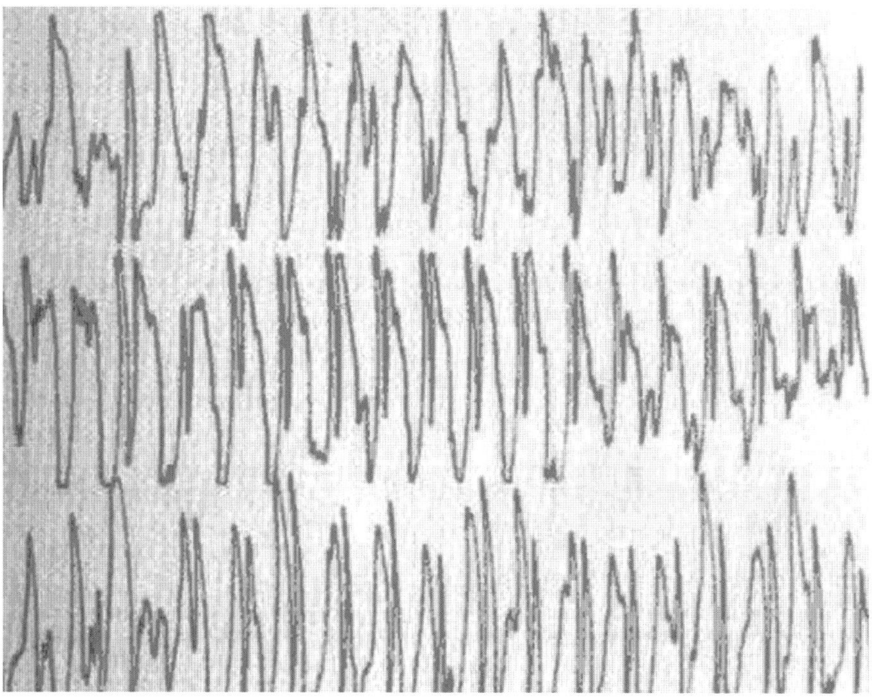

Figure 3.4 White noise

manages to preserve a uniform mean and variance no matter which "section" of the image one takes. The sections are thus interchangeable, they have the same "signature" and this can be confirmed using certain statistical procedures. If we were to extract any section and compare its mean and variance to the whole series or any other section then a simple statistical test would indicate that, with a very high degree of probability, we could declare that the two sections came from the same data population.

The graphic of white noise does have an interesting property, as will be discussed below, in relation to the Hurst coefficient. This measure, named after a British civil engineer, is being used by a growing number of financial analysts as a useful metric in understanding trend persistence in time series data. White noise has a Hurst coefficient value of 0.5 which satisfies the theoretical property of being essentially a random walk entirely lacking in trend persistence. Given the fondness for random walks amongst some advocates of the Efficient Markets Hypothesis (EMH), which will be discussed in much more detail in Chapter 10, there has been quite a lot of research undertaken predicated on data mining within historical databases of asset prices to see whether a Hurst value of 0.5 is found. The evidence indicates considerable variability especially across different asset classes and different geographical regions. Without delving too deeply into this research it has been found that, for example, equities in developing markets show much higher Hurst coefficients than equities in more developed markets. [15] More striking is the fact that recent research, as referenced in the article entitled "Is high-frequency trading inducing changes in market microstructure and dynamics?" [16] discussed above, is revealing that in recent years there has been a general increase across most asset classes for most instruments traded to exhibit increasing Hurst coefficient values. Part of this has been attributed to the proliferation of HFT as the article suggested, but much of it can also be seen to coincide with the risk on/risk off paradigm that has been our focus. It certainly is fair to say that when we switch to empirical data of asset price movements during the GFC and other critical episodes in financial markets, the assumption of EMH diehards of stationarity and randomness can easily be seen to be patently false.

Volatility clustering is one of the most easily observed characteristics of financial time series data and its existence violates the notion that price development and the changes from succeeding prices follow a random walk and are normally distributed. One of the underlying (Gaussian) assumptions about a normally distributed data series is that all of the data points are independent and identically distributed. This is the so-called i.i.d. assumption [17] and it is best illustrated by examples from games of chance; it rests on the notion that there is no "memory" in the sequence of independent events. The sequence of outcomes when we throw a fair dice or spin a roulette wheel exhibits the quality of i.i.d. in the sense that no inferences can be drawn from any repetitive patterns. If the spins of a roulette wheel lead to five red outcomes in a row, the very next spin has an equal chance of being a red or black outcome. There is no dependency between each outcome, and the outcomes theoretically will follow a normal distribution. If they do not follow this distribution this should be seen as a purely contingent feature of the particular sequence and no predictive patterns can be inferred. This is demonstrably not true in the case of a sequence of financial returns. Volatile returns will cluster and when we find one exceptionally volatile trading session we are much more likely than suggested by chance to find others in close proximity. This has far-reaching repercussions for the statistical analysis of financial data and for understanding the vulnerability of the financial system to bouts of illiquidity.

Figure 3.5 shows the daily changes for the S&P 500 between January 2, 1985 and mid-May of 2012. However only those returns which exceed, on an absolute basis, two standard

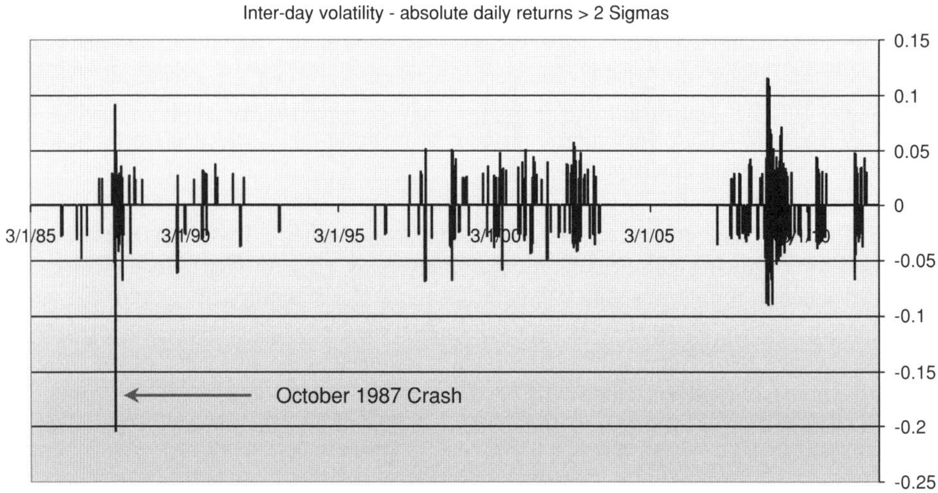

Figure 3.5 S&P 500 daily returns 1985–mid-2012 – volatility clustering

deviations (i.e. ± 2 sigmas) are included in the chart. The vertical y axis indicates the magnitude of the changes in percentage terms. By only plotting the more extreme periods it is clearly visible how the broad market index has had extended, quiescent periods and then periods where the incidence of large fluctuations (both above and below the x axis) cluster. Some obvious periods that stand out on the chart are the 1987 market crash, the period in the late 80s and early 90s that coincided with the S&L problems, recessionary forces, and the first Gulf War. There followed a period through the mid-90s where there were few instances of abnormal fluctuations. There are periods in the late 90s that correspond with the Asian market crisis in 1997, the Russian debt/LTCM crisis in 1998, and then a large cluster in the early part of the new millennium that is related to the collapse of the Nasdaq and the calamitous events of September 11, 2001. The period from 2003 through to mid-2007 is remarkably quiet and then there is the very large cluster of high sigma events which corresponds to the 2008 crisis and the aftershocks which have been experienced since.

During the 27-year period covered on Figure 3.5 there were almost 7000 data points and 409 or 4.6% of those that exceeded the threshold of ± 2 sigmas. That this frequency of 4.6% also concurs with the expectation from statistical theory that ± 2 sigma events should occur with approximately a 5% probability may be seen as validation of the theory that asset returns are normally distributed, but the problems arise when considering the frequency of the outliers and their distribution or tendency to cluster. As illustrated there is a pronounced tendency for abnormal moves to cluster and not be distributed haphazardly across the time line. This should not be surprising of course as prices are determined by human beings who have memories, fears, and emotions and when they are stressed and anxious their reactions to events are going to be more extreme and erratic. It is surprising that one has to even make this observation but unfortunately the fallacy of objectifying price behavior and misuse of statistical theory is still widespread. By thinking that it is the S&P 500 index itself which reacts to events rather than traders and market participants who are reacting to events and that it is their behavior which causes the S&P 500 to go up and down, there is a kind of anthropomorphic fallacy in reverse. The expression of judgments about events and decisions about whether to buy or sell based on such judgments *is represented* on a graph in the form of a trajectory but this should not be taken literally. Prices move but seeing these movements as being of the same kind as the movement of objects through three-dimensional space leads to an egregious misunderstanding of market behavior. This misunderstanding becomes most dangerous in relation to expectations about how likely extreme events are. As noted in Chapter 2, the normal distribution can be helpful in telling us how frequently we are likely to encounter an adult male who is more than 2 meters in height but not how likely it is that there will be a – 5 sigma event in the financial markets.

Failure to properly acknowledge the clustering of volatility and the feral quality of outliers (a reflection of the emotional upheavals being experienced by traders) have led many practitioners of financial orthodoxy to greatly underestimate the financial risks associated with the likelihood of abnormally volatile trading conditions. The probability calculus that is used in statistics, or at least that part of statistics that is widely used in calculation of Value at Risk (VaR), for example, [18] is based, in the final analysis, upon assumptions that financial returns data are normally distributed. But the clustering of volatility and the fatness of the tails of asset returns clearly demonstrate that this is not the case. Recklessly, many risk managers will simply import financial data into their models, apply various routines built on probabilistic functions stemming ultimately from a fundamentally mistaken view of the distribution quality of outlier events, and pull out bogus conclusions that are *precisely inaccurate* to 15 decimal places. Based upon a truly empirical approach in understanding financial markets we should abandon the probability forecasting derived from Gaussian assumptions and admit that *there is essentially no reliable statistical basis for determining when volatility outliers will occur or how severe they might be.*

Even supposedly sophisticated financial institutions such as JP Morgan have acted with remarkable ineptitude by relying upon VaR, even if their version of this metric goes far beyond a plain vanilla version (maybe that's part of the problem!). In May 2012 JP Morgan's CEO Jamie Dimon had to hastily convene a conference call to investors and analysts to explain why the bank had losses, estimated at the time of the conference call, at $2 billion from a failed derivatives strategy. Just one month earlier when challenged about rumored mishaps in the "hedging" activities of his CIO team Dimon had dismissed them as a "tempest in a teapot." The respected author Satyajit Das commented on this in an article entitled "Topiary Lessons – JP Morgan's $2billion loss": [19]

> Given JPM's vaunted risk management credentials and boasts of a "fortress like" balance sheet, it is surprising that the problems of the hedge were not identified earlier. In general, most banks stress test hedges to ensure their efficacy prior to implementation and monitor them closely.
>
> **While the US$2 billion loss is grievous, the bank's restatement of its VaR risk from $67 million to $129 million (an increase of 93%) and reinstatement of an older risk model is also significant, suggesting a failure of risk modeling.**
>
> During the conference call, Mr. Dimon conceded that the trades were "flawed, complex, volatile, poorly reviewed and poorly monitored . . . there are many errors, sloppiness and bad judgment."

As Das suggests the derivatives loss reflected a *failure of risk modeling.* Although it might have seemed to many observers that there has been sufficient criticism of the reliance on normal distribution assumptions in finance for notions like VaR to now be discredited, sadly this is far from being the case.

For Dimon, having to restate the VaR risk by almost doubling it from $67 mn to $129 mn may seem like a candid *mea culpa* but the problem is that it still provides an unwarranted kind of hubris that such measurements can be relied upon at all. It is not just an inability to precisely measure the magnitude of unlikely events that is the fallacy; it is the assumption that they can be measured with any precision at all. It is the latter point that this excursion into Statistics 101 and probability was intended to show.

The last section started off with the purpose of showing that to propose that asset prices wander aimlessly without any regard to where they have just been, is not only falsified by the evidence but really nonsensical when one considers that price developments do express the intentionality and emotions of market participants. When traders and investors are experiencing stressful circumstances the movement of prices will exhibit self-similar behavior as with the clusters of volatility seen. Also, and more importantly, the memories of recent events *in the minds of traders/investors* will be a key motivational factor explaining how prices evolve moving forwards after stressful events, and this vital component of price discovery will manifest itself in persistent trends which can be observed and measured. The global financial crisis provided the *ideal template* of abnormal market conditions which enables us to have exceptional insights into the characteristics of "abnormal" behavior by market participants.

3.2 HURST COEFFICIENT

The Hurst coefficient is named after the English civil engineer H E Hurst. Hurst studied the flooding patterns of the river Nile to determine whether there was evidence that the series of flood observations contained evidence of "memory" in the incidence of flooding. By plotting data on the irregular flooding patterns of the Nile delta over the period 622–1469 Hurst found that flooding exhibited a persistent pattern. Large floods were not only frequent, but came in clusters (as volatility does in asset markets). They had a long memory. Apart from the value of this particular insight with respect to the Nile itself, the methodology provided a transferable technique for detecting the presence of "memory" in the analysis of many other kinds of time series data sets. The following expresses in a succinct manner the key idea behind the Hurst coefficient or as it is often described the Hurst exponent: [20]

> A common theme in this research has often been the investigation of self-similarity and long-range dependence in the time series. The former is often measured by the Hurst exponent, H, which measures the relative degree of self-similarity from pure Markovian Brownian motion at $H = 0.5$ to complete self-similarity at $H = 1$.
>
> A value of $0.5 < H < 1$ is typically described by fractional Brownian motion which demonstrates self-similarity at multiple time scales of fluctuations in contrast to the independent fluctuations of Brownian motion.

A Hurst coefficient notably above 0.5, which as discussed has been observed in HFT dominated asset markets, implies fatter tails, self similarity and longer memories. The importance of this statement will become more evident as the discussion proceeds.

Figure 3.6 plots the path of three simulated price series with Hurst coefficients of 0.5, 0.7, and 0.9. [21] The simulation reveals that for the most extreme value – which as will be shown later in this chapter was actually observed in asset markets during 2008 – the trajectory is far less haphazard and erratic than for the neutral value of 0.5. Looking at the path taken by the H

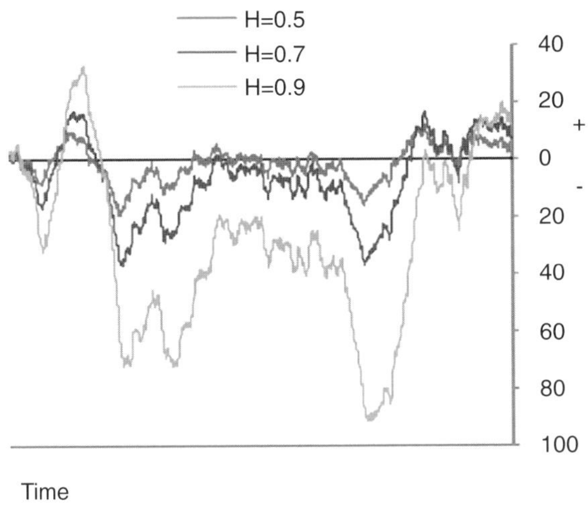

Figure 3.6 Hurst coefficient simulated
Source: Haldane, A G (2011), "The Race to Zero".

values of 0.7 and 0.9, they bear a much greater resemblance to those strongly trending patterns which were seen for financials, commodities, and certain currencies during the financial crisis and the calculations of their Hurst values confirm that extreme values were observed.

For those who are technically inclined the following is the method used to determine the Hurst value, for those less so the remainder of this paragraph can easily be skipped. The Hurst exponent is estimated by calculating the average rescaled range over multiple regions of the time series. To estimate the Hurst exponent using the rescaled range algorithm, a vector of points is created, where each point is the log of the size of the data region used to calculate each R/S average value, and y is the log of the R/S average value. The Hurst exponent is estimated by a linear regression line through these points. The slope which results from that linear regression is the estimate for the Hurst exponent. [22]

In essence the Hurst coefficient provides evidence of whether the constituents of a time series of price changes reveal interdependences as opposed to being independent of each other much like the way in which when a coin is tossed, the outcome of each toss is completely separate from the prior toss(es) of the coin. The coin, as an inanimate object, possesses no "memory" of previous outcomes (even though the person tossing it over a long series of "trials" clearly does retain a recollection of the previous outcomes). With respect to the probability of outcomes, it can be said that each trial is independent of any and every other trial and that there is no inherent reason why a series of heads should then tip the coin in favor on the next trial to be tails. In all likelihood a series of heads will be terminated or punctuated by the appearance of tails but this is not because the coin decides that there have been too many heads, and, that in order to maintain the semblance of being a "fair" coin, it should now switch to showing tails.

The language that had to be used to describe the coin as "deciding" on its next outcome is of course metaphorical and, at a distance, rather comical. It is reminiscent of the criticism that Nicholas Taleb uses in the following dismissal of the manner in which financial economists have tried to subsume the essential uncertainty of economic decision making under the cover of statistically quantifiable probabilities: [23]

> Life is not a laboratory in which we are supplied probabilities. Nor is it an exercise in textbooks on statistics. Nor is it an urn. Nor is it a casino where the state authorities monitor and enforce some probabilistic transparency.

The tendency to treat the movements of markets – or what might more meaningfully be described as price development – as akin to the tossing of coins or drawing of colored beads from an urn makes even less sense when considering the mounting empirical evidence that contradicts the view that asset returns are examples of "pure Brownian motion with a Hurst value of 0.5."

3.3 HURST VALUES REACHED EXTREMES DURING 2008

Following on from this theoretical detour and by way of demonstrating why such analysis is very useful to risk management, it can be shown that the critical events of 2008 provided ample evidence that when markets became stressed, much like in the case of volatility clustering already outlined, there was a notable persistence in trend for many asset markets. In particular those on the frontiers of the risk on/risk off dichotomy had a tendency to show the most extreme Hurst values when the financial crisis was at its peak

Figure 3.7 illustrates a remarkably elevated Hurst value of 0.68 revealed by five-day log changes in the daily Australian dollar/US dollar exchange rate from July 2007 to March 2010. There are more than 800 separate data points and the period selected is designed to cover the onset of the financial crisis up to the period preceding the Flash Crash of May 2010 which will be discussed in the next two chapters. The Hurst value is the gradient of the linear equation shown on the scatter diagram of Figure 3.7. Plotted on the scatter graph are log values for the rescaled range calculations on the vertical axis and the time period of those respective R/S calculations on the x axis. There are several methods for estimating the Hurst coefficient and

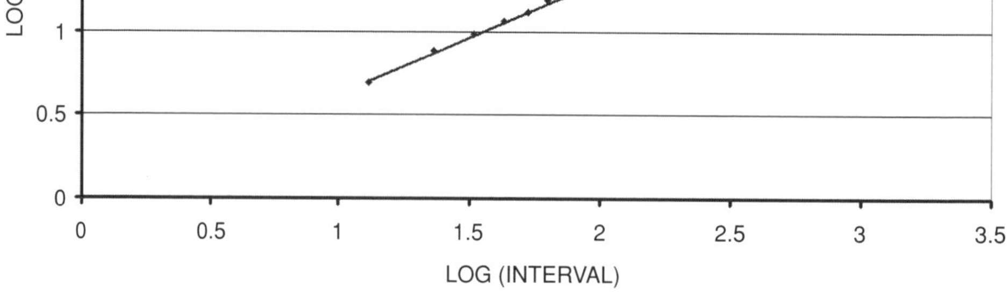

Figure 3.7 Hurst analysis for daily changes to AUD/USD – July 2007–March 2010

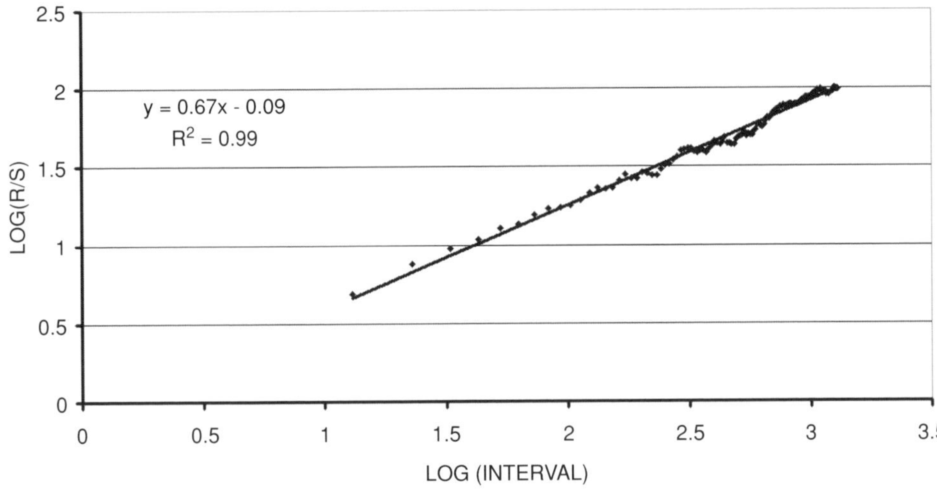

Figure 3.8 Hurst analysis for KBW Banking Index July 2007–July 2012

they can result in quite different values; the method used and a discussion of some alternative methods can be found in the endnotes. [24]

It is generally advisable to use a relatively large set of values from which to calculate the rescaled range metrics as shorter periods or fewer values will cause the Hurst coefficient to converge at a value which overstates the true value. At the same time if one wants to use the rescaled range technique for monitoring intermediate term market developments there is a necessary compromise involved as the rigor required by some versions of the analytical technique would insist on using such long data sets that it would prevent us from drilling down on certain critical time frames.

Figure 3.8 covers the five-year period for a widely followed index for the US financial sector, the KBW Banking Index. [25] By using an extended time period, in this case more than 1300 different data points, and also by retaining the logic of measuring the log changes based on five-day intervals, it is possible to find certain asset types which exhibit unusually high values. The gradient of the slope from the linear regression shown in Figure 3.8, which is the estimate for the Hurst exponent, has a value of 0.67. This value is considerably higher than that of a random walk which would be 0.5 (the white noise level) and suggests strong trend persistence and a fractal quality to the price development patterns. The presence of higher Hurst values for a significant class of key asset types reveals a significant shift in investor behavior in the post-crisis environment.

Specifically with regard to the US banking index the observed Hurst level of 0.68 demonstrates that investors and traders in the equities of US banks and brokers are not buying and selling these instruments in a haphazard fashion, as implied by the random walk hypothesis, but are revealing evidence of persistent concerns and sentiments regarding the sector.

Figure 3.9 shows the relative performance of the Australian dollar against its US dollar counterpart and also the KBW Banking Index, BKX, during the interval from July 2007 to the end of 2008 – which coincides with the acute period of the GFC. While the paths taken by each are far from identical, there is self similarity and clear evidence of strongly trending

Figure 3.9 Relative performance of AUD/USD and KBW Banking Index July 2007–end 2008

behavior for both. In particular the lighter tone line for BKX shows a remarkable downtrend which persists almost across the entire period captured in the chart.

Taking July 2007 as the base for both moves in Figure 3.9 it can be seen that the respective low values registered for each were in more or less the same time frame, i.e. November 2008. The financial services sector shows a decline of more than 70% from the July 2007 base value – which is itself quite an extraordinary decline and echoes the discussion in Chapter 13 regarding the substantial drops in value witnessed by major banks such as Citigroup, Bank of America, Deutsche Bank, and UBS.

The decline for the Australian dollar, shown in Figure 3.9, from the late July 2008 peak to the trough in October/November 2008 was approximately 30% but taking into account the fact that the Australian currency versus the US dollar had actually climbed by around 15% from its July 2007 level into the summer of 2008, the drawdown amount, which is measured from the peak to trough of the values shown on the chart, is in the region of 45%. The equivalent period drawdown for the benchmark index for US equities, the S&P 500, during that same period showed a very similar value.

The severity and duration of drawdowns is the real dimension of stress experienced by investors and traders. It is a far more realistic yardstick of the risk of holding assets than a probabilistic guesstimate as to the likelihood in the abstract of a tail event occurring which, in essence, is the severe methodological flaw of the VaR approach to risk management.

In Figure 3.9 the path followed by the KBW Banking Index, BKX, not only illustrates the presence of a persistent downtrend which is captured in the very high value for the Hurst exponent, but also it is possible to detect self-similar patterns or waves in sub series of the data. The other line in Figure 3.9 which represents the performance of the Aussie dollar against the US dollar shows a steady upward bias to the data until the peak in July/August 2008 and then the appearance of a very abrupt and persistent downtrend throughout the second half of 2008.

Translating what is evident from a visual inspection of the trends that are present within the data points seen in Figure 3.9 into a useful metric, the Hurst exponent provides a useful quantitative tool to assist in an explanation of the cognitive underpinnings of asset returns data. *Markets reveal their behavioral and emotional components most transparently when they are functioning under stress.* Just as individual human beings will provide their most reliable strengths and weaknesses (from the point of view of inter-personal relationships) when they are under pressure or stressed, so markets give up a lot of their mystery and roll back the opacity of their inner dynamics when there are macro-financial factors at work. The reason why the time series shows trend persistence is a reflection of the persistence of the anxieties being experienced by the investors who were being reminded on almost a daily basis of the fragility and instability of the financial intermediations during the unfolding credit crisis.

When seen in this context the actual underlying drivers of the observed behavior of financial markets become far more transparent. One could suggest that there is much more clearly a manifestation of a collective intelligence and set of emotions being expressed by market participants as they react to developments in the bursting bubble narrative. The narratives which are driving market prices under less stressed circumstances than the burst bubble scenario are more diversified and less uniform which is why under "normal" conditions there will be less of a coherent trend to price behavior. This will be reflected in much less extreme values for the Hurst exponent and is consistent with the view that *under normal circumstances* markets do exhibit fairly uncoordinated price action and an absence of strong trending behavior. But to extrapolate from what is normally true, and build a bogus view of the probability of extreme events, based on the idea that outliers will behave in accordance with a normally anchored distribution, is, as a result of the collectivization of the losses incurred by systemically threatening episodes like the GFC, extremely harmful to taxpayers' wealth. [26]

ENDNOTES

1. The emergence of ECNs has made it possible for retail investors to trade outside normal exchange hours. ECNs include Island, Archipelago, and Instinet amongst others.
2. Dark pools refer to the non-displayed or hidden nature of the buy and sell orders that reside in a crossing platform.

   One investment manager has described the appeals of dark liquidity pools as follows:

   > A dark pool is a very simple way you can hopefully capture lots of liquidity and achieve a large proportion of your order being executed without displaying anything to the market.

   In the US, the influx of crossing networks and alternative venues, and the rapid adoption of electronic trading technologies, has been driving the growth of dark pools for several years.
3. Andrew G. Haldane, *The Race to Zero* (see previous references to this article), http://www.bankofengland.co.uk/publications/Documents/speeches/2011/speech509.pdf.
4. See above for quotation that:

   > [a]s recently as 2005, HFT accounted for less than a fifth of US equity market turnover by volume. Today, it accounts for between two-thirds and three-quarters.

5. A Morgan Stanley report on changes in markets can be found referenced at some length in *Why The Market Is Slowly Dying*, zerohedge.com, April 14, 2012, http://www.zerohedge.com/news/why-market-slowly-dying
6. See above.
7. See above.
8. The following brief account of the work of Mandelbrot comes from Clive Corcoran, *Long/Short Market Dynamics* (John Wiley & Sons, 2007):

> Benoit Mandelbrot is largely responsible, through his classical work *The Fractal Geometry of Nature*, for the position that fractals now occupy in the intellectual landscape. Mandelbrot has written numerous articles about the unsuitability of Gaussian assumptions to the understanding of financial markets. The most accessible treatment of his views on markets is to be found in a book that he co-authored with Richard Hudson entitled *The (Mis)behavior of Markets* which carries the subtitle *A Fractal View of Risk, Ruin and Reward*. The book is a *tour de force* of all that Mandelbrot finds erroneous in the way that finance is still taught in universities and widely practiced in the investment community.

9. A good example of an online fractal generator can be found at http://www.fractalposter.com/fractal_generator.php
10. Reginald Smith, *Is High-frequency Trading Inducing Changes in Market Microstructure and Dynamics*? http://arxiv.org/pdf/1006.5490v3.pdf.
11. The quote is from *Is High-frequency Trading Inducing Changes in Market Microstructure and Dynamics*? See endnote 10.
12. The simple point that is being made is that a computer algorithm or function will create an output by following certain execution paths which are rule governed. The outcomes will often not be predictable or knowable in advance of the actual execution, but unless the algorithm possesses overall randomizing behavior, which is not a feature of (well behaved) HFT algorithms then outcomes will be, in a general sense, explicable by reference to the set of rules that have been programmed.
13. In *Long/Short Market Dynamics*, chapter 10 is entitled Regime Shifts and Stationarity pp. 221–38.
14. See for example Andrew Lo and Craig MacKinlay, *A Non-random Walk Down Wall Street* (Princeton University Press, 1999).
15. Carlos León and Alejandro Reveiz, *Portfolio Optimization and Long-term Dependence*:

> Trend persistence is typical of emerging markets' fixed income instruments (and of less-developed equity markets (e.g. Colombia, Turkey and Peru)). Developed equity markets and liquid emerging markets (eg Brazil, Mexico) show less incidence of persistent individual risk factors.

http://www.bis.org/publ/bppdf/bispap58e.pdf.
16. The quote is from *Is High-frequency Trading Inducing Changes in Market Microstructure and Dynamics*? For full reference see endnote 10.
17. In probability theory and statistics, a sequence of variables is independent and identically distributed (i.i.d.) if each variable has the same probability distribution as the others and all are mutually independent.

A paper entitled "Statistics, Distributions and the IID Assumption" (author is not identified) stipulates that the following three conditions need to be satisfied in order for a set of data to be independent and identically distributed:

- The data are randomly scattered about the center (median) of the data, that is, the points do not exhibit an increasing, decreasing, or otherwise systematic trend about the center over time;
- The data have a constant degree of scatter, that is, the amount of variability does not exhibit an increasing, decreasing, or otherwise systematic trend over time; and
- The data consist of independent observations.

http://www.rose-hulman.edu/~bryan/ma223/distn.pdf.

The discussions regarding clustering of volatility clearly indicate that asset returns do not have the i.i.d. property.

18. There is an extended discussion of Value at Risk and how it can be calculated in *Long/Short Market Dynamics*, pp. 266–80:

> The VaR calculation does not answer the question: What is the largest amount that one can lose during a month? Rather it provides the answer to the following question: What is the amount that one would expect to lose (under normal distribution assumptions) with a probability of $x\%$ for a specified period?
>
> Consider the problem of estimating how big a loss a portfolio could experience over the next month. Typically, the estimate of the maximum expected loss is defined for a given time horizon and a given confidence interval. Assuming for simplicity that the distribution of portfolio returns is normal, then a three standard deviation drop is possible, but not very likely. According to the probability density function it should arise only 0.3% of the time or once in approximately 300 months.

The reader may also want to have a look at Romain Berry, *Value-at-Risk: An Overview of Analytical VaR* (J.P. Morgan Investment Analytics and Consulting) which is available online at http://www.jpmorgan.com/tss/General/email/1159360877242:

> Suppose we want to calculate the Analytical VaR at a 95% confidence level and over a holding period of 1 day for an asset in which we have invested \$1 million. We have estimated[3] μ (mean) and σ (standard deviation) to be 0.3% and 3% respectively. The Analytical VaR of that asset would be:
>
> $$\text{VaR}_{95\%} = -(0.003 - 1.6449 \times 0.03) \times \$1 \text{ million} = \$46,347.$$
>
> This means that there is a 5% chance that this asset may lose at least \$46,347 at the end of the next trading day *under normal market conditions*. (author's emphasis)
>
> VaR calculates the worst expected loss over a given horizon at a given confidence level *under normal market conditions*. (author's emphasis)

The qualifications in the above quotations from the JP Morgan article – that VaR applies only under normal market conditions and also the underlying assumption of the methodology – that asset returns are normally distributed – are the key reasons why the VaR metric can be hazardous as a risk management tool, especially when markets are behaving abnormally.

19. Satyajit Das, *Topiary Lessons – JP Morgan's \$2billion loss*, available at http://www.nakedcapitalism.com/2012/05/satyajit-das-topiary-lessons-jp-morgans-us-2-billion-loss.html.
20. The following descriptions of the Sharpe ratio and the Sortino ratio come from Clive Corcoran, *Long/Short Market Dynamics* (John Wiley & Sons, 2007):

> The simplest method to calculate the Sharpe Ratio is to deduct the Risk Free Rate of Return [RFR] from the CAGR and divide the result by the annualized standard deviation of the returns. So the formula is simply
>
> $$[\text{CAGR} - \text{RFR}]/\text{Annualized Standard Deviation of Returns}$$
>
> There is a slightly different approach which is to deduct the average monthly return at the risk free T Bill rate from the average monthly return and divide the result by the monthly standard deviation of the returns. Once that figure is obtained the result is again multiplied by the square root of 12. The alternate formula is simply
>
> $$\{[\text{Average Monthly Return} - \text{Average RFR}]/\text{STD of Monthly Returns}\}^{*}12^{\wedge}0.5$$
>
> The assumption behind the calculation and the reason why the standard deviation is used as the denominator to the equation is that since investors prefer a smooth ride to a bumpy one the higher the standard deviation the lower will be the Sharpe ratio.

> The numerator of the Sortino ratio is the CAGR – the Risk Free Rate (as before for the Sharpe ratio), but the denominator is based on a calculation of the standard deviations of only those returns that are below a minimum acceptable level. There is some disagreement on how that minimum threshold should be set so we prefer to simply calculate, for the denominator, the standard deviation of all the negative returns. The Sortino ratio, as it is heralded, no longer penalizes the superior fund managers for spectacular upside returns.

21. *The Race to Zero*, Speech given by Andrew G. Haldane, Executive Director, Financial Stability Bank of England International Economic Association Sixteenth World Congress, Beijing, China, 8 July 2011, http://www.bankofengland.co.uk/publications/Documents/speeches/2011/speech509.pdf.

    Also see another of Haldane's presentations entitled *Tails of the Unexpected*, http://www.bankofengland.co.uk/publications/Documents/speeches/2012/speech582.pdf.

22. A good explanation of how the Hurst coefficient is measured, the various pros and cons of the measure, and some software tools which can be used to calculate the Hurst exponent is found at the useful website Long Memory.com which is maintained by Martin Sewell.

    There are some Excel files which can be used to calculate the Hurst value when asset log returns are entered into the spreadsheet, and there is a separate C++ source file which can be compiled to perform a similar calculation.

    > In 1906, Harold Edwin Hurst, a young English civil servant, came to Cairo, Egypt, which was then under British rule. As a hydrological consultant, Hurst's problem was to predict how much the Nile flooded from year to year. He developed a test for long-range dependence and found significant long-term correlations among fluctuations in the Nile's outflows and described these correlations in terms of power laws. This statistic is known as the *rescaled range*, *range over standard deviation* or *R/S* statistic.

    http://www.long-memory.com/.

    Another worthwhile document on the Hurst exponent and other related matters of time series analysis, authored by Martin Sewell, can be found in the research document entitled *Characterization of Financial Time Series* by Martin Sewell, 20 January 2011, http://www.cs.ucl.ac.uk/fileadmin/UCL-CS/research/Research_Notes/RN_11_01.pdf.

23. James Saft, *The Knightian Dog Ate my Recovery*, Reuters, August 31, 2010:

    > Nicholas Nassim Taleb has been properly excoriating academically minded policy-makers for being over-confident in their own systems, like the guy who bluffs in poker and then complains that you shouldn't have called him.
    >
    > "Life is not a laboratory in which we are supplied probabilities. Nor is it an exercise in textbooks on statistics. Nor is it an urn. Nor is it a casino where the state authorities monitor and enforce some probabilistic transparency," Taleb writes.
    >
    > "The more events matter, the worse our empirical knowledge about their properties."
    >
    > The amazing thing is that central bankers, or at least some of them, are just now getting the courage to admit how little they know and knew about the forces that caused the crisis and the ones that are still operating today.

    http://blogs.reuters.com/great-debate/2010/08/31/the-knightian-dog-ate-my-recovery/.

24. I am indebted to Craig Ellis at the University of Western Sydney for private correspondence relating to the various methods used for measuring the Hurst coefficient. One method of calculating the Hurst value depends on slicing the series of log changes into a series of ranges or boxes which start from an initial box size and then incrementally increases that box size until all of the available data has been covered. This method, known as the H-Hurst technique, is computationally expensive and for a large set of data, even with a fast processor, can take hours to calculate. An alternative method, known as the G-Hurst technique, is to divide the data set into a series of boxes based upon discrete samplings chosen at specific intervals across the entire range of data. This will involve far fewer calculations and will take much less time to compute.

As Ellis has observed "the rescaled range is an asymptotic statistic and is highly sensitive to short series lengths and small subseries lengths in the log (R/S) / log (n) calculations." Ellis recommends using the G-Hurst method and then recommends that this should be followed by a final adjustment algorithm which will correct any overestimations of the value derived from the use of inadequately sized data series. An excellent, but somewhat technically daunting, explanation of this technique can be found in Craig Ellis, "The mis-specification of the expected rescaled adjusted range," (2006) *Physica A*.

The document is available online at: http://www.finance.uts.edu.au/research/wpapers/wp69.html.

The algorithm that I have used to obtain the Hurst values is based on the G-Hurst method that was outlined above but without using the final adjustment logic that is outlined in Ellis's paper. I am satisfied that using this technique has considerable value when one is focused on relatively shorter time frames in contrast to the very extended periods which are required by certain Hurst estimation techniques. The algorithm used to produce the results shown in Figure 3.7, Figure 3.8 and also in Figure 8.10 has also been used to calculate values for a wide variety of asset types. For a significant subset of these asset types Hurst values have been calculated as lying in the range of 0.5 to 0.6 which is the range which would be "expected" from extensive historical back testing. It has also been observed that in the post-GFC financial environment there has been a general tendency across most asset types for higher Hurst values to be found than was the case in pre-GFC financial markets.

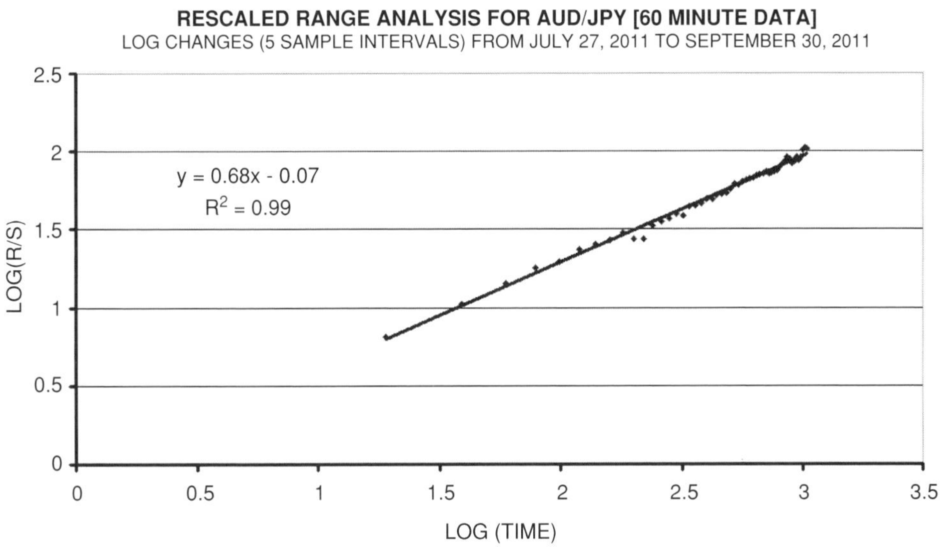

25. The following description of the KBW Banking Index comes from http://www.analyzeindices.com/ind/banks.htm:

> The KBW Bank Sector (BKX) is a capitalization-weighted index composed of 24 geographically diverse stocks representing national money center banks and leading regional institutions. BKX is based on one-tenth the value of the value of the Keefe, Bruyette & Woods Index (KBWI). Founded in 1962, Keefe, Bruyette & Woods is long recognized as the "banking industry experts," following more than 200 commercial banking and thrift industries on a daily basis.
>
> The index was initiated at the time of the firm's founding and was calculated retroactively to 1947. The index is evaluated at least annually by Keefe, Bruyette & Woods to review whether the composition is

highly representative of the banking industry. BKX was set to an initial value of 250 on October 21, 1991; options commenced trading September 21, 1992.

Bank of America Corp.	BAC
BB&T Corp.	BBT
Bank of New York Company	BK
Citigroup Inc.	C
Comerica Inc.	CMA
Fifth Third Bancorp	FITB
Golden West Financial Corp	GDW
JP Morgan Chase & Co	JPM
Keycorp	KEY
MBNA Corp	KRB
Mellon Financial Corporation	MEL
M&T Bank Corp	MTB
National City Corp.	NCC
North Fork Bank	NFB
Northern Trust Corp.	NTRS
PNC Financial Services	PNC
(New) Region Financial	RF
SunTrust Banks Inc.	STI
State Street Corp.	STT
US Bancorp	USB
Wachovia Corp	WB
Wells Fargo and Co.	WFC
Washington Mutual	WM
Zion Bancorporation	ZION

26. I am indebted to one of the reviewers of the manuscript for this book, John Lounsbury, for pointing out that the Hurst exponent is very fundamentally related to fractal dimensions. He drew my attention to a good, although somewhat technical, research note entitled "Stochastic Models That Separate Fractal Dimension and Hurst Effect" by T. Gneiting and M. Schlather which is available online at http://www.stat.washington.edu/research/reports/2003/tr425.pdf.

The authors also discuss software techniques for further investigating fractal dimensions and the Hurst coefficient:

> Time series, profiles, and surfaces have been characterized by their fractal dimension, a measure of roughness, and by the Hurst coefficient, a measure of long-memory dependence. Either phenomenon has been modeled and explained by self-affine random functions, such as fractional Gaussian noise and fractional Brownian motion. The assumption of statistical self-affinity implies a linear relationship between fractal dimension and Hurst coefficient and thereby links the two phenomena.

4

The Flash Crash

On May 6, 2010 just after 2.30pm Eastern Daylight Time, the Dow Jones Industrial Average (DJIA) plunged by about 1000 points – or about 9% – only to recover those losses within minutes. It was the second largest point swing, 1010 points, and the biggest one-day point decline, 998 points, on an intraday basis, in the index's history.

Temporarily, $1 trillion in market value disappeared. The stocks of several companies in the S&P 500 fell to one cent per share for a short time, including Accenture and Center Point Energy, while other stocks, including Sotheby's, Apple, and Hewlett-Packard, increased in value to over $100,000 in price. Procter & Gamble (PG) a component of the Dow Jones Industrial Average (DJIA) plummeted by 37% before rebounding, within minutes, back to more or less its original levels.

In order to understand the circumstances surrounding this event which has come to be known as the *Flash Crash* – although in truth it should better be described as a temporary systemic breakdown – it is necessary to give the reader a little background to the financial instruments that will be referenced in the ensuing analysis of the crash and also to make references to a document prepared by the US securities regulatory authorities who investigated this remarkable market event. The document entitled *Findings regarding the market events of May 6, 2010,* represents the report of the staffs of the CFTC and SEC to the Joint Advisory Committee on Emerging Regulatory Issues and was published on September 30, 2010. [1]

The E-Mini S&P 500 contract, often abbreviated simply to "E-Mini" is the most actively traded equity index futures contract in the world and is traded around the clock, five days a week, on the Chicago Mercantile Exchange's (CME) Globex electronic trading platform. [2] The notional value of one contract is US$50 times the value of the S&P 500 stock index. To further clarify the nature of this instrument, if one assumes that the S&P 500 index is trading at 1300 then the notional value of a single futures contract would be $65 000 although, as a leveraged futures position, the holder of such a contract may only have to post an initial margin of around $2500. The electronically traded version of the index futures contract has become the preferred instrument to trade by many institutions, especially by hedge funds, because, unlike the larger S&P 500 contract which is traded in the open outcry pits at the CME where there will be delays in execution, the Globex platform provides the capacity for real-time HFT algorithmic activity which is now the dominant form of trading for this contract as well as most other equity trading in the US.

As illustrated in Figure 4.1, on the day of the Flash Crash, the price of the E-Mini S&P 500 futures collapsed by 5% between 2:30pm and 2:45pm, on top of the almost 3% it had already retreated intraday. Between 2:30pm and 3:00pm, in excess of 1.1 million contracts were exchanged in the June 2010 futures version of the E-Mini contract alone. Across both futures and equity markets, according to the CFTC/SEC report "there was a complete evaporation of liquidity in the marketplace." It is worth quoting from the report at some length:

> At 2:32 p.m., against this backdrop of unusually high volatility and thinning liquidity, a large fundamental trader (a mutual fund complex) initiated a sell program to sell a total of 75,000 E-Mini contracts (valued at approximately $4.1 billion) as a hedge to an existing equity position.

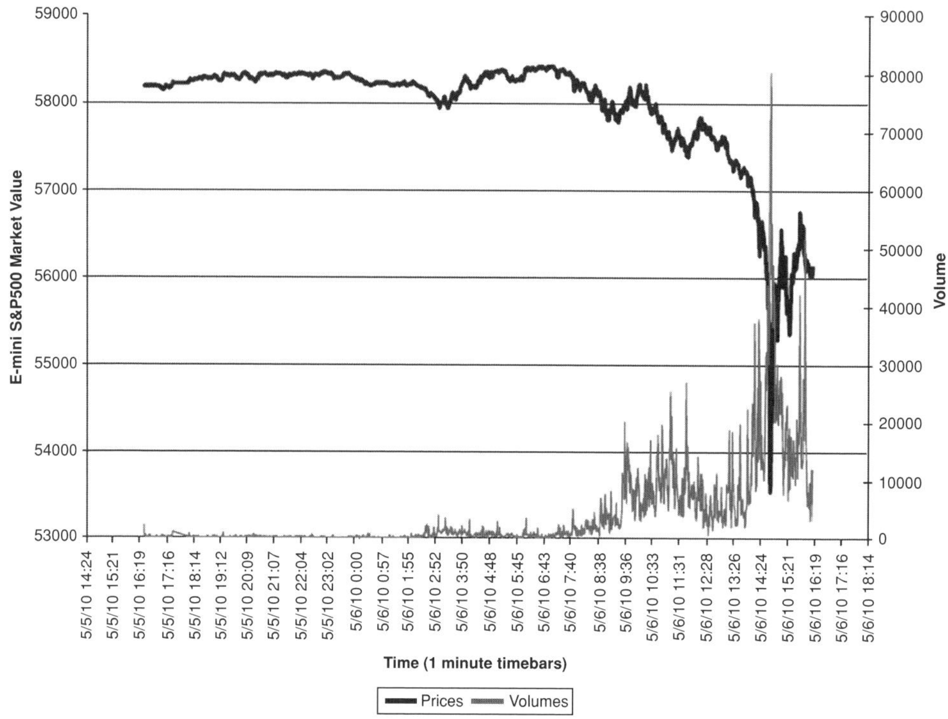

Figure 4.1 Flash Crash
Source: The Microstructure of the Flash Crash, Easley et al.

> This large fundamental trader chose to execute this sell program via an automated execution algorithm ("Sell Algorithm") that was programmed to feed orders into the June 2010 E-Mini market to target an execution rate set to 9% of the trading volume calculated over the previous minute, but without regard to price or time.
>
> The execution of this sell program resulted in the largest net change in daily position of any trader in the E-Mini since the beginning of the year (from January 1, 2010 through May 6, 2010). Only two single-day sell programs of equal or larger size – one of which was by the same large fundamental trader – were executed in the E-Mini in the 12 months prior to May 6. When executing the previous sell program, this large fundamental trader utilized a combination of manual trading entered over the course of a day and several automated execution algorithms which took into account price, time, and volume. On that occasion it took more than 5 hours for this large trader to execute the first 75,000 contracts of a large sell program.
>
> However, on May 6, when markets were already under stress, the Sell Algorithm chosen by the large trader to only target trading volume, and neither price nor time, executed the sell program extremely rapidly in just 20 minutes.

What is most striking about this account is the fact that the fundamental trader cited, i.e. a mutual fund (which has subsequently been identified as will be seen), decided to implement the sell algorithm very rapidly, unlike the more customary method of "slicing and dicing" trades to obtain better executions. There is an implicit suggestion that since "markets were already under stress" to use the report's own words, the large sell order in the E-Mini futures created a panic-like condition which precipitated a vicious feedback loop which then fed on itself. Whether or not the actions of the mutual fund can really adequately explain the resulting mayhem has been questioned as we will see. Moreover, the report unfortunately does not have too much to say as to why markets were, to use its own words, "already under stress," and as will be shown in later discussions, there is scant attention paid in the report to stressful events occurring in other asset markets coincidentally with the action in the E-Mini contract. [3] Nonetheless the report is a useful document in capturing the actual sequence of events that took place with regard to the E-Mini futures contracts as illustrated by the following quote from the report:

> HFTs and intermediaries were the likely buyers of the initial batch of orders submitted by the Sell Algorithm, and, as a result, these buyers built up temporary long positions. Specifically, HFTs accumulated a net long position of about 3,300 contracts. However, between 2:41 p.m. and 2:44 p.m., HFTs aggressively sold about 2,000 E-Mini contracts in order to reduce their temporary long positions. At the same time, HFTs traded nearly 140,000 E-Mini contracts or over 33% of the total trading volume. This is consistent with the HFTs' typical practice of trading a very large number of contracts, but not accumulating an aggregate inventory beyond three to four thousand contracts in either direction.

Financial intermediaries, executing predominantly in the form of HFTs, in other words, electronic market makers, upon seeing such unbalanced order flow, decided to reverse their normal mode of operation which is one of providing liquidity to other market "principals" and instead began consuming liquidity in order to avoid building an excessive inventory of long positions (i.e. they would have been taking an abnormally high amount of long positions as the other side to the execution of the mutual fund's sell algorithm). This gives rise to the crucially important observation regarding, not only the events of May 6, 2010 but also, in a more general sense, the relationship between the volume of trading and the liquidity of a market. [4]

> Although May 6th 2010 was the third-highest-volume-day in the history of E-mini S&P 500 futures, there is consensus in categorizing it as an extremely illiquid day. Indeed, the CFTC-SEC report stresses that "high trading volume is not necessarily a reliable indicator of market liquidity." That volume and liquidity need not be congruent is a reflection of the delicate symbiosis between *market makers* and *position takers* in a high frequency world.

The key phrase in the above is *high trading volume is not necessarily a reliable indicator of market liquidity* and there is a lot to de-compress in this short phrase. Quite a lot of the discussion in subsequent chapters will be concerned with elucidating the nature of algorithmic activity and making the vital distinction, for understanding contemporary markets, between volume as a quantitative measure and liquidity as a qualitative characteristic that markets either have or do not have.

The CFTC/SEC report did not identify the mutual fund which it refers to in the account, but according to articles published by both the Wall Street Journal and Bloomberg after the report's publication, the company in question was Waddell & Reed, a mutual fund company, based in Kansas. [5] Bloomberg interviewed several market analysts regarding this firm and the consensus view was that, given the rather parochial nature of the fund, it seemed to be a rather unlikely company to be blamed for the entire episode. Since the publication of the CFTC/SEC Report there have been numerous criticisms of their findings. For example, Scot Warren, managing director of equity indexes for CME, flatly contradicted the characterization of the sell algorithm that featured as one of the central elements of the SEC report's conclusions. According to the CME executive: [6]

> "This was a sophisticated algorithm that took time and price into consideration," said Warren, contesting descriptions of the trade as an emergency bet that helped spark a rout in stock prices. Warren said the session's activity revealed a "fundamental supply and demand imbalance" that spooked buyers from the market.

While this may be a valid observation, other criticisms have been made that even the purchase of a very large number of equity index put options by Universa Investments, a Santa Monica hedge fund, advised by Nicholas Taleb, [7] would not itself have been sufficient to cause the kind of dramatic sequence of events that unfolded in the thirty minutes from 14:30 – 15:00 on May 6, 2010. Probably the best that can be said about the CFTC/SEC report is that it threw quite a lot more light on the event than the initial explanation which was propounded by some commentators in the financial media who suggested that it was a "fat finger" event caused by a single trader hitting the wrong key on the keypad of a trading terminal.

In more general terms, there is a danger that from our common sense notions of causation there is a tendency to look for a large cause when there is a large effect. However the nature of markets is that they can be critically poised on the edge of disorder and it might well be a relatively minor contributory factor which causes them to enter into the kind of spiraling feedback loop which causes them to crash. In this context it is worth noting the comment made by Per Bak, a very influential physicist who was mentioned in the introductory chapter, with regard to the behavior of complex systems which can undergo rapid changes of state due to feedback loops, and in general, what is referred to as nonlinear dynamics:

> The assumption that a large effect must come from a large impact also represents a linear way of thinking. However, we may be dealing with highly non-linear systems in which there is no simple way (or no way at all) to predict emergent behavior . . .
>
> From Per Bak, *How Nature Works (The Science of Self Organized Criticality)* p. 131

Bak's experimental work with virtual sand-piles – they are software simulations – focuses on the manner in which very large scale disruptions in the form of avalanches can arise within the sand-piles following the gradual and incremental addition of a single grain of sand. Bak shows that it is not possible to anticipate exactly when the incremental grain added will cause a sudden avalanche, and the fact that such large scale consequences can arise from the addition of a single grain is noticeably counter intuitive. In other words, the addition of one more grain – a small event – when placed into a pile of sand which has reached a position of "self-organized criticality" or *latent stress* may then undergo a dramatic change of state in which it collapses. The "emergent behavior" of a system of sand grains in a pile or even a financial market which may also have reached a state of hidden stress can be abrupt and overwhelming. The notion of a tipping point has often been used to exemplify the character of these types of nonlinear dynamics.

As the preceding discussion suggests it is necessary to look at the background conditions within the equity markets – and specifically the E-Mini futures market – as well as the actual flow of orders and trading activity that transpired on May 6, 2010.

Some very illuminating research that has been undertaken by a group of academics at Cornell University on the micro-structure of markets, in general, and specifically the Flash

Crash has given rise to a metric known as VPIN. [8] Before describing this metric, which will be a central feature of Chapter 5, it is worth noting that the term VPIN has become a trademark of Tudor Investment Corporation, a large Connecticut based hedge fund which is owned and spearheaded by Paul Tudor Jones, one of the most successful global macro trader/investors over the last 20 years and who is listed amongst the top 40 richest individuals in the US. [9] His company uses various sophisticated, quantitatively based, procedures in its trading activities across multiple asset classes. That Tudor Investments has procured the trademark and access to the VPIN technology is a significant endorsement of its underlying methodology and reflects their view that the technology is very beneficial for market timing.

In essence, the VPIN metric is designed to capture the extent to which markets may have reached hidden stress levels resulting from large imbalances in the flow of trading orders, and these were very much in evidence prior to, and during the Flash Crash, and which could even provide an early warning system for regulators. [10] Using a statistical technique to estimate the probability of extreme values in order flow, [11] the metric provides a single value between 0 and 1 which captures the degree to which HFTs and electronic market makers may have become critically skewed or lopsided with respect to their short-term inventories of long or short positions (such as E-Mini futures) in an electronic market. Once market makers have reached a critical level – and this could be the culmination of several sessions of unbalanced order flow from the market makers' perspective – the HFTs and electronic intermediaries can abruptly *switch from being liquidity providers to liquidity consumers*. Recognizing that there is a high risk for them of being caught with an excessive holding of positions for which there is no demand but rather indefinitely large supply, these electronic intermediaries will want to rapidly exit their trades. As electronic market makers become price takers rather than price suppliers normal market liquidity can evaporate within seconds in an HFT world.

As explained in the CFTC/SEC report and elaborated within the Cornell University research work it is worth spelling out the nature of the HFTs in, for example, the trading of futures contracts such as the E-Mini. Many of the firms which employ HFT algorithms are best seen as acting as market makers or intermediaries to principals (for example hedge funds and the proprietary trading desks of investment banks, as such the latter can best be considered as *position takers*). Position takers may know more about the future direction of prices or have greater capital and/or different holding periods to those of the market makers. Position takers also need to operate within a market place where there is sufficient liquidity for them to be able to execute large trades. The electronic market makers under "normal circumstances" will provide this liquidity by being the *transient* counter-parties to the trades which the position takers wish to have executed.

Market makers make money through the bid/ask spread. By intermediating what it expects to be relatively haphazard order flow, the electronic market maker or the HFT firm can buy at the bid, i.e. the lower price, and sell at the ask, the higher price. The bid and ask are constantly changing quantities depending on fluctuating market conditions, and likewise the size of the spread itself can widen or narrow to reflect the depth of the orders flowing through the market. Market makers, more precisely HFT algorithms, will adjust the size of the spread to reflect their perceptions as to the changing nature in the volume of buy and sell orders, the degree of inventory which they are holding and also with regard to the quality of the order flow. Market making is highly competitive and in the rapid fire world of HFT algorithms there are several dimensions for potential disruption based on excess inventory accumulation, changes in the quality of order flow and so on.

4.1 MARKET MICROSTRUCTURE

Insightful explanations of the kind of extreme behavior seen during market crises can arise from a detailed examination of the micro-structure of markets. These insights, as revealed in a more detailed explanation of the VPIN metric which we will come to, will help to understand the causes of the extreme outlier phenomena which are a central theme of this book. So what is meant by this term micro-structure of markets? In her book *Market Microstructure Theory*, Maureen O'Hara, who is also one of the contributors at Cornell University to the development of the VPIN metric, defines market micro-structure as "the study of the process and outcomes of exchanging assets under a specific set of rules. While much of economics abstracts from the mechanics of trading, microstructure theory focuses on how specific trading mechanisms affect the price formation process." [12] The merit of this approach is that, in line with future discussions regarding profound limitations of mainstream macro-economic theory, the focus is very much on a strongly empirical approach to how markets actually behave rather than *deducing* how they behave from a flawed theory. In the same way that armchair speculation about the nature of matter by metaphysicians has been overwhelmingly replaced by the work of practicing scientists, so there is need for a paradigmatic shift and new economic thinking and investigation into the actual *modus operandi* of financial markets and the macro economy.

Observation and empirical data are the vital prerequisites for more accurate and robust types of explanations for the bubble/bust dynamics that are found at the macro-economic level, and it is contended that they can be very well informed by a better understanding of what happens at the micro level in the behavior of actual markets. Some macro-economists, as with the metaphysicians of yesteryear, engage in a lot of top down *a priori* reasoning about the nature of the global economy and its financial system but much of it has proven to be hopelessly ineffectual. It is not an exaggeration to say that there is a crisis in macro-economics [13] and equal criticisms can be leveled at orthodox theories of finance. There is a need, which is being addressed as will be seen in Chapter 10, to replace a lot of the outmoded conceptual baggage which underlies financial economics in particular. One of the useful building blocks in this task of reconstruction of outmoded concepts can be found in better understanding of markets at the micro-structural level.

In this chapter and in the next there will be a lot of attention to some innovative research that is taking place into the manner in which characteristics displayed in the workflow of markets – the behavior and functions of various participants on sophisticated trading platforms – can, when scaled up, provide useful heuristics for much better understanding of the financial economy at the macro level. One of the most valuable insights, and this was derived from a forensic analysis at the micro level of order flow during the Flash Crash, relates to the manner in which markets can become disproportionately unbalanced at extremes. Under such circumstances intermediation becomes dysfunctional – in other words those providing market liquidity suddenly *exit the market* – and, lacking basic liquidity, markets will crash. In an intricate and closely interwoven fashion that will be developed in later sections, it is not too much of an overstretch to suggest that the decisions by liquidity providers to exit the market as on May 6, 2010, bear a resemblance within a macro context to the reaching of a Minsky moment at the culmination of a bubble. [14]

In developing better frameworks, tools, and models for this enriched understanding it will be useful, following on from some of the Cornell research which will be the main focus of the next chapter, to propose a simple three-tiered schematic to capture the key structural elements of a contemporary financial market. The three layers or tiers – which may not always be in evidence in all markets – are as follows:

Table 4.1 Schematic for simplified market micro-structure

Tier	Description	Participants
One	Informed Traders	Principals, Prop Trading Desks, Hedge Funds, Large Institutional Investors
Two	Liquidity Enhancers, Market Makers	Market Makers, Liquidity Providers, HFT Electronic Intermediaries
Three	Uninformed Traders	Retail Investors, SME Financial Institutions, Small Pension Funds

Tier One is called Informed Traders. Sometimes this is referred to as "smart money" but I shall refrain from using that terminology as there is something rather circular and elitist about this notion. [15] If we are tempted to use the term smart money – which has entered the Wall Street folklore – we should ask the following question. Following an important market breakout when we are tempted to attribute this to accumulation and astuteness on the part of smart investors, can we identify the actual parties that were accumulating and showing astute tactics before the event? If not we are really saying little more than this – there was some accumulative activity prior to the price increase and since certain parties were correctly positioned to take advantage of the increase they must have been the "smart" money. But it doesn't take much reflection to realize that this is only true in a circular fashion. What is valuable about more recent research and better understanding of the underlying dynamics in trading activity is that we can avoid this circularity and be a lot more precise about the nature of each of the tiers in Table 4.1, including the informed traders/investors. Greater specificity as to how it is possible to differentiate the activities in each tier from the actual characteristics of orders and the quality of order flow will be the subject matter of the next chapter.

Going back to the schematic shown in Table 4.1, occupants of Tier One – the informed traders – may have superior knowledge regarding certain securities; these informed traders will be well capitalized and may, but do not necessarily, have longer holding period horizons than those in the next layer – the market makers.

Tier Two is best described as the market makers – in traditional markets this would be human beings including, for example, NYSE specialists, but in modern markets these are electronic "agents" and include firms which deploy HFT algorithms. Market makers are those, who, because of their position within the micro-structure of markets, have the ability to monitor order flow, volume, bid/ask spreads, and they therefore have a relative advantage over the third tier with respect to the likely development of price within relatively short time frames. Occupants of the second tier will typically have very short holding period horizons and may be thinly capitalized. They need to be nimble and apply strict inventory control protocols to ensure that their end-of-day inventories are neither greater nor more lopsided than is commensurate with their risk management experience.

Tier Three is called uninformed traders (I shall refrain from using other terms which have been used in this context such as "noise traders" or even the derisory term "the dumb money").

Occupants of the three layers would be typically as follows:

Tier One would comprise hedge funds, proprietary trading desks, and under certain circumstances and in certain markets, institutions such as central banks and sovereign wealth funds.

Tier Two would comprise liquidity providers or market makers and HFT firms. Most liquidity providers do not seek to make a directional bet, but instead participate on both sides of the order book in an attempt to maximize the turnover of their inventory. A typical HFT market maker could turn over its inventory several times a day. In addition, these market makers also will be looking to hold very small or even zero inventory positions at the end of each session as they do not want to incur either the expense or risk of carrying inventory over night and especially over a weekend or holiday period.

Tier Three would comprise retail investors, certain kinds of collective investment schemes – such as mutual funds, investment trusts – and I will propose that this category should include those pension funds and insurance companies that have not engaged a specialized broker to act as an advisor and execution agent with algorithmic trading expertise.

One of the key notions with this three-tiered model is that there is information asymmetry with respect to the different tiers of market participants. Expressed simply the informed traders will have the most advantageous position with respect to an estimation about the future trajectory to be taken during the process of *price discovery*. This advantage could arise because they are the largest players and they will often have superior knowledge through their commitment to investing in intramural research, and also via access to knowledge about the investment decision making of a broad cross-section of other market "principals" such as their corporate clients. It could, despite protestations to the contrary about the sanctity of *Chinese walls* in the world of banking, even stem from "front running" i.e. knowledge before the rest of the market of the intentions of large clients for whom a prime broker acts. As investment banks wear many hats as agents, prime brokers (not exactly the same as an agent but similar), and principals, the classic issues regarding principal/agent conflict of interest most certainly do apply, and there are sufficient cases on record to have to be very skeptical about the supposed lack of internal disclosures beyond Chinese walls.

The market makers, already characterized as electronic agents, have some information advantages but these are primarily derived from their knowledge of market internals – order flow, depth of order books, and certain knowledge that they may have derived from observing the actual logic of the software routines within competing algorithmic agents.

The uninformed traders are those who most probably will be lacking both the knowledge possessed by the informed traders because they may not have access to all of the high powered research of investment banks (for example it has not yet been published) or exposure to a wide range of sources of information from the multiplicity of clients that an investment bank may advise; also they will not have such detailed meta-market information, i.e. the internal market order flow data knowledge, which is possessed by the market makers.

4.2 PREDATOR PREY DYNAMICS

The archetypal occupants of the third tier in Table 4.1 are retail investors who have a pretty poor reputation as far as those who focus on investment analysis are concerned. Often perceived as herd-like with a tendency to buy when markets are fully priced – indeed they have traditionally been seen, again within the Wall Street parlance, as the "suckers" or "muppets" who come into the markets in the latter stages of a bubble and thus provide a fertile area for the informed traders to distribute what they accumulated when equities were out of favor – and sell in fits of despair when markets crash.

In fact one can even find literal expression within the academic literature on market microstructure of seeing, for example, the relationship between the relatively informed participants which would include the Tier One participants along with the market makers of Tier Two as opposed to the uninformed participants in Tier Three such as the retail investor, in the guise of a predator/prey model.

In a paper entitled "Time-Varying Arrival Rates of Informed and Uninformed Trades" published in 2002, [16] authored by some of the contributors at Cornell University to the development of the VPIN methodology which will be described later, make references to the notion that the informed traders have similar characteristics to the predators within an ecosystem or food web, and that the uninformed traders of Tier Three can be characterized as being their prey.

The following quotation comes from the introductory section to the paper just cited: [17]

> [A] useful construct is to view order arrivals as reflecting the behavior of sheep and wolves. In sequential trade models ... the uninformed act as sheep, meekly heading to market where they will be preyed upon by the more informed wolves. The informed traders, the wolves, also head to the market, driven by the need to feast on the gains from their private information.

I find this to be a remarkably candid and illuminating insight, at the micro-structural level, into the predatory nature of modern markets, and indeed in the enlarged sense and if scaled up to the macro level, it echoes some of the more polemical attacks on post-industrial capitalism. [18] Particularly striking is the notion that the informed traders – the wolves – *need to feast on the gains from their private information.* In their extensive review of the literature regarding the *modus operandi* of informed and uninformed traders the authors also note that even in more refined modeling approaches which have been undertaken by other researchers using computer simulations of market behavior there is still a clear sense that the uninformed traders – the sheep – are the victims of predation:

> [Other studies] ... allowed for more introspective sheep who timed their trades to avoid the presence of wolves. In these models, sheep herd by sending in orders when other sheep are known to be present; the wolves respond by trading when the sheep trade.

The nature of predatory/prey ecosystems has been the subject of a huge amount of research in the life sciences and beyond, and to do justice to this, even at the superficial level, would take us considerably beyond the core themes of this book. I will just allude to one of the more provocative ideas which has emerged from the interaction of predators and prey and its impact on population dynamics. [19] To summarize this rather simplistically it is contended that predator/prey systems have unstable dynamics where perturbations or disrupting events can easily shift a food web into feedback loops which will make it increasingly difficult for such food webs or ecosystems to maintain any kind of equilibrium conditions. For example, and to continue with the example of the wolves and sheep, any decrease in the population of sheep will inevitably destabilize the food chain leading to a reduction in the population of wolves. Once this instability is introduced into the ecosystem there is then the possibility that the population of sheep will be allowed to enlarge and this will pose additional instability until there is a commensurate increase in the number of wolves and so on. If one conducts simulations of such an unstable system and plots the changing dynamics and attainment of temporary equilibria states the results are quite extraordinary and the reader may be tempted to explore this fascinating area in more depth.

From the standpoint of political economy there are quite significant implications to the preceding discussion and especially in regard to the kind of disruptions that have resulted from the crisis of 2008. The dramatic shifts in wealth and the disappearance of income which are legacies of the bursting of the real estate bubble (and which will be discussed in Chapter 10) have resulted in fundamental changes to the nature of participants in each of the three tiers of Table 4.1. The exit from equity markets of many retail investors has reduced the importance of the Tier Three participants and in turn created more of a predator/prey dynamic between the occupants of Tiers One and Two. Perhaps more provocative is the notion that as there is an erosion in the depth of true liquidity in markets as opposed to algorithmic churn there is a greater potential for cannibalization at the Tier One level.

4.3 COMPUTER SIMULATIONS OF MARKET BEHAVIOR

The growing and fascinating literature on market micro-structure takes in a number of different areas of focus, but all of them revolve around the notion of "price discovery."

Computer scientists at the Santa Fe Institute, for example, [20] have set forth some very informative results from creating artificial markets populated by "agents" designed by software engineers to emulate the behavior of human agents in real markets. Somewhat ironically, given the prevalence of algorithmic routines as the underpinning of today's real markets, the distinction between humans and robot traders is becoming extremely blurred. The good news is that the ability of algorithms to follow programmed rules and decision procedures and conduct markets – at least a lot of the time – provides an opportunity to inspect the logic which drives the process of price formation or discovery. In at least one tier within a market, while not entirely deterministic – the algorithms can always be switched off, as they were on May 6, 2010 – the manner in which electronic market makers can go about their business according to the rules which have been programmed throws light on a key part of the intermediation process whereby liquidity functions and prices emerge from a complex interplay of other actors/agents within a financial market.

One of the leading exponents of applying computer simulations and what are generally referred to as agent-based modeling techniques to the study markets is Professor Doyne Farmer of the Santa Fe Institute in New Mexico, which is the home of the inter-disciplinary approach to complexity theory and the study of complex adaptive systems. Farmer also had a stint working for the Prediction Company as a co-founder, which was a company that was partly financed by UBS and whose mission was to apply sophisticated quantitative techniques designed to uncover exploitable patterns in financial time series. [21] In a paper entitled "Toward Agent-Based Models for Investment," first published in 2001, [22] Farmer outlines his agenda for the importation of software simulation techniques that had been used in numerous contexts at the Santa Fe Institute to the study of finance and investment. In the article we find a prospectus for the technique:

> An agent-based model involves a model for price formation and a model for agent behavior, including the models' information inputs and how the inputs behave, which could involve learning.

> From an investor's point of view, agent-based models represent a new direction that may or may not result in more practical investment models. From an academic's point of view, agent-based models are fascinating new tools that make it possible to investigate problems previously out of reach. [23]

Since this early work in the field Farmer has been joined by a growing number of practitioners that have made considerable progress in investigating the complex dynamics that emerge from relatively simple rules of engagement between traders within a simple market micro-structure. They have produced some important insights into the nature of the stylized facts (e.g. volatility clustering and the "fat tails" phenomenon) about markets that the more traditional/orthodox financial community had been unable to explain.

Another approach [24] suggests that markets will produce abrupt switches when too many traders are following momentum strategies based on technical factors and that the "switch" will cause the restoration of "normal" conditions that are the outcome of strategies and valuations more in accordance with the algorithmic traders that are following fundamentalist strategies. Although the model is simple and begs questions about exactly what constitutes a fundamentalist strategy, the broad conclusions that are extracted from the way that the model functions have a certain intuitive plausibility. In broad terms the findings offer additional insights into the building of bubbles and their subsequent collapse.

One further approach to the cognitive elements that are built into the software agents is worth attention as it rests on a large body of work that seeks to explain what is sometimes referred to as herding behavior. The concept of financial contagion has its roots in the use of the terminology that explains the process by which diseases are propagated to form epidemics. The spread of viruses can be extraordinarily fast in a highly networked world and for instantaneous forms of communication such as those upon which the capital markets are founded the contagion metaphor can be very apt to explain how crises can emerge and rapidly mesmerize the world's trading desks. Financial contagion models are usually based on the idea that traders occupy virtual "neighborhoods" and when enough of a trader's nearest neighbors are in the process of changing their views about the market or individual security there is a network feedback effect or "tipping point" reached in which the traders *en masse* suddenly form the same opinions. This is reminiscent of the discussion of how coherent behavior emerges as market sentiment becomes highly aligned. Another metaphor or model that has been used to explain the way in which an effect spreads through a network topology is the percolation model. The seminal work in this regard is a book by Dietrich Stauffer [25] which provides an insight into percolation logic when considered in its most general form.

Stauffer demonstrates that for a network conceived as a two-dimensional grid or lattice the theoretical percolation value can be precisely determined. The best way to imagine this is to think of the lattice as analogous to a forest with each of the trees occupying sites on the lattice or grid. If all of the sites in the grid are occupied a fire which begins on the forest's boundaries will eventually consume all of the trees within the forest. But what is the threshold amount that will ensure that the fire will eventually spread from one boundary to the furthest boundary? It turns out that the threshold amount is approximately 59%. So if only 50% of the sites in the forest (or lattice) are populated with trees the fire will not spread from one side to the other but above 59% it will.

Interested readers may wish to follow up on this work in network topologies and percolation because it is replete with novel insights into network dynamics. As traders in a binary trading environment form extremely aligned views about the near term direction of price development in financial markets there is a greater propensity to sudden and abrupt bouts of illiquidity.

ENDNOTES

1. *Findings regarding the market events of May 6, 2010*, which is easily accessible on the internet at http://www.sec.gov/news/studies/2010/marketevents-report.pdf.
2. The S&P500 E-Mini is a futures contract that tracks the S&P500 index. It is traded on the Chicago Mercantile Exchange (CME) via their Globex electronic platform. Trading is $23^1/_2$ hours a day, 5 days a week, using the symbol ES.

    Each 1 point move in the S&P500 index is worth US$50 per contract and the minimum move of the E-mini futures contract (tick size) is 0.25 index points or US$12.50 per contract.

    Weekly trading of the E-mini opens on Sunday at 5pm (CST) and closes on Friday at 3:15pm. Trading is almost 24 hours a day with a short break every day between 3:15pm and 3:30pm and then between 4:30pm and 5:00pm for any scheduled maintenance.

    Trade is broken into two sessions: the Day session and the After-hours session. The Day session trading starts at 8:30am (CST) and closes at 3:15pm. Then the After-hours session trading re-starts at 3:30pm and continues until the open of the Day session the next morning.

    The greatest activity and volume traded obviously happens during the Day session. However, data releases before the Day session open can often generate large activity, as can any important news out of Europe.

    With contract expiry every quarter E-mini contracts are very similar to other futures contracts. They expire quarterly in March, June, September and December and are denoted by the letters "H", "M", "U" and "Z" respectively. So ES11H (or ESH11) is the symbol for an S&P500 E-mini futures contract that expires in March 2011.

    Contract expiry is on the 3rd Friday of March, June, September and December. However, Contract rollover – when the majority of trading moves to the next contract – is on the 2nd Thursday of March, June, September and December (unless the rollover month starts on a Friday, in which case it is on the 1st Thursday of the month).

3. Graham Bowley, Stock Swing Still Baffles, Ominously, *The New York Times*, August 22, 2010, http://www.nytimes.com/2010/08/23/business/23flash.html:

    To some people, like Eric Scott Hunsader, the founder of Nanex, they suggest that the specialized computers responsible for so much of today's stock trading simply overloaded the exchanges.

    He and others are tempted to go further, hypothesizing that the bizarre patterns might have been the result of a Wall Street version of cyberwarfare.

    "It's just madness to say we don't know what caused it. We do," said Steve Wunsch, a market structure consultant. "The crash was an inevitable consequence of creating multiple market centers."

    That is one explanation. Others have pointed to the high-frequency traders, who use powerful computers to transmit millions of orders at lightning speed. Some of these traders, who now dominate the stock market, appear to have fled the market as prices went haywire.

    Then their computer programs might have dragged down exchange-traded funds, popular investment vehicles that fell sharply during the crash, said Thomas Peterffy, chief executive of Interactive Brokers.

> "Computerized arbitrage kicked in," he said.
>
> But if Nanex's theory is to be believed, computer algorithms might have been at work as well, knowingly or unknowingly wreaking havoc and creating data crop circles.

4. Cited in the CTC/SEC report, see endnote 1.
5. The Mutual Fund in the "Flash Crash," *Wall Street Journal*, October 6, 2010, http://online.wsj.com/article/SB10001424052748704689804575536513798579500.html;
   Flash-Crash Story Looks More Like a Fairy Tale, Bloomberg, May 7, 2010, http://www.bloomberg.com/news/2012-05-07/flash-crash-story-looks-more-like-a-fairy-tale.html.
6. Flash Crash Report Criticism Continues, PrefBlog, November 5, 2010, http://www.prefblog.com/?p=12867.
7. Universa Investments, a Santa Monica hedge fund, advised by Nicholas Taleb:

   > From their website: Universa is an investment management firm that specializes in convex tail hedging and investing, ranging from hedging stock market crashes and inflation to macro and equity options strategies. Universa portfolios are, by construction, exceedingly positively-skewed, robust to extreme risk assumptions, and non-linear to common risk factors (such as *beta*).

   http://www.universa.net/about.html.
8. David Easley is the Scarborough Professor and Donald C. Opatrny Chair, Department of Economics, Cornell University; Marcos M. López de Prado is Head of High Frequency Futures, Tudor Investment Corp. and Fellow at RCC, Harvard University; and Maureen O'Hara is the Robert W. Purcell Professor of Finance, Cornell University.

   > According to Bloomberg, the VPIN Flow Toxicity metric is the subject of a pending patent application filed by renowned Economics Professors Maureen O'Hara (Cornell University), David Easley (Cornell University) in collaboration with Tudor Investment Corporation, a large hedge fund.

9. Paul Tudor Jones II is the founder of Tudor Investment Corporation, which is the management company for his various private investment partnerships. As of March 2011, he was estimated to have a net worth of USD 3.3 billion by Forbes Magazine and ranked as 336th richest in the world.

   > The Tudor Group of companies is a group of affiliated entities engaged in the management of client and proprietary assets. Paul Tudor Jones II formed Tudor Investment Corporation, the first of the Tudor Group companies, in 1980. The Tudor Group manages assets across fixed income, currency, equity and commodity asset classes and related derivative instruments in the global markets for an international clientele. The investment strategies of the Tudor Group include, among others, discretionary global macro, quantitative global macro (managed futures), quantitative equity systems, discretionary equity long/short and growth equity.

   https://www.tudorfunds.com/TUDOR/WEB/me.get?dps.home.
10. E. Wes Bethel, David Leinweber, Oliver Rubel, and Kesheng Wu, *Federal Market Information Technology in the Post Flash Crash Era: Roles for Supercomputing*, Lawrence Berkeley National Laboratory, September 2011, http://www.lbl.gov/cs/html/CIFT-LBL-report.pdf.
11. The [C1] cumulative distribution function is a term within statistics to describe the probability that a given variable has a value above a specified threshold value. Accordingly a high value for the CDF of (say) 0.9 suggests that the probability is 90% that it would be below that value and only 10% that it would be above.

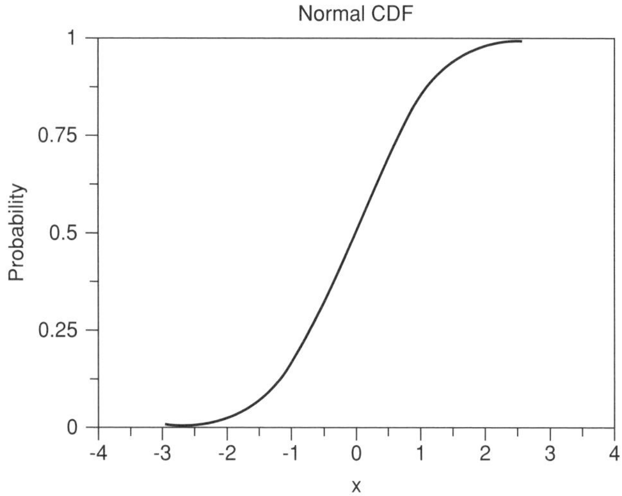

Simplified view of the cumulative distribution function

The horizontal axis is the allowable domain for the given probability function. Since the vertical axis is a probability, it must fall between zero and one. It increases from zero to one as we go from left to right on the horizontal axis.

12. Maureen O'Hara, *Market Microstructure Theory* (Blackwell, Oxford, 1995).
13. The State of Economics, The other-worldly philosophers, *The Economist*, July 16, 2009:

> The past 30 years of macroeconomics training at American and British universities were a "costly waste of time."

http://www.economist.com/node/14030288.

14. See Chapter 7, endnote 19.
15. There is a reference to the Smart Money Index in Clive Corcoran, *Long/Short Market Dynamics* (John Wiley & Sons, 2007) pp. 63–4.

One further and related approach to the issue of tracking the activity of smart money is to be found in the work of Lynn Elgert who initially expounded his views some years ago in an article that appeared in *Barrons* magazine. The procedure culminates in a market metric called the Smart Money Index and the basic idea behind its construction is that the dumb money is most active during the initial period of a market session whereas the smarter and more informed traders and investors are more active during the final hour of trading each day.

> The Smart Money Index is based on the idea that emotional, news-driven investors tend to trade during the first half-hour of trading, while the more rational, professional investors tend to trade during the final hour after evaluating the day's action in the markets. The Index is calculated by subtracting the change in the Dow-Jones Industrial Average during the first half-hour of trading from the change during the final hour, and then cumulating.

The concept of smart money seems to have lost favor amongst technical analysts.

16. David Easley, Robert F. Engle, Maureen O'Hara, and Liuren Wu, *Time-Varying Arrival Rates of Informed and Uninformed Trades*, March 13, 2002, http://www.bnet.fordham.edu/crif/WorkingPapers/crifwp02017.pdf.
17. As above.

18. Charles Ferguson, *Predator Nation: Corporate Criminals, Political Corruption, and the Hijacking of America* (Crown Business, 1st edn, May 22, 2012). See also Simon Johnson, *Predators and Professors*, Project Syndicate, June 18, 2012. Simon Johnson, a former chief economist of the IMF, is a professor at MIT Sloan. http://www.project-syndicate.org/commentary/predators-and-professors.
19. The Lotka–Volterra equations, also known as the predator–prey equations, are a pair of first-order, nonlinear, differential equations frequently used to describe the dynamics of biological systems in which two species interact, one a predator and one its prey.
20. The Santa Fe institute in New Mexico is renowned for its inter-disciplinary approach to the study of many kinds of complex systems. Pioneering work in artificial life, genetic algorithms, cellular automata, and finance and artificial markets has been conducted by the many scientific luminaries that have been associated with the Institute over the last 20 years. They have included Per Bak, Chris Langton, Stuart Kauffman, J. Doyne Farmer, W. Brian Arthur, John Holland, Murray Gell-Mann, and Duncan Watts.
21. There is a readable account of the Prediction Company's work to be found in Thomas A. Bass, *The Predictors* (Henry Holt, 1999).
22. J. Doyne Farmer, *Toward Agent-Based Models for Investment* (2001). Available online at http://www.santafe.edu/~jdf/papers/aimr.pdf.
23. As above.
24. Thomas Lux and M Marchesi, Volatility Clustering in Financial Markets: A micro simulation of interacting agents, (2000) *International Journal of Theoretical and Applied Finance* 675–702, http://www.ge.infm.it/~ecph/papers/marchesipapers/microsimul.pdf.
25. D. Stauffer and A. Aharony, *Introduction to Percolation Theory* (Taylor & Francis, 1992).

5

Detecting Mini Bubbles with the VPIN Metric

The key elements of the Flash Crash have been described in the previous chapter and an outline of the framework within which electronic market making takes place has been provided. Apart from its value in providing a possibility for a forensic analysis of this bout of systemic illiquidity there is an opportunity to build on the foundation stones provided by this type of micro-structural analysis to gain useful insights about macro-financial phenomena such as a full blown crisis.

The micro framework provides the opportunity for scaling purposes to enable us to gain much greater insight into the developments of imbalances which self-organize themselves into critical states and following which a tipping point is reached – a Minsky moment – and markets suddenly display dangerous non-linear dynamics (recall the sand-piles from Chapter 1). A big part of the difficulty in improving our theoretical assumptions in macro finance and economics can ultimately be traced back to erroneous views – allegedly from common sense – about the nature of causation and the need to find large causes for large effects. Understanding the logic of bubbles and the dynamics which allow them to become unsustainably large is vital to a new framework in finance and economics. This will be taken up as a challenge in the latter part of this book but it will be helpful at this stage to look at some groundbreaking work which fits the test for a new paradigm in macro finance.

During the discussion of market micro-structure in the previous chapter the point was made about the circularity issue with regard to Wall Street folklore about "smart money." I shall quickly summarize the circularity criticism of this folklore which has been unquestioningly adopted by many market commentators and, to some extent by "old school" technical analysts. [1] There is a presumption from the literature that by careful examination of certain market internals, for example volume indicators, that a certain accumulative activity has been taking place prior to a price breakout and this reveals the footprints of the smart money. All one has to do to be profitable in trading is to align oneself with the activity of the smart money But unless one can differentiate trading activity adequately, and since for every buyer there is a seller, it becomes very difficult, without the appropriate methodology, to identify exactly who the smart money is. If not we are really engaging in circular or tautological reasoning as was mentioned in the last chapter.

So how can we make a more robust analysis of the undoubted differential advantages which do exist within the three tiers identified in Chapter 4 without resorting to circularity? This is where the efforts of a group of researchers at Cornell University – who have developed something known as the VPIN methodology – provides a cornerstone on the way to a more robust understanding of macro finance and especially to a richer framework for analyzing bubble and bust dynamics in the macro economy. This is an exalted claim, but as we progress through an examination of the VPIN techniques, there is, in my mind at least, no doubt that its claim to importance is justified. Before embarking on this analysis it is worth noting that VPIN is an acronym for Volume Synchronized Probability of Informed Trading. The other great merit which it has shown is that it can act as a leading indicator to bouts of illiquidity. Best of all, the VPIN theory is falsifiable as it has predictive capacity to make precise and testable market timing calls. It remains to be seen whether future calls will be as reliable as they were at the time of the Flash Crash.

5.1 ADVERSE SELECTION AS THE BASIS FOR THE VPIN METHOD

In the previous section I made some strong claims for the VPIN method. One of its strengths lies in how order flow within contemporary markets can be monitored in such a fashion that it is possible to differentiate with respect to the actual behavior of informed and uninformed traders. As will be shown later a thorough testing of the VPIN methodology has been undertaken by an independent research team at the Lawrence Berkeley National Laboratory in California, and their findings on the efficacy of the VPIN techniques encouraged them (the Lawrence Berkeley team) to provide a strong endorsement of the VPIN metric in a report it was asked to submit to US regulators. [2] To begin our examination of the VPIN methods it will be helpful to start with a discussion of *adverse selection* since this topic is central to the efforts of the Cornell University researchers. [3]

The study of adverse selection is an interesting area within behavioral finance and can be illustrated in a number of ways. It arises precisely in the context of asymmetric information which it has been proposed is one of the distinguishing characteristics of the three-tiered market structure already discussed and illustrated in Table 4.1 of the previous chapter. Where there are information advantages possessed by one side of a market these will act to the detriment of the other side – this can best be characterized in the metaphor that there is not a level playing field. Although it does not follow that a market will become unstable because of asymmetric information – in other words a strong discordance in the resources and information possessed by opposing sides of a market – there is a high likelihood that instability will arise. When the asymmetry becomes extreme one side may wish to withdraw or switch its normal mode of behavior completely – for example when the liquidity providers become liquidity consumers – the market will become too lopsided to function properly, liquidity will evaporate, and a crash can occur. One rather different analogy would be to imagine what would happen to an ocean liner or even an airliner if everyone on board suddenly wanted to be on just one side of the vessel or plane – it would sink or crash.

The problem of adverse selection can be quite convincingly illustrated by taking the perspective of an insurance company. In this illustration the information asymmetry is that the insurance company stands ready to insure any customers but it is at a relative disadvantage in that not all of its customers will be uninformed about the likelihood that they will be making a claim against the company. The insurance company is at a relative disadvantage because the customers that are most likely to want to take out an insurance policy could well be the people who face the highest risks. Not only are these the people that insurance companies would least like to have as customers, but they are unable to do a proper actuarial assessment of the risk that they may have to make a payout on a claim. For example consider the following scenarios where there is a clear example of information asymmetry, and from the perspective of the insurance company, where it will suffer from adverse selection in that the customers are seeking to exploit the information advantage:

- The people who are most eager to buy health insurance are those who have reason to think that they are going to have an expensive illness.
- The people who are most likely to buy life insurance are those who have reason to believe that they are likely to die soon.
- The people who are most eager to buy annuities are those who have reason to believe that they will live for a long time.

Clearly insurance companies have taken steps to level the playing field by for example requiring medical checks, reviewing previous claims, and by basing their actuarial assessments on a long history of insurance claims made by their existing customers.

How does all of this apply to the role of the market makers? The key idea is that from the intermediaries' perspective they do not want to become the victims of a sudden change in sentiment or order flow from the more informed traders. Their predicament is made more critical because in today's markets, following the 2008 crisis, there is far less activity by the uninformed traders, so in essence the market makers themselves have become the relatively disadvantaged. How can the market maker become aware of this shift against them?

The market maker – usually algorithmic – may have a number of passive orders at any time on the market order book. As an example a stock may be trading at $40 and the market maker has limit buy orders at $39.95 and limit sell orders at $40.05. If we take the limit buy order the market maker is prepared to buy a specified amount at a lower price than the current price and would expect that order, and any other similarly priced limit orders, *to fill slowly if at all.* But if the market maker suddenly finds that there is an increase in sellers seeking out these passive buy orders – in other words the informed counter-parties are showing an enhanced desire to sell into a falling market – this signals to the market maker that it is being adversely selected by other market participants. Adverse selection in this scenario arises when there are more buyers than sellers when prices are rising – in which case the market maker could be accumulating too many short positions – or more sellers than buyers when prices are falling – in which case the market makers are building up an inventory of long positions in a downward trending market. In both cases the risk control procedures to prevent excess accumulation of inventory will be triggered and the market maker will want to adjust its spreads, cancel or revise limit orders, and under duress begin to operate more like a liquidity consumer than a liquidity provider. There is a good summary of the scenarios just outlined, which can be found in a research document authored by HFT developers at Goldman Sachs, [4] where it defines adverse selection with regard to electronic market making activity as follows:

> ... the natural tendency for passive orders to fill quickly when they should fill slowly and fill slowly (or not at all) when they should fill quickly. We define passive orders ... for example, as placing limit orders in electronic limit order books or pegged orders in dark pools. *We call it "natural" adverse selection because it arises out of the natural presence of more buyers than sellers when prices are rising and more sellers than buyers when prices are falling.* Unlike predatory practices like gaming and pinging that may affect some passive executions, natural adverse selection affects all passive executions.

To summarize, in a rising market passive buy orders will execute more slowly than passive sell orders so that the market maker's gain from selling in a rising market will not

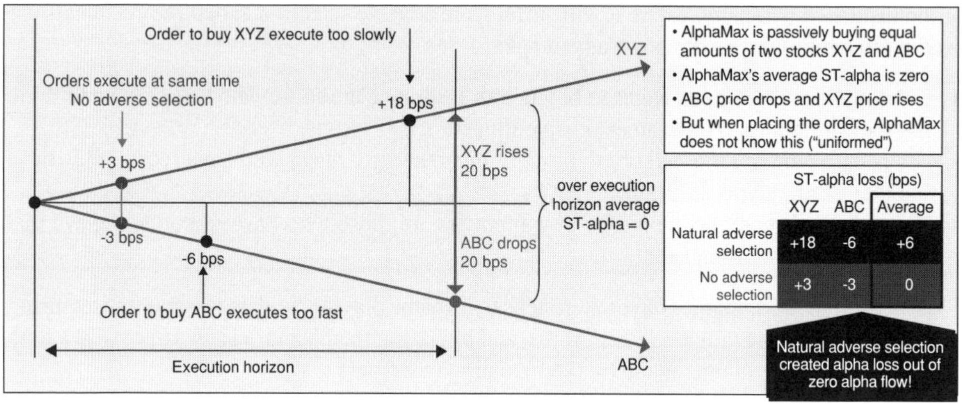

Figure 5.1 Algorithmic trading – natural adverse selection: a simple example
Source: ©Goldman Sachs by David Geria and George Sofianos, Vice Presidents of Goldman Sachs.

fully offset the market maker's loss from buying in a rising market. This is demonstrated in Figure 5.1.

Figure 5.1, which is included in the Goldman Sachs document, illustrates the problem of adverse selection, and although the exact details do not require a detailed explanation it should be clear from the left hand side of the diagram that the relative delay or mismatch in the filling of orders on the two sides of the order book will, if not addressed by the inventory accumulation logic of an algorithm, result in the market maker accumulating "alpha losses" which are not sustainable, especially in a fast moving market.

It is now possible to look more closely at how the notion of adverse selection can be used to identify order imbalances in financial markets and thereby provide the possibility of an early warning system for the kinds of illiquidity which are not only the central concern of this book but in a more general sense, a very large concern for financial regulators and policy makers. As already noted the US government commissioned a research project, undertaken by the Lawrence Berkeley National Laboratory in California, and the findings of which have been published in a very readable document entitled *Federal Market Information Technology in the Post Flash Crash Era: Roles for Supercomputing*. [5] A few observations from this report are worth repeating here.

Firstly on the prevalence of alternative trading venues and market fragmentation, which was covered in Chapter 3 of this book, the point is made that:

> [i]t is estimated that there are up to 100 market "fragments" for trading of stocks alone. The best known venues, the NYSE and NASDAQ have seen their market shares for their securities drop from more than 90% to the 20% range.

The research team at the National Laboratory in the Berkeley hills of California then examined all of trade data available from the Flash Crash – which poses significant data retrieval and access issues even for their supercomputers – and checked the findings reported by the Cornell University team and which gave rise to the VPIN metric. The findings will be quoted first and then explained in the next section. [6]

> VPIN measures the balance between buy and sell activities. An earlier version of this indicator is called Probability of Informed Trading (PIN). The key change in VPIN is to use bins with the

> same trading volume instead of bins with the same time span. The VPIN authors refer to this as measuring the buy-sell imbalance in volume-time instead of clock-time. Furthermore, instead of using the relative imbalance value directly, which can be different for different commodities, the authors normalized them using the function _ that defines the Cumulative Distribution Function of a normal distribution. Because of this normalization, a single threshold, T = 0:9, can be used for many different stocks. *With suitable parameters, the authors have shown that the VPIN reaches 0.9 more than an hour before the Flash Crash on May 6, 2010. This is the strongest early warning signal known to us at this time.* (emphasis added by this author)

The last sentence in particular is high level endorsement of the VPIN methodology and the recommendation to the US government is that implementation of a VPIN-based surveillance system within the micro-structure of very active markets such as the E-Mini S&P 500 futures market "could provide early warning signals" of impending crash-like events: [7]

> Is real-time high frequency monitoring needed? The SEC/CFTC has announced their intention to direct many billions from the financial industry to this effort, which has been criticized by others as unnecessary overkill. We ... have come to believe that it is not overkill. Current post Flash Crash regulatory approaches are based on "circuit breakers," which suspend trading when price or volatility triggers set them off. These are very "blunt instruments" that do not allow the market to self-correct and stabilize, and they can easily make a bad situation worse. Our tests showed that VPIN, and similar indicators could provide early warning signals for a more gradual "slow down, rather than stop" replacement for on/off circuit breakers.

A couple of the numerous and helpful graphics from the Berkeley Laboratory report highlight the nature of the extreme behavior which occurred during the Flash Crash. Figure 5.2, which is a highly granular chart showing one second intervals, reveals the massive drop in price for Accenture (NYSE:ACN) which for several seconds (as shown on the chart) had a bid of $0.01 per share, having traded within the preceding minutes at approximately $40 per share. The most apt description for Figure 5.2 during the few seconds commencing at 14:47:48, where the best bid drops like a stone, is the phrase that was seen quoted earlier in connection with the CFTC/SEC report on the crash [8] of "a complete evaporation of liquidity." The vertical lines shown on Figure 5.2 are the volumes registered at each second time slice and readable against the right hand axis. At 14:47:53 and in each of the next two seconds it can be seen that there were executions of orders in the low hundreds in terms of volume size, the typical order size for HFT trades (see Chapter 3).

A different perspective on the same stock – Accenture – is shown in Figure 5.3. Once again using a different technique for representing the data there is an excellent depiction of the disappearance of liquidity from both sides of the order book viewed on four different time scales. The top left hand graphic takes a full day perspective on the NYSE trading of Accenture and during the morning and early afternoon part of the session there is no evidence of the severe tapering in the depth of the order book which is clearly visible around 14:47 which would coincide with the alternative perspective as illustrated in Figure 5.2. The bottom right hand graphic which is the finest granularity in terms of the time frame highlights the trading between 2:40 and 2:55pm and in the middle of this chart segment there is virtually no activity or depth to the order book. The market makers had completely withdrawn, there was literally no liquidity on offer, and even ridiculously low bids were filled by some HFT algorithms that were not "clever" enough to realize that there was no market for the stock. Subsequently many of these extremely abnormal "fills" were cancelled by the exchanges. The Nasdaq Exchange, for example, announced that they would cancel all trades made between

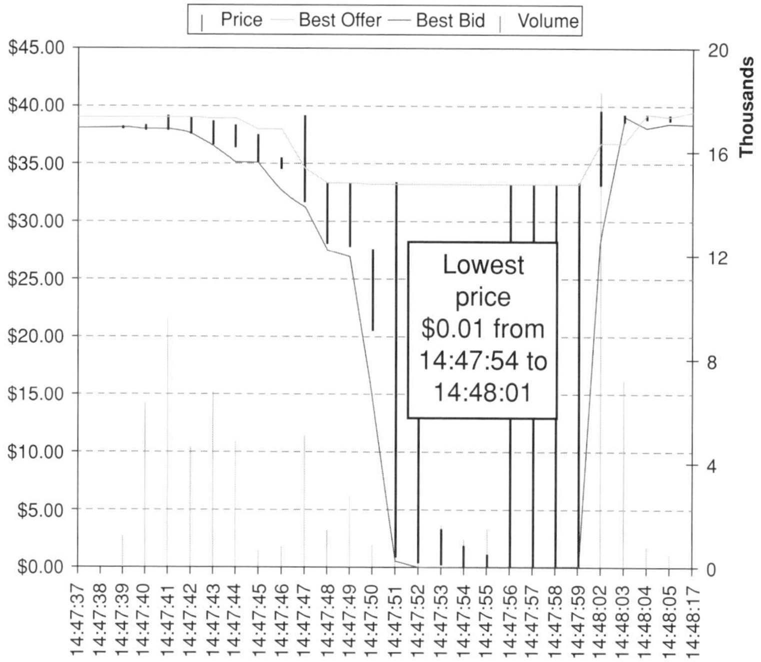

Figure 5.2 Performance of Accenture during Flash Crash
Source: Federal Market Information Technology in the Post Crash Era, Lawrence Berkeley Laboratory.

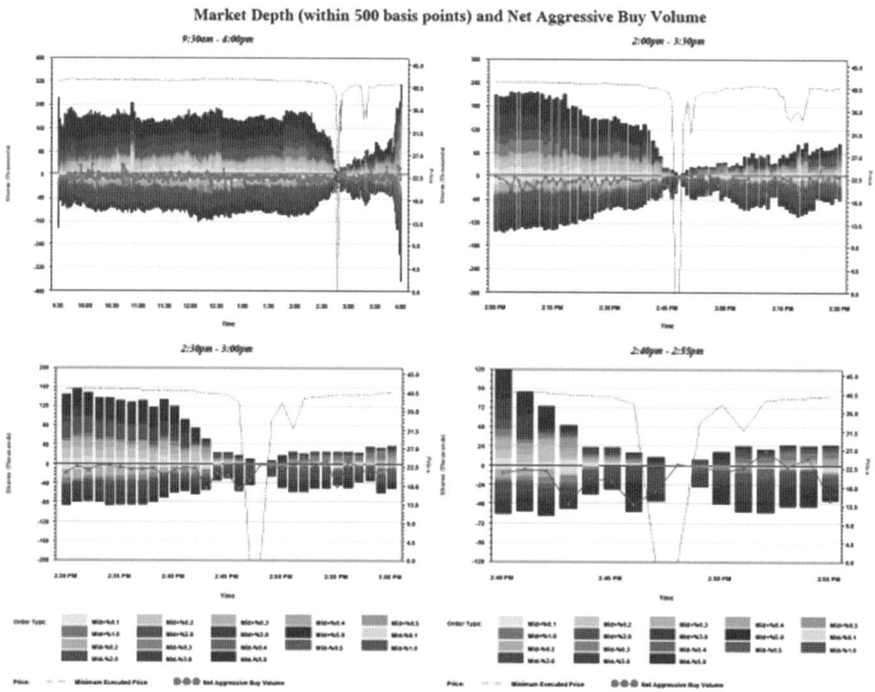

Figure 5.3 Accenture during Flash Crash – multiple time frames
Source: Federal Market Information Technology in the Post Crash Era, Lawrence Berkeley Laboratory.

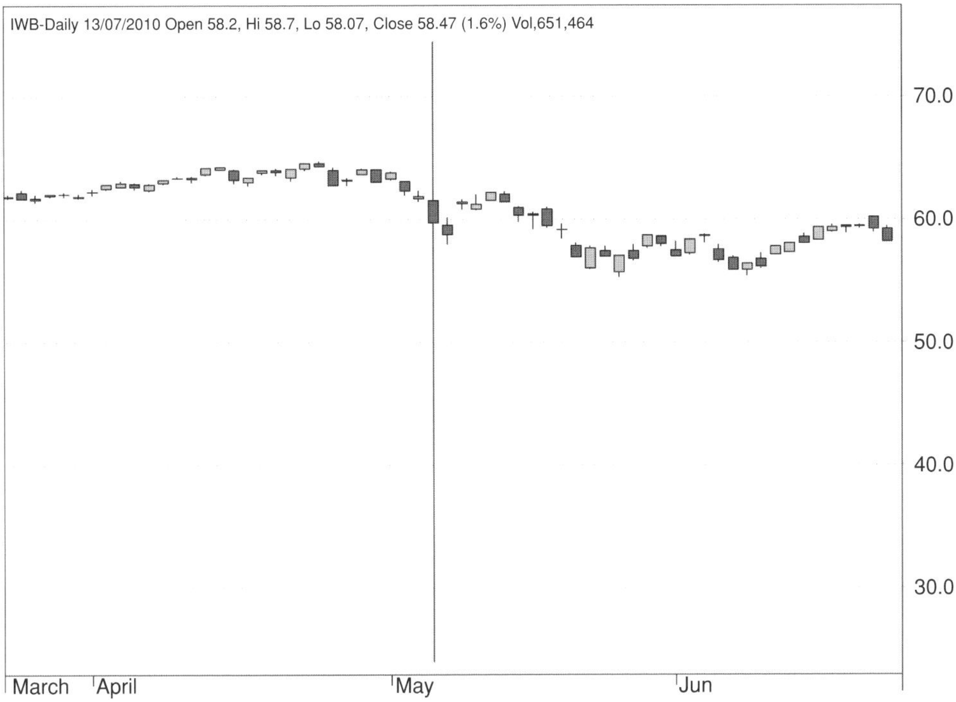

Figure 5.4 Russell 1000 ETF chart (IWB) for Flash Crash, May 6, 2010

2:40pm and 3pm on May 6 where the price varied by more than 60% from the last trade at 2:40pm. [9]

During trading on May 6, 2010 some of the largest price anomalies observed in the US financial markets were found in the trading of several exchange traded funds (ETFs) which trade on the NYSE Arca platform and which it is known are widely used by hedge funds in cross asset plays. Figure 5.4 represents the daily price activity over several sessions for IWB, an exchange traded fund which tracks the Russell 1000 index of stocks in the USA – as discussed in an earlier chapter with regard to cross-sectional correlations – the Russell 1000 index encapsulates more than 90% of the entire US equity market capitalization. [10]

The very long spikes both above and below the candlestick for May 6 are indicative of the high and low values at which trades took place. These are actual trade prices rather than bid or ask quotes which may have been even more extreme. IWB trades on an average daily basis around 1.2 million shares and is one of the more liquid ETFs traded. However during the Flash Crash there was no liquidity at all during the critical time frame which accounts for the dramatic intraday drop as registered on the chart. In another discussion below the consequences of this for traders and investors who had stop loss orders on this ETF could well have become quite alarming as will be demonstrated.

Reviewing the price charts for many ETFs for May 6, 2010 shows that there were several large and usually liquid instruments that experienced similar plunges. In fact by observing which ones experienced the most significant intraday ranges it is possible to determine which

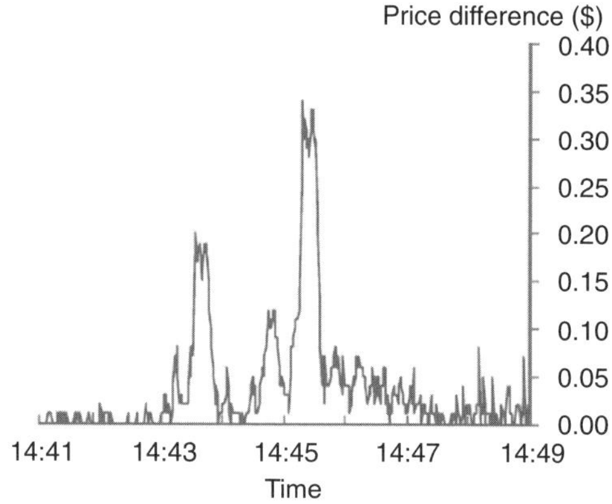

Figure 5.5 Difference in maximum and minimum prices for GE shares across exchanges during Flash Crash
Source: Haldane, A G (2011), "The Race to Zero".
Notes: Difference in bid prices across NASDAQ, NYSE and Pacific Exchange.

are the most frequently used instruments in the kind of cross asset strategies employed by many hedge funds that are using an inter-market algorithmic approach to trading.

It has been suggested by Andrew Haldane from the Bank of England [11] in a lecture entitled *The Arms Race* that the kinds of developments now taking place within the HFT world, where ever more proximate co-location to the exchange servers and obsession with reducing the speed in execution times is analogous to the arms race that was seen in the Cold War. Moreover Haldane suggests that some of the anomalies in pricing during the Flash Crash episode were aggravated by the increasing fragmentation of the platforms for executing trades. Even for the more established exchanges and for a highly liquid security such as General Electric, Figure 5.5 indicates that bid/ask spreads and actual executions were particularly sloppy during the height of the market disorder.

Returning to the methodology used in calculating the VPIN metric we are now in a much better position to understand how the technique is able to determine the quality of order flow and in turn how electronic market makers are able to detect the presence of adverse selection. The Cornell team describes the emergence and enlargement of the adverse selection experienced by the market makers as "toxicity": [12]

> When order flows are essentially balanced, high frequency market makers have the potential to earn razor thin margins on massive numbers of trades. When order flows become unbalanced, however, market makers face the prospect of losses due to adverse selection. The market makers' estimate of the toxicity (the expected loss from trading with better informed counterparties) of the flow directed to them by position takers now becomes a crucial factor in determining their participation. *If they believe that this toxicity is too high, they will liquidate their positions and leave the market.* (author's emphasis)

It is worth thinking through the implications of this quotation and specifically the italicized last sentence. Modern markets where large players can move billions of dollars in rapidly executing inter-market strategies have a paramount requirement for the liquidity provided by financial intermediaries. But if those electronic intermediaries detect that their risk of experiencing adverse selection has become too high they will exit the market with a concomitant collapse in liquidity and where asset prices can literally go to zero. The rather ominous predicament to which Andrew Haldane was alluding is found in the following summary of HFT driven markets from the Cornell University research team:

- Concentration of liquidity provision into a small number of highly specialized firms.
- Reduced participation of retail investors resulting in increased toxicity of the flow received by market makers.
- High sensitivity of liquidity providers to intraday losses, as a result of the liquidity providers' low capitalization, high turnover, increased competition, and small profit target.

The clearest statement of how the VPIN metric is calculated is found in this extract from the Cornell University research paper (see endnote [12] for source):

> For any time period, the VPIN metric is the ratio of average unbalanced volume to total volume in that period. Heuristically, *the VPIN metric measures the fraction of volume-weighted trade that arises from informed traders as the informed tend to trade on one-side of the market and so their activity leads to unbalanced volume (either more buy volume than sells volume or the reverse). In periods in which there is a lot of information-based trade, the VPIN metric will be large. During these periods, market makers are on the wrong side of the trade with the informed (i.e. buying when prices are moving down, and conversely), and so they will accumulate or lose inventory on the wrong side of the market.* As market prices move, market makers will make losses on their positions. If these losses accumulate, we would expect market makers to undo their positions, thus adding to the imbalance in trade and potentially leading to a crash. (author's emphasis)

The authors point to the fact that under "normal" market conditions the VPIN metric is relatively stable with a value of approximately 0.5 which is in accordance with the notion that it hovers around the levels associated with normal probability. [13] However, as can be seen on the right hand axis of Figure 5.6, the abnormality of the VPIN metric when in the vicinity of May 6 – as measured by how closely this value moves toward extreme values in terms of its cumulative distribution function – is quite striking.

Figures 5.7 and 5.8 show the actual day of the crash and the few sessions which preceded the crash. The Cornell authors' own commentary for the day of the crash explains what is depicted on the chart as clearly as possible:

> ... by 11:55am on May 6th, the realized value of the VPIN metric was in the 10% tail of the distribution (it exceeded a 90% CDF(VPIN) critical value). By 1:08pm, the realized value of the VPIN metric was in the 5% tail of the distribution (over a 95% CDF(VPIN)). By 2:30pm the VPIN metric reached its highest level in the history of the E-mini S&P500. At 2:32pm the crash begins according to the CFTC-SEC Report time line.

It is also notable that while the actual crash took place within a few minutes on May 6 it would have been possible to have been alerted to the increased likelihood of extreme behavior by monitoring the VPIN in the sessions before May 6:

> the VPIN metric for the E-mini S&P 500 future was abnormally high at least one week before the flash crash ... [Figure 5.8] ... shows the value of the E-mini S&P 500, the value of the VPIN metric, and, for each estimated value of the VPIN metric, the fraction of the empirical distribution that is less than this value of the VPIN metric, CDF(VPIN). This measure of the likelihood of the VPIN metric being less than or equal to the current value is volatile, but it was generally unusually high during the week before the flash crash. Such behavior must have placed market makers on the alert, as the toxicity of flow directed to them was gradually becoming more unpredictable.

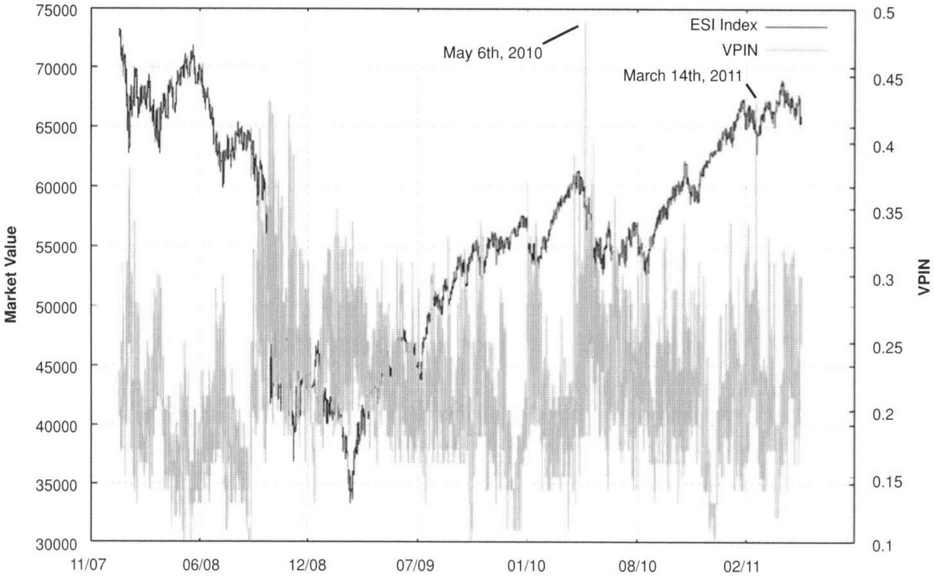

Figure 5.6 VPIN metric between January 1, 2008 and August 2011
Source: VPIN Flow Toxicity, Easley et al.

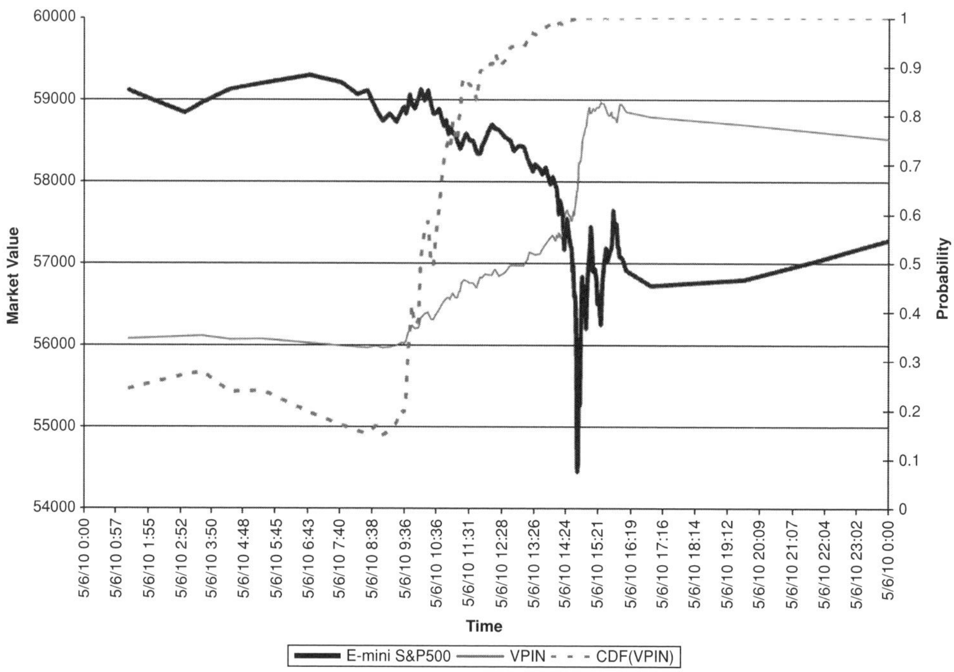

Figure 5.7 E-Mini S&P 500's VPIN metric on May 6, 2010

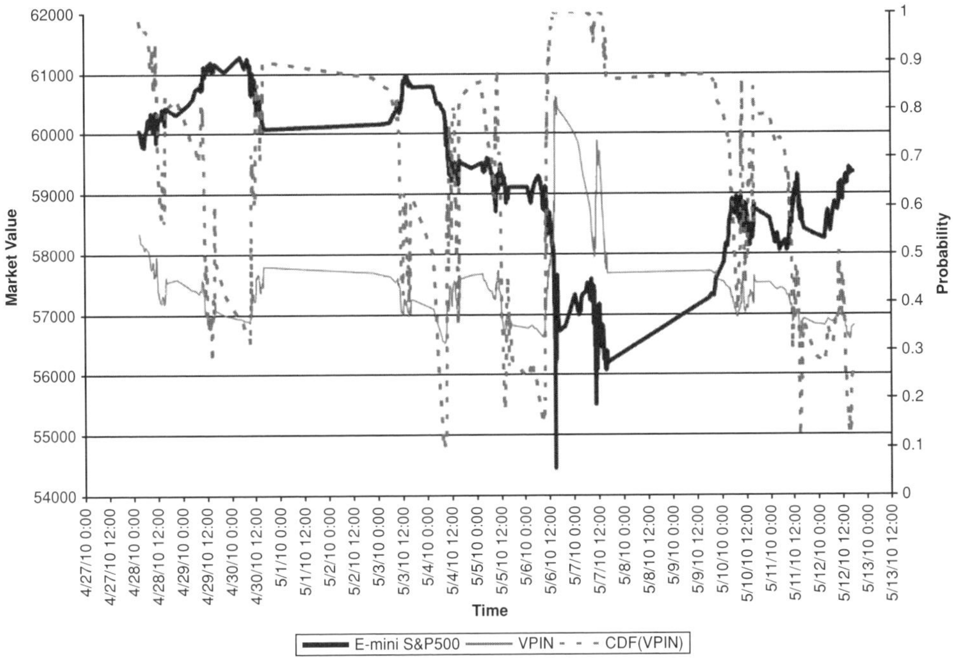

Figure 5.8 E-Mini S&P 500's VPIN metric one week before and after the Flash Crash
Source: The Microstructure of the Flash Crash, Easley et al.

Figure 5.9 shows the price development in the S&P 500 during the first few months of 2010. Extending the lookback period before the Flash Crash it can be seen that the S&P 500 had been rising almost without interruption from the beginning of February 2010 until just late April; as annotated by the multi period peak value registered on April 26. To state things simply, in the three months leading up to May 6, 2010 there had been an exaggerated and unsustainable risk on phase in asset markets and this is reflected in the straight line up move which is illustrated in Figure 5.9. This is crucial to an understanding of the underlying dynamics behind the actual crash – and this is entirely consistent with the findings of the VPIN developers and illustrated in their own graphic which is reproduced here as Figure 5.8.

What will be demonstrated in later chapters is that during extended risk on phases of financial markets – where there is a coordinated allocation by informed traders into risk assets which include US equities but also would include commodities and certain foreign exchange pairs – the market begins to develop a mini bubble where the order book has remained one-sided for an extended period. Under such circumstances there is an increased likelihood that it is not only the market makers that would have unbalanced inventories – which are much more likely to become critical in shorter time frames – but as one moves out to encompass longer time horizons – the informed traders may well have an exaggerated and unbalanced exposure to the risk on assets exactly at the time when the more immediate circumstances will create a rush for the exits and an evaporation of liquidity.

Under this type of explanatory model the market could be said to be revealing a fractal fragility in that the kind of imbalances which are of concern to the much shorter time frame

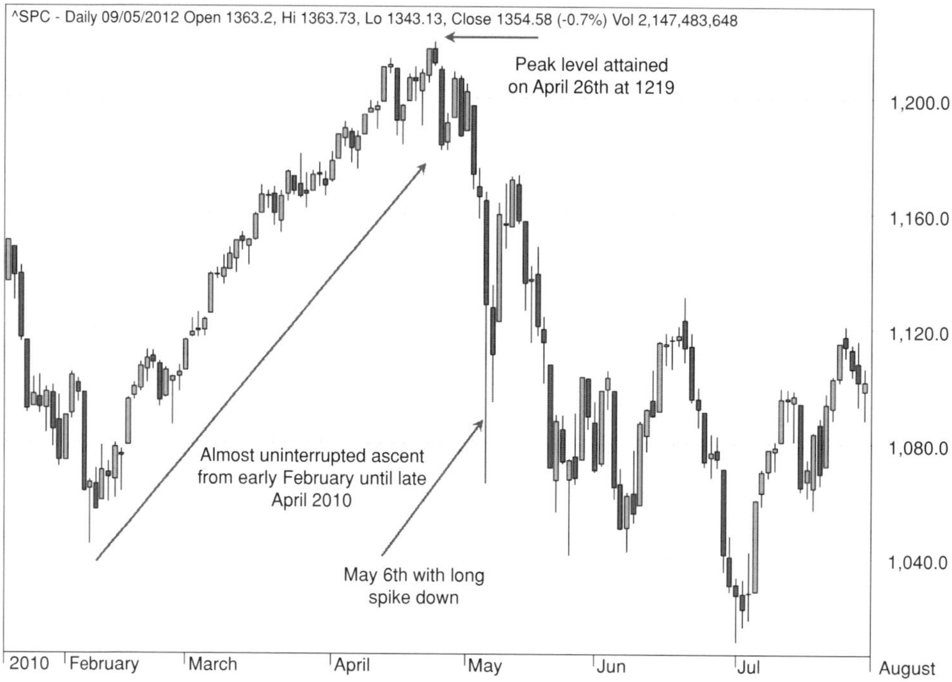

Figure 5.9 S&P 500 daily performance first half 2010

focused market makers are also shared by the longer time frame focused informed traders, i.e. the hedge funds and proprietary trading desks.

When considering the conclusion of the Berkeley team that were asked to report to the US government on the Flash Crash it was noted that there was explicit criticism of the notion of circuit breakers. The report opined that "[c]urrent post Flash Crash regulatory approaches are based on 'circuit breakers,' which suspend trading when price or volatility triggers set them off. These are very 'blunt instruments' that do not allow the market to self-correct and stabilize, and they can easily make a bad situation worse." Just how blunt these are can be seen in the context of the following which comes from the CFTC/SEC report referenced above: [14]

> Starting at 2:45:28pm, CME's Globex stop logic functionality initiated a brief pause in trading in the E-mini S&P 500 futures. This functionality is initiated when the last transaction price would have triggered a series of stop loss orders that, if executed, would have resulted in a cascade in prices outside a predetermined "no bust" range (6 points in either direction in the case of E-minis).

Despite the brief pause which resulted from the CME's Globex stop logic functionality, when trading resumed the S&P 500 continued its swift decline and this may have aggravated the decline as other markets were still active and various arbitrage activities between the cash and futures markets would have become even more mis-aligned. [15] There is a malignant feedback loop which can arise in the case of circuit breakers and stop loss orders. When prices cascade downwards and threaten to hit a large number of the stop loss orders that are sitting under the market the thinking of regulators is that it would be beneficial to have a "time out" during which traders can rethink their positions. This cannot be ruled out as a possible advantage, however as was seen in the case of the Flash Crash the magnitude of the order imbalances was such that the downward spiral and the elusive seeking out of liquidity by HFT and other algorithmic activity, which is ultimately self defeating, effectively continued until many of the HFT algorithms were switched off and human beings stepped in. [16]

From the perspective of an asset manager the unsophisticated use of stop loss orders when there is a panic resulting from the kind of order imbalances that occurred on May 6, 2010 could very likely lead to an exit from a position at the worst possible prices. How many stop loss orders might have been triggered during Accenture's plunge or even for the IWB exchange traded fund? The risk of an undefined or unlimited loss is explained by the fact that a stop loss order becomes a market order after the stop level has been violated. Beyond this limit specified in the stop loss order (unless a guaranteed stop loss order is available but these can be expensive) the potential losses are no longer confined to the calmly determined maximum risk level designed by the fund manager. As can be seen from the evaporation of liquidity there is a high likelihood that the stop loss could be executed at the worst possible exit time, i.e. when there are ludicrously low bids.

Although the severity of the "slow motion" crash which took place in most global equity markets during 2008 – including a 40% drop for the S&P 500 and DAX indices and more than 50% for indices such as Hong Kong's Hang Seng – far exceeded the magnitude of the declines experienced during an episode such as the Flash Crash, the realized losses resulting from incidents such as the latter could be more damaging to an investor. Even at the height of the 2008 crisis there were many sharp counter-trend rallies which would have enabled a distressed fund manager to exit losing positions at much better prices than if one had been filled via stop-loss instructions during a climactic sell-off such as that experienced on May 6, 2010.

As the writing of this book was being finalized an illustration of just how damaging aberrant trading sessions can be – resulting from the vagaries of HFT trading – was seen at the beginning of New York trading on August 1, 2012. Knight Capital Group, which is an electronic market maker responsible for more than 10% of all trades in US equities, suffered a software glitch which caused short-term pandemonium for the overall market and culminated in losses for the trading firm of $440 million. One report of the incident cited the following: [17]

> Knight's software executed in a matter of minutes a series of trades that were designed to be done over a period of days. This glitch is just one of a series that have plagued Wall Street in recent years.
>
> In May, the Nasdaq Stock Market botched Facebook Inc.'s initial public offering. The latest glitch is also an echo of the 2010 "flash crash" that terrified investors after high-speed trading went haywire and $1 trillion vanished from the stock market.
>
> In Washington, Knight's trading disaster has rekindled worries that new regulations haven't been effective in protecting investors.

Indeed, it is now being argued by investors and some policy makers that flash crashes and other HFT shenanigans which can happen in the space of 15–20 minutes may be far more damaging to investor morale and participation than the kind of protracted decline that was seen in H2, 2008.

5.2 THE ROLE OF THE JAPANESE YEN IN THE FLASH CRASH

Even though the work by the Cornell University team is an excellent forensic account of the market micro-structure processes which help to explain the manner in which the rapid disappearance of liquidity took place there is still a question as to what caused the actual crash on May 6, 2010. Do we simply claim that it was a "black swan" or "fat tail event," or can a more substantial explanation be provided? I believe that the answer is yes. But to answer the question it is necessary to engage in a more holistic, cross market approach to the circumstances in other asset markets which accompanied the crash, and in the days and weeks leading up to the crash. Specifically it will be very illuminating to look at the largest capital market – the foreign exchange market where more than $4 trillion (notional) is traded each day. [18] There will be an extended discussion of the foreign exchange market and the associated FX carry trade in Chapter 6.

Figure 5.10 shows two price progression patterns during the critical time frame on May 6, 2010 and, I believe, in many ways allows for an explanation of the precipitating factor which caused a fragile market to reach a tipping point – recall from our discussion above that the market was vulnerable, as reflected by the VPIN metric registering abnormal levels, for some days prior to the crash.

The black candlesticks in Figure 5.10 are two minute samplings of the US dollar versus the Japanese yen exchange rate, USD/JPY, and the lighter toned candlesticks are for the S&P 500 cash index (this would closely follow but not be identical with the ES futures contract – the E-Mini traded on the CME's Globex platform).

As annotated on Figure 5.10 at 14:02 EST the USD/JPY which had been trading in a very tight range – almost immobile for the previous hour or so – was registered at 91:58. The right hand vertical axis of the chart provides the values for the exchange rate and the left hand vertical axis is the scale for the equity index. The S&P 500 at this same time was around 1145. The next few candlesticks are the crucial ones to observe as the USD/JPY rate begins to plummet indicating increasing yen strength. It is clear from the chart that this move began

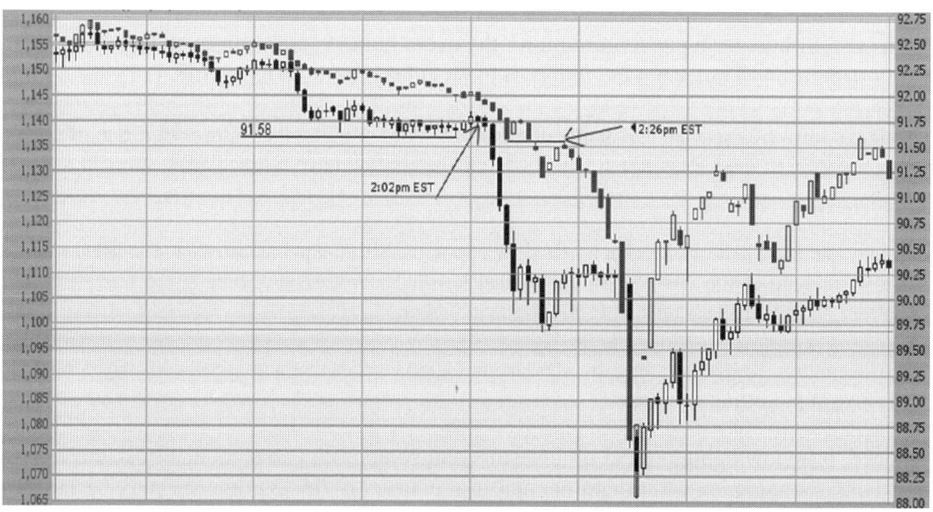

Figure 5.10 Performance of USD/JPY and the S&P 500 during Flash Crash of May 6, 2010

about 20 minutes before the stock market index began its plunge. As annotated on the chart the S&P 500 at 14:26 had fallen to 1135 but this was before the fireworks began. Meanwhile the USD/JPY rate had fallen to 89.75 or roughly *two big figures* [19] within 20 minutes which is a very sizable and abrupt move in the FX markets.

The next 30 minutes is the period during which events became so unstable and which have been described and shown in pictorial form in the previous discussion above. The yen continued to strengthen against the dollar as the USD/JPY rate dropped to 88 and the S&P 500 collapsed quickly to the 1070 level. One of the most remarkable features on the chart is that both instruments reached their trough levels in the same time frame, and both began to recover in tandem afterwards. It is hard to resist the conclusion that the big move in the FX market, affecting primarily the Japanese currency but with ripple effects elsewhere in FX cross rates, was the de-stabilizing factor which caused the equity market to go into a tailspin.

The CFTC/SEC report makes a passing reference to this in its narrative of the events leading up to the Flash Crash but in my estimation (as well as others [20]) the investigation should have drilled down to a far greater extent on the inter-relationship between the two markets. Unfortunately the "blinkered" decision to focus solely on what was happening with the E-Mini contract and the cash market for equities prevented the inquiry from seeing the large scale inter-market, cross asset correlations which have been the focus of this book. One needs to dig down into related markets, to conduct an extensive forensic analysis which goes beyond a single market topological diagnosis. It is vital to examine the forces/dynamics which are operating beneath the surface and across a wide spectrum of asset markets to properly understand the prevalence of, and predilection for, the kind of exaggerated bipolar risk on/risk off behavior, which was part of the build up to the Flash Crash.

So the reader might be asking the next obvious question which is why did the Japanese yen abruptly begin to strengthen and, even if Figure 5.10 provides compelling evidence of some type of correlated movement, why can't this be dismissed as a coincidence and not as a form of causation? These are excellent questions, and to answer them thoroughly it will be necessary to address the nature of the FX carry trade, and the manner in which risk on asset classes trade in such close alignment that in early May 2010 there was a disproportionately large allocation being made by informed traders – hedge funds and large proprietary traders – to the risk on trade, which included large exposure to both equities and to AUD/JPY in the FX market. A detailed analysis of the FX carry trade will be postponed until Chapter 6, but we can now address the question posed above in relation to the risk on imbalances which had accumulated in the run up to the Flash Crash.

In essence the explanation as to the unusual behavior of the yen against the US Dollar on the day of the Flash Crash, and the reason why I believe that it was the precipitating factor for the events that took place around 2.30pm that day in the E-Mini futures market have to do with a withdrawal by informed traders from an exaggerated exposure to the risk on class of financial assets.

In attempting to push even further with a forensic analysis of the Flash Crash, Figure 5.11 shows the relative performance, during the critical February–May period of 2010, of three key instruments – the S&P 500, the JPY/USD exchange rate, and the AUD/JPY exchange rate. The reason to invert the US dollar/Yen rate is to highlight the fact that in the three-month period leading up to May 2010 the yen had been declining steadily against the dollar and this is well illustrated in Figure 5.11. Observing the relative decline of the yen enriches our understanding of the AUD/JPY cross rate because it suggests that the accelerated upward move of Aussie/Yen – a key risk on instrument – as it tracked another key risk on instrument, the S&P 500, was

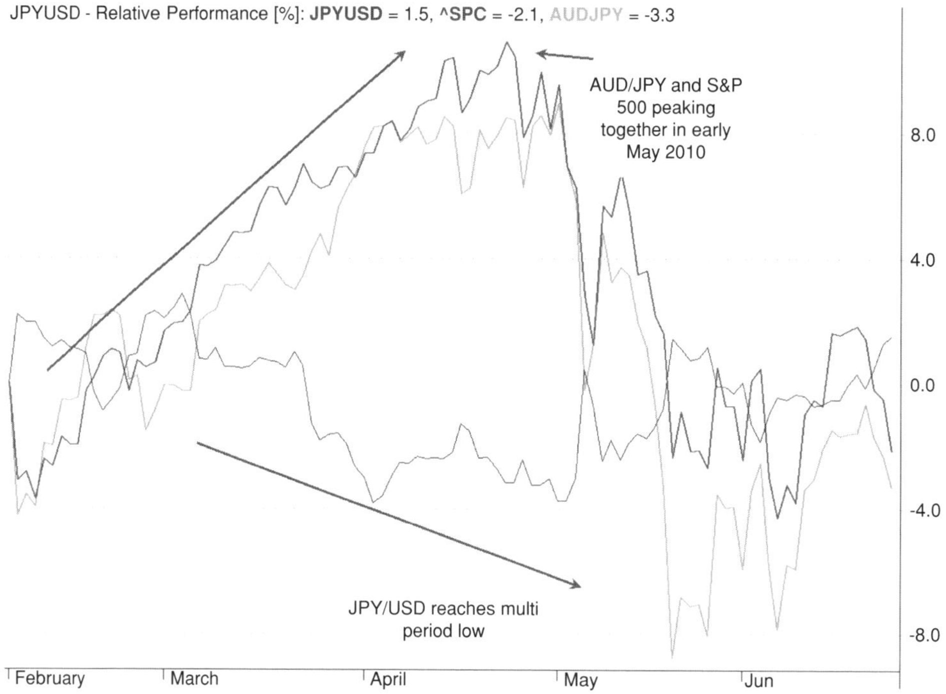

Figure 5.11 Performance of AUD/JPY, JPY/USD, and S&P 500 leading up to Flash Crash

not only a result of an increasing appetite for Australian dollars – itself an expression of risk on – but also a diminished appetite for Japanese yen – a risk off asset. When both elements to *the pivotal "risk on" exchange rate, AUD/JPY*, are going in diametrically opposed directions – and this can be deconstructed by using a common base and considering AUD/USD and JPY/USD separately – then there is further evidence, in addition to the strong move in the S&P 500 from February, that asset markets had reached an extremely unbalanced juncture, with a very large commitment to the risk on class of assets.

Figure 5.11 uses February 1, 2010 as a base. The AUD/JPY rate and the S&P 500 moved up in a very closely aligned fashion, with both reaching multi period peak values at the end of April. The lines moving up diagonally together on the left hand side of the chart show just how synchronized the price action actually was. During the same period the line on Figure 5.11 which is moving down on the left hand side tracks the JPY/USD exchange rate is in a steady down trend. The risk on trade had been prevalent for three months throughout February, March, and April and the yen had also been declining. At the beginning of May it was as if the risk on/risk off (the yen is the archetypal risk off asset class) dynamic had become overly stretched towards an extreme value. The suggestion is that at this point the "*risk on/risk off*" dialectic had reached a tipping point, or to express this in relation to the VPIN metric – the order flow to market makers was becoming increasingly "toxic" requiring market makers and even informed traders, as a consequence of the disappearance of liquidity provided by the market makers, to have to deal with inventory build-up of a disproportionally large kind. The way both dealt with disproportionate inventories was to try to liquidate at the same time. It is the paradoxical nature of systemic liquidity, attested to at the beginning of Chapter 1, that there is no liquidity when everyone needs it, and when there is a panic-induced rush for the exits, and no bids can be found, there will inevitably be a severe market disruption or crash.

For a moment it would be worth considering for a "fundamentals" perspective that the strong upward movement in the Japanese yen around at 2pm on May 6 could be explained partly as a result of capital flight from Europe which was immersed at the time with growing anxiety about a Greek default. [21] Some safe haven buying of yen in early May was definitely a contributory factor. However, my suggestion is that the binary dynamics which had fuelled the escalation in AUD/JPY and the S&P 500 (and other risk on assets), had reached a temporary exhaustion level in early May 2010. Perhaps through the antics of some hedge funds engaged in the very highly leveraged FX carry trade, realizing that the market had been making a one way bet in AUD/JPY and USD/JPY for several weeks, the tipping point had been reached. The seeking out of the yen as a safe haven amidst the worries about the deteriorating Greek situation could well have provided the excuse for a sudden switch into the yen which some of the more astute hedge funds would have realized could be the trigger for a rapid unwind of the exaggerated risk on positioning that had been taking place prior to May 6.

As hedge funds and carry traders witnessed the newly emerging upward trend in the Japanese yen on May 6 this set off alarm bells both for respective positioning in FX – overly long the Australian dollar and short the yen – and due to the cross asset class nature of more sophisticated algorithmic trading routines, there was a sudden rush for the exits in terms of quick liquidation of excessive inventories of risk on assets.

This is entirely consistent with the VPIN authors' explanation of the specific activity of market makers on May 6, but having augmented that explanation with a larger time frame analysis and extended the scope beyond just the E-Mini contract to take into consideration the inter-connectedness of multiple asset class portfolios, the explanatory power becomes even more compelling. Without, at this juncture, pursuing the HFT aspect any further, it is worth citing the following from the VPIN authors as an added dimension to the explanation provided which is reflective of the changing micro-structure of financial markets: [22]

> Based on our analysis, we believe that High Frequency Traders exhibit trading patterns inconsistent with the traditional definition of market making. Specifically, High Frequency Traders aggressively trade in the direction of price changes. This activity comprises a large percentage of total trading volume, but does not result in a significant accumulation of inventory. As a result, whether under normal market conditions or during periods of high volatility, High Frequency Traders are not willing to accumulate large positions or absorb large losses. Moreover, their contribution to higher trading volumes may be mistaken for liquidity by Fundamental Traders. Finally, when rebalancing their positions, High Frequency Traders may compete for liquidity and amplify price volatility.
>
> Consequently, we believe, that irrespective of technology, *markets can become fragile when imbalances arise as a result of large traders seeking to buy or sell quantities larger than intermediaries are willing to temporarily hold, and simultaneously long-term suppliers of liquidity are not forthcoming even if significant price concessions are offered.* (emphasis not in the original)

While the Flash Crash was an extraordinary event which has deservedly received a lot of attention – although the recognition of the role of the yen based carry trade has not – there have been other bouts of illiquidity in financial markets since May 6, 2010. [23]

The remainder of this chapter will be devoted to another example of how useful – from a forensic perspective – extreme events are for understanding what on most occasions are sub-surface phenomena and asset co-movements which can easily be overlooked as mere

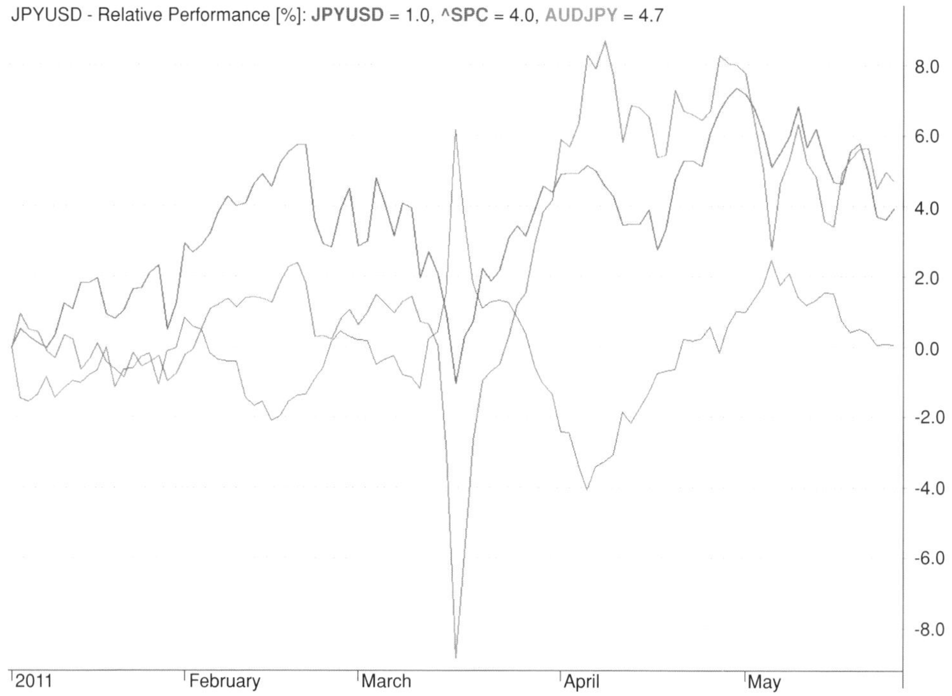

Figure 5.12 Performance of AUD/JPY, JPY/USD, and S&P 500 leading up to Japanese earthquake, March 2011

market noise. Throughout most of the discussion in this book – especially in regard to the macro-economic realm – the core proposition is that it is endogenous factors related to the expansion of credit and the dynamics of bubble/bust which should be used in explaining overall patterns of behavior within financial capitalism. Reaching out for exogenous factors is methodologically unsound and also has the cultural implications of removing the accountability burden for economists and policy makers to external shock events that enable excuses such as the most lame – no one could have seen the 2008 crisis coming. As is now well documented many analysts with a better intellectual framework did see the crisis coming and recognized that most of the Great Moderation of the early part of the millennium was based on the growth of credit and the completely unsustainable real estate bubble which in turn fed into the proliferation of structured financial instruments which led to even more euphoria about a new era where risk management had removed bubbles etc. As we now know the Minsky moments came in spades during 2007/8 and the hubris of many politicians (Gordon Brown the UK prime minister certainly comes to mind), mainstream economists, derivatives salesmen, and financial engineers has now been well documented. For the reader that has not encountered Michael Lewis's book, *The Big Short*, this is a strong recommendation to pick up a copy for a full account of the hubris and stupidity of the worst aspects of the global financial crisis. [24]

There are obviously some occasions when exogenous factors are clearly at work and produce quite dramatic financial consequences. One such event was the devastating earthquake and tsunami of March 11, 2011 which caused a massive amount of human suffering and economic dislocation to Japan. When examining the aftermath of that event from the same perspective that was seen under an endogenously caused crisis such as the Flash Crash it is remarkable that very similar behavior can be observed within the risk on/risk off paradigm from the Japanese natural disaster.

Figure 5.12 takes the same perspective on three instruments that were examined in the prior discussion. The base period is the beginning of 2011 and once again the three paths shown on the graphic are for the JPY/USD exchange rate, AUD/JPY, and the S&P 500.

During the early part of 2011 the trajectories for US equities and the risk on FX pair, AUD/JPY, are trending upwards while the yen is moving sideways. It is worth dwelling for a moment on the fact that unlike the previous analysis shown in regard to the Flash Crash and seen on Figure 5.11, the yen was not moving downwards during the first few weeks of 2011 and this may help to explain why AUD/JPY is less synchronized with the US benchmark index as was seen previously. The real drama on the chart is revealed in mid-March when the yen surged and AUD/JPY plunged – both as a direct result of the denominator of the pair increasing with yen strength, and also due to a severe shift in sentiment towards risk off as a result of a recalculation of global growth arising from the economic impact of substantial damage to Japanese economic infrastructure and GDP prospects. The impact on US equities was short lived as was the impact on the AUD/JPY pair when the sudden switch to risk off was re-evaluated and market participants became more sanguine about the ability of global growth dynamics to withstand the Japanese disaster. But with the ironic benefit of being able to observe the impact of the natural disaster on financial markets it is immediately apparent that a shock event resulted in a validation of the notion that the correlation between the AUD/JPY and other risk assets was temporarily impacted but then resumed its reinstated co-movement characteristics once the shock had been "discounted."

Some commentary from Dow Jones regarding the aftermath of the Japanese disaster and its extraordinary impact on the FX market is worth quoting: [25]

> Barclays Capital pulled yen prices off its Barx dealing system for a short period Wednesday, as the Japanese currency fizzed to its strongest levels on record ... In a spectacular move, the dollar collapsed against the yen at 2100 GMT Wednesday, sinking 4% to hit a record low of Y76.25. Most big banks' systems functioned normally during that hectic period, albeit with a markedly wider spread between where the banks were prepared to buy and sell the currency – a feature that reflected extreme market stress and uncertainty. But Barx was unavailable, a Switzerland-based user said.
>
> "All of the banks showed wide spreads – they went into panic mode," the Barx user said, speaking on condition of anonymity. "But I use six banks, and of them, only Barx was down," he said, adding that he was unable to trade yen on the system for an hour. A person familiar with the situation said that Barx didn't experience any technical difficulties, but the bank's traders decided to pull prices from the system to protect themselves during hectic trading conditions at what is normally a quiet time of day.

To conclude this discussion it has hopefully been of value to the reader to undertake the fairly detailed analysis of the events of May 6, 2010, and those of March 17, 2011 which were covered in a less thoroughgoing fashion, in order to gain an increased understanding of the nature of how suddenly markets can become illiquid. In turn this enables us to explore the very closely related phenomenon of severely unbalanced trader positions which can arise from an over emphasis on the risk on side of the dichotomy present in more binary markets.

Of the questions raised by the changes resulting from the increased focus on robotic trading there is less clarity about the way forward and what approach regulators need to adopt with respect to algorithmic trading. I have argued that May 6, 2010 was not a black swan event in the sense that it came out of nowhere and that accordingly we simply have to accept it as part of the tail risk of being an investor or trader in the financial markets. It can certainly be described in a short hand fashion as a tail risk event. However, not to appreciate the endogenously created background conditions that are part of the larger bubble and bust insights of such theorists as Minsky, is to fail to learn the important lessons as to how such events are by-products of the exaggerated manner in which markets embrace periods of impetuous optimism which lead to disproportionately large commitments to risk assets, and which will inevitably be followed by major corrections. In financial markets dominated by HFT these corrections can easily be amplified into severe crashes – albeit short lived ones. But the post-GFC financial system has seen the bullish and bearish sentiment becoming more polarized and transient with sudden shifts in a binary approach to risk. When there is an absence of widespread elevation of the "animal spirits" amongst the investing public at large, the games played by hedge funds and other large trading desks will create more intraday volatility and require different approaches to risk control. At the same time increased asset correlations make it easier to read the shifts in risk on and risk off behavior and to that extent could make it easier to trade in short time frames.

The second half of 2008 saw a dramatic drop in liquidity in almost all markets – with the exception of the safe haven markets such as the US Treasury market. When there is a coherent view, shared by almost all market participants about the near term direction of a market there is no scope for the normal fractiousness which enables two-way traffic and the market seizes up and becomes extremely illiquid. The problem becomes magnified in the shortest time frames by the prevalence of HFT algorithms as well. In fact, the reason why regulators have tolerated the mishaps that can arise from HFT (e.g. May 6, 2010) is precisely because high quality liquidity which used to be provided by households and the retail investors has disappeared as global financial markets have become the exclusive playgrounds for large institutional investors.

May 6, 2010 showed that machines don't panic – they leave that to us humans – but they just decide not to run their algorithms when certain parameters/thresholds are crossed. That may be an entirely logical response (the thresholds, of course, would have ultimately been set by the algorithm programmers), but, paradoxically, markets require fractiousness and emotions to function, and it was only when the machines were turned off and bottom fishing humans got involved that the free-fall ended.

Longer term systemic liquidity requires confidence that the playing field can produce winners and losers and that skill will be rewarded. If traders and investors sense that markets are not only casinos, but ones where an *Ocean's 13* type software crash can wipe out everyone, they will not want to play in them. [26]

ENDNOTES

1. See endnote 15 in Chapter 4.
2. E. Wes Bethel, David Leinweber, Oliver Rubel, and Kesheng Wu, *Federal Market Information Technology in the Post Flash Crash Era: Roles for Supercomputing* (Lawrence Berkeley National Laboratory, September 2011). The paper appeared in the 2012 Spring Issue of *Journal of Trading*. The more recent and an earlier version of the paper are also available online at http://www.lbl.gov/cs/html/CIFT-LBL-report.pdf; http://papers.ssrn.com/sol3/papers.cfm?abstract_id=1939522.

3. David Easley, Marcos M. Lopez de Prado, and Maureen O' Hara, *Flow Toxicity and Liquidity in a High Frequency World* http://papers.ssrn.com/sol3/Delivery.cfm/SSRN_ID2008486_code58370.pdf?abstractid=1695596&mirid=1.
4. Research note from Goldman Sachs entitled Street Smart Issue 33. The authors of the article are David Jeria, a Vice President at Goldman Sachs, and George Sofianos, a Vice President at Goldman Sachs.
5. See endnote 2.
6. *Findings regarding the market events of May 6, 2010,* which is easily accessible on the internet at http://www.sec.gov/news/studies/2010/marketevents-report.pdf.
7. See endnote 2.
8. See endnote 6.
9. *Thursday's Canceled Trades: Nasdaq*, Wall Street Journal, May 7, 2010:

   > Nasdaq reiterated that it had no technology or system issues, and said that it is going back and canceling some of the trades that resulted in the Flash Crash Thursday.

   http://s.wsj.net/public/resources/documents/st_canceled0507_20100507.html.
10. The Russell 1000 index is an index maintained by the Russell Investments:

    > The Russell 1000 Index measures the performance of the large-cap segment of the U.S. equity universe. It is a subset of the Russell 3000® Index and includes approximately 1000 of the largest securities based on a combination of their market cap and current index membership. The Russell 1000 represents approximately 92% of the U.S. market.

    http://www.russell.com/indexes/data/fact_sheets/us/russell_1000_index.asp.
11. Andrew G. Haldane, Financial Arms Races: April 14, 2012. Speech by Mr Andrew G. Haldane, Executive Director, Financial Stability, Bank of England, at the Institute for New Economic Thinking, Berlin, 14 April 2012 http://www.bis.org/review/r120426a.pdf.
12. David Easley, Marcos M. Lopez de Prado, and Maureen O'Hara, *The Microstructure of the "Flash Crash": Flow Toxicity, Liquidity Crashes and the Probability of Informed Trading*. The Journal of Portfolio Management, 37(2): 118–128. Winter 2011.
13. See endnote 11 in Chapter 4.
14. *Findings regarding the market events of May 6, 2010,* which is easily accessible on the internet at http://www.sec.gov/news/studies/2010/marketevents-report.pdf.
15. On page 4 of the report mentioned in endnote 14 the CFTC/SEC noted:

    > Still lacking sufficient demand from fundamental buyers or cross-market arbitrageurs, HFTs began to quickly buy and then resell contracts to each other – generating a "hot-potato" volume effect as the same positions were rapidly passed back and forth. Between 2:45:13 and 2:45:27, HFTs traded over 27,000 contracts, which accounted for about 49 percent of the total trading volume, while buying only about 200 additional contracts net.
    >
    > At this time, buy-side market depth in the E-Mini fell to about $58 million, less than 1% of its depth from that morning's level. As liquidity vanished, the price of the E-Mini dropped by an additional 1.7% in just these 15 seconds, to reach its intraday low of 1056. This sudden decline in both price and liquidity may be symptomatic of the notion that prices were moving so fast, fundamental buyers and cross-market arbitrageurs were either unable or unwilling to supply enough buy-side liquidity.

16. High-Frequency Trading, *New York Times*, October 10, 2011:

    > Regulators did not blame high-frequency traders for causing the sell-off. But some firms may have exacerbated the decline by switching off their machines and withdrawing from the market. As the number of buyers dropped drastically, so too did the stock prices.

    http://topics.nytimes.com/topics/reference/timestopics/subjects/h/high_frequency_algorithmic_trading/index.html.

17. For an account of the incident see for example, Knight Capital trading debacle shows Wall Street frailties, *Los Angeles Times*, August 3, 2012.

    The subtitle to the article is "A software bug leaves brokerage Knight Capital teetering on failure, raising fears of structural flaws in the financial system." The article, which is available online at http://www.latimes.com/business/la-fi-0803-trading-chaos-20120803,0,1527952.story, also includes a couple of pertinent observations regarding the effect on investor morale:

    > Knight's losses reaffirmed Los Angeles retiree Robert Altman's decision to pull nearly all of his investments out of stocks. Altman said his distaste for the market's wild swings and technical glitches may confirm industry fears that recent Wall Street technical mishaps could scare off retail investors.
    >
    > "I'm out of it," said Altman, 73, who has plowed his savings into municipal bonds. "The little guy has no business in the market anymore."
    >
    > One of Wall Street's biggest critics when it comes to high-speed trading, Joe Saluzzi, said it was only a matter of time before another glitch throws the market into turmoil.
    >
    > "Everyone is at risk," said Saluzzi, a partner in the brokerage firm Themis Trading. "There's no doubt it will happen again. It's just a matter of how severe it will be next time."

18. See endnote 2 to Chapter 6.
19. The stem, or whole dollar price, of a price quote. The term "big figure" is most often used in international currency markets, where it is often abbreviated to "big fig." For example, assume that the Japanese yen is trading versus the US dollar in the interbank spot market at 88.20 (bid)/88.25 (offered). While the big figure here is 88, interbank traders will quote the price as 20/25.
20. The connection between the coincidental drop in the S&P 500 and the increase in the Japanese yen is highlighted in an article entitled *Stepping Into An Empty Elevator Shaft*, which is to be found at the following website: http://www.tradersnarrative.com/stepping-into-an-empty-elevator-shaft-4032.html. A similar viewpoint is also provided in *The Yen Did It,* Bruce Krasting, personal blogsite, May 6, 2010, http://brucekrasting.blogspot.co.uk/2010/05/yen-did-it.html.
21. Greece's Debt Crisis May Spread, Agency Warns, CBS Money Watch, May 6, 2010, http://www.cbsnews.com/2100-500395_162-6465221.html
22. See endnote 3.
23. Discussed for example in Andrew G. Haldane, *Financial arms races*, April 14, 2012.

    Speech by Mr Andrew G. Haldane, Executive Director, Financial Stability, Bank of England, at the Institute for New Economic Thinking, Berlin, 14 April 2012, http://www.bis.org/review/r120426a.pdf.
24. Michael Lewis, *The Big Short: Inside The Doomsday Machine* (Allen Lane, 2010).
25. Yen volatility is too much for one bank, *FT Alphaville*, March 18, 2011, http://ftalphaville.ft.com/blog/2011/03/18/519736/yen-volatility-is-too-much-for-one-bank/.
26. For those who have not seen the movie Ocean's 13, directed by Stephen Soderbergh, it was one of a series of Ocean's films, and featured George Clooney, Brad Pitt, Al Pacino, and Matt Damon among others.

    Without revealing too much of the narrative there is an elaborate swindle perpetrated against a casino in Las Vegas in revenge for a broken promise. The swindle is accomplished by hacking into the sophisticated software systems which are used to run the casino. The movie includes scenes of mayhem including a simulated earthquake and pandemonium for all of the gamblers at the various games and tables in the casino.

6

Foreign Exchange and the Carry Trade

Conventional wisdom regarding portfolio management has neglected the role of foreign exchange or FX as an asset class in its own right. Not only in finance textbooks but also in conversations one might have with many hands-on fund managers, FX exposure is often seen as an incidental feature of portfolio construction and risk management; a kind of by-product of selecting different assets which are denominated in different currencies. The presumption which would typically accompany such a viewpoint is that it is incumbent on asset managers to "manage" FX risk, through the application of hedging techniques to avoid adverse movements of the currency in which the primary assets are denominated *vis-à-vis* the domestic or base currency. Under such a constrained view there are two main drawbacks.

Firstly, hedging the foreign exchange "risk," to the extent that it can be achieved (see endnote 6 for discussion of covered interest parity), will neutralize the investments so that from a base currency point of view the exposure to either positive or adverse currency movements has been removed. When adopting this circumscribed view of FX, which sees it very much as an unintended by-product of owning an asset, there will be a failure to take into account the positive contributions to portfolio construction which can arise from favorable FX movements. More radically it will be shown in Chapter 10 that, rather than hedging FX risk, the use of outright positions in currencies, as an asset class in their own right, can actually be used as a protective hedge strategy for substantially reducing drawdowns and tail risk in a portfolio. This was especially the case in the 2007/8 financial crisis where a short position for example in the Australian dollar on a matched dollar basis for an equity portfolio would have achieved a more effective hedge than most other traditional hedging instruments. [1]

Secondly, there is ample evidence that certain FX pairs demonstrate strong influence and co-movement catalysts to other asset classes. Rather asset managers should open their minds to the possibility of seeing a lot of FX price development as being an *instigator for movements* across financial markets, and, in general, be ready to monitor FX markets for directional cues in the same way that financial spreads, CDS prices, and other meta-market indicators are treated.

In the remainder of this chapter, and a recurring theme throughout, the contention is that price developments in the forex market can act as an early warning system and vital barometer of what can be called *macro risk* perception in financial markets. Distinguishing between cause and effect in the mood swings of markets, characterized as binary or bipolar, is no easy task. Fortunately we don't need to take a position on this. It suffices for our purposes in what follows to recognize that the exchange rate dynamics of certain key currency pairs, most notably those which will be discussed in relation to the FX carry trade, are demonstrably interwoven within the context of the behavior of the wider class of *risk on* and *risk off* asset classes.

Furthermore the exercise in quantifying the nature of asset correlations with certain currency pairs can be very useful in ascertaining macro risk appetite and its flip side macro risk aversion. Within the new trading paradigm where asset classes can be aligned along a risk on/risk off frontier, the co-movement of certain asset classes and currency pairs, ultimately related to the FX carry trade, can act as remarkable precursors to under the surface price patterns that are still not manifesting themselves to the overall market. Before beginning an examination of the FX carry trade a brief primer on the nature of the foreign exchange market itself will provide a useful background.

6.1 PRIMER ON THE FOREX MARKET

The foreign exchange market is an example of a de-centralized market which has no trading exchanges *per se* or venues. Rather trading occurs on a distributed electronic platform or virtual network with nodes or screens scattered across the world. The primary real time or spot market in foreign exchange (see below) is accessible from different trading terminals on different platforms, and hundreds of thousands, if not millions of investors and traders will be found monitoring the changing exchange rates for most major currencies throughout the global trading day. The major participants in the 24-hour-a-day market are the large commercial banks and increasingly the "shadow banking system" in the form primarily of hedge funds.

The principal kinds of FX transactions can be categorized as follows:

Spot transactions are single outright (cash) transactions that involve the exchange of two currencies at a rate agreed to on the date of the contract. Delivery and settlement is typically within two business days.

Outright forwards involve the exchange of two currencies at a rate agreed to on the date of the contract for value or delivery at some time in the future. This category also includes non-deliverable forwards (NDFs), and other forward contracts for differences.

Foreign exchange swaps involve the exchange of two currencies on a specific date at a rate agreed to at the time of the contract, and a reverse exchange of the same two currencies on a future date also at a rate agreed to at the time of the contract.

Currency swaps involve the exchange of fixed or floating interest payments in two different currencies over the lifetime of the contract. Equal principal amounts based on the initial spot rate are typically exchanged at the beginning and close of the contract.

Foreign exchange options are contracts that give the right to buy or sell a currency with another currency at a specified exchange rate during or at the end of a specified time period.

The Bank for International Settlements (BIS) publishes a triennial survey of the FX market and the most recent was published in September 2010. [2] Table 6.1 shows the breakdown of activity in each of the categories listed above and also gives a historical dimension to the data. The most recent BIS figure shows that the total turnover for all transactions with FX instruments was more or less \$4 trillion per day. Estimates have even suggested that the figure in mid 2012 could have reached \$5 trillion per day. [3] It is important to realize that this is the notional amount of all trading and that very high leverage is available in the trading of FX. However, it is fair to say that the FX market is the largest and most liquid of the world's financial markets.

The BIS triennial reports provide a comprehensive analysis of the types of participants in the FX market and the respective shares of the market for each of the major currencies.

Here are some of the key findings in the 2010 survey:

- Among the 10 most actively traded currencies, the Australian and Canadian dollars both increased market share in the 2010 survey. The Australian and Canadian dollars both increased their share by around 1 percentage point, to 6.6% and 5.3%, respectively.

Table 6.1 BIS Foreign Exchange Market Triennial Survey, September 2010

Triennial Central Bank Survey of Foreign Exchange and Derivatives Market Activity in April 2010

Global foreign exchange market turnover by instrument[1]

Average daily turnover in April, in billions of US dollars

Instrument	1998	2001	2004	2007	2010
Foreign exchange instruments	**1,527**	**1,239**	**1,934**	**3,324**	**3,981**
Spot transactions[2]	568	386	631	1,005	1,490
Outright forwards[2]	128	130	209	362	475
Foreign exchange swaps[2]	734	656	954	1,714	1,765
Currency swaps	10	7	21	31	43
Options and other products[3]	87	60	119	212	207

- Sterling and the Swiss franc trades declined marginally from the 2007 survey.
- The market share of emerging market currencies increased, with the biggest gains for the Turkish lira, Korean won, Brazilian real, and Singapore dollar.
- In the 2010 survey banks located in the UK accounted for 37% of total turnover as compared to 35% in 2006. Turnover in other centers was as follows: USA (18%), Japan (6%), Singapore (5%), Switzerland (5%), Hong Kong (4%), and Australia (4%).
- EUR/USD remained by far the dominant pair with a 28% share.
- USD/JPY responsible for 14% of total FX turnover.
- Trades involving euro account for 39% of all transactions.

Figure 6.1 includes data supplied by the CLS Bank in New York which is owned by the major participants in the FX market, the large banks, and is the settlement system for the

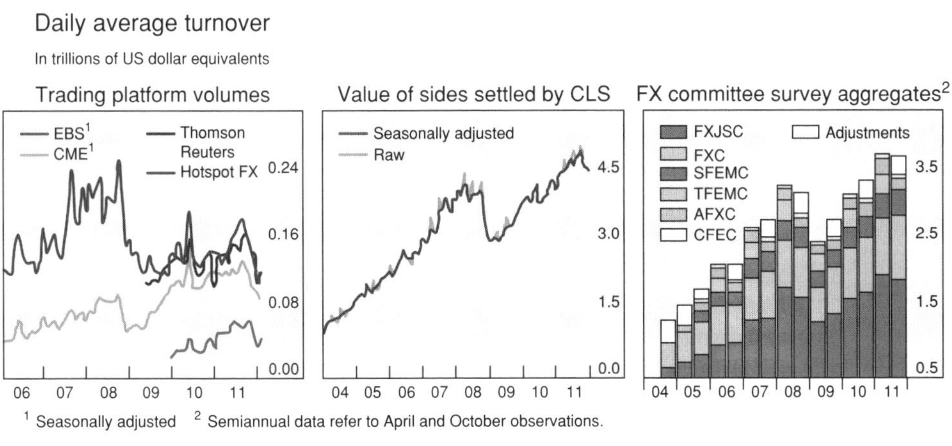

Figure 6.1 FX turnover
Sources: CLS Group; CME.

great majority of FX transactions except OTC swaps. The system is designed to ensure that settlement takes place according to a strict payment versus payment protocol so that there is no counter-party risk as arose in the 1970s. [4]

6.2 THE FX CARRY TRADE

The FX carry trade can be seen as a standalone foreign exchange trade or part of an integrated macro strategy which is often practiced by large investment banks or within the shadow banking system by hedge funds and other proprietary trading firms. Although not strictly an arbitrage, the FX carry trade relies upon there being a possibility to exploit interest rate differentials which are provided in the international money markets and applicable to lending and borrowing transactions in different currencies. For example if the LIBOR rate to borrow yen is at 50 basis points (on an annualized basis) and the equivalent rate which can be earned on an Australian dollar denominated deposit or money market instrument is 400 basis points, there is 350-basis-point spread and accordingly an opportunity to earn carry.

In general, one would sell or go short (borrow) a low yielding currency such as the yen, Swiss franc or, since 2008, the US dollar (as a result of the ZIRP policy [5] implemented by the Federal Reserve) and buy or go long (lend) a high yielding currency – typically the Australian or New Zealand dollar. In its pure form the carry trade is motivated by a desire to earn the spread by exploiting the interest rate differential, and this is what provides the carry. There is, of course, a risk to this trade which is that the relative values of the two currencies will fluctuate and that when the carry period terminates and it is time to repay (say) the Japanese yen which were borrowed and "swapped" into the other currency (say) the Australian dollar, the exchange rate may have moved against the carry trader to such an extent that the carry earned on the interest rate differential is more than offset by a decline in the Aussie dollar with respect to the yen.

In spread trading it is the size of the spread which matters and either the yen could have increased, the Aussie dollar declined, or a bit of both from the rate applicable at the time of entering the carry trade. It doesn't matter which of the preceding actually happens, but if the pure FX spread moves the wrong way then there is the potential for substantial losses which would eradicate the carry. It may be possible to hedge the currency exposure, but, in an efficient market with covered interest parity, [6] it should not be possible to do so using simple forward agreements or futures contracts. An article in *The Economist* with the provocative title "Crash and Carry" spells out the difficulty in hedging the pure exchange rate risk: [7]

> If markets were truly efficient, carry trades ought not to be profitable because the extra interest earned should be exactly offset by a fall in the target currency. That is why high-interest currencies trade at a discount to their current or "spot" rate in forward markets. If exchange rates today were the same as those in forward contracts, there would be an opportunity for riskless profit. Arbitrageurs could buy the high interest currency today, lock in a future sale at the same price and pocket the extra interest from holding the currency until the forward contract is settled.

Even with tailored swaps there will be difficulty in reaching outside the covered parity box to provide effective hedging. Should it be possible to find a vehicle for some hedging of the currency exposure there will be a cost associated with this, and, in turn, this diminishes the return to be gained on the carry earned from the difference in the interest rates. For this reason it is often the case that there is a lot of activity within the traditional FX carry pairs such as AUD/JPY which are in the form of a straightforward long/short strategy which expects to gain on one or both of the currency legs, without implementing an associated strategy to earn interest carry.

Given that there are very well capitalized banks and hedge funds which are seeking to earn the carry, there is undoubtedly a strong motivation by pure FX traders to see opportunities in just trading the relevant FX pairs. Arguments have been put forward that global macro hedge funds have used the carry trade to "create" investable funds. [8] This can be achieved because of the extreme leverage of 100:1 (or even greater) which can be applied in the FX part of the carry trade. In addition, for the full blown carry trade, designed to earn the interest rate carry, considerable leverage is also available through prime brokers and other intermediaries prepared to accept on margin the high grade collateral such as short-term securities borrowed or deposited with the funding currency, e.g. JPY and the target currency, e.g. AUD. The availability of this kind of trading has been criticized by some critics of the shadow banking system on the basis that it is a method of greatly enhancing the amount of "hot money" which lies "offshore" and beyond the jurisdiction and control of the central banks, although this criticism is often made by people who fail to appreciate the manner in which the onshore banking community is able *to create money out of thin air* as well. A war of words on the World Wide Web between Professor Paul Krugman, Professor of Economics and International Affairs at Princeton and Nobel Laureate, who is also an active blogger via the *New York Times*, and Professor Steve Keen from the University of Western Sydney, among others, in April 2012, was based on exactly this issue. [9] References to this debate will also be made in Chapter 10 when considering critiques of mainstream macro-economic theory.

6.3 DOES THE CARRY TRADE POSE A RISK TO THE FINANCIAL SYSTEM?

This question has been asked by many critics of the shadow banking system and has generated a lot of academic research, some of which will be touched on later in this chapter. The IMF has opined on the matter [10] and in broad terms concluded that, although large scale movements in FX, possibly the result of the stressed unwinding of carry trades, can be disruptive they seem reasonably relaxed about the risks posed to financial markets. It seems to be almost worth turning the question around and asking the following question: If the financial system is de-levering how much risk is there in the carry trade? The answer to the latter question actually is more instructive than the former because for highly leveraged trades which involve the Japanese yen as a component, there is a real risk of substantial appreciation in that funding currency when markets are entering a stressful state. The yen is a safe haven play as will be demonstrated more thoroughly in later discussions. This flight to safety quality of the yen and the Swiss Franc was clearly seen in the summer of 2007 when the sub-prime crisis was peeking above the parapet, at least for those participants in the shadow banking system who were "close to the action," and resulted in an abrupt exit and unwinding of the major FX carry pairs.

In Chapter 9 we will revisit the early warnings provided by the major FX carry pairs in the days leading up to the first severe liquidity crisis which occurred in August 2007. In that chapter we will look at AUD/JPY and also GBP/JPY as sterling was also an attractive target currency for the trade in that time frame with short-term rates above 5% in the UK. It will be seen that the main carry trade pairs dropped abruptly in the last week of July 2007.

For present purposes, Figure 6.2 shows the dramatic drop of the New Zealand dollar against the Japanese yen, which is one of the better known carry pairs, in the summer of 2007.

Figure 6.2 The New Zealand dollar/Japanese yen exchange rated during second half of 2007

AUD/JPY topped on July 22 (see Figure 8.6) and then began to sell off abruptly and the NZD/JPY drop was just one day later with the peak value registered on July 23 2007 at 96.6. As the chart in Figure 6.2 shows the downside momentum was rapid and the New Zealand dollar fell almost 25% in the next three weeks reaching an intraday low of 76.22 on August 17, 2007. This quite extraordinary price move was a clear indicator to those paying attention that the shadow banking system was reacting quite drastically not only to a changed perception of the viability of their carry trade positions but also, in more general terms, to margin calls from prime brokers and the inevitable de-leveraging consequences that they would have to undertake as troubles in the asset backed securities markets began to mount.

Remaining vigilant to the sudden appearance of these painful episodes in the carry trade, as will be seen below, provides an excellent insight into the kinds of liquidation under stress scenarios which are often foreshocks of a more systemically threatening event which is still beneath the surface. To summarize, there are very few canaries in the coalmine in the financial markets but close observation and an understanding of FX carry trade movements will be a rewarding exercise offering an early warning system to broader price development trends across most asset classes.

It is convenient to illustrate the dynamics which drive the FX carry trade by considering Figure 6.3. The exchange traded fund (ETF) known as *Powershares DB G10* can act as a simple proxy for the FX carry trade. The fund tracks the performance of the Deutsche Bank G10 Currency Future Harvest Index – Excess Return, a bit of a mouthful but in essence it shows the result of holding long futures positions on the three G10 currencies which have the highest interest rates and short futures positions on three currencies associated with the lowest

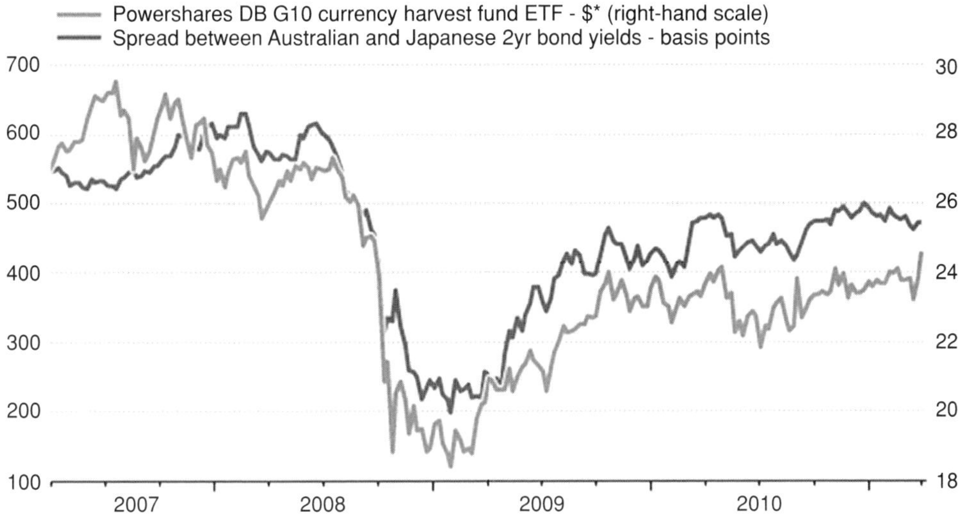

Figure 6.3 DG10 Currency Harvest Exchange Traded Fund (DBV) and spreads between Australian and Japanese short-term bonds
Source: Thomson Reuters.

interest rates. By diversifying the trade to three currency pairs on either side of the spread there is less possibility that an adverse move in just one of the FX pairs, such as AUD/JPY caused by abrupt moves in the yen, will be detrimental to the trade. However it is likely that non-specific changes to the dynamics for the carry trade in general are likely to be felt across all three pairings.

Figure 6.3 shows on the left hand scale the spread between the yields of the funding currency in this example, the Japanese yen, and the target currency, the Australian dollar, and two-year bond yields have been chosen. The yield spread moved to almost 700 basis points in early 2007 which is a powerful inducement for putting on the carry trade. Moving into the late July and early August of 2007 there was a big unwinding of all of the FX carry trades – as captured also by Figure 6.2 the NZD/JPY chart – and this is reflected in the noticeable dip of the lighter toned line on the chart about one third over from the left hand side. The yield spread at this juncture was still moving upwards – in fact the two lines are going in opposite directions in Q3, 2007. This could suggest that position unwinding in just the FX pairs was the dominant factor in the sudden move towards risk off. As the global financial crisis unfolded into 2008 there was a steady convergence of both paths on the chart below with both basing in Q3, 2008 when the yield spread had fallen to 200 basis points. As the recovery began in the spring of 2009 and the yield spread widened again so the performance of the exchange traded fund, which trades under the symbol of DBV, also moves again in close alignment with the lighter toned line.

The Powershares DB G10 Currency Harvest exchange traded fund can provide access to the FX carry trade for retail investors. An alternative exchange traded fund to DBV which acts in a similar manner to the one based on the Deutsche Bank index is based on the Barclays Intelligent Carry Index, and trades under the symbol ICI. It is however less liquid than the DBV fund. Figure 6.4 shows the relative performance of both ETFs since July 2008 and indicates that the performances are relatively similar with the exception of the deeper fall of DBV during the height of the GFC. The chart also shows that the returns from the carry

Figure 6.4 Comparison between two different ETFs which represent carry trade – ICI and DBV

trade – using the methods employed by both of the indices tracked by the funds – have moved in a sideways pattern after returning to the more normal post-GFC levels since October 2009.

For the large institutional investors there are more exotic FX carry pairs which can be constructed and targeting other high yielding currencies such as the Indonesian rupiah, the Brazilian real, and the Russian ruble. However when the target currencies become more exotic and the yields on offer become more elevated there is an increased risk of rapid depreciation in the exchange rate of the target currency. Referring back to the article in *The Economist* cited above, it also makes the following relevant comment in this regard: (see endnote 7)

> ... although it makes sense for traders to buy currencies with fat yields, it may be dangerous past a certain point. After all, a high interest rate can be a symptom of a currency in distress ... the link between profits and yields (is) likely to be "non-linear" (i.e. its strength alters as the interest rate of the target currency climbs) ... This non-linearity applies to a currencies' values, too: the likelihood of a crash escalates as a currency becomes ever dearer.

Even when confining the selection of the target currency to the less exotic variety such as the Australian and New Zealand dollars, there are substantial risks for the FX carry trader. This feature has been well documented in some useful research on the risks inherent in the carry trade conducted by a research team at the University of California at Davis. [11] One of their more attention grabbing remarks is the following:

> By the fall of 2008 attention was grabbed by an even more brutal squeeze on carry traders from bigger yen moves e.g., up 60% against the AUD over 2 months, and up 30% against GBP (including 10% moves against both in five hours on the morning of October 24). Money managers on the

> wrong side saw their funds blowing up, supporting the June 2007 prediction of Jim O'Neill, chief global economist at Goldman Sachs, who had said of the carry trade that "there are going to be dead bodies around when this is over."

The research authors have undertaken a very comprehensive analysis of the returns and risk characteristics of the FX carry trade over an extended period and found that while the strategy does, overall, generate positive returns it does so with high risk. Reflecting the "crash"-like behavior to the returns seen in 2008 and covered in the previous quotation they also make the point that the returns from a simple carry trade strategy have a very low Sharpe ratio (around 0.2) as the denominator to apply to the modest returns in the numerator of this ratio, [12] which is the standard deviation of the returns, is very high reflecting a high degree of volatility in the returns:

> The international financial crisis of the second half of 2008 effectively undid the majority of the persistent carry trade returns observed during the previous five to ten years. Strategies based on arbitraging interest rate differentials across countries under the belief that it was equiprobable for exchange rates to appreciate or depreciate displayed consistently positive average returns. But these returns were volatile and subject to occasional crashes (negative skewness) ... more sophisticated strategies that incorporate information about the fundamental equilibrium exchange rate can deliver positive returns with high Sharpe ratios and zero or even mildly positive skewness.

In concluding this chapter and to pursue a little further the risk/reward profile of the FX carry trade there is another study entitled *Downside risk in carry trades* by Philip Marey of Rabobank which was published in October 2009 and which contains some useful discussion and some helpful graphics. [13]

Table 6.2 displays a table from the Rabobank research note, and captures the average carry trade returns of five G10 currencies as the target currencies; in each case the Japanese yen was the funding currency. The period covered is from August 1993 to November 2008 so it covers the most acute period of the GFC. The table also separates the two components which contributed to the total return as expressed in the right hand column – the average carry return and the average exchange rate return. One simple conclusion to draw from the table is that there is a remarkable homogeneity to the average returns for each of the five target currencies.

It is also interesting to note from the findings shown in Table 6.2 that "the exchange rate loss is too small to wipe out the positive carry. In other words, uncovered interest parity does not

Table 6.2 Average monthly carry trade returns 2003–8

Average monthly carry trade returns (annualized percentages)			
Against JPY	Average carry	Average exchange rate return	Average carry trade return
USD	3.67	−0.61	3.07
CAD	3.59	−0.36	3.22
AUD	5.17	−0.95	4.20
EUR	3.37	0.12	3.50
GBP	4.90	−0.37	4.53

Source: Downside risk in carry trades, Philip Marey, Rabobank October 2009.

Monthly observations of one-month LIBOR fixings and one-month exchange rate returns, annualized rates. Sample: August 1993–November 2008. *Source:* Reuters Ecowin.

hold. Instead – the carry trade returns are positive, on average, despite modest depreciations in target currencies." The conclusion that uncovered interest parity does not hold can actually be cited as a counter instance to the notion that in efficient markets there can be no possibility of a successful currency hedge which was alluded to in the earlier discussion (see endnote 6).

Another important insight provided in Philip Marey's article relates to liquidity issues which have already been the focus of our attention in previous chapters. The FX market is renowned for its depth and liquidity, especially during the London trading session which spans the two other time zones of Asia in the morning and North America during the afternoon from a GMT perspective. Liquidity which, in this guise, can be measured in terms of the bid/ask spread is especially narrow with regard to the quotations in the spot and forward markets of the most actively traded pairs such as EUR/USD and USD/JPY. In normal market conditions one would expect to see a minimal pip spread on either side of the market (a pip is equal to 0.0001 units of the quote currency). However, as with other capital markets there was a very noticeable illiquidity – observable in terms of much wider spreads – which developed at the height of the GFC. Figure 6.5 shows this in relation to the bid/ask spreads being quoted in the three-month forwards market for the dollar/yen exchange rate. The lighter toned line on the graph – which is related to the left hand vertical scale – shows the steady decline of the dollar against the Japanese currency throughout the period shown on the graph. The decline became acute in the August–October 2008 time frame and is visible on the chart. The right hand vertical scale provides an insight into the width of the bid/ask spreads throughout the period as well. In "normal" conditions the spreads were minimal but during the critical time period just cited they spiked and remained much wider than normal. Stresses within the FX market for the Australian dollar, as evidenced by much wider bid/ask spread, are also noticeable in

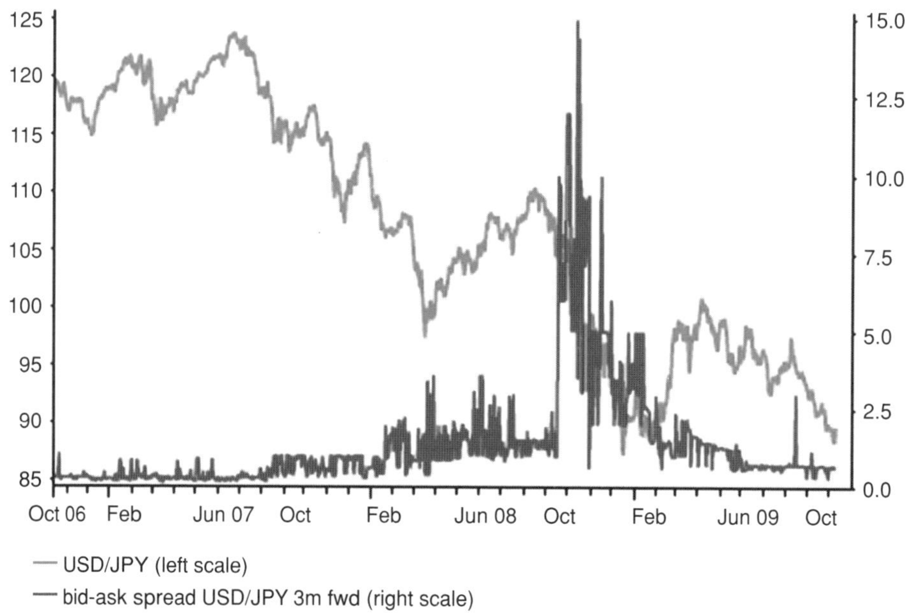

Figure 6.5 Liquidity, carry trade unwinding, and target currency depreciation
Source: Downside risk in carry trades, Philip Marey, Rabobank October 2009.

the second half of 2008 and contributed to disruptive and turbulent conditions for carry traders and risk on markets in general.

Echoing the findings of the two academics from the University of California at Davis, Marey's own conclusion provides a good summary of the FX carry trade in general:

> The distribution of carry trade returns has a positive mean, but is also characterized by fat tails and negative skewness. This means that carry trades are profitable on average, but extreme returns occur relatively frequently. More importantly, extremely negative returns occur more often than extremely positive returns, so downside risk prevails. Carry trades may generate positive returns as long as investors jump on the bandwagon, but sudden large scale unwinding of carry trades results in a sharp depreciation in the target currency, which could lead to substantial losses.

ENDNOTES

1. There is a discussion of how the use of outright FX positions, especially a short position in the Australian dollar/Japanese yen, provides effective hedging and shock absorption for a portfolio with risk assets in Chapter 13.
2. Triennial Central Bank Survey Foreign exchange and derivatives market activity in April 2010 Preliminary results, published in September 2010. Coordinated by the BIS, participating institutions collect data from some 1300 reporting dealers on turnover in foreign exchange instruments and OTC interest rate derivatives. The triennial survey has been conducted every three years since April 1989, and has been modified since April 1995 to include OTC interest rate derivatives, http://www.bis.org/publ/rpfx10.pdf.
3. *Currency Trading At $5 Trillion A Day Surpassed Pre-Lehman High, BIS Says*, Bloomberg, April 12, 2012:

   > Currency trading may have risen to a record $5 trillion a day in September, surpassing the peak reached before Lehman Brothers (LEHMQ) Holdings Inc.'s collapse in 2008, according to the Bank for International Settlements. Trading then declined to about $4.7 trillion a day in October and is likely to have fallen considerably in early 2012, the Basel, Switzerland-based bank said in a report. The BIS said it derived its estimates from supplementing the data in its foreign-exchange survey, which is undertaken every three years, with information collected from central banks and electronic-trading platforms.

   http://www.bloomberg.com/news/2012-03-11/currency-trading-at-5-trillion-a-day-surpassed-pre-lehman-high-bis-says.html.
4. Settlement risk is sometimes called "Herstatt risk," named after the failure of the German bank Herstatt. On June 26, 1974, the bank had taken in its foreign currency receipts in Europe, but had not made any of its US dollar payments when German banking regulators closed the bank down, leaving counter-parties with the substantial losses.

   Settlement risk was a problem in the FX market up until the creation of continuously linked settlement (CLS), which is facilitated by CLS Bank International, which operates with a matched payment versus payment (PVP) protocol ensuring a safer forex market.
5. ZIRP policy is associated with a policy stance adopted by the Bank of Japan and has been summarized as follows "In February 1999, the Policy Board of the BOJ assigned staff a new guideline for money market operations to 'flexibly provide ample funds and encourage the uncollateralized overnight call rate to move as low as possible' and the BOJ adopted the so-called zero interest rate policy."

   From *Monetary Policy under Zero Interest Rate: Current Situation and Future Perspective*, by Kunio Okina, Director, Institute for Monetary and Economic Studies, Bank of Japan, http://www.imes.boj.or.jp/research/papers/japanese/ko0006.pdf.

   In mid-2012 the US Federal Reserve has a 0.5% federal funds rate, the Bank of England has a base rate of 0.5%, and the Bank of Japan's uncollateralized overnight call rate is 10 basis points.

6. The best way to illustrate the concept of covered interest parity is to consider the method by which forward rates are calculated for foreign exchange transactions. The table below indicates that the current spot rate for GBP/USD is $1.585. In this (simplified) quotation a person with £1 would be able to exchange that for $1.585. GBP or sterling is the base currency and the US dollar is the quote currency. The annual interest rates available on deposits in each currency are shown in the table.

Present Spot Rate	Annual Interest Rate	One Year Forward
£1,000.00	4.00%	£1,040.00
1.585		
$1,585.00	1.50%	$1,608.78
One Year Forward Rate		$1.5469
Forward Rate =	Spot Rate x	(1 + R[Quote currency]) / (1 + R[Base currency])

Calculating FX forward rates

The example shows that if one started with £1000 in a sterling deposit at the end of one year that would have grown to £1040. Alternatively one could have exchanged at the spot rate and obtained $1585 and earned the dollar deposit for one year, i.e. 1.5% and the amount at the end of the year would be $1608.78. The one-year forward rate would be the ratio between the quote currency – the US dollar – and the base currency – sterling. In the example this would be at the discount to the spot rate of $1.5469.

The illustration shows that an investor should be indifferent between the available interest rates in each of the two currencies because the forward exchange rate sustains an equilibrium condition whereby the dollar return on dollar deposits is equal to the dollar return on the sterling deposit. If this was not the case there would be an opportunity for covered interest arbitrage profits; rational pricing theory suggests that in efficient markets this would not arise.

7. Economics Focus: Crash and carry, *The Economist*, May 18, 2012, http://www.economist.com/node/15065320/print 2/4.
8. Tim Geithner, Financial Crisis Amnesia, *Wall Street Journal*, March 1, 2012, http://online.wsj.com/article/SB10001424052970203986604577253272042239982.html.

   US Treasury Secretary, Tim Geithner, who authored the article, makes several related points:

   > A large shadow banking system had developed without meaningful regulation, using trillions of dollars in short-term debt to fund inherently risky financial activity. The derivatives markets grew to more than $600 trillion, with little transparency or oversight.
   >
   > The failure to modernize the financial oversight system sooner is the most important reason why this crisis was more severe than any since the Great Depression, and why it was so hard to put out the fires of the crisis.

9. See for example the following two summaries of the debate:

   Steve Keen vs. Krugman/The Science of Economics, zerohedge.com, April 3, 2012, http://www.zerohedge.com/contributed/2012-14-03/steve-keen-vs-krugmanthe-science-economics. The Economics Spring, Renegade Economist, April 5, 2012, http://www.renegadeeconomist.com/blog/from-a-renegade-correspondent/the-economics-spring.html.
10. G Plantin and H Shin, *Carry Trades, Monetary Policy and Speculative Dynamics*, January 2011, http://www.imf.org/external/np/seminars/eng/2011/res2/pdf/gp.pdf.

11. Oscar Jorda and Alan M. Taylor, *The Carry Trade and Fundamentals: Nothing to Fear But FEER Itself* (Department of Economics, University of California, Davis, November 2009), http://www.econ.ucdavis.edu/faculty/jorda/papers/JTcarry_110609_at.pdf.
12. Quoted in *The Carry Trade and Fundamentals: Nothing to Fear But FEER Itself.* See endnote 11.
13. Philip Marey Rabobank, *Downside Risk in Carry Trades*, October 2009. Not available on the internet.

7

The Enigmatic Performance of the Japanese Yen

As one looks across the performance of globally significant asset classes there are a number which appear to be counter intuitive; one of the most surprising must be the performance of the Japanese yen against the US dollar. Figure 7.1 displays the price development of the yen against the dollar – it is inverted to show the yen as the base currency unlike the more customary pattern of USD/JPY (as it is typically quoted in forex transactions).

Figure 7.1 covers the period from January 1998 until the end of April 2012, during which time the yen strengthened by approximately 62% against the US currency. A fair characterization of the pattern from the beginning of 1998 up until August 2007, the "unofficial" onset of the financial crisis, would be to describe it as one of being range bound between approximately 75 and 100. But as the annotation on the chart makes clear there is a noticeable inflection point in August 2007 from which level the yen has moved consistently upwards against the dollar. Just one further comment on the chart is to note that in the first half of 2009 the yen retreated back to a re-test of the 100 level, which was the break out level from the previously mentioned range, and the re-test validated the yen's strength; clearly the previous resistance level had now become a key support. Since this re-testing of the 100 level, the yen has moved up by more than 30% against the US dollar to the level seen on the right hand side of the chart.

By way of a brief recap of recent economic history related to our excursion regarding the enigma of the strong yen, the Japanese economy has experienced 20 years of deflation in what Richard Koo, Chief Economist at Nomura Group in Tokyo, [1] has described as a profound balance sheet recession. It is quite astonishing that as of July 2012 the broadest gauge for prices of Japanese equities, the Nikkei 225 index, is down more than 75% since the index reached its historic high of almost 40 000 on the last trading day of 1989.

In a presentation to the INET Conference in Berlin in April 2012 (there will be quite a lot more to say about the INET organization in Chapter 10), Nomura's Koo documented the nature of the Japanese experience – characterized as a balance sheet recession – and its parallels to what is now unfolding in other parts of the world, particularly in the US, UK, Spain, Ireland, and Italy, since the GFC. Figure 7.2, taken from Koo's presentation, shows the remarkable similarities in the trajectories taken by real estate prices in Japan and the US during their respective property price bubbles.

For Japan the prices for both Tokyo and Osaka condominiums are based in December 1985 as the Japanese bubble started to become rampant during the second half of the 1980s; for the US composite index of 10 major US cities the base period selected is January 2000, which can be considered comparable in relation to the boom that developed.

Extending backwards along the time axis for both Japanese and US real estate the three lines track each other in a striking fashion with the 15-year lag which is evident from the legend shown on the horizontal scale. In both cases the peaks came at approximately the same interval from the dates shown on the left hand side of the time axis, and the degree of the bubble was

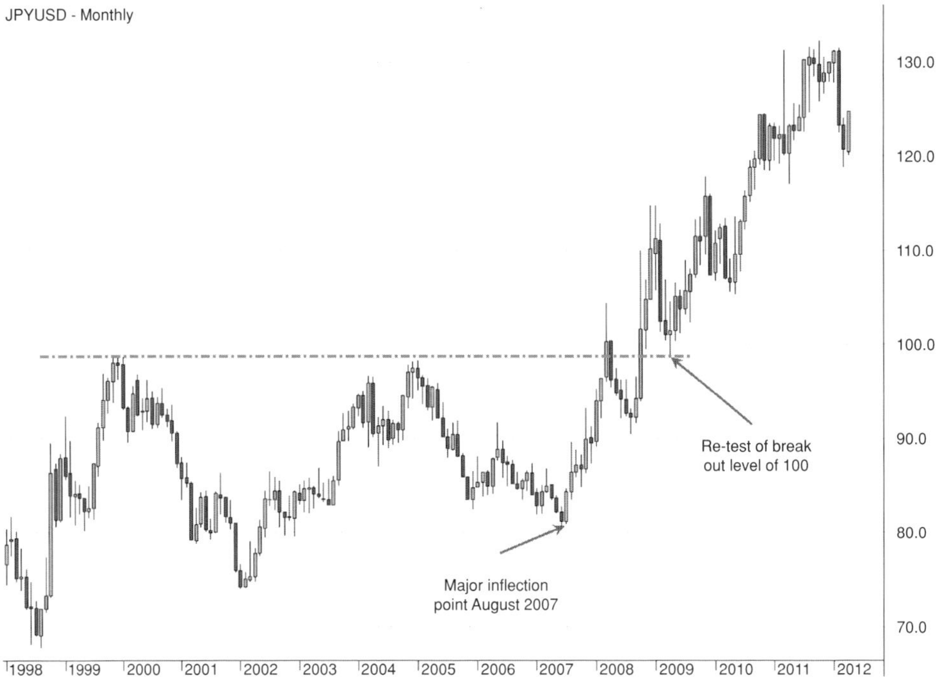

Figure 7.1 Japanese yen/US dollar exchange rate monthly since 1998

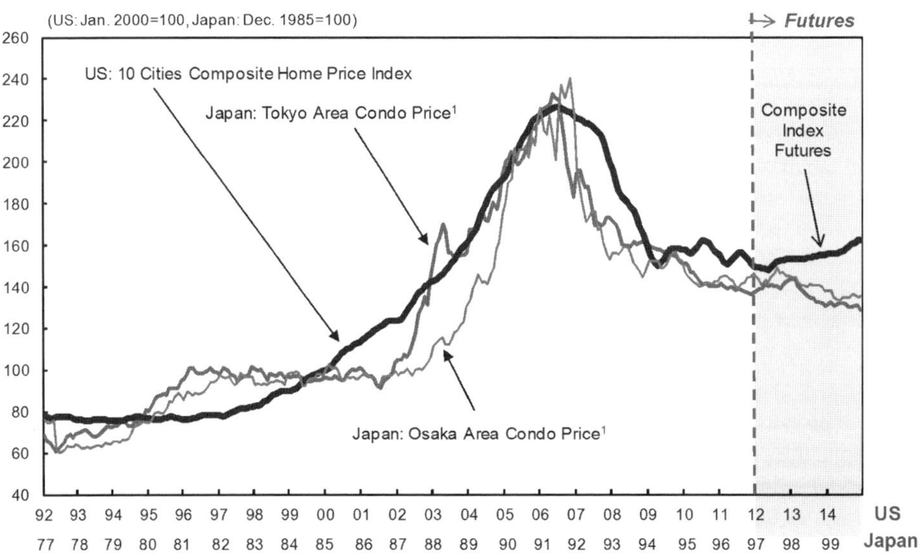

Figure 7.2 US housing prices are moving along the Japanese experience
Source: The World in Balance Sheet Recession, Richard Koo INET Berlin April 2012.
Note: per m^2, 5-month moving average.

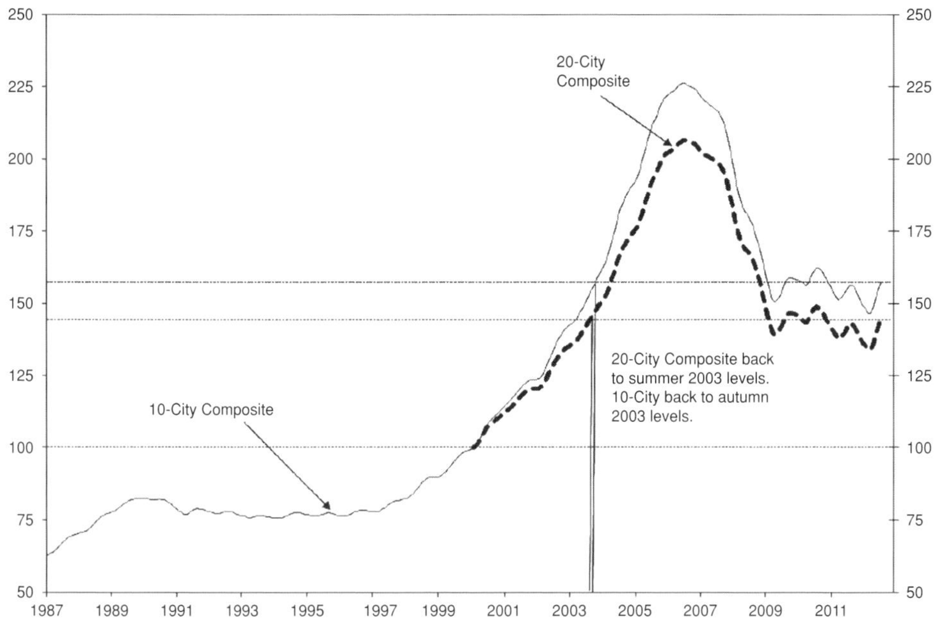

Figure 7.3 S&P Case-Shiller Home Prices Indices March 2012
Source: S&P Dow Jones Indices and Fiserv.

remarkably similar with an approximate 225 reading on the index values for each of the three trajectories. In fact the price of Osaka condos reached a level of 240. So the magnitude of the price escalation (bubbles) in the cases of both Japan and the US was extraordinarily similar, as also was the time taken for the peaks to be reached in each market.

For the Japanese data, and following Koo's trajectories, there was a 90% retracement of the gains seen from the top of the market to the levels seen at the end of 1999. Looked at from the perspective of someone who had bought a condo in Osaka at the height of the Japanese property bubble, that condo would have lost approximately 40% of its value within eight years and the bulk of the drop would have occurred within the first three or four years. The US example shows a slightly smaller drop – those who bought at the top have seen somewhere in the vicinity of a 35–40% erosion in their investment from 2007 to 2011, but there is still time to run before making the exact comparison with the timeline for Japan.

According to the S&P/Case-Shiller Home Price Indices, the 10 and 20 Cities Composites Indices had both returned to 2003 levels in July 2012. [2] Figure 7.3 shows the index levels for the 10-City and 20-City Composite Indices within the US. The following quotation from the report indicates the magnitude of the declines across the US as a whole; regional variations can be even more striking as subsequent discussion will show:

> As of July 2012, average home prices across the United States are back to their summer 2003 levels for the 20-City Composite and to autumn 2003 levels for the 10-City Composite. Measured from their June/July 2006 peaks, the decline for both Composites is approximately 30% through July 2012. For both Composites, their July 2012 levels are approximately 7.5–8.0% above their recent early 2012 lows.

What clearly emerges from the Case Shiller research and from Figure 7.3 is the quite extraordinary and abnormal amplification of the 2003–2007 real estate bubble, and the fact that five years later the entire bubble has been deflated, leaving in its wake about 16 million US households which, as of mid-2012, owe more on their homes than their current valuations. [3] This amounts to a multi-trillion dollar loss of wealth and a major contributor to the disappearance of income and marginal propensity to borrow which will be discussed in further detail in Chapter 10.

Released in May 2012 the Zillow Negative Equity Report [4] includes some startling facts about the aftermath of the real estate mania which is not only still acting as a major drag on a recovery in the USA but also acts as a deflationary dynamic for the global economy:

> Nearly one-third (31.4 percent) of U.S. homeowners with mortgages – or 17.7 million – were underwater on their mortgage in the first quarter of 2012. Collectively, underwater homeowners owed \$1.2 trillion more than their homes were worth. Nearly 40 percent of underwater homeowners, or 12.4 percent of all homeowners with a mortgage, owe between 1 and 20 percent more than their home is worth. An additional 21 percent of underwater homeowners, or 6.6 percent of all homeowners with a mortgage, owe between 21 and 40 percent more than their home is worth. [Nationally] . . . about 2.4 million or 4.7 percent of all homeowners with mortgages owe more than double what their home is worth.

Regional variations within the US real estate bust show that some cities and states have been hit especially hard – often the so-called sun-belt states which saw a large population influx as baby boomers began retiring in the early 2000s. In the Las Vegas metro area 26.8% of homeowners with mortgages owe double what their properties are worth. [5] On a state level, Nevada has the highest percentage of negative equity, with more than two-thirds of all homeowners with mortgages underwater. Arizona, Georgia, Florida, and Michigan also have extraordinary levels of homeowners in negative equity.

The correction in residential property prices in the aftermath of the GFC is still unfolding and it is not possible yet to estimate the eventual damage done to the global economy by the real estate fuelled bubble which burst in 2007/8. However it is very instructive to look again at the Japanese experience as there have been more than 20 years to witness the wealth destruction which has resulted from the bursting of their bubble in 1990. Again Richard Koo is the pre-eminent commentator on this, and another of the charts from his INET presentation is well worth a full examination. [6]

Figure 7.4 uses a base of 100 for September 1990 by which time the Nikkei 225 had already lost more than 40% of its peak value from the end of 1989 although the impact for Japanese equity holders is not actually displayed on the chart. However on the right hand side it can be seen that Koo's figure of 1500 trillion yen for wealth destruction since the base period is estimated at 87% from the top. Interestingly, and perhaps taking into account the 40% decline already commented on in the Nikkei 225 as of September 1990, a ball park estimate in the region of a 90% total drawdown is not dissimilar to the magnitudes of the drawdowns which have been observed elsewhere in this book when other bubbles have burst, particularly for those dot com and high tech companies which lost more than 95% of their bubble valuations (in many cases 100%) in the aftermath of the Nasdaq crash which began in 2000.

Over and beyond the staggering degree of wealth destruction – actually, in better terminology, the evaporation of the phantom wealth that didn't really exist in the blowing up of the Japanese bubble of the 1980s – the trajectory followed by real GDP is perhaps the most illuminating. During the 1980s real GDP – itself subject to the mirage of asset inflation – doubled

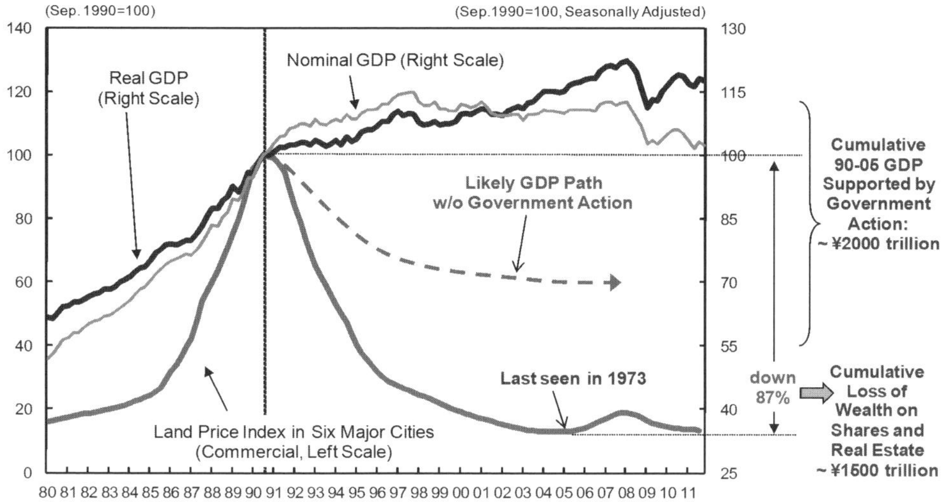

Figure 7.4 Japan's GDP grew in spite of massive loss of wealth and private sector deleveraging
Source: The World in Balance Sheet Recession, Richard Koo INET Berlin April 2012.

on an inflation adjusted basis which is the translation for "real" versus "nominal" GDP in Figure 7.4 and which is shown as separate trajectories on the graphic. Following the relentless decline of asset values which has persisted since 1990 the Japanese economy has *only managed to increase its real GDP by 15% since 1990.* Koo has indicated that if it had not been for the massive amounts of public investment – in the region of 2000 trillion yen – the real GDP by his estimate would be 30% less than it was at the peak of the bubble. Given the massive amount of asset depreciation and the debt deflationary dynamics prevailing in what must surely have been the largest balance sheet recession prior to the GFC, the Japanese government decided, through a variety of public investment expenditures, to increase its total debt/GDP ratio to the highest level in the world at approximately 240% [7] to stave off a truly desperate depression. Without these large scale investments underwritten by the public balance sheet, the Japanese economy, according to Koo's estimates, would be operating at two-thirds of its capacity in relation to the 1980s. Private asset holders who were not diversified and held only Japanese assets – primarily stocks and real estate – would be about 90% less well off than they were at the end of 1989.

7.1 THE NIKKEI 225 AND THE YIELD ON THE US TREASURY TEN-YEAR NOTE

As part of our examination of the intriguing properties of the Japanese yen in asset markets as highlighted in our discussion of the Flash Crash there is another question which poses itself: How can one explain the extraordinarily high correlation in the movements of the Nikkei 225 and the yield on the US Treasury 10-year note?

Figure 7.5 depicts the relative performance of both assets with a base period established as of July 1992. Apart from the base chosen there is another point on the chart where the paths

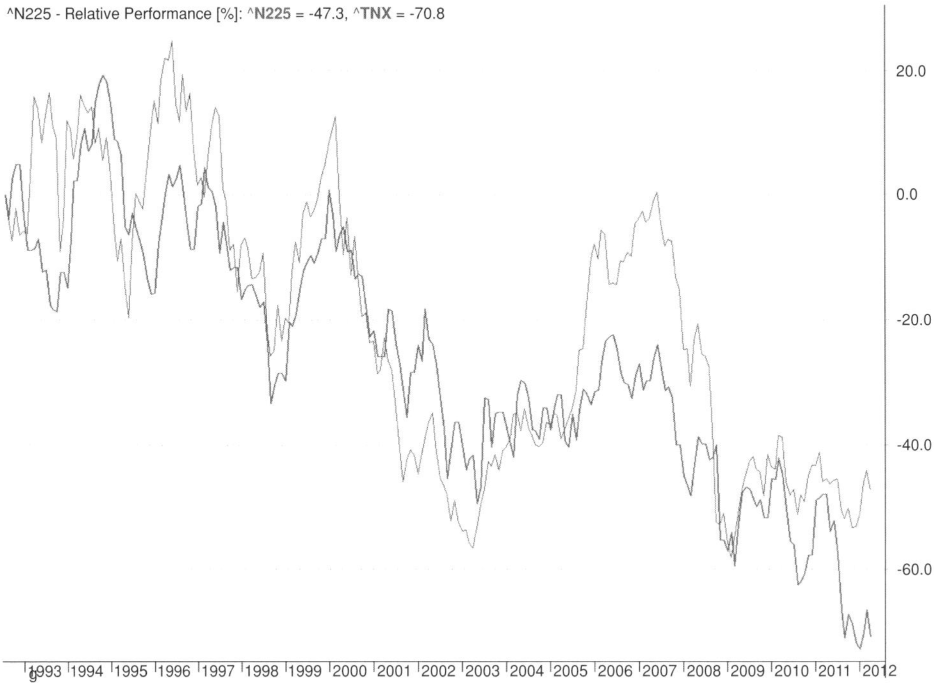

Figure 7.5 Performance of Nikkei 225 and yield on 10-year US Treasury Note mid-1992–mid-2012

followed by each are exactly at the same value on the right hand axis, and that is in March 2009 when both have fallen to a value of −60%. The journeys taken by each up to that point were remarkably aligned and as a general comment it is notable that each time the Nikkei 225 began to move upwards out of its close alignment with the 10-year yields the direction taken by the latter predominated and brought the Nikkei back downwards in a reversion to the declining yields. This is most conspicuous in the 2006/8 period where Japanese equities in harmony with other global stock indices were enjoying their last hurrah before the GFC. Despite reaching back to the baseline in the latter part of 2007, the Nikkei then sank back down by approximately 60% with respect to the baseline and rejoined the path taken by the 10-year yields. It may be premature to be making this comment but in examining the right hand side of the chart there is another divergence developing where the Nikkei is moving away from the path taken by the 10-year Treasury note yields; the continuing move down in yields is perhaps suggesting that once again there is a little too much "optimism" built into Japanese equity prices. Another possibility is that the yield on the 10-year note may be basing and that the leading indicator could be moving to the Nikkei – but only time will tell whether the pattern shown across the rest of the inter-relationship is sustained or whether the degree of correlation, and the evidence that the 10-year yield is the leading indicator, is finally breaking down.

What is clear is that there has been an understandable absence of any speculative fever or enhanced "animal spirits" at work in relation to the Nikkei 225. Describing the Japanese predicament as one of subdued speculative fever is a classic understatement. A number of followers of that economy would more accurately characterize it in less flattering terms including the allegation that Japanese banks, with their seriously impaired balance sheets, are effectively "zombies." [8] Alluding to a possible parallel with woes in the Eurozone, a prominent investment strategist has made the following observation: "[T]he eurozone's banking sector may ultimately go the way of Japan's 'zombie system', where banks have an economic net worth of less than zero but continue to operate as their ability to repay debts is shored up by the government." [9]

Japanese private investors are not only still repairing their balance sheets from the collapse in 1990 – itself an indication of the long lived nature of recovery from a "once in a generation" burst bubble – but there has been little appetite from overseas investors for the Japanese stock market. This could reflect at least two separate viewpoints. Firstly overseas fund managers would be discouraged from taking positions in the Nikkei 225 if they do not see much supporting evidence that domestic investors and traders will be seeking out capital gains and helping to drive any upward momentum in Japanese assets in general. Secondly, and perhaps most acutely, there is what might be construed as a negative feedback loop (in a worst case a no-win dynamic) at work with respect to the price of Japanese equities and the external value of the yen. And this brings us back to the enigmatic question regarding the strength of the yen which began this discussion.

To pursue this investigation further it will be useful to examine another remarkable correlation that is pertinent in understanding Japan's predicament; that between the exchange rate of the yen to other currencies – especially to the US dollar and then in turn to the Chinese renminbi which, relatively speaking, is pegged to the dollar – and Japanese equities, as reflected in the Nikkei 225 benchmark.

Figure 7.6 shows, from a normalized perspective, the paths taken by the Nikkei 225 and the yen against the dollar from mid-2007 until late July of 2012 and on most of the chart – especially during 2011 – there is a clear inverse correlation. As the yen strengthens so the Nikkei weakens; the inverse relationship is expressed in a correlation coefficient value as of mid-2012 of −0.48. Being an export driven economy the rise of the yen has a negative impact on the prospects for large Japanese corporations such as Sony, Mitsubishi etc. in two key

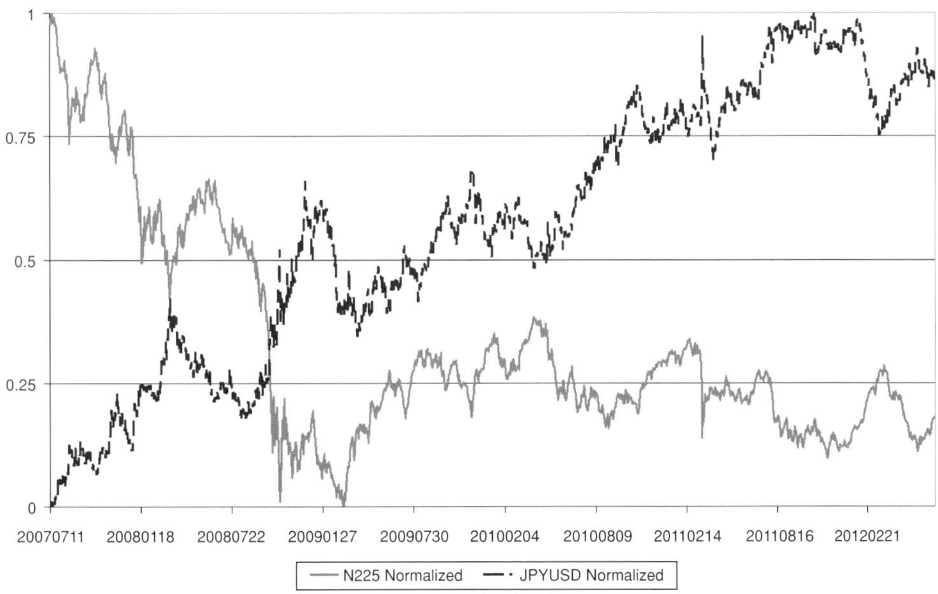

Figure 7.6 Normalized Nikkei 225 and Japanese yen/US dollar mid-2007–mid-2012

respects. Firstly, the price of Japanese manufactured goods – especially in comparison to those made in China – will become less competitive in world markets as the yen strengthens. In fact the cynical argument regarding the undoubtedly huge FX trading activities of the PBOC (with its estimated $3.4 trillion of reserves) is that China, for mercantilist reasons, favors an elevated rate for the yen against the US currency. The PBOC can be very instrumental in ensuring an elevated yen by purchasing the currency and Japanese money market instruments in its external market operations. In this regard it is worth citing a comment made by George Soros in a BBC radio interview in 2011, heard by this author, which included the remarkable statement that "the PBOC effectively controls the foreign exchange market." Alas the interviewer failed to question Mr Soros further on this very provocative statement. [10]

The second depressing aspect for the income statements of Japanese corporations is that, with an appreciating currency, its overseas revenues – which for many large Japanese corporations are the bulk of its sales – are being earned in currencies which are losing value with respect to their domestic currency of account. This will directly impact the profitability of Japanese corporations and is part of the explanation for the dire performance in recent years of companies such as Sony. [11]

In addition to the factors cited above which have encouraged the PBOC to want a strong yen there is further evidence that many central banks have been boosting their holdings of yen-based assets amidst the uncertainties surrounding the future of the euro. Also the Swiss National Bank, in its activities related to the pegging of the Swiss franc to the euro, has been shifting its newly acquired euros partly into yen. An article from Bloomberg entitled "*Yen-Denominated Assets at Central Banks at Record, BOJ Data Show*" underlines both the safe haven appeal which the Japanese currency has and why this poses ongoing problems for companies like Sony: [12]

> Foreign central banks boosted their holdings of yen-denominated assets to the highest level in at least a decade, an indication Europe's debt crisis has bolstered the currency's appeal as a haven.
>
> The holdings rose 26 percent to 44 trillion yen ($555 billion) in Dec. 2011, the highest since comparable data were made available in 2002, according to a Bank of Japan document obtained by Bloomberg News. Bonds made up 40.7 trillion yen of the total, the document showed.
>
> Increased demand for Japanese assets overseas underscores the difficulty authorities are having in limiting currency gains since the yen surged to a post-World-War-II high against the dollar in October. Japan sold 14.3 trillion yen last year, the third-highest ever, to limit the damage a stronger yen inflicts on the profits of the nation's exporters.

Given this negative feedback loop there is a further disincentive for foreigners to take great interest in Japanese equities. In order for the profitability of Japanese corporations to improve, and for there to be a more positive environment for the Nikkei, the yen will have to weaken. Apart from the suspicion that this is not what is on the horizon given the desire on the part of other Asian trading nations (especially China of course) to "prefer" a strong yen, even if it should come to pass, then translating the possible gains in yen-based assets back into (say) a US dollar accounting base would once again have characteristics of a no-win bind.

This bind can also be seen, by switching the perspective from a foreign investor in Japanese equities to one of a Japanese investor holding overseas assets, for example, US equities.

The predicament for the Japanese investor holding US equities is well exemplified in Figure 7.7. During the second half of 2007, which represented the "blow off" of the financial bubble in the US market, the yen was still trading within the range of 75-100 noted above

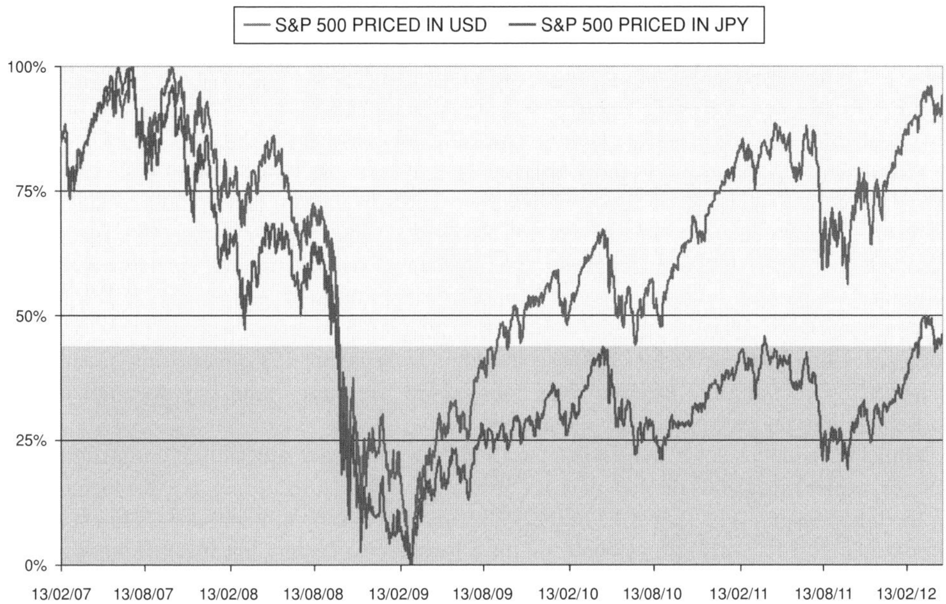

Figure 7.7 Returns of S&P for US dollar and Japanese yen based investor

in the more detailed attention given to the yen/dollar cross rate. Usefully from the point of making the historical comparison of the relative performance of US equities as experienced by a dollar and yen-based asset manager there is a close approximation from a temporal perspective in that both trajectories of Figure 7.7 are extremely close during the second half of 2007. The paths taken by both lines during the next 18 months are also closely inter-related with both registering their lowest values coincidentally during March 2009. But the pathways taken since then diverge considerably. To put it simply, for a US dollar-based investor (and that does not obviously mean only US residents) the equity index has almost returned towards the levels seen in the second half of 2007, whereas for a yen-based investor the S&P 500 is still less than halfway towards recovering its yen value as seen in the latter part of 2007. To express that in terms of actual return percentages it is only necessary to refer back to the point of departure above – which is the difference in the exchange rate of approximately 30% which is the decline of the US currency against the yen. Just to spell it out, *a Japanese pension fund would still be nursing a 30% loss if they had bought US equities in late 2007, whereas a US fund manager would more or less be back to where they were in the same period.*

As part of the explanation for the high degree of correlation between the Nikkei and the yield on the US 10-year, the contention is that there is more or less no speculative froth or bubble traits incorporated into the valuation of Japanese equities. While the Nikkei 225 has declined steadily over the last 20 years, as the process of paying down debt and deleveraging of the financial system has taken place, the case for buying on the "fundamentals" is not a compelling one and with an absence of any bubble dynamics Japanese equities are unlikely to attract "hot" money, i.e. momentum seeking capital. Indeed it is precisely because the private sector in Japan had to undergo such deleveraging and deflation that the Japanese government was required to spend the enormous amounts which are an integral part of Richard Koo's highly persuasive thesis about possible lessons to be learned by other governments from the

Japanese experience. It is not so much that there is risk aversion implied by the unwillingness of overseas investors to purchase Japanese equities – although there may still be a residual hangover effect from those who indulged too much in Japanese speculation in the 1980s – but rather there is a void with regard to risk appetite and expectations that there will be any "exciting" developments with regard to this asset class.

With respect to the yield on the US Treasury this is more complex and there are various strands to disentangle. One or two relatively straightforward comments can be made in the context of an "explanation" for the strong co-movement that has been observed. It has been observed that for risk-averse Japanese asset managers – such as their pension funds and insurance companies – after their very substantial commitment to domestic JGB's the US Treasury market is a major target for their asset allocation decision making. [13] To further underscore this propensity for Japanese investors to seek out US government securities it is instructive to track the external ownership of US Treasuries (and this does not include participation in the various agency securities).

While it is widely acknowledged that the Chinese are the most substantial foreign holders of US government securities the Japanese are very close behind. According to a disclosure made by the US Treasury as of July 2012 of the $5.4 trillion of US government debt held externally, approximately $1.15 trillion was held by the Chinese government but this was very closely followed by the Japanese who held approximately $1.12 trillion. Together these two nations hold about 47% of the total held by foreigners, and their combined holdings by far out-shadow the next category of stakeholders which is the oil exporting nations who hold about $260 billion. It is also worth noting that from July 2011 leading up to the most current reading (at the time of writing) Japan increased its holding of USTs from a total of $885 billion to $1117 billion, whereas the PRC decreased its holdings from £1315 billion in July 2011 to $1149 billion in July 2012. [14]

Given the steady decline in yields of UST's, and especially with regard to the longer dated securities such as the 10-year note, the Japanese asset managers will have experienced quite substantial capital gains on their holdings of USTs (however this has to be offset by the losses, leaving aside currency hedging, incurred by the drop in the value of the dollar with respect to the yen). Frustratingly however the quid pro quo for the Japanese asset managers is that they have been a victim of the *disappearance of income* malaise, a discussion of which will be found in Chapter 10.

For Japanese pension funds that are holding USTs through to maturity in order to match their liabilities, the mark to market gains on their portfolio of Treasury bonds is not really of much comfort especially when taking into account the fact that in their purchases of more recently issued 10-year notes they are receiving only a 2% coupon during the time that they will be holding them.

Moving beyond the more obvious direct relationship between Japanese investors and USTs there is also a strong case to be made that the parallel between the Nikkei and the 10-year yield is a case study in subdued "animal spirits" or passive investing stemming from risk avoidance. There are numerous dynamics which have resulted in the steady decline in UST yields and surely one of them has been a diminution in the role played by the so-called "bond vigilantes." This latter group who wielded much greater power in earlier periods such as the 1990s, which prompted the famous remark from Bill Clinton's advisor James Carville that he wanted to be reincarnated as the bond market so he could intimidate everybody [15], as they have been superseded by the more acquiescent approach of large sovereign wealth funds who need to recycle their current account surpluses into "safe" US capital assets.

Table 7.1 US Treasury security holdings of foreigners

	MAJOR FOREIGN HOLDERS OF TREASURY SECURITIES (in billions of dollars) HOLDINGS 1/ AT END OF PERIOD							
Country	Jul 2012	Jun 2012*	May 2012*	Apr 2012*	Mar 2012*	Feb 2012*	Jan 2012*	Dec 2011*
China, Mainland	1149.6	1147.0	1164.0	1164.4	1144.0	1155.2	1166.2	1151.9
Japan	1117.1	1110.1	1108.9	1089.8	1082.5	1090.6	1082.8	1058.0
Oil Exporters 3/	262.3	268.2	258.4	259.9	260.0	267.6	267.5	261.1
Brazil	253.0	244.3	245.8	245.9	238.1	228.4	228.2	226.9
Carib Bnkng Ctrs 4/	246.2	244.2	243.0	237.3	234.3	231.7	223.5	226.2
Taiwan	196.1	196.4	190.0	187.3	190.1	183.7	178.4	177.3
Switzerland	190.1	171.8	154.9	150.1	150.5	145.3	146.4	142.3
Russia	154.3	163.8	156.3	155.4	151.1	144.8	145.7	149.5
Belgium	144.2	144.5	132.0	132.3	141.6	125.1	131.4	135.2
United Kingdom 2/	140.9	137.8	136.2	135.8	125.3	118.0	115.5	113.7
Hong Kong	136.7	136.0	143.8	145.0	140.3	141.8	134.3	121.7
Luxembourg	128.3	138.3	130.9	130.0	140.0	140.9	140.0	147.6
Singapore	92.7	86.9	83.1	82.5	84.7	84.6	74.8	75.1

China, Japan, OPEC, Brazil, and Taiwan among other sovereigns feature right at the top of the list of external holders of US Treasuries. An examination of Table 7.1 will show that those nations which have visible trade surpluses with the US are some of the largest holders of US capital assets. In itself that is not surprising as it reflects the recycling of the US currency earned by major exporters to the US market. However, what is not so widely recognized, even by many economists, is that the reason why the ongoing demand for US Treasuries has not suffered as a consequence of apprehensions about the growing public debt of the US, the fiscal impasse, the declines in the US dollar, and the outlook for inflation etc. – but rather more pragmatic arithmetic by the surplus nation to provide *vendor financing* to the US in order to prolong that country's predilection for being home to the *consumers of last resort*. The nature of this form of vendor financing will be discussed again in Chapter 10.

Just within the excerpt shown in Table 7.1 of the larger table, which comes from the one which is published by the US Treasury each month, [16] it is possible to account for about $4 trillion dollars, or 80% of the total amount held by foreigners. When one considers that about 50% of USTs are held externally it is simple arithmetic to see that a large determining factor in the demand/supply equation for the US Treasury is (to put it politely) passive acceptance of the need to buy on favorable terms from the point of view of the issuer – hence part of the solution to the riddle of keen demand for USTs despite declining yields.

Hopefully this thread of our discussion will have helped to throw more light on the peculiarly strong co-movement of the Nikkei 225 index and the yields on US Treasury 10-year note. For reasons outlined, but far from being a comprehensive account, the two assets represent the deflationary and risk avoidance stance which is part of the twin dynamics that are observable within the risk on/risk off paradigm.

Recalling the inverse relationship between the USD/JPY exchange rate and the Nikkei 225, the suggestion is that it is the pursuit of safe haven assets such as the yen and US Treasuries that is revealed by markets when they become risk averse. The seeking out of these safe haven assets is in direct contrast to the tendency during the risk on phases of price development to move out of such "flight to safety" assets and walk the tightrope of the riskier side of the boom/bust dichotomy by deploying funds to equities, commodities, and the other classes of risk on assets. Switching in and out of safe harbor assets such as the Japanese yen and US Treasuries on the one hand, and risk on assets on the other, is the primary driver of the correlation which has captured our attention throughout. As all good statisticians will recite strong correlation is not evidence of causation and highly correlated movements may well be explicable by reference to a third "governing" variable. Evidence presented in this chapter suggests that the dominant variable which appears to be guiding or governing the abrupt changes into risk off assets is the decision by many traders during heightened perceptions of macro risk, to align themselves with those asset classes that have either *already* been most subjected to, or are most likely *in the future* to be the beneficiaries of, the forces of deflation. The major asset class which will benefit from the twin concerns of deflation and default risk is the bond issuance of highly rated sovereigns. This explains the attraction not only of US Treasury instruments, UK gilts, and German bunds, but also, at least at the time of writing, the perceived safety of Japanese government bonds (JGBs) especially as far as Japanese pension funds are concerned. [17]

To summarize, when market participants are reminded of the massive risk of drawdowns when financial markets wobble precariously, and may be susceptible to systemic liquidity evaporation, the safest place to be is in those asset classes which have either already been massively deflated, or those which are expected to be the most resilient to deflationary forces. The Japanese yen and the US 10-year note, each in their separate ways, are two such instruments and the account given hopefully explains why both play such a key role within the fearful polarity of risk on/risk off market dynamics.

If the behavior of the yen/dollar exchange rate is "connected" to the performance of the pricing of long-term US Treasury instruments one would expect a positive correlation between the notional pricing of long-term USTs and the value of the yen. Correspondingly if we flip both instruments over one would expect to see a high degree of co-movement between the yield on long dated US Treasury bonds (the inverse of the price) and the relative weakness of the US dollar against the yen (which is the inverse of yen strength). Figure 7.8 shows the pattern of price movement for both of these instruments since the end of 2002 and in this instance the yield of the 30-year US Treasury bond has been taken (although the picture for the 10-year yield is not radically different).

Rather than citing a set of statistical data to support the claim that the yen is in fact the common determinant for the enigmatic co-movement which has been under the microscope in this chapter, the intention here is to establish the case that in understanding the special role within the motivation which leads to (a) a flight to safety by taking positions in US Treasury instruments and the yen and (b) a recognition of the powerful deflationary forces which will remain prevalent while Richard Koo's balance sheet recession scenario unfolds beyond Japan, it is well worth focusing on following and analyzing the movements in currency pairs involving the Japanese yen, and in particular, as was seen in Chapter 6, the relationship of the yen and the Australian dollar, AUD/JPY.

The final diagram for this chapter, Figure 7.9, is taken from Richard Koo's earlier work. [18]

The diagram provides one of the best illustrations of a bubble/bust cycle and in many respects can act as a template to the events which unfolded largely after the first publication of Koo's book in 2007. There are some questionable issues in the diagram, one being the second box down on the left hand or Yin side of the chart which suggests that monetary tightening

Figure 7.8 Peformance of yield on US 30 Treasury Bond and US dollar/Japanese yen exchange rate 2003–2012

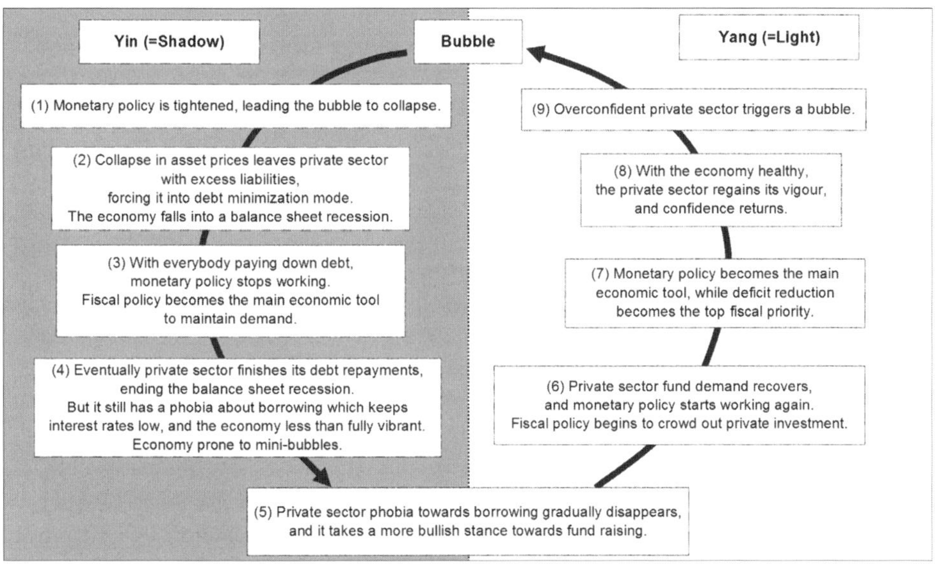

Figure 7.9 Yin-yang cycle of bubbles and balance sheet recessions
Source: Richard Koo, *The Holy Grail of Macroeconomics: Lessons from Japan's Great Recession*, John Wiley & Sons, Singapore, April 2008 p. 160.

is what will lead to the bursting of the bubble. This might be the case, as was true in the Japanese example of the late 1980s, but the situation prior to the GFC does not fit this part of the template. The precipitating factors in 2007/8 were more diverse as we have seen, and should perhaps best be expressed by reference to a term which has entered common parlance and which will be examined again later, the Minsky moment. [19]

However the remaining elements of Koo's diagram provide a very useful schematic for the stages of the bubble/bust cycle informed by the Japanese experience but which can very much act as a *pro forma* for further iterations of the cycle which lie in our future.

ENDNOTES

1. Richard Koo, *Balance Sheet Recession: Japan's Struggle with Uncharted Economics and its Global Implications* (John Wiley & Sons, October 2003). See also the following article on growing interest in Koo's prescriptions for the Eurozone: German leaders warm up to lessons from Japan's "lost decade," *Wall Street Journal*, Market Watch, July 4, 2012:

   > Germany's politicians could be warming to the idea that they may need to borrow a page from Japan's playbook in dealing with the euro-zone crisis, according to a noted economist.
   >
   > Nomura Research Institute Chief Economist Richard Koo, who coined the term "balance sheet recessions" to explain Japan's prolonged economic malaise, said in research distributed to reporters Wednesday, that he encountered a more receptive attitude among officials who attended a recent presentation he gave in Berlin.
   >
   > The mood in the room was different from a year earlier, Koo said, noting that policy makers at that time were "brimming with confidence" in their policy approach to the crisis.
   >
   > "German politicians are starting to question the strongly held beliefs that have brought them this far," Koo said in the note.

   http://blogs.marketwatch.com/thetell/2012/07/04/german-leaders-warm-up-to-lessons-from-japans-lost-decade/.
2. S&P/Case-Shiller Home Price Indices. The S&P/Case-Shiller Home Price Indices are the leading measures for the US residential housing market, tracking changes in the value of residential real estate both nationally as well as in 20 metropolitan regions, http://www.standardandpoors.com/indices/sp-case-shiller-home-price-indices/en/us/?indexId=spusa-cashpidff–p-us—-.
3. Zillow Negative Equity Report Shows 1 in 3 Mortgage Holders Underwater, Zillow, May 24, 2012, http://www.zillow.com/blog/2012-05-24/zillow-negative-equity-report-shows-1-in-3-mortgage-holders-underwater/.
4. See endnote 3.
5. See endnote 3.
6. Richard Koo, *The World in Balance Sheet Recession: What Post-2008 West Can Learn from Japan 1990–2005*, INET Conference Berlin April 2012. The slides for this presentation are available at http://ineteconomics.org/sites/inet.civicactions.net/files/koo-richard-berlin-slides.ppt.
7. Japan's Debt Sustains a Deflationary Depression by Gary Shilling, Bloomberg, June 5, 2012, http://www.bloomberg.com/news/2012-06-04/japan-s-debt-sustains-a-deflationary-depression.html
8. Zombie bank threat haunts Eurozone, City Wire money, January 12, 2012:

   > Cazenove European manager Chris Rice has upped his exposure to defensive stocks in preparation for what he predicts will be a difficult year for European equities.
   >
   > Rice says that German chancellor Angela Merkel's plans to solve the Eurozone crisis are unlikely to be achievable. He believes the euro zone's banking sector may ultimately go the way of what he calls Japan's "zombie system", where banks have an economic net worth of less than zero but continue to operate as their ability to repay debts is shored up by the government.

   http://citywire.co.uk/money/zombie-bank-threat-haunts-eurozone/a557435.
9. See endnote 8.

10. George Soros, interviewed on the BBC Radio 4 program Today (October 9) can be heard in the clip referenced below making the rather striking assertion that the "Chinese effectively control the entire world's currency system." http://news.bbc.co.uk/today/hi/today/newsid_9076000/9076763.stm

    The assertion comes around 1:40 into the interview segment. Notice how the interviewer completely fails to grasp the true significance of what Soros is alleging and moves on with the interview in a prosaic manner to talk about re-valuation of the yuan against the dollar.
11. Sony Revises Expected Loss to $6.4 Billion, *New York Times*, April 10, 2012, http://www.nytimes.com/2012/04/11/business/global/sony-revises-expected-loss-to-6-4-billion.html.
12. Monami Yui, Hiroko Komiya and Toru Fujioka, *Yen-Denominated Assets at Central Banks at Record, BOJ Data Show*, Bloomberg, June 28, 2012, http://www.bloomberg.com/news/2012-06-29/yen-denominated-assets-at-central-banks-at-record-boj-data-show.html.
13. Japan's $1.4 trillion Government Pension Investment Fund is the world's largest public pension fund and according to its 2011 Annual Report its asset allocation was approximately 63% for domestic bonds and 9% for international bonds which are not further itemized.

    2011 Annual Report available at: http://www.gpif.go.jp/en/fund/pdf/2011_0.pdf.

    During 2012 there were reports that Japanese institutions were lightening up on their JGB exposure due to poor returns. See for example *World's Biggest Pension Fund Sells JGBs to Cover Payouts*, Bloomberg, July 26, 2012. Available online at http://www.bloomberg.com/news/2012-07-25/world-s-biggest-pension-fund-sells-jgbs-to-cover-payouts.html.
14. Major Foreign Holders of Treasury Securities, US Treasury website, http://www.treasury.gov/resource-center/data-chart-center/tic/Documents/mfh.txt
15. At the beginning of the Clinton administration in the early 1990s, adviser James Carville was stunned at the power the bond market had over the government. If he came back, Carville said: "I used to think if there was reincarnation, I wanted to come back as the president or the pope or a .400 baseball hitter. But now I want to come back as the bond market. You can intimidate everybody," *Wall Street Journal* (February 25, 1993, p. A1), http://en.wikiquote.org/wiki/James_Carville.
16. See endnote 14.
17. Japanese Government Bond yields have moved steadily downwards since 1990 as shown on the graphic below:

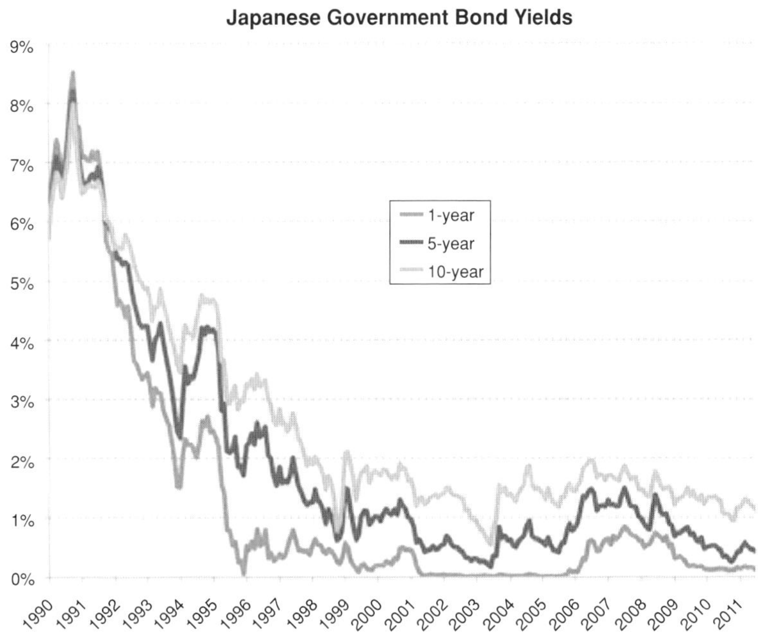

Japanese Government Bond yields for different maturities 1990–mid-2012

18. See endnote 1.
19. In Time of Tumult, Obscure Economist Gains Currency, *Wall Street Journal*, August 18, 2007:

> It was Mr. McCulley at Pacific Investment, though, who coined the phrase "Minsky moment" during the Russian debt crisis in 1998.
>
> "We are in the midst of a Minsky moment, bordering on a Minsky meltdown," says Paul McCulley, an economist and fund manager at Pacific Investment Management Co., the world's largest bond-fund manager.
>
> At its core, the Minsky view was straightforward: When times are good, investors take on risk; the longer times stay good, the more risk they take on, until they've taken on too much. Eventually, they reach a point where the cash generated by their assets no longer is sufficient to pay off the mountains of debt they took on to acquire them. Losses on such speculative assets prompt lenders to call in their loans. "This is likely to lead to a collapse of asset values," Mr. Minsky wrote.

http://online.wsj.com/public/article/SB118736585456901047.html.

8

The Aussie/Yen Connection

A central theme of this chapter will be to demonstrate that the Australian dollar can be seen as an excellent proxy for the *risk on* phases in contemporary asset markets. On the contrary, the Japanese yen can be seen as a proxy for *risk off* behavior for reasons which we have already touched on in the previous chapter.

To begin our exploration of the connection between these two diametrically opposed financial instruments our initial focus will be on the Australian dollar. The currency has enjoyed its status as a beneficiary of global growth and positive economic fundamentals as a result of being buoyed by the demand for its mining and resources from China and other rapidly developing markets. To the extent that such demand from China and other emerging market (EM) economies remains buoyant this is a "bullish" macro dynamic and thus a driving force for positive risk appetite characteristics. Moreover, short-term tactical implementation of FX carry trade inspired strategies by hedge funds reveals the risk on/risk off dynamics in the movement of such key FX pairs as AUD/JPY and AUD/USD (given the very low rates now applicable in the USA, the US dollar has become a funding currency). [1]

In the discussion of the VPIN metric and the precipitating factors that triggered the Flash Crash of May 2010 there was a discussion of the role played by the large move in the exchange rate of the yen against the US dollar immediately prior to the large moves down in the S&P 500 E-Mini future which created pandemonium across global equity markets during the ensuing 30 minutes or so. As suggested in that discussion the role of the yen certainly appears to have been a major contributory factor to the crash and the reasons for that were related to the disproportionately large position which had been accumulated in risk on assets in the weeks prior to the crash. A further piece of the puzzle was proposed in that the critical currency movement on May 6, 2010 may have had as much to do with the AUD/JPY exchange rate as the USD/JPY rate, although the two rates are inextricably linked.

Figure 8.1 provides a very convincing visualization of the unusually strong interconnectedness of the AUD/JPY exchange rate and the S&P 500. The values for each can be read off on the two vertical scales to the diagram but it is quite self-evident that there is a very strong fit or co-movement between the paths taken by each instrument during the first half of 2010. The alignment of the trajectories taken in the lead up to the May 6 crash and especially following the crash is quite extraordinary and substantiates the case that what we are witnessing is the performance of two very closely aligned "risk on" assets.

Taking a different perspective on this association and to quantify the covariance a linear regression can reveal the degree to which the two variables are correlated. Figure 8.2 covers all of the data points that were used in the rendering of the graphic in Figure 8.1. The box on the chart reveals that the R^2 value is 0.72 which indicates that the correlation coefficient is approximately 0.85 for the period which is exceptionally high for an FX pair and a benchmark equity index. Interestingly also the beta value from the box of 0.96 – which is the gradient of the line of best fit – shows that not only was there a high degree of directional symmetry in the paths taken by both instruments but that the magnitudes of the percentage changes from day to day were extraordinarily well matched.

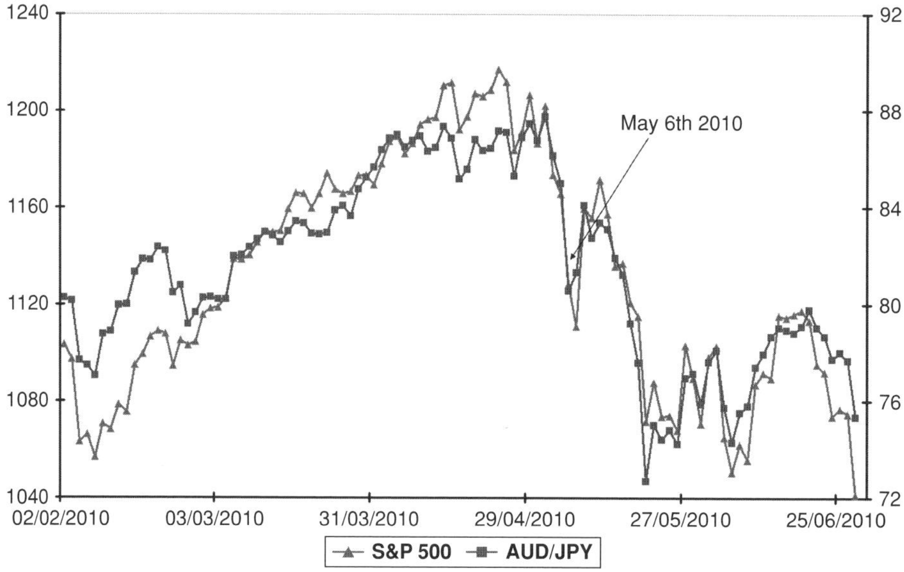

Figure 8.1 Daily performance of Aussie/yen and S&P 500 February 2010–end of June 2010

Although this topic was discussed in Chapter 5 it will, I believe, be worthwhile to look again at one of the more interesting precursors to the Flash Crash which was the exact performance of the two currency elements to the AUD/JPY exchange rate in the period leading up to the crash. It will be suggested that the Aussie/yen connection, as this chapter is called, has shown itself to be such a good precursor to periods of financial stress that it should be included

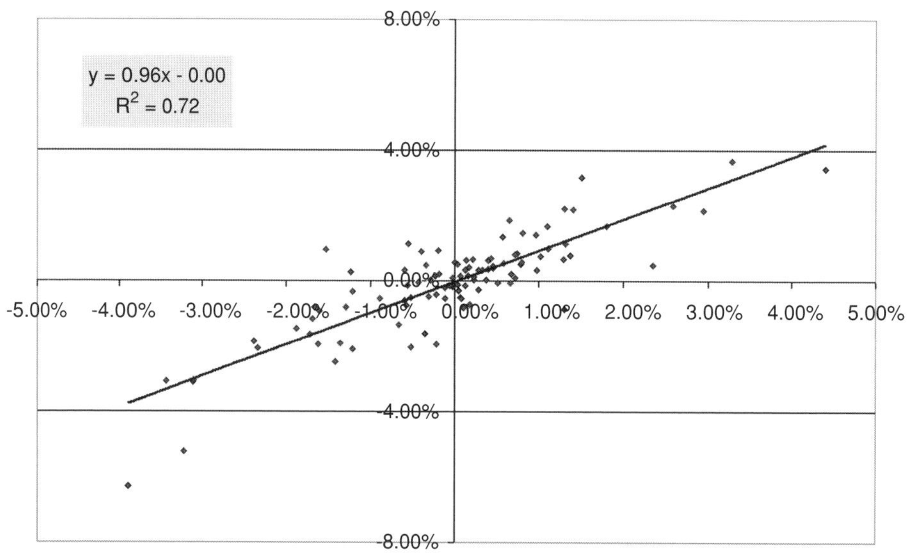

Figure 8.2 Linear regression of daily changes of AUD/JPY and S&P 500 February 2010–June 2010

as a key component in any market timing toolkit. As will be seen later in this chapter the performance of the FX pair in the summer of 2007 acted as an early warning system to the critical events which took hold in August 2007 and the role it played in May 2010 has already been alluded to in Chapter 5. Spelling out further the Aussie/yen connection will also be a useful introduction to some material, developed by this author and which will be discussed in the next chapter, where heat maps of correlations between a large number of assets with the AUD and JPY elements show promise with respect to anticipating the timing of significant inflection points in many asset markets.

As with all exchange rates the manner in which a currency pair performs can be decomposed into separate elements which can be seen via both of their relationships to a common base, which for convenience can be the US currency. When considering how AUD/JPY performs it is possible to think not just in terms of that specific cross rate itself but also whether the reasons for the strength of the pair are related specifically to the relative strength of the Australian dollar – which can be monitored via the AUD/USD exchange rate – or alternatively weakness in the Japanese yen versus the US dollar – which in turn can be monitored via the USD/JPY rate. Using a very simple analogy from physics the AUD/JPY rate is the resultant force of changes both to the numerator currency and the denominator currency – which will manifest itself as either opposing or complementary forces – in other words, either moving directionally together or opposing each other. As will be seen digging out the resultant of the numerator/denominator forces is not an idle abstraction but provides a basis for testable hypotheses and a framework for anticipating market illiquidity.

The hypothesis to test is as follows. When the Australian dollar is gaining *and* the Japanese yen is declining against the US currency, and also there is evidence from price action of an increasing appetite for risk on assets such as equities and commodities which endures for some extended period, the nascent bubble will tend to feed on itself as traders climb on the bandwagon and that at some point (a mini Minsky moment) the risk on trade will have become so skewed that a significant correction – or in more fragile liquidity conditions a crash – will become increasingly probable. The hypothesis would appear to be entirely validated by the market action in the three-month period from early February 2010 right up to the May 6 crash event. Figure 8.3 which has been repeated from Chapter 5 provides the best explanation – a visual one – of the template conditions under which a market correction might be expected and which is taken up again with the heat map techniques to be outlined in the next chapter.

Looked at with regard to the risk on/risk off paradigm, a strengthening of the AUD/JPY rate will typically be driven by increased appetite for the Aussie currency and reflected in an increased appetite for equities, emerging market assets (including EM currencies and EM fixed income instruments), commodities and an associated reduction in exposure to the types of assets which are linked to a more downbeat outlook for the "animal spirits." On the contrary, weakness in AUD/JPY will often be associated with a decline in the appetite for the numerator currency – the Australian dollar – and also weakness in equities particularly those of resource-based economies, commodities, and so on. Weakness for AUD/JPY will also be driven by flight to safety and risk aversion behavior which it has been demonstrated will lift the bid for the Japanese yen, US Treasuries, and other perceived safe haven assets. The flight to safety will also induce the selling of the risk on assets just outlined so one would expect to see weakness in equities in general, and particularly for EM markets, weakness in resources and commodities and an increased propensity for fund managers to seek out protective strategies which will be reflected in increased option premia, as reflected by increases in the VIX and other volatility instruments.

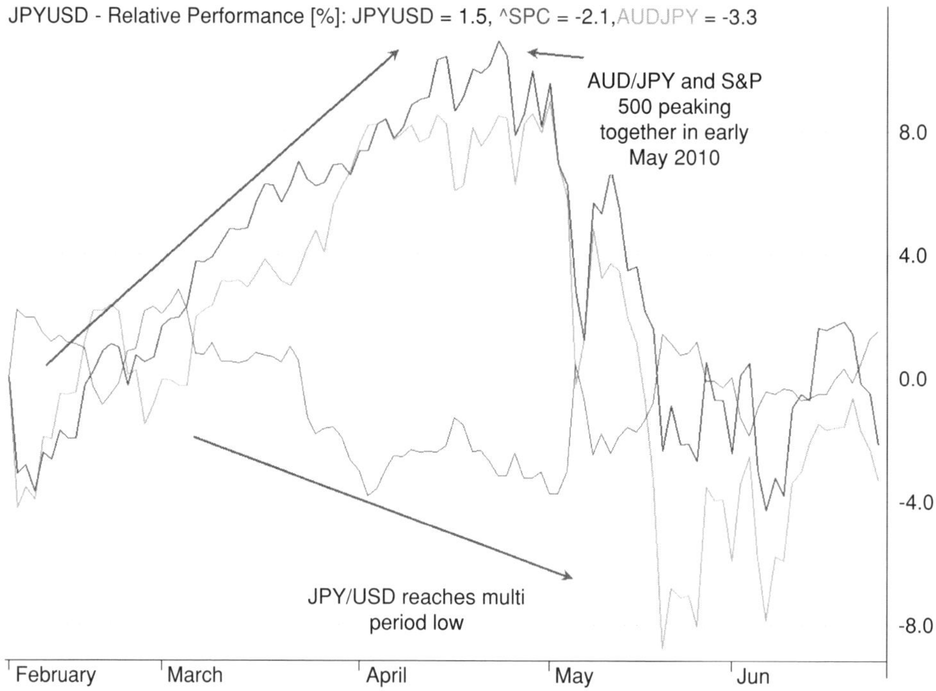

Figure 8.3 Performance of AUD/JPY, JPY/USD, and S&P 500 leading up to Flash Crash

The testable hypothesis which has been suggested with regard to the underlying tension between the two constituents of the AUD/JPY relationship hinges on the degree to which the macro trends within the financial markets during sessions (or even intraday time periods) when the market is turning up the risk control lever and exhibiting bullish behavior towards the riskier assets and vice versa, can be associated with changes in the AUD/JPY cross rate. Although the discussion in this book is focused on daily and low granularity time frames there is additional evidence from the author's research that the AUD/JPY relationship can act as an early warning system for significant inflections in higher granularity time series contexts such as real time intraday trading.

The relevance of movements in the FX market involving cross rates with the yen and specifically the AUD/JPY pair to events of May 2010 has now been well documented. We can now shift attention to the onset of the financial crisis in the summer of 2007 where once again there were very useful signals and clues as to what lay ahead provided by the Aussie/yen pair. A review of the charts for AUD/JPY, and other pairs involving the Japanese yen as the base currency, [2] reveals that those trades which integrally involve the concept of carry outlined in Chapter 6 began to lose their appeal in July 2007 due to a combination of factors which can be briefly summarized as follows:

- A decline in the overall degree of leverage which was commonly found prior to 2007.
- The diminution in the relative interest rate differentials between the funding currency rates and the high yielding rates (as these began to decline).
- Risk aversion began to cause the FX movements to go in exactly the wrong direction for each leg of the FX relationship.

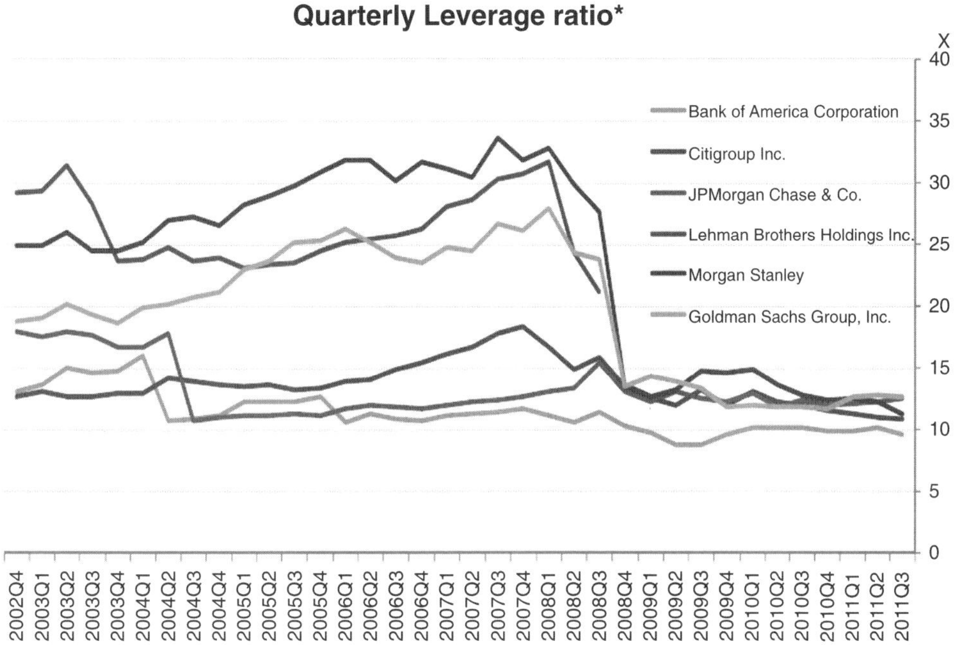

Figure 8.4 Declining leverage of investment banks 2007
Source: Shadow Banking and Financial Instability, lecture by Adair Turner delivered at the Cass Business School, London, in March 2012.

Statistics are not readily available for the degree of leverage employed within the shadow banking system, particularly by hedge funds, but Figure 8.4 [3] shows quite clearly that for Morgan Stanley and Citigroup the degree of leverage, as determined by the ratio of total assets to total equity, peaked in the second half of 2007 and for the other institutions shown the decline became very abrupt in the first half of 2008. It is worth noting that the line for Lehman Brothers – which terminates in Q3, 2008 – was the last to peak and reached a ratio of approximately 33:1 during the second quarter of 2008.

Figure 8.5 [4] provides further background evidence to the perception by market participants of the dramatically increased risk of financial firms during the late summer of 2007. The inflection point for the almost vertical ascent of the credit default swap rates (CDS) for the wide assortment of global financial services firms listed at the bottom of the graphic took place in July 2007.

Within the financial sector there were several developments in the summer of 2007 which were serving as a major alarm signal regarding the potential for a meltdown in the mortgage-backed securities market, but these events were not yet widely acknowledged by other sectors within the broader market. Michael Lewis, among others, has provided an excellent time line of the major incidents in his book *The Big Short*. [5] I shall confine myself here to just mentioning a few that are pertinent within this time frame. In June 2007, liquidity pressures at two hedge funds sponsored by Bear Stearns Asset Management, brought about the imposition of gates on investor redemptions, [6] sudden increases in margin calls, and sudden falls in asset prices. In August 2007, there were major losses at hedge funds which the market had thought were following low-risk market-neutral strategies, as a result of knock-on consequences from

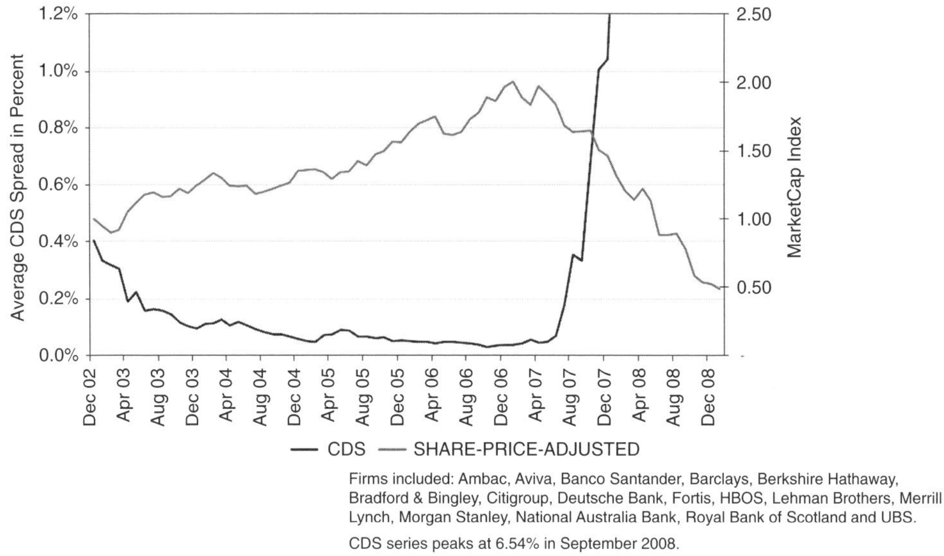

Figure 8.5 Financial firms: CDS prices and share prices 2007
Source: Shadow Banking and Financial Instability, lecture by Adair Turner delivered at the Cass Business School, London, in March 2012.

margin calls in structured credit portfolios. For example both the Global Alpha Fund and GEO fund of Goldman Sachs are estimated to have lost more than 20% just during the month of August 2007, and this prompted the following remark from the firm's CFO David Viniar: [7]

> "What we have to look at more closely is the phenomenon of the crowded trade overwhelming market fundamentals," he said. "*It makes you reassess how big the extreme moves can be.*" (author's italics)

Figure 8.6 shows the daily activity of the Australian dollar versus the Japanese yen during the period from April through to mid-November of 2007. The zenith actually arises at a rate just shy of the 108 level and took place during trading on July 20, 2007. The sharp sell-off which occurred at the end of July saw the rate drop to below 88 by the middle of July which corresponds to a drop of almost 20%. On August 16 alone the Aussie dollar weakened against the Japanese yen by almost 6% which is an unusually large daily move in the foreign exchange market.

With regard to those engaged in the FX carry trade the currency move observed in the graphic is an extremely adverse development and illustrates the point made earlier that returns in this trade suffer from being very volatile and negatively skewed. The Japanese yen as the funding currency would have been borrowed (i.e. the hedge funds were short the yen and long the Australian dollar) and these borrowings would need to be paid back with proceeds from the sale of the assets denominated in the much depreciated target currency.

Reinforcing the notion that those engaged in the FX carry trade began a major unwinding of highly leveraged positions, following the problems with the Bear Stearns hedge funds (and other issues) and just prior to the more widespread problems in August 2007, Figure 8.7 highlights the coincidental performance of UK sterling against the Japanese yen. During 2007

Figure 8.6 AUD/JPY during 2007 illustrating unwind of carry trade

Figure 8.7 GBP/JPY during 2007 illustrating unwind of carry trade

short-term rates available within the UK money markets and on short dated gilts were in the vicinity of 5% and were thus an alternative target for funds borrowed once again in the Japanese currency where short-term rates were a matter of 20/30 basis points.

The apogee for the GBP/JPY cross rate – as seen on Figure 8.7 – also, coincidentally with AUD/JPY, occurred on July 20 – with an intraday high during that session just above the psychologically key level of 250. Although 250 was not *per se* a technically vital level it is often the case that targets are set at round figure levels and then act as an attractor for price action.

During the week from August 9 to August 16 UK sterling dropped by almost 10% against the yen. In turn this would have resulted in similar adverse consequences for those having to repay their Japanese currency borrowings, i.e. the funding currency, with assets denominated in sterling which were rapidly depreciating in value against the yen (for the purpose of keeping the illustration as simple as possible, the assumption is that the FX exposure had not been hedged). The very abrupt nature of the correction during the first two weeks of August 2007 provided an early warning – for those paying attention to the FX carry trade footprints – that there was more dislocation and financial distress on the horizon.

Figure 8.8 covers the period from the beginning of January 2007 through to mid-2009 and normalizes the daily closing prices for the S&P 500 and also for the AUD/JPY exchange rate. As can be seen both instruments were at their peaks during 2007 and both reached their respective trough values during the latter part of 2008; AUD/JPY reached its lowest value before the S&P 500 but then went back and revisited this level again in close proximity to the S&P 500 which registered its lowest value on March 6, 2009 (as a matter of record the intraday low was 666). The paths taken by both instruments are very closely aligned across the whole period with the exception of the summer of 2008 in which the currency pair drifted away from the equity index as the latter began to sell off. However, once the selling gained momentum as the fall of 2008 progressed, the two paths became synchronized to a very noticeable degree

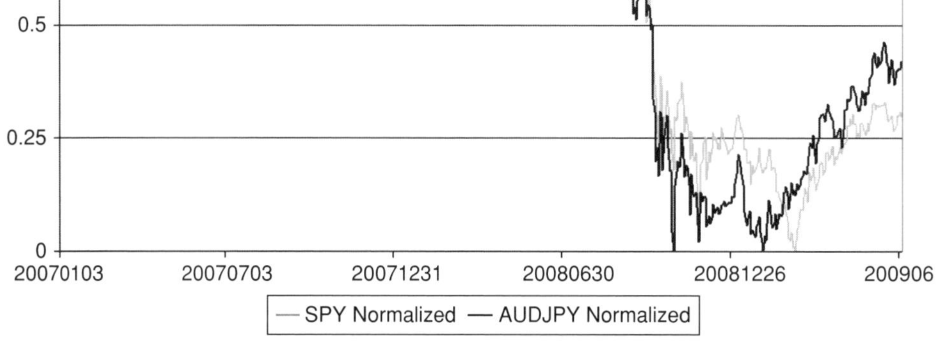

Figure 8.8 AUD/JPY and S&P normalized from January 2007–July 2009

and they remained in a strongly aligned co-movement throughout the rest of the period shown on the chart. It is fair to point out that no other currency pair exhibits such a strong correlation with the way in which prices on the S&P 500 developed from the second half of 2008 and throughout 2009. [8]

Figure 8.8 reveals very clearly that, in this period of extraordinarily negative price action, the expected behavior of AUD/JPY discussed earlier with respect to providing a proxy for risk and investor sentiment is demonstrably validated by its very close co-movement with the broadest indicator of risk appetite versus risk aversion – the price performance of US equities as embodied in the benchmark index.

It is often observed that when placed under stress or confronted with very difficult circumstances, individuals will tend to reveal their true nature. When normal composure and polite behavior are pushed aside by the need to deal with adversity a person's character will be more transparent than at other times and this will enable another to make more reliable judgments about their real personal qualities. In a similar vein, the contention is that markets reveal more about their internal dynamics during critical periods, and the period captured in Figure 8.8 surely qualifies as one of the most momentous in modern financial history. One by-product of the global financial crisis is that we now have a vast amount of data regarding how asset classes performed under extreme duress. Following on from this it has enabled students of markets to undertake forensic analysis which throws light on inter-dependencies and correlated behavior which is not so readily observable when markets are operating under more normal conditions.

8.1 THE ROLE OF AUSSIE/YEN IN INTER-MARKET STRATEGIES

When we examined the CFTC/SEC findings into the circumstances of the Flash Crash in Chapter 5 it was noted that their failure to account for the interplay between the rapid appreciation of the yen in the FX market and the subsequent drop in the S&P 500 futures meant that much of the work done in seeking an understanding of, and possible remedies for, the aberrant behavior is significantly deficient. This becomes ever more apparent when realizing the extent to which those hedge funds and trading desks engaged in multiple asset class algorithmic trading strategies. Such funds are carrying positions in equities, FX, commodities etc. and where fast moving asset allocation decisions, implemented at the micro-structure level by algorithms, are, at the programmatic level, being driven by sampling market internals on the shifting emphasis on macro level risk on/risk off conditions.

Sophisticated fund managers aided by carefully programmed routines which are constantly monitoring meta-market information – order flow, bid-ask spreads, the pattern of price developments, volume and liquidity, inter-market correlations, and so on – are able to switch and change directional plays rapidly in accordance with the opportunities presented. However, one of the side effects of this preoccupation with trading based on monitoring market internals and the high degree of cross asset correlations that are evidenced each day in the markets, is that from time to time, at inflection points, uniform and destabilizing decisions can be reached (both by humans and metaphorically speaking by algorithms) about near term market direction. When a consensus view develops that the market has become vulnerable to a market correction, and when cross market correlations are abnormally high, the uniformity of opinion about where price is headed next leads to a highly unbalanced market in which market makers rather than providing normal service become risk averse and unwilling to take on new transient inventory (because they fear they may have to *take it home* with them). When such aversion to further inventory accumulation arises liquidity providers become liquidity consumers and therefore overall market liquidity evaporates. Discerning the patterns in market internals and using the binary logic which arises from the risk on/risk off paradigm to reach certain short-term directional decisions – which is so much a feature of high frequency trading – can easily lead to rather an unpleasant feedback loop which, if overall liquidity becomes hard to find, will produce the kind of crash seen on May 6, 2010.

It has not been widely recognized but these bouts of illiquidity are more frequent (at a limited scale) than reported, but the evidence that they are occurring is being chronicled by a number of companies which specialize in studying the micro-structure of markets such as Nanex and has even entered the radar of the Bank of England's Financial Stability Division [9].

Association can be measured statistically as in the methods used to calculate the correlation coefficient we have seen, but high correlation does not imply causation. It can also be daunting in trying to identify which is the independent variable and which is dependent in any "explanation" of strong co-movements between asset classes. Nevertheless the evidence for strong association is compelling for risk on assets and the AUD/JPY foreign exchange rate, and this strong association will help to illuminate the kinds of trading and market timing strategies which are being implemented by many hedge funds, proprietary trading desks, and independent traders in today's markets. As suggested earlier there is ample evidence that the association does not only hold when considering end of day data based on closing prices but is also evident in intraday time frames. For large trading desks and hedge funds the association is actually computed on a tick by tick basis and when certain alignments become distorted or too unbalanced, as they were in May 2010, there can be sudden and abrupt intraday changes in the risk on/risk off complexion of asset markets.

The kind of bipolar switching which has been documented primarily using end of day data so far is also manifest on shorter time frames such as 60-minute, 15-minute, and even sub-minute time segments. There is a truly fractal quality to the binary behavior of financial markets showing that it operates across multiple time frames, and this can be illustrated by returning again to the Flash Crash and presenting time series data of a higher granularity to support this claim.

The unusually high correlation between the S&P 500 and AUD/JPY based on intraday data is very well depicted in Figure 8.9 which uses 15-minute sampling during the days leading up to May 6, 2010.

Figure 8.9 shows how the trajectories of the S&P 500 Cash index (upon which the E-Mini futures contract is based) and the AUD/JPY spot market rate tracked each other very closely during the period immediately prior to May 6, 2010 and on the actual day itself. Previously a normalized chart was shown, but in this case as the very tight co-movement is so readily seen, and as the time axis is for a relatively short period, the chart above shows each instrument on a different vertical axis.

The left hand axis of Figure 8.9 shows the price of the S&P 500 which on May 3 actually penetrates above the 1200 level temporarily and then over the next three days including the brief period on May 6 between 2.30 and 3pm EDT, when the crash occurred, the index drops almost to the 1080 level – a 10% move within three market sessions, and for the Dow Jones Industrials the almost 1000 point move during the crash was the largest intraday points movement in its history. The right hand axis of Figure 8.9 provides the key to the AUD/JPY exchange rate and during the same time interval the FX rate drops (as the Aussie dollar weakens against the yen) from above 87 to below 79 which itself is a 10% drop for the currency pair.

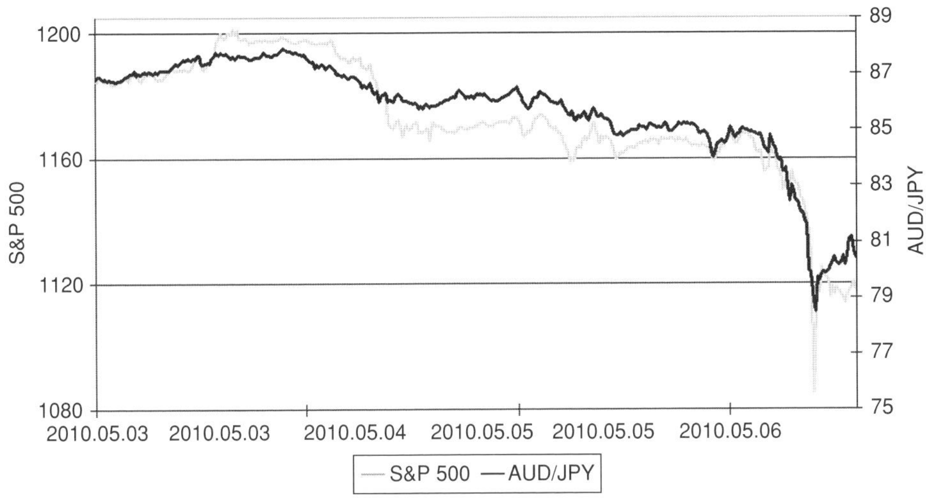

Figure 8.9 S&P 500 and AUD/JPY in early May 2010 – 15 minute data

The most prominent feature of Figure 8.9 is the almost synchronized paths taken by both assets over the entire period – both in the lead up to the crash and then during the crash. Both instruments fell very abruptly and in tandem during the initial phase of the crash, but the FX pair managed to avoid sinking to the bottom of the very steep V shaped plunge (the light gray line on the chart) traced out by the equity index. What is not evident from Figure 8.9 is any indication as to which may have had any causative influence over the other. In essence the manner in which both are moving in a very tight alignment suggests, especially during this critical market episode, that the FX pair is an excellent proxy or tracker for the overall bullish/bearish dynamics which operate in equities and across many other asset classes.

Returning again to the Hurst coefficient which was discussed in Chapter 3, an application of the software tools to the log returns for intraday samplings of the AUD/JPY cross rate pair produces the remarkable Hurst value which is shown in Figure 8.10.

To set up the context, the period covered in Figure 8.10 is from the end of July 2011 to the end of September 2011. There are more than 1300 such 60-minute samplings and the period chosen coincides with a period of market stress brought on by concerns about peripheral sovereign debt in the Eurozone and especially the deterioration in the outlook for Greece. The summer and fall of 2011 was a period which saw a sharp increase in risk aversion and there was a very noticeable transition towards risk off asset allocation throughout the period which also saw, as previously commented, historically high correlations in the returns across many asset classes.

The elevated Hurst value of 0.68 helps to underline the fact that Aussie/yen occupies a very unusual position in the financial domain. Figure 8.10 should remove doubts about the value of tracking the Aussie/yen rate as a precursor to inflection points in the spectrum of risk on/risk off behavior. That a currency pair can exhibit such trend persistence, evidenced even with high granularity samplings of intraday prices over a 60-day period, suggests that there are peculiar dynamics at work which relate to the manner in which markets switch back and forth in a binary fashion between embracing risk and shunning risk. It would appear that this switching

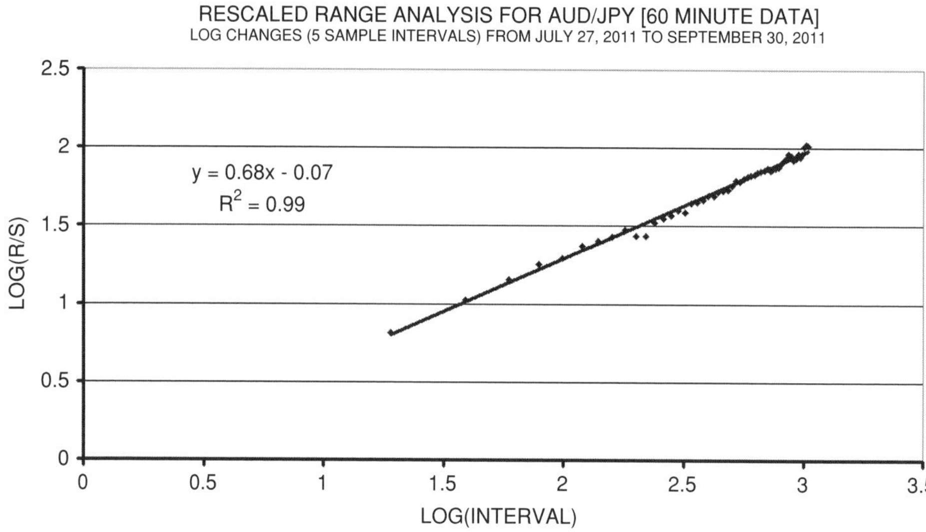

Figure 8.10 Hurst Coefficient for AUD/JPY [60 Min data] July–September 2011

behavior is invariably accompanied (the question of any causation link is left as a moot point) by very pronounced and persistent trends in the Aussie/yen rate.

Figure 8.11 shows the result of using a linear regression to drill down on the critical time frame from just before the crash and through to the immediate recovery. The changes registered for each variable have been tracked at 15-minute intervals and then plotted on the scatter graph. The value for the gradient of the linear equation of the regression is 1.1 which can be referred to as the beta value for the covariance of each variable and the R^2 value of 0.72 is almost

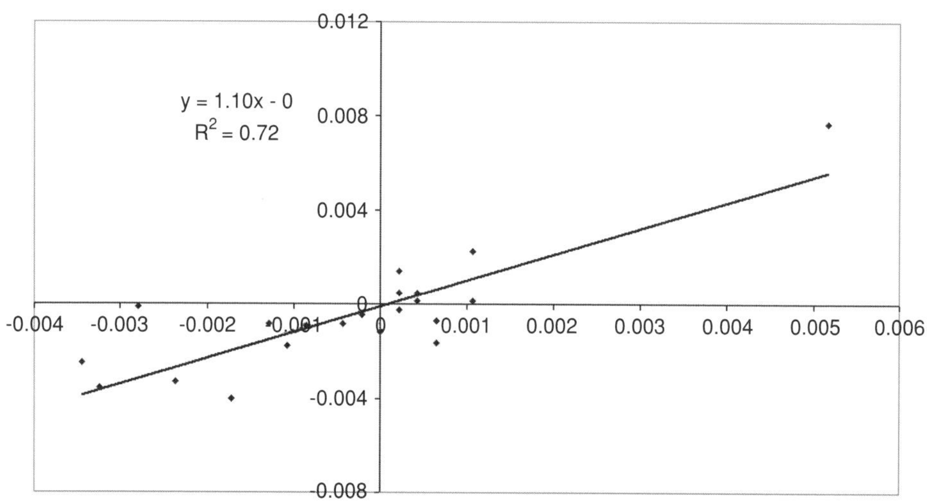

Figure 8.11 Linear regression of 15-minute changes in AUD/JPY and S&P 500 on May 6, 2010

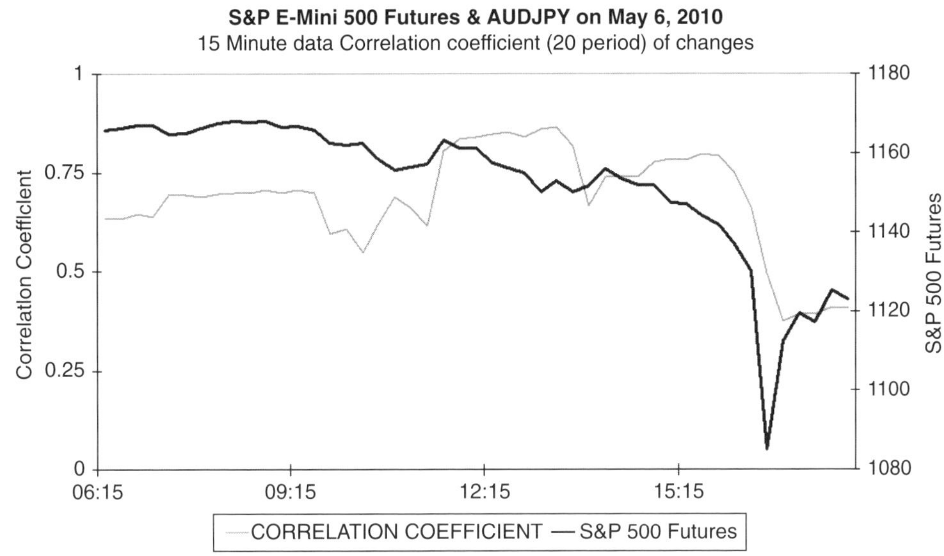

Figure 8.12 Linear regression of trailing 15-minute changes to S&P 500 E-Mini & AUD/JPY on May 6, 2010

identical to the value seen in Figure 8.2 earlier in this chapter which is a regression conducted on daily data and covering a much longer time frame. The fact that the two key statistical values shown on Figures 8.2 and 8.9 – the gradients or beta values and the R^2 values – are almost identical is strong evidence that market participants are making allocation decisions across multiple time frames where decisions to buy or sell both instruments are closely coordinated.

One final chart will complete our examination of the Aussie/yen connection and takes a slightly different view to that which is shown in Figure 8.10. The linear regression shown in Figure 8.12 captures a static one-off view of the correlation throughout the critical period of May 6, 2010. The method employed to prepare Figure 8.12 uses a developing or historical approach and takes the same critical time frame but samples the correlation (using a trailing twenty 15 minute period) and then renders them across the graph as the trading day progressed.

Once again a 15-minute sampling of the relevant price levels for the S&P 500 has been tracked in Figure 8.12, and the right hand scale simply shows the level of the S&P 500, as depicted by the black line, as it started the trading day and then suffered the crash in the mid-afternoon. The light gray line traces the degree of correlation which is shown on the left hand scale (the correlation is measured across a 20-period lookback window). What emerges from this more detailed probing of the correlation is that, in the period coincidental with the crash, the correlation is reaching its most elevated levels with readings above 0.8. In fact it would seem that even after the S&P had begun to plunge there is a further tightening of the correlation. This provides further support for the view that the kinds of cross asset trading strategies, touched upon earlier, were not cast aside during extreme market behavior but were in fact consistently followed, rather than abandoned, even while such a critical event was unfolding.

More contentiously, the tendency for assets to become so segregated and demarcated as either *risk on* or *risk off* by many fund managers and algorithmic firms, and then to be so systematically deployed in a tightly coupled and closely aligned fashion, depending on the prevailing complexion of the market, can itself become a contributory factor to the "evaporation of liquidity" explanation which has been correctly applied to a diagnosis of events like those of May 6, 2010. The algorithmic implementation of such a high degree of alignment and tight coupling between risk on assets may well turn out to be the Achilles heel which could, if not itself create a systemic liquidity crisis on its own, certainly aggravate one that has been set in motion by institutional factors such as any further collapses in the banking system or an unraveling of the euro currency.

For those who sit at a trading terminal each day this may not be significantly newsworthy – although I suspect it will be for many who do not adopt a cross market approach and monitor the foreign exchange market closely. For those who do not have the inclination or time to devote to monitoring markets in real time or who have not contemplated the association between such apparently diverse instruments as the US benchmark index for equities and the slightly off the beaten track currency pair that has been front and center in this chapter, the results shown in Figures 8.9, 8.10, 8.11, and 8.12 could be quite surprising.

I would also suggest that by paying closer attention to the correlation between these diverse instruments there will be a far richer understanding of the nature of the binary trading and investment behavior of modern financial markets.

ENDNOTES

1. Conventionally the US dollar would not have been used as a funding currency as under more normal market conditions there would not have been a significant difference in the interest rate paid to borrow in the US currency and the rate available to lend in the target currency. Since 2008, with the Federal Reserve operating a more or less zero interest rate policy, this is no longer the case.
2. With regard to the manner in which an exchange rate is quoted, the first currency to be quoted in a currency pair is known as the base currency and the second currency is known as the quote or, less commonly, the counter currency. The value of the quote currency is expressed in terms of one unit of the base currency. For example, if the exchange rate is the EUR/USD the exchange rate indicates that the value of the US dollar is being expressed in terms of one euro. For example, if EUR/USD has been quoted at 1.30 this would mean that it would take US $1.30 to purchase one euro.

   In the case of the USD/JPY exchange rate the value of the US dollar would be expressed in terms of one Japanese yen. For example if the USD/JPY exchange rate is quoted at 80, it would take 80 Japanese yen to buy one US dollar.
3. *Shadow Banking and Financial Instability*: Lord Turner speech to the CASS Business School, Adair Turner, March 14, 2012, http://www.fsa.gov.uk/library/communication/pr/2012/027.shtml.

   Slides for the above speech can be found at http://www.fsa.gov.uk/static/pubs/speeches/0314-at.pdf.
4. See above.
5. Michael Lewis, *The Big Short: Inside The Doomsday Machine* (Allen Lane, 2010).
6. A description of the rationale for gates on redemptions can be found in Lawrence Cohen and Thomas M. Griffin, *Run On Hedge Funds: Redemption Strategies and Responses*, December 30, 2008:

   > The global economic crisis has had a significant impact on the hedge fund world. One of the most striking developments has been the rush by many investors to redeem their holdings. Individual and institutional investors alike, in reaction to dismal returns on their investments (the average fund has lost 20% this year),

> have engaged in a classic run on the bank. In response, dozens of hedge funds have suspended or restricted redemptions – if such actions were authorized by their governing documents.
>
> Preventing an investor from exiting a fund, unless the investor had a reasonable justification (e.g., a legal requirement or financial emergency), was once anathema to all but the weakest funds, as it was often taken as a sign that the fund was in distress and might even collapse.

http://www.finalternatives.com/node/6474.

7. David Viniar Goldman's CFO quoted in Peter Thai Larsen, Goldman pays the price of being big, *Financial Times*, August 13, 2007:

> "What we have to look at more closely is the phenomenon of the crowded trade overwhelming market fundamentals," he said. "*It makes you reassess how big the extreme moves can be.*"

http://www.ft.com/cms/s/0/d2121cb6-49cb-11dc-9ffe-0000779fd2ac.html.

8. Correlation analyses performed by the author have not revealed any stronger correlations between major FX pairs and other mainstream assets than that for the Australian dollar/Japanese yen pair.
9. Nanex, a small company based near Chicago, publishes various documents and white papers concerning extraordinary occurrences within the US markets arising from HFT activity. They have some interesting graphics relating to the Flash Crash of May 2010, http://www.nanex.net/FlashCrash/OngoingResearch.html.

9

Precursors to Illiquidity

More than anything the 2007/8 global financial crisis showed how *the proper functioning of capital markets cannot take place without systemic liquidity.* Since markets began their recovery in the spring of 2009 there have been a number of occasions when the threat of system-wide illiquidity resulted in highly charged and disruptive market episodes. The Flash Crash of May 6, 2010 was one and in late July/early August of 2011 when the Eurozone woes took a major turn for the worse there were other sessions when large drops in equities, both intraday and inter-day, and other risk on assets arose. The fearful specter of the fragility of markets when liquidity evaporates has now been etched deeply into the collective psyche. There is good reason to believe that apart from all of the structural hurdles that need to be overcome, this emotional scarring will be a significant dampener to the "animal spirits." One of the lingering doubts as to how long it may take to emerge from the kind of balance sheet recession which is still very much with us, can be traced back to the question: How long does it take for market participants to get over this residual fear about systemic instability and of markets "seizing up"?

In a proper theoretical framework which can explain the nature of systemic liquidity risk, it would be a major sign of progress for there to be a separation of the different types of factors which can contribute to market dislocations and the ensuing periods of economic contraction. There are cyclical downturns which have arisen historically, for example, from periods of inflation and where central banks have hiked interest rates to slow the economy down – not a very good metaphor but it is convenient shorthand for the types of contraction that have been seen such as in the early 1980s and again in the early 1990s. Much less frequent but more devastating are the kinds of downturns which come after the collapse of major asset bubbles such as that seen in the 1930s and that which we are living through in the second decade of the 21st century.

Significant progress could be made towards such a theoretical framework if there was a greater consensus amongst economists that the current weak global environment, the duration of which has exceeded any prior recovery, is *not a cyclical downturn* but rather a more insidious and chronic financial recession. One would have thought that it should be obvious to any macro-economist that a "normal" cyclical upturn is not going to wondrously eradicate the asset deflation and debt overhang which is the most enduring outcome of the implosion in 2007/8 of the massive credit bubble that built steadily in the prior ten years.

Given the fetish for quantification for all aspects of the financial economy, the allusion above to the *scarring of the collective psyche* brought on by the near collapse of the banking system in 2008 will probably be downplayed by mainstream economists as an example of "emotional baggage" which is not relevant to a scientific discipline. Encouragingly however, at the INET conference held in Berlin in April 2012 and attended by a growing constituency of new paradigm economists, quite a lot of attention was placed on the need for a proper recognition of the emotional side of finance. There will be an examination of some of the emerging ideas in emotional finance in Chapter 15 along with some more speculative suggestions as to how and why, despite and perhaps because of the GFC, there is still a kind of cognitive dissonance of the "collective mind" which could, at short notice, lead to a new systemic liquidity crisis. In addition the nature of the emotional and cognitive dissonance that will be clarified as the discussion proceeds will provide more validity to the extended notion that the risk on/risk off binary paradigm can equally be considered as a bipolar predilection with respect to the behavior of a large section of traders and investors in contemporary markets.

While this type of speculation at the level of group psychology is fascinating and worthy of a discussion in its own right, I want now to introduce a more grounded and empirically based approach to the examination of cross asset correlations which has shown considerable promise with respect to signaling when financial markets might be on the threshold of bouts of illiquidity. The motivating idea behind the development of the techniques to be outlined below was the special position that the Aussie/yen occupies within the risk on/risk off matrix of asset class correlations which was the subject of the last chapter.

9.1 USING HEAT MAPS FOR FX AND OTHER ASSET CORRELATIONS

In order to explore the cross-sectional correlation between AUD/JPY and JPY/USD with other different asset classes, geographically diverse indices, and economic sectors, I have developed a technique for quantifying and visualizing the relationships. The output from the analytical tools is shown in Figure 9.1 and is in the form of a heat map; the benefits of this technique

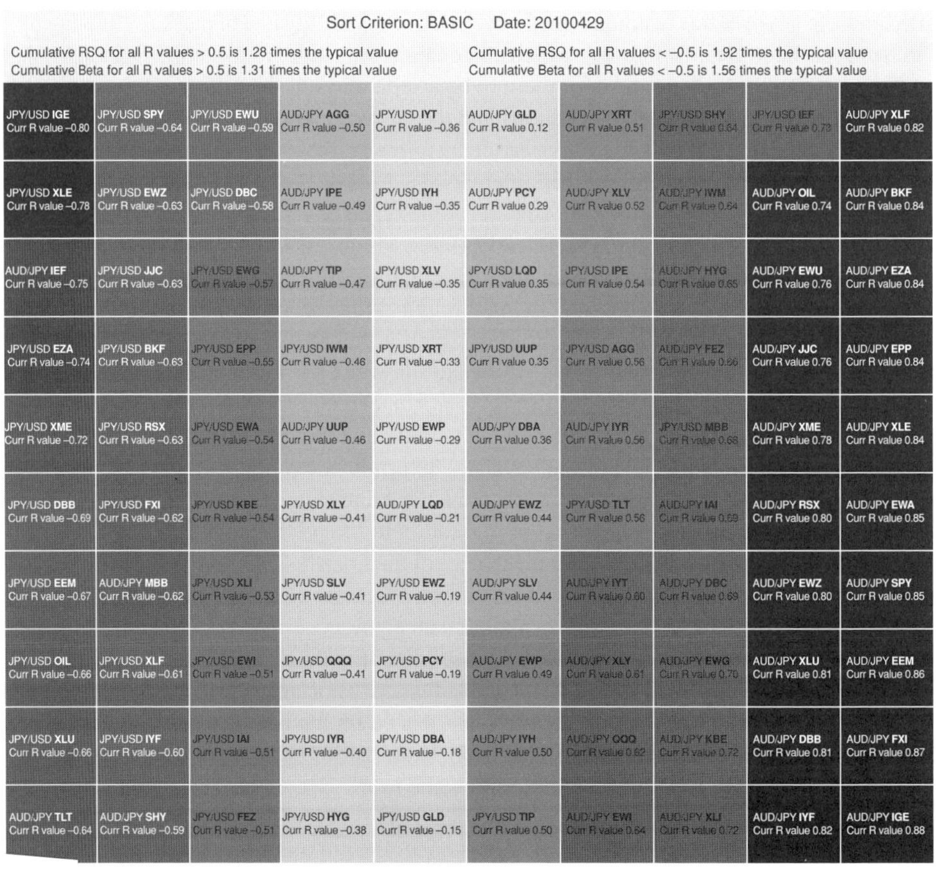

.1 FX/ETF heat map for April 29, 2010 uses ranking based on the prevailing correlation nt values

were outlined in Chapter 2. By way of a quick refresher the real advantage of using the heat map technology is that it enables one to perceive relationships quickly and intuitively in a way that is far more accessible (and user friendly) than displaying data in numerical form in a tabular format.

Figure 9.1 shows the correlations between 50 different assets (see the Appendix for a complete listing) and each of the two FX pairs. In all, there are one hundred cells displayed on each of the heat maps displayed in the remainder of this chapter. The cells are ranked according to the observed correlation between each pair of instruments from the most negative correlation which is in the top left hand cell to the highest positive correlation which appears as the bottom right hand cell. The ranking moves from the top left hand cell and then moves vertically down that column, then moves across to the top of the adjacent column and then down that column and so on. The number in each of the cells of Figure 9.1 is the R value or correlation coefficient for each of the assets identified in each cell as of the date shown at the top of the heat map. The correlation coefficient is calculated from taking the percentage daily changes for each pair shown in the cell using a trailing 21-day lookback period.

In what follows there will be a description invoking colors as these are a fundamental feature of heat maps and since the figures in the book will be reproduced in grayscale the reader will have to use their good sense to transpose the colors to the appropriate shades of gray. The key idea is that one starts with the coldest values in the top left hand corner – the dark blue values and as one moves across the heat map the values become progressively hotter moving through different hues of blue, green, yellow, orange and towards dark red. The simplest method of ranking the output from the correlation calculations is the one used in Figure 9.1 and is based on ranking by the correlation coefficient. There are several variations to the ranking which can also be applied such as a ranking based on the changes in the R value (or more precisely the R^2 value as this makes comparisons easier) from the current period to some prior period such as the value from five trading sessions previously. This delta approach will enable one to detect the changing nature of the correlations across time rather than a static snapshot of the current correlations which is the default approach shown in Figure 9.1. With alternative ranking approaches, as will be seen, the cell color which is based on the current correlation will be preserved but the heat map will follow a different sequence, and where the interpretation of the pattern with respect to the new ranking criteria can reveal useful information in a visually intuitive fashion.

Dark Blue – strong negative correlation
Green – weak negative correlation or uncorrelated
Yellow – weak positive correlation or uncorrelated
Dark Red – strong positive correlation.

The legend or color key shown above provides a key to the R values and for most purposes it is less vital to know the specific R value in numerical terms than where it is situated on the color spectrum of possible values for the correlation coefficient which extends from -1 to $+1$ – with values just above and just below zero being indicative of very weak correlation. [1]

By way of example the top left hand cell of Figure 9.1 shows the following information:

JPY/USD IGE with a current R value (i.e. the correlation coefficient) of -0.80. In deciphering this, reference to the Appendix will show that IGE is an exchange traded fund which captures the total return of the S&P North American Natural Resources Sector Index. The value of -0.80, which is the current correlation as of the date on the map, is the most extreme negative correlation of the 100 cells and indicates that the movements of JPY/USD and this sector fund move, to a very large degree, in opposite directions; in other words, there is a strong inverse correlation between the two different instruments. This is what one would expect from the discussion so far in that when JPY/USD is moving higher – typically a *risk off* market move – then the performance of the resources sector which typifies *risk on* assets would be expected to go in the opposite direction and *vice versa*. Moving to the other side of the heat map, the bottom right hand cell shows the correlation between AUD/JPY and IGE is effectively tracking the degree of co-movement between two notable *risk on* assets. In this case the value is 0.88 which demonstrates, as would be expected, very strong positive correlation.

To further illustrate the manner in which the cross asset correlations are reflective of the binary risk on/risk off mode of tactical asset allocation, let us consider the third cell down from the top left hand corner. This cell shows AUD/JPY and IEF with an R value of −0.75.

Reference to the Appendix will show that IEF is a sector fund which tracks the price and yield performance of the Barclays Capital 7–10 Year US Treasury Bond Index. Once again this is intuitively plausible as strength in the Australian dollar against the yen – reflective of a propensity for greater risk appetite – would tend to equate inversely with performance of a risk off asset such as the total return (including the yield) in the middle of the US Treasury yield curve.

There are many different cells that are worthy of comment but a couple of observations are worth noting as follows. There is a very high correlation between AUD/JPY and FXI – which is an index for 25 of the largest and most liquid Chinese companies – of 0.87 which fits again into the risk on/risk off characteristics which are dominant in the post-GFC markets. To the extent that Chinese growth remains strong with firm demand for resources from such economies as Australia (and the CARBS nations generally) [2] then this will translate into more risk on behavior where it has been shown that AUD/JPY is the best proxy for risk on in the realm of foreign exchange.

On the right hand side of the heat map the cells in the first column, all with high negative correlation values, are predominantly a variety of fixed income instruments and include AGG which tracks price and yield performance of investment grade corporate bonds in the US and TIP which tracks inflation-protected public obligations of the US Treasury. *What the heat map technology underscores is the fact that in tactical asset allocation decision making – especially in the contemporary paradigm of risk on versus risk off – there is a clear separation of those asset classes which move either in the same direction or opposing directions.*

Additional insights can be derived from the heat map methodology and these involve the values which are shown at the top of the table in the caption. The first point to note is the date on which the heat map is current. For the heat map shown in Figure 9.1 the date is 20100429 which when translated is April 29, 2010. [3] This date has been chosen deliberately to provide additional context to the analysis of the Flash Crash of May 6, 2010. In fact the date of the heat map coincides with the multi period high for USD/JPY (the inverse of course of JPY/USD) following a steady ascent over the preceding three months and which coincided within a day or so of the multi period peak seen on US equities (again following an almost uninterrupted ascent in the prior three month period). Charts reflecting this can be seen in Chapter 8.

A more detailed discussion of the methods used in calculating the values which are seen in the heat maps is provided in the Appendix, but some guidance will also be addressed here. How then to interpret the statement in the caption of Figure 9.1 that the "cumulative RSQ value for all R values > 0.5 is 1.28 times the typical value"? RSQ relates to R^2 which is simply the squared value of R which is seen in each cell. The reason for squaring it is to enable comparison of the degree of correlation for all possible values but where they are all positive. In other words the sign of the correlation coefficient is "neutralized" by squaring and only the magnitude of the degree of correlation is compared. This makes sense as extreme values of R – either positive or negative – are revealing behavior which is either one of directionally similar moves or directionally opposed moves. In either case there is useful information conveyed in the magnitude of the co-movement irrespective of the sign value of directionality, i.e. whether it is negative or positive in the directionality.

Calculating the R values (and by implication the RSQ values) on any particular date is very instructive but a reference back to a benchmark value throws even more light on whether that currently observed value is above, below, or in close proximity to typical values observed over an extended period of time. For instance, we can ask were the aggregated correlation values observed on April 29, 2010 – just prior to the Flash Crash – more elevated than normal or less so? This question can be resolved by reference to the historically observed correlation values of each pair of assets which is captured in each cell of the heat map. The technique used is to average the RSQ values observed on the trailing 21 period lookback basis over the prior three years of data points. This has an advantage over simply taking a single reading of the correlation coefficient for the entire set of data points over the preceding three years, because the R value (and in turn the R^2 value) fluctuates and by smoothing out all of the many 21 period correlation values observed over the time frame a more reliable value can be calculated to represent the *typical or normal* value for the degree of correlation.

Given this background, the question posed above in connection with the information expressed at the top of the heat map can now be answered. On April 29, 2010, for all of those relationships exhibited in the one hundred cells of the heat map, and where the current correlation is more than 0.5, the sum of all those values is 1.28 times the historically observed values for that same set of cells. This enables an inter-temporal comparison and adds an extra dimension of heat to the underlying heat map.

It is now possible to say that using the temperature analogy the values just prior to the Flash Crash were about 25% hotter or higher than the typical values for the most positively correlated values. Looking to the other side of the caption it can be seen that for the more negatively correlated relationships the observations just prior to the Flash Crash revealed that they were much colder than the typical values observed; in fact they were almost twice as cold as the typical values, with a value of 1.92.

Some explanation of this latter value might prove helpful in better understanding the value of the heat map methodology. It will be recalled from the discussion in the last chapter that there is merit in deconstructing the AUD/JPY relationship into its constituents – the AUD part and the JPY part – and this can be done by using the common base of the US currency and seeing what contribution is made to the AUD/JPY rate by changes in AUD/USD and JPY/USD. In essence this is why the decision was made to use the JPY/USD rate within the heat maps. Figure 8.3 (which may be one of the most useful graphics in the book) shows that in the period prior to the Flash Crash the JPY/USD rate had been declining indicating that the yen was sliding against the dollar. It was also seen that the AUD/JPY rate was closely tracking the S&P 500 (our *ideal proxy for risk on assets*). The point was made that the strong performance of both the S&P and AUD/JPY between February and late March of 2010 was indicative of a strong appetite for risk on assets. What was equally important was that the decline in the yen during the same period – accessible via the JPY/USD rate – indicated that there was a shunning of risk off assets during the period which was in excess of what might be seen where just appreciation of the Australian currency was doing most of the work in driving up the AUD/JPY rate. If the denominator of the AUD/JPY pair – the JPY – had been stable and the increase was largely due to the increase in the numerator it would still have been appropriate to call this increase a positive for the risk on side of the market. However when the AUD/JPY rate was being driven higher by the cooperation of a declining denominator – the decline in the yen – then there is an even more pronounced manifestation of committed bullishness in the movement of the AUD/JPY pair.

The cooperation of a declining denominator is revealed in the heat map shown in Figure 9.1 by the fact that the aggregate of RSQ values for the correlations which were less than −0.5 was twice as high as it had been in the prior three years. Since most of these negatively correlated pairs shown in Figure 9.1 in the left hand column involved JPY/USD against the various ETFs shown, this suggests that there was a strongly biased positioning not only in favour of risk on but also (via short positions) a strongly biased positioning against risk off. Such disproportionate skew in the relationships was a contributory factor to the Flash Crash and also helps to illustrate how paying attention to the dark blue cells in the heat maps is just as important as focusing on the dark red cells.

In general terms, by making day to day comparisons of these references of the current RSQ values back to an historical benchmark it becomes easier to observe the overall delta or rate of change in the degree of cross-sectional correlation. In turn this provides valuable information on the extent to which market participants may be creating a lopsided market in which the risk on asset alignments are becoming too tightly coupled giving rise to the kinds of order imbalances that were commented on in Chapter 5 with respect to the VPIN metric.

The fact that the negative correlations are becoming much colder, especially given the prevalence of red across the heat map shown in Figure 9.1, is actually symptomatic of unbalanced tactical asset allocations by fund managers where there is too much tension and fragility – via more tightly coupled polarities – than would be expected in more normal market conditions with less critically poised asset allocations. In simpler terms the heat map shows that during the period prior to the Flash Crash fund managers had been loading up on risk assets, and coincidentally either the same fund managers or others had also been taking on large long bets with the risk on currency AUD/JPY pair and short bets on the risk off currency pair, JPY/USD (or what amounts to the same, a long bet on USD/JPY). In moving away from a more evenly balanced and neutral equilibrium level the seeds were being sown for a disruptive outbreak of market instability.

The heat map techniques can thus provide early warnings, as they will reveal the emergence and development over time of minor and more systemically threatening "bubbles" within risk on assets. To the extent that there is increasing heat of the red cells and increasing coldness of the blue cells as they become extreme, there is heightened likelihood of abrupt corrective behavior and increased volatility. It is worth recalling that even though after all of the fireworks seen on May 6, 2010 and the fact that markets recovered much of the severe fall by the end of that trading day, in the weeks following May 6 both US equities and AUD/JPY suffered from serious corrections. From values above 1200 at the end of April 2010 the S&P 500 reached an intraday low of 1010 on July 1 and AUD/JPY dropped precipitously from 87.19 on April 29 to touch values close to 72 in June and early July. Given what ensued, the Flash Crash is improperly characterized as a freak event – some dismissed it at the time as a "fat finger" day. Seen in the larger context of the way that price developed in the months following the event of May 6, 2010 it can more accurately be described as providing the tip-off that risk on assets had taken on the semblance of a bubble during the period which equities, commodities, and risk on FX pairs ran up steadily (too steadily!) from early February to the end of April 2010.

A further illustration of the tighter couplings between the risk on assets – and conversely the increase in the magnitude of correlations for the risk off assets (notwithstanding that this

Sort Criterion: BASIC Date: 20100505

Cumulative RSQ for all R values > 0.5 is 1.4 times the typical value
Cumulative Beta for all R values > 0.5 is 1.95 times the typical value

Cumulative RSQ for all R values < –0.5 is 2.05 times the typical value
Cumulative Beta for all R values < –0.5 is 3.92 times the typical value

AUD/JPY **IEF** Curr R value –0.85	JPY/USD **SPY** Curr R value –0.65	AUD/JPY **AGG** Curr R value –0.59	JPY/USD **XLY** Curr R value –0.53	JPY/USD **XRT** Curr R value –0.40	JPY/USD **LQD** Curr R value 0.05	AUD/JPY **SLV** Curr R value 0.56	AUD/JPY **XLY** Curr R value 0.73	AUD/JPY **IAI** Curr R value 0.76	AUD/JPY **XLU** Curr R value 0.85
AUD/JPY **TLT** Curr R value –0.78	JPY/USD **FXI** Curr R value –0.64	JPY/USD **OIL** Curr R value –0.58	JPY/USD **EWI** Curr R value –0.51	JPY/USD **IYH** Curr R value –0.39	AUD/JPY **GLD** Curr R value 0.12	AUD/JPY **EWZ** Curr R value 0.58	AUD/JPY **FEZ** Curr R value 0.73	AUD/JPY **DBB** Curr R value 0.77	AUD/JPY **EWA** Curr R value 0.87
JPY/USD **IGE** Curr R value –0.78	JPY/USD **EEM** Curr R value –0.61	JPY/USD **IAI** Curr R value –0.57	AUD/JPY **IPE** Curr R value –0.51	JPY/USD **XLV** Curr R value –0.38	JPY/USD **UUP** Curr R value 0.26	JPY/USD **TLT** Curr R value 0.58	AUD/JPY **DBC** Curr R value 0.73	AUD/JPY **KBE** Curr R value 0.77	AUD/JPY **SPY** Curr R value 0.87
AUD/JPY **MBB** Curr R value –0.77	JPY/USD **KBE** Curr R value –0.61	JPY/USD **EPP** Curr R value –0.56	AUD/JPY **UUP** Curr R value –0.51	JPY/USD **SLV** Curr R value –0.34	AUD/JPY **PCY** Curr R value 0.30	AUD/JPY **XRT** Curr R value 0.59	AUD/JPY **IWM** Curr R value 0.74	AUD/JPY **XME** Curr R value 0.77	AUD/JPY **BKF** Curr R value 0.87
JPY/USD **XLU** Curr R value –0.76	JPY/USD **HYG** Curr R value –0.61	JPY/USD **IWM** Curr R value –0.56	AUD/JPY **TIP** Curr R value –0.50	JPY/USD **EWP** Curr R value –0.30	AUD/JPY **DBA** Curr R value 0.41	AUD/JPY **EWP** Curr R value 0.60	AUD/JPY **IYT** Curr R value 0.74	AUD/JPY **XLI** Curr R value 0.79	AUD/JPY **EZA** Curr R value 0.87
JPY/USD **XLE** Curr R value –0.76	JPY/USD **RSX** Curr R value –0.60	JPY/USD **DBC** Curr R value –0.55	JPY/USD **EWZ** Curr R value –0.49	JPY/USD **DBA** Curr R value –0.29	JPY/USD **AGG** Curr R value 0.46	AUD/JPY **IYR** Curr R value 0.67	AUD/JPY **HYG** Curr R value 0.75	AUD/JPY **EWZ** Curr R value 0.80	AUD/JPY **EPP** Curr R value 0.87
AUD/JPY **SHY** Curr R value –0.73	JPY/USD **IYR** Curr R value –0.59	JPY/USD **XME** Curr R value –0.54	JPY/USD **IYT** Curr R value –0.49	JPY/USD **PCY** Curr R value –0.29	JPY/USD **IPE** Curr R value 0.48	JPY/USD **MBB** Curr R value 0.69	AUD/JPY **EWU** Curr R value 0.76	JPY/USD **SHY** Curr R value 0.80	AUD/JPY **XLE** Curr R value 0.88
JPY/USD **EZA** Curr R value –0.66	JPY/USD **EWU** Curr R value –0.59	JPY/USD **EWA** Curr R value –0.54	JPY/USD **FEZ** Curr R value –0.48	JPY/USD **EWJ** Curr R value –0.27	AUD/JPY **XLV** Curr R value 0.50	AUD/JPY **JJC** Curr R value 0.71	AUD/JPY **OIL** Curr R value 0.76	AUD/JPY **RSX** Curr R value 0.83	AUD/JPY **EEM** Curr R value 0.89
JPY/USD **IYF** Curr R value –0.66	JPY/USD **XLI** Curr R value –0.59	JPY/USD **EWG** Curr R value –0.54	JPY/USD **QQQ** Curr R value –0.46	AUD/JPY **LQD** Curr R value –0.10	JPY/USD **TIP** Curr R value 0.52	AUD/JPY **QQQ** Curr R value 0.72	AUD/JPY **EWG** Curr R value 0.76	AUD/JPY **IYF** Curr R value 0.84	AUD/JPY **FXI** Curr R value 0.91
JPY/USD **XLF** Curr R value –0.66	JPY/USD **BKF** Curr R value –0.59	JPY/USD **DBB** Curr R value –0.54	JPY/USD **JJC** Curr R value –0.44	JPY/USD **GLD** Curr R value –0.02	AUD/JPY **IYH** Curr R value 0.54	AUD/JPY **EWI** Curr R value 0.73	JPY/USD **IEF** Curr R value 0.76	AUD/JPY **XLF** Curr R value 0.84	AUD/JPY **IGE** Curr R value 0.91

Figure 9.2 FX/ETF heat map for May 5, 2010 uses ranking based on the prevailing correlation coefficient values

represented itself in higher negative correlations) can be seen by a comparison between the heat map shown in Figure 9.1 from April 29, 2010 and that from a few days later which captures the picture of correlations on May 5, 2010 – shown as Figure 9.2 which was the trading session before the Flash Crash.

The information in the caption for Figure 9.2 shows that the positively correlated cells had become even more correlated moving from 1.28 times the typical value for such cells as of April 29 to a reading of 1.44 on May 5. For the negatively correlated assets the movement was from 1.92 times to 2.05 times. Nearly all of the dark blue cells in Figure 9.2 are on the one hand pairings of AUD/JPY against the more defensive, safe haven fixed income assets. On the other hand they are pairing of JPY/USD – the risk off pair – against the ETFs which are typically more associated with increased risk appetite. In general terms there are more dark blue cells on the later date heat map and the dark red cells have become even darker or hotter. The great advantage of depicting the correlations in this format is that it is immediately visible when the tug of war between risk on and risk off is reaching extreme levels.

It is also worth noting that on Figure 9.2, the May 5 heat map, 7% of the cells are registering R values below negative 0.75 whereas on Figure 9.1, the April 29 heat map, only 3% are below this threshold. Also in terms of outliers, on April 29 only three pairs have an R value greater than 0.85 whereas on the eve of the Flash Crash there are 10 pairs registering an R value above this elevated level.

One final comment can be made in the transition over the few trading days between the two dates shown which is in relation to the information regarding the beta values shown in the captions to Figures 9.1 and 9.2. The beta values represent the degree to which the currency pairs are responding to, or sensitive to, changes in the sector values. Increased beta values are pointing to the fact that there is more sensitivity and, in a sense, more volatility present in the relationships. In turn the greater sensitivities can be pointing towards more instability which is creeping into the matrix of correlations with a greater disposition towards disruptive behavior. The beta value for the correlated pairs with more than a 0.5 value for R is twice the historical value in the heat map for May 5 as opposed to 1.3 times for the earlier heat map of April 29 and for the negative values the uptick in beta is even more acute on the eve of the Flash Crash registering a value of almost four times the historically observed average value as opposed to 1.5 times for the April 29 heat map. Yet again there is an indication from the correlations matrix not only that asset markets had become precariously skewed but also that there was a stronger likelihood of disruptive volatility brewing beneath the surface.

Alternative versions of the heat maps can display different rankings of the cells based on different criteria. One variation which is useful is to rank the cells according to the change or delta in the RSQ value from a prior period. In all other respects the calculations are in accordance with the explanation of the techniques provided above (and described in more detail in the Appendix), but the method of ranking is, in this case, based on the ratio of the current RSQ value compared to its value one week prior (this is an adjustable parameter, but one week prior appears to be a useful value). The color displayed in the cells is still the current correlation coefficient or R value but by sorting on another criterion than the R value itself, the manner in which the cells are displayed enables a quick two dimensional comparison over time. The overall temperature dimension of the heat map is still reflected in the intensity of the different colors, but there is an added dimension which is most readily apparent by focusing attention on the outlier values in the new ranking, and in particular by the make-up of the cells in the right hand column.

In the heat map shown in Figure 9.3 from May 5 the right hand column is populated solely with dark blue cells which is actually implicit in the previous discussion and also echoed in the increased deviation from the historical benchmark of the R values below negative 0.5. The preponderance of dark blue cells on the right, in the context of a ranking of the deltas in the RSQ value, is strongly indicative of an impending correction.

We have scratched the surface of the capabilities of this type of methodology and inspired by suggestions from one of the reviewers of the manuscript for this book, it would be very useful to be able to see the various heat map patterns developing over time by means of an animation. I hope to implement this on an interactive platform.

To conclude this chapter it can be observed that, in what I shall refer to as the build-up of the bubble phase (the term "bubble" is used relatively and relates in the case of daily heat maps to near term lopsidedness where the market has become overly exposed to risk on assets), there should be a gradual increase in the intensity of the red values in the right hand column. There will also be evidence of increased negative correlations appearing in the left hand column. In more general terms one would expect to see evidence of increased couplings of the risk on assets and risk off assets as expressed in the caption values.

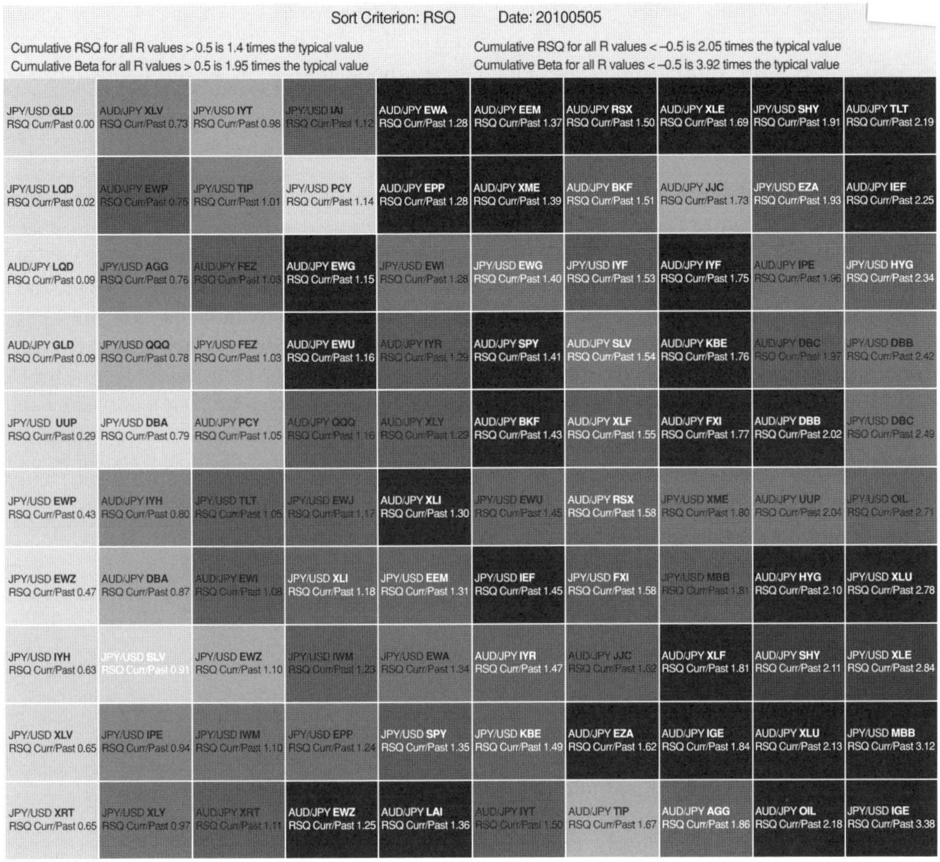

Figure 9.3 FX/ETF heat map for May 5, 2010 uses ranking based on change in RSQ value

At critical points when the market has become too stretched in one direction with respect to the risk on/risk off polarities the heat maps can provide a combination of warning signals. Firstly, the overall temperature of the heat map should have deviated quite significantly from that seen under more typical conditions. Therefore one would expect to see the values in the caption to be registering quite far from the historical benchmark values. To simplify matters, the further that these values have deviated from the more typical values, the more stretched the market has become and the more likelihood that the correction following the bubble build-up phase could be quite severe accompanied by large portfolio drawdowns. It is worth pointing out that the values seen on May 5 are some of the highest seen from using the heat map technology.

The second clue as to how to interpret the displays from a market timing perspective relates to the versions of the heat maps when the ranking criterion is based on the delta of the RSQ – in other words the degree of change for the current reading from a recent reading, and as shown in Figure 9.3. Under this ranking criterion a warning of an increased likelihood that the overall financial market is reaching a critical impasse will be evidenced by more dark blue cells in the right hand column, and in more general terms where nearly all of the intensely colored cells – red and blue – will be concentrated on the right hand side of the heat map with the paler colors – the yellow and green cells – appearing primarily on the left hand side.

ENDNOTES

1. The limiting cases for the coefficient of correlation are –1, which would be perfect negative correlation, and +1, which would be perfect positive correlation. The closer that the actual value is to either of the limiting cases, the stronger the correlation is; so a positive value 0.92 and a negative 0.92 are both very strong correlation, but in the positive case the two variables will be directionally aligned, and in the negative case the directions taken by each variable will be the inverse or in opposite directions.

   Theoretically the limiting case of no correlation would be where the coefficient had a value of zero. In practice it would be highly unlikely to find such a relationship between the returns for two assets, as it would suggest that they move entirely independently of each other. One way of simulating zero correlation is to generate two sets of random numbers and then create a scatter diagram and find the line of best fit. The line should be a very poor fit and the correlation coefficient should be close to zero.
2. The CARBS nations are mentioned in the following article: *"Carbs" Commodity Nations Are A New Asset Group, Citigroup Says*, Bloomberg, November 11, 2011:

   > Commodity-rich nations Canada, Australia, Russia, Brazil and South Africa between them control commodity assets worth nearly $60 trillion and 29 percent of the world's landmass, and represent a distinct asset class, according to an e-mailed note from Citigroup Inc. (C)
   >
   > The nations produce between a quarter and a half of most major commodities, according to the note, citing Kingsmill Bond, an analyst at Citigroup based in Moscow.

   http://www.bloomberg.com/news/2011-11-21/-carbs-commodity-nations-are-a-new-asset-group-citigroup-says.html.
3. The method used in the construction of the heat maps is discussed in the Appendix. The date format is the year followed by the month and then by the day. Using this format it is easier to rank dates in a programming environment.

10

Mainstream Financial Economics Groping Towards a New Paradigm

One of the more severe consequences of a failure to have an appropriate explanatory framework for the booms and busts so evident in economic history and, to use Richard Koo's nomenclature, the current global "balance sheet recession," is a lamentable disregard for the insidious dynamics which have led to a *disappearance of income*. In addition to addressing this malaise of recent economic times it will also be useful to consider some other macroeconomic phenomena which are poorly, if at all, explicable in the mainstream theory of financial economics. This chapter will examine some of these hard to explain and awkward predicaments, and, in the latter section, we can turn to some new initiatives that are being shown by a growing number of macro-economists who are proclaiming that a new paradigm of economic thinking is emerging to supersede the fundamentally flawed orthodoxy which still prevails.

The naïve view expressed by "laissez faire" economics, is that, to simplify matters, but not indefensibly so, the economic system can be best understood using concepts that are essentially similar to those outlined in the textbooks of 19th and 20th century classical economics. This is a world, familiar to anyone who has studied even high school economics, of demand and supply diagrams, markets which tend towards equilibrium, and where individuals, as economic agents, seek to maximize their utility – itself an imprecise concept borrowed from 19th century British philosophers such as Jeremy Bentham and John Stuart Mill. [1] Although the footnotes in the literature of such economists will pay lip service to the fact that the real world is different from their idealized diagrams, there is often a quick and not so subtle sleight of hand by such advocates in which the theoretical entities presupposed in the classical tradition, are deemed to be applicable in the real world. There is still an implicit supposition that the economic and financial market place can be entirely understood by using the demand/supply diagrams from legacy text books.

Simplifying again, for the purposes of this adventurous discussion, there are tacit assumptions, to be taken as givens, that firms supplying to markets are price takers, that they compete with each other vigorously and on a level playing field, and that all consumers have perfect information and access to goods and services and provide an unfettered demand function to which suppliers respond. Furthermore, the disruptive events which we have spent much time considering in this book arise because markets are not allowed to "clear" properly. Within the neoclassical tradition there is a canonical belief that if returns to the various factors of production were frictionless, and if they were allowed to respond according to the simple laws of demand and supply, then the periodic booms and busts would either not arise or the process of clearing them through market mechanisms would be far less disruptive. One strand of this admittedly cursory outline (a more detailed outline will come later) leads to an ivory tower detachment which would claim that, to the extent that governments have hindered the free flow of economic forces, to criticize the neoclassical premises is misguided since we do not live in a world that their conceptual framework is designed to explain. Rather than amending the premises, many "laissez faire" ideologues would prefer to carry on describing a world that should exist and blame policy makers for lacking the vision to see this. [2]

However there are a number of different kinds of asymmetry present in a sophisticated financial economy which would prevent the alleged efficacy of market-based mechanisms envisaged by the neoclassical economists from satisfactorily dealing with bubble and bust dynamics.

A fundamental asymmetry which is awkward for the "frictionless" assumptions of mainstream economic theory is that debt is sticky in a way in which equity is not. [3] It is clearly the case that owners of capital are not exclusively, or perhaps even primarily, engaged in the financing of enterprises and investment projects through the provision of equity or, as it is properly characterized, through risk capital. Equity can and will rise and fall exponentially in a bubble/bust cycle. But many providers of finance are rentiers or creditors – they provide financing via bonds and debt instruments. Generally speaking, other than in cases of debt re-structuring, the claims held by creditors are considered to be immune from downward adjustment. It is not just the case that creditors want to be protected – "saved harmless" – from widespread asset writedowns but also public policy makers find themselves in a compromised position in many cases as a result of the Too Big to Fail "gotcha". However, as will be seen in the next section, the consequences of the "stickiness of debt" and the survival of the full-blown debtor's obligation has created a zombie-like and moribund household sector in many developed economies. Most of those who over-borrowed during the inflation of the real estate bubble, which took place in the lead up to the GFC, are now suffering from not just a decline in their net worth but also in their disposable income.

10.1 DISAPPEARANCE OF INCOME

For most people the biggest hit to their net worth in the wake of the GFC can be attributed to the (phantom) value destruction in real estate. Prices of homes in many (but not all) developed economies have declined substantially since 2007. [4] A large number of owners of homes, that during the early years of the new millennium were registering double digit percentage annual increases in value, are in 2012 much less wealthy than they thought they were in 2006/7. Many owe more on the mortgages of their homes than that property is currently worth – which is a separate topic pursued elsewhere in this book. [5]

The person who borrows money in the form of a mortgage has a fixed liability – from the perspective of the mortgage provider this is the same thing as saying that the bank or mortgage provider sees itself as having a fixed and non-adjusted (post crash) IOU for the principal value. But the homeowner has an asset which may well be worth less, sometimes drastically less, than her liabilities. From a personal balance sheet perspective that person is *upside down* and has to either default or engage in repairing her balance sheet, i.e. through paying down debt and thereby postponing consumption. This will contribute, especially from a macro-economic perspective, to a *disappearance of disposable income*. Defaulting causes an immediate loss of credit worthiness, negative equity ensures a serious drop in the marginal propensity to provide collateral, and the negative impact on "animal spirits" actually suggests that there will most likely be zero or minimal marginal propensity to want new credit. An alternative formulation of this consequence, often more realistic from the perspective of the lender, is that the individual has none or very limited marginal propensity to provide suitable collateral for borrowing even should they wish to take on new debt.

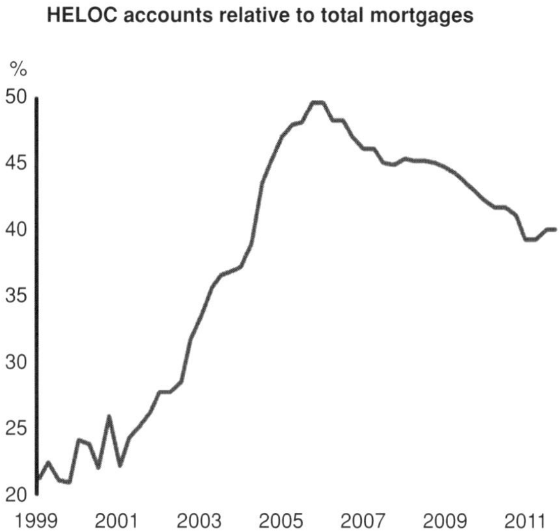

Figure 10.1 Home equity lines of credit accounts relative to total mortgages in US
Source: Nomura Report Slow healing of US household finances April 2012.

A study by Nomura entitled *Slow Healing of US Household Finances*, published in April 2012 [6] addresses the issues raised in the last paragraph as they apply to households in the United States. A good summary of the big picture predicament of many US households is found in the following extract:

> Severe imbalances in the household sector's financial condition have played a unique role in the economy's anemic performance in this business cycle. In particular, households accumulated debt – especially mortgage debt – at a feverish pace to fund investment in residential real estate. The resulting speculative real estate binge lifted housing prices to unsustainable levels that far exceeded the "fair value" of the stream of the "services" associated with housing. The inevitable home price "correction" that ensued left the household sector with crippling debt. By the peak of the previous business cycle (Q4 2007) the aggregate value of mortgage debt exceeded the equity value of owner-occupied real estate. Despite a net reduction in mortgage debt, declining housing prices have widened that gap further and at the end of 2011, mortgage debt exceeded housing net equity by $3.7 trillion.

Graphically the situation experienced by many US households since the turn of the millennium is illustrated in Figure 10.1. The term HELOC is an acronym for home-equity lines of credit and is effectively a second charge against a property which was used during the bubble years as a way of funding a lifestyle which was in excess of one's current income. As the Nomura report observed: [7]

> During the housing boom, households increasingly tapped the accumulated equity in their real estate holdings by taking on home-equity lines of credit. When refinancing existing loans, households also increasingly extracted equity from their appreciating real estate holdings. But since the housing bubble has burst, that pattern has changed markedly. Instead of withdrawing equity by increasing the size of the mortgage when homeowners refinanced, many homeowners have been compelled to inject equity ("mortgage equity injections") when they have refinanced in a housing market characterized by falling home values.

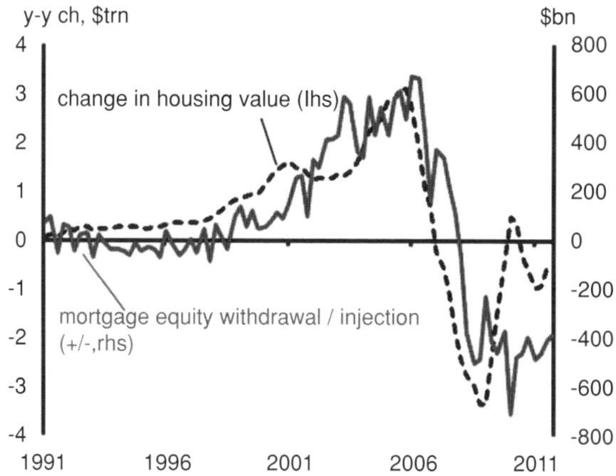

Figure 10.2 Changes in housing wealth and mortgage equity withdrawal/injections in US
Source: Nomura Report Slow healing of US household finances April 2012.

From its peak during 2005 when US households had tapped into their HELOCs to the extent that these second charges totaled in aggregate about 50% of the outstanding first mortgages – surely an indication that a lot of this household "wealth" was ephemeral – the retirement or pay-down of the HELOCs had brought this down to a level of about 40% at the end of 2011.

Figure 10.2 shows that Mortgage Equity Withdrawal (MEW), which is essentially what is reflected in Figure 10.1, has gone into reverse since the peak of the housing bubble in 2006. The zero line in Figure 10.2 indicates whether households were deciding to cash in on the "wealth effect" from increased valuations of their homes. At the peak during 2006 US households in aggregate, based on the increased value of their homes (shown on the left hand vertical scale), had withdrawn almost $800bn of "equity" from their real estate holdings to finance their own "booms," and in turn further inflating the macro-economic bubble that many central bankers and politicians mistakenly perceived as "real prosperity". Rubbing salt into the wound was the hubris that accompanied the era of the "Great Moderation". Boom and bust, it was often contended, had been eradicated by the pursuit of inspired monetary policies and by the proliferation of instruments enabling precision financial engineering.

Interestingly after the bubble burst and home-owners were required to pay down their HELOC's, or effectively inject mortgage equity, the correction at the trough in 2011 saw the entire $800bn having to be returned. There is not much better evidence that the process of wealth destruction so often lamented by economic commentators was actually no more than the creation of phantom wealth during the bubble and its subsequent collapse and restoration to normal as the bust took hold.

The conclusion to the Nomura report, suggesting that the process of balance sheet repair has a long way to go is as follows: [8]

> Consequently, more adjustment will be necessary but a dysfunctional foreclosure process will likely continue to delay aggregate debt reduction and thereby remain a restraint on spending for several more years. The speed and extent of further balance sheet repair – ultimately reflected in rising net worth – will depend on the pace of recovery in real estate values. We expect that price recovery to evolve only slowly so that debt reduction will remain the primary and "slow road" to balance sheet repair and one that will likely continue to restrain the growth in spending.

In addition to the reduction in the wealth effect from reduced valuations (sometimes drastically reduced) of their homes there will be many households that will also have suffered from the severe slumps or drawdowns in their holdings of equities. These holdings can come in two varieties through either direct ownership of securities – which as was seen in Chapter 3 has been on a downward trajectory especially since 2000 – or through indirect ownership via participation in collective investment vehicles such as mutual funds, and, less obviously, through being part of a pension scheme.

For an individual who has purchased equities on margin (either directly or through a collective scheme) he or she is also "committed" to a rigid liability but with assets which now have a lower and uncertain future value. If the asset owner has been subject to a margin call they are then faced with the classic liquidity trap which is one of needing to raise cash in illiquid markets where their efforts to "stop the rot" will only contribute to further markdowns in the assets which they are trying to turn into cash – the deflationary negative feedback loop. This loop echoes the symmetry perfectly, from a risk capital perspective, between asset bubbles amplified and inflated in a positive feedback loop on the way up, and the depressing and deflationary dynamics which characterize the process of restoring equity to a balance sheet. This process will, of course, be magnified to the extent that the purchase of the assets (on margin) was the result of using financial leverage.

Needless to say realized losses and the sale of other collateral will have a similar negative wealth affect of diminishing the animal spirits leading to a postponement of consumption, which will itself, via a multiplier effect, contribute indirectly to a disappearance of disposable income at the micro and macro level. One further consequence of having to liquidate some assets is the replacement of dividend paying securities with cash which in essence is a zero coupon perpetual security – *hence further disappearance of income.*

The third and probably the least obvious way in which there is asymmetry for the equity or risk capital participants in the aftermath of a crash comes about as a result of the exposure of individuals to the increasing poverty of their pension funds. Traditionally pension fund managers have seen equity as an asset class to which they should have substantial exposure. Since their obligations to pay out to the pensioners (their liabilities) are long lived, the *buy and hold* mantra which has prevailed in investment management for many decades has resulted in large exposure to equities. The funds that have been holding equities for almost any 10-year horizon since the late 1990s have sustained capital losses; some have seen the dividend income diminish especially following the 2001/2 recession and particularly following the 2007/8 crash. For those pension funds which had to sell equities during the last few years and crystallize a capital loss, the returns available via a fund to the future pensioner, i.e. the value of the pension pot from which an annuity has to be purchased will have diminished. This alone will lead to a protracted disappearance of income to pensioners as their annuities are declining.

While addressing annuities there are two further issues to address. One is demographic which is that increasing numbers of "boomers" are now reaching pension age and the fact that life expectancy is increasing. As a result of extremely accommodative monetary policy the yield on government bonds and short-term money market rates have dropped to levels which mean that the ability of pension fund managers to augment the losses on the equity part of their portfolios with coupon income has also suffered in an asymmetric fashion. This is yet a further illustration of the disappearance of income – at the first order level in the lower coupon income being provided by newly issued bonds. At the second level the life insurance companies that typically convert a diminished pension pot into an annuity are also unable to provide generous future cash flows. It has been estimated, for example, that since 2007 the amount that a 65-year-old man in the UK (although very similar reasoning would apply in much of the developed world) could expect to receive via an annuity from a £100k pension pot has fallen from approximately £7k per annum to around £5k per annum.

It is also worth pointing out that the purchase of an annuity is a one off event, and for those who have had to face that decision in the post-crash period the enduring effects of much reduced annuities will influence their future purchasing power for the rest of their lifetimes. It was also noted that loss of dividend income and the need to repair personal balance sheets through paying down debt will have the result of enforcing savings and postponing current consumption, Moreover, reduced coupon income from recently issued government and corporate bonds directly impacts on annuities, and is yet another contributing factor to an overall disappearance of discretionary income for a very wide cross-section of the populations of most developed economies. So the disappearance/diminution of income from the deployment of capital by the equity owning sector of the economy is multi-faceted.

One further large component to the macro condition of diminishing income arises from diminishing returns for the provision of labor. To cite just one relevant statistic in this regard, according to the Bureau of Labor Statistics in the US, approximately 15% of the US labor force is either unemployed or under-employed – this can be seen in each month's employment reports as the U6 statistic – and therefore unable to derive any or an adequate income from employment. [9]

To return to our central theme, one of the largest and most relevant asymmetries which is not properly addressed by conventional macro finance/economics is that between debt and equity. There are two broad disadvantageous consequences which follow from those participating via providing finance through equity or risk capital. One is that the capital losses sustained in the aftermath of a crash will be matched in a more or less symmetrically commensurate fashion with the capital appreciation during the bubble phase. In the current period this is especially true in the case of those who participated in the bubble through purchases of real estate (which of course is a much larger constituency than those who participated via direct purchases of equities). However, as the discussion of pension funds highlighted the indirect effect felt by those with relatively modest pension pots will be experiencing the disappearance of income via reduced annuities for a long time to come.

The next focus should be on the manner in which the credit providers are incommensurately protected from the real downside during the bursting of the bubble. The providers of credit to both the private and public sectors – which includes the commercial banks and private owners of capital – will not have seen a reduction in their asset values. To a great extent the existence of Too Big to Fail (TBTF) institutions and the fact that the write downs of asset values on the balance sheets of such institutions have been transferred to, or underwritten by the public sector, has ensured that the returns to the debt capital providing constituencies still have the same principal value claims against the debtors as they had before the bust.

Surely it is necessary to address the question of fairness regarding the fact that providers of debt financing have not, with few exceptions, had to suffer from write downs or haircuts, especially if they are of the TBTF variety. It could well be claimed that since those holding debt instruments had no participation in the upside of asset revaluations during the bubble phase, it is entirely consistent in terms of the risk/reward trade off, that they should not be penalized on the way down either. The most telling criticism of this assertion is that it fails to take into account the external costs that are imposed on the rest of society from the fact that the lending was reckless and irresponsible.

To point to such externalities and even use a term such as "irresponsible" is likely to invite an acrimonious rejoinder not only from rent seeking debt holders but also from mainstream economic theorists.

Fortunately there is a growing constituency that is debunking the revisionist mythology that parts of the private banking sector stood above the GFC and did not impose any negative externalities on the economy at large. The revisionists, led by Jamie Dimon at J.P. Morgan, as well as the CEOs from Wells Fargo and Goldman Sachs, would like to maintain that when the TARP program was unveiled in the US they were reluctant recipients of taxpayer funds and had to receive them as Treasury Secretary Paulson insisted that they should. They have also made the claim that they have never been the recipients of public subsidies and would have survived the financial crisis simply based on their own fortress balance sheets. This last assertion, for example, was made by Jamie Dimon in testimony he gave to two Congressional committees in the spring of 2012. [10]

On the morning of his testimony to the House Financial Services Committee on June 19, 2012 [11] the editors of Bloomberg.com took the unusual step of publishing an open statement which had the title *Dear Mr. Dimon, Is Your Bank Getting Corporate Welfare?* [12]

The unusually frank article contained suggestions that JP Morgan, along with other banks, has in fact been the recipient of taxpayer funded corporate welfare and the article is worth quoting at some length:

> JPMorgan receives a government subsidy worth about $14 billion a year, according to research published by the International Monetary Fund and our own analysis of bank balance sheets. The money helps the bank pay big salaries and bonuses. More important, it distorts markets, fueling crises such as the recent subprime-lending disaster and the sovereign-debt debacle that is now threatening to destroy the euro and sink the global economy.
>
> With each new banking crisis, the value of the implicit subsidy grows. In a recent paper, two economists – Kenichi Ueda of the IMF and Beatrice Weder Di Mauro of the University of Mainz – estimated that as of 2009 the expectation of government support was shaving about 0.8 percentage point off large banks' borrowing costs. That's up from 0.6 percentage point in 2007, before the financial crisis prompted a global round of bank bailouts.
>
> To estimate the dollar value of the subsidy in the U.S., we multiplied it by the debt and deposits of 18 of the country's largest banks, including JPMorgan, Bank of America Corp. and Citigroup Inc. The result: about $76 billion a year. The number is roughly equivalent to the banks' total profits over the past 12 months, or more than the federal government spends every year on education.
>
> JPMorgan's share of the subsidy is $14 billion a year, or about 77 percent of its net income for the past four quarters. In other words, U.S. taxpayers helped foot the bill for the multibillion-dollar trading loss that is the focus of today's hearing. They've also provided more direct support: Dimon noted in a recent conference call that the Home Affordable Refinancing Program, which allows banks to generate income by modifying government-guaranteed mortgages, made a significant contribution to JPMorgan's earnings in the first three months of 2012.

Needless to say there was no acknowledgment from Dimon at the testimony or subsequently that the Bloomberg editors' suggestion that via corporate welfare there was an imposition of a direct burden, or external cost, on the public balance sheet by the private banking system in the US which they were even able to quantify by reference to the academic research. As the article continued the Bloomberg editors pointed to the market distortions that will arise when public subsidies are provided and which, to return to the central theme of this chapter, undermine the foundation stones of those that would describe financial capitalism, especially as it is found in the US as the embodiment of all that is admirable within a more or less *laissez faire* environment.

> Like all subsidies, the taxpayer largesse distorts supply. If the government supports corn farmers, you get too much corn. If the government subsidizes banks, you get too much credit. As of March, households, companies and government in the U.S. had amassed debts of $38.6 trillion, or 2.5 times the country's gross domestic product. That's up from 1.3 times in 1980. The picture is similar in the euro area, where debt outstanding is 1.8 times GDP, double the level of 1995.
>
> The oversupply of credit – also supported in the U.S. by government-backed lenders Fannie Mae and Freddie Mac, and by tax breaks on mortgage interest – encourages risky behavior. People buy houses they can't afford, companies borrow too much for acquisitions, and banks employ excessive leverage to boost the returns they can offer their shareholders. The result is a bloated finance industry: As of 2011, the sector accounted for 8.3 percent of the US economy, compared with 4.9 percent in 1980.

The concluding section of the Bloomberg editors' intervention is also worth quoting in full as it contains prescriptive suggestions as well as referencing the huge lobbying pressures that the private banking sector exerts in Washington and which are designed to preserve the status quo in the face of regulatory initiatives which would limit the riskier sides of investment banking and remove the bailout burdens to public balance sheets.

> The solution: Minimize the subsidy. Require banks' shareholders to put up enough capital to make bailouts highly unlikely (we advocate 20 percent of assets). Allow some creditors to take losses when a bank gets into trouble, so they won't assume they're safe (an approach regulators in the U.S. and Europe are considering). Cut off subsidies to traders, such as the folks in London who lost billions for JPMorgan, by forbidding speculative trading activity at banks (the goal of the Volcker rule in the US and financial ring-fencing in the UK).
>
> Why hasn't this been done? One partial explanation can be found in the amount of money banks put into election campaigns and into lobbying, which has recently included efforts to water down the Dodd-Frank financial-reform legislation. According to the nonprofit Center for Responsive Politics, the broad financial industry – a category that includes real estate companies and insurers – has spent $285 million on political giving in the 2012 election cycle. That's much more than any other industry spends.
>
> Lawmakers and regulators need to recognize just how costly business as usual will be. When Dimon pushes back against capital requirements or the Volcker rule, it's worth remembering that he's pushing for a form of corporate welfare that, left unchecked, *could lead to a crisis too big for the government to contain.* (author's italics)

The final paragraph of this all encompassing critique of the state of play within the US banking sector – perhaps more shocking since it is four years on from the GFC – is perhaps the most telling. Most troubling perhaps is the suggestion that the enormous efforts mounted by the banks to try to subvert the demand for greater capital and the spirit of the Volcker rule [13] – which would essentially prohibit proprietary trading by banks which have an implicit government guarantee – *could lead to a crisis too big for the government to contain.*

One of the other radical proposals that is contained in this provocative Bloomberg piece and which resonates with some earlier discussion in this book is the proposal that would see "some creditors ... taking ... losses when a bank gets into trouble, so they won't assume they're safe." This goes right to the heart of the asymmetrical manner in which equity holders and debt holders are presently treated, and which underlies the classic statement of moral hazard by Walter Bagehot in the 19th century but which is as applicable today as it has always been with regard to financial risk taking. [14]

Some further thoughts on the cultural and political implications of the types of reform being advocated by the Bloomberg editors will be elaborated upon in the concluding chapter.

10.2 VENDOR FINANCING

The reciprocal nature of vendor financing is another of those feedback loops which is not adequately addressed by mainstream macro-economic thinking. Many mainstream economists have pronounced that one of the dynamos for the aggrandizement of the bubble in US real estate (and that seen in the UK, Ireland, and Spain amongst others) during the first few years of the new millennium was the mis-pricing of credit. According to this criticism the providers of such credit – primarily those exporters with trade surplus accounts with the US – were acting irrationally and setting the global financial system up for the subsequent bust as asset inflation based on increasing leverage turned into a deflationary rout of deleveraging. However such critics appear to have overlooked the subtleties of the feedback loop which underlies vendor financing and mercantilist *realpolitik* – and the symbiotic dependencies between sovereign creditors and debtors.

10.3 GLOBAL IMBALANCES AND THE MARTIN WOLF THESIS

An examination of the consequences of vendor financing will help to explain what appears paradoxical to many mainstream economists and commentators, and which can best be expressed in the form of the following question. Why has the US government been able to finance increasing deficits so readily with declining yields with background conditions of what is widely perceived to have been fiscal and monetary policy mis-management? A supplementary question might well be added which is: How was this achieved with the further unattractive feature to this financing, suggesting it should have been an even harder "sell," in that it was accompanied by a benign neglect by the Federal Reserve, despite their protestations to the contrary, for the external value of the US dollar?

To address these questions it is vital to consider the magnitude and pivotal role of the vendor financing schemes which have tacitly been followed by capital surplus countries during the last decade. The rationale behind these schemes becomes more compelling and intelligible in light of the massive imbalances in the balance of payments accounts for surplus and deficit nations. Vendor financing has operated especially with respect to the USA by China and OPEC, and interestingly in a parallel, with regard to its neighbors within the peripheral states of the Eurozone, by Germany. [15]

The bulleted points below, which address the questions posed above, summarize arguments contained in Martin Wolf's excellent book entitled *Fixing Global Finance* [16] which was first published in 2007 and before the onset of the full blown GFC. Wolf's account provides key insights into the ramifications of vendor financing:

- The Asian countries and oil exporters were unwilling to counteract persistent export strength and surpluses with rising exchange rates.
- Rather exchange rates were "managed" and effectively pegged to the US dollar.

- The result was the continuing accumulation of surpluses and US dollar reserves.
- Surplus economies had little choice but to recycle these surpluses back to the US.
- One method for correcting such persistent global imbalances would have resulted if the US had undertaken monetary policy leading to a domestic recession.
- Instead the US financial sector saw an opportunity to re-purpose the funds being lent at abnormally low interest rates by the surplus nations to create an extended boom, which inevitably led to the real estate bubble.
- Wolf suggests that, since orthodox lending activities were unable to fully tap the enormous amounts of under-priced credit made available to the US, Wall Street created *unorthodox* ones – sub-prime mortgages, CDOs e.t.c.
- Aided by light touch regulations and a boom in financial engineering, the US financial sector took full advantage and had no problem in absorbing the savings from emerging markets and oil exporters.
- To that extent, it could be contended, the US was an innocent victim of a global savings glut.

To return to the mistaken notion that the mis-pricing of credit was an act of irrationality by the lenders – which is the only consistent type of explanation that can be provided by someone with a more orthodox approach to macro-financial economics – misses the point that the lenders had ulterior motives in their cost/benefit calculations. Those motives, of course, had unintended consequences from a macro perspective, but just as the true external costs are rarely if ever charged properly to those operating at the micro level, i.e. individual firms and governments, so the logic of the feedback in vendor financing became one where the payoff to be earned by being a provider of cheap financing to facilitate the voracious appetites of consumers in the deficit countries was very rewarding right up until the point where it wasn't. The myopia of localized self-interest, coupled with willing ignorance or blindness to the unintended consequences and macro-financial externalities, is one of the root causes of the bubble/bust syndrome which, pessimistically perhaps, seem to be endemic to macro-economic behavior.

The core ideas in Wolf's book have also been echoed in the writings of Nouriel Roubini who also distinguished himself as being one of very few academic economists who anticipated the magnitude and inevitability of the GFC. Pursuing similar themes to those outlined above by Wolf, Roubini argued, in harmony with one of Wolf's key ideas – the rigidity of exchange rates and the managing of these by surplus nations – that there was no alternative to the US becoming the destination for huge amounts of overseas capital. The scale of reserve accumulation within the surplus nations shows quite clearly that these countries refused to adopt the freely floating exchange rates which would have restrained and inhibited the development of the severe global trade and capital account imbalances which are so much a feature of the contemporary world economy. Rather than allowing exchange rates to move freely and provide a more stabilizing force with respect to the build-up of imbalances, the principal surplus nations – exemplified by China – chose to keep their exchange rates pegged to the US dollar at rates which were far below what would be expected in the absence of a controlled exchange rate regime. In a similar fashion to the reasoning developed in Wolf's fine book, Roubini, in essence, was making the similar and logically consistent point that if a substantial constituency in the world economy is generating huge current account surpluses, other nations – the deficit countries – have to be running substantial offsetting deficits.

A further refinement to the argument is that the accumulation of large quantities of net foreign liabilities is easiest for countries able to borrow freely in their own currencies. Such an advantage would apply most readily to the US, UK, Australia, and New Zealand, and the consequence of which is the fact that each of these nations have had chronic balance of payments deficits financed by exports from their capital accounts in the form of financial assets (i.e. government bonds) and financial services. In slightly different terminology, the conclusion reached is that through the logic of mercantilist self-interest, vendor financing, and the propensity to engender asset bubbles, the US inevitably had to emerge as the world's chief deficit country. As consumer of last resort the US government and household sector became the world's "borrower of last resort." This way of stating matters is not quite the same description as seeing the US economy and financial system as the *innocent victim* of a global savings glut, and is actually preferable for reasons discussed directly below, but, in highlighting the symbiotic motivations and dependencies of the relevant parties, it comes close enough.

Rather than looking for heroes and villains, which is why the term "innocent victim" is not really appropriate, the explanatory power of the argument is to be found in the realization that different entities and economic agents acting in an entirely cogent and purposeful manner from the limited confines of their short-term self-interest, will produce adverse consequences in the fullness of time, often with extraordinarily high external costs. To the extent that economic agents are either unable to quantify the magnitude of these costs, or wish to remain willfully ignorant of them, bubbles will inevitably be followed by busts. This may not entirely capture the central theme of Hyman Minsky's seminal contributions to financial economics, but it does emphasize that in our anxiety to avoid a debt/deflation spiral by re-activating the animal spirits in order to have flourishing enterprises and reduction of idle capacity, paradoxically we will be sowing the seeds for the next bubble and its eventual collapse.

What is intellectually appealing about the Wolf/Roubini thesis is that it removes the moralizing which is so often found, for example, in discussions of Sino-American economic and political relations. This is especially the case in the often acrimonious nature of the dialogue regarding the value of the renminbi. Once one recognizes the inter-dependence of surplus and deficit nations and the nature of the debtor and creditor entanglement, aptly expressed in the aphorism that it always takes two to tango, there could be a greater understanding of the symbiotic dynamics of the special relationship between China and the US. One consequence of this appreciation would be a realization that the price that the US might have to pay for an alleged boost to US manufactured goods in overseas markets from a more "fairly" priced exchange rate with the renminbi (RMB), is that its capital exports, i.e. US Treasury bonds, will be less in demand as the Chinese trade surplus shrinks and that if US investors have to pick up the slack in demand for domestic debt issuance there could be a resurrection of the bond vigilantes alluded to in an earlier chapter.

Over the long haul as the much hoped for expansion in consumer demand within surplus countries materializes, what might turn out to be a benefit to US exporters of manufactured goods, could well result in higher yields that will need to be offered to attract domestic investors for US public debt. This re-alignment should it come about – and one senses that in the longer term it must –will produce yet more unstable dynamics as the re-pricing of US public sector obligations, for example, will not be easily accomplished given the high level of both private and public sector debt.

In those countries which have been persistently high deficit nations – both with respect to their international trade as well as their propensity to run large public deficits (in fact following the logic from above they are inextricably inter-related) – the financing of deficits will become far more problematic, should the chronic surpluses of China and Germany, for example, begin to ease owing to their higher domestic consumption in the future. Some would argue that the latter would be a nice problem to have as it would impose much more discipline on the debtor nations if their access to global capital flows required them to pay a higher rate of return to savers. But it remains to be seen just how fragile, and accident prone, the re-balancing of the global economy, as envisaged by Martin Wolf, might be.

10.4 PROJECT EVALUATION AND THE COST OF CAPITAL

A further anomaly that poses difficulties for the explanatory framework of mainstream financial economics relates to an inability, under the orthodox theoretical framework, to properly account for the role of the speculative element in project and investment evaluation by entrepreneurs. In addition this needs to be supplemented by a proper recognition of how vital is their determination of where one is in the boom/bust cycle, and how this will inform their judgments regarding a true and properly grounded appraisal of the cost of capital. Conventional macroeconomic tools fail to provide for an adequate understanding of the real world concerns and aspirations of entrepreneurs facing an appraisal of investment prospects. Any account of this critical feature of economic life will be found wanting if it is provided by financial economists who are not equipped with a conceptual repertoire that incorporates a deep understanding of entrepreneurs' estimations as to the outlook for future speculative sentiment and their access to creative forms of credit financing. These are just two of the insights from Hyman Minsky and others that should by now have been incorporated into mainstream financial economics.

Using a standard discounted cash flow model for determining the feasibility of a new investment under the rational expectations model of mainstream economics, there is a paradox relating to the cost of capital or discount rate and the attractiveness of the investment. The lower the cost of capital, or the lower the discount rate to apply to the future cash flows, the less onerous will be the required cash flows to sustain the project or investment. The length of the payback period and ultimately the profitability of the investment should be that much more attractive.

However owing to the paradoxical nature of the financial economy (which is really only explained in economic theory by Hyman Minsky or, enigmatically, by the Keynesian notion of the "animal spirits") the reason why the discount rate or cost of capital is so low is because investors are risk averse and central bankers are doing their utmost to spark a new speculative phase which will drive the expectations of future asset appreciation.

In fact the last sentence raises very succinctly the problem with the discounted cash flow modeling which is that it fails to take into account the expectation of the investor as to the possibility of the resale value of the underlying asset rising substantially, i.e. the possibility of capital gains and the pure speculative element – not just the cash flows from the use of the asset.

The payback period can be considered as the safety interval – it represents the most cautious scenario by an investor that is uncertain whether to add to long-term inventory of assets. In cash flow projections – using a low discount rate – the presumption is that the payback period must reduce if the projections remain constant but (at least) three elements could undermine this notion that the attractiveness of a reduced payback period should make an investment more compelling:

1. The cash flow projections must be scaled down to reflect the fact that there is an inverse relationship between cost of capital and risk appetite (in a leveraged economy which is being "nursed" by an accommodative central bank).

2. The lack of asset price speculation and expectation that the capital value of the project will be increasing acts as a disincentive to impatient and short-term oriented managements that are bonus focused and lack the ability to financialize or securitize the project.
3. The counter-party risk, i.e. with respect to the cooperating "partners" in the development of the project (investment), will most likely be perceived as having increased. The "confidence" in the reliability of others to perform in accordance with stated obligations has diminished. If one extends this notion to the expectation that final demand will be as forecasted this ties back to point #1.

Expressed in very simple terms the third of the bulleted points comes down to the difference between return of capital versus return on capital, and to the old joke that one should not so much be concerned with the return on capital as with the return of capital.

Anticipating some of the discussion that will come later in the book, the payback period can be considered as a fractal for inter-temporal commitments in that it operates in multiple time frames ranging from the long run for a project evaluation, in the case just seen, to the very short run as in the case of an overnight money market transaction. The common thread which explains this multiple time frame view has to do with different liquidity horizons at each time frame and expectations as to asset enhancements or depreciations depending on where one is within a bubble/bust cycle. What can be paradoxical and inexplicable from a neoclassical perspective can, hopefully, become far more susceptible to a robust explanation within the framework which has been developing during the last few chapters.

From this perspective it is precisely the uncertainty as to current and future collateral values which will inhibit or enhance inter-temporal commitments – almost irrespective of the cost of capital and surface viability of such commitments. A more generalized (and philosophical) concept of the *financing of an interval* will be picked up again as the main thread of Chapter 15.

10.5 TOWARDS A NEW PARADIGM IN ECONOMIC THINKING

At this point it would be useful, from a theoretical and conceptual vantage point, to continue further with a critique of orthodox theory in finance and economics and to draw attention to the emergence of a new paradigm in economic thinking. This new paradigm – that term is particularly associated with Thomas Kuhn's *Structure of Scientific Revolutions* [17] – and the term revolution do not appear to be exaggerated in the context of the radical new thinking which is taking shape in relation to macro-economics and which will be sketched in the remainder of this chapter.

To begin it will be helpful to return briefly to the epistemic issue which pivots on the difference in mindset of those who would consider it appropriate to say that financial market prices from day to day have no "memory," and those who would claim that in so doing one is committing a cognitive category mistake in much the same way as it would be nonsensical to make the statement "Mondays are green." [18]

How could we know that price development does not exhibit "memory"? Prices do not develop "out there" in an objective world where we are merely bystanders sampling prices at various intervals and taking measurements to plot on a graph. The notion of price as a trajectory is a useful heuristic but there is a further risk in sliding into another category mistake if we think that such a trajectory literally exists. By exploring, firstly, the nature of such category mistakes and conceptual (metaphorical) fallacies it will become more readily apparent where the fundamental flaws in orthodox financial economics are, and how that discipline needs to be thoroughly overhauled.

While quantum physicists have given up on the notion that we can make truly objective observations, many trained in economics and finance seem not to have moved on from this fallacy. Market prices result from the interaction of tiers of human participants who are constantly creating and updating a view of the relative values of different kinds of financial instruments. The instruments will reflect views regarding the underlying values, merits, and risks of certain assets but once again the determination of such valuations is the result of human judgments. It is not as if there are unambiguous facts which all market participants are observing. Indeed the essence of a market is that without there being a difference of opinion or disagreement about what the "facts" *show* there would be no reason for an ongoing dialogue, conducted through formalized market interactions, to determine the appropriate pricing for assets. If the facts were uncontroversial, judgment free, the adversarial dynamics and fractiousness which are pre-conditions for a normal functioning and liquid market would be absent.

It goes much deeper than this however. The nature of markets is that they are complex forms of organized behavior where differences of opinions, of conflicting value judgments, have to be interpreted within the context of larger narratives relating to macro-economic factors. It is useful to consider the benefit of thinking about markets as similar to a competitive and adversarial game or even a narrative of conflict. From an epistemological perspective, the different ways in which the "facts" can be interpreted and how market participants can "internalize" different narratives is perfectly exemplified by the easy way in which we understand the difference between those of a bullish outlook versus those of a bearish persuasion.

The following thought experiment will hopefully be instrumental in illustrating the interdependency of reporting an observation and, at the same time, its *sine qua non* – an understanding of the proper context to that observation. In essence what I want to spell out in the thought experiment is that perception is not a passive process of observing something which is "out there" but is much more of an active process which is *informed* by the appropriate framework for *making sense* of what is being perceived. The actual terminology of "making sense" conveys the notion through the operative word *making,* that perception is an *act* – it is a process of framing *raw sensory data* in terms of a narrative and the relevant spatial, temporal, and semantic coordinates. Only by imposing terms of reference and a cognitive framework are we able to make meaningful *perceptual judgments.* [19]

Suppose you are a visitor from another planet and have been told about the game of chess. Due to different DNA and a different biochemistry, however, your sensory apparatus only allows you to see one square on the chess board. Over the course of the game any, or all, of the pieces might arrive on the single square which you can see.

You might see any one of the chess pieces arrive on the single square – a Knight or a Bishop; a Rook or a Queen or a Pawn – but you would never know where it had come from nor where it had gone to when it disappeared. Due to the difference in your sensory perspective you would never get enough information to envision the entire board or have any understanding of the *concept of the game.*

Instead of imagining an alien in the above one can easily substitute the idea of an observer who is unable to frame the coordinates of any particular value in a time series as part of a rich interplay between participants in the game of financial markets. Not much of a stretch is required to see that this is the epistemic standpoint of the disengaged or unentangled observer of a series of random, independent moves which possess no "memories" of what has come before and what could be expected in the future. Because this disengaged observer has no knowledge of the rules of the game of chess and no comprehension of expectations – *from the point of view of intentionality rather than probability* – they are essentially clueless as to the purpose, value, and meaning of their observations. They are unentangled. Unentangled here is used in contradistinction to entangled in the sense that various philosophers, such as Hilary Putnam, and quantum scientists have used it in relation to epistemology, the theory of knowledge. According to this view our knowledge of scientific "facts" relies fundamentally on epistemic *value* judgments; therefore, facts, theoretical frameworks, and value judgments are inherently *entangled*. [20]

To continue with the thought experiment, suppose that the King arrives in the square which the unentangled observer is monitoring and then there is an indefinitely long interval before anything else happens. Should the observer keep monitoring those coordinates in order to register any new activity or has the game finished due to a checkmate? Would the unentangled observer even have any comprehension of what it would mean to be in checkmate or that the game (?) is now over?

Let us slightly rearrange the thought experiment. A node within a network – to the extent that it is at all meaningful to say this – would be the passive recipient of all kinds of messages/ inputs – and these would then be relayed on to other nodes. Passage through the particular node could be recorded and a time series of the activity of all the nodes in the network could be registered in some kind of notation which would show the pattern of the "development" of inputs and outputs within the network. But how would one display this time series without knowing what the purpose of the network is? Does it make any sense to say that the series of changes in state of network are either random or exhibit memory? From which perspective, that of the network or that of the observer, would it even be intelligible to ask such a question? What would be the appropriate values to use for our visual representation?

What has just been described could actually be likened to the activity of a CPU and RAM module in a computer. While a computer device is executing instructions in software code there are a staggeringly large number of electrical pulses taking place within the hardware of the computing device which enables it to perform a task such as calculating the value of pi to thousands of decimal places or rendering a complex architectural diagram on a screen. There is no problem, from a metaphorical perspective, to describe the behavior of the system, as observed by a human being, as exhibiting intelligence, but it would be a fairly radical claim to maintain that the machine is actually thinking and literally recalling information from its memory. [21] The language used to describe the behavior of a computing device is *anthropomorphic* – it needs to be understood, as in much of epistemology, as ultimately metaphorical. The converse of anthropomorphism, but with grave conceptual difficulties, is the fallacy of econophysics which seeks to depersonalize all financial behavior and consider it as susceptible to explanation within a theoretical framework similar to that used in the natural sciences. Notwithstanding the fact that contemporary physicists are no longer infatuated with an obsession for *raw facts* and closed physical systems, the mania for such *elusive objectivity* surely reaches some kind of absurdity when claiming that financial time series data exhibits no memory, and is best understood as a random walk.

One could even be agnostic on the merits of orthodox macro-economic theory, which we shall examine shortly, and yet still have serious disputes with the orthodoxy in mainstream finance. This orthodoxy advocates the use of probabilistic reasoning based upon, in the opinions of the dissenters, the mis-application of statistical methods which assume that the outcome of human interactions in the financial realm are susceptible to analysis using a normal distribution. It goes even deeper than that and, even though this may not always be openly articulated, the real basis of dissent from distinguished commentators such as George Soros and many others, is best understood as committing what elsewhere [22] I have referenced as the econophysics fallacy.

Let me try briefly to outline the econophysics fallacy as it is closely related to themes which I discussed in a previous book, *Long/Short Market Dynamics* and which is referenced in endnote 22. The principal motivation of advocates of econophysics is the desire to see economic behavior as being *driven by* or, better still, *generated by* fundamental dynamic forces which are the outcome of human agents acting together. Although it is admitted by practitioners of econophysics that these interactions are highly complex, they are still founded upon what might be described as *algorithmically deterministic* behavior. Under this guise human economic agents are regarded as rational information and utility processors and possess some kind of probabilistic calculus which governs all of their choices and modes of economic behavior. Steve Keen, one of the foremost critics of mainstream financial economics, in lecture notes at his website [23] has some very pertinent observations and amusing insights from computational theory as to how misguided and ultimately ludicrous such a model is.

Keen shows how long it would take to complete a shopping trip for an individual confronted with choices in which they have to make a rational decision and undertake a utility maximization exercise based on exploring a multi dimensional space of utility comparisons. To jump ahead slightly Keen suggests if one is entirely consistent in applying a completely rational approach to utility maximization for the weekly shopping excursion, such a chore could take more than three and a half years to complete!

For a relatively small problem involving a choice between just two or three different products which could be combined into a shopping basket the set of mental (rational) computations required is just about feasible to comprehend and compute. However once one examines the possibility of going to a supermarket where, for the sake of the exercise, there are 50 possible products that one could purchase, there is an exponential explosion to the number of calculations that would need to be computed. As Keen suggests, according to the completeness requirement of revealed preference theory which is part of the conceptual baggage of neoclassical economics and part of the econophysics fallacy, one would need to examine all of the possible permutations for such a shopping expedition. Assuming that one assigned the value 0 or 1 to whether or not one was going to purchase each item, there would be 2^{50} possible combinations to consider which is equivalent to 10 million billion combinations.

Keen has more fun with this model by considering a "neo-classically rational" computer that could examine all of the separate permutations at the rate of one in every 10^{-7} seconds. (Under such an assumption it would be possible to do 10 million calculations in each and every second.) For a 50 product combination there would, as already indicated, be 2^{50} calculations required and as Keen remarks, even at the rapid rate available to the neoclassical ratiocination device, it would take approximately 3.5 years to deliberate on the utility maximizing combination of products 100^{10}. The obvious conclusion to be drawn from this is that, to be polite, this is not how human agents behave in the real world and that we should abandon such a conceptual framework as ludicrously unfit for purpose.

10.6 RATIONAL AND EFFICIENT MARKETS

The efficient market hypothesis is associated with the idea of a "random walk," which is a term loosely used in the finance literature to characterize a price series where all subsequent price changes represent random departures from previous prices.

The logic of the random walk idea is that if the flow of information is unimpeded and information is immediately reflected in stock prices, then tomorrow's price change will reflect only tomorrow's news and will be independent of the price changes today. But news is by definition unpredictable, and, thus, resulting price changes must be unpredictable and random. As a result, prices fully reflect all known information, and even uninformed investors buying a diversified portfolio at the prices given by the market will obtain a rate of return equivalent to that achieved by the informed investors or "experts."

The efficient market hypothesis was first expressed by Louis Bachelier, a French mathematician, in his 1900 dissertation, *The Theory of Speculation*. His work was largely ignored until the 1950s when a small number of academic studies proposed that US stock prices and related financial series followed a random walk model, which was essentially the view expressed by Bachelier. [24]

The underlying idea of Bachelier's thesis was that price movements within markets are essentially random and have similar characteristics to, what in physics is called, Brownian motion, and which is integrally related to the "white noise" which was encountered in Chapter 3. This means that there is no pattern or signature to the development of price in a time series. If there are no underlying patterns or trends to price movements, then the way that asset prices move over time is a matter of "chance" rather than intention. But if this is the case there would seem to be no basis for prediction or anticipation of the way in which a market is going to behave in the future. Bachelier came to the conclusion that "[t]he mathematical expectation of the speculator is zero."

If the manner in which prices move within markets is purely a chance process with no underlying *intentionality*, then, it is alleged that many of the activities of the financial and specifically technical analysts would be akin to those who look for patterns in the winning number sequences for lottery draws.

The efficient markets hypothesis (EMH) is an integral part of mainstream financial economics and its corollary view regarding how rational markets function is also a cornerstone of macro-economic theory based on rational pricing. In essence EMH states that it is impossible to "beat the market" because, at any time, prevailing share prices will always incorporate and reflect all relevant information. There are different flavors of the EMH [25] but it will suffice for present purposes to simply express the EMH as the view that securities always trade at their fair value in financial markets, making it impossible for investors to either purchase undervalued stocks or sell stocks for inflated prices. As such, it should be impossible to outperform the overall market through expert stock selection, technical analysis, or market timing. If one accepts this view the only way an investor can possibly obtain higher returns is by purchasing riskier investments. This would be in accordance with the view of the CAPM that only higher beta stocks will deliver higher returns, but with increased risk. [26]

Professor Andrew Lo, currently at MIT, and Craig MacKinlay published *A Non-random Walk Down Wall Street* in 2001 [27] in which very convincing arguments were presented that asset prices do not follow a random walk and many academics have now become persuaded that, even if a lightweight version of the EMH is valid, to go the extra distance and talk about prices and asset returns behaving randomly just does not fit the facts.

The global financial crisis has led to renewed scrutiny and criticism of the hypothesis. Market strategist Jeremy Grantham has claimed that belief in the hypothesis caused financial leaders to have a "chronic underestimation of the dangers of asset bubbles breaking." [28]

Roger Lowenstein, who wrote a definitive account of the Long Term Capital Management debacle of 1998, [29] declared in 2009 that "[t]he upside of the current Great Recession is that it could drive a stake through the heart of the academic nostrum known as the efficient-market hypothesis."

Advocates and defenders of the EMH do not dismiss the possibility of anomalies in the market that result in the generation of superior profits. In fact, market efficiency does not require prices to be equal to fair value all of the time. Prices may be over- or undervalued but they eventually revert back to their mean values. As such, because the deviations from a stock's fair price are in themselves random, investment strategies that result in beating the market cannot be consistent phenomena. Furthermore, the hypothesis argues that an investor who outperforms the market does so not out of skill but out of luck. EMH followers say this is due to the laws of probability: At any given time in a market with a large number of investors, some will outperform while others will remain average. The following quote from Burton Malkiel, a firm advocate of the EMH and the view that markets follow a random walk, is quoted below: [30]

> What I do not argue is that the market pricing is always perfect. After the fact, we know that markets have made egregious mistakes, as I think occurred during the recent Internet "bubble." Nor do I deny that psychological factors influence securities prices. But I am convinced that Benjamin Graham (1965) was correct in suggesting that while the stock market in the short run may be a voting mechanism, in the long run it is a weighing mechanism. True value will win out in the end.

Just how many financial economists still adhere to a robust form of the Efficient Markets Hypothesis (EMH) is unclear but, judging from the persistent and uncritical acceptance of the fundamentally flawed notion that VaR can provide reliable guidance as to the magnitude and likelihood of extreme risk, there is reason to be very uncomfortable that it is widespread. This is just one element to the critique of a central theme in macro finance which is not, taken on its own, sufficiently powerful to be dismissive of the whole body of mainstream finance. But it does suggest that the cornerstone axioms are far more unstable and error prone than is appreciated by many professional and lay investors.

The shortcomings of mainstream macro-economics have been widely catalogued by several writers, and especially by Steve Keen (see endnote 23) and Yves Smith (see endnote 2). Before examining some of the main theoretical flaws it is worth making note of the obvious point that macro-economists, with some obvious exceptions outside the neoclassical mainstream, failed to recognize the unsustainable nature of the huge bubble that burst in 2007/8. To this day most of them have neither provided an entirely plausible account of why bubbles arise nor prescriptively what can and should be done to avoid the incalculable damage done by episodes similar to the GFC from happening again.

To pose the core issue which appears to be at the root of the criticisms from such contemporary economists as the aforementioned Steve Keen, Yves Smith, and L Randall Wray, and from legacy economists such as Hyman Minsky, [31] I shall simplify greatly by asking the following question:

> Are the dynamics which lead to bubbles and crashes the result of endogenous or exogenous macro economic factors?

The mainstream neoclassical school, which sees economic and financial behavior as being the outcome of a kind of utility optimizing function which expresses the seeking out of economically stable equilibria by a collection of rational economic agents, has, as one of its cornerstones, the view that financial crashes are due to exogenous factors. That is, within the modeling tools that they use to explain system-wide economic circumstances, there is no explanation, other than abnormal shocks, which are "outside" the scope of their models, to explain why bubbles become unsustainable and eventually burst resulting in very damaging financial crashes. Mainly because they lack a proper framework for explaining the role of money and credit creation within modern financial capitalism, they can only resort to something extraneous to account for the disequilibrium crash events which have punctuated economic history.

The alternative school, often referred to as Modern Monetarist Theory or MMT and inspired by the writings of Hyman Minksy and latter day disciples, starts out from a very different premise. Expressed simply that premise is, to use Minsky's own words: "Financial instability is a deep seated characteristic of a capitalist economy with a sophisticated financial system ... Any economy with private ownership of capital assets, private investment, and a complex financial system will be unstable." [32]

The foundations of the MMT view can best be expressed in a couple of quotes from *Stabilizing an Unstable Economy*, the seminal work of Hyman Minsky who also wrote a definitive account of the writings of John Maynard Keynes and perhaps understood the latter's work better than most economists who claim to be his followers. [33] The first quotation brings out this misinterpretation of Keynes's work by most who call themselves Keynesians:

> Unfortunately for the development of economic theory, for an understanding of how our economy works, and for the design of policy to improve the performance of our economies, Keynes's investment theory of business cycles and his financial theory of *investment in the face of uncertainty* [author's italics] were lost as the standard interpretation of Keynes's General Theory evolved into today's orthodox theory. What had started as an inspired flash of understanding into basic relations guiding our economy was reduced by the interpreting economists who followed into a banal set of prescriptions for guiding aggregate output.

Perhaps the most important ingredient in the critique of the neoclassical school is in regard to the function of money and credit within the macro economy. The neoclassical school is unable to explain the nature of credit and its role in the development of asset bubbles precisely because it fails to offer a satisfactory account for endogenous credit creation and the role of credit/debt in financing investments which can and will lead to unsustainable bubbles. Minsky outlines his intention to remedy this critical defect in the neoclassical tradition early in his book *Stabilizing an Unstable Economy*: [34]

> We will develop a theory explaining why our economy fluctuates, showing that the instability and incoherence exhibited from time to time is related to the development of fragile financial structures that occur normally within capitalist economies in the course of financing capital asset ownership and investment.

A pithy statement of the opposition to the neoclassical tradition and its marginalization of the insights which Hyman Minsky had with respect to the role of financing in a modern economy – and its associated instability – is revealed in this quote which comes from Steve Keen in a US television interview. [35] It also alludes to the dispute with Paul Krugman which was mentioned previously:

> You can't model the economy without including the role of banks, debt, and money. And Krugman's part of the economic establishment, which for thirty or forty years has got away with arguing that you can model a capitalist economy as if it had no banks in it, no money, and no debt ... You just don't have a model of capitalism if you don't include those components.

With this brief summary of the adversarial schools let us turn to one further critic of mainstream economics. The man who can lay claim to be the greatest global macro investor of the last 40 years, George Soros [36] is a proponent of the view that current macro-economic orthodoxy is based on fundamentally mistaken notions which fail to capture the role of human *reflexivity* in economic decision making and investment behavior. Not content to write several books on the matter and be a leading critic of the economic orthodoxy in numerous broadcasts and publications, he launched and contributes to the ongoing funding of the Institute for New Economic Thinking or INET. The mission of INET can be briefly summarized by the following extract from the Institute's website: [37]

> The Institute for New Economic Thinking (INET) was created to broaden and accelerate the development of new economic thinking that can lead to solutions for the great challenges of the 21st century.
>
> The havoc wrought by our recent global financial crisis has vividly demonstrated the deficiencies in our outdated current economic theories, and shown the need for new economic thinking – right now.
>
> INET is supporting this fundamental shift in economic thinking through research funding, community building, and spreading the word about the need for change.
>
> NET stages a series of conferences and regional meetings held around the world that bring people from different fields and schools of thought together to debate on vital issues and questions that urgently require new economic thinking.

The INET website is a vital resource for those who are dissatisfied with mainstream economic thinking and who believe that not only have orthodox academic economists failed to properly account for key aspects of modern financial capitalism, but are also unable to comprehend the nature of the bubble/bust dynamics – so well portrayed by Hyman Minsky.

In contrast, there is a vacuum within the neoclassical tradition for any account of the manner in which credit/debt is created and most tellingly there is no explanation for the feedback loops between the amount of credit (or indebtedness) available to consumers of assets and the increasing valuations of such assets.

The logic of bubbles remains a mystery to a traditional macro-economist.

ENDNOTES

1. The concept of utility was introduced into the philosophical literature by Jeremy Bentham (1748–1832) in *An Introduction to the Principles of Morals and Legislation*:

   > By utility is meant that property in any object, whereby it tends to produce benefit, advantage, pleasure, good, or happiness, (all this in the present case comes to the same thing) or (what comes again to the same thing) to prevent the happening of mischief, pain, evil, or unhappiness to the party whose interest is considered: if that party be the community in general, then the happiness of the community: if a particular individual, then the happiness of that individual.

   http://www.econlib.org/library/Bentham/bnthPML1.html.

   The concept of utility was subsequently the foundation of much of John Stuart Mill's work such as *On Utilitarianism*.
2. Yves Smith, *ECONned: How Unenlightened Self Interest Undermined Democracy and Corrupted Capitalism* (Palgrave Macmillan, 1st edn, March 2, 2010).

Yves Smith discusses the manner in which much of economic theory descending from Paul Samuelson reveals this tendency. To cite just one extract from page 43:

> To make the preferred formal apparatus work, economists assume a Panglossian outcome, namely, that not only does the economic system tend to self correct on an aggregate level and come to a stable outcome ... but the end result is the best possible place an economy can be – full employment!

Also similar discussion can be found in John Gray, *False Dawn – The Delusions of Global Capitalism*, (Granta Books, London, 2002):

> The ***free-market*** is not – as today's economic philosophy supposes – a natural state of affairs which comes about when political interference with the market exchange has been removed. In any long and broad historical perspective the free-market is a rare, short-lived aberration.

3. The stickiest price from the Interfluidity blog of Steve Randy Waldman, http://www.interfluidity.com/v2/910.html. Also see endnote 32 for Chapter 1.
4. The following graphic reveals the declines in markets which experienced banking crises versus those which did not.

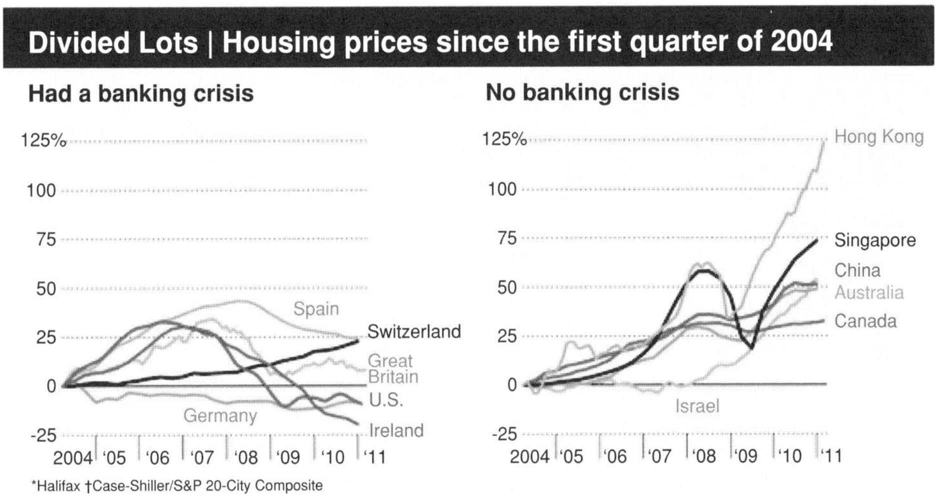

Impact of banking crisis on real estate prices
Source: Thomson Reuters.

5. See discussion in Chapter 7 and also endnote 4 regarding the Zillow Negative Equity Report.
6. A study by Nomura entitled "Slow Healing of US Household Finances," published in April 2012, http://www.scribd.com/doc/91550405/Nomura-Special-Housing.
7. As above.
8. As above.
9. In the Bureau of Labor Statistics Employment Report the U6 classification indicates the number of persons who are unemployed and under-employed. U6 is defined as "total unemployed, plus all marginally attached workers plus total employed part time for economic reasons, as a percent of all civilian labor force plus all marginally attached workers."

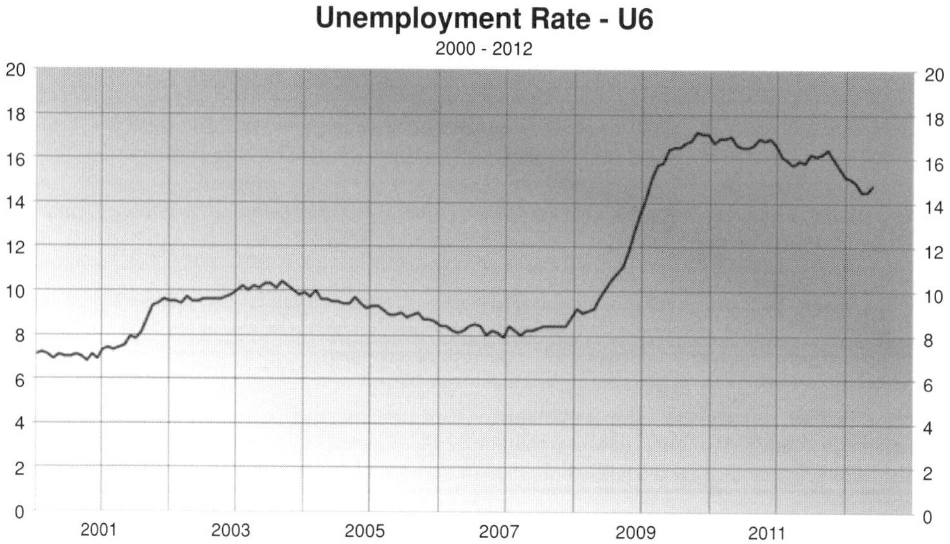

Percentage of labor force which is unemployed or under-employed
Source: US Bureau of Labor Statistics.

10. This last assertion, for example, was made by J.P. Morgan CEO Jamie Dimon in testimony to both Congressional committees which he appeared at in the spring of 2012.
11. J. P. Morgan's CEO Jamie Dimon gave testimony to the House Financial Services Committee on June 19, 2012:

    > As the House Financial Services Committee hearing into recent failures at JPMorgan waned, bank CEO Jamie Dimon finally said what had already been obvious to everyone – he didn't want to be there. "These are complex things that should be done the right way, in my opinion in closed rooms," Dimon said. "I don't think you make a lot of progress in an open hearing like this."

    http://www.npr.org/2012/06/20/155418887/the-nation-jamie-dimon-finally-takes-some-heat.
12. Dear Mr. Dimon, Is Your Bank Getting Corporate Welfare? http://www.bloomberg.com/news/2012-06-18/dear-mr-dimon-is-your-bank-getting-corporate-welfare-.html.
13. The Volcker rule refers to a specific part of the Dodd–Frank Wall Street Reform and Consumer Protection Act and relates to the initiative promulgated by Paul Volcker, a former chairman of the Federal Reserve, to restrict the role of speculative trading activities by systemically significant financial institutions. There has been considerable controversy regarding exactly how the rule is to be implemented as there is a debate about how to distinguish between hedging activities by banks – which would not be restricted by the rule – and proprietary trading activities which would be curtailed. The difficulties in distinguishing clearly between these two kinds of activities was highlighted in regard to the losses experienced by J.P. Morgan in the first and second quarters of 2012. Specifically the losses of approximately $6bn were incurred by a trader known as the "London whale" through the use of fixed income derivatives contracts which it was claimed were designed to protect J.P. Morgan's exposure to its large holdings of corporate bonds. However the division that was responsible for trading in these derivatives had also previously been a key profit center for the bank and raised questions as to whether its activities could correctly be characterized as hedging.

    A good collection of articles regarding the activities of the "London whale" can be found at the following online link: http://ftalphaville.ft.com/blog/series/jpm-whale-watching-tour/.

14. Walter Bagehot in the 19th century is acknowledged to be the originator of the notion that moral hazard will arise when there is an absence of penalty or adverse consequences with regard to financial risk taking.

    Those who made the risky bets have diverted the risk to others: taxpayers or the general public who holds currency. The gains from the bets are private, and theirs to keep, but all the losses are distributed to the public via government bailouts or money-printing. The first shifts the losses to the taxpayer, and the second shifts the losses to everyone holding the currency being devalued.

    Still less should it give peculiar favour to any one, and by entrusting it with the Government account secure to it a mischievous supremacy above all other banks. The skill of a financier in such an age is to equalise the receipt of taxation, and the outgoing of expenditure; it should be a principal care with him to make sure that more should not be locked up at a particular moment in the Government coffers than is usually locked up there. If the amount of dead capital so buried in the Treasury does not at any time much exceed the common average, the evil so caused is inconsiderable: it is only the loss of interest on a certain sum of money, which would not be much of a burden on the whole nation; the additional taxation it would cause would be inconsiderable. Such an evil is nothing in comparison with that of losing the money necessary for inevitable expense by entrusting it to a bad bank, or that of recovering this money by identifying the national credit with the bad bank and so propping it up and perpetuating it. So long as the security of the Money Market is not entirely to be relied on, the Government of a country had much better leave it to itself and keep its own money. If the banks are bad, they will certainly continue bad and will probably become worse if the Government sustains and encourages them. *The cardinal maxim is, that any aid to a present bad bank is the surest mode of preventing the establishment of a future good bank.*

15. Yves Smith, The Eurozone vendor financing scheme, nakedcapitalism.com, November 8, 2011, http://www.nakedcapitalism.com/2011/11/the-eurozone-vendor-financing-scheme.html
16. Martin Wolf, *Fixing Global Finance* (Yale University Press; Expanded and updated edition, April 13, 2010).
17. Thomas S. Kuhn, The Structure of Scientific Revolutions (University of Chicago Press, 3rd edn, December 1996).
18. For a philosophical treatment of category mistakes see Gilbert Ryle, *The Concept of Mind* (Kessinger Publishing, June 2008).
19. Only by imposing terms of reference and a cognitive framework are we able to make meaningful *perceptual judgments*. This is very much the view of Immanuel Kant throughout the *Critique of Pure Reason* as the following quotes from it will demonstrate:

    Both space and time and our conceptual principles and processes pre-structure our experience.

    Kant believed that causality is a conceptual organizing principle that we impose upon nature, albeit nature understood as the sum of appearances that can be synthesized according to our a priori concepts. In other words, space and time are a form of perceiving and causality is a form of knowing.

    Things as they are "in themselves", the noumenal world, is unknowable. For something to become an object of knowledge, it must be experienced, and experience is structured by our minds – both space and time being the forms of our intuition. For Kant, intuition is the process of sensing or the act of having a sensation, or a perception, and it is the unifying, structuring activity of our concepts. These aspects of mind turn things-in-themselves into the world of experience. We are never passive observers or knowers.

20. Hilary Putnam, An example of Putnam's work where facts and values are entangled can be found in *The Collapse of the Fact/Value Dichotomy and Other Essays* (Harvard University Press, March, 2004):

    When and where did a Nazi and an anti-Nazi, a communist and a social democrat, a fundamentalist and a liberal, or even a Republican and a Democrat, agree on the facts? Even when it comes to one specific policy question [. . .], every argument I have ever heard has exemplified the entanglement of the ethical and the factual. There is a weird discrepancy between the way philosophers who subscribe to a sharp fact/value distinction *make* ethical arguments sound and the way ethical arguments *actually* sound.

> One may not wish to go as far as the author of a fascinating article which can be found in the online publication Global Economic Intersection, but undoubtedly there is a tendency for each of us to "frame" our perceptions of the "real world" by reference to our beliefs and our underlying ideologies. See the following article *Manufacturing Public Opinion*, June 5, 2012, which is available online at: http://econintersect.com/b2evolution/blog2.php/2012/06/05/manufacturing-public-opinion.

The author of this provocative piece, who prefers to remain anonymous, makes the following comments:

> Perception is the relationship between external sensory evidence and internal mental representation and interpretation so pure "objective" observation is logically and practically impossible. But with dedicated effort we can learn to recognize which parts of our perceptions are interpretation and which parts are evidence, and we can at least approach objectivity in our observations. In order to see clearly we must dissolve the parameter walls of our conceptual worldview, of all worldviews, and start with a fresh perspective, a virgin mind.
>
> If we claim we "know" how this world "should be", so that we judge them wrong and us right, then we are guilty of conceptual realism, of knowing first then trying to make the world and other people conform to how we "know" they're "supposed to" be. Objectively, reality is what it is, "real", and reality cannot be right or wrong. What's real and not real is the "judge" of right and wrong. "Ideas" about reality can be right or wrong, and ideas that contradict observed reality are probably wrong ideas.

21. The Turing test is described well in the *Stanford Encyclopedia of Philosophy*:

> The phrase "The Turing Test" is most properly used to refer to a proposal made by Turing (1950) as a way of dealing with the question whether machines can think. According to Turing, the question whether machines can think is itself "too meaningless" to deserve discussion (442). However, if we consider the more precise – and somehow related – question whether a digital computer can do well in a certain kind of game that Turing describes ("The Imitation Game"), then – at least in Turing's eyes – we do have a question that admits of precise discussion. Moreover, as we shall see, Turing himself thought that it would not be too long before we did have digital computers that could "do well" in the Imitation Game.

http://plato.stanford.edu/entries/turing-test/.

22. Issues related to the econophysics fallacy are discussed in *Long/Short Market Dynamics*. See for example pp. 207–20 and for reference to book see below.
23. Steve Keen has an excellent collection of lecture notes at his personal website and these can be found at: http://www.debtdeflation.com/blogs/lectures/.
24. The following comment on Louis Bachelier comes from Clive Corcoran, *Long/Short Market Dynamics*:

> Louis Bachelier, a French mathematician, wrote his Ph.D. dissertation on the nature of speculative markets at the turn of the 20th century. Largely unnoticed at the time, the underlying ideas of his thesis were that price movements within markets have similar characteristics to what is called Brownian motion and which, in effect, means that there is no pattern or signature to the development of price in a time series. It follows that if there are no underlying patterns or trends to price movements, then price development over time is a matter of "chance" rather than intention. But if this is the case there would seem to be no basis for prediction or anticipation of the way in which a market is going to behave in the future. Bachelier came to the conclusion that "*The mathematical expectation of the speculator is zero*."

25. There are three common forms in which the efficient market hypothesis is stated:
    - Weak-form efficiency;
    - Semi-strong-form efficiency;
    - Strong-form efficiency.

    In weak-form efficiency, future prices cannot be predicted by analysing price from the past. Excess returns cannot be earned in the long run by using investment strategies based on historical share prices or other historical data. Technical analysis techniques will not be able to consistently produce excess returns, though some forms of fundamental analysis may still provide excess returns.

In semi-strong-form efficiency, share prices adjust to publicly available new information very rapidly and in an unbiased fashion, such that no excess returns can be earned by trading on that information. Semi-strong-form efficiency implies that neither fundamental analysis nor technical analysis techniques will be able to reliably produce excess returns.

In strong-form efficiency, share prices reflect all information, public and private, and no-one can earn excess returns. If there are legal barriers to private information becoming public, as with insider trading laws, strong-form efficiency is impossible, except in the case where the laws are universally ignored. To test for strong-form efficiency, a market needs to exist where investors cannot consistently earn excess returns over a long period of time.

Even if some money managers are consistently observed to beat the market this does not detract from strong-form efficiency. The rejoinder from the advocate of the theory is simply that with hundreds of thousands of fund managers worldwide, even a normal distribution of returns (as efficiency predicts) should be expected to produce a few dozen "star" performers.

The key piece of evidence supporting the EMH, at least in its weak version, is that studies have revealed that over time the performance of most fund managers fails to "beat" that of passively investing in an index-tracker fund.

26. See for example the discussions on the CAPM in Clive Corcoran, *Long/Short Market Dynamics* (John Wiley & Sons, 2007):

> One theme which is often used by fund managers in tactical asset allocation that hinges on market timing is to adjust the beta value (β) of the portfolio. If the fund manager believes that the overall market is under-priced and wishes to take advantage of the expectation that other investors/traders will recognise this and move prices higher, then the best way to increase returns in the short term, in anticipation of higher prices ahead, is to increase the beta of the portfolio. By holding relatively higher beta stocks, for example, these stocks will outpace the overall market on the upside if the fund manager's judgment about increasing prices is correct. Of course, if the converse is true, high beta stocks are not the place to be if the market is about to decrease in value.

27. Andrew Lo and Craig MacKinlay, *A Non-random Walk Down Wall Street* (Princeton University Press, 1999).

28. Jeremy Grantham, *Obama and the Teflon Men, and Other Short Stories. Part 1* (GMO Quarterly Letter, January 2009):

> Ingenious new financial instruments certainly facilitated and exaggerated these weaknesses, but they were not the most potent ingredient in our toxic stew. That honor goes to the economic establishment for building over many decades a belief in rational expectations: reasonable, economically-induced behavior that would always guarantee approximately efficient markets. In their desire for mathematical order and elegant models, the economic establishment played down the inconveniently large role of bad behavior, career risk management, and flat-out bursts of irrationality.
>
> Never underestimate the power of a dominant academic idea to choke off competing ideas, and never underestimate the unwillingness of academics to change their views in the face of evidence. They have decades of their research and their academic standing to defend. The incredibly inaccurate efficient market theory was believed in totality by many of our financial leaders, and believed in part by almost all. It left our economic and governmental establishment sitting by confidently, even as a lethally dangerous combination of asset bubbles, lax controls, pernicious incentives, and wickedly complicated instruments led to our current plight. "Surely none of this could happen in a rational, efficient world," they seemed to be thinking. And the absolutely worst aspect of this belief set was that it led to a chronic underestimation of the dangers of asset bubbles breaking – the very severe loss of perceived wealth and the stranded debt that comes with a savage write-down of assets.

29. Justin Fox, Lowenstein's comments can be found in a review of *The Myth of the Rational Market: A History of Risk, Reward, and Delusion on Wall Street* (Harper Business, Reprint edn, February, 2011).

The review can be found online at http://www.washingtonpost.com/wp-dyn/content/article/2009/06/05/AR2009060502053.html.

30. Burton G. Malkiel, The Efficient Market Hypothesis and Its Critics (2003) 17(1) (Winter 2003) *Journal of Economic Perspectives* 59–82, http://www-stat.wharton.upenn.edu/~steele/Courses/434/434Context/EfficientMarket/malkiel.pdf.
31. The following are the seminal works from each author cited:
    Yves Smith, *ECONned: How Unenlightened Self Interest Undermined Democracy and Corrupted Capitalism* (Palgrave Macmillan, Reprint edn, 2011); Steve Keen, *Debunking Economics – Revised and Expanded Edition: The Naked Emperor Dethroned?* (Zed Books, 2nd edn, October 2011); L. Randall Wray, *Understanding Modern Money: The Key to Full Employment and Price Stability* (Edward Elgar Publishing, June 2006).
32. Hyman Minsky, *Stabilizing an Unstable Economy* (McGraw-Hill, April 2008).
33. Hyman Minsky's review of the works of Keynes can be found in Hyman Minsky, *John Maynard Keynes* (McGraw-Hill, April 2008):

    > Unfortunately for the development of economic theory, for an understanding of how our economy works, and for the design of policy to improve the performance of our economies, Keynes's investment theory of business cycles and his financial theory of *investment in the face of uncertainty* [author's italics] were lost as the standard interpretation of Keynes's General Theory evolved into today's orthodox theory. What had started as an inspired flash of understanding into basic relations guiding our economy was reduced by the interpreting economists who followed into a banal set of prescriptions for guiding aggregate output.

34. Hyman Minsky, *Stabilizing an Unstable Economy* (McGraw-Hill, April 2008).
35. Steve Keen appeared on Capital Account with Laura Lyster, April 4, 2012, http://www.youtube.com/watch?v=lnwEGeMQRCs.
36. George Soros has authored a number of titles and just three are mentioned below:
    The Alchemy of Finance (Wiley Investment Classics) (Wiley & Sons, July 29, 2003); *The Crash of 2008 and What it Means: The New Paradigm for Financial Markets* (Public Affairs, Revised edn, March 30, 2009); *Financial Turmoil in Europe and the United States: Essays* (Public Affairs, 1st edn, February 7, 2012).
37. INET website etc., http://ineteconomics.org/about; http://ineteconomics.org/conference/berlin/speakers.

11

Could a Eurozone Breakup Trigger Another Systemic Crisis?

For reasons which can be and are overlooked in the concerns expressed about the threats posed by the macro-economic woes of the 17 countries which share the single currency, it will be suggested that the difficulties within the Eurozone have the capacity to create a true systemic crisis which could dwarf the problems seen in 2008. The reason I make this claim is that there is a political dimension to the threat of financial contagion which could easily develop over the coming months and years which was not in the spotlight when the financial system teetered on the edge back in 2008. At that point the financial crisis had more of a cathartic effect on policy makers and the population at large. After many years of relative "prosperity," sometimes referred to as the "Great Moderation," the shock of the GFC had an unfamiliar and mesmerizing effect on sophisticated market practitioners and the layman alike. Today such "innocence" has gone.

Despite clearly articulated hostility towards the various rescue programs such as TARP by a significant part of the US electorate, the populace was less cynical and indeed far less well educated in all of the mistakes and improprieties that had brought on the crisis. One of the true growth businesses since 2008 has been a proliferation of books, films, and commentary on what went wrong in the events leading up to the financial crisis. Now with so much knowledge of the recklessness, stupidity, profligacy, and other associated dirty laundry in the public domain, it is much harder for politicians and other policy makers to find any kind of consensual resolution for policy initiatives to address new potential threats to the integrity of the financial system. The new divisiveness and polarization of views amongst electorates can be attributed partly to a widespread contempt for bankers, a general view that nothing has really been changed and that no one has been really held to account since the more obviously acute phase of the crisis has passed. In addition despite the onset of crisis fatigue there is still the nagging suspicion widely held that there could be much further to go and perhaps an even bigger crisis on the horizon. [1]

Hostility towards politicians and bankers is especially deep seated in the peripheral territories of the Eurozone where there is a great reticence to embrace austerity programs which appear, at least at the time of writing, to be considered as the necessary therapy for the overly indebted condition of the relevant sovereigns and most of their citizens. Much of the debate regarding a growth agenda versus an austerity agenda is actually quite vacuous and sees these as mutually exclusive goals. It is also not clear exactly how and why politicians should be believed when they claim to have any robust solutions as to how to execute a growth strategy. [2]

In Europe there is a much greater problem than that which confronted the US Congress in the fall of 2008. When US Secretary of the Treasury, Henry Paulson, took a three-page memo to ask Congress for $700 billion which became the TARP program – although it was initially rejected – he essentially had to persuade only one legislative body that unless his request for a financial bailout was accepted, the consequences for the US (and global) economy would be catastrophic. Constitutionally the United States is a federation with a centralized fiscal system (admittedly the states can levy taxes as well) and a financial system which is implicitly one with *joint and several responsibility* for all liabilities arising within a truly integrated financial and political union. The Eurozone has no such federal underpinnings – although it has a single currency, a single interest rate setting European Central Bank (ECB), and some elements of a federal-like bureaucracy in Brussels – it is fundamentally not a federation.

Just one of the major differences between the Eurozone and the USA is that there is *de jure* no joint responsibility for the obligations and liabilities of the member states which make up either the Euro area or the larger European Union. Indeed, as will be shown, the 10 member states, out of the 27 EU states in total, that are not within the Eurozone, have no responsibility with respect to the financing obligations and potential losses that might be suffered by the ECB. The absence of joint responsibility or debt mutualization was purposefully incorporated into the Maastricht Treaty and any proper analysis of the systemic risks posed by the distressing problems faced by the Eurozone has to examine some of the consequences which flow from the legal framework which underlies the ECB and its operations with respect to the Eurosystem – a term which will be clarified in the following discussion.

Fortunately, as it would not be too entertaining for the reader, or necessary, as there are other very good sources where the various EU related treaties can be found, it will not be a priority to delve too deeply into the constitutional arrangements and legal framework upon which the European System of Central Banks or ESCB is based. This chapter will be less concerned with the macro-economic difficulties of the Eurozone – the strains arising from the fact that such a heterogeneous group of states has markedly different cost structures, labor laws, and public benefits programs – rather the focus will be on architectural flaws in its organizational structure. Our central theme in this chapter will be the system threatening macro-financial plight which ultimately hinges on the absence of joint responsibility by all of the member states to guarantee the obligations incurred by each and every other EZ member state.

The ESCB comprises the ECB and the national central banks or NCBs of all 27 EU member states. Since not all of the current 27 EU states have joined the euro, the ESCB could not be used as the monetary authority of the Eurozone. For this reason the Eurosystem (which excludes all the NCBs which have not adopted the euro) became the institution in charge of those tasks which in principle had to be managed by the ESCB. In accordance with the treaty establishing the European Community and the Statute of the European System of Central Banks and of the European Central Bank itself, the primary objective of the Eurosystem is to *maintain price stability in the medium term.* That last italicized phrase will resonate with anyone who has watched the press conferences which follow the monthly meetings of the Governing Council of the ECB, as hosted formerly by Monsieur Trichet and now by Signor Draghi.

The shares of the national central banks (NCBs) in the ECB's capital structure or key as it is called, as seen in Tables 11.1 and 11.2, are a reflection of each of the member states' shares in the total population and gross domestic product of the EU, in equal weightings. Eurosystem NCBs are required to pay up their subscribed capital in full, whereas, and this is significant, the non-euro area NCBs only have to pay up a minimal percentage of their subscribed capital as a contribution to the operational costs of the ECB, currently the amount is 7%.

Table 11.1 Euro area NCB's contributions to the ECB's capital

NCB	Capital key %	paid up capital (€)
Nationale Bank van België/Banque Nationale de Belgique	2.4256	220,583,718.02
Duetsche Bundesbank	18.9373	1,722,155,360.77
Eesti Pank	0.1790	16,278,234.47
Central Bank of Ireland	1.1107	101,006,899.58
Bank of Greece	1.9649	178,687,725.72
Banco de España	8.3040	755,164,575.51
Banque de France	14.2212	1,293,273,899.48
Banca d'Italia	12.4966	1,136,439,021.48
Central Bank of Cyprus	0.1369	12,449,666.48
Banque centrale du Luxembourg	0.1747	15,887,193.09
Central Bank of Malta	0.0632	5,747,398.98
De Nederlandsche Bank	3.9882	362,686,339.12
Oesterreichische Nationalbank	1.9417	176,577,921.04
Banco de Portugal	1.7504	159,181,126.31
Banka Slovenije	0.3288	29,901,025.10
Národná banka Slovenska	0.6934	63,057,697.10
Suomen Pankki-Finlands Bank	1.2539	114,029,487.14
Total[1]	**69.9705**	**6,363,107,289.36**

The net profit and losses of the ECB are allocated among the euro area NCBs in accordance with Article 33 of the Statute of the European System of Central Banks and of the European Central Bank (see the →legal framework):

Table 11.2 Non Euro area NCB's contributions to the ECB's capital

The EU's ten non-euro area NCBs are required to contribute to the operational costs incurred by the ECB in relation to their participation in the European System of Central Banks by paying up a small percentage of their share in the ECB's subscribed capital. Since 29 December 2010 their contributions have represented 3.75% of their total share in the subscribed capital. The capital paid to the ECB by the non-euro area NCBs amouts €121,176,379.25 and breaks down as follows:

Non-euro area NCBs' contribution to the ECB's capital

NCB	Capital key %	Paid-up capital (€)
Българска народна банка (Bulgarian National Bank)	0.8686	3,505,013.50
Česká národní banka	1.4472	5,839,806.06
Danmarks Nationalbank	1.4835	5,986,285.44
Latvijas Banka	0.2837	1,144,798.91
Lietuvos bankas	0.4256	1,717,400.12
Magyar Nemzeti Bank	1.3856	5,591,234.99
Narodowy Bank Polski	4.8954	19,754,136.66
Banca Naţională a României	2.4645	9.944,860.44
Sveriges Riksbank	2.2582	9,112,389.47
Bank of England	14.5172	58,580,453.65
Total[1]	**30.0295**	**121,176,379.25**

The non-euro NCBs not entitled to receive any share of the distributable profits of the ECB, nor are they liable to fund any losses of the ECB.

Table 11.1 shows the capital key percentage of each of the Eurozone NCBs which is directly proportional to the population and weighting of the respective GDPs of the states in terms of the total European Union GDP.

The bottom line of Table 11.1 shows that for the 17 member states the proportion of their capital commitment to the ECB is just shy of 70% of the total, and as previously noted their paid in capital amount, absent the 7% of the non EZ NCBs, is about 93% of the total.

When examining the various financing structures which have been rolled out by the EU Commission the capital key percentages from this table are crucial in two respects. Firstly, the 70% total for the Eurosystem NCBs has to be scaled up to 100% for the obligations which each of the 17 have, for example, to the European Financial Stability Facility or EFSF and to the European Stability Mechanism or ESM. Accordingly, while the capital key percentage for Germany's Bundesbank is showing in Table 11.1 at 18.93% this rises to just over 27% when scaled up to 100% to reflect the fact that the non-Eurosystem NCBs play no part in guaranteeing the obligations incurred by the EFSF. This also applies to all present and future special purpose vehicles to augment or replace the EFSF, and specifically to the European Stability Mechanism or ESM, about which there is more to come. Just to complete the capital key structure, the following table, Table 11.2, shows the other 10 NCBs which are not on the hook at all for guaranteeing the EFSF liabilities.

In terms of the capital key percentage the most notable non-euro area NCB is the Bank of England which has a percentage of 14.5%. The footnote to Table 11.2 also spells out what is made very clear in the legal articles underpinning the ESCB: that none of the non-EZ NCBs *are liable to fund any losses of the ECB*. Not only then have these ten NCBs been excluded from any liability with respect to the EFSF but they are also excluded from any losses which could be incurred by the ECB itself. Some might argue that the latter point is a bit academic since the ECB is in a position to issue sufficient euro currency to ensure that it would never have to realize any losses on its balance sheet. However academic that may seem to some it seems to be a constant source of anxiety to the financial elite in Germany, and especially within the hierarchy at the Bundesbank.

Returning to the legal and structural flaws within the Eurosystem the obligations and responsibilities of the 17 member states are *several but not joint*. In a lot of the discussion about the possible financial contagion arising from further deterioration of many of the sovereigns and the health of the private sector banks within those jurisdictions, the fact that the obligations of the rescue mechanisms are not joint can easily get overlooked. Yet the *de facto* limitation of the obligations to the pro rated basis in the capital key ratios discussed above are fundamental to, for example, the EFSF's funding protocols. Put very simply, under the legal terms of the ESCB framework, Germany is not fully liable for all of the financing obligations to which it is a party either within the EFSF, ESM, or even to the ECB – its obligations are *pro rata or several*.

The following comes from an article written by this author on this subject in 2010 regarding the key legal flaw in the underpinnings of the euro currency and it remains as a valid observation even in mid-2012: [3]

> There is a flaw in the legal/constitutional framework that underpins the way the Eurozone is organized. It needs to be confronted without the usual shenanigans of smoke and mirrors that give most observers a false sense that it's just a matter of more meetings that will solve the problems besetting the EMU currency union.
>
> The essence of the problem lies within the legal architecture which surrounds the whole Eurozone project and specifically the EFSF (or its successors). The best way to get a handle on the structural

flaws is to consider the difference between joint obligations and several obligations. The EFSF has several obligations on the member states that are guaranteeing the obligations of the facility, but critically, not a joint obligation.

In simple terms, the best way to contrast the difference is to consider the nature of a partnership – a form of business organization which used to prevail in the professional world, including until the 1980's in the domain of investment banking.

A firm based upon a partnership deed is bound together legally under the concept of joint and several responsibility for all of the obligations of the firm or partnership. All of the partners are each fully liable for all of the sums that the firm could be obliged to pay out in the case of a financial mishap. There is not a pro rata agreement which says that the liability of each member of the partnership is limited in any fashion – for example, in proportion to that partner's net worth or other assets. If there is a judgment against the partners, requiring the obligations to be honored, theoretically the onus for meeting those obligations could fall on just one of the partners if he or she is the only one left standing after the others may be insolvent or may have declared personal bankruptcy. Admittedly this would be a limiting case but the key idea about joint responsibility – which overrides the notion of several responsibility – is that each and every person in the partnership is liable up to the full amount of the relevant obligation.

The manner in which the EFSF structure was established only provides for several responsibilities in which the liability of each of the Eurozone member states is limited to their capital contributions to the ECB.

The following tables show the commitments of each of the 17 member states to the current EFSF facility. Table 11.3 shows the guarantee commitments of all 17 Eurozone member states. Table 11.4 confines itself to the percentage guarantees of the four AAA states at the time of writing: [4]

Table 11.3 Capital commitments to EFSF – all Euro area member states

Member State	Percentage of Total
Federal Republic of Germany	27.13%
French Republic	20.38%
Kingdom of the Netherlands	5.71%
Kingdom of Belgium	3.48%
Republic of Austria	2.78%
Republic of Finland	1.80%
Slovak Republic	0.99%
Republic of Slovenia	0.47%
Grand Duchy of Luxembourg	0.25%
Republic of Cyprus	0.20%
Republic of Malta	0.09%
Italian Republic	17.91%
Kingdom of Spain	11.90%
Hellenic Republic	2.82%
Portuguese Republic	2.51%
Ireland	1.59%
Estonia	0.30%
Total Guarantee Commitments	100%

Table 11.4 Capital commitments to EFSF – AAA rated Euro area member states as of July 2012

Member State	Percentage of Total
Federal Republic of Germany	27.13%
Kingdom of the Netherlands	5.71%
Republic of Austria	2.78%
Republic of Finland	1.80%
French Republic	
Kingdom of Belgium	
Slovak Republic	
Republic of Slovenia	
Grand Duchy of Luxembourg	
Republic of Cyprus	
Republic of Malta	
Italian Republic	
Kingdom of Spain	
Hellenic Republic	
Portuguese Republic	
Ireland	
Estonia	
Total Guarantee Commitments	37%

The EFSF is structured as an off-balance-sheet vehicle that issues debt backed by the guarantees of all 17 euro-zone countries, less the recipients of aid programs. The formal arrangements require that every EFSF bond will be backed by up to 165% of its size in guarantees, so under EFSF version 2.0 the EFSF can borrow a maximum of €440 billion (€440 billion x 1.65 = €726 billion). This over-collateralization feature was provided as a credit enhancement provision designed to encourage the credit ratings agencies (CRAs) to give the EFSF an AAA rating. When designing the architecture of the fund it was decided in effect to emulate the structure of a CDO with some features that would make the ratings agencies look benignly on the risk parameters for the SPV. Credit enhancement features, especially over-collateralization, were introduced into the capitalization model. In essence the fund is over-collateralized by 20% so that the relative contributions of each guarantor are actually 20% above the available funds that the facility can borrow against.

The design of the facility achieved the required goal as all of the three major CRAs did give the EFSF an AAA rating when the facility was first launched in 2010. However, when Standard & Poor's downgraded the sovereign ratings of France and Austria on January 13, 2012 they soon afterwards reduced their rating on the EFSF by one notch to AA+ citing the fact there were not enough AAA rated guarantors for the fund to maintain its top rating.

In the context of the EFSF, and ultimately with regard to the ECB's capital structure, the predicament really arises with regard to the undue burden expected of the most creditworthy member states. But of course given the absence of *de jure* joint obligations one has to wonder just whether counter-parties have undertaken a thoroughgoing due diligence to fully quantify the risks of purchasing and holding EFSF or ESM bonds. More ominous would be the consequences of any kind of disorderly breakup of the European Union or its subset the Eurozone.

Figure 11.1 is designed to illustrate a worst case scenario where there was an inability to perform on the part of the non-AAA rated guarantors of the liabilities of the EFSF and where

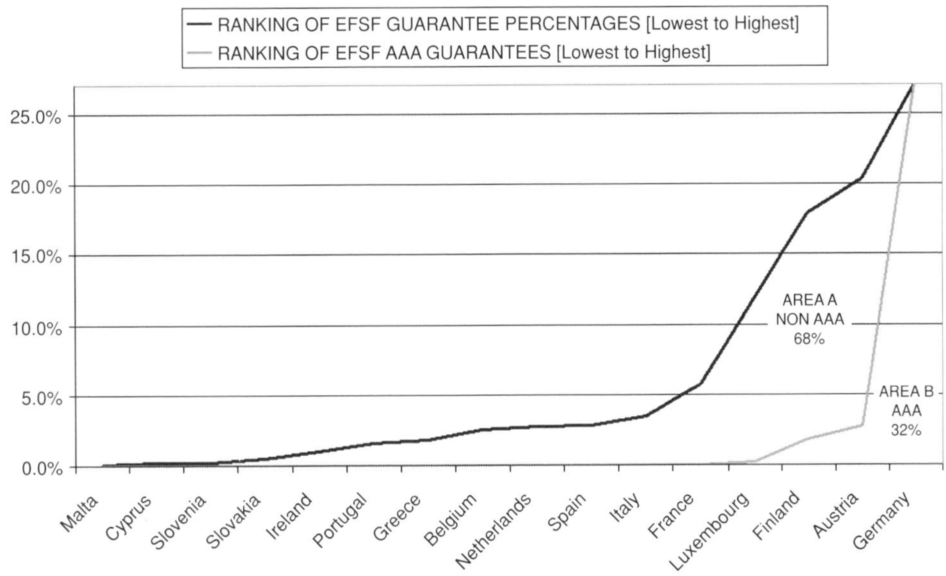

Figure 11.1 Illustrating the GINI coefficient for EFSF: AAA guarantors and non AAA rated guarantors

the remaining states adhered to the principle of a *pro rata* obligation only in accordance with their ECB capital key ratios.

One simple method of depicting the degree of imbalance or skew of a distribution is to use the Gini coefficient, and this has been employed in the construction of the diagram in Figure 11.1. This coefficient ranges between 0 and 1 (or it can also be expressed as a number from 0 to 100) and is given by the ratio of the areas:

$$\text{Gini Coefficient} = \frac{A}{A + B}$$

If A is a very large area, which logically implies that B must be very small, then the Gini coefficient will approach a value of one, and when used in its more commonplace context, a high reading means that there is very uneven distribution of income or wealth. Although the coefficient has primarily been used to illustrate the degree of inequality with respect to income or wealth distribution, more generally the coefficient can illustrate any potentially unstable distributions where a relatively small proportion of a population (in the statistical sense) have a disproportionate role – either they have too much wealth or too much of a financing obligation in the case of the EFSF or ESM – *vis-à-vis* the whole. For the population breakdown graphic the values for A and B are 234 million and 96 million respectively which would give a Gini coefficient of 234/330 or 71%. Although not shown the breakdown in analogous fashion for GDP of each EZ state would show values for A and B of Euro 11.333 trillion and Euro 3.005 trillion which would give a Gini coefficient of 11.333/9.338 or 68%.

It will be recalled that when CDOs were issued by US investment banks they also had credit enhancement features – such as "guarantees" from monoline insurers like AMBAC. It may be redundant to point out at this stage that far from AMBAC being able to honor its commitments made to enhance the creditworthiness of CDOs, the company filed and declared for Chapter 11 bankruptcy in New York on November 8, 2010. [5] There was also the not insignificant problem confronting the US Treasury when it was faced by honoring all of the guarantees made by AIG under various swaps and instruments designed to enhance the massive issuance of CDOs during the 2003–7 period in the US and elsewhere.

The over-collateralization feature built into the EFSF was certainly a cosmetic sweetener providing an additional buffer of capital and gave the EFSF more breathing room if things got tight. But the troubling issue with over-collateralization and the concept of several obligation which is part of the legal fabric of the EFSF and its successor facility the ESM, is extraordinarily similar to the problem that arose for mortgage-backed securities.

Just as in the case of the CDO debacle with real estate mortgages as collateral, where the possibility that real estate all over the US could suddenly decline in a uniform fashion was seen as a statistically insignificant "outlier," it also appears to have been assumed by the CRAs that the chances of several sovereigns running into difficulties and suffering impaired creditworthiness at the same time is equally as remote. However, a default by even one major sovereign, with its cascade of impairments to the balance sheets of the major private sector banks in the core territories such as Germany and France, could trigger the ultimate systemic meltdown.

How should we model the systemic risk of a failure of the euro? On the one hand from macro-economics we could try to pretend that it is relatively contained by citing the fact that EU contribution to total GDP is about 20% and that the weighting of EU equities in the MSCI World Index is about 15%. However, if we fail to take into account the financial domain and consider FX reserves which are estimated to be about 30% for major central banks, the amount of outstanding euro denominated debt issues, the counter-party risk from swap agreements that are based on either the euro currency itself or where one (or both) of the counter-parties may be a European institution which is unable to perform then the default and liquidity risks explode to a very different order of magnitude. In fact it is hard to imagine a more systemically threatening event than the disorderly collapse of the euro currency.

It is hard not to take a more cynical view of either the EFSF or the ESM in that, even if a member state is not actually a current recipient of assistance – for example, in April 2012 the EFSF sold euro 25 billion of Floating Rate Notes which were forwarded to Greece to provide funding for the recapitalization of its banking system [6] – there is validity in having doubts about how viable it is to take at full face value the guarantees made by countries that could well become candidates themselves for rescue in the future. As can be seen from Table 11.3 Spain and Italy make up almost 30% of the guarantee and there are grounds for believing that their ability to perform, even in *pro rata or several guarantee* fashion that is embedded in the EFSF and the ESM structure, may not be a safe assumption. Such doubts are becoming more manifested as 2012 progresses as concerns are mounting that the size of the guarantees will have to be increased, and more ominously that either or both of these two member states appear to need some form of rescue. One of the sad ironies of the EFSF and ESM structures is that included amongst the guarantors of the funding are several states which have already proven themselves to be junk credits – Ireland, Portugal, Cyprus, and Greece, and several, including Spain, which appear to be headed for that status. In headline terms there are just four AAA countries, at the time of writing in mid-2012, which have several guarantees for only 37% of the total obligations of the fund.

It is debatable – should circumstances ever become so distressing as to require guarantees to be called upon – whether those capable of fulfilling their pledges would, despite the lack of a joint guarantee *de jure,* in fact decide to honor in full the obligations incurred by the EFSF and the ESM. This is not just of academic interest to the various parties that are buying bonds from both structures – which include Japanese pension funds and Asian sovereigns.

11.1 THE EUROPEAN STABILITY MECHANISM (ESM)

Up to this point the focus has been primarily on the EFSF as that is the vehicle, at the time of writing, which is actually operational, has issued bonds, provided financial assistance to troubled states, and has been officially sanctioned by all of the member states of the Eurozone.

Attention should now be turned to The European Stability Mechanism (ESM), which is designed to supersede the EFSF in mid-2013, and also to a brief sketch of the Outright Monetary Transactions (OMT) program – outlined by the ECB in September 2012, but which, at the time of finalizing this book, had not been implemented. As with many of the ECB's initiatives the exact manner in which the OMT program will operate, either as a stand-alone facility or in conjunction with the activities of the ESM when it gets under way, remains somewhat opaque.

OMT was launched as part of Mario Draghi's stated objective in the summer of 2012 to "eliminate", for private sector investors, the "tail risk" attached to the euro currency and thereby address a big part of their aversion to holding peripheral sovereign debt. Under the OMT program the ECB is prepared to offer unlimited support to the bond issuances of troubled EZ states provided that such states agree to strictly adhere to the conditional undertakings stipulated by the ECB, IMF and European Commission when they apply for aid under the ESM mandate. This strict conditionality, which enabled Draghi to persuade Angela Merkel to bypass the objections to the OMT program voiced by her own Bundesbank, requires troubled EZ states to comply with specified targets and budgetary discipline. Any recipient of assistance, under the OMT program, which fails to adhere to the conditionality, would (theoretically at least) lose the ECB's further support. To the extent that such failure would in fact be "punished" by it being cut off by the ECB from further OMT support. The predicament for the delinquent sovereign would appear to be a really worse case scenario since not only would it be shunned by the private sector it would also have no recourse to any ECB safety net, and accordingly there would seem to be no way to avoid a default and a probable exit from the EMU. On the other hand, an unwillingness by a sovereign – Spain for example at the time of writing – to request assistance from the ESM would prevent the ECB from offering OMT support, resulting in an unresolved purgatory like condition that almost certainly could not endure. It remains to be seen whether the OMT program will be able to deliver on its promise and overcome the limiting case scenarios just described.

Some useful background to the ESM can be found at the European Commission's website [7]:

> In July 2013, the ESM will assume the tasks currently fulfilled by the European Financial Stability Facility (EFSF) and the European Financial Stabilisation Mechanism (EFSM).
>
> The ESM's initial maximum lending volume, after the EFSF has been completely wound down, is set at €500bn. Its capital stock of €700bn will ensure that lending can effectively be made up to this amount and consists of €80bn in paid-in shares and €620bn in callable shares. National contributions are established with a contribution key and would increase automatically if a non-euro-area country were to join the euro area.

From the above it is clear that the total facility that will be available for financial assistance is pegged at €500 billion and there have been numerous assertions, particularly from the German Finance Minister and the Bundesbank, that this is a hard number and will not be increased. Only time will tell, of course, whether this total commitment amount is as hard a number as German policy makers would have us believe.

One other important statement by the European Commission (EC) regarding the role of the ESM is also worth quoting: [8]

> The ESM will provide financial assistance to euro-area Member States following mutual agreement and under strict conditions. *Financial assistance will only be provided if it is considered as necessary to ensure the financial stability of the euro area as a whole.* Any euro-area Member State receiving assistance must implement a macro-economic adjustment programme and a rigorous analysis of public-debt sustainability, and foresee IMF participation in liaison with the ECB. *The ESM may, exceptionally, decide to purchase bonds issued by an ESM Member on the primary market if this maximises the cost efficiency of the financial assistance.*

The two italicized sentences from this statement of intent which was published on the EC website in 2011 are worthy of close attention as they are the "small print" which could have significant ramifications for the way in which the ESM operates and also the way in which market traders may, inadvertently, think that more is on offer from the ESM than may turn out to be the case.

As has been a pattern with all of the European Commission's initiatives and the numerous EU summits there have been a succession of quick rallies following communiqués released after the summits and these have usually subsided rather quickly.

One cynical view which has been levelled at the new arrangements, which are designed to be the ESM, which doesn't yet exist, agreed to lend money which it doesn't yet have, to member states who claim that they don't really need it. Such is the level of skepticism surrounding so many of the day to day news flows which emanate from the Eurozone.

The major difference with regard to the ESM as opposed to the EFSF is that when the facility is fully funded (over five years and assuming that it is funded!) the provision of financial assistance will not require the issuance of further bonds via the EFSF which has the limitations previously discussed. However it is vital to note that the ESM, like its predecessor, still does not have a joint undertaking – the ultimate backstop supplied by the German government – that many private investors in the securities issued by the EZ governments would like to see.

Unless private investors, including the commercial banking sector, the Chinese sovereign wealth fund, PIMCO, and many other larger providers of capital, are willing to reappraise their decision not to be participants in the market for debt issuance by the troubled states it remains highly problematic for the EZ sovereign debt difficulties to be contained. This predicament is underlined by a review of Table 11.5 which outlines the re-financing needs of two critical sovereigns – Spain and Italy – during the period when the ESM has a euro 500 billion ceiling.

Table 11.5 Refinancing needs of Spain and Italy 2012–2016

	Refinancing needs of Spain and Italy 2012-2016 Euro billions					
	2012	2013	2014	2015	2016	TOTAL
SPAIN	161	132	107	99	102	601
ITALY	427	230	201	194	139	1191
TOTAL	588	362	308	293	241	1792
Cum Total	588	950	1258	1551	1792	

Sources: Spanish Treasury, Italian Treasury, IMF.

11.2 IMPACT OF MONETARY UNION

Although the euro currency did not completely replace the old European coins and notes until 2002, it was January 1, 1999 that the euro became the official currency of the Eurozone in the financial markets. Figure 11.2 shows just how dramatic the impact of the official monetary union – the EMU – was to be for the sovereign bond issuances of the member states. The left hand side of the chart prior to the formal implementation of the EMU in 1999 shows the disparate yields of the five sovereigns listed, i.e. Portugal, Spain, Ireland, France, and Italy. The actual yields are not shown but rather the spread in basis points of the 10-year bond of each sovereign over the equivalent German bund yields. As the 1999 introduction approached the yields converged and then for almost all of the next 10 years there were negligible spread values with German bunds for each of the sovereigns. This could be called the golden era for the Eurozone in which member states benefitted from the perception amongst fixed income investors that there was no difference in credit quality for each of the issuers. In many respects it has all of the required characteristics which justify its description as the Eurozone mega bond bubble.

The convergence in yields was actually anticipated by large institutional bond purchasers, and in particular many European banks, and the arbitrage trade of buying the higher yielding bonds of sovereigns such as Greece, Spain, and Portugal and then selling an equivalent euro amount of German bunds became one of the favorite trades of the lead-up to, and early period of, the EMU. The trade was greatly facilitated by the fact that all of the different sovereign bonds were denominated in a single currency which removed the need to hedge the currency risk and the possibility that one of the issuers might devalue its currency against the old

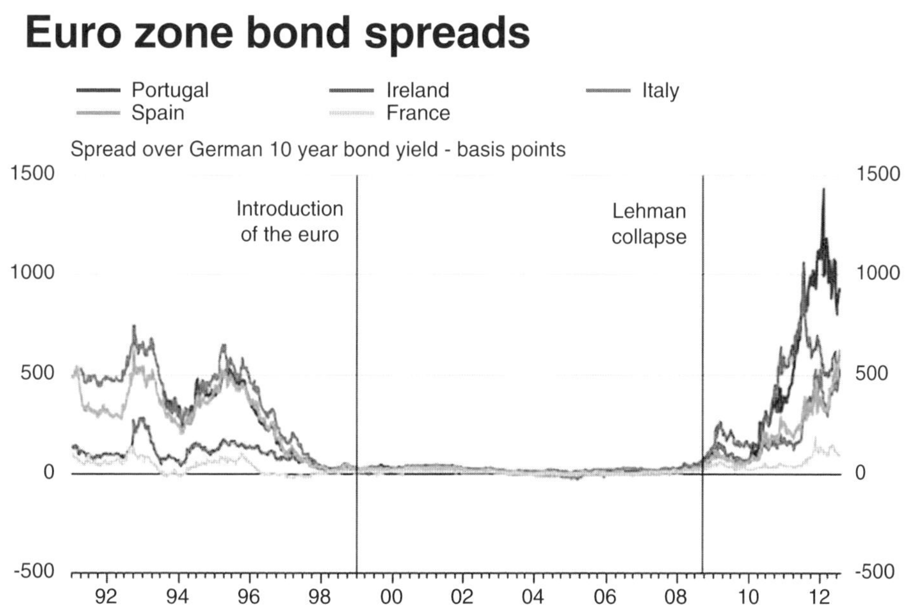

Figure 11.2 Bond spreads for selected Euro area sovereigns July 2012
Source: Thomson Reuters.

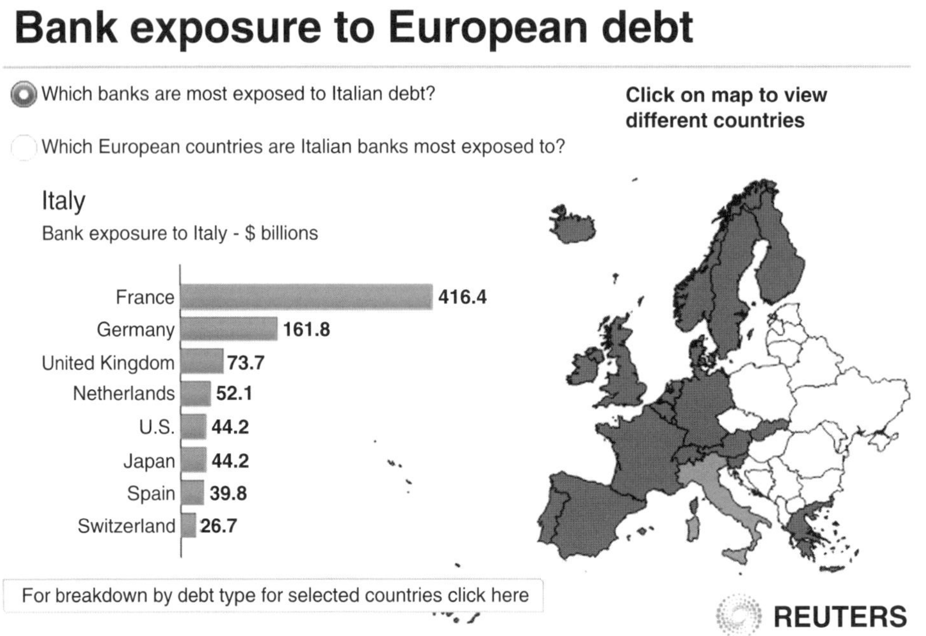

Figure 11.3 Private bank sector exposure to Italian debt
Source: Thomson Reuters.

deutschemark. Some of the very precarious positions that a number of major European banks now have are a direct legacy of the fact that the trade became so widespread.

Many French, German, and some UK banks decided to invest heavily in this convergence trade and when the yields started to diverge abruptly as shown on the right hand side of Table 11.2 there resulted considerable stress to the balance sheets of many banks.

Figure 11.3 is a good echo of the extent to which European banks engaged in the convergence trade as it shows the exposure of the private banking sector of several EU states to Italian debt – most of which is Italian government debt. As can be seen the French banks were, by some considerable margin, the largest participants in this trade and also have substantial exposure to other peripheral EZ debt. This helps to explain why the CDS spreads for Société Générale, Banque Paribas, and Crédit Agricole are some of the highest for the European banking sector. Figure 11.3 also helps to explain why both the French and German governments have been especially keen, with such delicate matters as the re-structuring of Greek sovereign debt, to prevent a disorderly default by any of the distressed peripheral sovereigns as the next step following a major crunch at one of the very large commercial banks within their respective jurisdictions would be a publicly funded bailout. In a political climate which is becoming increasingly hostile to bailouts this is not the kind of measure that French or German politicians would want to present to their electorates.

In hindsight it seems even more remarkable that the complacent perception which gave rise to the convergence of yields during the 10-year period after the implementation of the EMU failed to take into account one of the central flaws of the EZ architecture. The flaw is so fundamental that it is hard not to conclude that the architects either were willfully blind

Table 11.6 Comparison between bank lending and capital market financings for US and Europe

	United States	Europe
GDP 2012	\$15 trillion	\$18 trillion
2012 GDP growth forecast	2.20%	0%
Size of Banking System (Total Assets)	\$12 trillion	\$62 trillion
Ratio bank assets to GDP	80%	344%
Size of Capital Market for Corporate Lending	\$5 trillion	\$1 trillion
Total Corporate Lending Market (Banks vs Capital Markets)	~25%	~85%
Size of securitization market	\$9 trillion	\$3 trillion

to it or totally incompetent. To take the first option, one of the suggestions which has been advanced by some commentators, including George Soros and David Marsh in his excellent history of the single currency *The Euro: The Politics of The New Global Currency*, [9] is that the architects anticipated that there would eventually be a crisis. Their reasoning is that whereas it would have been unpalatable to attempt true fiscal integration back in 1993 at the time of the finalization of the Maastricht Treaty, once the single currency had become a *fait accompli* the citizens of Europe would wish to preserve the monetary union at all costs and when a crisis arose their representatives would have no choice but to amend treaties in order to create something akin to a United States of Europe. Just how mistaken that line of reasoning was remains to be seen but all of the contemporary evidence suggests that far from instigating a move towards federalism and the possibility of built in fiscal transfers from the core to the periphery, the opposite is happening where the citizens of the core are becoming increasingly disenchanted with the grand European experiment. The problem is further aggravated as it is becoming more evident that with a new recession affecting most of the European economies it is increasingly difficult to even separate a strong northern core from a weak southern periphery.

In relation to the broader question of where the potential for system threatening risk from an escalation of the financial crisis in Europe might reside, the third row of Table 11.6, which was presented at the Milken Institute Global Conference held in Los Angeles in May 2012, [10] is particularly disturbing. The total European Union has a higher nominal GDP than the US and expectations of zero GDP growth in 2012 (and that may be an optimistic outlook with the benefit of hindsight), but its private banking system has five times as many assets (i.e. loans) as those for the private sector banks in the US. Reviewing the other rows of the table it can be clearly seen that European enterprise is far more dependent on the banking system than its American counterparts. That the banks play a much larger role in the funding of corporations in Europe than the capital markets helps to explain the much larger asset base for the European banking sector but it has two consequences which could feed the negative feedback loop dynamics that have arisen from the debt overhang and austerity programs widely implemented across the EZ states.

From the bankers' perspective for every asset, that is for every loan, there should be some collateral supporting the valuation of those loans on their balance sheet. Given their exposure to sovereign debt and also to questionable real estate in many troubled markets, Ireland and Spain especially, but also there have been concerns expressed about property values in France, [11] and also to deteriorating credit conditions for some European SMEs, there are legitimate and ongoing concerns about the solvency of some of the large European commercial banks.

Certainly very few of these banks either have the balance sheet or the appetite to lend new funds and consumers and SMEs have little or no unencumbered collateral to be seeking new financing either. The real risk that arises from these disproportionately large balance sheets for European banks relative to their GDP and to their US counterparts is that as the governor of the Bank of England has observed "banks live globally but die locally." [12]

In a worst case scenario where there could be a run against say one of the large French banks the Banque de France and the French government would almost certainly have to take control of that bank and transfer the assets (it should of course be remembered that the other side of those assets on the balance sheet is liabilities) to the public sector. Needless to say this would act as a further destabilizing factor at the very core of the Eurozone.

11.3 THE DEBT DEFLATION TRAP IN THE EUROZONE

One of the most astute global macro investors, George Soros, made the following remarks during a visit to Davos, Switzerland in January 2012: [13]

> "The policies that Germany is pushing on the eurozone strict fiscal austerity, it is creating a deflationary debt spiral because it puts pressure on wages and profits. So as the GDP declines, the debt ratio goes against you, then you need more austerity and that makes the economy decline some more and that is the trap we are caught in . . . "

> "the weaker members of the euro zone are relegated to the status of third world countries that became highly indebted in a foreign currency," he said. "Germany is acting as the task master imposing tough fiscal discipline. This will generate both economic and political tensions that could destroy the European Union."

One does not, necessarily, have to go along with the scathing criticism that Soros has leveled against the Bundesbank and the Merkel government, augmented in additional comments elsewhere, to see that there is a rather apocalyptic tone to these candid remarks. Soros has an intuitive grasp of the destructive dynamics that are present in the Eurosystem framework which many economists and commentators who are preoccupied with just GDP data, measures of productivity etc. (not that these are unimportant) fail to fully comprehend. He is surely right to suggest that the peripheral nations – the GIPSI states [14] are effectively imprisoned within a foreign currency which may seem to be just attention grabbing and without substance. But for a country like Greece which has a very uncompetitive economy when expressed in euro terms the possibility of restoring some of that non-competitiveness through currency devaluation is not available unless the country decides to abandon the euro.

Willem Buiter, formerly professor at the London School of Economics and currently Chief Economist at Citigroup, has suggested that any benefit to Greece from a devaluation would be very short lived – he is actually on record as saying sardonically it would probably only be a benefit for about two weeks [15] – as costs, primarily labor costs in a structurally unsound economy such as that of Greece, would jump quickly by demands from labor unions to counter the loss of purchasing power suffered from much higher import costs. But this view has to be counterbalanced against the no-win problem which Greece currently is experiencing and is revealed in Figure 11.4. The data is obtained from the IMF World Economic Outlook for 2011 and has been superseded in 2012 by even more depressing data for each of the three countries shown on the chart, but the presentation style of the chart is still valuable in showing the nature of a debt deflation spiral. If one abides by the Debt to GDP ratio which seems to be the

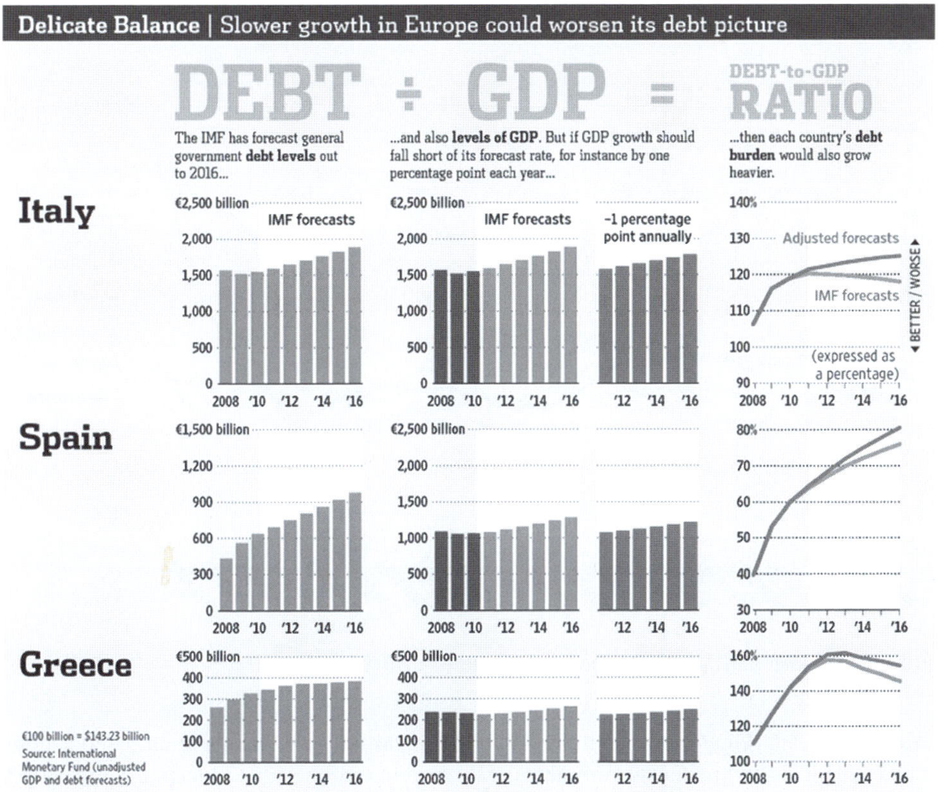

Figure 11.4 Debt to GDP ratios and growth projections for Spain, Italy, and Greece
Source: Wall Street Journal.

preferred statistic for each of the three major CRAs it is necessary to look, as is well illustrated by the layout of Figure 11.4, at the dynamics which drive both the numerator, i.e. Debt, and the denominator of that ratio, i.e. GDP, and more pertinently the rate of increase/decrease of each. It is worth just noting that, although the three most established credit ratings agencies pay close attention to the Debt/GDP ratio, this is not the view taken by the "new kid on the block" CRA, Egan Jones, which focuses on the ratio of debt service costs to government revenues (primarily taxation) and which more fits the methodology by which corporations are rated. [16]

In essence a debt deflationary spiral is a negative feedback loop which is especially evidenced by the data shown for Greece at the bottom of Figure 11.4, and with more current data is becoming evident also for Spain, and to a somewhat lesser extent for Italy. [17] Even after a re-structuring of Greek sovereign debt in early 2012 [18] the ratio is above 160% and if, as the graphic supposes, the old IMF forecasts are far too optimistic then the path taken in the rightmost segment of the chart will show that the ratio will continue to increase. This deterioration is due to a combination of increased debt service – Greece is still paying double digit coupons on its more recent bond issuance since its major debt re-structuring – further borrowing which will almost certainly have to be undertaken, and also to a dramatically declining GDP (estimated to be around a 7% contraction in 2012 alone).

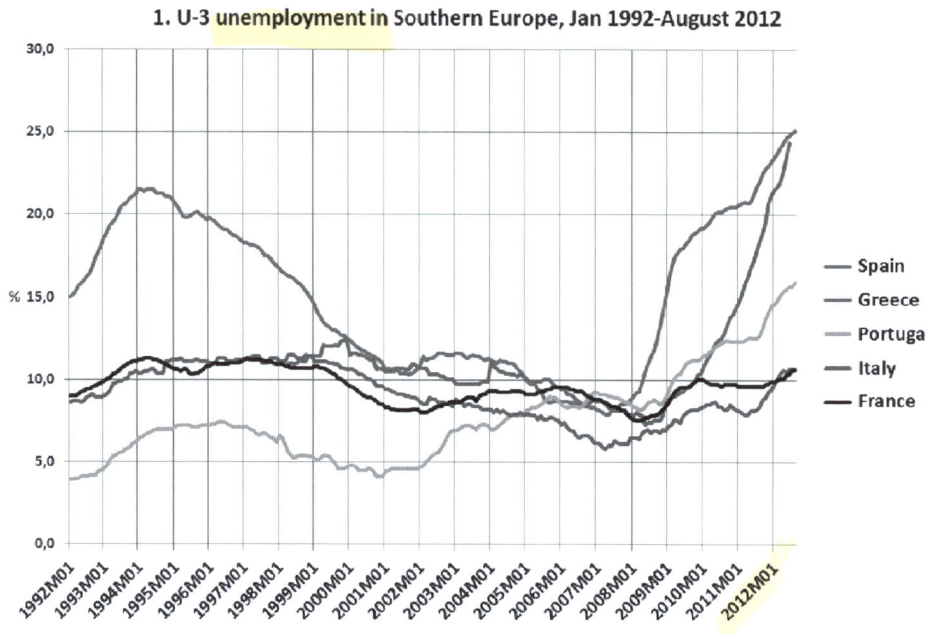

Figure 11.5 Unemployment in Southern Europe 1992 – August 2012
Source: Eurostat.

The simple debt/GDP model presented for Spain and Italy also needs to take into account the fact that yields on Spanish government debt have been rising in 2012 (despite a brief respite resulting from the ECBs two LTRO programs) and have exceeded 7.5% on 10-year maturities, and not quite so acutely (at least at the time of writing) the yields on 10-year Italian government bonds have been above 6% on occasions, and been consistently above 5% during 2012.

A further very sobering set of statistics which underscore the human capital costs arising from the flawed structure of the Eurozone can be seen in Figure 11.5 and Figure 11.6. For the most troubled EZ states total unemployment rates, according to Eurostat, in August 2012 can be seen in Figure 11.5. Spain and Greece are both showing rates of approximately 25%, with Portugal around 17%. Most forecasts suggest that these rates are only likely to increase as the evidence from Eurostat, the IMF and others is suggesting as of Q4, 2012 that the Eurozone's recession is deepening. More alarming are the statistics shown in Figure 11.6 which focus on unemployment amongst the under 25s in some of the EU states. Both Greece and Spain have disturbing rates in excess of 50% and even for the less troubled states such as France and the UK (the latter is not of course an EZ member state) the rates for youth unemployment exceed 20%.

The economic damage which is being inflicted across a generation of young people in Europe is hard to estimate. Even more concerning should be the disaffection and disengagement that such young people are developing with respect to European institutions. Without any real stake-holding in the future of their respective national economies, and with growing disrespect for pan European political structures, there is increased risk that more extreme political ideologies may become more appealing.

The debt spiral in Spain is further aggravated by the constant pressure on Spanish banks from their need to accept substantial write-offs from real estate loans which are becoming

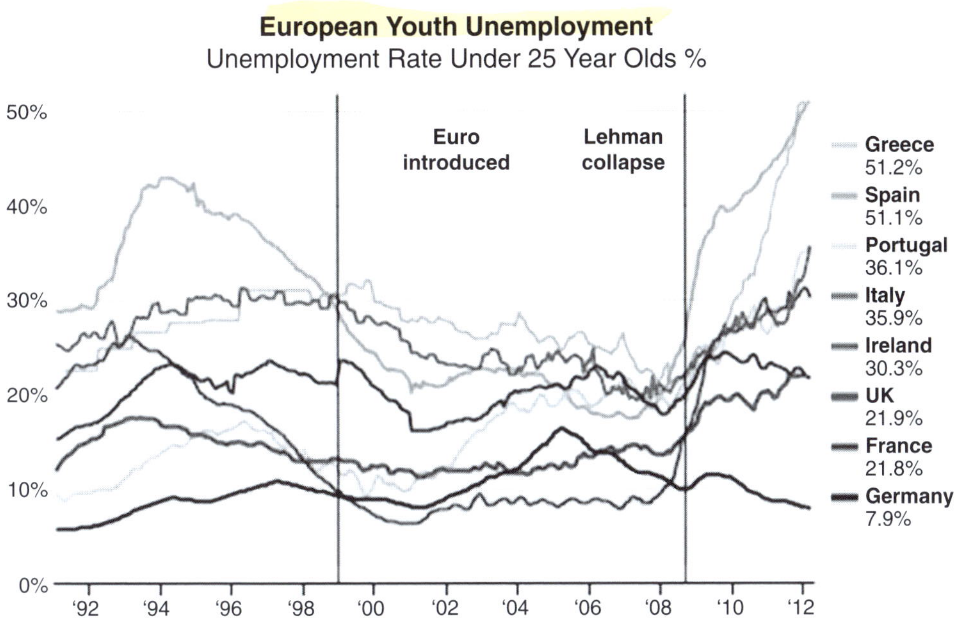

Figure 11.6 Youth unemployment in Eurozone February 2012
Source: Thomson Reuters.

delinquent. Additional pressures on Spanish banks are coming from capital flight in which increasing numbers of Spanish depositors are withdrawing funds from onshore banks and moving them to other jurisdictions, such as Germany, Switzerland, and the UK. It does not require a feverish imagination to contemplate the worst case scenario for Spain if it should have to bail out its banking system, thereby massively increasing the obligations on the public balance sheet. This raises the worst fear of the eurocrats which is that Spain is too big to save! It should be factored as one of the largest potential risks to a future systemic crisis.

Surely the ECB would not allow Spain to implode and create enough financial contagion to threaten the survival of the euro currency and the Eurozone itself? I pose this as a rhetorical question but Figure 11.7 shows just how much fire power from its balance sheet the ECB has had to employ over the last two years especially in its attempt to convince private investors that they should not throw in the towel with respect to their holdings of the sovereign debt of the peripheral states. Of each of the four central banks shown on the graphic the ECB now has the highest ratio of assets to GDP, having surpassed Japan which has suffered its own version of the debt deflationary spiral for a lot longer than Europe. With more than 30% assets to GDP there must be some question mark over the long-term credibility of the ECB's convalescence strategy. PIMCO's Paul Gross has remarked that central banks are the places where bad bonds go to die, [19] so it may be that the ECB is actually running a morgue rather than a convalescence home.

One thing which is becoming more and more apparent is that the LTRO programs of late 2011 and early 2012 in which Spanish and Italian banks have been buying up the debts of their sovereigns has provided an excellent exit strategy for other private sector banks who are not only on a buyer's strike but are liquidating as much of their exposure as possible to the debt of the troubled EZ states. [20]

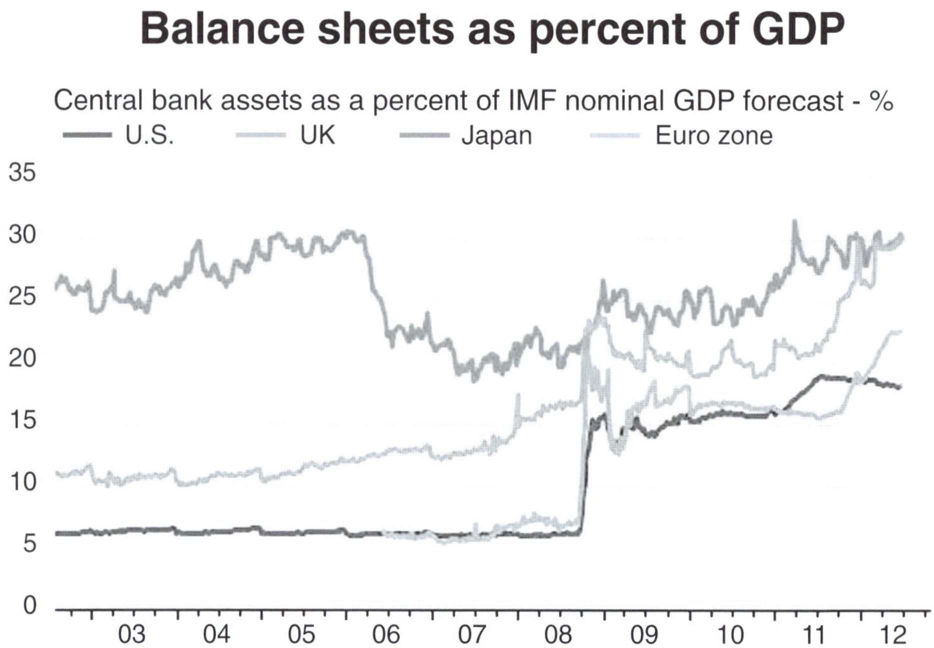

Figure 11.7 Central bank balance sheets as percentage of GDP July 2012
Source: Thomson Reuters Datastream.

11.4 EUROBONDS

There is a large and quite vociferous constituency amongst not only Eurozone policy makers but also amongst asset managers and analysts who suggest that the best way to convince the private sector to re-engage with the sovereign debt issuance of the peripheral member states would be for the EZ to issue Eurobonds. In part this is a response to the recognition of the difficulties of designing a new architecture for rescuing the solvency of distressed EZ states based on the limitations of structures such as the EFSF and its successor the ESM. The Merkel government in Germany and the Bundesbank however have also been just as vocal in shooting down this idea. The German Constitutional Court has also declared that any such initiative would directly contravene the German constitution and perhaps most critically a decision to introduce Eurobonds would almost certainly require a new EU treaty which would be tantamount to opening a can of especially wriggly and unattractive worms. Apart from the fact that electorates would have to be convinced, at least in the more democratic member states which would want to put this issue to a referendum, which is no small task (that is to understate the problem by several orders of magnitude I would surmise), the process could take many years and is not likely to solve the near-term problem that the private sector has a very limited appetite for stepping in and replacing the ECB as the buyer of last resort for Spanish, Italian etc. sovereign bonds.

The reason why Germany is so reluctant to even discuss the matter is that to do so would have the unintended consequence of highlighting the legal flaw considered already in connection with the discussion of the absence of joint liability in the current EU framework. Additionally, to give that issue a full airing would run the twin risk of antagonizing the German electorate even more than they are, and that having the required debate would almost certainly bring about even more vitriolic anti-Germany attacks from citizens in other member states.

Interestingly an outspoken critic of Eurobonds was the former ECB president, Jean Claude Trichet, as this quotation makes clear: [21]

> The European Central Bank maintains its position that eurobonds with a "joint and several" guarantee would not be appropriate given the present circumstances in the European economies, ECB president Jean-Claude Trichet said Monday.
>
> "In the ECB, as you know, we are not in favour of European bonds in which the European countries would be joint and several. We don't consider it is something that would be appropriate in the present circumstances," Trichet told the European Parliament's Economic and Monetary Affairs Committee on Monday.
>
> Just to be totally clear and unambiguous on the matter – never something that a central banker should really do – the following direct quotations from M. Trichet are also on the record of the European Parliament:
>
> "We are not ourselves in favour of issuing securities, treasuries that will be joint and several," Trichet told the European Parliament.
>
> "We consider it is good that each particular state, each particular treasury has its own refinancing and has its own way of being on the market."

In an interview with the French newspaper *Le Monde* in May 2012 Jens Weidmann, President of the German Bundesbank and member of the ECB Council, expressed a categorical repudiation of the notion that Eurobonds would be acceptable to Germany, and Angela Merkel in June 2012 stated in the Bundestag that there will not be Eurobonds "while I am still alive." [22]

A good summary of Weidmann's position and indeed the overall objection to Eurobonds on the part of the German government and financial establishment is found in the following: [23]

> "The belief that Eurobonds could solve the current crisis is an illusion," he said, reflecting the opinion of his compatriots, an astounding 79% of whom were dead set against them, grasping how insidious these bonds would be for German taxpayers.
>
> Eurobonds, which would spread liability for one country's sovereign debt across all Eurozone countries, could only happen, if at all, "after a long process that would among other things have to include changing the constitution of several countries, modifying treaties, and having more of a budgetary union," he said. "You don't entrust someone with your credit card if you cannot control how much he spends."
>
> Communalizing national debts across the Eurozone would require "federalism," he said. "But even in countries where governments clamor for Eurobonds, such as France, I see neither public debate on, nor popular support for the transfer of sovereignty that must accompany them."
>
> "In the US, certain people believe that the ECB should buy more sovereign debt like the American Federal Reserve. But we're not a federal state, and the Fed doesn't buy the debt of California or Florida." And he vetoed in advance any new Long Term Refinancing Operations (LTRO) through which the ECB late last year and earlier this year had lent banks €1 trillion for three years at 1%.

"Like morphine, they relieve the pain but don't cure the disease," he said. "And there are side effects, such as delaying the reform of the banking sector."

If Eurobonds are a non-starter, and if the Germans are only committed to a pro-rated liability for anything that can go wrong within the Eurozone states, the capital markets may well be moving towards the ultimate test of the solvency of certain sovereigns. Once again, there is a danger in thinking, as for example Christine Lagarde, head of the IMF appears to think [24] that traders would be dissuaded by larger "firewalls" from calling the bluff of the Troika – the EU Commission, the ECB, and the IMF. The fallacy is to think that traders have always been testing only the size of the rescue facilities, whether they be the capital commitment to the EFSF or to the ESM, the size of the LTRO programs, and even the activities of the ECB's SMP program. [25] Far more seriously they appear to be testing the nature of the legal guarantee behind the facility.

To be more direct about it I shall state a view, which is that the euro currency bloc faces an almost impossible dilemma. On the one hand, over the longer term (maybe five years, maybe more) the Eurozone is almost certainly doomed, unless the German government is willing to underwrite a bailout system which makes them joint and several guarantors for all of the debt of the Eurozone nations collectively. On the other hand, there is increasing evidence that the German electorate wants no such thing.

The question that really needs to be confronted by the politicians of Germany – given that the ECB is now expanding its balance sheet and incurring obligations on behalf of the citizens of the Eurozone's member states – is who stands behind the debt of the ECB?

Does the principle of several liability realistically apply there? I see this as somewhat similar to the situation that the US faced with Fannie Mae and Freddie Mac in which there was not an explicit US guarantee until the whole edifice came tumbling down in 2008 at which point the holders of GSE bonds needed an answer right away – are these things federally guaranteed or not? The US decided that the public safety net would be put in place to cover them and another possible trigger for a systemic meltdown was averted. The simple rule of thumb that the US government has taken since the financial crisis of 2008 has been, to return to the main motif, we're all in this together and the debt holders will be protected by the full faith and credit of the US government.

If a truly Darwinian outcome were to befall the Eurozone and capital flight from the banks of troubled peripheral states were to gravitate towards the center, would Germany stand tall and agree to fully underwrite or backstop Eurobonds? This is the really hard question for which the only sane answer might be that it is better for Germany to get out of this commitment sooner while the going is good, rather than later when the entanglement is so great that there is no way out.

The Germans are effectively snookered on this issue. Unless they agree that they are totally committed to supporting the euro – with all of the nasty political consequences that would flow from that, including even the possibility of German civil unrest – then the euro's next crisis may be its final one as, to paraphrase W.B Yeats' classic line from *The Second Coming*, the center may not hold. [26]

The architectural flaws of the EZ currency club are almost too numerous to mention but can be framed essentially in the following question: How does one expect a "union" to survive under a common currency, which has to be supported by a central bank, when any and all of the member states are free to issue as much debt in the collective currency as they deem necessary? A more pointed way of expressing the same sentiment can be found in the comments made by Jens Weidmann to *Le Monde* in May 2012 and which are referenced in endnote 22 to this chapter: "You don't entrust someone with your credit card if you cannot control how much he spends."

11.5 THE VISCERAL DIMENSION TO THE EUROZONE'S PROBLEMS

In concluding this chapter, and to take a more emotive and visceral perspective with regard to the ongoing saga of difficulties facing the single currency and the matter of closer political integration which may well be resisted by European electorates, the following is a slightly modified extract from an article published by the author in 2010 and which is only offered as an optional addendum to the reader: [27]

> There has been a lot of criticism from various German and French politicians and other eurocrats that the markets have been displaying irrational behavior and "have it in for the euro." Once again, when stripped down to the bone, these kinds of statements need to be understood as the utterances of individuals coming from cultures which are highly competitive and which have had a troubled history.
>
> Part of this resentment is tinged with a certain hostility (and perhaps envy) toward the pre-eminence of "Anglo Saxon finance" (whatever that means!) with London and New York clearly outranking Paris and Frankfurt as financial hubs. Again to pursue the more emotive side of this envy and anger at the Anglo Saxon axis, there is considerable antagonism expressed by many continental bankers at what they perceive as financial engineers in London and New York embodying the "Wild West" of modern finance.
>
> However, one of the hardest things for such critics to explain is how and why some of the largest purchasers of questionable structured products were banks within their own domiciles. Furthermore to accuse traders in markets as being subject to bouts of irrational behavior is like complaining that your national football team should have won the game because they played more skillfully. The height of folly and hubris of the technocratic mindset would be to imagine that these bouts of non-rational behavior can be eliminated by clever regulators and regulations.
>
> The same kinds of strongly visceral responses are pervasive in the EZ crisis. Why should the German electorate agree to a new EZ architecture which would include, among other devices leading to more "integration," provision for fiscal transfers, and where amongst the recipients would be Greek citizens who can retire in their early fifties on a state pension? West Germans had to extend considerable generosity to twenty million fellow countrymen/women in 1990 after the Berlin Wall was removed and the old GDR was absorbed into the new German Federation. The fiscal transfers and re-structuring based upon accepting the old East German mark at parity with the old Deutschemark, while it was portrayed (correctly) as an exciting re-unification by German leaders, for a lot of ordinary German citizens there was a lot of disgruntlement about the drop in living standards and increased taxes that were involved in the process.
>
> To expect German voters to elect politicians who would consent to treaty changes within the EU which would allow fiscal transfers to the peripherals may be as far removed from the real world as is the belief that an enlarged EFSF or ESM is going to solve the structural flaws in the EMU.
>
> However the continuing use of the term "uncertainty" with regard to the outlook for the Eurozone puts me in mind of another term which has been used to describe the aftermath of the bursting of the Japanese real estate/equities bubble of the 1980s which is "zombie." A zombie financial

system is one in which uncertainty is omnipresent as participants continue to deny that there really is a problem and try to find comfort in *pretend and extend* stratagems which will hopefully make insolvency problems go away.

In conclusion and to enlarge the context, for the fiscal problems of the US are not that dissimilar in many respects to those being seen in much of Europe, there is a real question mark as to how long we can all continue to kick the can down the road and believe that in the long run we will muddle through without dealing with our demons.

ENDNOTES

1. *Crisis has barely begun, says GLG hedge fund manager*, Reuters, June 20, 2012:

> The global financial crisis has barely started and is likely to last for at least another 15 to 20 years as major economies cut debt levels, according to Jamil Baz, one of Europe's most prominent hedge fund managers.
>
> Baz, chief investment strategist at GLG Partners, told the GAIM 2012 conference in Monaco that total debt levels in a number of major economies had actually risen since 2007 and had much further to fall before reaching "a semblance of equilibrium".

   http://www.reuters.com/article/2012/06/20/uk-hedgefunds-gaim-glg-idUSLNE85J00C20120620.
2. The ECB website can be found at http://www.ecb.int/home/html/index.en.html.
3. Clive Corcoran, *The Eurozone Crisis: The Visceral and the Cerebral*, http://seekingalpha.com/article/241235-the-eurozone-crisis-the-visceral-and-the-cerebral.
4. The following outline of the EFSF is found at its website:

> The European Financial Stability Facility (EFSF) was created by the euro area Member States following the decisions taken on 9 May 2010 within the framework of the Ecofin Council.
>
> The EFSF's mandate is to safeguard financial stability in Europe by providing financial assistance to euro area Member States.
>
> EFSF is authorised to use the following instruments linked to appropriate conditionality:
>
> Provide loans to countries in financial difficulties
> Intervene in the debt primary and secondary markets. Intervention in the secondary market will be only on the basis of an ECB analysis recognising the existence of exceptional financial market circumstances and risks to financial stability
> Act on the basis of a precautionary programme
> Finance recapitalisations of financial institutions through loans to governments.
>
> To fulfill its mission, EFSF issues bonds or other debt instruments on the capital markets.
>
> EFSF is backed by guarantee commitments from the euro area Member States for a total of €780 billion and has a lending capacity of €440 billion.

   http://www.efsf.europa.eu/about/index.htm.
5. Special Report: Standard & Poor's Actions On Eurozone Sovereigns Publication date: February 17, 2012, http://www.standardandpoors.com/ratings/articles/en/us/?articleType=HTML&assetID=1245329040931.
6. Bond insurer Ambac files for bankruptcy, Reuters, November 8, 2010, http://www.reuters.com/article/2010/11/08/us-ambac-idUSTRE6A75EW20101108.
7. Some useful background to this new entity ESM can be found at the European Commission's website: http://ec.europa.eu/economy_finance/articles/financial_operations/2011-07-11-esm-treaty_en.htm.

8. Wolfgang Schaeuble is German Finance Minister and is quoted as follows in an article entitled "Schaeuble: No euro bonds in my lifetime either," Reuters June 29, 2012:

    German Finance Minister Wolfgang Schaeuble echoed Angela Merkel's pledge that Europe would have no common euro bonds in her lifetime, saying on Friday they wouldn't happen as long as he lived either unless other radical reforms occurred first.

    "Euro bonds, if understood as euro bonds without common liability and without common financial policy, are something that I don't want in my lifetime either," Schaeuble said.

    http://www.reuters.com/article/2012/06/29/us-eurozone-bonds-schaeuble-idUSBRE85S18P20120629.
9. David Marsh, *The Euro: The Politics of The New Global Currency* (Yale University Press, May 2009).
10. Slide shown at the Milken Institute Global Conference in Los Angeles, May 2012, http://www.milkeninstitute.org/gc2012/.
11. French Real Estate: A Little Bubbly, WSJ Online, September 14, 2011:

    It is a mistake to treat real estate as a safe haven, says Hervé Boulhol, the Organization for Economic Cooperation and Development's France economist, as such an underestimation of risk can, in turn, inflate a bubble. Until the end of 2009, the OECD had been able to explain price movements in the French market with fundamental factors, but in 2010 their usual econometric calculations based on factors such as cohabitation rates, credit conditions and household incomes failed to explain what was going on.

    "This may signal a bubble phenomenon, as a bubble is a disconnection with fundamentals," Mr. Boulhol says.

    http://online.wsj.com/article/SB10001424053111903532804576568573122088718.html.
12. The attribution of the remark to Mervyn King has been cited by a number of commentators including in the following speech entitled *The Future Shape of Banking* which presented by Bill Williams at the BBA's Annual Banking Conference on 29 June 2011. The speech can be found online at http://www.kpmg.com/uk/en/issuesandinsights/articlespublications/pages/future-shape-banking-bill-michael-speech-bba-annual-banking-conference.aspx.
13. *Remarks at the World Economic Forum at the Central Sporthotel, Davos, Switzerland* by George Soros, January 25, 2012, http://www.georgesoros.com/interviews-speeches/entry/remarks_at_the_world_economic_forum_at_the_central_sporthotel_davos_switzer/.
14. Here is a comment from Wikipedia on the adoption of the alternative acronym to the often used PIGS

    PIGS is an acronym used to refer to the economies of Portugal, Italy, Greece and Spain. Since 2008, the term has included Ireland, either in place of Italy or with an additional I.

    Originally, the term referred to Portugal, Italy, Greece and Spain, which were notable as similar economic environments. Since the European sovereign debt crisis, with the addition of Ireland, the term is used to group European economies facing particular financial crisis. Some news and economic organisations have limited or banned use of the term because of criticism regarding perceived offensive connotations.

    http://en.wikipedia.org/wiki/PIGS_(economics).
    See also Hey, Jamie Dimon, You Sure About that Acronym? WSJ Blogs, January 14, 2011:

    Europe hasn't been thrilled about being called "PIIGS" — the acronym that refers to the pain points of the Continent's sovereign debt troubles: Portugal, Ireland, Italy, Greece and Spain.

    Then this morning, J.P. Morgan CEO Jamie Dimon instead referred to his bank's exposure to the "GIPSI" countries, or Greece, Ireland, Portugal, Spain and Italy.

> The moniker – which even diehard Europhiles at Deal Journal HQ had never heard – also sounds like the word "Gypsy," a term for an ethnic group sometimes known as Roma. The term Roma is preferable in many, but not all, quarters in Europe.
>
> Seeking Alpha contributor Carlos X. Alexandre claimed credit in November for coining the "GIPSI" shorthand for the frazzled countries in Europe. But the turn of phrase doesn't seem to have caught on widely, at least outside of J.P. Morgan's Park Avenue offices.
>
> One advantage of "GIPSI" over PIIGS, as Alexandre pointed out: It reflects the order of risk severity for each country, with Greece first and Spain and Italy bringing up the rear.
>
> J.P. Morgan declined to comment.

http://blogs.wsj.com/deals/2011/01/14/hey-jamie-dimon-you-sure-about-that-acronym/.

15. The comment was made during a panel discussion at the Milken Institute Global Conference in Los Angeles, May 2012. The panel was entitled *Where Will Economic Growth Come From?* More details including a link to the video of the panel discussion can be found at the following location: http://www.milkeninstitute.org/events/gcprogram.taf?function=detail&eventid=gc12&EvID=3126.
16. Egan-Jones Ratings is an independent NRSRO and not paid by corporations issuing bonds. Our only mission is to assist our buy-side institutional clients through accurate, risk averse, market sensitive credit ratings with predictive value.

> Our business model is different. *We're paid by investors, we have to earn our keep every single year. Basically we have to provide value to those investors or else they're not going to sign up again.* S&P and Moody's are being paid by the issuers of debt, and they don't have the pressures to be as timely and as accurate as we do with our ratings.

http://www.zerohedge.com/contributed/2012-06-15/sean-egan-europe-and-why-they-are-always-out-front-other-ratings-agencies.

Debt fears lead to US downgrade, FT.com July 18, 2011, http://www.ft.com/cms/s/0/b13d5d56-b16a-11e0-9444-00144feab49a.html.

Egan-Jones has become the first US rating agency to downgrade the country's sovereign credit rating from triple A to double A plus as it focuses on the rapid rise in outstanding debt over the past five years.

http://www.egan-jones.com/.

17. The problem with Italy's debt is its size, *Daily Telegraph*, November 9, 2011

> Italy is Europe's third biggest economy and the world's third biggest sovereign borrower. It's public debt stands at €1.9trillion (£1.6 trillion) – around five times the size of Greece's.

http://www.telegraph.co.uk/finance/financialcrisis/8878970/The-problem-with-Italys-debt-is-its-size.html.

18. Greek Debt Restructuring Leaves Dissent Question, *Wall Street Journal*, April 25, 2012, http://online.wsj.com/article/SB10001424052702303990604577365992964156550.html.See also Greece inches closer to €206bn debt deal, *Financial Times*, March 7, 2012; http://www.ft.com/cms/s/0/4fc58c98-67b7-11e1-b4a1-00144feabdc0.html.
19. PIMCO's Paul Gross remarked on Twitter that "central banks are where bad bonds go to die." http://www.indexuniverse.com/sections/news/11506-gross-reintroduces-trxt-to-world-as-bond.html.
20. An article on the buyer's strike in Eurozone bonds can be found at the English edition of Der Spiegel online: Euro Zone on the Brink: A Continent Stares into the Abyss, November 18, 2011, http://www.spiegel.de/international/europe/euro-zone-on-the-brink-a-continent-stares-into-the-abyss-a-800285-2.html.

21. ECB Trichet: Maintains Opposition To Joint Eurobond, *Market News International*, June 10, 2010, http://www.forexlive.com/blog/2010/06/21/ecb-trichet-maintains-opposition-to-joint-eurobond/. See also Trichet against European omnibond, FT Alphaville, December 8, 2008, http://ftalphaville.ft.com/blog/2008/12/08/50177/trichet-against-european-omnibond/.
22. Jens Weidmann, Bundesbank President, *ECB Has Reached The Limit Of Its Mandate* (May 25, 2012):

> FRANKFURT (MNI) – The European Central Bank has reached the limit of its mandate, especially in the use of its non-conventional measures, ECB Governing Council member Jens Weidmann said in an interview published Friday morning.
>
> "In the end, these [measures] are risks for taxpayers, most notably in France and Germany," the Bundesbank chief told France's daily Le Monde.
>
> Commenting on the ECB's longer-term refinancing operations, Weidmann said that the measures had bought time, but have not resolved the structural issues of the crisis.
>
> "It's like morphine," Weidmann said. The LTROs "provide relief from the pain, but are not a cure for the illness. They could even have side effects, including delayed adjustments in the banking sector, for example."
>
> Weidmann also reiterated his opposition to the idea of granting a banking license to the European Stability Mechanism so that it could obtain funding directly from the ECB. He opposes such a move, he said, because it would amount to "subjugating monetary policy to budget policy, which greatly harms the credibility of the ECB. And also because monetary financing of states, for good reasons, is strictly prohibited by the [EU] treaties."

23. The President of the Bundesbank lashes out, May 27, 2012, http://mobile.businessinsider.com/the-president-of-the-bundesbank-lashes-out-2012-5
24. ÌMF Chief Lagarde Seeks Stronger Firewall to Protect Growth, *The Independent* (Ireland), April 13, 2012:

> A STRONGER firewall is needed to protect the world economy from Europe's debt crisis but the International Monetary Fund may not need as much money as it thought just a few months ago, the head of the global lender said yesterday.
>
> Speaking ahead of meetings of finance chiefs in Washington on April 20–21, IMF Managing Director Christine Lagarde said a deal among countries on ponying up more money for the Fund would take time, signaling an agreement may not be sealed next week.

    http://www.independent.ie/business/world/mf-chief-lagarde-seeks-stronger-firewall-to-protect-growth-3080188.html.

25. An outline of the ECB's programs of non-standard monetary measures can be found at the following link at the ECB website: http://www.ecb.int/mopo/liq/html/index.en.html.
26. "Things fall apart; the centre cannot hold" from the poem by WB Yeats, The Second Coming (1919):

> Turning and turning in the widening gyre
> The falcon cannot hear the falconer;
> Things fall apart; the centre cannot hold;
> Mere anarchy is loosed upon the world,
> The blood-dimmed tide is loosed, and everywhere
> The ceremony of innocence is drowned;
> The best lack all conviction, while the worst
> Are full of passionate intensity.
>
> Surely some revelation is at hand;
> Surely the Second Coming is at hand.

The Second Coming! Hardly are those words out
When a vast image out of Spiritus Mundi
Troubles my sight: somewhere in sands of the desert
A shape with lion body and the head of a man,
A gaze blank and pitiless as the sun,
Is moving its slow thighs, while all about it
Reel shadows of the indignant desert birds.
The darkness drops again; but now I know
That twenty centuries of stony sleep
Were vexed to nightmare by a rocking cradle,
And what rough beast, its hour come round at last,
Slouches towards Bethlehem to be born?

27. Clive Corcoran, *The Eurozone Crisis: The Visceral and the Cerebral,* See endnote 3.

12

China, Commodities, and the Global Growth Narrative

From the global macro perspective there are several *key drivers* and motivational narratives which can be seen at work in the financial markets on a day to day basis. Being better equipped to discern these key narratives, along with the kinds of patterns in cross asset movements which have been our focus, will provide valuable clues as to the current predilection of the overall market with respect to its appetite or aversion to macro risk. Amongst the narratives which most contribute to market perceptions, and manifestations of the prevailing risk on/risk off sentiment, are pronouncements by respected China analysts and pundits regarding the outlook for the global economy based on the growth dynamics within the world's most populous nation. Given the anemic recovery in the USA since the global financial crisis, the seemingly endless mishaps in the Eurozone, and the concerns about the debt overhang and associated de-leveraging of the banking system, a boost for the global growth bulls and a rally in risk assets can often be attributed to positive economic news regarding China. FT Alphaville has somewhat cynically referred to this phenomenon as "the world's biggest put option – the China growth story." [1]

Obviously in a single chapter of a book, which is covering a large enough terrain, there will be need for selective brevity in consideration of the vital macro-economic characteristics of the world's second largest economy. The focus in this chapter will be on the significant inter-relationship between the changing sentiments regarding China – whether its economy is continuing to achieve the elevated expectations on the one hand or whether it is heading for a hard landing on the other – and the pricing of industrial commodities. However a broad sketch of the main economic fundamentals will be our starting point.

The National Bureau of Statistics of China reported that the nation's GDP in the first quarter of 2012 was almost 11 trillion yuan: a year-on-year increase of 8.1%. In US dollar terms the most recent GDP figure on an annualized basis translates into approximately $7 trillion. According to more or less contemporaneous statistics available from the IMF's April 2012 *World Economic Outlook* this compares with total GDP for the United States in 2011 of approximately $15 trillion and, in third place behind China, the GDP of Japan is approximately $5.8 trillion. On a GDP per capita basis the People's Republic of China (PRC) with $8400 per annum only manages a world ranking of 92 according to the 2011 IMF statistics. This divergence between the overall global GDP ranking, and the far more modest ranking in terms of per capita income distribution, echoes an observation from PIMCO's Mohammed El Erian that "China has become globally systemically important despite the fact that it is not rich on a GDP per capita country basis." [2]

An indication of the spectacular growth in the GDP of China since 1995 is reflected in the steep gradient of the path taken in the middle chart on the top row in Figure 12.1. The increase in GDP from less than $1 trillion in 1995 to $7 trillion in 2011 represents a compounding annual

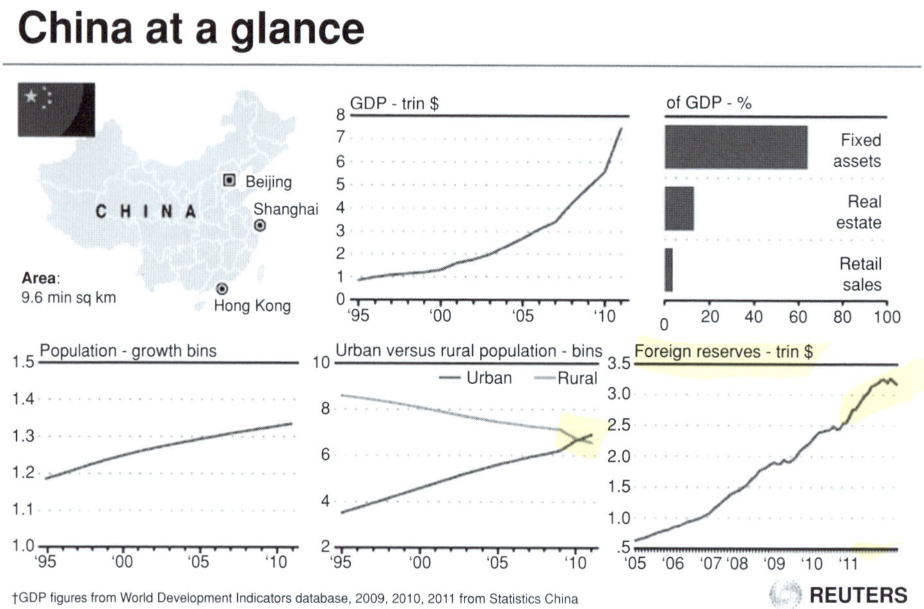

Figure 12.1 China – key economic metrics January 2012
Source: Thomson Reuters.

growth rate of more than 12%. Longer term charts dating back to the 1960s reveal almost parabolic growth of China's GDP and these older charts would also reflect more dramatically than is indicated in the middle graphic on the bottom row of Figure 12.1 the increasing urbanization of the Chinese population. In 1995 approximately 25% of the population lived in cities and 75% in rural communities but by 2010 the composition had shifted so substantially that more than half of China's 1.3 billion people now live in cities with a corresponding drop below half for those in rural areas. This dramatic shift poses quite profound policy issues for the Chinese central planners as they try to allocate resources effectively and, for example as will be discussed below, attempt to maintain affordability of residential accommodation for the huge influx of their citizens into the new sprawling conurbations, as exemplified by Shanghai, Beijing, and Chongqing. [3]

The bottom row right hand chart of the useful graphical overview from Reuters and provided in Figure 12.1 illustrates the quite remarkable accumulation of foreign reserves by the PBOC since 2005. In early 2012 these reserves have been estimated at about $3.25 trillion and this stockpile has quadrupled since just 2005. The simple explanation for the rapid growth in this extraordinary war chest available to China's central bank – which as was noted earlier in this book enables them to have a very large footprint in the FX and money markets [4] – is the persistence of current account surpluses registered by the PRC in recent years. By way of illustrating the size and persistence of these surpluses, Figure 12.2 is taken from a 2011 document from the IMF entitled *The Regional Economic Outlook Asia and Pacific: Managing the Next Phase of Growth* [5] and shows China's current account balances from

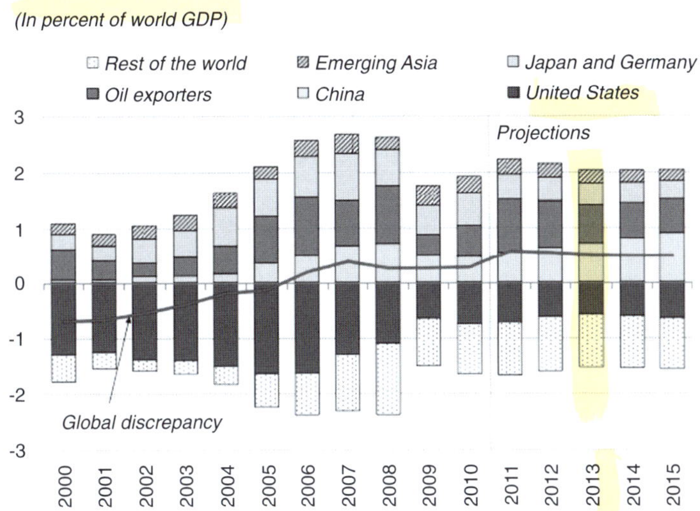

Figure 12.2 Global current account balances
Source: IMF Regional Economic Outlook Asia and Pacific April 2011.

2000 and, as of the time of preparation in 2011, the IMF's projected surpluses through until 2015.

Alongside the oil exporting nations which have had the most persistently large surpluses since 2000, as illustrated in Figure 12.2, China's current account surpluses have been growing steadily especially since 2005 and, according to the 2011 IMF projections, were expected to reach almost one percent of *total global GDP* by 2015. However, the IMF has tempered its assessment of the scale of the surpluses and in its *World Economic Outlook* published in April 2012 made the following observation which is indicative of a widely held and more cautious outlook regarding China's medium-term growth potential:

> It has long been challenging to forecast China's current account, given the economy's rapid structural change, the uncertainties surrounding prospects for the terms of trade, the *World Economic Outlook* forecast assumption of a constant real exchange rate, and the volatility of the global economy in recent years.
>
> Overall, the conclusion is that growing domestic investment, worsening terms of trade, weakening external demand, and a rising real effective exchange rate (REER) explain a large share of the post-crisis decline in the current account surplus.

As a consequence of the factors just cited, which are reflected in the revised forecast as illustrated in a graphic from the April 2012 *World Economic Outlook* [6] and which is shown as Figure 12.3, some have taken the view that, based on these revised IMF forecasts as well as several other indicators, such as declining PMI data [7] released in the first half of 2012, there are grounds for concern that China may be slowing more rapidly than previously

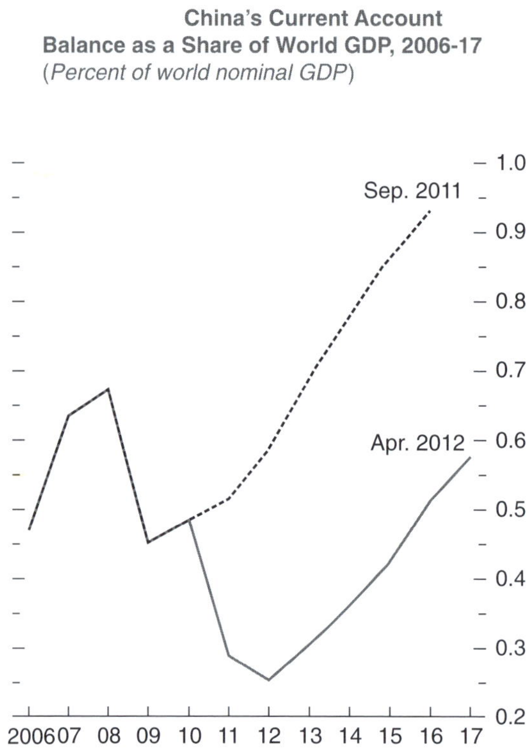

Figure 12.3 IMF's revision to China's current account from WEO 2011 to April 2012
Source: IMF WEO April 2012.

anticipated. To the extent that China's current account surplus is diminishing owing to reduced demand from the Eurozone economies in particular and, in general, a weaker global growth outlook, some concerns are well founded. However there is an alternative and more benign way of construing the double edged quality to the IMF comments – an example of disambiguating the glass is half full versus half empty dichotomy which will be discussed further in Chapter 15 – which is also spelled out further in the IMF WEO report:

> China has the potential for domestic consumption, rather than investment, to drive future declines in its current account surplus. This would ultimately be a more lasting transformation that would increase the welfare of the Chinese people and contribute significantly to strong, sustained, and balanced global growth.

The two very different paths taken in the IMF WEO forecasts in just the period from September 2011 to April 2012 as shown in Figure 12.3 highlight the precarious nature of macro-economic forecasting and bring to mind the old joke that macro-economists have the dubious distinction of making astrologers look good. There is an inherent uncertainty in economic forecasts and notwithstanding the undoubtedly useful work which is done by the statisticians at the IMF, I would suggest that, from a methodological perspective, the best way to position oneself from an investment perspective with respect to China's contribution to global growth is to continue looking at linkages in price movements across the relevant asset classes, i.e. prices of metals, industrial commodities in general, certain FX rates, and other risk assets and this will be the main focus of the remainder of this chapter. From the point of view of a global macro investor there is a daunting challenge posed by the combination of the sheer magnitude of the influence exerted by China's centrally planned allocation decisions and at the same time the opacity of its internal decision making apparatus. The manner in which perceptions amongst traders and investors regarding the dynamism of the Chinese economy can shift quite quickly, and the observable tendency for financial markets to react quite abruptly and with heightened sensitivity to the release of important Chinese economic data, is yet another indication of, and contributory factor to, the sudden binary switches which are so evident in contemporary markets.

While there plenty of cheerleaders on the prospects of the Chinese economy – Jim O'Neill, Chairman of Goldman Sachs Asset Management and the originator of the BRIC acronym being one of the best known – there are also a number of prominent China bears as well. Amongst the most vociferous of these bears are Jim Chanos, president and founder of Kynikos Associates, a US based hedge fund, Michael Pettis, a professor at Peking University's Guanghua School of Management, where he specializes in Chinese financial markets, and Hugh Hendry of Eclectica Asset Management. [8] The degree of bearishness expressed by the preceding pundits ranges from the milder form expressed by Michael Pettis who believes that the previous stunning growth rates in GDP (in 2007 estimated at 13%) have peaked and will decline in coming years towards a new normal level of around 3%, to outright gloom and doom bearishness, as expressed by the outspoken hedge fund manager Hugh Hendry. [9] Hendry believes that the Chinese banking system, based on over leveraged exposure to Chinese property, is a major accident waiting to happen.

One does not have to be as bearish as Hendry however to be concerned about the sustainability of residential real estate prices in the major Chinese cities. In July 2011 the International Monetary Fund published a separate case study on China which is rich in informative statistical data on the Chinese economy and can be accessed at the IMF website. [10] One of the more striking and contentious charts to be found in the IMF report, and shown as Figure 12.4, illustrates the non-affordability of residential properties in Beijing, Shanghai, and especially Hong Kong. Although on a national basis China has a ratio of five with respect to the price of a 70 square meter home as a multiple of annual household disposable income, which is not dissimilar to current ratios in the UK and Singapore, the ratio for Beijing is at 20 times and for Hong Kong the figure jumped towards 25 in 2010 from an already elevated level of 20 in 2001/2. These ratios can easily conjure up alarming scenarios of a real estate bust perhaps more severe than that seen in western economies in 2007/8 and underscore the fact that there is growing evidence of discontent among Chinese workers at income inequality and their inability to participate in the fruits of the nation's economic success story.

For the reasons already alluded to this chapter will not be focused on deliberating about the macro-economic data which emanates from China. To be candid, I do not believe that with such an enigmatic and opaque economy it is possible to have strongly held convictions on either a bullish or bearish outlook, and accordingly I will confine the discussion in the rest of this chapter to a study of the price action as revealed in the markets involving the complex

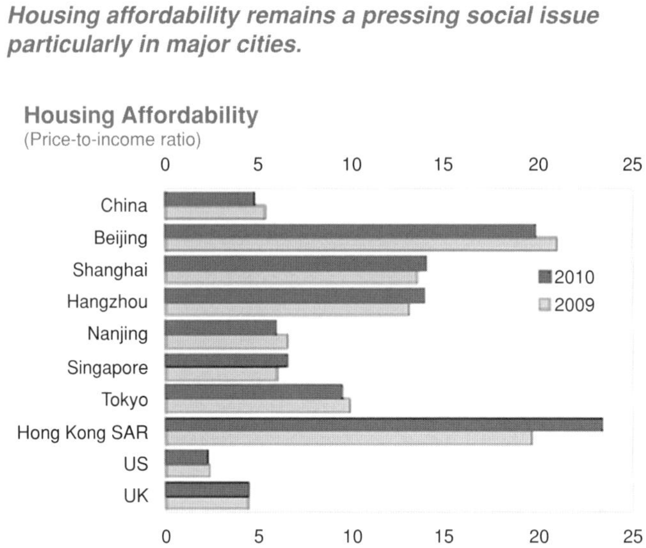

Figure 12.4 Housing affordability in China
Source: IMF Country report on China July 2011.
Note: Price of a 70 sq.m. home as a multiple of annual household disposable income.

matrix of asset class movements which hinge on *prevailing sentiment* regarding the vitality or otherwise of China.

In a nutshell the sequence of events which is observable on a continuing basis in global capital markets is that positive news regarding China – for example an uptick in PMI data or more robust GDP growth statistics – will have an immediate impact on the price of industrial commodities and especially on base metals. In turn this will have a positive impact on equities in the resource economies, and in the FX market there will be an increased bid for resource economy currencies and most especially for the Australian dollar. Flipping that over, and given the lack of transparency of actual macro-economic conditions within China, a reliable guide to more negative sentiment regarding the global growth story and the vigor of the Chinese economy can be seen in weak price action of the industrial commodities and more bearish action in the resource currencies and especially the Australian dollar.

There are different indices which can be used to track the performance of Chinese equities including that of the country's main exchange, the Shanghai Composite Index. The main drawback to using this index is that there are limitations on the extent to which global investors can participate in all of the securities listed there. Another possible instrument to analyze is the Hang Seng Index in Hong Kong which, of course, is now part of the PRC but has a long history of being available to global investors. The Hang Seng Index is however a "special case" as it includes listing for various multi-national companies which are not directly representative of what is happening within the domestic Chinese economy. The preferred vehicle for this discussion will be the FTSE China 25 Index, and this can be accessed readily via the exchange traded fund FXI which trades on the NYSE Arca platform. The FXI fund consists of 25 of the largest and most liquid Chinese companies, and is useful as a proxy for those Chinese large

Figure 12.5 Chinese large cap equities and MSCI Australia Index – FXI and EWA normalized

cap equities which are available to international investors. The average daily volume for the FXI exchange traded fund is approximately 18 million shares and the ETF has net assets in excess of $6 billion.

Figure 12.5 shows the extraordinary correlation and linkage between the performance of FXI and that of Australian equities. The chart is normalized and shows the co-movement of the FTSE China 25 Index, and the MSCI Australia Index (as represented by another exchange traded fund, EWA). The period chosen is from the end of the global financial crisis in the early part of 2009 until late July of 2012 and there is a very notable tendency for movements in both equity indices to be closely aligned.

Applying the linear regression technique for the FTSE China 25 Index and Australian equities during the period covered in Figure 12.5, shows strong correlation with an R^2 value of 0.69 as indicated in Figure 12.6 which reflects a positive correlation across the whole period of more than 0.8. As demonstrated previously the correlation coefficient for the whole period is a useful statistic, but it can conceal a lot of variability and most importantly it will not provide valuable information as to what is likely to happen with respect to outlier events.

In order to assess the behavior within the tails of the covariance, a stress regression has been undertaken for the period from the end of January 2009 until July 25, 2012. In all 900 pairs of daily data points were examined and the focus was on the 5% of extreme values, in other words only the 45 pairs of data points were included in the stress regression analysis. The results of focusing just on the outliers is displayed in Figure 12.7.

It is evident from Figure 12.7 that the bulk of the datapoints (between the arrows) have been excluded as these fall within the ±5% moves which account for 95% of the observations. A

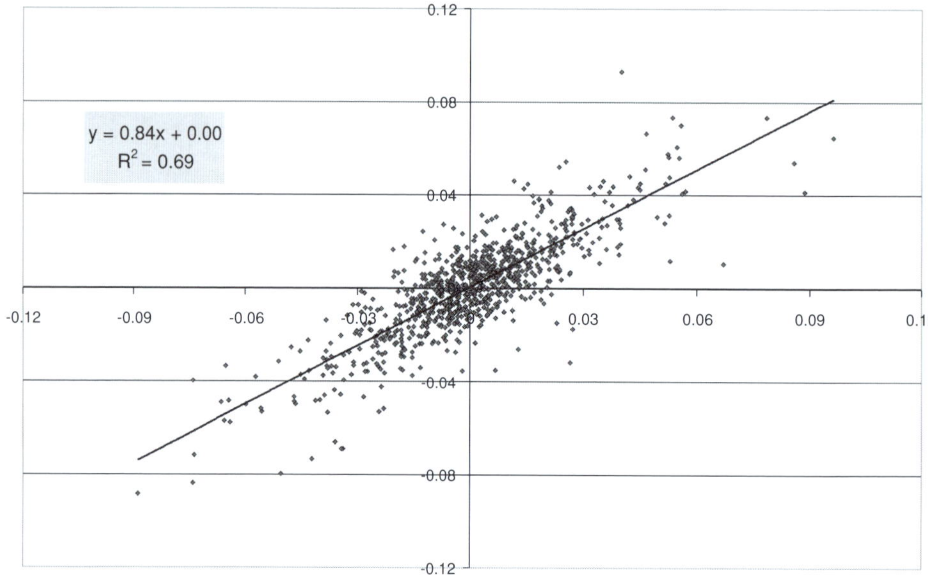

Figure 12.6 Linear regression of daily changes to Chinese large cap equities and MSCI Australia Index – FXI and EWA

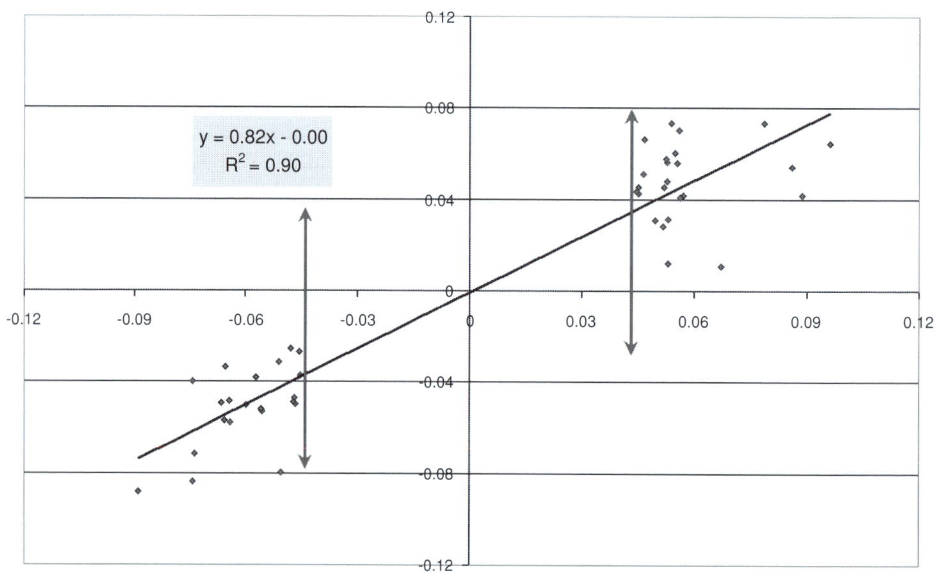

Figure 12.7 Stress regression for outlier changes to Chinese large cap equities and MSCI Australia Index – FXI and EWA

regression has been performed on the outliers and the relevant values are shown in the table below:

Independent Variable: FXI Dependent Variable: EWA
Period covered from 20090130 to 20120725

Independent Variable Performance 40.02% Dependent Variable Performance 118.13%
****
OUTLIER CORRELATIONS, BETA AND RSQ VALUES
****
Outlier absolute change threshold: 4.44%
n Extreme Moves 45 percentage of data points 5.0%
Extreme Correlation Coefficient: 0.95
Correlation coefficient for whole period: 0.83

Extreme Beta: 0.82
Average Beta (based on rolling window period of size 21): 0.85
Beta for whole period: 0.84

Extreme RSQ: 0.90
Average RSQ (based on rolling window period of size 21): 0.66
RSQ for whole period: 0.69

Taking into account the entire period the correlation coefficient or R value is 0.83. Confining the analysis to the outlier events and screening out the 855 values which fall within 95% of the distrubution, the R value jumps to 0.95. The beta values have not undergone a significant variation under the normal and stress scenarios but in regard to the last three rows of the output in the table above there is a rather notable variability.

Comparing the more accurate average RSQ value of 0.66 which is computed using a rolling lookback window of 21 periods (see the Appendix for an explanation of the methodology), there is a pronounced tightening of the RSQ or R^2 value to 0.9 for the outlier moves. From the perspective of portfolio construction and risk controls, an asset manager who was holding these two sector funds would be much more prone to a substantial drawdown in "abnormal" market conditions than with two other assets which had less closely aligned risk on/risk off characteristics.

The great advantage of using the tails or stress regression analytical tool is that it enables one to identify which financial instruments are similarly positioned and aligned under stressful circumstances. In accordance with our general theme, an examination of market correlations under stress conditions provides extremely useful information as to the enhanced macro risk dynamics which have become so ubiquitous in bipolar markets.

12.1 CHINESE CONSUMPTION OF BASE METALS

Table 12.1 provides a rather startling insight into the almost insatiable demand that China has for base metals while it continues the rapid expansion of its economic infrastructure. In the earlier periods shown on the table of 1995–2002 and 2003–07 (the latter was a period of double digit GDP growth for China and as the table shows the increase in China's industrial

Table 12.1 Global consumption of base metals
Source: IMF WEO 2011.

	Growth in Consumption of						World GDP	China's Industrial Production
	Aluminum	Copper	Lead	Nickel	Tin	Zinc		
1995–2002 World	**3.2**	**3.4**	**3.1**	**2.2**	**1.5**	**3.7**	**3.4**	**10.9**
Of Which:								
China (percent)	46.1	57.5	54.5	29.4	14.9	39.6	6.8	...
Other Emerging Markets[1] (percent)	13.5	19.3	29.2	−8.9	14.5	11.2	...	...
2003–07 World	**8.0**	**3.8**	**4.7**	**3.0**	**6.0**	**3.8**	**4.7**	**16.6**
Of Which:								
China (percent)	67.6	67.4	94.2	130.3	95.7	99.3	9.4	...
Other Emerging Markets[1] (percent)	7.7	19.7	−0.7	−5.6	0.6	11.2	...	...
2008–10 World	**1.9**	**2.1**	**3.6**	**3.6**	**1.7**	**2.9**	**2.4**	**13.1**
Of Which:								
China (percent)	159.5	226.3	175.5	153.0	104.3	166.7	12.3	...
Other Emerging Markets[1] (percent)	5.2	−12.8	−9.3	−7.7	41.0	−0.3	...	...

Sources: World Bureau of Metal Statistics, *World Metal Statistics Yearbook* (various issues).
[1] Brazil, India, Mexico, and Russia.

production during this period was 16.6%) there is a strong and noticeable uptrend in the incremental consumption of all the key base metals by China. In the period from 2008–10, as shown in the lower part of the table, the increases in consumption of base metals became quite extraordinary with copper consumption, for example, having more than doubled in the period. Consumption of all of the other base metals has impressive increases as well. This table can act as illustrative of the decision made by the Chinese government to provide a counter-cyclical boost to the world economy following the global financial crisis, and some would argue, not only a willingness to be the industrial consumer of last resort but also to take advantage of depressed metals prices owing to depressed demand from the North Atlantic economies. But probing questions are being asked in mid-2012 as to whether the Chinese buying spree has created problems of excess inventory accumulation and over capacity for the world's second largest economy as the ensuing discussion will consider.

China uses more than 50% of the world's iron ore, 40% of steel, aluminum and coal, and is by far the world's largest user of copper. According to the IMF, [11] global consumption of copper increased by 15% from 2003–09; if, however, China is removed from the equation world copper consumption declined by 14% over the same time period.

Some other useful statistics to keep in mind regarding copper specifically are as follows:

- The average single-family home uses 439 pounds of copper in construction, an air conditioner uses 52 pounds, and a refrigerator uses 4.8 pounds.
- The average vehicle contains more than 50 pounds of copper.

Concerns have been raised [12] that copper stockpiles in China are approaching 20% of the nation's annual consumption. Should the global economy slow down more drastically than is currently forecast by the IMF, and be headed for a recession, there could be a substantial nward impact on copper prices as well as other metals. As the previously pertinent alances in supply and demand for many industrial commodities begin to fade away,

Figure 12.8 Shanghai futures exchange copper deliverable stocks
Source: Bloomberg.

China's excess reserves of base metals matched with decreasing demand could lead to a severe slump for prices of these metals and also the share prices of mining companies. This will in turn act as a depressing influence on equity prices in the resource economies and helps to explain the very close alignment in performance of large cap Chinese equities and those of Australia and South Africa.

A lot of the copper that China has purchased has not been put to use and is being accumulated in warehouses. The notable China bears already cited, and those with a negative view regarding the intermediate macro-economic prospects, are keen to point out that this stockpiling of copper and other metals could easily lead to a situation where the accumulating stocks at the Shanghai Futures Exchange warehouse, as depicted in Figure 12.8, could make their way back into the market and result in plummeting prices for copper and other metals.

On the other hand the bullish case for copper prices in particular does not necessarily only hinge on the demand and supply considerations, but rather one can point to the Chinese government's alternative motivations for stockpiling. China's State Reserves Bureau (SRB) has been buying copper and other industrial metals since 2009 on a scale which goes beyond the usual rebuilding of stocks for commercial reasons. The head of Taiwan's TMT group, which ships commodities to China, said Beijing is trying to extricate itself from dollar dependency owing to their disdain for overly accommodative US monetary policy, and that accumulation of base metals is integral to this strategic objective [13] as expressed in the following comments:

> China has woken up. The West is a black hole with all this money being printed. The Chinese are buying raw materials because it is a much better way to use their reserves. They get ten times the impact, and can cover their infrastructure for 50 years. The next industrial revolution is going to be led by hybrid cars, and that needs copper. You can see the subtle way that China is moving into 30 or 40 countries with resources . . .

The SRB has also been accumulating aluminum, zinc, nickel, and the so-called rare earth metals such as titanium, indium (thin-film technology), and rhodium (catalytic converters). Rare earth metals are considered to be of strategic significance to Chinese manufacturing and demand for them is likely to remain buoyant as they are widely used in mobile communications technology [14].

As previously observed, the Chinese consumption of copper – or at least from the cynical point of view, its increased stockpiling – has gathered momentum since the recovery from the GFC began in early 2012. The PRC's stated desire to re-inflate the world economy in the very subdued economic environment which prevailed in early 2009, it could be argued, is well illustrated in Figure 12.8. Beginning in 2009 reported copper stocks at the warehouse of the Shanghai Futures Exchange began an upward movement which took them to historically high levels, and despite a pull back in 2011 the uptrend has continued to the highest level seen in the recent 10-year period.

In addition to the elevated levels of reported copper stocks in Shanghai there has been a notable global shift in the accumulation of copper stocks at the other principal warehouses as is well illustrated in Figure 12.8. The three principal metals exchanges and their associated warehouses are in London at the LME, in New York at the COMEX, and at the Shanghai Futures Exchange (SHFE) as shown in Figure 12.9. At the end of March 2012 the SHFE was holding 39% of the world's stockpile and as the trend on the chart shows, the gain has come at the expense of declining inventories at the London Metals Exchange. The most recent few months are showing a widening of the relative shares between the SHFE and the LME. However several commentators believe that the accumulation in Shanghai is unsustainable. [15]

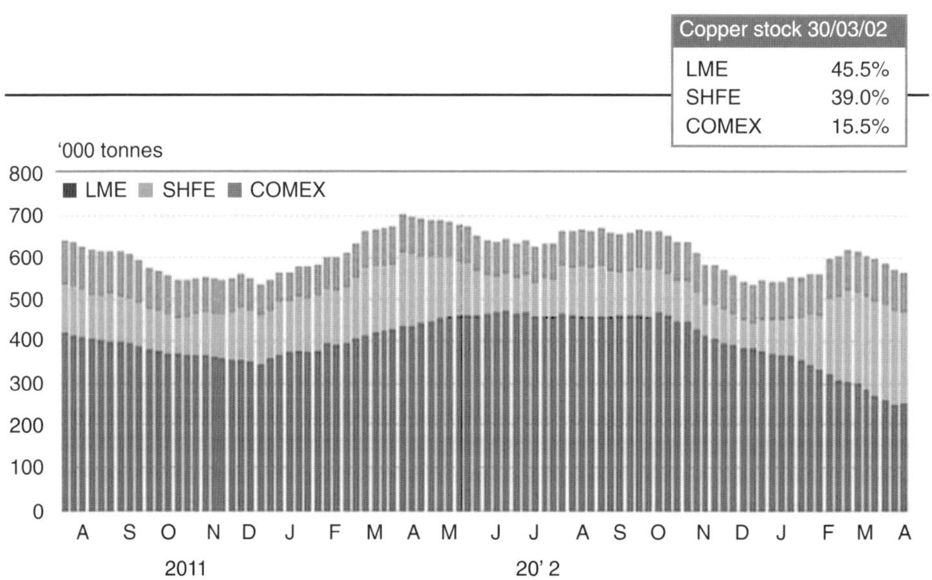

Figure 12.9 Global copper stocks April 2012
Source: Reuters.

Figure 12.10 China's copper warehouses are full as domestic demand weakens
Source: Carlos Barria, Reuters.

An April 2012 article by Isabella Kaminska at the FT Alphaville blog site has the deliberately attention grabbing headline *China is being buried alive in copper.* [16] The provocative article has a number of good photographs showing huge stockpiles of copper which were taken by analysts from Standard Chartered Bank. The article quotes the SCB analysts: (see endnote 16)

> On a routine trip to examine copper inventories in the bonded area in eastern Shanghai last week, we were astounded by how much copper is being stored in warehouses. We visited one of the biggest warehouse operators (which holds nearly one-third of the inventory in Shanghai's bonded area) and saw some interesting sights. Copper plates were piled to the maximum allowable height (based on weight so as not to damage the land it is sitting on). The covered warehouses were full. The staff car park was used to store copper. The driveway between warehouses was blocked by copper. The warehouse operator told us that it cannot accept additional inventory until existing inventory is shipped out.
>
> We estimate that total copper inventory in China, which includes inventory outside of the bonded areas, has reached about 1mn tonnes.

Figure 12.10 illustrates the predicament where copper stocks are being stacked to the maximum permitted height. The opinion expressed by the SCB analysts is also worth citing but it remains to be seen whether their implied upbeat expectations for the second half of 2012 will in fact materialize:

> While we believe that excess inventory in China, which consumes about 40% of global copper, is a clear near-term headwind for price increases, we caution investors not to be too bearish – especially in regard to price expectations for H2. Risk appetite could suddenly turn positive, especially if our expectation of stronger global economic growth in H2 proves to be accurate.

Before leaving the topic of China's voracious appetite for copper stocks I want to return to the allusion previously that Beijing may have made a strategic decision to stockpile metals as an alternative to accumulating ever more paper assets such as foreign bonds and currency reserves. A commentary from UBS has also suggested this as a motivation for continued stockpiling: [17]

> We're very surprised by Chinese demand. They are buying much more copper than they will need this year. If this is strategic, there may be no effective limit on the purchases as China's pockets are deep.

A number of Chinese government officials have been very vociferous in their condemnation of the Quantitative Easing (QE) policy initiatives followed by the US Federal Reserve. With more than $1 trillion of US Treasuries to protect, in addition to huge holdings of US dollar reserves, there would seem to be a lot of credence in the notion that the stockpiling of metals involves more than just a desire to protect strategic industrial interests but also is motivated by the need for an alternative store of value for its wealth than just reliance on financial instruments. To illustrate this further Zhou Xiaochuan, the PBOC governor, has called for a world currency modeled on the "bancor," an interesting financial vehicle which was first floated by Keynes at the Bretton Woods conference in 1944. Mr Zhou said such a currency would prevent the sort of "credit-based" excess that "has brought the global finance to its knees." [18]

To pursue the PBOC governor's thinking further, from China's perspective there have been clearly articulated benefits of recycling China's enormous capital surpluses into metals instead of relying on purely financial assets. The following benefits could be cited. Firstly, it relieves pressure on the USD/RMB currency pair which will help to alleviate the stream of complaints from policy makers in Washington. Secondly industrial metals are easily stored in warehouses, unlike oil. Thirdly, the value of holdings of base metals are likely to rise over the very long term since the earth's crust is gradually depleting its accessible ores. Finally and just as strategically vital, the ongoing accumulation safeguards China's industrialization while the West may one day face a supply crisis.

The focus on the Chinese demand for commodities also needs to be seen in the context of a very different view of commodities as an asset class in recent years. There is a lot of folklore related to outmoded notions of global business cycles that used to suggest that from the perspective of asset class diversification there were counter-cyclical advantages in having commodity futures, for example, in a well balanced portfolio. It will be worth simply summarizing the traditional view on the role of commodities and the contemporary view.

The traditional view regarding commodities can be found expressed as recently as in an academic paper from 2004. [19] The authors make the following points, all of which are contradicted by strong evidence involving the much larger footprint on the macro-economic stage of China and the other emerging economies. In fact to adhere to the views outlined below could be hazardous to one's wealth in a much more globalized economy:

- Fully-collateralized commodity futures have historically offered the same return and Sharpe ratio as equities.
- While the risk premium on commodity futures is essentially the same as equities, commodity futures returns are negatively correlated with equity returns and bond returns.
- The negative correlation between commodity futures and other asset classes is due, in significant part, to different behavior over the business cycle.

- In addition, commodity futures are positively correlated with inflation, unexpected inflation, and changes in expected inflation.

In contrast to this outmoded view, the evidence of the last decade is increasingly pointing to the fact that there has been a de-coupling in the performance of emerging economies and the advanced economies. Moreover, the *business cycle* is no longer a unified global phenomenon and although China, India, Brazil, Indonesia etc., are not immune from financial system crises, they are much less subject to the same cyclicality as the advanced economies. Accordingly the consumption of commodities – both industrial and agricultural – have become de-coupled with the economic conditions in the North Atlantic and Japanese economies and are far more correlated to emerging market GDP growth dynamics. There is a debate about whether these de-coupling dynamics will become a permanent feature of the global economy but certainly current evidence from observing actual price patterns in markets suggest that strategic commodities are following patterns that would not have been expected under a more traditional application of the notion of business cycles.

Figure 12.11 provides further support to the highly coupled nature of the demand for industrial commodities, specifically metals and mining in this instance, and the performance of the largest Chinese equities. It will be useful again to use two exchange traded funds to make the comparison as both are traded contemporaneously in the US equity markets and being dollar based there are fewer obstacles for a correlation analysis. As previously the FXI sector fund is used to represent large Chinese corporations and the XME fund employs a replication strategy in seeking to track the performance of the S&P Metals & Mining Select Industry Index. Over the entire period from early 2009 until late July of 2012 shown on the normalized chart of Figure 12.11 the two instruments have moved in close alignment but the right half of the chart reveals that this has been especially the case since early 2011.

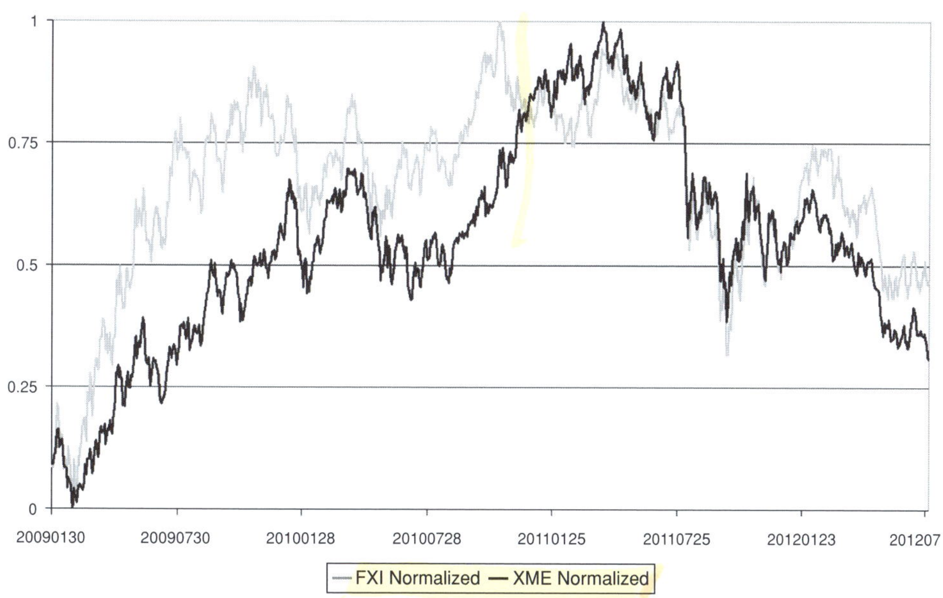

Figure 12.11 Chinese large cap equities and S&P Metals and Mining Index – FXI and XME normalized

Independent Variable Performance 40.02% Dependent Variable Performance 46.08%

****
OUTLIER CORRELATIONS, BETA AND RSQ VALUES
****
Outlier absolute change threshold: 4.44%
n Extreme Moves 45 percentage of data points 5.0%
Extreme Correlation Coefficient: 0.96
Correlation coefficient for whole period: 0.77

Extreme Beta: 1.07
Average Beta (based on rolling window period of size 21): 0.99
Beta for whole period: 1.03

Extreme RSQ: 0.92
Average RSQ (based on rolling window period of size 21): 0.54
RSQ for whole period: 0.60

The output from a stress regression analysis which covers just the outlier events that are depicted in Figure 12.11 can be seen in the table above. There is strong evidence as would be expected from the preceding discussion that, when just considering the outliers, there will be a marked increase towards a tightening of the correlation. The average RSQ value for the entire period is 0.54 but when screening out 95% of the data points and focusing on the co-movement for the remaining 5% of data the RSQ value has accelerated to 0.92. Similar observations could be made regarding the value of this insight for portfolio construction and risk management. In the coming years the real challenge for China, which it is actively tackling already, will be to move beyond being the world's largest consumer of commodities, and through its substantial investments in Africa and other territories, become the owner and operator of resource extraction businesses. According to the *Economist* in an article entitled "The Chinese in Africa" in 2010, about 14% of China's investment abroad found its way to sub-Saharan Africa. However as the article points out the recipients of this outward investment have not necessarily welcomed this with open arms: [20]

> The ambiguities in China's relationship with Africa have created fertile ground for politicians. Opposition parties, especially in southern Africa, frequently campaign on anti-China platforms. Every country south of Rwanda has had acrimonious debates about Chinese "exploitation." Even in normally calm places like Namibia, antipathy is stirring. Workers on Chinese building sites in Windhoek, the capital, are said to get a "raw deal." In Zambia the opposition leader, Michael Sata, has made Sino-scepticism his trademark.
>
> Suspect above all is the type of transfer that China offers to African countries. Most loans and payments are "tied" – i.e., the recipient must spend the money with Chinese companies. (Japan, Spain and others followed a similar model until fairly recently.) But tied aid leads to shoddy work. With no competition, favoured firms get away with delivering bad roads and overpriced hospitals. Creditors and donors often set the wrong priorities.
>
> Worse, the Chinese government is anything but transparent about its money. Aid figures are treated as state secrets. China Exim Bank and China Development Bank, the main lenders, publish no figures about their vast loans to poor countries. The Democratic Republic of Congo was persuaded

at the last minute by international advisers to scale back a Chinese lending facility from \$9 billion to \$6 billion.

12.2 THE INTERNATIONALIZATION OF THE RENMINBI

The final section of this chapter will briefly examine the evidence, which is appearing through a number of channels, that the PRC authorities are anxious to relax capital controls for both foreign inward investment and also for Chinese nationals to invest in overseas markets/economies. A very important part of this attempt to develop capital markets within China, that is befitting the world's second largest economy, is now being focused on the internationalization of the renminbi, and this seems to be proceeding at a faster pace than many observers expected.

The following article entitled "China to Let in more Foreign Investment" appeared in the *Financial Times* in April 2012 and indicates that the initiatives with regard to loosening the capital controls are moving ahead in a coordinated fashion: [21]

> China has almost tripled the amount of money foreign institutions can invest in its capital markets, in the latest move aimed at loosening strict capital controls and internationalizing the renminbi. The China Securities Regulatory Commission announced on Tuesday that international fund managers would be allowed to invest a combined total of \$80bn in China's onshore capital markets – up from the previous limit of \$30bn – in an expansion of the so-called qualified foreign institutional investor (QFII) scheme. Beijing also increased the total amount of renminbi that foreign investors can raise in Hong Kong for investment back on the mainland, from Rmb20bn (\$3.2bn) to Rmb70bn. Together the moves will allow global financial institutions to play a more active role in China's largely closed domestic equity markets and breathe life into a market that was one of the world's worst performing last year.
>
> ... Dai Xianglong, China's former central bank governor and the man now responsible for managing the country's biggest pension fund, said China should lift capital controls more quickly. "China should speed up renminbi convertibility on the capital account to make it become a currency that can be used for the purpose of investment," Mr Dai said at a conference in southern China. One crucial precondition for full convertibility of the currency will be liberalization of government-capped interest rates in China, something policymakers have been debating fiercely over the last year.

In 2003, the People's Bank of China (PBOC) and the Hong Kong Monetary Authority (HKMA) came to an agreement to allow Hong Kong banks to conduct business in renminbi. The renminbi trades on the Chinese mainland and is known as the CNY and offshore via the HKMA known as the CNH, but it trades at slightly different rates. The size of the market is still relatively small but the steady growth of this portal and recent evidence of relaxation of capital controls by the Chinese authorities [22] suggest that the timetable for convertibility and cross border trade with the renminbi is moving at a faster rate than the more cautious estimates would suggest. Alongside the offshore and onshore currency, there is also a dollar settled non-deliverable forward (NDF) as well as the trade-settlement exchange rate used by offshore corporations.

Figure 12.12, which is featured in a useful report on Internationalization of the RMB by The Reserve Bank of Australia [23], outlines the structure for both traditional RMB trade settlement as well as the portal, which the Chinese authorities established in conjunction with the Hong Kong Monetary Authority and which has enabled the development of an Offshore

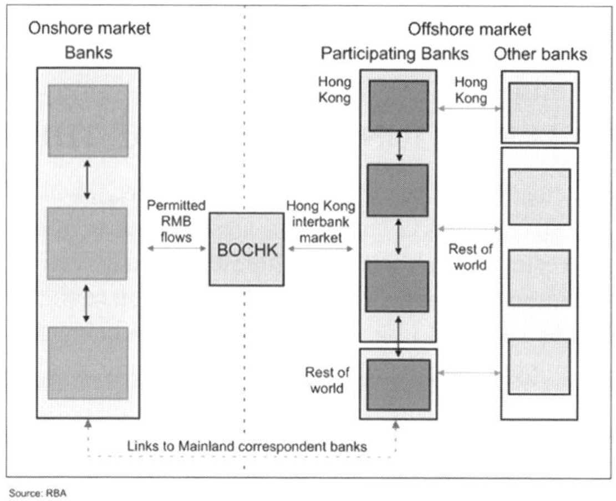

Figure 12.12 Structure of the offshore RMB market and RMB trade settlement
Source: Reserve Bank of Australia.

RMB market known as CNH. For offshore exporters and banks that settle directly with a mainland correspondent bank (the dotted line at the bottom of Figure 12.12) the RMB will remain onshore – part of the CNY market – and subject to applicable regulations from the Chinese perspective. On the other hand, if the settlement takes place via the Bank of China Hong Kong (BOCHK on the diagram) the RMB can then remain in the offshore CNH deposit market. In addition to enabling foreigners to directly hold the RMB currency and thereby perhaps benefit from appreciation of the exchange rate, the Hong Kong portal also provides an impetus to the liberalization of Chinese capital markets through the expansion of the offshore RMB denominated (dimsum) bond market. The difference between the valuation of the offshore and onshore renminbi is dictated by the ease with which cross border transfers can be made.

Along with the development of trade settlement via the Bank of China Hong Kong (BOCHK) that was just discussed there has been a sizable expansion in offshore RMB deposits. Figure 12.13, also from the Reserve Bank of Australia, shows that in the two year period until June 2012 the amount of RMB deposits in Hong Kong has risen from about USD $15 billion to about USD $90 billion. The RBA also noted in its report [24]

> A sign of the maturation of the deliverable RMB market has been the quoting of a CNH fix by the Treasury Markets Association since mid-2011. This has been supported in recent months by the quoting of interbank interest rates by eight major banks in Hong Kong.

Not only is the offshore RMB market growing in Hong Kong but there is a nascent RMB deposit base being established in London. The following comments are from a speech by the UK Finance Minister, George Osborne in April 2012 [25] and provide further evidence that the process of liberalization and internationalization of the renminbi is gathering momentum:

> I am delighted to be here today to celebrate London as a centre for international renminbi (RMB) business. This is a significant moment. This morning, we saw the launch of the first RMB bond outside of Chinese sovereign territories. And it happened here in London. This builds on the progress London has already made toward becoming the western hub for RMB.

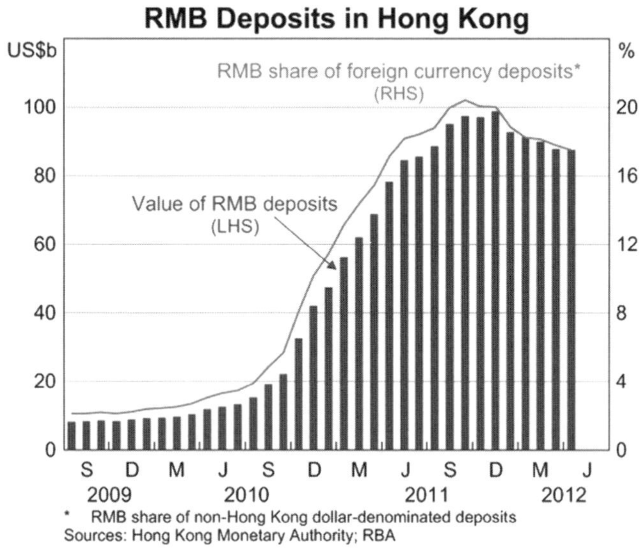

Figure 12.13 RMB deposits in Hong Kong
Source: Reserve Bank of Australia.

> By the end of last year, the volume of RMB deposits in London had already reached 109bn RMB – equivalent to around 11bn pounds, of which 35bn RMB – around 3.5bn pounds – are customer deposits.
>
> The annual trading volume in offshore RMB bonds had reached 28 billion RMB – around 3 billion pounds. And London already represents 26% of the global offshore RMB spot forex market – the majority is based in Hong Kong. This is a market which grew by over 80% last year.
>
> Let me be clear – London is not in competition with Hong Kong, it is a complement – providing a Western hub for RMB business.
>
> These developments are the culmination of a team effort by global banks with operations in London and Hong Kong, strongly supported by the UK, mainland Chinese and Hong Kong Authorities.

Further evidence of the escalation of the movement towards the internationalization of the renminbi can also be seen in a statement from JP Morgan's operation in China which notes in general terms that "China is acting on its plan for the RMB to become an international reserve currency. In the past few months, there have been large advances in progressing towards that goal": [26]

> In March 2012 The People's Bank of China (PBOC) announced an expansion of the Renminbi cross-border trade settlement scheme in a move expected to further promote the RMB as an international trade settlement currency. What initially started with 365 pilot companies and in limited geographic scope was in subsequent years expanded to cover over 60,000 qualified Mainland Designated Enterprises throughout China. The new rules announced by the regulators will allow all mainland firms with import and export licenses to conduct trade settlement in Renminbi.

ENDNOTES

1. The quote comes from Izabella Kaminska, *Why China's RMB Exodus IS the Story*, May 16 2012:

> China's capital outflow problem is the real ticking time-bomb for markets.
>
> If China fails to plug this problem sharpish, the world's biggest put option – the China growth story – could quite genuinely come undone.

http://ftalphaville.ft.com/blog/2012/05/16/1002681/why-chinas-rmb-exodus-is-the-story/.

2. The comment was made during a panel discussion featuring PIMCO's Mohammed El Erian at the Milken Institute Global Conference, Los Angeles April/May 2012. The panel was entitled *Where Will Economic Growth Come From?* More details including a link to the video of the panel discussion can be found at the following location: http://www.milkeninstitute.org/events/gcprogram.taf?function=detail&eventid=gc12&EvID=3126. See also endnote 15 in Chapter 11.
3. Only created as a municipality in 1997 Chongqing now has a total population of approximately 30 million. For a discussion of the challenges posed by increasing urbanization in China see the following article which is available online at http://www.bbc.co.uk/news/magazine-16761784:

> Professor Kam Wing Chan of the University of Washington in the United States, who has made a career out of correcting people's exaggerated claims about Chinese population statistics, explains that what China calls a municipality or city is better understood as a province.
>
> Many of the 30 million people who are said to live in the city of Chongqing are actually agricultural workers living in a rural setting, he says.
>
> "And if you were to travel from the downtown area to some of the peripheral areas where those 30 million live, it might take a day or two because the road conditions are not that good. So, this cannot be possibly called a city. Because when we call a place a city the general understanding is that we're talking about a commuting zone."

4. George Soros, interviewed on the BBC Radio 4 program *Today* (October 9) can be heard in the clip referenced below making the rather striking assertion that the "Chinese effectively control the entire world's currency system." http://news.bbc.co.uk/today/hi/today/newsid_9076000/9076763.stm.

   The assertion comes around 1:40 into the interview segment. Notice how the interviewer completely fails to grasp the true significance of what Soros is alleging and moves on with the interview in a prosaic manner to talk about re-valuation of the yuan against the dollar.
5. IMF Regional Economic Outlook Asia and Pacific Managing the Next Phase of Growth, April 2011. The entire report can be downloaded from the following link: http://www.imf.org/external/pubs/ft/reo/2011/apd/eng/areo0411.pdf.
6. HSBC services PMI shows weakest growth in 10 months, Reuters, July 4, 2012:

> BEIJING, July 4 (Reuters) – China's services firms grew at their slowest rate in 10 months in June, easing back from May's 19-month peak, as new order growth cooled albeit while marking 43 months of consistent expansion, a private sector survey showed on Wednesday.
>
> The China HSBC services purchasing managers index (PMI) stood at 52.3 in June, down from 54.7 in May, indicating a marginal expansion of activity that capped job creation at a three-month low and bolstering expectations that Beijing will deliver further policy measures to boost growth.
>
> "Services activities softened in June due to slowing new business flows, which translated into only marginal growth of employment," Qu Hongbin, the Hong Kong-based chief China economist at survey sponsor, HSBC, said in a statement.
>
> "This, plus the ongoing slowdown of manufacturing sectors, points to growing pressures on the jobs market – the last thing Beijing policy makers want to see. But with inflation also falling fast, we believe Beijing has sufficient room to step up easing and revive domestic demand," Qu said.

> The HSBC index, compiled by UK data provider Markit and tracking smaller firms mainly in the private sector, completes the series of China PMI releases for June that broadly leave investors anticipating more policy easing in the near future.

http://in.reuters.com/article/2012/07/04/china-economy-hsbcservicespmi-idINL6E8I33MX20120704.

7. IMF World Economic Outlook, April 2012. The entire report can be downloaded from the following link: http://www.imf.org/external/pubs/ft/weo/2012/01/pdf/text.pdf.
8. Michael Pettis challenges The Economist, global economic bragging rights and sweet gig for Chinese band at stake, FT Alphaville, March 28, 2012. The article makes reference to a bet that Pettis made with *The Economist* that China would not surpass the USA as the nation with the largest GDP.

   At the end of last year, *The Economist* predicted that Chinese GDP would surpass US GDP at market exchange rates in 2018. Still, this 2018 prediction deserves I think more than a little questioning – it requires that nominal Chinese GDP growth in dollars outpace nominal US GDP growth by 12% a year. Pettis has long argued that Chinese GDP is overstated because it's failed to account for misallocated investments and environmental degradation.

   http://ftalphaville.ft.com/blog/2012/03/28/941451/michael-pettis-challenges-the-economist-global-economic-bragging-rights-and-sweet-gig-for-chinese-band-at-stake/.
9. Hendry's bearish forecast for China can be seen in the Eclectica Asset Management newsletter for April 2012 which is not available as a download but can be found at the zerohedge.com website as referenced below. The following is a short extract:

> There is a near consensus that China will supplant America this decade. We do not believe this. We are more bullish on US growth than most. The momentous nature of recent advances in shale oil and gas extraction and America's acceptance of the unpleasantness of debt and labour price restructuring looks to us as if it is creating yet another historic turning point. By embracing his inadequacies and leaping on his luck, the strong man may have finally broken the binds that had previously held him back. *We are also more pessimistic on Chinese growth than ever. This makes us bearish on most Asian stocks, bearish on industrial commodity prices*, interested in some US stocks, a seller of high variance equities and deeply concerned that Japan could become the focal point of the next global leg down. On the plus side we also believe that we are much closer than before to the beginning of a bull market of perhaps 1982, if not 1932, proportions. We just need the last shoe to drop. (author's italics)

http://www.zerohedge.com/news/hugh-hendry-back-full-eclectica-letter.

10. *IMF Country Report No. 11/192 PEOPLE'S REPUBLIC OF CHINA*, July 2011. The entire report can be downloaded from the following link: http://www.imf.org/external/pubs/ft/scr/2011/cr11192.pdf.
11. See endnote 10.
12. China's towering metal stockpiles cast economic shadow, Reuters, May 18, 2012:

> Commodity markets are used to seeing China's inventories swell in the first quarter, when manufacturing slows down due to the Lunar New Year holidays, and then gradually decline during the second quarter when industrial activity picks up.
>
> This year, however, is different.
>
> Copper stocks in Shanghai's bonded storage, the biggest in China, are now double the 300,000 metric tons (330,693 tons) average of the past four years and iron ore stocks are about a third more than their 74 million metric tons average.
>
> For copper, Chinese traders appeared to have misjudged the fundamentals and embarked on a massive shopping spree in November, expecting demand to rebound after the Lunar New Year.
>
> But the buyers never materialized in bulk and China is now left with up to 1.4 million metric tons of copper, the most since 2009. In the past month, stocks have fallen 3.5 percent, half the pace from the same period a year ago, according to data from the Shanghai Futures Exchange.

13. This is a quotation from the article cited in endnote 17.

14. China "stockpiling rare earths for strategic reserves," *Daily Telegraph*, July 5, 2012:

> China has already started the purchase – using state funds – and storage of rare earths for strategic reserves, the *China Securities Journal* said, but did not say exactly when the initiative was launched.
>
> The country produces more than 90pc of the world's rare earths, which are used in hi-tech equipment ranging from iPods to missiles, and it has set production caps and export quotas on them.
>
> Major trading partners last month asked the World Trade Organization (WTO) to form a panel to resolve a dispute over China's export limits on rare earths after earlier consultations through the global trade body failed.
>
> The European Union, the US and Japan claim China is unfairly choking off exports of the commodities to benefit domestic industries.
>
> The newspaper said current low prices for rare earths had prompted the start of strategic buying and the reserves could be used to address future shortfalls of the resources.

15. Izabella Kaminska, What happens if the Chinese government cracks down on all copper 'financing deals'? *FT Alphaville*, May 16, 2012: http://ftalphaville.ft.com/blog/2012/05/16/1002881/what-happens-if-the-chinese-government-cracks-down-on-all-copper-%E2%80%98financing-deals%E2%80%99/.
16. "China is being buried alive in copper," http://ftalphaville.ft.com/blog/2012/04/26/975511/china-is-being-buried-alive-in-copper/.
17. Ambrose Evans-Pritchard, A "Copper Standard" for the world's currency system? *Daily Telegraph*, April 15, 2009:

> Hard money enthusiasts have long watched for signs that China is switching its foreign reserves from US Treasury bonds into gold bullion. They may have been eyeing the wrong metal.

http://www.telegraph.co.uk/finance/comment/ambroseevans_pritchard/5160120/A-Copper-Standard-for-the-worlds-currency-system.html.

18. Mr Zhou's comments were reported in the article mentioned in endnote 17. With regard to Keynes's idea regarding a bancor the following is a good summary: http://prosperityuk.com/2003/05/how-keynes-bancor-international-trade-currency-would-work/:

> Keynes proposed a new, neutral unit of international currency – the 'Bancor' – and a new institution – the International Clearing or Currency Union (ICU). All international trade would be measured in Bancors. Exporting would accrue Bancors, importing would expend Bancors. Nations were expected to maintain, within a small percentage, a zero account with the ICU. *This would indicate that they had an overall equivalence of imports and exports.* Each nation's Bancor account would also be related to its currency through a fixed, but adjustable, exchange rate.
>
> The key feature of Keynes proposal was that it placed an equal obligation on creditor and debtor nations to maintain a balance of trade . . .
>
> Nations that imported more than they exported – debtor nations – would pay a small interest charge to the Clearing Union on their overdrawn account. This would encourage those nations to promote exports by a range of domestic policies as well as marginal currency devaluation. Equally, nations that ran an aggressive trade policy and exported more than they imported would also be charged by the Clearing Union for their surplus account. This would encourage those nations to find ways to spend their excess Bancors back in debtor nations – or gradually lose that surplus.
>
> The efforts of debtor nations to promote exports was intended to coincide with the efforts of creditor nations to expend their otherwise worthless Bancor surplus. These charges were intended not so much as a deterrent or punishment, but as a benign 'feedback' mechanism, ensuring that, over time, trade remained in balance.

19. Gorton & Rouwenhorst, *Facts and Fantasies about Commodity Futures* (Wharton and Yale, 2004).

20. Economist in an article entitled "The Chinese in Africa" in 2010, http://www.economist.com/node/18586448.
21. China to let in more foreign investment, FT.com, April 3, 2012, http://www.ft.com/cms/s/0/c755b3ba-7d9b-11e1-81a5-00144feab49a.html.
22. A KPMG note for clients in August 2012 made the following observation on relaxation of capital controls:

> August 20: China Securities Regulatory Commission issued guidance that revises the general regulation governing the qualified foreign institutional investment (QFII) program, to permit foreign investment in PRC listed securities.The new QFII regulation (issued 27 July 2012) is viewed as a step towards relaxation of China's strict capital controls on inbound equity portfolio investments, in that it significantly lowers the threshold for QFII license applications and allows "smaller" foreign investors, private equity funds, and other institutions to enter the market for the first time.

http://www.kpmg.com/global/en/issuesandinsights/articlespublications/taxnewsflash/pages/china-foreign-investment-in-prc-listed-securities.aspx.

23. *Internationalizing the Renminbi*, Bulletin June Quarter 2012, by Lynne Cockerell and Michael Shoory, The Reserve Bank of Australia. Available online at http://www.rba.gov.au/publications/bulletin/2012/jun/9.html.
24. The RBA report also makes the following pertinent observation regarding the size of the offshore RMB market:

> The rapid accumulation... [of RMB deposits in Hong Kong]... initially reflected both the growth of RMB trade settlement and the relative lack of alternative options in the developing offshore market. The recent decline in deposits corresponds to a certain extent with the increased ability to transfer RMB between the onshore and offshore markets. While the offshore deliverable RMB foreign exchange market has grown substantially in terms of size and liquidity since mid-2010, with average daily turnover of around US$4 billion last year, this is still below turnover in the dominant offshore non-deliverable forward RMB market (which settles in US dollars) and the onshore market (estimated in 2010 at US$23 billion and US$10 billion per day, respectively).

25. Speech by the Chancellor of the Exchequer, George Osborne, at the City of London RMB launch event, H M Treasury, April 18, 2012, http://www.hm-treasury.gov.uk/speech_chx_180412.htm.
26. China Internationalization of Renminbi (RMB) at J.P. Morgan website, http://www.jpmorgan.com/tss/General/China_Internationalization_of_RMB/1288220029583.

13

Drawdowns and Tail Risk Management

It has been noted earlier that the widely discussed phenomenon of tail risk needs to be situated within the broader context of enhanced left tail dependencies, statistical terminology which illustrates the propensity for many asset classes to become more highly correlated as they all fall in unison when markets are experiencing crises. The propensity for the co-occurance of severely abnormal or left tail events, at the micro level of individual securities, is one of the defining features of a liquidity crisis. Moving to the macro level, and given the heightened degree of cross-sectional asset correlations discussed in Chapter 2, there will be a further accentuation of these left tail dependencies resulting in an increased risk of systemically threatening events. Taken together this combination became the signature of the financial crisis of 2008. However, instances of heightened left tail dependencies across multiple asset classes are certainly not confined to the 2008 crisis and can be observed at several other periods in financial history.

In this chapter I want to demonstrate the severity of drawdowns for a variety of securities that occurred both in 2008 and also during the bursting of the Nasdaq bubble in 2000/1. The longevity of adverse price developments leading to sustained drawdowns, which may include a fat tail event or trigger, but not necessarily so, needs to be distinguished from the notion of the isolated tail risk as a very rare event – a black swan – which is typically associated with the kind of banking crisis seen in 2007/8.

Severe and long lived drawdowns for individual assets are relatively commonplace and pose a much greater threat than is often acknowledged for long-term investors who subscribe to the view, attributed to Benjamin Graham and often espoused by Warren Buffet, "that in the short term markets are voting machines but in the long term they are weighing machines." [1] On a long enough time line, at least in recent financial history, there have been rewards to patient investors in equities, and Mr Buffet is certainly a testimony to that, but as the ensuing discussion will reveal there can be drawdowns which will test the fortitude of even the most patient investors. Later in the chapter I will consider various techniques and strategies, one of which has not, to my knowledge, been featured in mainstream finance, which can ameliorate the alarming magnitude of drawdowns and, in general, address the question of how one can preserve wealth in a post-GFC environment.

Figure 13.1 illustrates quite dramatically the stomach wrenching "ride" for a buy and hold investor in the stock of Bank of America (NYSE:BAC) in just 21 months, starting in the summer of 2007 and lasting through until Q1, 2009. As a reference point for this chart the market capitalization for the bank in the summer of 2007 was approximately \$250 billion and by the early part of 2009 this had fallen towards \$40 billion. As can be seen the stock price when adjusted for dividends experienced its maximum drawdown during this period of more than 93%. To spell out further the drastic disappearance of dividend income for a buy and hold investor in Bank of America, which echoes previous discussions on this important consequence of the global financial crisis, the quarterly dividend paid in July 2008 before the crisis was \$0.64 and following the share price collapse at the end of 2008 this has been at one cent ever since. Not only would there have been a huge capital loss for an investor but also a drastic disappearance of the income from the dividends.

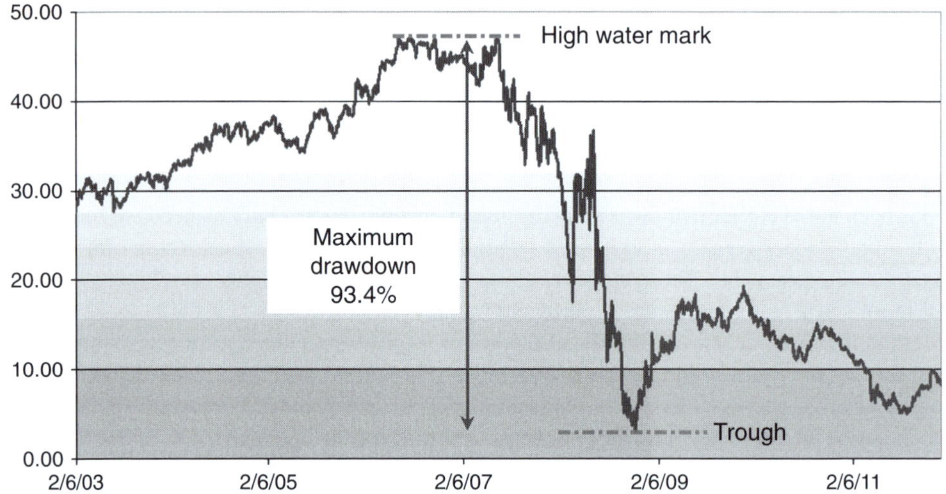

Figure 13.1 Bank of America June 2003–April 2012 illustrating maximum drawdown

Figure 13.1 illustrates the method for measuring the maximum drawdown value, which is the actual experiential discomfort to an investor; the extreme severity of this drawdown can easily be neglected in the more theoretical treatment of the tail risk phenomenon.

The impact of the financial crisis of 2007/8 on the shares of financial institutions is strikingly illustrated by Figure 13.2. Six firms with a variety of different offerings within financial services have been selected and the data shown are the monthly prices adjusted to have a base value of 1 as of the end of March 2009. This date was selected as marking the nadir of the crisis – at least as far as the US equity markets were concerned – and it also marks quite well (but not exactly) the troughs for each of the firms during the period displayed. The starting point is June 1993 for four of the firms Bank of America (BAC), American Express (AXP), Barclays (BCS), and General Electric (GE). Two other firms, Deutsche Bank (DB) and Union Bank of Switzerland (UBS), have slightly less data – the price history is taken from the trading of each institution on the NYSE in order to be in US dollars and thus consistent from a foreign exchange point of view and in regard to the synchronicity of daily closes on the same exchange.

The key features to notice about Figure 13.2 are the manner in which all of the companies coincided approximately with registering their trough values at the end of Q1, 2009 and that most of them also attained their peak values, for the period displayed, during Q2, 2007. By far the most exaggerated performances within the "bubble" period are shown by Bank of America and Barclays which increased in value by factors of six and nine respectively, during the period from 2003 to Q2, 2007.

General Electric (GE) which is included in the chart has the least of the drawdowns shown and was included because its GE Capital division offers commercial loans and leases, home loans, credit cards, personal loans, and other financial services. It is also a widely diversified business with a foothold in many other businesses including broadcasting and technology. While the stock shows the smallest drawdown on the chart, because of its exposure to the financial sector, its losses during the 2007/8 were in excess of those seen for many other large conglomerates which did not have significant exposure to financial services. Inclusion of the

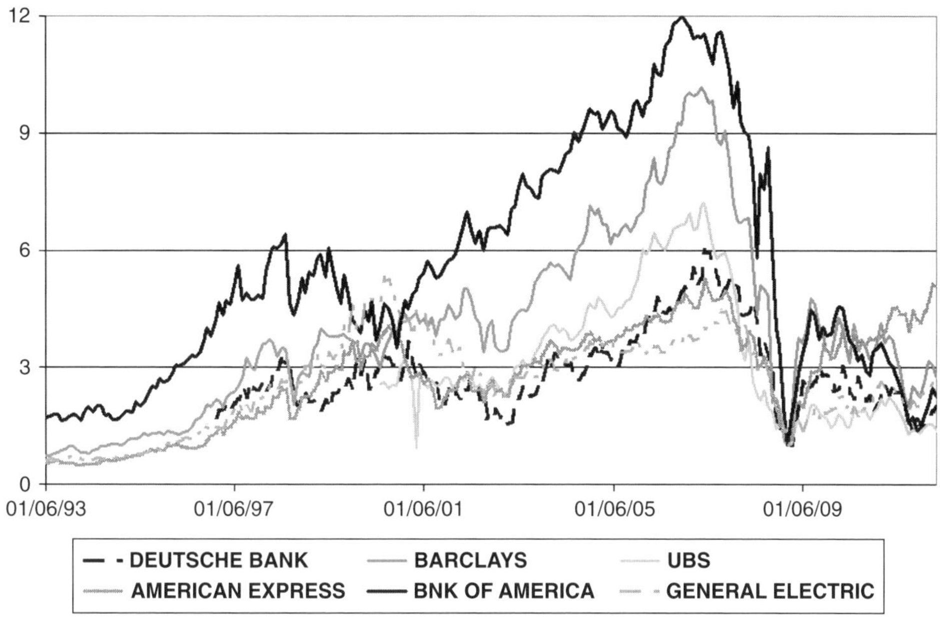

Figure 13.2 Relative performance of financial firms 1993–April 2012

GE stock also helps to provide a comparative scale to highlight the severity of the drawdowns of some of the pure investment banks including Deutsche Bank and UBS.

Table 13.1 is designed to provide a comprehensive perspective on the risk and reward trade-off experienced by investors in various firms within the financial services sector during the period commencing in June 2003 and concluding in April 2012. This covers approximately 10 years and most pertinently the focus of the analytical framework is on the financial crisis of 2007/8. As seen in regard to the previous graphic, Figure 13.2, most of the firms will have seen their peak values during the summer of 2007 and many but not all saw their trough values during Q1, 2009 (notable exceptions are Goldman Sachs which reached a turning upward from the trough inflection in November 2008 and Morgan Stanley which registered its lowest value for the period in September 2011).

The method used to compare relative performance on a consistent basis is able to accommodate the fact that not all peaks and troughs are exactly coincidental. The maximum price reached during the 10-year period is the first row of Table 13.1, and it is important to note that all of the monthly prices have been adjusted to incorporate the payments of dividends by each of the companies shown and for any stock splits. [2] For example, Deutsche Bank registered its peak monthly close of $150.74 as of the beginning of May 2007 and coincidentally Morgan Stanley registered its peak close in the same month at a price of $65.28.

The base prices for each company are for June 2003, and row 8 of the table expresses the growth from the base to the peak value. For example in the case of the left most column of the table which is for Goldman Sachs the multiple of growth from base to peak is 3.08 indicating that the price has just more than tripled. The Compound Annual Growth Rate (CAGR) [3] from this respective base to the peak is shown in row 11 which has the designation “CAGR from base to peak.” Continuing with the example for Goldman Sachs the rate shown is 29.7% which indicates that from the base value of $76.90 to the maximum value of $237.02, the

Table 13.1 Summary of key drawdowns and recovery ratios for financial firms 2003–2012

		Goldman Sachs Adj Close	Wells Fargo Adj Close	Deutsche Bank Adj Close	Barclays Adj Close	UBS Adj Close	Citigroup Adj Close	Bank of America Adj Close	General Electric Adj Close	Morgan Stanley Adj Close	US Bancorp Adj Close	American Express Adj Close
1	Peak Price	$237.02	$35.34	$150.74	$49.88	$65.24	$503.06	$46.75	$34.53	$65.28	$33.86	$58.95
2	Trough Price	$76.17	$11.72	$25.09	$4.90	$9.05	$14.98	$3.90	$7.77	$13.43	$13.69	$11.28
3	Price June 2003	$76.90	$19.84	$56.08	$21.71	$27.56	$339.87	$29.70	$21.34	$30.56	$18.14	$31.99
4	Price April 2012	$112.44	$33.00	$49.79	$13.60	$12.41	$33.89	$8.77	$19.14	$17.48	$31.29	$57.45
5	Date of Peak	01/10/2007	01/09/2008	01/05/2007	02/04/2007	01/05/2007	01/12/2006	01/11/2006	03/09/2007	01/05/2007	01/09/2008	01/05/2007
6	Date of Trough	04/11/2008	02/02/2009	02/03/2009	02/02/2009	02/02/2009	02/02/2009	02/02/2009	02/02/2009	01/09/2011	02/02/2009	02/02/2009
7	Date of Base	02/06/2003	02/06/2003	02/06/2003	02/06/2003	02/06/2003	02/06/2003	02/06/2003	02/06/2003	02/06/2003	02/06/2003	02/06/2003
8	Growth from Base	3.08	1.78	2.69	2.30	2.37	1.48	1.57	1.62	2.14	1.87	1.84
9	Interval from Base	4.33	5.25	3.92	3.84	3.92	3.50	3.42	4.26	3.92	5.25	3.92
10	Ratio April 2012 to Peak	0.32	0.33	0.17	0.10	0.14	0.03	0.08	0.23	0.21	0.40	0.19
11	Cagr From Base	29.7%	11.6%	28.7%	24.2%	24.6%	11.9%	14.2%	12.0%	21.4%	12.6%	16.9%
12	Time Interval Peak to Trough	1.10	0.42	1.84	1.84	1.76	2.18	2.26	1.42	4.34	0.42	1.76
13	Cagr Peak to Trough	0.35	0.07	0.38	0.28	0.33	0.20	0.33	0.35	0.69	0.12	0.39
14	Recapture Peak Multiple	2.82	13.68	2.65	3.53	3.07	5.03	3.00	2.86	1.44	8.55	2.56
15	Recovery Rate Required	29.9%	23.4%	58.1%	83.1%	65.6%	172.8%	106.8%	42.0%	49.8%	18.8%	52.6%
16	Ratio Cagr Down/up	1.01	2.01	2.02	3.43	2.67	14.58	7.53	3.51	2.33	1.49	3.11
17	Ratio Cagr up/down	0.99	0.50	0.49	0.29	0.38	0.07	0.13	0.29	0.43	0.67	0.32
18	Time Interval Mtn to April 2012	3.41	3.16	3.09	3.16	3.16	3.16	3.16	3.16	0.59	3.16	3.16
19	Cagr Trough Price to April 2012	12.1%	38.7%	24.9%	38.1%	10.5%	29.4%	29.2%	33.0%	56.8%	29.9%	67.3%
20	Ratio Achieved Cagr to Required Recovery Rate	40.4%	165.6%	42.8%	45.8%	16.0%	17.0%	27.3%	78.6%	114.1%	158.7%	128.0%

geometric annual mean was 29.7% and the exact interval during which this growth occurred (shown as row nine of Table 13.1) was 4.33 years.

At the risk of stating the obvious, but in order to make the table as accessible as possible, the calculation of $76.90 times $1.29^{\wedge 4.33}$ (i.e. 1+ 0.29) will provide the peak value of $237.02 (which is an uplift of 3.08 or 308% as shown in row 8 of the table). Row 10 shows the decay from the peak and is represented as the ratio of the trough to peak value and is effectively the multiple which can also be considered as the drawdown – in the case of Deutsche Bank, for example, the value is 0.17 which when subtracted from the value one indicates a percentage loss of 83%. The CAGR or geometric mean of decay required to produce this drawdown can be calculated by considering this drawdown or decay expressed relative to the time interval of 1.84 years during which the peak to trough occurred (as shown in row 12 of the table). The result of 0.38 (as shown in row 13) should be subtracted from unity and then expressed in percentage terms as $\approx$ 62%.

Row 14 is a key row of the table, designated as the Recapture Peak Multiple and the value, for example, for Deutsche Bank is 2.65. In order for that multiple to be achieved during a similar period to the period which generated the peak value from the base value (i.e. 3.92 years), the CAGR recovery rate required would be 58% (as shown in row 15). Once again to spell out the matter, it would take a CAGR rate of 58% to be applied for 3.92 years to recover from the trough value of $25.09 and to regain the peak value of $150.74.

It now becomes possible to determine the risk/reward ratio for this scenario by calculating the ratio of the damaging drawdown experienced during the "bust" phase to the work required during a recovery phase. Once again for clarity, the ratio for Deutsche Bank from row 15 of Table 13.1 is 58% and from row 11 is 28.9%, so the ratio is 0.58/0.29 and is equivalent to 2.02. Expressed in slightly different terminology the downside was twice as severe as the upside on a *temporally pro-rated basis*. An alternative way of thinking about the risk/reward ratio in the case of Deutsche Bank is to take the reciprocal of 2.02 which is 0.49 (and shown as row 17 of the table) and to realize that the upside was approximately 50% as rewarding as the subsequent downside. Expressed in simpler terms the pain was twice the gain.

Looking across row 17 of the table for each of the companies analyzed it can be seen just how unrewarding it would have been to have held Citigroup during the critical period with an upside/downside ratio of only 7%. The ratio for Goldman Sachs is the most attractive with a ratio of almost 1 which suggests that the recovery momentum required is almost identical to the drawdown momentum; in other words, again on a *temporally pro-rated basis*, there would have been a similar amount of pain to gain for long-term holder of shares in Goldman Sachs.

The final two rows of Table 13.1 are also instructive as they consider the return rates (CAGR) which have been achieved for each institution since the trough date until the time period that the table was prepared in April 2012. For example, in the case of Citigroup a compounding annual return of 29.4% has been achieved between the trough (which occurred in February 2009) and the cut-off date in April 2012. The final row of the table (row 20) then expresses the ratio achieved in row 19 in relation to the required CAGR to recover the previous high water mark which is seen in row 15. As can be seen the very high risk/reward characteristics for Citigroup reveal that even with the attractive 29.4% rate achieved in a little over three years from trough to April 2012 this rate still falls far short of equaling the spectacular demise of the stock from a value at the high water mark of $503.06 to the trough value of $14.98.

The value of Table 13.1 – in terms of revealing the true magnitude of the boom/bust experienced by investors in the financial sector during the global financial crisis – is well illustrated by row 20 of the table. In general terms there is a clear demarcation between those institutions which were more heavily engaged in the mortgage-backed securities and associated derivatives and which employed substantial leverage on their balance sheets – the investment banks – and those institutions which were more focused on mainstream and retail banking activities. To the extent that they all had a substantial degree of real estate exposure, the business models of companies such as US Bancorp, American Express, and Wells Fargo were far less damaged by the calamities arising from "cutting edge" financial engineering (which proved to be far more hazardous than most realized, or admitted to having realized – which is not the same thing of course). Those institutions such as Citigroup, Deutsche Bank, UBS, and Bank of America that had become so deeply enmeshed in highly leveraged *bets* within structured finance, were the main casualties when the unraveling of leverage brought on by the collapse of the bubble occurred. Most, if not all, of the latter category would have gone to the undertakers rather than into the intensive care unit had it not been for the largesse shown by policy makers in underwriting their solvency via public balance sheets.

Figure 13.3 provides a different perspective on the massive drawdowns which were experienced by equity holders of many of the companies included in Table 13.1. The chart displayed as Figure 13.3 shows – this time using daily data rather than monthly – the severity of the drawdown for an investor who purchased Bank of America stock in June 2003 and held it through April 2012. As can be seen there were several small declines during the initial four-year period up until the middle of 2007, but in the ensuing year and a half the investor would have seen a capital loss from the high water mark to the trough on March 6, 2009 of 93.4%. Even on the far right hand side of the chart, which is more than three years since the trough, the investor would still be "under water" if they had bought BAC in 2003 to the tune of about 80%.

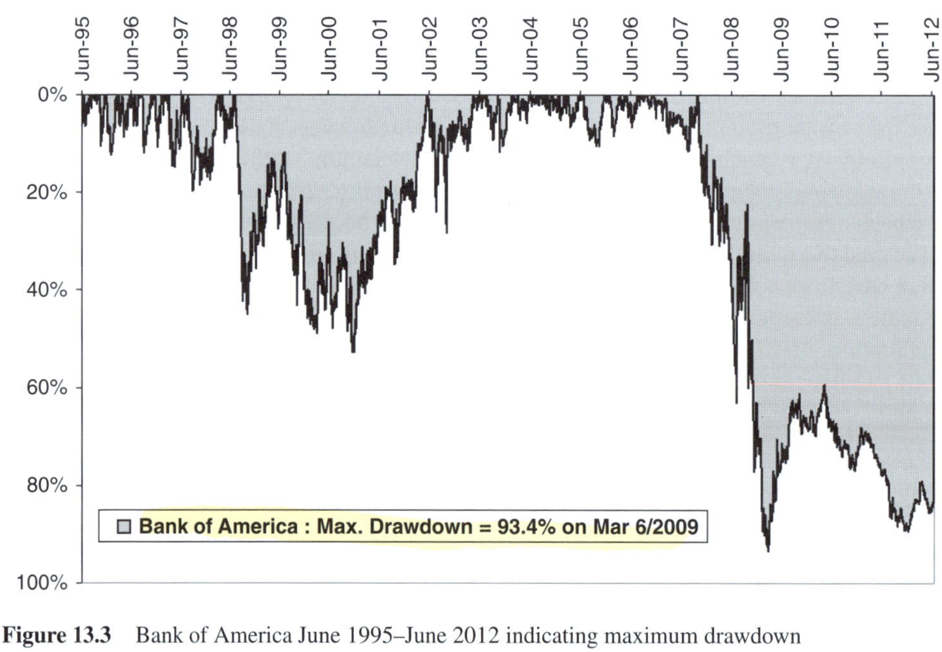

Figure 13.3 Bank of America June 1995–June 2012 indicating maximum drawdown

Figure 13.4 Nasdaq Composite Index monthly closes 1993–mid-2012

So far the discussion of drawdowns has focused on the 2007/8 crisis but there have been other periods in recent financial history when drawdowns of similar magnitude have been experienced by a wide variety of equities. The collapse of the Nasdaq Composite Index is strikingly illustrated in Figure 13.4 as are the epic proportions of the bubble which inflated in the latter period of the last millennium. The index rose from the 1300 level at the beginning of 1997 to more than 5000 during the course of March 2000 which by far surpasses the bubble which developed in the financial services sector between 2002 and 2007 where prices of a cross-section of financials as captured by the KBW Banking Index [4] "only" doubled.

Investor euphoria, manifested at times in an almost maniacal appetite for internet-based companies and other high technology firms, which characterized the dot com era of the late 1990s, gave rise to some quite stupendous looking price charts. During the height of the truly manic phase of high tech and internet mania, partly exaggerated by the phantom Y2K phenomenon, [5] the charts of companies such as webvan.com and pets.com which are some of the better known internet casualties, along with other high tech ventures such as Global Crossing, Juniper Networks, and Alcatel Lucent would make even the performance of the Nasdaq Composite Index, as seen in Figure 13.4, seem "restrained" by comparison. To cite just three examples of "fallen angel" companies which are still trading today: Juniper Networks (JNPR) reached a price of $232 in October 2000 and in just two years – by October 2002 – it was trading at less than $5 – a collapse of 98%; JDS Uniphase (JDSU) reached a price of $1227 in early 2000 and at its worst dropped by 99.8% and in mid-2012 trades at around $10; [6] and Alcatel-Lucent (ALU) traded above $80 in 2000 and is trading in mid-2012 at less than $2.

An article published by the US periodical *Barrons* on March 20, 2000 makes for very interesting reading as it appeared about a week after the Nasdaq Composite Index saw its "blow off top" value of 5132 reached on March 10, 2000 (see Figure 13.4) which was rapidly followed by a 10% drop during the next few days. The *Barrons* article observed that "America's 371 publicly traded Internet companies have grown to the point that they are collectively valued at $1.3 trillion, which amounts to about 8% of the entire U.S. stock market." [7] When one recalls that many of these publicly traded dot com companies had insignificant revenues and negative net earnings it is not too surprising (although it clearly was to those in 1999 and early 2000 who were enjoying spectacular daily returns in companies such as Amazon.com) that the subsequent collapse saw the most overly inflated stocks lose 95% or more of their pre-crash market capitalization within a few weeks, and of course many are no longer with us.

The disappearance of companies through bankruptcy introduces an important methodological limitation for back-testing in general terms, and historical analysis of tail risk and drawdowns in particular, which is known as the *survivorship bias* phenomenon. Any contemporary time series analysis of, for example, the constituents of the Nasdaq Composite Index, conducted with a view to determining historical performance, will be confined to those companies which are still in existence, in other words those which have survived. For those that died along the way the time series data is not easily accessible.

The main issue with survivorship bias is that historical back-testing, unless conducted with all time series data included – even for those companies which failed – will understate the risks to an investor since they could well have been holding shares in the companies that went bankrupt and where there was effectively a 100% drawdown. After looking at the chart for the Nasdaq Composite Index it is sobering to note that those who had heavy exposure to the dot com and even high tech sectors could have had an even worse experience than suggested by the index itself. In this regard one might spare a thought for those who owned shares in telecommunications company Nortel at the turn of the millennium. Nortel's market capitalization fell from Canadian $398 billion in September 2000 to less than Canadian $5 billion in August 2002. The company declared bankruptcy in 2009 and the stock was then worthless.

Figure 13.5 is intended to reflect not only the severe drawdowns during the GFC but also the fact that large losses were experienced in the early 2000s by most technology related stocks. Intel's shares dropped (on a dividend adjusted basis) from $60 attained in 2000 to $10 in 2002. As raised at the beginning of this chapter in connection with a patient buy and hold investor in the stock of Bank of America, the actual experience for a similarly inclined investor in Intel would also have been one of suffering an alarming drawdown and the chart in Figure 13.6, illustrating the drawdown during the entire period from 1995 to June 2012, is testimony to the severity. It is worth commenting that in mid-2012 Intel's stock is trading around $25 which means that it is still quite a lot less than 50% of its peak value. For an investor that had held Intel throughout the last 17 years, in addition to the plunge in 2000/1, there would have been another major retreat in the stock to have endured during the global financial crisis when the stock went below $12 in 2008 and early 2009.

Figure 13.6 indicates the longevity of the drawdown for an investor who had purchased shares in Intel Corporation in June 1995 and held the stock throughout the entire period until June 2012, as shown in the former chart. It will be seen from the annotation on the chart that the maximum drawdown of 82% occurred in October 2002 but was then almost matched again in December of 2008. Despite receiving a dividend for some of the period in question, a patient, long-term investor who had followed Warren Buffet's advice that "the ideal holding

Figure 13.5 Daily closes for Intel Corporation June 1995–June 2012 (adjusted for dividends)

period is forever" [8] and held shares in Intel since the mid 1990s would still have a capital "loss" as measured from the price peak in 2000 of more than 50% as is evidenced by the drawdown level on the right hand side of Figure 13.6.

The previous discussion has revealed just how brutal and long lasting drawdowns can be for a buy and hold investor. They can also be hazardous to a more tactical short-term trader or portfolio manager that gets his or her timing wrong. One further metric which can be useful in highlighting the changing nature of investor sentiment to the "fundamentals" of a company can be seen in the following table which contrasts the market capitalizations for a subset of

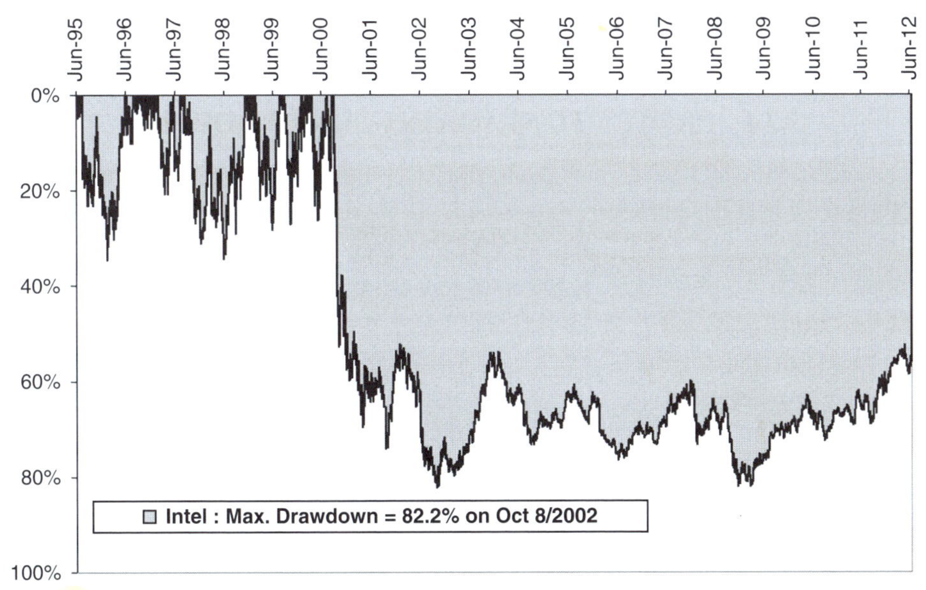

Figure 13.6 Intel Corporation June 1995–June 2012 (Adjusted for dividends) – maximum drawdown

Table 13.2 Declining market capitalizations for six large cap US companies 2000 vs 2012

Company	Market Capitalization $bn 2000	Market Capitalization $bn 2012	Percentage Change
Microsoft	586	250	-57.3%
General Electric	474	203	-57.2%
Cisco	349	91	-73.9%
Intel	278	135	-51.4%
Lucent	238	4	-98.3%
Citigroup	250	82	-67.2%

the Top 10 blue chip companies, at least as they were in 2000, and where their market caps are in mid-2012. [9]

The right hand column of Table 13.2 which shows the percentage changes in the market capitalization values since 2000 for the subset of companies should act as a precautionary advisory to the adage quoted at the beginning of this chapter that in the long run the stock market is a weighing machine, with the implication that investors over the long haul are rewarded for holding companies with strong valuation fundamentals. It is not surprising that more asset managers are becoming less focused on the long haul and more focused on market timing and tactical asset allocation. In turn this more opportunistic and pragmatic stance becomes a contributory factor to the shifting tides of risk on and risk off market movement as patterns which are descriptive of contemporary investor behavior.

13.1 PROTECTING AGAINST DRAWDOWNS

There are a variety of strategies which can be shown to soften the blow of the kinds of massive drawdowns that have been touched upon in the previous sections of this chapter.

Broad approaches to protection against crises drawdowns or tail risk can be summarized as falling into the following categories:

- Long Volatility Strategies
- Tail Risk Protection Indices
- Credit Quality Strategies
- Option Strategies
- Foreign Exchange Strategies
- Switching from risk on to safe haven assets.

Through extensive back-testing [10] it is possible to examine the efficacy of each one of these strategies, not only with regard to the events of 2007/8 but also to longer historical time frames. However, there are several authoritative studies on the mechanics and benefits of hedging in general, and especially in regard to the application of options strategies, [11] so an extensive and detailed examination of each would go beyond where I need to go in this book; accordingly the ensuing analysis will be somewhat selective and focus on strategies which have been less widely discussed in the risk management literature.

If an asset manager has long exposure to risk on assets – primarily equities, both from the developed world and emerging markets, as well as commodities and high yield debt – then a long volatility component included within the portfolio, which will be negatively correlated with those risk on assets, will act as a shock absorber during critical market episodes. Inserting a long volatility component into a portfolio can be achieved in a number of ways using derivatives – indeed volatility is considered to be an asset class in its own right. [12] Investment banks, via the over the counter swap market, can provide specifically tailored volatility-based structured instruments which will, to a varying extent, perform the required shock absorption. Alternatively a fund manager can use various futures contracts based on volatility metrics to offset the losses arising during periods when markets are very stressed. One of the most widely used volatility metrics is the VIX which is an acronym for the CBOE Volatility Index. [13]

The VIX tracks the implied volatility of premiums for the series of options on the S&P 500 index which are traded during each session on the Chicago Board Options Exchange. Fortunately there is a good data series for the VIX values dating back to 1990, and the values registered for the VIX as well as some key milestones in recent financial history are illustrated in Figure 13.7. The movements of the VIX are a good proxy for equity-related risk even beyond the US markets (evidence shows that movements in the VIX are well correlated with other global indices and critical episodes [14]). It should be immediately apparent from

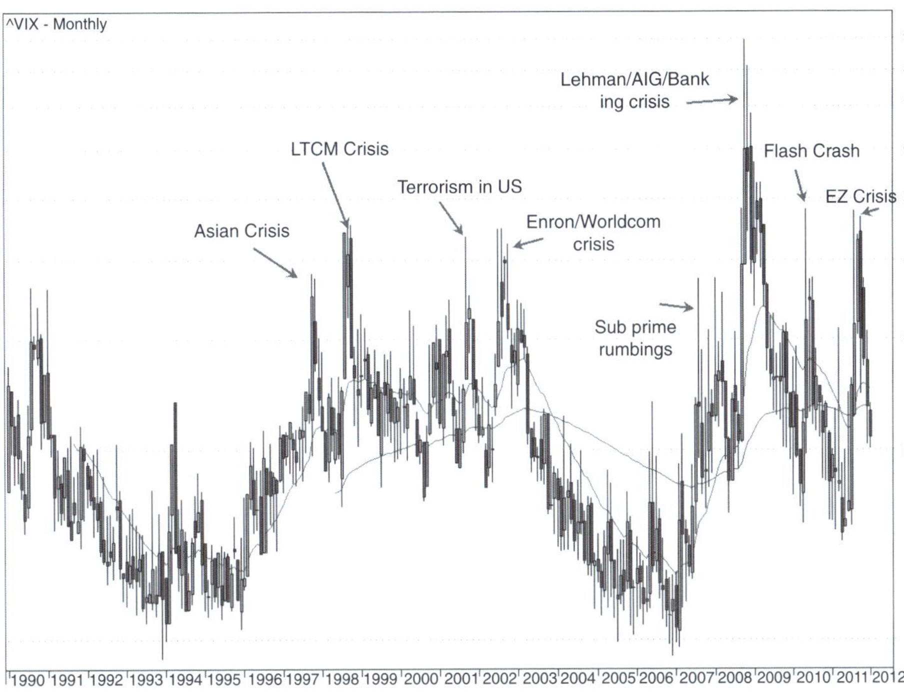

Figure 13.7 Long-term monthly chart of CBOE Volatility Index (VIX)

Figure 13.7 that numerous critical episodes of heightened financial risk coincide with upward spikes on the market's perception of implied volatility.

The VIX is a very useful barometer of macro or systematic risk – it is sometimes referred to as the fear gauge – but it will tend to be a reactive rather than a leading indicator. When risky assets in general experience the kinds of dramatic declines which have been illustrated at the beginning of this chapter, the implied volatility in options prices will invariably increase dramatically as well. Many fund managers will anxiously seek out protective index puts in an attempt to minimize damage to their portfolios and will be contributing to the escalation in premium prices. A consequence of postponing the decision to purchase puts on an index until a crisis has already commenced is that the efficacy of the protection can be considerably diminished. The payoff from the put should gain from the fact that its return will be inversely related to the downward direction of the long portfolio, but a substantial portion of the investment in the protection will be consumed by the gradual decay in the elevated volatility premium which has been purchased when investor sentiment may have been at its most negative.

The following is the output from a stress regression analysis of the co-movement or association of the S&P 500 (via its proxy, SPY) and the VIX which was undertaken after the market close of June 22, 2012. It covers almost six years of data points.

Independent Variable: SPY Dependent Variable: VIX
Period covered from 20060807 to 20120622

Independent Variable Performance 19.69% Dependent Variable Performance 20.68%

Current Rolling Correlation −0.817185
Current Rolling Beta −5.678221
Beta from one week ago −5.625741
****
OUTLIER CORRELATIONS, BETA AND RSQ VALUES
****
S&P 500 - outlier absolute change threshold: 3.15%
n Extreme Moves 75 percentage of data points 5.0%
Extreme Correlation Coefficient: −0.84
Correlation coefficient for whole period: −0.77

Extreme Beta: −2.86
Average Beta (based on rolling window period of size 21): −5.30
Beta for whole period: −3.60

Extreme RSQ: 0.70
Average RSQ (based on rolling window period of size 21): 0.70
RSQ for whole period: 0.60

A couple of points are notable. Firstly the correlation coefficient or R value for the whole period is −0.77 and there is no notable difference in the average rolling RSQ value and the extreme RSQ value. Secondly the average rolling beta value is −5.3 which is very highly negative and shows that the VIX will be very sensitive to changes in the S&P 500, and moves

Figure 13.8 Drawdown for portfolio of S&P 500 (SPY) 90% and VIX 10%

will be inversely amplified by a multiple of five. Further complicating the issue of how effective the use of a VIX hedge to a portfolio will be, and the actual calculation as to how many futures contracts need to be used in hedging [15] is the fact that the beta reading, i.e. during the 5% of outlier moves for the S&P 500, undergoes a significant reduction at market extremes. Given the unusual beta relationship between the pair and the very strong inverse correlation, the key issue with using a long volatility strategy relates to the timing of the purchase of the VIX futures, the precise value of the contracts purchased relative to the size of the portfolio, and most critically the decision about when to remove the hedge.

The pros and cons of using a long volatility strategy are well exemplified in the very simple approach which has been taken in the preparation of Figure 13.8. What is shown is a portfolio which holds a 90% long position in the S&P 500 – the risk asset – and a 10% allocation to the actual value of the VIX (futures were not used due to the term structure of volatility which is discussed below). The VIX was "purchased" in June 2007 and the period covered is up to June 2012. The benefit of having the protection in place as early as June 2007 is the flip side to the avoidance of buying protection when option premiums are elevated as previously discussed. An examination of Figure 13.8 shows that at the height of the financial crisis in the latter part of 2008 there was virtually no drawdown to the long risk portfolio but as the crisis receded – or to be more precise in this context, the implied volatility as expressed by the VIX dropped substantially – the long position in the VIX dragged the portfolio down quite significantly. In fact the largest drop from the high water mark (or the maximum drawdown) in the early part of 2009 is approximately 30%. The problem with the strategy is that if the VIX hedge is not removed, as a result of the very strong inverse correlation and the very high negative beta value for the pair – even with only a 10% allocation to the VIX component – the portfolio will struggle to make upward progress.

Figure 13.9 Daily closes for SPY and VIX – September 2007–mid-2012

Figure 13.9 provides a different perspective on the relationship between the S&P 500 and the VIX with left hand scale providing the guide to the equity index and the right hand scale the values for the VIX. The stress regression output which has already been considered for the period shown in Figure 13.9 reveals in statistical values what is visible on this chart. In particular, the chart highlights the strongly inverse correlation as well as the reduced beta values during the second half of 2008 due to extraordinarily large moves being experienced by both variables during the height of the crisis – where the bulk of the outlier moves are to be found.

A further factor to consider when adopting a long volatility strategy with VIX futures is that typically the term structure of volatility is steeply upward sloping. Essentially the forward curve for VIX futures resembles the "normal" yield curve for fixed income instruments in that options with a short time to maturity will typically trade at relatively lower implied volatility compared to options with a longer time to maturity. This is demonstrated in Figure 13.10 which is a graphic available from the CBOE's primer on the VIX. [16] As a consequence of this steep upward slope the roll return, i.e. buying more futures contracts on a rolling basis as the existing ones mature, will be negative, This challenge requires further financial engineering skills and raises efficacy considerations for this kind of long volatility strategy in addition to those witnessed in consideration of Figure 13.8. [17]

Being long puts is the simplest option strategy but there is the cost of the premiums to consider and the same reasoning about the timing of the long volatility strategies would apply as option premiums will become more costly as the markets become more volatile and an option premium is a decaying asset. One advantage of puts versus the long volatility strategy is that being long VIX futures could result in indeterminable losses when the protection is no longer required as the VIX falls, whereas the amount of the option premium is the maximum loss that can be sustained by a fund manager that uses options as the protection strategy.

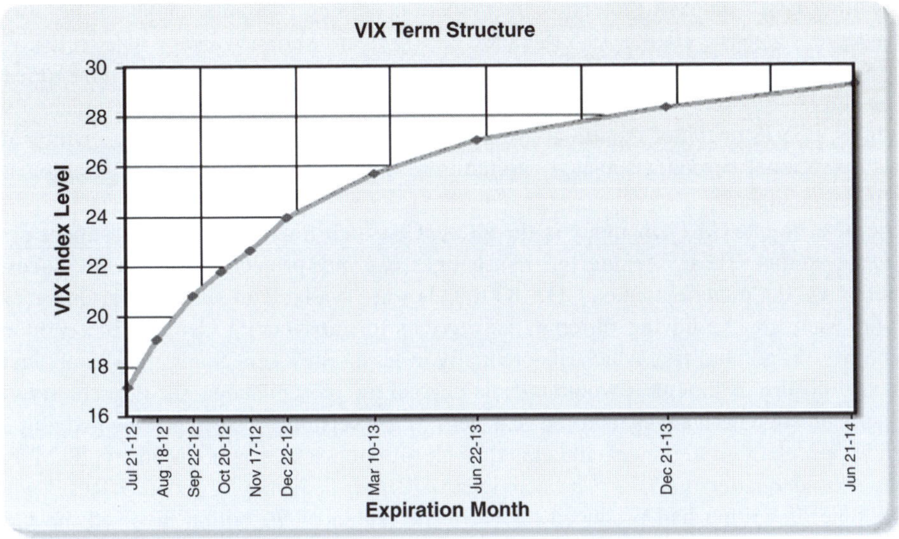

VIX Volatility Index values ganerated at: 06/20/2012 15:14:55

Trade Date	Expiration Date	Vix	Contract Month
6/20/2012 3:14:55 PM	21-Jul-12	17.17	1
6/20/2012 3:14:55 PM	18-Aug-12	19.10	2
6/20/2012 3:14:55 PM	22-Sep-12	20.84	3
6/20/2012 3:14:55 PM	20-Oct-12	21.81	4
6/20/2012 3:14:55 PM	17-Nov-12	22.65	5
6/20/2012 3:14:55 PM	22-Dec-12	23.98	6
6/20/2012 3:14:55 PM	16-Mar-13	25.72	7
6/20/2012 3:14:55 PM	22-Jun-13	27.05	8
6/20/2012 3:14:55 PM	21-Dec-13	28.34	9
6/20/2012 3:14:55 PM	21-Jun-14	29.25	10

Figure 13.10 The term structure of volatility
Source: CBOE.

13.2 THE TAIL RISK PROTECTION BUSINESS

Several investment banks have recognized the demand for tail risk protection and, given the declines in other areas of their businesses, have seen an opportunity to create various products which can be purchased either "off the shelf" for smaller fund management companies or which can be custom crafted for clients with more exacting requirements.

A variance swap is an over-the-counter financial derivative that allows one to speculate on or hedge risks associated with the volatility of some underlying product, such as an exchange rate, interest rate, or stock index. In a variance swap, two parties enter a contract on forward realized variance. At maturity it pays the difference between the realized variance and the pre-agreed variance strike. Variance swaps provide pure exposure to the underlying price volatility, without the complication of delta risk, which is present in options.

Volatility-based tail risk protection indices are becoming a popular choice as equity tail risk hedges. Deutsche Bank's ELVIS Index uses forward variance swaps to effectively go long S&P 500 implied volatility, which avoids the volatility "risk premium" embedded in option prices. Deutsche Bank's promotional materials claim that "[c]ontrary to many other strategies, ELVIS does not require active management to maintain protection – which alleviates operational burden associated expiration/rolling – and is structured in a simple and transparent manner."

The most liquid US CDS index is the CDX.IG, which references 125 investment grade corporate credits. Those seeking tail risk hedges can buy protection on specific slices of the index via the tranche market. CDX.IG tranches are available in slices of varying seniority with each tranche having different sensitivities to idiosyncratic default risk, economic downturn risk, and tail risk which, theoretically at least, allows for fine-tuning to obtain the desired exposure. Although it would take us beyond the present scope, the opportunities for mishap with such derivatives, and the fuzziness of the separation between true hedging and outright speculation, were well illustrated in the trading losses announced by JP Morgan in the second quarter of 2012. The activities of Bruno Iksil, the "London Whale," which at the time of writing had produced losses in the region of $6 billion involved the firm's traders taking massive positions in the CDX.IG derivatives. In fact it appears, in what was a highly complex trade involving separate components, that Iksil was selling huge tranches of derivatives on the CDX.IG, as he believed that economic conditions were improving and that this would be favorable for corporate bonds. So what appears to have begun as a hedge turned into a doubling of bets on the strength of the underlying JP Morgan portfolio of corporate bonds. Bruno Iksil along with several other traders involved in the debacle resigned from JP Morgan in July 2012. [18] The intricacies of the trade are discussed in a very useful article entitled "JP Morgan and the London Whale: Understanding the Hedge That Wasn't." [19]

Alternative strategies for diversifying a portfolio to include components which will reduce the skew and kurtosis characteristics [20] of a long portfolio in equities is provided in a research report published by Credit Suisse in April 2012 and which has been referenced earlier in this book. [21]

By examining the risk/reward characteristics from the universe of hedge funds available the Credit Suisse team explored the statistical properties of co-skewness in the beta with the S&P 500 and co-kurtosis in the beta with reference to the S&P 500 of all of the well known hedge fund strategies using an extended historical database.

Using a weighting technique for the three hedge fund strategies which prove to be beneficial – Global Macro, Managed Futures, and Multi Strategy – by combining these with only a 50% long exposure to the S&P 500 (and 25% for the Managed Futures, 16.5% for the Multi Strategy, and 8.5% for the Global Macro components) the results shown in the right hand box within Figure 13.11 show that a significant reduction in risk has been achieved plus a higher return having been achieved. In fact the risk is almost one half of that experienced by the 100% long S&P 500 portfolio. Also very significant is that the maximum drawdown has dropped from more than 50% of the long S&P 500 only portfolio to less than 30% for the portfolio balanced with the hedge fund strategies. The changes in the VaR and the other statistical values, given the caveats and reservations about their reliability that have been a recurrent theme of this book, also represent noticeable improvements in the risk characteristics of the balanced portfolio.

Display 12: Combine select asset classes to reduce skew and potentially increase risk-adjusted returns

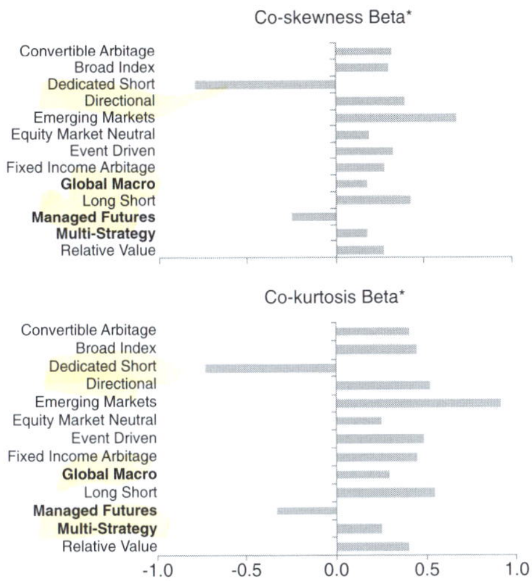

Portfolio Statistics	100% S&P 500	CVaR Optimization
S&P 500	100.00	50.00
Managed Futures	-	25.00
Multi-Strategy	-	16.50
Global Macro	-	8.50
Total	100.00	100.00
Historical Return	8.05	8.36
Historical Risk	15.72	8.83
Return per Unit of Risk	0.51	0.95
Return per Unit of CVaR	0.23	0.48
Annualized Value at Risk	-27.13	-11.92
Maximum Drawdown	-50.95	-29.29
Kurtosis	0.96	0.22
Skewness	-0.66	-0.42

Figure 13.11 Combination of different assets to reduce skew in portfolio
Source: Credit Suisse: Is the (Fat) Tail Wagging your Portfolio?

13.3 RAISING CASH AND SWITCHING TO SAFE HAVEN ASSETS

For a fund manager that becomes concerned about the imminence of systemic illiquidity, raising the cash component of a portfolio should offer an element of tail risk protection. However even if a fund manager had become more defensive, and liquidated a portion of the portfolio prior to the systemic crisis of 2007/8, there would still have been quite significant drawdowns. Wealth preservation was particularly challenging during the financial crisis and as the after shocks of the GFC continue to be felt, and for reasons related to the binary and bipolar nature of contemporary markets, there is need to explore innovative approaches to risk management. One of the suggestions that will be made, based upon the stress regression methodology which has been outlined, is that in asset selection it is vital to consider the way that normal market correlations can become much more tightly coupled when markets are stressed and illiquid.

On the one hand from the long only perspective one would want to avoid the diversification fallacy which arises from combining assets which ordinarily or normally would appear to be weakly correlated, but which when markets are behaving abnormally will exhibit much greater tail dependency and in the limiting case will effectively have correlations approaching unity. Alternatively by using the insights provided from stress regression analysis it becomes possible to find those assets where the extreme correlation and beta values are so linked when critical episodes arise that long/short strategies with suitable risk on and risk off characteristics can be used in portfolio construction to provide more safety in crises. The evidence from the cross correlations between certain sectors and asset classes with key FX pairs provides the motivation for using short positions in FX, implemented when timing signals are triggered

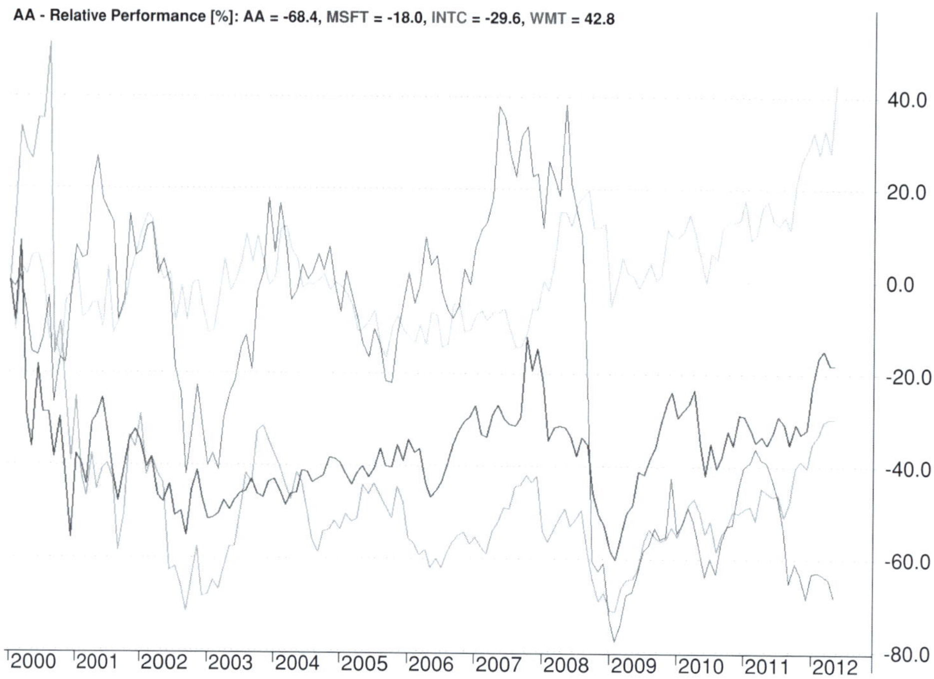

Figure 13.12 Relative performance of four large cap US equities 2000–mid-2012

from the heat map techniques outlined in Chapter 9, to provide some of the most effective methods of side stepping the most damaging drawdowns.

To begin this discussion there will be a review of some assets which are widely perceived as being safe havens and thus qualified for defensive positioning especially during very challenging market conditions. As will be seen some of the assets, contrary to popular belief, may not be fit for purpose.

Figure 13.12 illustrates the relative performance of four large cap multi-national corporations which trade in the US equity market, but since they are all global businesses they could be said to provide a cross-sectional view of the blue chip equity universe. The four companies selected are Alcoa (AA), Intel (INTC), Microsoft (MSFT), and Wal-Mart (WMT), all of which are consitutents of the Dow Jones Industrial Average, and the paths taken by each are from a base date of January 2000 until mid-2012.

Only the world's largest retailer, Wal-Mart, shows a positive return on a price basis over the 12-year period with a capital return of 42.8% which is tantamount to an approximately 3% compound annual growth rate or CAGR. The buy and hold investor who had purchased the other three well known companies at the beginning of the new millennium would have quite significant (unrealized) capital losses and in the case of Alcoa this would have amounted to more than a two-thirds depreciation of capital.

It could be claimed that the four securities selected are quite arbitrary as indeed is the start date for the exercise, and that by selecting different companies and setting a purchase date of spring 2003, for example, there would be substantially different returns. This is incontestable, but the purpose in showing the performances displayed in Figure 13.12 was simply to underline

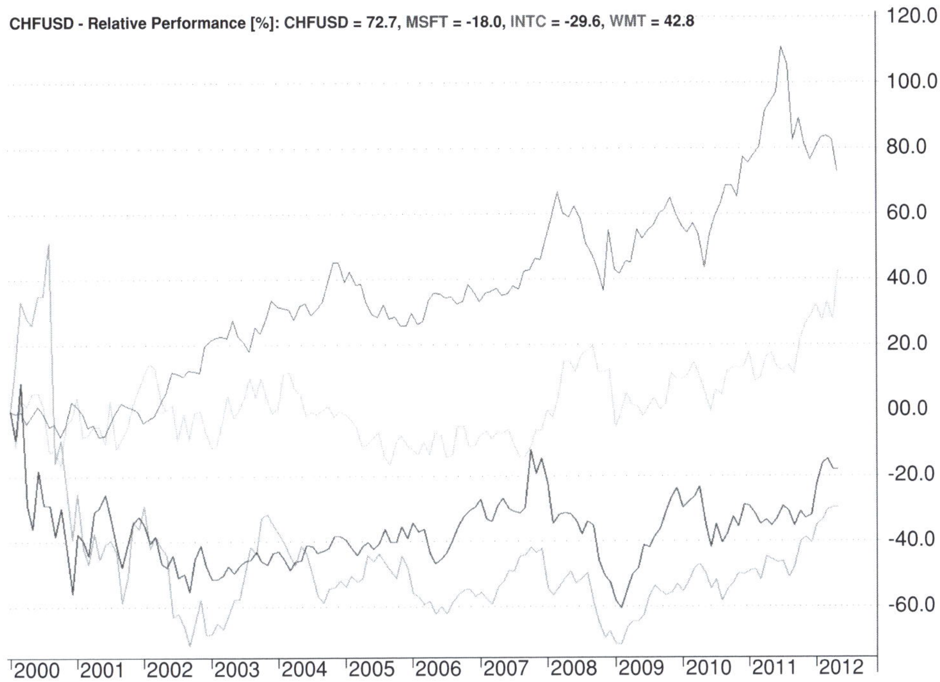

Figure 13.13 Relative performance of three large cap US equities and Swiss Franc 2000–mid 2012

the point that *blue chip equities are not inherently safe haven assets* and that there can be a high degree of risk associated with holding them uncritically over an extended period.

The safe haven characteristics of the Japanese yen have already been noted in Chapter 7 and another currency which has a well deserved status as a safe harbor or refuge when there is a flight to safety is the Swiss franc. Figure 13.13 introduces the Swiss franc versus the US dollar (CHF/USD) onto the previous graphic although Alcoa has been removed for the sake of simplicity. The Swiss franc's performance over the 12-year period exceeds all of the previously cited blue chip equities with a return of 72%. At one point in 2011 the Swiss currency had actually doubled against its US counterpart since the 2000 base, but following the Swiss National Bank's decision in September 2011 to peg its currency to the euro, [22] the movement for the Swiss currency has been locked against the EZ currency and diminished along with the decline of that currency.

Notwithstanding the more recent peg, which may eventually be removed, the path taken by the Swiss franc has been one of steady ascent since 2000 and despite a very minor retracement at the height of the GFC its safe haven and defensive characteristics suggest that for a well balanced global portfolio there are good reasons for an allocation to the currency directly or major Swiss corporations such as Nestle and Novartis which are denominated in the currency. Swiss government securities are considered such a safe haven that on May 31, 2012 the yield on five-year maturities actually dipped below zero and as Bloomberg reported in July 2012, the two-year note traded during that month at an historic low of a negative 46 basis points. [23] In other words for investors fixated on return of their investment rather than return on their investment it is considered worthwhile to pay the Swiss government to lend them money.

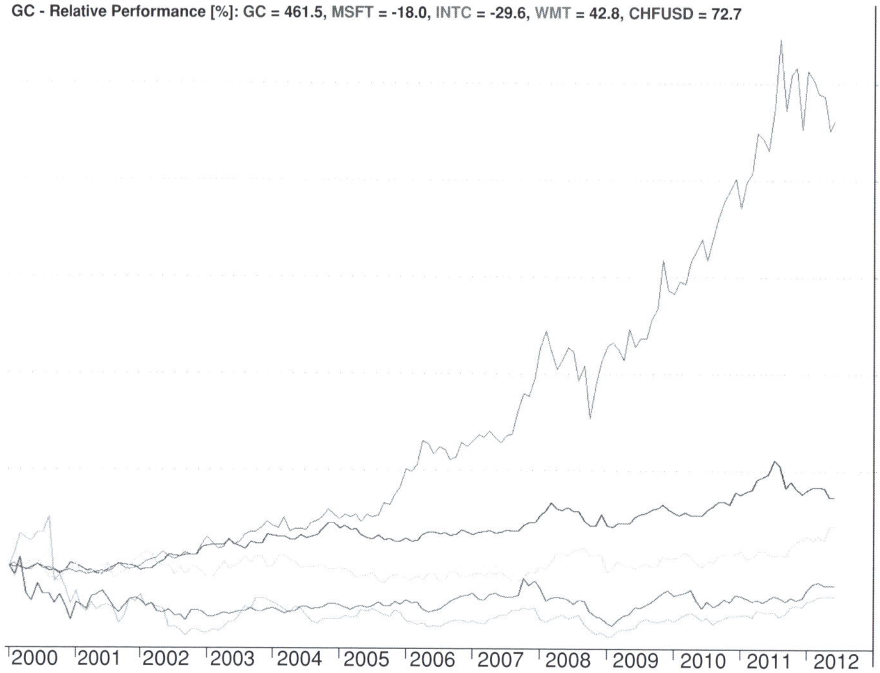

Figure 13.14 Relative performance of three large cap US equities, Swiss Franc and gold 2000–mid-2012

The gold price, as represented by a continuous futures contract for COMEX gold and shown in the chart as GC, has been introduced into Figure 13.14. The returns for the precious metal completely dwarf the returns on the other instruments with a gain of approximately 460%, or a compound annual growth rate or CAGR of more than 13%.

13.4 IMPLEMENTING DRAWDOWN PROTECTION STRATEGIES

One of the more interesting and useful discussions on dealing with substantial drawdowns is to be found in a research note from GMO and authored by James Montier. The white paper was published in June 2011 and is entitled *A Value Investor's Perspective on Tail Risk Protection: An Ode to the Joy of Cash.* [24]

The approach taken by Montier is very much in accordance with the approach taken throughout this book which is to focus on drawdowns as the vital risk metric to be managed. This is refreshing within most of the literature on this topic as it goes beyond so many of the strategies proposed by others which are based upon the misuse of statistical tools, especially those based on the seriously flawed VaR metrics.

Figure 13.15, which appears in the GMO article just cited, illustrates the risk component, or the drawdowns, of four different investment strategies tested by GMO for the period from 2005 through to 2011; the reward or rates of return are discussed later and shown in Figure 13.17. The first strategy which is shown at the top of the legend to Figure 13.15 is essentially one without any tail risk protection at all, as it represents a portfolio which is 100% invested

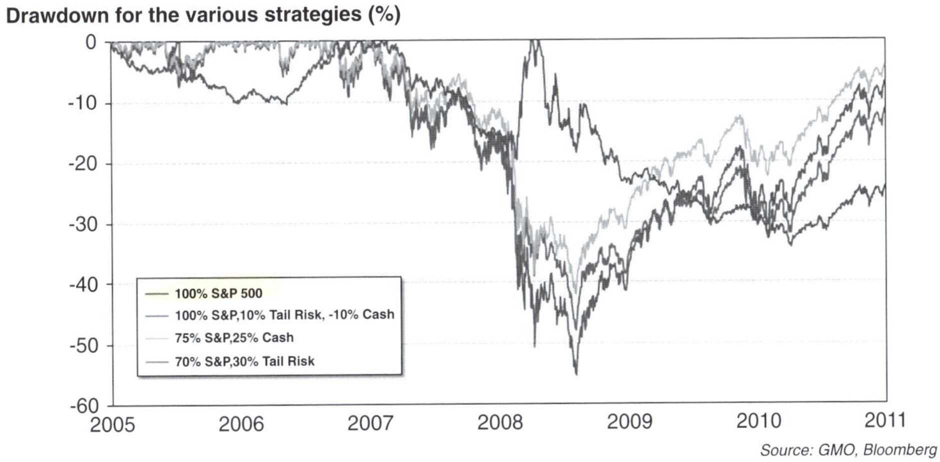

Figure 13.15 Drawdown for various tail risk protection strategies
Source: GMO.

in the S&P 500 which will be taken as a proxy for risk assets. The second strategy is similar to the one I examined from my own research in the earlier discussion but with some subtle variations. This approach retains a 100% exposure to the S&P 500 but includes a 10% long volatility position which is implemented using short-term VIX futures (effectively financed by shorting cash which is not a vital consideration for present purposes). The third strategy is for a reduced position in the S&P 500 of 75% and an allocation to cash of 25%. The fourth strategy shown is for a 70% allocation to the S&P 500 and a 30% long volatility strategy – again implemented with short-term VIX futures.

The worst case scenario in Figure 13.15 illustrates the severe drawdown to a 100% long position in the S&P 500 during the critical period of 2007/8. The drawdown exceeded 50% and if one had been required to crystallize such losses – for example as a result of a leveraged portfolio being subject to a margin call – the time to recovery for this strategy would be unattractive.

The darkest line on the graphic shows a substantial improvement. How was this achieved? As indicated in the legend of the chart the mix of the portfolio in this instance was 70% for the S&P position and 30% of tail risk protection.

Montier proposes that tail risk protection can be introduced into a portfolio by three main approaches. The first is simply to have a 25% cash position to sit side by side with the 75% exposure to equities via the S&P 500 holding. From Figure 13.15 it can be seen that this combination would have softened the drawdown in 2008/9 to about 40% in contrast to the 50% plus amount of drawdown for 100% exposure to equities. Although such a reduction is not to be ignored the discomfort to the investor would still have been severe. In Figure 13.16 which shows the overall returns from the four strategies considered by GMO's Montier the returns seen on the right hand side of the chart indicate that the use of cash as a shock absorber did relatively little to the performance in the post-2009 recovery with both a 100% S&P 500 position and one with a cash component performing very similarly.

The most useful takeaway from Figure 13.16 is in relation to the 70% S&P and 30% tail risk component. Retaining the 30% tail risk protection beyond the 2008 collapse – where it

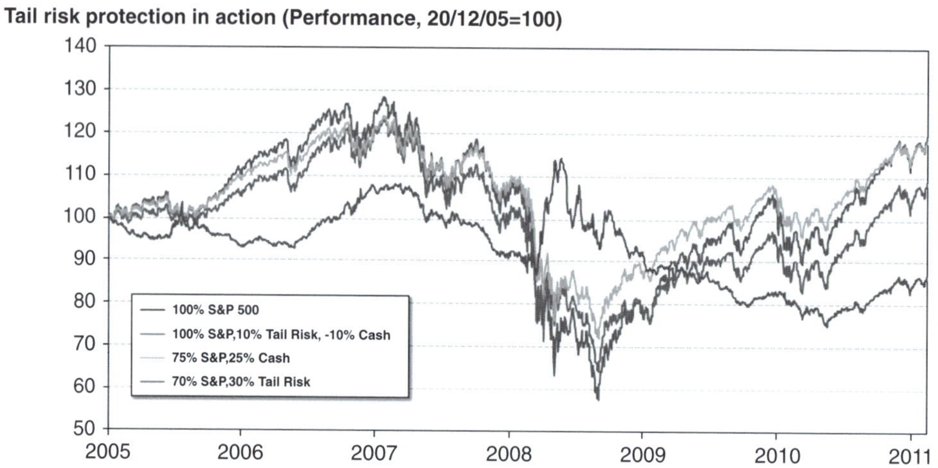

Figure 13.16 Overall performance for various tail risk protection strategies
Source: GMO.

would have sheltered the portfolio from any drawdowns as seen above – would have removed any upside portfolio and in fact brought it progressively underwater in comparison to a 100% position in equities. As shown in Figure 13.16 the outright equity portfolio would have risen to the 120 level on the right hand side (as compared to 100 at the base in December 2005), whereas retaining the tail risk protection after the 2009 recovery began would have resulted in an index value of about 85 on the right hand side of the chart. Timing of when to apply tail risk protection and when to remove it is clearly of paramount importance.

In the final section of this chapter an alternative strategy for protection will be suggested, and for this strategy market timing is not a concern.

The GMO study considers two further protection strategies in addition to using a cash cushion. On the one hand, as previously discussed, a Long Volatility strategy will be negatively correlated with the risk on assets such as holdings in the S&P 500. On the other hand one can use a credit spread strategy. This is based on the observable characteristic that when markets become critically stressed investment grade bonds will substantially outperform sub-investment grade bonds or junk bonds as they are disparagingly called. The GMO implementation of the Long Quality/Short Junk strategy is based on the returns of the top one third of investment grade credits versus the bottom one third of junk corporate credits in a universe of the largest 1000 US corporations.

Figure 13.17, which again comes from the GMO study, contrasts the contributions that each of these two approaches would make when employed as tail risk protection. At the height of the financial crisis there would have been a very close correspondence in the performance of each strategy and to that extent one could have been indifferent as to which one would have implemented as the 30% component in the preceding discussion.

With regard to the recovery phase on the right hand side of Figure 13.17, if the protection had not been removed the Long Quality/Short Junk strategy would have acted as less of a dampener on the upside returns to risk on assets than continued use of the Long Volatility strategy. As other evidence from Figure 13.16 suggested, the use of a Long Volatility strategy to soften the blow of drawdowns is not an effective instrument on an extended basis as its inverse

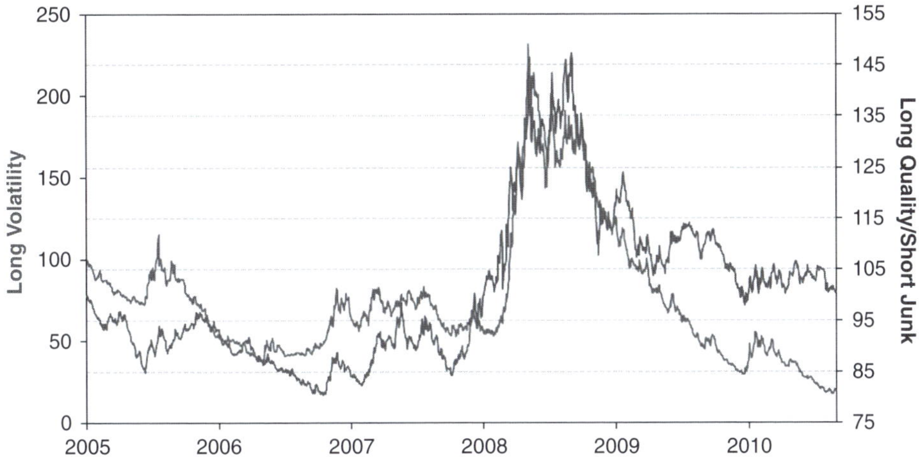

Long Volatility series = SPXSTR (first and second month contracts)
Long Quality/Short Junk series = return spread between quality companies (top 1/3) and junk companies (bottom 1/3) in a universe of the largest 1,000 U.S. companies. Quality and junk are based on the following metrics: profitability, leverage, and volatility of profitability.

Figure 13.17 Comparison of long volatility and Investment Grade versus Junk Bond strategies
Source: GMO.

correlation to risk on assets is too strong, and since volatility has very high beta characteristics this would make it unattractive except as protection in the most severe circumstances.

13.5 TAIL RISK PROTECTION FROM OUTRIGHT FX POSITIONS

One further strategy which is very much supported by the evidence presented in this book is to use the FX market as a way of hedging a portfolio of risk assets. Even if the portfolio does not require currency hedging *per se*, because it may not include assets denominated in currencies other than the accounting base currency, *the idea is to use FX as an asset class just for hedging purposes*. It has been demonstrated that in severe risk off phases since the GFC there has been a marked tendency for weakness in the commodity currencies, e.g. Australian dollar, South African rand, Canadian dollar during flights to safety. In particular using a short position with regard to the Australian dollar – either by selling AUD/USD or even more effectively, selling AUD/JPY, there will be an asset class component which will move, on a reliable basis, in an inverse fashion to the risk on elements of the portfolio. The stress regression tests which have been performed in earlier chapters show that there is a very clearly noticeable tightening in the correlations of, for example, AUD/JPY with both the S&P 500 and the MSCI Emerging Markets Index, as well as many other risk on assets.

One of the great advantages of the stress regression methodology is that it enables a fund manager to investigate those pairs which have experienced the greatest degree of convergence when markets are exhibiting extreme or outlier behavior. Since the correlation coefficient for AUD/JPY and the S&P 500 have shown a tendency to move towards unity during critical episodes, and moreover the beta values remain reasonably stable at close to one even under stress, there is a very straightforward tactic to employ. A matched exposure on a dollar adjusted basis would be to sell AUD/JPY against the long equity exposure. Given the high correlation – which will survive even when markets have passed through a crisis and are becoming less volatile – maintaining a hedge along these lines should create a shock neutralizing portfolio. However this will be preferable to hedging using a long volatility strategy or the credit quality spread as this will not be market neutral but will actually bring losses when markets are becoming calmer.

By experimenting with varying allocations to different asset classes and including a short AUD/JPY position in a portfolio alongside a core holding of equities, it is possible to find a combination which has the twin characteristics of low drawdowns and reasonably impressive returns. This would result in a high Calmar ratio which has the benefit of using portfolio drawdowns as the denominator in calculating the reward/risk trade off in asset allocations. [25]

Experimenting with different allocations reveals that the performance results are impressive for the following portfolio constituents:

- 20% Long US Treasury 7–10 years total return (via the IEF exchange traded fund)
- 50% Long S&P 500 via SPY
- 10% Long Gold
- 20% Long JPY/AUD (which is effectively short AUD/JPY).

The return for the above components in the five years from June 2007 is in excess of 45% as shown in Figure 13.18. Critically, the maximum drawdown for the whole period, as revealed in Figure 13.19, is less than 13.3%.

The combination of assets shown across the legend at the bottom of Figure 13.18 has produced a return of 47% in the five years from June 2007 which is a very respectable return over the period, especially considering that the equity market was at a peak in the third quarter of 2007 – just after the back-test period begins. It also achieved this reasonable return without

Figure 13.18 Performance of portfolio hedged with short AUD/JPY position

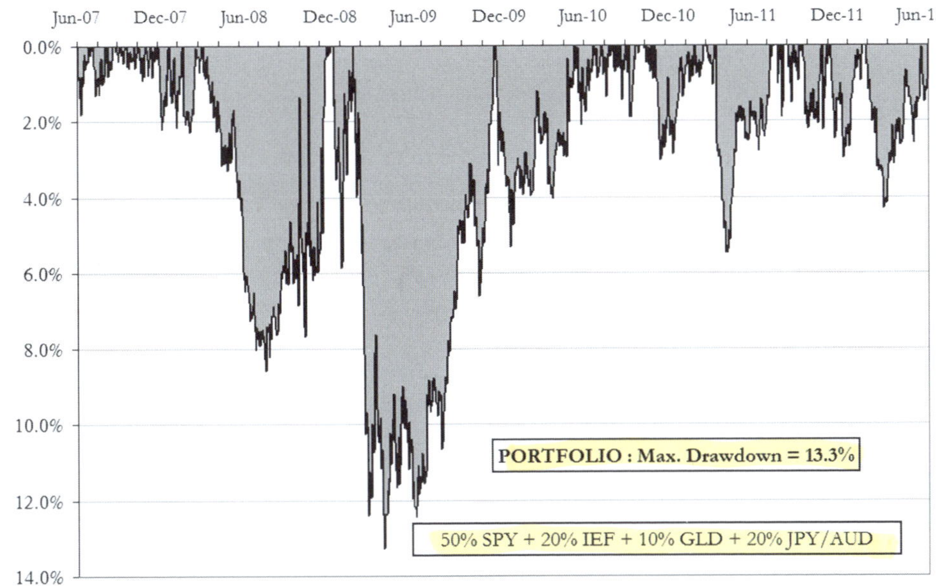

Figure 13.19 Maximum drawdown of portfolio hedged with short AUD/JPY position

subjecting the portfolio holder to the kinds of discomforting drawdowns that many other more traditionally crafted portfolios would have done as can be seen in Figure 13.19. The maximum drawdown of 13.3% for the portfolio composition shown in Figure 13.19 occurred in Q1, 2009 and was followed by a swift recovery.

If we now switch attention to portfolios without the built shock neutralization provided by the short FX position there are, of course, many permutations of constituent assets which could be reviewed from a back-testing exercise. The one which will be selected somewhat arbitrarily from the many available is shown in Figure 13.20 and this contains a fairly orthodox allocation of 70% to equities and 30% to medium/long-term US government bonds. The total return over the five-year period shown on the chart is 17% but as can be seen from the large drop in the path taken during 2008/9 there was a period when the portfolio was substantially below the water line.

Figure 13.21 focuses on the drawdowns for the combination of 70% equities and 30% medium-term US government bonds and the portfolio reached its nadir in March 2009 – which was exactly when the S&P 500 reached its final leg down – and the drawdown pike at this point was almost 33%.

Having highlighted the superior performance of a model portfolio which has been internally hedged through the use of an outright forex position it is also instructive to consider two variations on the exact nature of the forex hedge. In previous discussions it has been shown that the yen/Aussie combination is particularly fit for purpose as it embraces the twin polarities of the risk on/risk off dichotomy. The Japanese yen, for the various reasons noted in Chapters 7 and 8, has been a robust and reliable example of a safe haven currency where its behavior in times of stress is to strengthen against all other currencies. On the contrary the Australian dollar has, for reasons also cited in earlier chapters and specifically in relation to the China growth narrative, been one of the most adventurous currencies helping both to drive and respond to risk on phases of market activity.

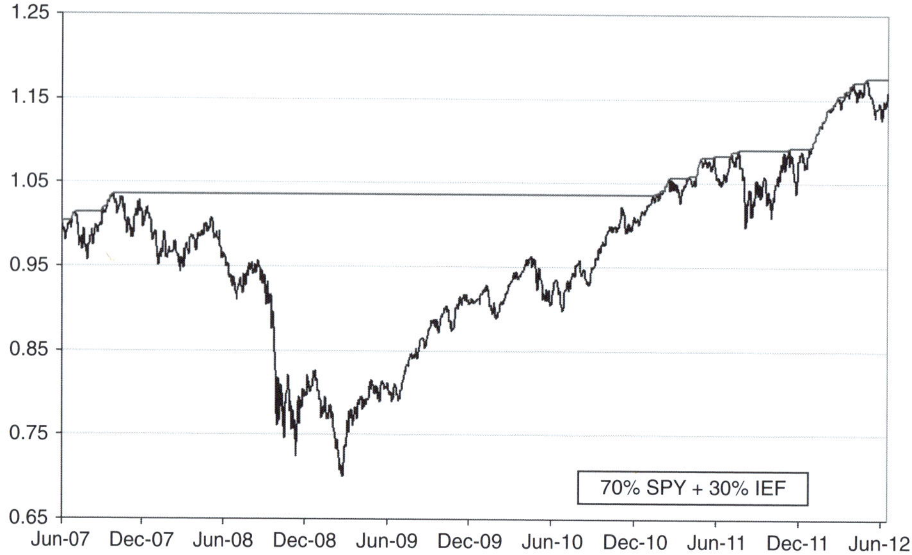

Figure 13.20 Performance of portfolio without FX hedging

The contribution of the short AUD/JPY component of an investment strategy designed to circumvent damaging drawdowns – even when this FX component is set at the 20% level – leads to a Calmar ratio superior to most other combinations and makes this an attractive option in portfolio construction. It is also an innovative approach which has not been covered previously in the risk management literature. Before concluding this chapter a couple of variations to the long JPY/AUD position (effectively short AUD/JPY) will be considered so

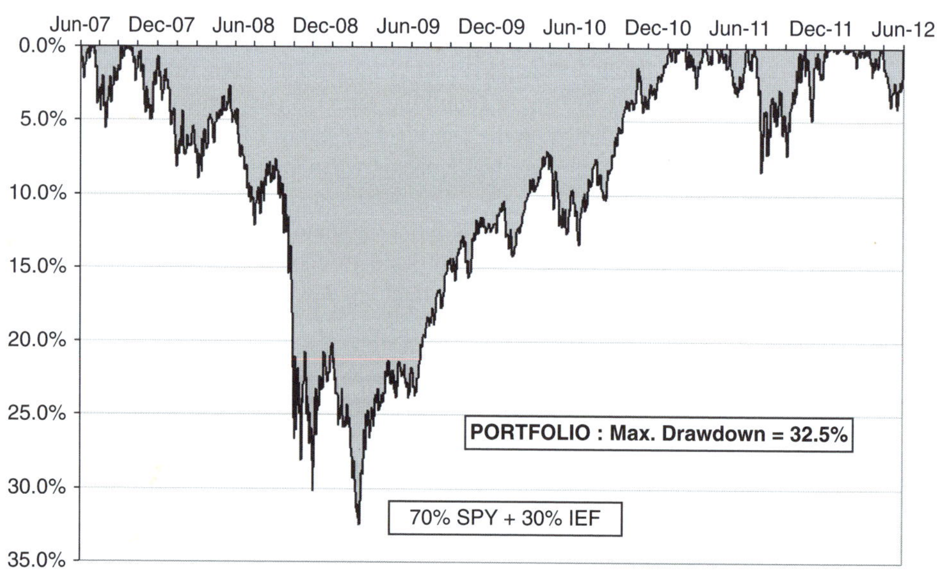

Figure 13.21 Maximum drawdown of portfolio without FX hedging

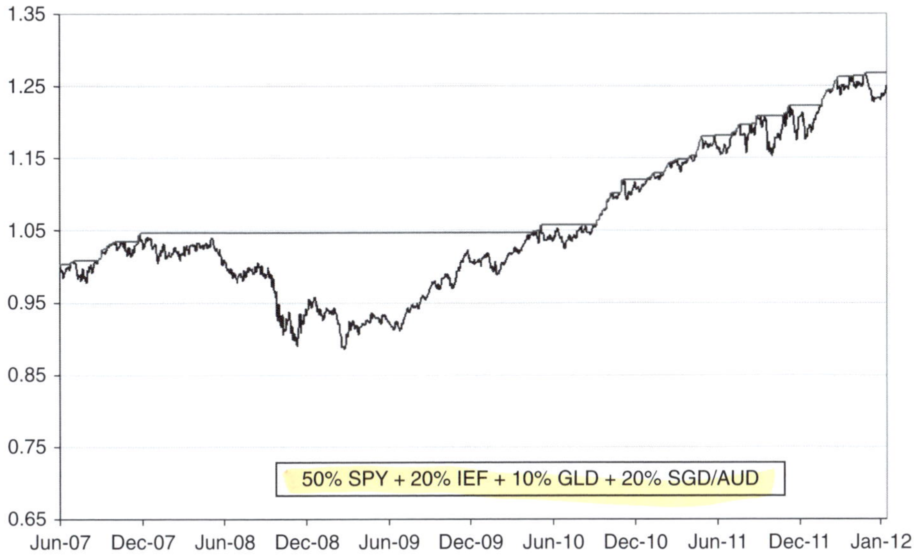

Figure 13.22 Performance of portfolio hedged with short AUD/USD position

that there can be some accommodation for special circumstances that may have impact on the yen side of the FX pair. As already suggested most of the tail risk protection benefits will derive from the fact that the Australian dollar is the most liquid and historically proven risk on asset which lends itself to being short in a portfolio designed to sidestep steep drawdowns. The two alternatives which are provided in diagrammatic form with little commentary are seen below.

Firstly, a portfolio (as before) with 20% US medium-term Treasuries, 50% S&P 500, and 10% gold has been supplemented with a 20% exposure to a long US dollar and short Australian dollar position – once again the Australian dollar is being shorted. Figure 13.22 reveals that this portfolio would have achieved a 23% return over the period from June 2007 to June 2012 – which is not dramatically dissimilar to the 33% return achieved with a long JPY/AUD position. Figure 13.23 reveals that the maximum drawdown will have risen to 14.3% as opposed to the 9.5% maximum drawdown for the comparable portfolio with a long JPY/AUD component.

The results of using another variation of a short position in the Australian dollar but this time matched against a long position in the Singapore dollar are to be seen on the final two diagrams which cover exactly the same time period as above.

Figure 13.24 shows that the long SGD/AUD approach achieves a slightly better return of about 28% and Figure 13.25 indicates a slightly higher drawdown than the AUD/USD approach at 16.9%. Nonetheless the drawdowns with each of the three FX variations as part of the asset allocation technique have performed remarkably well in comparison to the drawdowns seen with no drawdown protection afforded by using FX positions or even in comparison to other tail protection strategies outlined in earlier discussions of this chapter.

Finally, if one wished to avoid any idiosyncratic issues which might arise with respect to the long FX elements – the yen, the US dollar, or the Singapore dollar – a blended approach with equal exposures to each of the three variations (within the 20% FX component) would still exhibit similarly favorable characteristics to that seen with the optimal arrangement involving the JPY/AUD combination.

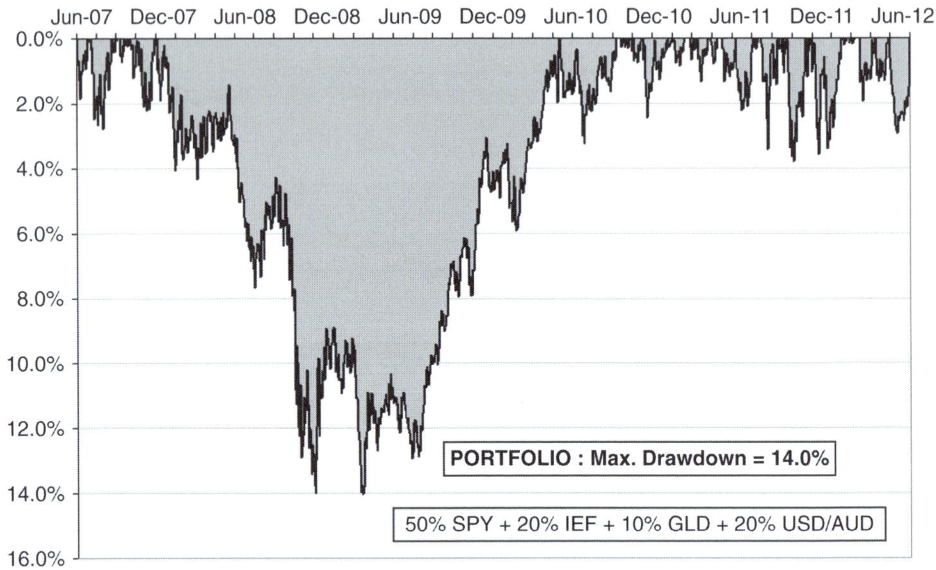

Figure 13.23 Maximum drawdown of portfolio hedged with short AUD/USD position

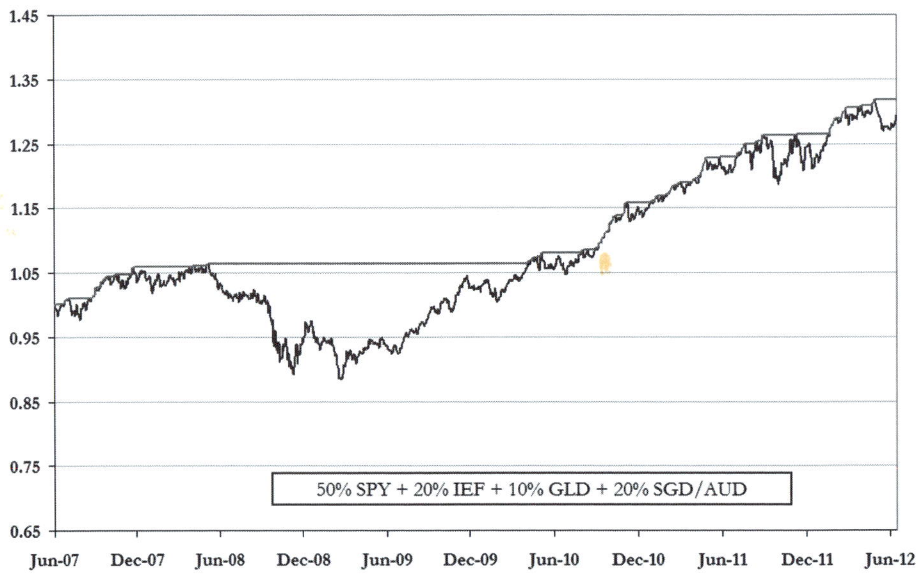

Figure 13.24 Performance of portfolio hedged with short AUD/SGD position

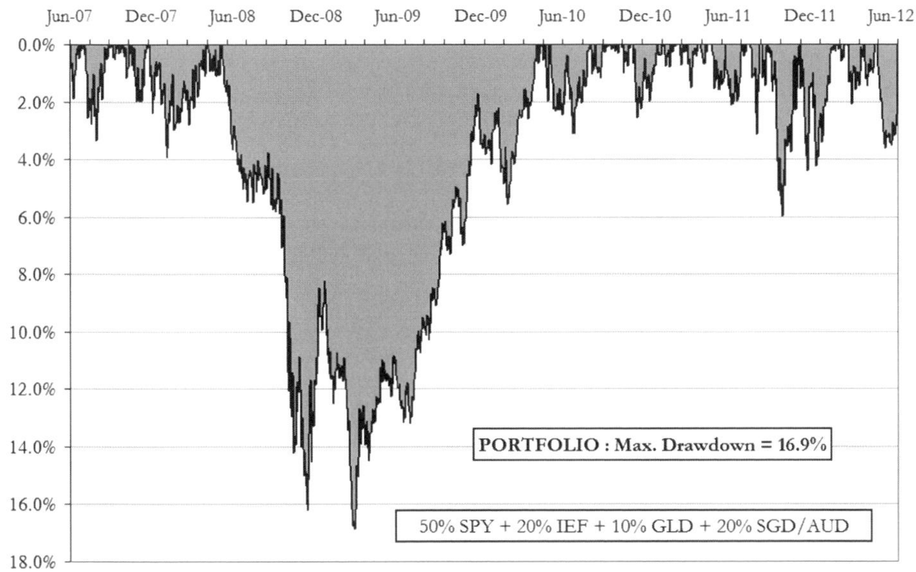

Figure 13.25 Maximum drawdown of portfolio hedged with short AUD/SGD position

ENDNOTES

1. Benjamin Graham and David Dodd, *Security Analysis* McGraw-Hill Professional; New edition of 1934 edition (1996) p. 23.

   One lesson which Warren Buffet has pointed to in his admiration for the writings of Benjamin Graham is well expressed in the following aphorism from the Sage of Omaha: "Rule Number One: Never lose money and Rule Number Two: Never forget rule one." As instructive and as amusing as this advice is, the context within Chapter 10 for this endnote suggests that this is not so easy to achieve in practice.
2. The data used for constructing the charts is known as the Adjusted Close and is provided to show the close price adjusted for all splits and dividends. Adjusted Close provides the closing price adjusted for all applicable splits and dividend distributions. Data is adjusted using appropriate split and dividend multipliers, adhering to Center for Research in Security Prices (CRSP) standards.
   - Split multipliers are determined by the split ratio. For instance, in a 2 for 1 split, the pre-split data is multiplied by 0.5.
   - Dividend multipliers are calculated based on dividend as a percentage of price, primarily to avoid negative historical pricing. For example, when a $0.08 cash dividend is distributed on February 19 (ex-date), and the February 18 closing price was 24.96, the pre-dividend data are multiplied by (1-0.08/24.96) = 0.9968.
3. When measuring asset price returns over an extended period it is preferable to use the Compound Annual Growth Rate since this applies the notion of growth (or decay) to a principal which is itself growing. It is customary to use the geometric mean of 1 plus each year's return (i.e. +3% becomes 1.03 and -2% becomes 0.98), and from this calculation one then subtracts one. The CAGR is also called a "smoothed" rate of return because it measures the growth of an investment as if it had grown at a steady rate on an annually compounded basis.
4. The KBW Banking Index, which trades under the ticker symbol BKX, is weighted according to capitalization and represents 24 major money center banks from across the US. Mathematically, the index is based on a tenth of the value of the Keefe, Bruyette and Woods Index (KBWI). BKX was

set to an initial value of 250 on October 21, 1991. The index includes Bank of America, Citigroup, J P Morgan, Wells Fargo, and other money center banks but does not include the "pure" investment banks such as Goldman Sachs and Morgan Stanley.

5. The Y2K or millennium bug is well characterized in this short piece from Computerworld, http://www.computerworld.com/s/article/9142555/Y2K_The_good_the_bad_and_the_crazy:

> While the world pondered dire predictions of massive global infrastructure failures – everything from elevators to air traffic control systems was rumored to be vulnerable – the specter of a total paralysis of business operations resulting from cascading Y2K failures galvanized organizations into a frenzy of activity. For many CIOs, the unprecedented size and scope of addressing Y2K problems was the biggest project of their careers.
>
> And then it was over. On Dec. 31, 1999, the world held its breath – and nothing happened. Jan. 1, 2000 came in just like any other day. There were no major failures to report anywhere. In the aftermath, or non-aftermath, some pundits said all the preparation had been overkill. Others maintained that only the hard work of IT pros, many of whom did not sleep that night, kept the information systems of the world on track.

6. The curious case of JDS Uniphase, http://www.cnbc.com/id/35663686/The_Curious_Case_of_JDS_Uniphase:

> Back in the late '90s, when tech stocks were flying high, JDS Uniphase capped out at $1,227 a share, giving it a bigger market cap than both Cisco Systems and Intel have today. But then the bubble burst, taking JDSU down 99.8% and changing its name on Wall Street from "Just Don't Sell Us" to "Just Don't Sue Us."

7. Jack Willoughby, Burning Up, *Barrons*, March 20, 2000. Available online at http://online.barrons.com/article/SB953335580704470544.html.
8. From the chairman's letter *To the Shareholders of Berkshire Hathaway Inc* in 1988, http://www.berkshirehathaway.com/letters/1988.html.

   The full quote is as follows:

> In fact, when we own portions of outstanding businesses with outstanding managements, our favorite holding period is forever.

9. The market capitalizations for 2000 were calculated by the *Financial Times* as of March 31, 2000 and can be found in the following article: http://en.wikipedia.org/wiki/List_of_corporations_by_market_capitalization.

   The market capitalization values for mid-2012 can be found at http://finance.yahoo.com.
10. Back-testing can be conducted by simulating how portfolios would have performed under different market scenarios by experimenting with differently constructed portfolios and parameters and then testing their performance against historical data for various asset classes. Certain trading platforms and software tools such as TradeStation are very useful for back-testing different investment and trading strategies.
11. See for example, Michael Mullaney, *The Complete Guide to Option Strategies: Advanced and Basic Strategies on Stocks, ETFs, Indexes and Stock Index Futures* (John Wiley & Sons Ltd, May 2009).
12. Israel Nelken, *Volatility as An Asset Class* (Risk Publications, September 2007).

    For a contrary view see Roger Nussbaum, Volatility is not an Asset Class, *Seeking Alpha*, March 27, 2012, http://seekingalpha.com/article/460821-volatility-is-not-an-asset-class
13. There is a detailed discussion of the CBOE Volatility Index or VIX at the CBOE website and a white paper which can be found at the following location: http://www.cboe.com/micro/vix/vixwhite.pdf:

> In 1993, the Chicago Board Options Exchange® (CBOE®) introduced the CBOE Volatility Index®, VIX®, which was originally designed to measure the market's expectation of 30-day volatility implied by at-the-money S&P 100® Index (OEX®) option prices. VIX soon became the premier benchmark for

U.S. stock market volatility. It is regularly featured in the Wall Street Journal, Barron's and other leading financial publications, as well as business news shows on CNBC, Bloomberg TV and CNN/Money, where VIX is often referred to as the "fear index."

Ten years later in 2003, CBOE together with Goldman Sachs, updated the VIX to reflect a new way to measure expected volatility, one that continues to be widely used by financial theorists, risk managers and volatility traders alike. The new VIX is based on the S&P 500® Index (SPXSM), the core index for U.S. equities, and estimates expected volatility by averaging the weighted prices of SPX puts and calls over a wide range of strike prices. By supplying a script for replicating volatility exposure with a portfolio of SPX options, this new methodology transformed VIX from an abstract concept into a practical standard for trading and hedging volatility.

14. The following comment comes from a useful statistical survey published by the ECB on global crises and their correlation with various indicators:

"... different measures of global risk aversion ... in particular ... are all strongly correlated with the VIX."

15. Maurizio Michael Habib and Livio Stracca, *Getting Beyond Carry Trade. What makes a safe haven currency?* by ECB Working Paper Series No 1288/January 2011, http://www.ecb.europa.eu/pub/pdf/scpwps/ecbwp1288.pdf.
16. The term structure of implied volatility is the curve of implied volatilities for periods extending from the current date to different future dates, e.g. March 19 to April 12, March 19 to April 13, and so on. Points of the curve at different terms can be estimated from option prices with matching expirations. One method is to find the Black-Scholes implied volatilities of at-the-money options. Alternatively, the implied volatilities can be calculated from the prices of strips of out-of-the-money options which replicate the variances, the "VIX Calculation."

Similar to the term structure of interest rates, the term structure of implied volatility is generated by spot and forward volatilities, more precisely by spot and forward variances since it is the variances which add up, not their square roots. In light of this, VIX and VIX futures prices can be squared and pieced together to yield alternative estimates of various points of the term structure of implied volatility.

http://cfe.cboe.com/education/vixprimer/Features.aspx.
17. Opportunities in the Volatility Term Structure, *Seeking Alpha*, September 14, 2010, http://seekingalpha.com/article/225039-opportunities-in-the-volatility-term-structure.
18. *JP Morgan trader "London Whale" leaves London.* Departure of Bruno Iksil confirmed as JP Morgan chief Jamie Dimon presents second-quarter results, *Guardian*, July 13, 2012, Available online at http://www.guardian.co.uk/business/2012/jul/13/jp-morgan-trader-london-whale-bruno-iksil.
19. *JP Morgan Chase and the London whale: Understanding the hedge that wasn't* by Ron Rimkus, May 17, 2012. The following is an extract from the article in which the author deconstructs the London Whale's trade:

Iksil had three discrete components to his trading strategy, which I will call packages A, B, and C as follows:

(A) JPM purchased credit default swaps (CDS) on high-yield bonds in which JPM would make money if high-yield bonds went down.

(B) JPM wrote substantial amounts of CDX.NA.IG.9, which is a basket of CDS on investment-grade bonds from 121 different issuers.

(C) JPM bought CDS on investment-grade bonds.

Package A (long CDS on high-yield bonds) could in fact act as a hedge on a loan book, but it is unknown how directly or indirectly related the derivatives are to its actual loan book. It is likely that the basis risk is

> high given that high-yield bonds are not a mainstay of JP Morgan's commercial loan book. In any event, these trades went against Iksil as the economy appeared to show some improvements.
>
> Recognizing that package A was performing poorly, Iksil created package B. Package B was possibly intended to act as a hedge on package A, but it is closer to the truth to call it a discrete proprietary trade. Writing CDS on investment-grade bonds is intended to take advantage of the improving economy that Iksil thought he recognized. Whether or not he was right about an improving economy is a separate issue, as the trading of CDS (or any security, for that matter) can move counter to an investor's hopes in the interim. While it is theoretically possible that JP Morgan was trying to hedge some future obligations (letters of credit, future loan growth, etc.) for which the firm is naturally short, Dimon's exit from this position suggests otherwise.
>
> It appears that once Iksil realized that the market was moving against package B, he sought to make up for it with trades on package C, rather than unwinding package B. It is unknown how much basis risk is introduced by package C, relative to either package B or to JP Morgan's actual loan book. Nevertheless, all of this is like a dog chasing its tail, and that shouldn't happen with true hedges.

The article is available online at http://seekingalpha.com/article/596871-jpmorgan-chase-and-the-london-whale-understanding-the-hedge-that-wasn-t.

20. Skew and kurtosis are defined in the article referenced in endnote 21 as follows:

> Skew is the degree to which a distribution departs from symmetry around its mean value (i.e., asymmetric return distributions). A distribution that is negatively skewed has returns concentrated on the right, with a longer left tail. In this scenario, the mean return is less than the median. Conversely, a positive skew shows the majority of returns on the left, with a mean return that is greater than the median.
>
> In a concept similar to skewness, kurtosis is the degree of "peakedness" of a distribution compared to the normal distribution with the same variance. A high kurtosis value means more of the variance is the result of infrequent extreme deviations.

21. *New Normal Investing: Is the (Fat) Tail Wagging Your Portfolio*? Credit Suisse Asset Management White Paper, April 2012. Available online at https://www.credit-suisse.com/asset_management/downloads/marketing/new_normal_investing_white_paper_042012.pdf.
22. The Swiss National Bank in effect devalued the franc, pledging to buy "unlimited quantities" of foreign currencies to force down its value. The SNB warned that it would no longer allow one Swiss franc to be worth more than €0.83 – equivalent to SFr1.20 to the euro – having watched the two currencies move closer to parity as Switzerland became a "safe haven" from the ravages of the Eurozone crisis.

> "That was the single largest foreign exchange move I have ever seen ... The Swiss franc has lost close on 9% in the past 15 minutes. This dwarfs moves seen post-Lehman brothers, 7/7, and other major geo-political events in the past decade," Cook said.
>
> The SNB pledged to enforce a "substantial and sustained weakening of the Swiss franc", adding that it might move to an even lower exchange rate against the euro if needed.
>
> "The current massive overvaluation of the Swiss franc poses an acute threat to the Swiss economy and carries the risk of a deflationary development," said Switzerland's central bank.

http://www.guardian.co.uk/business/2011/sep/06/switzerland-pegs-swiss-franc-euro.

23. Swiss haven status pulling 10-year borrowing costs toward zero, Bloomberg, July 26, 2012. The article makes the following observations:

> Swiss borrowing costs for seven years slid to a record-low 0.151 percent on July 23, according to data compiled by Bloomberg. They're following the course of five-year yields, which turned negative on May 31 for the first time since Bloomberg began collecting the data in 1994.
>
> Swiss five-year notes yielded 0.01 percent at 5:39 p.m. in London, after closing at minus 0.007 percent yesterday. The two- year yield was at minus 0.406 percent, after falling to a record of minus 0.462 percent two days ago. Ten-year bonds yielded 0.527 percent.

http://www.bloomberg.com/news/2012-07-26/swiss-haven-status-pulling-10-year-borrowing-costs-toward-zero.html.

24. James Montier, *A Value Investor's Perspective on Tail Risk Protection: An Ode to the Joy of Cash*, published June 27, 2011, http://www.gmo.com/America/GMOInsights/.
25. The Calmar ratio is discussed in *Long/Short Market Dynamics* by the author and the following is an extract from that discussion (see pp. 260–4):

> The Calmar Ratio may be the best measurement of the risk/return relationship as it most matches the requirements of the active trader, and it is also becoming increasingly favored by some academics who are concerned with the limitations in the Sharpe ratio. Very simply it is the CAGR divided by the absolute value of the Maximum Drawdown for the period under consideration. The higher the ratio the better is considered to be the trade off between risk and reward.
>
> A brief discussion of the Calmar Ratio will help in better understanding the interpretation

	CAGR	Max Drawdown (Absolute Value)	Calmar Ratio	Expected Maximum VAMI	Expected Minimum VAMI
Fund A	25%	10%	2.5	1250	900
Fund B	40%	30%	1.33	1400	700

> Although an investor in fund B has a potential upside VAMI of 1400 this must be seen within the context that the drawdown figures show that Fund B also has the capacity to deliver a final or interim VAMI of 700 for any particular holding period. In terms of the reward/risk ratio this is less attractive than the expectations for an investor in Fund A which will not potentially deliver as big an upside as Fund B but which does not expose the investor to as much potential downside risk. Using the Calmar ratio an investment in Fund A is to be preferred.

14

Liquidity and Maturity Transformation

In this chapter we will explore the fundamental and important inter-dependence of market liquidity and maturity transformation. The procedures and legal framework that have been developed within global money markets to facilitate the spanning of funding intervals which can be very short, i.e. overnight, to very long term, and which enable maturity transformations, are indispensable to the smooth functioning of the private sector banks and the integrity of the entire credit system. Later in the discussion there will be a more robust explanation of maturity transformation but an initial outline will be useful now.

William Dudley, the President and Chief Executive Officer of the Federal Reserve Bank of New York, gave an influential speech in November 2009 in which he addressed the problems within global money markets, particularly centered on those in the US, which had arisen at the height of the financial crisis, and most acutely following the collapse of Lehman Brothers. He provided the following useful starting point for our discussion of systemic liquidity and maturity transformation: [1]

> The need for maturity transformation arises from the fact that the preferred habitat of borrowers tends toward longer-term maturities used to finance long-lived assets such as a house or a manufacturing plant, compared with the preferred habitat of investors, who generally have a preference to be able to access their funds quickly. *Financial intermediaries act to span these preferences, earning profits by engaging in maturity transformation* –borrowing shorter-term in order to finance longer-term lending. (author's italics)

During his presentation Dudley pointed to the negative feedback loops which have been touched on in previous chapters and which hinge on the mutually reinforcing or spiral like effects between the bursting of the real estate bubble and the associated collapse of trust in the complex derivatives which were used to "finance" this bubble. As more and more Wall Street firms were suspected of holding assets that were hard to value, illiquid, and distressed, this led to a viciously iterative process where leveraging abruptly went into reverse, distressed selling begat more distressed selling, and there was virtually a complete unwillingness of financial intermediaries to engage in even overnight repo transactions. In a number of passages of his speech Dudley pointed to the contagion effect by which the negative feedback loop was accelerated since it not only became a judgment call by one party with respect to the possible insolvency about a counter-party but the second order issue of how others would perceive that solvency question. The need to factor in the second order and even orders beyond – the meta level judgments of one's potential counter-parties – echoes the classic analogy expounded by Keynes regarding investing judgments being similar to a decision one might make about the potential winner of a beauty contest. [2] The smartest judgment would not be to base a decision on one's own opinion about which contestant one thought was the most beautiful, but on an estimation of what one believed average opinion of all of the judges would be. The importance of needing to evaluate the meta level perceptions and judgments taken from the beauty contest heuristic are amply demonstrated, especially when markets are behaving erratically. After factoring in the tendency of stressed markets to exhibit the *lack* of wisdom of crowds in such a scenario, the *pragmatic* stance would be to align oneself with the consensus view regarding a potential counter-party's solvency or otherwise. In September 2008, after the collapse of Lehman Brothers, there were very few cool heads and precious little scope for calm, dispassionate judgments. Rather, as Dudley's speech reminds us, the prevailing emotion of market participants was one of escalating fear and paralysis against a backdrop of risk contagion:

> However, once Lehman Brothers failed many commercial banks and other financial institutions encountered significant funding difficulties. News that the Reserve Fund – a large money market mutual fund – had "broken the buck" due to its holdings of Lehman Brothers paper led panicked investors to withdraw their funds from money market mutual funds. This caused the commercial paper market to virtually shut down. This hurt bank holding companies and other large financial firms that depended on the commercial paper market for short-term funding.
>
> The result was a widespread loss of confidence throughout the money market and interbank funding market. *Investors became unwilling to lend even to institutions that they perceived to be solvent because of worries that others might not share the same opinion.* Rollover risk – the risk that an investor's funds might not be repaid in a timely way – became extremely high. (author's italics)

From these brief citations from an influential speech by the CEO of the New York Federal Reserve we can now cross the Atlantic and consider another useful contribution on the subject matter of this chapter from a prominent UK banking expert, Lord Adair Turner. Turner, at the time of writing, is head of the Financial Services Authority in the UK, although this regulatory body will become defunct at the end of 2012, and he is one of the leading candidates to be the next governor of the Bank of England when the current governor retires in mid-2013. [3] Turner gave a provocative presentation on the shadow banking system in 2011 at the Cass Business School in London, [4] and in that lecture he focused on maturity transformation and its critical importance to the smooth functioning of the financial system. The following extract from his comments will serve as a good way of supplementing the initial definition from William Dudley and turn our attention, in broad terms, on to the two main methods of conducting maturity transformation:

> Maturity transformation is a key function of the financial system, enabling non-financial agents – corporates and households – to hold longer-term financial liabilities than assets. The transformation is achieved either:
>
> 1) via the intermediation of a financial sector balance sheet (most typically a bank's) whose assets are of longer contractual maturity than its liabilities; or
> 2) via a liquid traded market, in which a contractual long-term liability can be treated by investors as a short-term asset, because it is sellable in a liquid market.

The ability to span the interval between the demand for short-term liquidity – such as short-term calls on a bank's liabilities when depositors are wanting to take their cash out, or when banks are needing to fund themselves in the money markets – has to be juggled in accordance with the fact that a bank's assets, i.e. its loans, are long lived and in most cases cannot be liquidated quickly. The manner in which the juggling is done can be more or less complex. Perhaps one of the simpler and more effective methods of facilitating maturity transformation is the provision of protection to depositors and this is accomplished in most jurisdictions by government-backed schemes such as the FDIC scheme in the US and the Financial Services Compensation Scheme (FSCS) in the UK. [5] A more sophisticated enabling apparatus, as the second point in Turner's explanation suggests, is that the actual tightrope which allows the chasm to be crossed in maturity transformation is to be found through the mechanism of the money markets. Repo transactions [6] and the issuance of various forms of short-term notes, when rolled forward on an ongoing basis, are the enabling mechanism for the long-term illiquid assets of banks and corporations to be continuously matched with the requisite short-term liquidity.

As Turner suggests, what is required for this type of interval spanning to be possible is "a liquid traded market, in which a contractual long-term liability can be treated by investors as a short-term asset, because it is sellable in a liquid market." Markets, as we have seen, are not always liquid and when placed under stress, as they were in the summer of 2007 and the fall of 2008, "market liquidity completely evaporated" to use the terminology used by the CFTC/SEC report in regard to the events of May 6, 2010 discussed in Chapter 4. In the third quarter of 2008, those sections in economics and finance textbooks discussing the role of central banks as the *lender of last resort*, which may have seemed to readers of such texts prior to 2008 to have been somewhat arcane, suddenly took on a compelling new significance. The profile of central bankers in 2007/8 became even more elevated as their role was seen not only to include the vital function of determining short-term interest rates, but literally as one of providing a safety net and liquidity back stop to avert the implosion of the global money markets.

It would not be an over-statement to suggest that maintaining relatively normal liquidity conditions in financial markets is the single greatest imperative of central bankers and the financial establishment in general. Liquidity begets solvency and when all is said and done about the collapsing of the real estate bubble, the vagaries of NINJA loans (no income, no job, and no assets), sub-prime mortgages, and convoluted CDO structures etc., the greatest threat to the global economy in 2008 was the threat of a systemic meltdown based on a complete inability to conduct any form of maturity transformation. In case one is uncomfortable about alluding to a systemic meltdown, and feels that such talk is tainted with hyperbole or melodrama, one just has to recall the febrile atmosphere of the second half of 2008 and some of the alarming comments from several critically placed individuals at that time. Here are some reminders of the gravity of the problems confronting the financial system from that period: [7]

> On Thursday, Sept. 18, 2008, the astonished leadership of the U.S. Congress was told in a private session by the chairman of the Federal Reserve that the American economy was in grave danger of a complete meltdown within a matter of days. "There was literally a pause in that room where the oxygen left," reported Senator Dodd. [from the film Inside the Meltdown]
>
> "Intensifying solvency concerns about a number of the largest US-based and European financial institutions have pushed the global financial system to the brink of systemic meltdown," said Mr Strauss-Kahn.
>
> "This is the most serious financial crisis we've seen at least since the 1930s, if not ever," warned the Bank's Governor, Sir Mervyn King.

Far from being melodramatic, and in view of inertia and complacency on the part of regulators and policy makers which has been developing as we move further away from 2008, it is actually more dangerous to indulge in revisionist hindsight and understate the severity of the GFC. My suggestion is that it should be a matter of much greater urgency for public policy makers to insist that there is a much better framework for monitoring systemic liquidity, better understanding of the kinds of metrics which could be useful in assessing the likelihood of

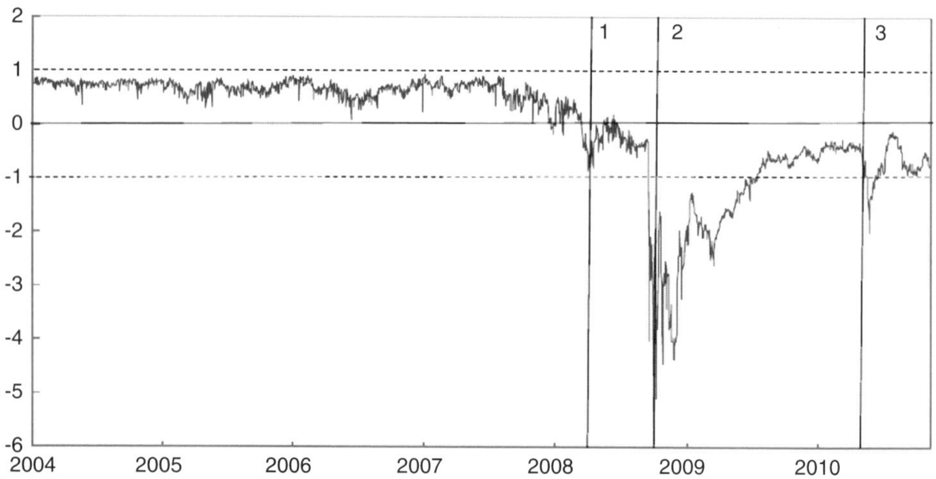

Figure 14.1 Systemic Liquidity Risk Index (SLRI) developed by IMF
Source: IMF Global Financial Stability Report (GFSR) April 2011.
Note: The dotted band depicts +/− standard deviation around the zero line. Dates of vertical lines are as follows: 1—March 14, 2008, Bear Steams rescue; 2—September 14, 2008, Lehman Brothers failure; and 3—April 27, 2010, Greek debt crisis.

systemically threatening events, and a mandate for central bankers to be vigilant and proactive in heading off unsustainable asset price bubbles. Despite protests from central bankers that pricking bubbles is not part of their mandate, willful ignorance in this regard could have momentous consequences if (when) we see a re-run of the events of 2008.

The IMF has proposed a Systemic Liquidity Risk Index (SLRI) and has developed an analytical framework and various monitoring tools designed to measure the pulse of the inter-bank market and various key spreads in the money markets with a view to providing an early warning system for future bouts of extreme illiquidity. The IMF characterizes this innovative index as follows: "a market-based index of systemic liquidity based on violations of common arbitrage relationships" [8] and, as this chapter is designed to illustrate, such arbitrage activities broke down completely during the global financial crisis and have a predisposition to do so again when circumstances lead to what is commonly called financial contagion.

Figure 14.1, which comes from the IMF study, provides an intriguing perspective on the highly abnormal values seen in the SLRI in the wake of the Lehman Brothers bankruptcy and which to a lesser extent were revisited in April 2010 at the onset of the Greek crisis. The IMF's work on the SLRI is important and groundbreaking in some respects and deserves to be more widely acknowledged by those engaged in the financial services sector.

In Chapter 1 a definition of systemic liquidity risk was given, and it is worth repeating it again here and augmenting it with further elaboration from the IMF study: [9]

> Systemic liquidity risk is the risk that multiple institutions may face simultaneous difficulties in rolling over their short-term debts or in obtaining new short-term funding through widespread dislocations of money and capital markets.

This quotation helps to position the nature of systemic liquidity risk, as discussed previously, as an holistic or emergent characteristic of the financial system. It goes far beyond the liquidity problems which may be encountered by a single institution but rather focuses on "simultaneous difficulties" experienced by all or most financial institutions. The pivotal difference is that the methods applicable to measuring tail risk for a standalone entity or issuer of securities are no longer applicable in determining the financial risk of multiple simultaneous tail risks. The collapse in system-wide liquidity feeds into a vicious spiral or feedback loop whereby tail dependencies become more elevated and the ability to model joint risk through the use of normal statistical tools (recall the discussion of copulas [10]) becomes hopelessly inadequate. The IMF recognizes the nature of the escalation of tail dependencies in a systemic crisis, the inter-linkages across the banking system, and how this is not adequately addressed under the Basel III guidelines:

> ... the Basel III rules do not address the additional risk of such simultaneous shortfalls arising out of the interconnectedness of various institutions across a host of financial markets. More needs to be done to develop macro-prudential techniques to measure and mitigate systemic liquidity risks.

Perhaps this is stating the obvious, but the reason why this is so important is that it explains why the methods used in stress testing commercial banks have proven to be so misleading and why, for example, banks tested in Spain in 2011 and granted a clean bill of health were in need of a bailout in 2012. [11]

A further enlargement of the IMF's outline of systemic liquidity risk is also worth quoting at some length as it points to the "negative externalities" associated with the aftermath of a systemic liquidity crisis whereby public balance sheets become the maturity transformation facilitators of last resort. The notion of liquidity risk being "under-priced" goes to the core of these externalities and is one of the most over-looked features of the GFC. [12]

> Systemic liquidity risk is the tendency of financial institutions to collectively under-price liquidity risk in good times when funding markets function well because they are convinced that the central bank will almost certainly intervene in times of stress to maintain such markets, prevent the failure of financial institutions, and thus limit the impact of liquidity shortfalls on other financial institutions and the real economy. If they ignore the tendency to under-price liquidity risk prior to the emergence of shortfalls and then intervene during times of systemic stress, central banks will reinforce these negative externalities and give financial institutions an incentive to hold less liquidity than needed.

Not shown on Figure 14.1, as the IMF report was published in early 2011, would be the bout of extreme illiquidity which occurred in regard to adverse developments within the Eurozone in late July and early August of 2011. The escalation of concerns about peripheral sovereigns and a second Greek bailout were even more disruptive than the initial Greek bailout in 2010 and would have seen values for the SLRI of more than two sigmas below the mean being registered. As the crisis in the summer of 2011 became more acute there were substantial drawdowns in equities and a rapid deterioration in money market spreads which are the primary indicators monitored by the IMF in the compilation of the SLRI.

Table 14.1 is an extract from a table contained in the IMF report which provides a good cross-sectional view of the types of indicators and financial variables that the IMF uses in calculating the SLRI. A detailed examination of these indicators would take us too far from our path but a brief examination of some key money markets would be a useful detour in this chapter.

Table 14.1 Fragment of table from IMF's indicators used for the SLRI

	Indicators for (Systemic) Liquidity Risk Monitoring				
Indicators	Unsecured interbank rate	Interest rate derivatives	Repo spread	Margins and haircuts on repo collateral	Forex swap rate
Examples	LIBOR-OIS spread, Euribor-OIS spread, TED spread, LIBOR rate spread-UST repo rate spread.	The probability distribution of LIBOR-OIS spread using derivatives (e.g. interest rate cap).	UST-repo rate, agency MBS repo rate-UST repo rate, U.S. asset-backed CP yields-UST.	Margins and average haircuts for various repo collateral assets.	Short-term foreign exchange swap implied interest rate-LIBOR, longer-term cross-currency basis swap-LIBOR.
Primary type of liquidity risk	Funding liquidity.	Funding liquidity.	Funding liquidity.	Funding and market liquidity risk.	Foreign exchange funding risk.
Pros	Widely used, easily available in most countries.	Provides probability assessment of liquidity stress events, forward looking.	Measures funding costs that are almost free of counterparty concerns.	Indicate the linkages between market liquidity of collateral and funding liquidity.	Indicates currency funding mismatch.
Cons	Influenced by counterparty risks. Not a representative measure of funding costs where repos are widely used.	Influenced by counterparty risks.	Influenced by market liquidity risk of collateral assets. Limited data availability (most are traded over the counter).	Difficult to collect and aggregate data. Difficult to disentangle liquidity and counterparty risks.	Influenced by counterparty risks.

Source: IMF Global Financial Stability Report (GFSR) April 2011.

14.1 MONEY MARKET SPREADS

The IMF summarizes the guiding principle behind the indicators it monitors for the SLRI in the following somewhat compressed manner: [13]

> However, in turbulent markets, arbitrage can break down. During the recent financial crisis, many arbitrage relationships were violated for relatively long periods. In currency markets, violations of covered interest rate parity (CIP) occurred for currency pairs involving the U.S. dollar. In interest rate markets, the swap spread, which measures the difference between Treasury bond yields and LIBOR swap rates, turned negative. In interbank markets, basis swaps that exchange different maturity LIBOR rates (for example, three-month for six-month) deviated from their close-to-zero norm. In credit markets, the CDS-bond basis, which measures the difference between credit default swaps (CDS) and implied credit spreads on cash bonds, turned negative.

Paraphrasing this, and before de-compressing some of the arbitrage and spread relationships alluded to, the IMF's SLRI is an attempt to grapple with the circumstances when financial intermediaries no longer want to intermediate – the maturity transformation chasm is not crossed and the juggling of long-term assets and short-term funding grinds to a halt – the markets have entered a potentially system threatening liquidity crisis.

Covered interest parity or CIP as referenced in the IMF quotation has been previously addressed in Chapter 6 but let us now turn to a review of some of the spread relationships that are also cited in Table 14.1. It should be noted at the outset that they are, to some extent, coincidental rather than leading indicators; they become seriously misaligned after the onset of a financial crisis although careful analysis of incipient trends before the onset can provide useful clues as to the imminence of liquidity troubles ahead. Indeed, this is why they are closely followed by those working at the sharp end of the financial markets and why we should have a look at them.

A good starting point for this section will be one of the most long-standing spread relationships which are used as a barometer of strains and counter-party risk within the banking system – the TED spread. The acronym derives from the spread between the inter-bank dealings in US dollars which are not conducted within the US money market specifically. The term eurodollar in this context thus has nothing to do with the FX rate between the US dollar and the EZ single currency, but relates to the much earlier use of the term "euro" as it relates to the development of offshore money market transactions (i.e. outside the native jurisdictions) conducted initially in US dollars in the 1960s but now in many currencies. This market historically and even today is based in London. Figure 14.2 shows the TED spread during the period from 2008–11 and the dotted line is the difference between the annualized rate of interest on three-month LIBOR-US and the annualized rate of return on three-month T-bills issued by the US Treasury – often regarded as the risk-free rate.

When markets are not stressed the normal TED spread is usually to be found in the range of 10–25 basis points. The T-bill rate is essentially risk free whereas the LIBOR rate is the rate applicable in the inter-bank market where commercial banks will borrow/lend to each other on an *unsecured basis*. During "normal" times, with a spread in the range just cited, one could surmise that there is a large degree of comfort by participants in the money markets since, in their dealings with each other they are not demanding a high premium above the risk free rate to engage in unsecured transactions. In turn this enables the maturity transformation merry go round continue to function smoothly. On October 10, 2008, the TED spread reached the extraordinarily high level of 457 basis points which can be observed as the peak reading on

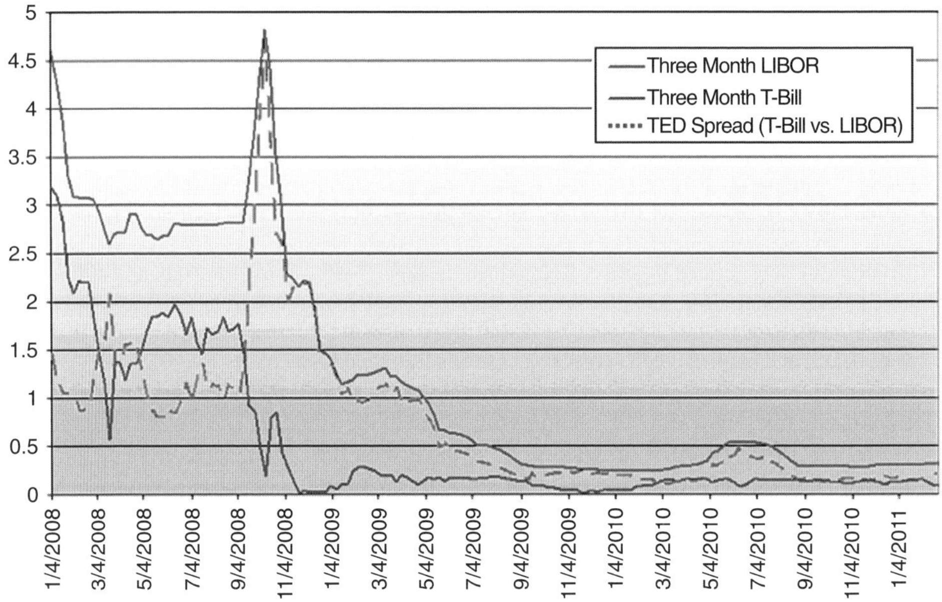

Figure 14.2 TED spread 2008–2011

Figure 14.2. Clearly banks were extraordinarily uncomfortable about dealing with each other on an unsecured basis. Very few were willing to deal at all.

A drastic widening of a similar money market spread, more relevant within the European banking system, can be seen in Figure 14.3 also indicating overwhelmingly negative views about counter-party risk at an extreme level in 2008 – at 180 basis points – but also notably elevated in the second half of 2011 as well. A description of the Euribor/OIS spread follows after some contextual background.

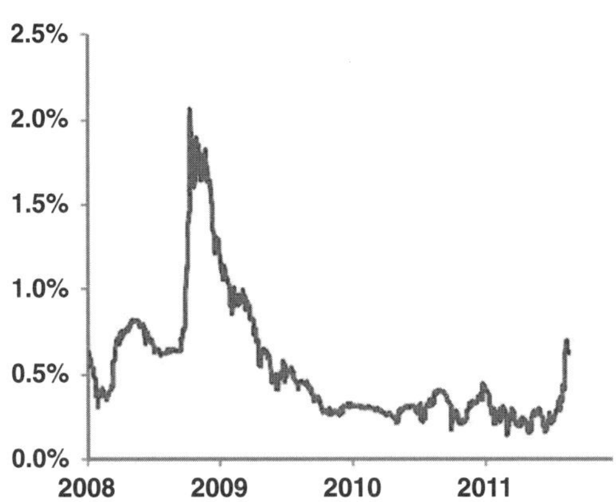

Figure 14.3 Three-month EURIBOR-OIS spread

Euribor rates are based on the interest rates, as deliberated upon by a panel of 57 European banks, and these rates are those at which banks borrow funds denominated in euros from one another. In the calculation, the highest and lowest 15% of all the quotes collected are eliminated. The OIS rate, or overnight index swap rate, referenced in the caption to Figure 14.3 is a measure of the market's expectation of the overnight funds rate over the term of a swap contract. There is minimal default risk in the OIS market because with such swap arrangements there is no exchange of principal; funds are exchanged only at the maturity of the contract, when one party pays the net interest obligation to the other. The spread shown in Figure 14.3 is similar to the TED spread in that, since one form of borrowing is unsecured, i.e. the Euribor rate, and the other has minimal risk, i.e. the OIS rate, the size of the spread can act as a gauge of the extent to which banks are comfortable or otherwise in engaging in unsecured transactions. In generic terms, any Libor-OIS spread is a measure of the health of banks because it reflects what commercial banks believe is the risk of default associated with lending to each other. The former Chairman of the Federal Reserve is on record as stating that the "Libor-OIS remains a barometer of fears of bank insolvency." [14]

The final spread that will be examined from the extended list monitored by the IMF in its calculation of the SLRI is the euro/dollar cross currency basis swap rate and before describing what it is a quick review of Figure 14.4 will show that the swap rate became extreme in both windows of the graphic – in 2008 and also notably in the second half of 2011. It should be noted that the vertical axis to the spread is actually inverted so that the elevated levels are really indicative of high negative values. As shown in Figure 14.4, in 2008 the one-year swap rate for euro principal and interest exchanges for US dollar principal and interest and reached a negative 120 basis points and in 2011 the rate reached around a negative 100 basis points.

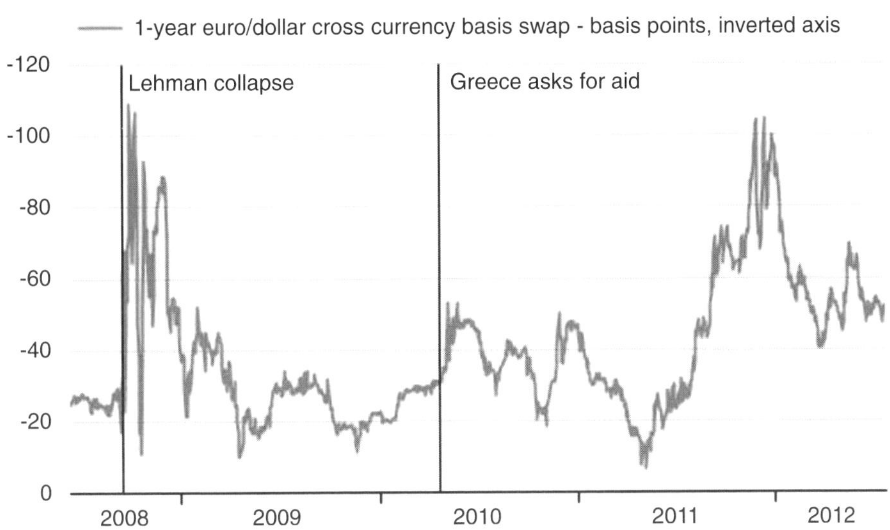

Figure 14.4 EUR/USD cross currency basis swap July 2012
Source: Reuters.

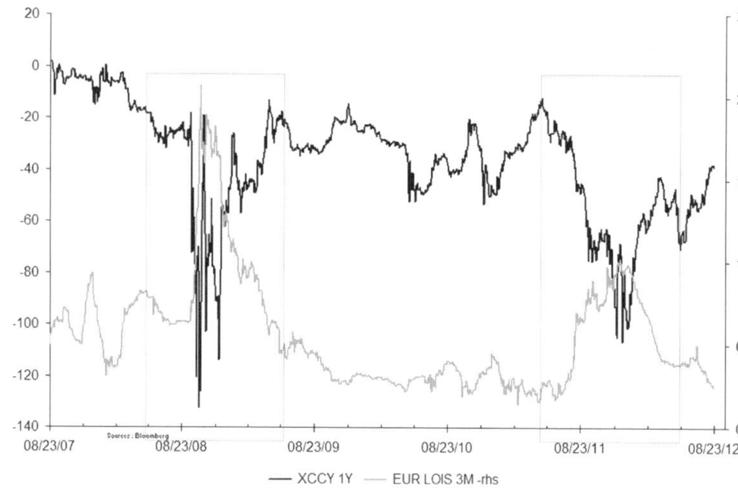

Figure 14.5 Sharp declines of the EUR/USD cross currency basis are contemporaneous to strain on European banks
Source: Evariste Lefeuvre, Natixis North America.

By way of explanation the swap rate refers to the rate at which banks will engage in swap arrangements with counter-parties where there is an exchange of each currency at the beginning and end of the swap and then interest payments are made in each currency and reference the appropriate LIBOR rates for the respective currencies involved in the swap. The fact that there was a substantial discount or a highly negative rate to the swap indicates that European banks were so eager to obtain dollars from US banks (the latter, in turn, were reticent to engage in lending out dollars to any institution let alone a European bank with a currency risk) that they were prepared to get paid at a discount to what would be applicable under "normal circumstances."

Towards the end of 2011 and to alleviate the stresses within the European banking system swap lines were established by leading central banks including the ECB and the Federal Reserve which made US dollar funding more accessible and cheaper [15] and this has enabled the cross currency basis swap to rise to less extreme levels. In mid-2012 the three-month rate is in the vicinity of -50 basis points.

The final graphic for this section, Figure 14.5, is useful in bringing two key spreads monitored by the IMF together onto the same chart. On the right hand side of the chart, in August 2011, which was when the graphic was prepared by Nomura Securities [16] there is clear evidence of increasing steepness to the three rates which marked the beginning of the heightened tensions in the European money markets which remained largely in effect until the ECB mounted its first LTRO operation in December of 2011. [17]

14.2 LIQUIDITY

In the most general sense, as used by accountants, balance sheet liquidity has to do primarily with the ability of a business to turn assets into cash. Liquidating inventories, for example, is more problematic for a company that needs to raise cash in the short term, than liquidating its holding of government securities such as Treasury bills. The latter are deemed to be highly liquid – "near cash" – as there is a very active and highly liquid market for these securities. Inventories are far less liquid and in adverse economic conditions there may be little or no market for liquidating inventory and it may need to be sold at "fire sale" prices or not at all.

Liquidity is defined by the Basel Committee as "the ability of a bank to fund increases in assets and meet obligations as they come due, without incurring unacceptable losses." [18]

Ability to conduct arbitrage is also a vital feature of liquid markets. A sizable portion of active participants in financial markets will be focused on exploiting temporary mispricings between different securities, such as those in the spot market and those trading in associated derivatives markets. For example if the spot price of a currency pair moves away from "fair price" alignment with the price for a futures contract for that same pair trading on the IMM at the Chicago Mercantile Exchange, an arbitrageur can make a quick profit from simultaneously selling the overpriced instrument and buying the underpriced instrument and waiting for the two to revert to the fair price and then again exiting the "spread" trade simultaneously to gain the benefit from a correction to the temporary mispricing anomaly. Just a little more explanation of this kind of activity will be helpful in understanding some of the material which lies ahead.

The spread trade initiated by the arbitrageur is one where, *under normal market conditions*, the existence of a mispricing between the cash or underlying market and the derivatives market for the instruments traded in the spot or cash market, once identified, should lead to a risk free arbitrage opportunity. If the mispricing suggests that the spread is too wide then by *buying the spread* – it doesn't really matter which one of the two legs to the trade is long and which is short – the trade will be profitable when the spread narrows as the market becomes more "efficiently" priced. The second important characteristic of this type of trading is that it is vital to the arbitrageur that the entry of the trade – which involves taking offsetting positions, i.e. matched long and short positions on the two "legs" of the spread – can be conducted simultaneously, and that, likewise, the exit from the two legs can also be executed simultaneously. Any interval or delay between the executions, especially during the exit from the two legs, can introduce *interval risk* to the arbitrageur.

14.3 REPO FINANCING AS THE SAFEST FORM OF INTERVAL CONFIDENCE

The following is a brief primer on the most common form of interval funding which is known as a repo or sale and repurchase agreement. A repo is often a short-term transaction between two parties in which one party borrows cash from another, which might be a central bank or other commercial bank, and pledges a financial security such as a highly rated bond as collateral. The standardized legal framework for such a transaction, which lies at the heart of the day to day financing in the money markets, ensures that if the borrower fails to repay the loan the counter-party has the collateral – legal title has been transferred via a "sale and repurchase agreement" – and can liquidate that security, should it wish, to replace the cash which they lent. The cash provider enters into a "purchase and resale agreement," or, in short, a *reverse repo*. Hence, every repo is also a reverse repo and vice versa. The perspective depends on who is the seller and who is the purchaser.

Overnight repos constitute the majority of repo transactions, and most of them are open, i.e. they roll over automatically until either party chooses to exit. Other repo transactions, called term repos, have terms longer than one day but shorter than one year, although the vast majority have maturities of three months or less. The difference – if any – between the values of the collateral and loan is called the "haircut" or margin. The haircut – if any – is a protection against the counter-party risk in the transaction. In principle either the cash or the collateral provider may be subject to a haircut. When the cash provider is subject to a haircut, then the haircut is the margin required by the collateral provider as protection against the potential value gain of the collateral in case the cash provider fails to deliver the collateral on the purchase date so that the collateral provider has to buy a substitute. When the collateral provider is subject to a haircut, then the haircut is the margin required by the cash provider as protection against the potential value loss of the collateral in case the collateral provider fails to come back, and the cash provider has to take ownership of the collateral, sell it, and recover the loss.

One important feature of the US repo market is that all transactions that fall under the umbrella of repos are exempt from the automatic stay in bankruptcy and therefore *all repo transactions can be liquidated following a bankruptcy filing*.

One of the triggers for the global financial crisis in the summer of 2007 was a "run" on two Bear Stearns hedge funds which were speculating in illiquid sub-prime mortgages and funding themselves via the US repo market. When questions were raised about the quality of the collateral that they could pledge, the "haircuts" that should be applied, and mounting evidence that there could be substantial counter-party risk they had to seek alternative funding which eventually entangled Bear Stearns in a negative "creditworthiness" feedback loop and the demise of the company in March 2008.

In his analysis of the failure of Bear Stearns, the Federal Reserve Chairman Ben Bernanke observed: [19]

> Until recently, short-term repos had always been regarded as virtually risk-free instruments and thus largely immune to the type of rollover or withdrawal risks associated with short-term unsecured obligations. *In March, rapidly unfolding events demonstrated that even repo markets could be severely disrupted when investors believe they might need to sell the underlying collateral in illiquid markets.* Such forced asset sales can set up a particularly adverse dynamic, in which further substantial price declines fan investor concerns about counterparty credit risk, which then feed back in the form of intensifying funding pressures ... *Future liquidity planning will have to take into account the possibility of a sudden loss of substantial amounts of secured financing.*

A good article which was prepared for the Federal Reserve Board's research conference on *Central Banking: Before, During and After the Crisis*, on March 23–24, 2012, [20] addresses the systemic consequences for the concerns that were raised in Bernanke's comments which were surely aimed at the problems encountered by Bear Stearns (Bernanke's comments were made in May 2008). The authors propose that there has been a mistaken notion that secured repo funding is relatively riskless; when there is financial stress and contagion assets *held predominantly by the financial sector are rendered illiquid* then the risk is *inherently systemic risk*. Their key findings are worth summarizing:

- To summarize, unlike the liquidity risk that unsecured financing may become unavailable to a firm (a risk largely specific to the credit risk of the firm), *the liquidity risk that secured repo financing may become unavailable to a firm is inherently a systemic risk, materializing in circumstances where other financial firms are also experiencing stress and the markets for assets held predominantly by the financial sector are rendered illiquid.*

- This leads to the problem that while in good times, financial firms may not fully internalize the costs imposed on the system by being excessively financed through short-term repo markets, in bad times, they charge excessively high haircuts on repo financing and do not internalize the pecuniary externalities imposed on other firms through the resulting fire sales of assets.
- Indeed, to support financial firms facing a repo freeze or to support the assets directly, the likely lender of last resort would only accentuate a problem that firms ignore in good times – namely, the systemic risk associated with repo financing.
- Viewed this way, in good times, there is a case for subjecting repo-financed risky securities to a capital charge – effectively a *regulatory haircut* – which takes into account the security's systemic risk and maturity mismatch relative to the repo tenor.

Interval risk arises because of the possibility of an unanticipated interruption or gap between the executions of separate but integrally connected legs of an arbitrage trade. In essence it was exactly this type of risk which caused the collapse of Long Term Capital Management (LTCM) in 1998 – which at the time was considered to have been a systemically threatening event. [21] If a single institution is faced with interval risk because it is unable to find a counter-party or counter-parties willing to engage with it in executing the two legs of an arbitrage simultaneously this can be so threatening to its liquidity that the institution may collapse. Systemic risk is the much greater problem which is that all (or certainly very many) institutions are unable to execute such trades because *there are no willing counter-parties*. This gives rise to the notion that the only antidote to a potential systemic meltdown is that the central banks have to become the counter-parties of last resort.

The important insight is to recognize that there are nonlinear dynamics in play which will lead to a phase shift (or tipping point) in considering the *qualitative difference* between the failure of a single institution, even one which is systemically important, and the kind of *seizing up of all counter-party activity* as was seen after the collapse of Lehman Brothers in September 2008. Rescuing single institutions can be a messy affair but when all institutions are so closely inter-linked that there is a complete breakdown in trust and willingness to conduct normal arbitrage and maturity transformation, there is only one antidote to a systemic meltdown which is that central banks have to provide the public balance sheet as the ultimate back stop to potentially huge losses from system wide "broken" trades. Unfortunately there is not a smooth continuum along which one can situate the possibility of an isolated failure as distinct from a systemic failure. The rapid escalation of the crisis in 2008 attests to the abrupt discontinuity in the "normal" functioning of the maturity transformation process and its complete breakdown.

As a further illustration of the inadequate modeling of the transition from isolated failure to systemically threatening failure it is worth contemplating the fundamental flaw which was at the heart of many structured financial products in the lead up to the GFC. The flaw can be best expressed in the question: How can we measure the total risk of the *combination* of a group of assets where we will only have some useful metrics for measuring the separate risks of the individual constituents? Is the risk additive or does it take on entirely separate degrees of freedom so that it essentially becomes unquantifiable?

The overly simplistic use of a technique known as the Gaussian copula which was used, for example, to assess the likelihood of a package of mortgages all defaulting together – considered highly unlikely owing to the limitations of the risk modeling methodology – has subsequently been thoroughly discredited. [22]

In more general terms the failure of most of the quantitative tools that were used by the creators of structured financial products, and even more alarmingly by the credit ratings agencies in assessing their risks, can be attributed to their inability to recognize the *network effect*. Complex systems theory provides insightful accounts for *emergent properties* of networks which have characteristics which are of a different order of magnitude and which exhibit very different *qualities* than would be expected from using an additive approach towards the lower level properties of that network. [23] The combination of mortgages in a CDO or the estimation of total risk to a party which is holding several separately priced CDS contracts with inter-linked parties are good examples of why an appreciation of the network effect is so vital and why it is sadly lacking in conventional risk management modeling tools.

14.4 TOWARDS NEW MODELS OF NETWORK OR SYSTEMIC RISK

It is actually even more disconcerting for those that have a fetish for quantifying the likely magnitude of critical episodes in that there are, in principle, no reliable quantitative tools for estimating the severity of price drops in asset markets, their likely duration, and the knock on effects of disruptive behavior of one market on the rest of markets in such a highly inter-connected world.

The micro-structure of markets was considered in some depth in Chapter 4 and there is now a rich and expanding literature which focuses not only on an empirical analysis of the patterns of trading in contemporary capital markets, but also on the "ecology" of markets. The term "ecology" may seem rather vague and vacuous but in what follows I hope to show that the types of participants and the way that they interact have similar characteristics to a food web – or more pejoratively they mimic in a fairly simplified manner the predator/prey ecosystem models which have been the focus of a huge amount of research in the life sciences.

In addition to the empirical studies, there has been much work done by more theoretically minded academics in terms of "agent" theory in understanding the interactions of programmatically designed "participants" in artificial simulations of real markets. Computer scientists such as J. Doyne Farmer from the Santa Fe Institute in New Mexico [24] have been working in this area for many years and have produced articles which have deepened the understanding of the manner in which the interplay of actors, their reactions to changing parameters such as the flow of orders into the market, the manner in which certain participants – separately identified as "informed traders.," "noise traders," market makers etc. – can at the individual transaction level produce a variety of liquidity conditions which will impact the exact methods of "price discovery" in a market.

Although the agent theorists are modeling markets there is a sense in which even an artificial market as a pure virtual market will not be radically different from a real market. Increasingly electronic markets are themselves virtual and have many artificial agents acting within them in the form of miniature computer programs which trade without human supervision but in accordance with algorithmic logic which has been pre-programmed. Even though there is an essential difference between the artificial agents in the simulations created by Farmer and others, since their agents or "bots" have a relatively limited set of "responses" to changing inputs and background conditions, unlike human beings with more complex response patterns, the distinction is becoming harder to draw. When the prevalence of algorithmic trading is taken into consideration, as much as 70% of market activity [25] can now be attributed to the activities of "bots" and artificial price makers and takers; there is much less to distinguish the nature of "real" markets and their "artificial" counterparts as generated by computer scientists.

14.5 THE SHADOW BANKING SYSTEM AND LIQUIDITY RISK

The lecture given by Adair Turner on the shadow banking system and which contains a good discussion of maturity transformation has already been cited earlier in this chapter. [26]

As Turner observed maturity transformation (as already defined) has great social value enabling "the non-financial sector to hold longer-term financial liabilities than assets, it is both directly welfare enhancing (because it enables households to smooth consumption over time) and potentially conducive to longer term investment. *But it introduces major financial stability risks*" (emphasis in the original).

These risks are well characterized by Turner and have already appeared in similar contexts elsewhere in this book. The following extract comes from Turner's address to the Cass Business School in 2011: [27]

> When performed via bank balance sheets, it creates the risks of liquidity runs – since not all depositors can simultaneously get their money back at the contractually due date.
>
> And when performed via liquid markets, it creates the risk of self-reinforcing downward spirals of falling prices and collapsing liquidity, if investors who collectively account for a large percentage of the market simultaneously seek to sell their contractually long-term commitments.
>
> ... [since] ... the financial system is a complex web of banks and other financial institutions – linked via repo and interbank markets, and interconnected with a system of market based maturity transformation – our ability to understand how much maturity transformation the total system is performing, and how that level that is changing, is seriously impaired.

Turner explains the idea of "the complex web of banks and other financial institutions" further in his elucidation of the shadow banking system which he describes as "a turbo charged variant of non-bank credit intermediation." There are additional risks posed by the shadow banking system however as Turner observes: "Securitization and shadow banking dramatically changed the scale of such non-bank credit intermediation, and changed its nature and riskiness in crucial ways. It introduced leverage and maturity transformation, the classic functions of banks, into the non-bank intermediation channel, with money market mutual funds performing large scale maturity transformation, with hedge funds employing leverage, and with SIVs both leveraged and maturity transforming."

14.6 MATURITY TRANSFORMATION IS SPANNING AN INTERVAL

The essence of any arbitrage is that the timelines for both entry and exit must be exactly co-extensive. If risk becomes too high and the arbitrageur loses faith in his or her ability to span an interval with simultaneous entries and exits on both sides of the trade a vital source of liquidity within markets will disappear. Earlier crises such as the LTCM crisis of 1997 showed that even with relatively riskless strategies such as spread trading between "on the run" US Treasuries ("on the run" means those most recently issued) and "off the run" instruments, an arbitrage which under normal market conditions can generate consistent profits – as it did for LTCM during its initial phase of operation and did previously for the traders from Salomon Brothers which staffed the hedge fund – when markets become severely stressed as they were in August 1997 after the Russian debt default – suddenly became horrendously loss making. The excellent book *When Genius Failed* [28] documents the fashion in which exiting the two legs of the US Treasury arbitrage sketched above could not be performed simultaneously and the hedge fund proprietors were faced with mounting losses in which they sold what they could and not what they wanted to. LTCM sustained losses of more than $5 billion (compared to the losses incurred by large financial firms in 2008 this now seems almost a laughably small sum) and required a bailout by the Federal Reserve Bank of New York in concert with several other investment banks (ironically Bear Stearns was the only major bank not to participate in this bailout!).

There is a disconcerting circularity about the explanation given for the collapse of LTCM which helps to illustrate the really deep problem about financing any kind of arbitrage when markets are unsettled. At the height of the 2008 crisis even the conducting of routine repo transactions became highly problematic as a result of a breakdown in trust by banks for each other. Counter-party risk was perceived to be at a limiting value where nobody trusted anybody else. Ironically it could be argued that for each CEO of a major money market participant when they reviewed how bad their own balance sheets were looking, they could not believe that their competitors and normal counter-parties were not suffering as much and were maybe in an even worse state. The circularity which I alluded to is that arbitrage requires liquid markets but when arbitrageurs and repo financing is absent market liquidity collapses. This is the classic chicken and egg problem and the suggestion is that it can only be explained by reference to the fact that the solvency/insolvency dichotomy does not permit any shading – it is purely a black and white or binary issue. There is no fuzziness when making a determination, under stressful conditions, as to whether a counter-party may or may not be solvent. When massive potential losses are at stake any doubt about solvency is going to err on the side of a complete unwillingness to engage with a troubled firm where *the perception is that they might be insolvent.*

At the market micro-structure level it has already been seen that during the height of the Flash Crash there were periods when there was a complete absence of two-way trading conditions and liquidity for individual stocks. Accenture, under normal conditions a very liquid stock, at one point had literally a complete breakdown in the bid/ask spread. It was also noted that the SEC/CFTC findings made the point that market liquidity and high volume can coincide and that the existence of high volume during crashes illustrates the fact that many participants are selling in panic and in the absence of proper bid/ask spreads there is little or no liquidity. The period of maximum loss when everyone was selling coincides with the highest volume but since the market was completely tilted to the sell side there was no liquidity.

Returning to the earlier analysis of the Flash Crash I shall conjecture the following idea. The longer the accumulation phase by short-term informed traders (e.g. hedge funds, prop trading desks, large speculators) in the absence of real depth to market liquidity (which is primarily provided by long exposure of institutional investors such as pension funds and mutual funds) the shorter the interval tolerance (i.e. the willingness to sit with inventory) when the market becomes unbalanced.

For risk managers and portfolio managers in general there are related questions upon which the notion of the duration of or interval is paramount:

- What is the worst drawdown possibility within a specified time interval?
- What is the expected recovery time?
- What is the waiting time for more "normal" circumstances to resume?

This begins to highlight one of the key differentiators between tail risk and the uncertainty of increasingly severe drawdowns. For an unleveraged asset manager with a long enough holding period, episodic tail risks – even of severe magnitude – may be considered as not ultimately threatening to a portfolio since the assets can be kept in convalescence long enough to recover. For leveraged portfolios which have to be marked to market on a daily basis there is always the risk of the call from the prime broker for more margin which can then instigate the vicious spiral of having to sell into a declining market. This sets off the vicious downward spiral where selling at fire sale prices causes more decay in the collateral values which will in turn lead to requests for further maintenance margin and further liquidations in a nasty wealth destroying feedback loop.

But if one can avoid the margin calls by not being leveraged and not being dependent on the need to enter into the risk of interval funding in illiquid markets, which, in essence is the real consequence of leverage, then given a suitably long-term holding horizon one can ride out very turbulent markets. The key terms there were a "suitably long term holding horizon" and this will depend a lot on the patience and fortitude of the investors in a managed fund or the depths of the pockets and confidence of a wealthy principal. The best placed long-term convalescence home for keeping assets when markets are extremely distressed is a central bank.

Far more unsettling however to the long-term investor is the uncertainty as to whether a series of fat tail events portends further critical episodes in the future. If one takes a gloomy view that the 2007/8 GFC was just the first in a continuing series of rolling crises which might culminate in an as yet even more unnerving systemic crisis then there will always be a temptation to cut losses before they become overwhelming. The emotional trade off between tolerating adversity, on the supposition that it is transient, and ultimate preservation of wealth, when evidence suggests it may be chronic, is one of those peculiarly non-rational elements in investment decision making.

To make this more concrete one has only to consider what the appropriate holding period would be for the following two scenarios. Apple, at the time of writing, is the world's most valuable company, but for an early stage investor in that company would it have been entirely rational to have held that stock throughout the 1990s when the company appeared to be on the verge of bankruptcy and traded in single digits? Even more strikingly what should have been the appropriate holding period for a fund manager who had bought Japanese equities or real estate in 1988?

Questions regarding the appropriate holding period and the estimation of returns across a time interval are not just relevant to a fund manager holding a portfolio of existing securities; they also arise in regard to the decision making by entrepreneurs about the viability of new capital investments in general. When seen in the context of the recovery process following a dramatic market collapse this takes on even more significance than usual and once again the shortcomings of much mainstream thinking in economics and finance is underscored.

But the key elements which are lacking in orthodox economic theory regarding the decision making process undertaken by enterprises and entrepreneurs contemplating the viability of a new investment go far beyond a simple evaluation of calculating the net present value of the future cash flows. Such considerations involve psychological questions regarding entrepreneurs' expectations for future asset growth, which, in turn, hinge on conjectures regarding the likely emergence of new "bandwagons" giving rise to new bubble-mania. Also relevant are such matters as whether or not there is a dynastic component to investment appraisal. For example, a firm with short-term oriented hired guns will have a very different perspective to a family or legacy business where the founders are focused on inter-generational wealth creation. However, in the post GFC environment the most important variable would seem to be persistent questions and uncertainties regarding the overall integrity of the financial system.

ENDNOTES

1. *More Lessons from the Crisis: Remarks at the Center for Economic Policy Studies (CEPS) Symposium*, Princeton, New Jersey by William C. Dudley, President and Chief Executive Officer of the Federal Reserve Bank of New York November 13, 2009: http://www.newyorkfed.org/newsevents/speeches/2009/dud091113.html:

   > William C. Dudley became the 10th president and chief executive officer of the Federal Reserve Bank of New York on January 27, 2009. In that capacity, he serves as the vice chairman and a permanent member of the Federal Open Market Committee (FOMC), the group responsible for formulating the nation's monetary policy.
   >
   > Previously, Mr. Dudley served as executive vice president of the Markets Group at the New York Fed, where he also managed the System Open Market Account for the FOMC.

2. The often cited example comes from J.M. Keynes, *General Theory of Employment Interest and Money* (1936):

   > It is not a case of choosing those [faces] that, to the best of one's judgment, are really the prettiest, nor even those that average opinion genuinely thinks the prettiest. We have reached the third degree where we devote our intelligences to anticipating what average opinion expects the average opinion to be. And there are some, I believe, who practice the fourth, fifth and higher degrees.

3. Jim O'Neill would shake up Bank of England if he became Governor, *Daily Telegraph*, June 22, 2012:

   > Among the leading candidates are Paul Tucker, the current deputy Governor; Lord Turner, chairman of the Financial Services Authority (FSA); Lord O'Donnell, the former Cabinet Secretary; and Sir John Vickers, a former Bank of England chief economist and chairman of the Independent Commission on Banking that recently proposed broad reforms to the financial sector.

   http://www.telegraph.co.uk/finance/economics/9350013/Jim-ONeill-would-shake-up-Bank-of-England-if-he-became-Governor.html.
4. Shadow Banking and Financial Instability: Lord Turner speech to the CASS Business School, Adair Turner, March 14, 2012, http://www.fsa.gov.uk/library/communication/pr/2012/027.shtml. Slides for the above speech can be found at http://www.fsa.gov.uk/static/pubs/speeches/0314-at.pdf.
5. Deposit insurance schemes are provided by various national government agencies including the following for USA, UK and Germany.

   The Federal Deposit Insurance Corporation (FDIC) is a United States government corporation operating as an independent agency created by the Glass-Steagall Act of 1933. It provides deposit insurance, which guarantees the safety of deposits in member banks, up to $250,000 per depositor per bank as of January 2012.

   The Bundesverband deutscher Banken (Federal Association of German Banks) is the association of private banks in Germany. Deposits are insured up to Euro 100,000.

   In the UK the FSCS guarantees the safety of deposits in UK member banks, up to £85,000 per depositor per bank as of June 2012.
6. A primer on how repo transactions work is to be found later in this chapter.
7. Here are some reminders of the gravity of the problems confronting the financial system from that period:

   > On Thursday, Sept. 18, 2008, the astonished leadership of the U.S. Congress was told in a private session by the chairman of the Federal Reserve that the American economy was in grave danger of a complete

> meltdown within a matter of days. "There was literally a pause in that room where the oxygen left," reported Senator Dodd [from the film Inside the Meltdown].

http://www.youtube.com/watch?v=I6xw2gd4kMg.

IMF in global "meltdown" warning, from BBC News website, October 12, 2008, http://news.bbc.co.uk/1/hi/7665515.stm.

James Kirkup, World Facing Worst Financial Crisis in History, Bank of England Governor Says, *Daily Telegraph*, October 6, 2011, http://www.telegraph.co.uk/finance/financialcrisis/8812260/World-facing-worst-financial-crisis-in-history-Bank-of-England-Governor-says.html:

> Sir Mervyn King was speaking after the decision by the Bank's Monetary Policy Committee to put £75 billion of newly created money into the economy in a desperate effort to stave off a new credit crisis and a UK recession.
>
> Economists said the Bank's decision to resume its quantitative easing [QE], or asset purchase programme, showed it was increasingly fearful for the economy, and predicted more such moves ahead. Sir Mervyn said the Bank had been driven by growing signs of a global economic disaster.
>
> "This is the most serious financial crisis we've seen, at least since the 1930s, if not ever. We're having to deal with very unusual circumstances, but to act calmly to this and to do the right thing."

8. Global Financial Stability Report: Durable Financial Stability: Getting There from Here, IMF, April 2012, http://www.imf.org/external/pubs/ft/gfsr/2011/01/pdf/text.pdf.
9. As above.
10. A well written account of the Gaussian copula is to be found in Felix Salmon, Recipe for Disaster: The Formula That Killed Wall Street, *Wired*, February 23, 2009, http://www.wired.com/techbiz/it/magazine/17-03/wp_quant.
11. Europe's Banking Regulator Reveals Eight Banks Fail Stress Tests, *Daily Telegraph*, July 15, 2011. Although five Spanish banks failed to pass the stress test, Bankia was not amongst those, http://www.guardian.co.uk/business/2011/jul/15/european-banks-stress-test.
12. The International Monetary Fund considers the underpricing of liquidity risk to be the defining characteristic of systemic liquidity risk. The following quote comes from Chapter 2 of the IMF's Global Financial Stability Report, *How to Address the Systemic Part of Liquidity Risk*, April 2011:

> Systemic liquidity risk is the tendency of financial institutions to collectively underprice liquidity risk in good times when funding markets function well because they are convinced that the central bank will almost certainly intervene in times of stress to maintain such markets, prevent the failure of financial institutions, and thus limit the impact of liquidity shortfalls on other financial institutions and the real economy. If they ignore the tendency to underprice liquidity risk prior to the emergence of shortfalls and then intervene during times of systemic stress, central banks will reinforce these negative externalities and give financial institutions an incentive to hold less liquidity than needed.

The relevant part of the IMF report is available online at: http://www.imf.org/external/pubs/ft/gfsr/2011/01/pdf/chap2.pdf.

13. See endnote 8.
14. Greenspan's Libor Barometer Shows Markets Stay Frozen, Bloomberg, February 23, 2009:

> "Libor-OIS remains a barometer of fears of bank insolvency," former Federal Reserve Chairman Alan Greenspan said in an interview. "That fear has been substantially reduced since mid-October, but the decline has stalled well short of any semblance of normal markets."

http://www.bloomberg.com/apps/news?pid=newsarchive&sid=aUi9ZqasnjRY.

15. Central Banks Cut Cost Of Borrowing Dollars To Ease Crisis, Bloomberg, November 30, 2011:

> Six central banks led by the Federal Reserve made it cheaper for banks to borrow dollars in emergencies in a global effort to ease Europe's sovereign-debt crisis.

> The premium banks pay to borrow dollars overnight from central banks will fall by half a percentage point to 50 basis points, the Fed said today in a statement in Washington. The so-called dollar swap lines will be extended by six months to Feb. 1, 2013. The Fed coordinated the move with the European Central Bank and the central banks of Canada, Switzerland, Japan and the U.K.
>
> The six central banks also agreed to create temporary bilateral swap programs so funding can be provided in any of the currencies "should market conditions so warrant." Those swap lines were also authorized through Feb. 1, 2013.

http://www.bloomberg.com/news/2011-11-30/fed-five-central-banks-lower-interest-rate-on-dollar-swaps.html.

16. The graphic is found in Funding stress revisited, *FT Alphaville*, August 3, 2011, http://ftalphaville.ft.com/blog/2011/08/03/642501/funding-stress-revisited/.
17. The acronym LTRO stands for Long-Term Refinance Operations. The ECB conducted two such operations, one on December 21, 2011 and another on February 29, 2012. They were designed to boost the European banking system by lending more than euro 1 trillion to at least 800 banks for a term of up to three years.
18. Quoted in the IMF report mentioned in endnote 8.
19. Bernanke: Repo was thought to be risk free, *Repo Watch*, May 29, 2008:

> Until recently, short-term repos had always been regarded as virtually risk-free instruments and thus largely immune to the type of rollover or withdrawal risks associated with short-term unsecured obligations.

http://repowatch.org/2008/05/29/906/.

20. *Central Banking: Before, During and After the Crisis*, March 23, 2012, Chairman Ben S. Bernanke, At the Federal Reserve Conference on Central Banking: Before, During, and After the Crisis, Washington, D.C.

    http://www.federalreserve.gov/newsevents/speech/bernanke20120323a.htm.

    Another document which is useful in this regard is entitled "Shadow Banking" by the Federal Reserve Bank of New York Staff Reports, Staff Report No. 458 February 2012. The document can be found online at http://www.ny.frb.org/research/staff_reports/sr458.pdf.

    Adair Turner makes several references to this piece of research and uses diagrams from it in his own presentations on the Shadow Banking System – see endnote 4.

    The FRBNY document makes the following pertinent observation with regard to liquidity and maturity transformation as conducted within the shadow banking system:

> Over the past decade, the shadow banking system provided sources of funding for credit by converting opaque, risky, long-term assets into money-like, short-term liabilities. Arguably, maturity and credit transformation in the shadow banking system contributed to the asset price appreciation in residential and commercial real estate markets prior to the 2007–09 financial crisis. During the financial crisis, the shadow banking system became severely strained and many parts of the system collapsed. Credit creation through maturity, credit, and liquidity transformation can significantly reduce the cost of credit relative to direct lending. However, credit intermediaries' reliance on short term liabilities to fund illiquid long-term assets is an inherently fragile activity and may be prone to runs.

21. Roger Lowenstein, *When Genius Failed: The Rise and Fall of Long-Term Capital Management* (Random House, September 2000). The following is a brief description from the publisher:

> LTCM began trading in 1994. The fund would seek to earn a tiny spread on thousands of trades, "as if it were vacuuming nickels that others couldn't see," in the words of one of its Nobel laureate partners, Myron Scholes. And nickels it found. In its first two years, LTCM earned $1.6 billion, profits that exceeded 40 percent even after the partners' hefty cuts. By the spring of 1996, it was holding $140 billion in assets. But the end was soon in sight, and Lowenstein's detailed account of each successively worse month of 1998, culminating in a disastrous August and the partners' subsequent panicked moves, is riveting.

22. See endnote 10.
23. A readable account of how complex systems create emergent properties is found in John H Holland, *Emergence: From Chaos to Order* (Addison Wesley, 1998).
24. J. Doyne Farmer from the Santa Fe Institute in New Mexico.
25. *The Race to Zero*, Speech given by Andrew G. Haldane, Executive Director, Financial Stability and member of the interim Financial Policy Committee, International Economic Association Sixteenth World Congress, Beijing, China, 8 July 2011:

    > As recently as 2005, HFT accounted for less than a fifth of US equity market turnover by volume. Today, it accounts for between two-thirds and three-quarters.

    http://www.bankofengland.co.uk/publications/Documents/speeches/2011/speech509.pdf.
26. See endnote 4.
27. *Leverage, Maturity Transformation and Financial Stability: Challenges beyond Basel III*, A speech by Adair Turner at the Cass Business School, March 16, 2011.
28. See endnote 21.

15

Emotional Finance and Interval Confidence

How can investors that have been so traumatized by the complete absence of normal liquidity conditions that they were unable to engage even in short-term arbitrage opportunities, where the interval spanned is just a matter of hours or days, be persuaded (or persuade themselves) to become confident again and to engage in long-term investing and investment decisions? The reason for inserting the parenthetical phrase "or persuade themselves" in the formulation of the question raises the difficult matter of the human mind's propensity to have selective recall and on occasion to engage in a form of self-deception. Without becoming too philosophical, there is a behavioral trait which human beings have – perhaps because of the mystery of their mortality – to screen out and "ignore" certain unpleasant memories and deep seated fears in order to function normally and go about their daily business. However the fact that within an individual's consciousness there is both knowledge of those unpleasant memories and fears – and the recollection of the events that may have precipitated such discomforting memories – and at the same time an ability to overlook them (at least much of the time), suggests that our capacity for tolerating cognitive and emotional dissonance is considerable and enigmatic.

Understanding the psychological processes involved in the recovery from a crisis – both in the obvious sense of the emotions experienced directly as a result of a financial crash but more commonly from a multitude of other causes – the timeline for rebuilding confidence, and a willingness to engage again in risk seeking behavior, is a fascinating topic about which books have been written and which would take us far beyond our present focus. In a sense the questions that arise in this context go to the heart of the "animal spirits" which Keynes wisely decided to leave as vaguely defined.

The rebuilding of interval confidence, in other words the willingness to have confidence in inter-temporal commitments of human emotions and physical resources, will be the focus of this chapter. In many ways it has been one of the undercurrents of much of the discussion so far. In the early stages of rebuilding confidence it is most likely to be incremental and a gradual process but, after a suitable recovery time which will be an extremely variable period depending on the specific circumstances, there can then be abrupt and dramatic shifts in the willingness to embrace risks and make commitments in the face of a similar kind of uncertainty which had previously been unacceptable. In essence this highly compressed description encapsulates the boom/bust psychology. It should also be apparent that the process described is a process which leads to qualitative changes. The emotional transitions in the process can be likened to phase shifts and as such are not readily susceptible to explanation by reference to any simple quantitative scalar. They are similar to the nonlinear dynamics and network effects which were outlined in previous chapters.

The following citation echoes a lot of the thoughts in this chapter and comes from Menzie Chin, a professor of public affairs and economics at the University of Wisconsin who has served on the staff of the Council of Economic Advisers: [1]

> During the financial crisis of 2008, the asymmetry of information regarding each institution's financial situation was so pronounced that lending fell precipitously as trust dissipated. These informational problems were only exacerbated as lending fell further. Eventually, no interest rate could induce lending and price failed to clear the credit market. Restoring the functioning of the credit markets required mitigating those information asymmetries, essentially by way of short-term government guarantees.
>
> It is a mistake to think information problems of this nature will disappear as memories of the crisis recede. In fact, when times are good, then each loan seems like a sure bet, and firms that were previously constrained from borrowing can borrow – and over-borrow. Easy access to credit further reinforces the good times, and an unsustainable lending boom ensues – unless it is constrained by regulation or some sort of countervailing policy. The crisis highlighted the existence of these self-reinforcing feedback loops, and we ignore them at our peril.

The observation that "the asymmetry of information regarding each institution's financial situation was so pronounced that lending fell precipitously as trust dissipated" captures the issue raised above that trust/distrust and solvency/insolvency are all or nothing propositions. They are unlike most dichotomies in that there are no shades of gray.

15.1 CONSTRUCTIVE AMBIGUITY

The concept of information asymmetry has been explored in Chapter 4 in the context of the informed and uninformed agents within the micro-structure of markets. As a follow on from that discussion I want to pursue an associated concept which hinges on the presence of ambiguous elements in messages and information conveyed within a financial context. Ambiguous signals are those which may have intentionally been framed as open to two (at least) interpretations, or that is the way that they are received and interpreted by a consumer of that information. On the one hand it may simply be that two different individuals will find alternate meanings in the same message or, more stressfully, that an individual will perceive that the information is pregnant with alternate meanings. This will give rise to the kind of cognitive dissonance that was alluded to at the beginning of this chapter, and at the limits, this dissonance has the capacity to lead to a breakdown in interval confidence that is manifested in liquidity crises.

Ambiguity in a financial context is exemplified by considering what can arise in connection with a release of some economic data such as unemployment statistics or data relating to the CPI and inflation. On the one hand "facts" are being presented and, to that extent, it could be claimed that they are open to different interpretation *but* in essence they should be free of ambiguity. However the situation is more nuanced than this would suggest.

The Bureau of Labor Statistics (BLS) is the agency of the US government which publishes the Non-Farm Payroll report at the beginning of each month. [2] The BLS presents a huge amount of data in each report which is designed to show the state of the labor market and employment as of the month before the data is released. The data is collected in a variety of ways and there are so many different metrics presented that it is not easy to render the level of unemployment, which is the most widely followed metric, in an easily digestible single number. There are issues related to seasonality, other issues related to participation rate of the labor force, and a myriad of other factors such as those in employment that are currently working part time but who would prefer to be full time etc. There is even a methodological tool known as the births/deaths adjustment – which has nothing to do with actual births and deaths but which is the BLS's guesstimate as to the creation of new businesses which it is not easy to discern from the method of collecting the data. [3]

Suppose that one reads a headline to the effect that unemployment has declined by a certain percentage point or that 120 000 new jobs were created, how is one to interpret that "fact"? What if the participation rate has declined by 250 000 during the same month – does that mean that the fact that the new jobs created has to be adjusted to reflect the fact that more workers have become discouraged from actually looking for work? These are questions that can be, and are, debated by most economic commentators. In fact it is worth pointing out that the *actual number of people employed in the private sector* in the US has remained at a fairly constant level since 2000 [4]. The essential point is that even the data is open to such widely different interpretations that it could justifiably be claimed to be inherently ambiguous, and that is before the various analysts and commentators add their own "spin" to the data.

Spin, it is contended, is actually the deliberate introduction of ambiguity and a narrative bias to data which itself may already be ambiguous! Any data, whether it is unemployment data or earnings announcements by companies can be construed as being fundamentally positive or negative, as bullish or bearish. When markets are functioning normally the bulls will run with a positive interpretation, and the bears with a negative interpretation. It is precisely their disagreement that will be reflected in an adversarial contest or battle regarding prices. The resulting battle of wills will be a sign that the market is functioning in a healthy, normal, and liquid manner (it is noteworthy that in this context these separate adjectives are more or less synonyms)

In the wake of the extreme evaporations of liquidity discussed in this book, I want to go the further step and make the claim that *markets need to be provided with ambiguous information* from central bankers/policy makers in order to lubricate the adversarial dialectic of the bulls and the bears. This lubrication of fractiousness and the presence of disagreements between those who want to sell at the current price and those who would rather buy at the current price are vital requirements for two-way, liquid markets.

When markets are unwilling or unable to accept ambiguous signals – because for example there are questions about solvency – the markets lack the prerequisite degree of fractiousness. Market participants become much more coherent and uniform in their views and, somewhat counter-intuitively this uniformity of opinion gives rise to *macro illiquidity* which is the instigator and defining characteristic of systemic crises, fire sales of assets, and the onset of deflationary spirals. One might recall the extended discussion regarding the VPIN metric from Chapter 5 where at the microcosmic level the Flash Crash contained the right ingredients for a bout of systemic illiquidity. Uniformity of judgment about the over-extended nature of risk on inventory accumulation, arrived at in exactly the same time segment by the uninformed and informed agents in the market, led to a mass withdrawal of liquidity. Even though it was a relatively brief episode on the day itself – May 6, 2010 – it was followed in ensuing weeks by a sizable retreat from risk on assets. [5]

In such circumstances market participants are unable or unwilling to have interval confidence as that term was defined above. Questions are posed about the liquidity–solvency continuum, and whenever such questioning takes place and there is an absence of strong counter-parties willing to take an alternative view, there arises a strong inclination towards exiting a market, and this has severely disruptive effects for liquidity and maturity transformation. At such times there is a need for the uniformity of opinion which gave rise to the crash to be superseded by a novel injection of information asymmetry, and this is often in the form of a new ambiguity.

It is now appropriate to introduce the concept of "constructive ambiguity" which is a term that has been applied to the way in which difficult international diplomacy can be conducted. It is a term which has been used in describing the manner, for example, in which Henry Kissinger conducted foreign policy and diplomacy during his tenure as US Secretary of State under both Presidents Nixon and Ford in the 1970s. [6] Constructive ambiguity means phrasing an idea in such a vague way that no one is quite sure what is being said. Unlike unintentional ambiguity which is really a sign of not being precise enough in expression and a consequence of uncritical thinking, constructive ambiguity is almost the opposite in that it is intentional – it is cunning and designed to obfuscate and keep the persons to whom the message is communicated off balance. In this sense "off balance" should best be understood as expressing the same notion as that conveyed by the term non-uniform. As was argued earlier uniform markets are too highly correlated with too many participants sharing the same viewpoint which can then become extremely skewed (lopsided) and crash. If it is helpful one might recall the analogy of all passengers moving to the same side of an ocean liner or airplane.

With regard to the application of constructive ambiguity in financial communications, the suggestion is that for central bankers, policy makers, and even corporate executives and their PR advisors a lot of information is deliberately designed to be ambiguous. It is crafted in such a fashion to keep investors and traders in a state of uncertainty and disagreement about future direction of prices which is a vital pre-requisite of market liquidity. This is its *raison d'être* as the need for fractiousness and market liquidity is paramount. There is a vital need to create "incentives" for market participants to differentiate between the longer term and the shorter term. This preserves the necessary longevity in interval confidence.

As long as there is ambiguity in the information being supplied to markets there is legitimate scope for dissenting opinions to arise which, it has been argued, is vital to the preservation of systemic liquidity. As an heuristic to help this intuition, if we consider a certain "fact," such as a glass which has been filled to the 50% level with a liquid, those who see that glass as half full, perhaps guided by positive contextual information, are as justified in reaching their conclusion as others who see the same fact, but within a less benign context, as showing that the glass is half empty.

Because politicians, regulators, and central bankers have a deep fear of illiquidity, for valid reasons that have only been too well exemplified by the financial meltdown of late 2008, the imperative to promote the right conditions in the financial economy as well as the cultural world (including the media/blogosphere) which will enhance and sustain market liquidity, will drive financial policy measures as well as political debate.

At times of crisis those providing liquidity to principals will begin to notice that their normal threshold for ambiguity toleration will drop and that ambiguity aversion becomes more dominant. This will manifest itself, at the microstructural level of market behavior, in qualitative changes to order flow. This manifestation will often result in a radical change in the signal to noise ratio with respect to the ratio of declining bids/declining asks, as well as a widening of the bid/ask spread. The widening of the bid/ask spread is itself a reflection of risk aversion as market makers are less willing to hold inventory across the interval. The presence of uncertainty and deep seated anxiety as to current and future collateral values is precisely the "wild card" variable which enervates the *animal spirits*, and reduces confidence in financing of the interval.

15.2 DOUBLE BINDS AND EMOTIONAL FINANCE

In the fall of 2008, after the collapse of several blue chip names in global finance, there was a period during which the investor community suffered from a complete lack of information asymmetry. The state of the collective mind (which can act as a metaphor for the markets) was one of a symmetry of fear and ignorance. It would not be unreasonable to say that there was almost *unanimous* opinion about how to value risk on securities and assets. That unanimity or uniformity expressed itself, in essence, in the stance that these securities were over-valued, unattractively risky and that this was not the time to be an heroic buyer of distressed assets for which there was no liquid market – why step forward to catch a falling knife? The coherent and almost unanimous decision to step aside created a liquidity trap in which those forced to sell kept selling into a declining market, and when selling begets more selling the financial system stares over the precipice to contemplate freefall into total collapse.

Emerging from a liquidity trap is not primarily about having central banks injecting limitless amounts of liquidity into the financial system. This mistaken belief lies at the root of the ineffective measures that central bankers have been trying with very little success since 2008. Moving beyond the emotional scarring left by a systemic liquidity crisis is principally a matter of restoring interval confidence from which there will be a willingness to engage in inter-temporal commitments (initially of the short to medium term variety) of resources and emotions. Eventually these inter-temporal commitments must become longer term and involve large scale commitments of risk capital and this is ultimately how the economy emerges from the bust phase and a band wagon gets started for a new investment boom.

In April 2012, while this book was being written, there were some fascinating topics presented at the INET Conference in Berlin. In the keynote session accompanying remarks from George Soros, there was a short presentation by Perry Mehrling which touched on the growing interest within INET in a new discipline being called Emotional Finance. [7] This very useful addition to the body of work within finance is exemplified by the work of David Tuckett, a London-based professor of psychoanalysis, who is a recipient of a research award from INET. [8] In words which echo the concept of spanning the interval discussed above, Mehrling makes the following observations which were inspired by Tuckett's work which will be considered in a moment:

> The interlocking structure of credit is a bridge that we build from the present out into the unknown future, from the present shore out over the void toward shores only imagined. The credit system privileges some visions of the future over others; that's how the bridge gets started on one direction rather than another, but there is always a bridge.
>
> David Tuckett teaches us that fantastical objects play a key role in the way fund managers handle their jobs, which require them to make myriad consequential decisions under conditions of radical uncertainty. But the situation of the fund manager is just a more extreme version of the situation we all face.

The first observation in the above quotation uses the metaphor of a "bridge" getting started to capture exactly the kind of regaining of interval confidence that is so vital to the rejuvenation of the animal spirits following a financial crash. In seeking a better understanding of the role of "fantastical objects" referenced above, in the emergence of new financial bandwagons, it will be very useful to consider the writings of David Tuckett.

David Tuckett's book *Minding the Markets*, [9] is based on an empirical study using interviews with a large number of hedge fund managers in New York, London, and elsewhere. Tuckett has attempted to unravel from a psycho-analytical perspective the emotions experienced by them throughout the investment life cycle. His findings are very informative and can be characterized simply as being dualistic whereby the fund managers would experience both elation and depression based upon their performances and their perception of market conditions and their current holdings. His notion of a "fantastical object" referred to in the above quotation reflects the full blooded expression of the animal spirits in which a certain asset is elevated to an abnormally high pedestal by the fund managers and for which there then develops an almost obsessive attachment. [10]

> A feature of making decisions under uncertainty is that they involve hope and risk – the risk of getting it wrong and then of having to pay the consequence. In the investment environment this means not just financial loss, but also risk to your job. Insofar as the future is inherently unknowable, painful anxieties are evoked which the decision-taker can do nothing "rational" to abate. Because taking risk creates both excitement and anxiety, it ushers in the opportunity to split off the good "exciting" experience from the bad "painful" thought of loss.
>
> The formal recognition of the equation "investment = uncertainty = anxiety," along with the proposition of the two mental states in which decisions are evaluated, the depressive and paranoid-schizoid states of mind, are we believe key contributions of emotional finance. The process of investing means that the investor enters into an emotional attachment, whether conscious or not, with something that can easily let him down.

It is the need for investors to have a kind of fantasy about the investment prospects for the desired asset that provides a primal and visceral motivating force in investment behavior. However as Tuckett observes there can be abrupt mood swings in the emotions of investors and traders and these need to be factored to a much greater extent in an analysis of investor behavior. An article written by Tuckett entitled "Emotional Finance: Understanding what drives investors" which appeared in the Autumn 2007 edition of *Professional Investor*, contains a brief but illuminating insight into the emotional and mental states that are almost certainly confronted by the typical investor and trader (even though they themselves may not admit to them): [11]

> Melanie Klein, a leading British psychoanalyst, describes two basic oscillating mental states. In the depressive state of mind we experience ourselves, and others, more or less as we are, complex with attractive and unattractive characteristics, good and bad, and ultimately frail, i.e. we're real. Feelings of "trust" are a feature of this state. In the paranoid-schizoid state of mind we avoid the pain of reality by splitting good and bad experience. "Distrust" is a feature of this state.
>
> There is a direct relationship, we suggest, with financial markets and investment decisions where emotions and uncertainty interact. There is a constant tension between "realistic" judgment made in a depressive state of mind, and the tendency towards "fantastic" judgment, made in a paranoid-schizoid state.

Without venturing too far beyond my expertise or even inclination, I want to pursue a little further the kinds of personality characteristics and emotional responses which are being described in the above quotation. There is a clear reference to the kind of bipolar characteristics that Tuckett observed in the emotional behavior of the fund managers he interviewed.

Bipolar disorder is a term that is often applied indiscriminately by certain medical practitioners, and sometimes there is a failure by such practitioners to differentiate between a certain degree of bipolarity or susceptibility to mood swings which is quite "normal" and a more pathological condition of manic-depressive behavior which is abnormal and which can be debilitating. Clearly many people have a mild condition of bipolarity; in fact it could quite reasonably be claimed to be a fairly common behavioral trait. I would go on to say, and it would seem implicit in the second paragraph of the quotation from Tuckett above, that "where emotions and uncertainty interact" there is a tension which can and will arise when it comes to decision making about financial investments. Earlier on the term "dissonance" was used and in many respects this will give rise to the tensions that arise between the differing interpretations we put on reality. To use again the analogy of the glass which under certain conditions or moods could be said to be half full, and under other conditions or moods could be described as half empty ... which is right? Does that question even have a simple answer? What is actually being illustrated in the posing of the question is the interaction of emotions and "reality" and, tying back to the earlier discussion, the fact that the human mind is capable of embracing ambiguities and even self-contradictory propositions. The really interesting issues arise when one tries to determine what are the limits or threshold beyond which these kinds of dissonance and self contradictions can lead to pathological behavior?

From the evidence of abrupt switches in investor sentiment and from the extensive discussion of the binary risk on/risk off dynamics that have become entrenched in the macro behavior of market participants, it is more than tempting to conclude that there is a bipolar quality driving the collective consciousness which manifests itself in financial markets. The financial markets can be seen metaphorically at least as a collective mind and the kind of behavior which has been described throughout this book is one of increasing bipolarity. The suggestion is that when considering the difficulties presented by some of the almost impossible dilemmas confronting policy makers, central bankers, and investors this may well be a lot more than just a transient form of investor behavior. Indeed a strong argument could be made that, at its core, the tendency for markets to go through booms and busts is a collective manifestation of the oscillating mental states described by Melanie Klein and which appear in the above quotation from David Tuckett.

In a more extreme form the kinds of mood swings which are experienced by someone with a bipolar disorder can manifest themselves in a psychiatric condition known as schizophrenia. It certainly is *not* part of my agenda here to suggest that there is evidence of widespread pathological behavior in modern markets. However, as an heuristic or explanatory tool for the emotional and cognitive dissonance which are becoming more prevalent for investors it will be useful to have a look a little more closely at a framework which has been used in understanding psychopathology.

One of the psychiatric tools and a framework that has been proposed for understanding how some individuals placed in stressful circumstances can be prone to acting in a schizophrenic fashion is known as the concept of the double bind. To state things rather simplistically the psychiatric notion of the double bind condition is one of being in a state where an individual is inescapably bound in a kind of mind knot that can lead to that individual suffering a breakdown in their ability to function and behave "normally." Using slightly different language it can also be characterized as an archetypal *no-win scenario* in which an individual, placed in certain conditions where information and perceptions of messages are contradictory and irreconcilable, is unable to resolve cognitive and emotional conflicts and is prone to breakdowns and aberrant behavior.

The essential hypothesis of the double bind theory is that the "victim" finds himself or herself in a communicational matrix, in which messages contradict each other, the contradiction is not able to be communicated or overruled and the person is not able to disengage from the situation. In such a situation if a person "successfully" responds to one message it necessarily means that they will be failing with respect to the other and vice versa, so that the person will automatically be wrong regardless of response. A simplified way of expressing this bind is that the person is in a "no-win" situation.

The following describes the more extreme kind of torment that could be experienced by someone who has faced existential no-win situations for most of their lives.

> Some people who have been soaked in a soup of double binds have lived with the pain and the confusion rather than giving in to it and conforming to the evidently impossible situation. For some of these people life simply gets more and more difficult and confusing. Until they resolve the environment in which the contradictions exist they see the world as a collection of catch 22 situations or a series of inter-locking double binds. Constant arguments are going on inside the victims mind. Every thing they do seems to be wrong or they simply fail. They anticipate criticism and eventually they start even hearing the relentless voices as if they were someone else. It is exhausting and debilitating. At some point they might be diagnosed as schizophrenic. [12]

The term "double bind" was introduced into the psychological lexicon by Gregory Bateson in the mid 1950s. [13] Bateson's work, which was influenced by his exposure to information theory and cybernetics, precedes the more recent views that schizophrenia has organic origins and is best treated as a form of mental illness. In fact, most contemporary practitioners of psychiatry have reached the conclusion that the use of the double bind theory is no longer valid as a diagnostic or prescriptive tool in the treatment of mental illnesses such as schizophrenia. [14] In a sense that conclusion liberates us from having to tread carefully in the use of the double bind concept in the more limited confines of aiding our understanding of the kinds of emotional and cognitive dissonance which are found within financial markets. By sidestepping the matter of whether or not I am misusing a redundant methodology for the understanding of psychopathology, it becomes possible to show that there is some explanatory power from the double bind metaphor in expressing the increasingly impossible dilemmas that are faced by central bankers, politicians, and investors.

The best way to consider the double bind model for explanation, and the reason why I believe it has some relevance to the subject matter of this chapter, is that it considers the difficulties encountered by individuals who experience stress because of their inability to escape from certain *impossible to reconcile* propositions. If, as suggested in earlier discussions, there are only very bad choices available in the "solution" to many financial and economic problems there can be a growing sense of unease of finding oneself in an impossible or no-win situation.

As already indicated, but for the avoidance of any doubt, the use of the double bind model in this context is only as an heuristic device to throw some light on the nature of a nexus or matrix of conflicting messages faced by today's investors. When experienced by a vulnerable individual such as a child growing up within a dysfunctional family, intensely conflictual messages can lead to pathological behavior and mental breakdowns. But within the context of financial decision making and investor behavior we can simply focus on the matrix of dissonant messages and ambiguity without dwelling on the more extreme accompaniments within a dysfunctional family unit that might lead to pathological personality disorders.

To apply the model just outlined with the confined intention of using it as an heuristic device, it could be argued that a bipolar market is the appropriate response to a deeply conflicted matrix of economic circumstances and policy initiatives. In other words, the binary risk on/risk off trading behavior, which is so evident in contemporary financial markets, arises precisely because the dilemmas facing policy makers and strategically placed decision makers, and the messages that are being communicated from them, are *inherently conflict laden and contradictory* and create *irresolvable* cognitive choices and emotional dissonance for investors in financial markets. In this bizarre sense a binary, bipolar risk on/risk off pattern of market activity is a legitimate, sane, and pragmatic response to a market which is perceived to be either in, or approaching, a no-win predicament.

The following extract from an article by Charles Hugh Smith who has a quite radical, financially oriented blog by the name of *Of Two Minds* (the title reflects a predilection to the manner of reasoning in the preceding section) expands on this psychoanalytical approach to conditions in the Eurozone and employs the conceptual framework of the double bind in an insightful way. The following is an extended excerpt from an article entitled "Euro Double-Bind: Both Paths Lead to Disintegration": [15]

> The euro's handlers are in a double-bind: whatever path they choose, Germany has no choice but to renounce the euro as an act of self-preservation.
>
> Is there anything that hasn't already been said about the Eurozone's structural flaws and the absurdity of the half-baked "solutions" tossed together by its frenzied, fumbling leadership? Perhaps not, but we can fruitfully boil the mess down to a simple double-bind.
>
> The double-bind can be stated thusly:
>
> 1. If the European Central Bank (ECB) tries to save the private banks and bondholders by printing trillions of euros to buy up the mountain of hopelessly impaired sovereign bonds, then Germany will rebel and renounce the euro as an act of self-preservation.
>
> Germany knows that money-printing robs savers and the productive via the stealth theft of inflation, and its people will not stand idly by while their wealth is destroyed by ECB euro-printing.
>
> 2. If the ECB renounces money-printing, then the only economy solvent enough to fund the 3-trillion-euro bailout with actual cash is Germany, which will rebel against this debt-serfdom by renouncing the euro.
>
> **There are only two paths, and they both lead to the same end-state: dissolution of the euro and the EU's monetary union.** The situation is truly binary; there are no other real solutions. The half-life of theatrical, fantasy "solutions" is shrinking fast; where a meeting, a resolution or a vote once sparked a three-month rally, now it powers a meager three-day rally at best.
>
> Soon the rumor-fantasy-"solution" rallies will last three hours, not three days. Once the zero line is reached, then rallies invert to crashes, and the markets will go critical, i.e. implode. This is the nature of intrinsically unstable systems.
>
> The only real question left is when the criticality occurs. Can it be staved off until 2012? How long will it take for Germany and the rest of Europe to grasp the end-state of this simple double-bind? Months? Or will it be weeks or even days?
>
> Once you realize the only two paths left both end at the same destination, then the only rational action is to move your cash out of euros and the doomed banks, and liquidate your euro-denominated assets into some other currency as fast and as furiously as possible.

Somewhat apocalyptic maybe, but sometimes overstatement helps to sharpen the mind to seeing what in a more complacent manner is only half perceived if at all.

In another article written by this author and published in May 2009 [16] a similar type of reasoning was applied to the very stressful dilemma faced by the chairman of the Federal Reserve in regard to his desire to reflate asset prices – in particular equities – which has since become an officially stated policy of the Fed, [17] without causing inflationary concerns that would spook the bond market. It is worth remembering that when this piece was written and published there had not been any announcements by the Fed chairman about quantitative easing.

> So a real nasty split-personality market is developing where sentiment is improving because equities are going up (pleasantly circular too – until it isn't), but under the surface the ploy about how the Administration is going to prudently navigate the public finances through their current "difficulties" is looking more and more suspect.
>
> Even if the Fed can't actually manipulate long end rates they can help to calibrate the tone of the equity market's perception of risk. A well timed comment from Dr. Bernanke here, or a well placed announcement about some new initiative there, and before all of the *other people's money* can get back safely to the sidelines, risk aversion moves up the agenda rapidly with an ensuing rush into the "safety" of Treasuries and the S&P 500 has a 7 as its first digit again. Surely the Administration wouldn't want to see stocks go down in a hurry again! Well – er ... no, but actually er ... they could dust off the "irrational exuberance" mantra and talk about the need for a more "measured" market reaction to what are after all only the first signs of improving fundamentals. Not a difficult speech to write for a seasoned Fed professional. The big problem facing the Fed is that, more than ever, it has too many constituencies, with different agendas, to please right now (including, amongst a very long list, the Chinese government) and their room for maneuver is getting more compromised as the debt grows and the need to keep an orderly market in Treasuries becomes critical ... the Fed faces a dilemma ... Actually it's worse than a dilemma in my opinion, and it would be better to see that, given the nature of the Fed's position, its efforts to craft a coherent and internally consistent policy and to communicate its intentions to the market, will place investors/traders in what is sometimes called a "double bind." A manic-depressive market is probably *the appropriate response* to such a deeply conflicted policy.
>
> We had better get used to this split personality dynamic because I suspect it's going to be with us for quite some time.

Another example of analysis regarding the "impossible situation" which Ben Bernanke is in can be found in the following article by Mark Gilbert of Bloomberg which was actually written in 2007 before the housing bubble had burst: [18]

> Evidence is building that the U.S. economy is slowing sufficiently to warrant a soothing reduction in interest rates from the Federal Reserve. That poses an interesting dilemma for Fed Chairman Ben Bernanke.
>
> Cut too soon, and he will stand accused of ignoring inflation in an attempt to rescue the housing market. Leave it too late, and he risks tainting his second anniversary at the helm of the world's biggest economy by overseeing a recession.
>
> All four legs of the U.S. housing market are wobbling precariously. The mortgage lenders who funded the boom are going bust or shutting up shop. The homebuilders who slapped together the bricks and mortar are seeing their earnings plummet. The financial alchemy used to repackage home loans into tradable securities is starting to unravel.

> Targeting asset prices is anathema to the current generation of monetary-policy guardians, who invoke the risk of moral hazard – the danger that investors will throw caution to the wind in the belief that central banks will always bail out their risky adventures by making money cheaper.
>
> "I do want to emphasize that we have not shifted away from an inflation bias," Bernanke told Congress. As the crisis engulfing the subprime mortgage market worsens and the contagion threatens the wider U.S. economy, though, *the Fed chief may find he's damned if he does cut, damned if he doesn't.*

One more example of the possibility of a no-win dilemma for Fed policy is revealed in this different perspective on the predicament that Bernanke faces. The following extract comes from an article by Lawrence B. Lindsey published in the *Wall Street Journal* in May 2011: [19]

> Right now, thanks in large part to Federal Reserve policy, Uncle Sam can borrow at an average cost of just 2.5 percent. The average borrowing cost over the last three decades was 5.7 percent. Our debt is now $14 trillion and scheduled to grow to $25 trillion by the end of the decade. If interest rates normalize over that period the added interest costs in 2021 alone will be $800 billion—more than 20 times the mere $37 billion in budget cuts that tore up Congress in March. It would take virtually all of the cuts in the Ryan budget just to cover that added interest, much less to start bringing down the national debt. *Unfortunately, the Fed is now in a fiscal box.* A normalization of interest rates would break the Treasury. *Hence, a normalization of rates really can't happen—we're stuck in a world in which the Fed must keep rates artificially low in order to prevent a budget disaster.*

The language used is slightly different in the above article – "the Fed is now in a fiscal box" but the nature of the impossibility of resolving matters in a manner which is not self-defeating is implicit in this observation.

I suggest that the fact that many commentators are resorting to language which expresses the view that there is a no-win prospect for Fed policy, while it may ultimately prove to be faulty, does capture a meme which is germinating not just within the blogosphere but amongst financial professionals and investors in general. It is not so much the question of whether or not there is a win-win solution to the problems which have been articulated in the above citations – one can be doubtful but that remains to be seen – rather it is the perception that there may not be a politically plausible solution. It is the lack of a palatable solution which creates the conditions of a double bind and the bipolar response.

As a final example of reference to impossible dilemmas and this time within the Eurozone the author of this piece makes reference to "a bank-fiscal twin bind": [20]

> The arithmetic of debt deflation is relentless. High real interest rates deflate asset prices, but bank liabilities in the form of deposits are fixed nominally. The pressure is on European bank balance sheets. The banks are in a bind because they hold a lot of European sovereign debt, which is deflating in value as real interest rates rise. The European problem is a bank-fiscal twin bind in which the governments have to bail out the banks, while their own fiscal debt overhang is the root of further deflation.

The reason to absorb these citations is that they are expressing a common set of problems which have arisen in the aftermath of the global crisis. There is an old joke regarding the naïve person who remarks "One day I am going to borrow enough money to get myself completely out of debt." Of course the self-referential and paradoxical nature of this utterance is obvious. But what if the person is not naïve but is actually a macro-economist who under admittedly a crude interpretation of the need for constant stimulus and public deficits to overcome a debt deflationary spiral makes statements that to the logic seeking mind seem self-contradictory.

The essence of a paradoxical remark is that it is irresolvable without apparent contradiction. Philosophy is replete with examples of paradoxes which range from the classic paradox of Zeno to some of the more enigmatic examples from Bertrand Russell. [21] I shall not repeat the famous paradox of the tortoise and the hare but one of the more puzzling and bewildering examples known as the barber paradox is attributed to the philosopher/mathematician Bertrand Russell and runs as follows. One is asked us to consider the following statement: In a village, the barber shaves everyone who does not shave himself, but no one else. The question that is embedded within the paradox is this: Who shaves the barber? *No matter how we try to answer this question, we get into trouble.* Expressed differently we are in a bind and if we persist in trying to unravel the paradox, rather than seeing it as an amusing artifice, we could find ourselves, metaphorically speaking, in danger of slipping over the edge.

Consider further the following situation. If someone says, "I am lying," how can this be correctly understood? The paradox, which will lead to a kind of mental knot, is that the statement "I am lying" is false if it is true. The command "Don't follow this command!" is another example. However you interpret this statement seems to violate the command. In order to obey it you must disobey it, but in disobeying it, you seem to obey it. Yet one further example is expressed in the following sign where the paradox speaks for itself.

One of the more radical contentions of this book is that many of the situations which confront us in the realms of contemporary finance are essentially in the form of irresolvable dilemmas and conflicts. They bring on the kind of cognitive dissonance which is analogous to the contemplation of a paradox or a catch 22 predicament. Whilst we can find amusement in the contrived paradoxes just outlined it is far less amusing to contemplate different real world situations with regard to the inherently contradictory choices faced within the Eurozone outlined in Chapter 11, the dilemma faced by central banks that they are trying to cure a patient from addiction to debt by prescribing more debt, and the fact that the only way of exiting from the damaging nature of bubble/bust cycles is to create the conditions for a new bubble.

15.3 PATIENCE AND INVESTMENT DECISION MAKING

The final section of this chapter will consider the nature of maturity transformation from a slightly alternative perspective to that which was considered in Chapter 14. Within the context of the discussion above regarding the psychological and emotional dimension to investor behavior it will be useful to examine briefly another motivation which can be explained within the context of interval confidence, but this time with reference to the patience or impatience of an investor.

The standard text book rationale for maturity transformation, and its social and economic value, is that it enables well-capitalized institutions which, *under normal market conditions*, have strategies for managing their assets and liabilities to provide financing for less well-capitalized individuals and firms to engage in activities and enterprises where the long-term commitments being made extend beyond their ability to fund them out of current income or cash flows.

There is a different perspective that could be created for the role of the kind of financial intermediation that is described in the preceding paragraph. Suppose that one wants to account for the different manner in which certain investors have a propensity to hold investments for the long term – often called a buy and hold strategy – whereas others are much less patient and would typically have a holding period horizon of a few hours or days rather than a few years. There are many permutations that could be created from such different stances and I shall only focus on one which brings out the nature of the patient versus the impatient investor. One of the reasons for so doing is that in the discussion of market micro-structure, which was the subject matter of Chapter 4, some have characterized the distinction between the informed and uninformed traders as being one also of patient and impatient investors or traders. To conflate the separate issues may seem disingenuous but there is evidence, as hopefully will become apparent, that the personality characteristics of the hypothetical informed and patient investors are in marked contrast to those of the hypothetical uninformed and impatient investors. This does not have to be the case because the essential difference in the ecology of the market place may rest much more on the access to capital and the asymmetry of information than on anything to do with patience. But to slightly reformulate the model presented in Chapter 4 it is not difficult to imagine that that one tier of a market ecology consists of principals, not only with more capital but also with longer time frames for holding assets and who are applying a lower discount rate to future cash flows. They will be prepared to take into inventory those assets which have fallen out of favor and which more impatient holders of such assets are either keen to disgorge or who maybe have limited capital or are meeting margin calls. The essential element in this somewhat crude characterization has to do with the extent to which different personality types discount the value of stock and future cash flows.

Highly recommended in this regard is some research undertaken by Ersner-Hershfield et al. (2009). [22] The observed fact that different individuals have very different approaches to inter-temporal discounting suggests that this must be connected with different psychological profiles of individuals. Their research conducted with students at the New York University Stern School of Business, shows that those individuals who have the *most connected view of themselves* both in the present and in the future are likely to be more patient and less willing to discount future flows:

> In our view, a person values future outcomes in proportion to how much she feels, at that moment, that the current self's important psychological characteristics will persist in the future self. When people feel highly connected to the future self, benefits received by the future self are valued much as if they were received by the present self. However, when a discontinuity in identity is perceived, deferred benefits accrue to a disconnected future self (i.e., a somewhat different person), and this outcome is valued less than having those benefits consumed by the present self.
>
> Thus, when people are faced with explicit inter-temporal tradeoffs, their allocations of benefits to the future selves are driven, in part, by how psychologically connected they feel to those future selves. As a result, decisions that might appear short-sighted (i.e. decisions characterized by a low decision weight on future consequences or an inflated discount rate) may instead merely reflect this notion of inter-temporal selfishness – an unwillingness to share resources with a future self who is evaluated to be substantially different from the current self.

The following extract in particular deserves attention as it expresses the degree to which a "joined up" and stable view of self-evolution – perhaps not so readily available to those who have become pessimistic in a post-GFC world – is likely to encourage an outlook with less inter-temporal discounting:

> . . . those people for whom thinking about the current self most resembled thinking about the future self (in terms of the neural activation elicited) tended to show less devaluation of monetary rewards over time . . . there is also present evidence that people who report having accrued greater total assets – more money invested in a home, in securities, in other material goods, and in the bank – tended to rate themselves as more similar to who they would be in 10 years than people who had fewer assets. These findings provide initial evidence that individual differences in perceived future self-continuity can promote valuation of future rewards. Specifically, the extent to which individuals perceive the present self as similar to a future self is associated with less discounting of future rewards in the laboratory and greater financial assets in the real world. From a pragmatic standpoint, enhancing future self-continuity might encourage people to save for the future. From a philosophical standpoint, individuals who see their future selves as similar may be more likely to sacrifice present pleasure for the benefit of that potential person.

Before concluding these remarks on different psychological profiles it is also worth briefly mentioning some other research which shows that people who discount the future quite heavily appear to have a higher predisposition to becoming drug users and compulsive gamblers (the latter is probably not too surprising). [23] Intriguing as this research is it is possible to ask the following question: Which way round is the causation process? For example does one who is predisposed toward severe discounting of the future, i.e. present biased and/or impatient, have a higher likelihood of becoming a gambler or drug user? Or is the causation process the other way around?

Finally as a parting shot on this conjectural chapter the question could be asked whether another contributory factor leading to the kind of binary investment behavior discussed throughout this book could also be that there are far fewer patient investors in today's markets. In general terms, the buy and hold approach has not been rewarding for many long-term investors and asset managers. Certainly for most passive investors in North American and Western European equities, the returns generated for a buy and hold approach with respect to the majority of 10-year holding periods since the late 1990s would have failed to keep pace with inflation. [24]

ENDNOTES

1. Menzie Chin, The Role of Reality in Prices, *New York Times*, April 4, 2012.

   Menzie Chin is professor of public affairs and economics at the University of Wisconsin, http://www.nytimes.com/roomfordebate/2012/04/01/how-to-teach-economics-after-the-financial-crisis/the-role-of-reality-in-prices.
2. The Bureau of Labor Statistics of the U.S. Department of Labor is the principal Federal agency responsible for measuring labor market activity, working conditions, and price changes in the economy. Its mission is to collect, analyze, and disseminate essential economic information to support public and private decision-making, http://www.bls.gov/.
3. Technical Information: Estimation Methods for Business Births and Deaths, Bureau of Labor Statistics:

   > The Current Employment Statistics (CES) program, also known as the payroll survey, produces nonfarm employment, hours, and earnings series each month based on a monthly sample of nearly 400,000 business establishments nationwide.

Why CES uses non-sample methods to account for business births and deaths – Although the CES sample is very large and follows standard design principles, it alone is not sufficient for estimating the total employment level because each month new firms generate employment that cannot be captured through the sample. There is an unavoidable lag between a firm opening for business and its appearance on the CES sample frame. The sample frame is built from Unemployment Insurance (UI) quarterly tax records. These records cover virtually all U.S. employers and include business births, but they only become available for updating the CES sampling frame 7–9 months after the reference month. After the births appear on the frame, there is also time required for sampling, contacting and soliciting cooperation from the firm, and verifying the initial data provided. In general, the CES can not sample and begin to collect data from new firms until they are at least a year old.

There is a parallel though somewhat different issue in capturing employment loss from business deaths through monthly sample collection. Businesses that have closed are less likely to respond to the survey and data collectors may not be able to ascertain until after the monthly collection period that firms have in fact gone out of business. As with business births, hard information on business deaths eventually becomes available from the lagged UI tax records.

Difficulty in capturing information from business birth and death units is not unique to the CES; virtually all current business surveys face these limitations. Unlike many surveys, CES adjusts for these limitations explicitly, using a statistical modeling technique. Other surveys that do not explicitly adjust for business births and deaths are implicitly using the continuing sample units to represent birth and death units. This approach is viable when the primary characteristic of interest is an average measure of some type. However, because the goal of the CES program is to estimate an employment total each month and business births and deaths are important components contributing to these totals, CES uses a model-based adjustment in conjunction with the sample. Without the birth/death model-based adjustment, the CES nonfarm payroll employment estimates would be considerably less accurate.

http://www.bls.gov/ces/cesbdtech.htm.

4. According to the St Louis Federal Reserve the Total Private Non-Farm Payroll in December 2000 was 111.57 million and in September 2012 was 111.4 million.

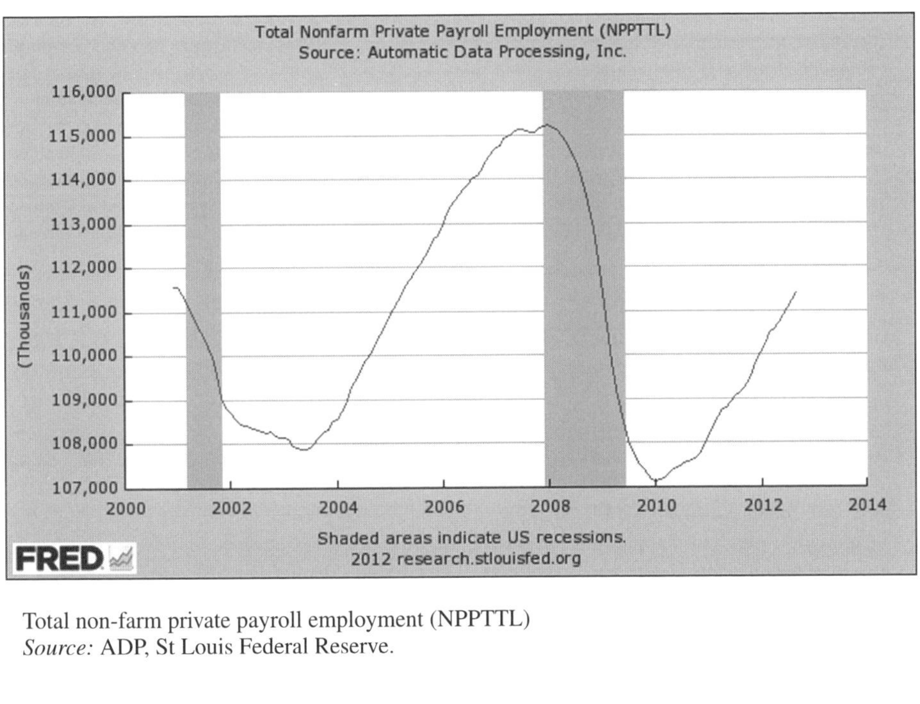

Total non-farm private payroll employment (NPPTTL)
Source: ADP, St Louis Federal Reserve.

5. For example the S&P 500 closed at 1165 on May 5, 2010 and on July 2, 2010 it closed at 1022, registering a drop of 13% in less than two months. The Nasdaq 100 Index closed at 1958 on May 5, 2010 and at 1728 on July 2, 2012. The Nikkei 225 closed at 10 696 on May 6, 2010 and closed at 8824 on August 31, 2010, registering a drop of almost 18% in less than three months.
6. Kissinger conducted foreign policy and diplomacy during his tenure as US Secretary of State under both Presidents Nixon and Ford in the 1970s. Heinz Alfred "Henry" Kissinger (born May 27, 1923) is a German-born American writer, political scientist, diplomat, and businessman. A recipient of the Nobel Peace Prize, he served as National Security Advisor and later concurrently as Secretary of State in the administrations of Presidents Richard Nixon and Gerald Ford. After his term, his opinion was still sought by many subsequent presidents and many world leaders.
7. Perry Mehrling is Senior Advisor at the Institute for New Economic Thinking, Professor of Economics, at Barnard and has also held visiting positions at the Sloan School of Management at MIT, and at Boston University.

   A video of the opening session of the INET Conference in Berlin 2010 can be found at the following link: http://ineteconomics.org/conference/berlin/george-soros-challenging-foundation.
8. David Tuckett is Professor in the Psychoanalysis Unit, Research Department of Clinical, Educational and Health Psychology, University College London:

   > Professor David Tuckett has been awarded nearly $250,000 to research the role of emotions in economics. The Institute for New Economic Thinking (INET) grant will enable Professor Tuckett to examine how unconscious processes can cause swings in the financial markets.
   >
   > The research, which will take place over 2.5 years, will be based on interdisciplinary insights into the social and psychological context that trading financial assets create and in which decisions are made.
   >
   > In 2006 David Tuckett was awarded a Leverhulme Senior Research fellowship to conduct a Psychoanalytic Study of Investments. The study aimed to provide a description of the work of asset fund portfolio managers and the processes of thinking and judgment they bring to their work. An interview method was developed to research how implicit unconscious theories and emotions might enter into and influence the working methods and judgments of fund managers. It was hoped that insights would assist fund managers in reflecting on their task and provide an indication of the future value of this combination of interdisciplinary work for the further understanding of financial markets, facilitating the development of appropriate methodologies to enable any desirable future investigation. Work began at the end of September 2006 and interviewing proper began in Boston in January continuing until the end of August. 52 managers eventually took part working for 16 of the world's leading investment houses. They were based in Boston, Edinburgh, Paris, Philadelphia, New Jersey, New York, London and Singapore and represent a global sample.

9. Minding the Markets: An Emotional Finance View of Financial Instability, David Tuckett, Palgrave Macmillan (July, 2011).
10. From the above book: http://www.huffingtonpost.com/dr-prudence-l-gourguechon/fantastic-objects-excited_b_988770.html.
11. Emotional Finance: Understanding what drives investors which appeared in the Autumn 2007 edition of *Professional Investor*, http://www.ucl.ac.uk/psychoanalysis/unit-staff/pi_emotional_finance_article_%2009_07.pdf.
12. The quotation was found at the following website: http://www.toxicdrums.com/double-bind.html.
13. Gregory Bateson (1904–1980) was an anthropologist, social scientist, linguist, and cyberneticist who developed an inter-disciplinary approach to epistemology and the understanding of human behaviour. His views regarding the "functioning" of the human mind were much influenced by concepts from

communications and systems theories. Two of his most influential books were *Steps to an Ecology of Mind* (1972) and *Mind and Nature* (1979).

14. Most practitioners in the psychiatric profession are no longer convinced of the usefulness of the double bind theory with regard to understanding the origins, or aiding in the treatment, of schizophrenia. An important contribution leading to the diminished importance of Bateson's work was the publication of *Schizophrenia Genesis: The Origins of Madness*, by Iriving Gottesman (W. H. Freeman 1st edn, September 15, 1990).
15. Charles Hugh Smith, Euro Double-Bind: Both Paths Lead to Disintegration, Of Two Minds, November 2011, http://www.oftwominds.com/blognov11/EU-double-bind11-11.html.
16. Clive Corcoran, Calling Dr. Bernanke: Market Now Exhibiting Split Personality, Seeking Alpha, May 2, 2009, http://seekingalpha.com/article/134764-calling-dr-bernanke-market-now-exhibiting-split-personality.
17. Ben Bernanke gave a speech on October 15, 2010 in which he stated that "[t]he FOMC is prepared to provide additional accommodation if needed to support the economic recovery, and to return inflation, over time, to levels consistent with our mandate." *Monetary Policy Objectives and Tools in a Low-Inflation Environment*, speech given at the Revisiting Monetary Policy in a Low-Inflation Environment Conference, Federal Reserve Bank of Boston, Boston, Massachusetts, http://www.federalreserve.gov/newsevents/speech/bernanke20101015a.htm.

    He has also on other occasions suggested that higher equity prices – asset inflation – is one of the goals of a very loose monetary policy.
18. Mark Gilbert, Fed Risks Moral Hazard as Housing Market Melts, Bloomberg, March 29, 2007, http://www.bloomberg.com/apps/news?pid=newsarchive&refer=columnist_gilbert&sid=apKbQNSz4iXs
19. Lawrence B. Lindsey, The Sharp Pencil Test: Time for a real growth agenda, June 13, 2011, http://www.weeklystandard.com/keyword/Sharp-Pencil-Test.

    Also republished in the *Wall Street Journal* and can be found at the following: http://online.wsj.com/article/SB10001424052702304259304576379244129176386.html.
20. Andrew Sheng, The Battle for Europe: The State versus the Market, December 13, 2011, http://www.fungglobalinstitute.org/index.php?option=com_zrticles&id=212&view=publication.
21. For a useful discussion of the barber paradox and how it is an example of Russell's difficulties with naïve set theory the reader may wish to look at the following: http://www.suitcaseofdreams.net/Paradox_Russell.htm.

> The paradox considers a town with a male barber who shaves all and only those men who do not shave themselves.
>
> The question is: Who shaves the barber?
>
> When one thinks about whether the barber should shave himself or not, the paradox begins to emerge.
>
> If the barber does not shave himself, according to the rule he must shave himself.
>
> If he does shave himself, according to the rule he will not shave himself.
>
> Russell's paradox: The set M is the set of all sets that do not contain themselves as members. Does M contain itself?
>
> If it does, it is not a member of M according to the definition.
>
> If it does not, then it has to be a member of M, again according to the definition of M.
>
> Therefore, the statements "M is a member of M" and "M is not a member of M" both lead to contradictions.
>
> The paradox was discovered by Bertrand Russell in 1901. The paradox arises within naive set theory. It showed that naive set theory (set theory as it was used by Georg Cantor and Gottlob Frege) contained contradictions. After the discovery of the paradox, it becomes clear that naive set theory must be replaced by something in which the paradoxes can't arise.

22. Ersner-Hershfield et al., Don't Stop Thinking about Tomorrow: Individual differences in future self-continuity account for saving (2009) 4(4) *Judgment and Decision Making*, http://people.stern.nyu.edu/hhershfi/resources/Research/2009-Ersner-Hershfield.pdf.
23. See also Bartels and Urminsky, On Inter-temporal Selfishness: The Perceived Instability of Identity Underlies Impatient Consumption, https://marketing.wharton.upenn.edu/mktg/assets/File/Bartels-Job%20Paper%202%20of%202.pdf.

    The authors make the following pertinent observations:

> The degree of concern one has for one's future self should be scaled by the degree of "psychological connectedness" – overlap in personality, temperament, major likes and dislikes, beliefs, values, ambitions, life goals, ideals, and so on – held between one's current and future self.
>
> In our view, the greater the perceived connectedness to the future self, the greater people's willingness to defer benefits to the future self, all else equal. Conversely, feeling disconnected from the future self will undercut the general underlying motivation to preserve resources for the future self, resulting in a reduction in patience that is distinct from other factors which affect valuations of present and future outcomes.

24. Floyd Norris, A 10-Year Stretch That's Worse Than It Looks, *New York Times*, February 6, 2009.

> In the last 82 years – the history of the Standard & Poor's 500 – the stock market has been through one Great Depression and numerous recessions. It has experienced bubbles and busts, bull markets and bear markets.
>
> But it has never seen a 10-year stretch as bad as the one that ended last month.
>
> Over the 10 years through January, an investor holding the stocks in the S.& P's 500-stock index, and reinvesting the dividends, would have lost about 5.1 percent a year after adjusting for inflation, as is shown in the accompanying chart.

See also Floyd Norris, A Historical Cycle Bodes Ill for the Markets, *New York Times*, January 7, 2012:

> At the turn of the last century, it was widely accepted that American stocks were virtually certain to be good long-term investments. Now, far fewer people are confident of that.
>
> A major reason for the earlier confidence was that in the 15 years from the end of 1984 through the end of 1999, the total return of the Standard & Poor's 500-stock index was more than 740 percent, even after adjusting for inflation. That amounted to a compound annual real return of more than 15 percent.
>
> At the end of 2011, by contrast, the 15-year return – from the end of 1996 – was just 3 percent. And most of those gains came in the first three years of the period. Since the end of 1999, the stock market has not come close to keeping up with inflation.

http://www.nytimes.com/2012/01/07/business/economy/a-historical-cycle-bodes-ill-for-the-markets.html.

See also Is the Buy & Hold Stock Strategy Officially Dead? CNBC.com: http://finance.yahoo.com/news/buy-hold-stock-strategy-officially-182631835.html:

"I speak with retail investors every day and I can tell you that more than ever, they believe that the stock market is a casino for the large and well-connected investors," said Mitch Goldberg, ClientFirst Strategy in Woodbury, NY. "Of course, different investment styles go in and out of favor every so often, so to be a long term investor, you'd need a ton of patience and very thick skin. Eventually, the Graham and Buffett way will be back in favor and I think that is what will encourage the retail investor to step back into the market."

16

Adjusting to More Correlated Financial Markets

The previous chapter contained some provocative views as to the nature of the emotional and cognitive kinds of dissonance which manifest themselves in the day to day gyrations of modern markets. The bipolarity of the risk on/risk off paradigm can be seen at the surface level as the outcome of several empirically observable developments in the financial world following the global financial crisis. Undoubtedly the directly observable changes in market behavior are a large part of the explanation for the increased correlations, greater outlier risks, and the binary risk on/risk off paradigm. Much of the evidence presented in this book – the detailed and forensic analysis of price developments and the review of changes in market microstructure – have focused on these direct observables.

A quick summary of the most pertinent observables in financial markets would have to include the following: lack of institutional participation as reflected in the decline in the volume of real trading on exchanges as contrasted with the now almost ubiquitous presence of algorithmic "churn"; the fact that monetary policy has been "unorthodox" for several years; the anxieties regarding a potential breakup of the Eurozone; the growing importance of China in a globalized economy; and the prevalence of highly coordinated and correlation based trading strategies in many markets have all been featured prominently in the discussion.

The more conjectural underpinnings to the new characteristics in markets (or at least to old characteristics but now being expressed in more extreme variations) were touched on in Chapter 15. In that chapter we looked at the current difficulties more from a psychoanalytical perspective, in which traders and investors have to resolve ambiguities and self-contradictory messages being conveyed either directly by policy makers and central bankers, or indirectly by the information conveyed from actual price patterns and the risk on/risk off dynamics of price discovery. The difficulty in resolving conflicting policy objectives and the dilemmas faced by central bankers could both be a cause of a more binary pattern to price discovery and also a symptom of the kind of emotional and cognitive dissonances that have been discussed. That these ideas are conjectural should not be taken *per se* as undermining their validity if they have increased explanatory power in accounting for the very difficult circumstances and choices which, it is widely agreed, face all of us – investors and citizens – in the coming years.

Central bankers themselves are faced with almost impossible dilemmas where there is a real possibility that, even with the most careful regard to not making any missteps, their decisions *might* ultimately lead to at best a quandary and at worst a no-win situation. Such a bleak scenario could come about as a result of growing civil unrest, a collapse in the confidence of fiat currencies, and rampant inflation, all of which could be well beyond the tipping point for even the most resilient and patient investors.

One of the dilemmas faced by central bankers is best captured by the question: what will be their exit strategy from what has been christened ZIRP or a persistent zero interest rate policy? Ben Bernanke alluded to an exit strategy several times in testimony to the US Senate in 2010 when outlining the rationale for quantitative easing. It is interesting to note that in the wake of the first round of QE he felt the need to alleviate potential criticism that the inevitable expansion of the Federal Reserve balance sheet could reach levels where the institution's credibility was at stake. Here are his final remarks for the speech he prepared as testimony to Congress in February 2010: [1]

> The economy continues to require the support of accommodative monetary policies. However, we have been working to ensure that we have the tools to reverse, at the appropriate time, the currently very high degree of monetary stimulus. We have full confidence that, when the time comes, we will be ready to do so.

It is notable that, in the two years since this testimony was prepared, Bernanke rarely mentions an exit strategy as that could spook markets. In fact there has been a rather notable shift away from a focus on an exit strategy to one of prolongation of the super accommodative monetary; indeed his expressed intention has been one of trying to encourage some degree of asset price inflation. [2]

Constructive ambiguity has a role to play in diplomacy and commercial negotiations and also, now that sufficient time has elapsed from the panic that came from contemplating a collapse of the banking system in late 2008, it may be a required policy stance in maintaining and promoting the degree of systemic liquidity required to keep markets functioning properly. But having had a glimpse at the abyss there may be, under the surface, a compelling curiosity in the process of price discovery to see just how far markets can be trusted again. As discussed in Chapter 11 with regard to the critical flaws in the Eurozone's organizational architecture and legal framework, the suggestion was made that traders and investors may ultimately want to put to the test the question of whether the absence of joint responsibility for the huge financings being undertaken by the ECB, EFSF, ESM, and whatever other acronym bearing bodies come on the playing field, could mean that their guarantees should not be relied upon. Would Germany be prepared to underwrite the entire obligations of a much enlarged ECB balance sheet? In the game of chicken being played out between the various constituencies that want complete mutualization of the debt obligations of the EZ states, and the Bundesbank on the opposing side, will Germany ultimately blink first? Indeed, does Germany even have the wherewithal to back stop the whole thing? And would the Federal Reserve be willing (able) to step in and contain the systemic fallout if the Eurozone begins to unravel? These questions are posed as a way of sharpening the focus on some very hard decisions that will almost certainly need to be addressed in the foreseeable future.

One of the most notable characteristics about day to day price discovery in markets is that traders are constantly testing price levels for support and resistance, and in the constant battle between bulls and bears there is continual probing for stop losses set by adversaries. In addition to their role in allocating capital to enterprises, the business of markets is to operate on the frontiers of pricing, to go where prices have not gone before, to find just how far a certain price can be pushed (in either direction). With questions of solvency hanging over so many financial intermediaries and, as previously observed, the unwillingness of investors to tolerate any kind of constructive ambiguity with respect to questions regarding solvency, it is not surprising that traders and investors will want to test and retest any doubts about the financial soundness of a potential counter-party – including the ultimate counter-parties which are the central banks.

Much of the time, during non-critical phases, participants in financial markets will tolerate the ambiguities in the information provided by corporate executives, central bankers, and policy makers. This will be considered as "spin" by many and for others it will contribute to the background "noise" which will encourage the basic disagreements about price and value amongst traders and investors which promote market liquidity. The adversarial dimension to investment decision making is precisely what allows for the kind of two-way traffic and depth to a market which allows maturity transformation to take place smoothly and for markets to perform their necessary functions. In "normal" circumstances there is no urgent demand for transparency or unequivocal clarification of systemic information. Risk appetites and complacency levels are relatively high.

From time to time, when a disruptive event occurs or when markets have moved into a critical phase (e.g. unexpected macro-economic developments or a major default), market participants will immediately press for disambiguation on as many fronts as possible. Risk aversion moves to center stage, equivocation is rejected and ignored, and the fractiousness which facilitates liquidity is replaced by a coherent viewpoint which results in markets becoming precariously unbalanced and lopsided with a subsequent (and sudden) drop in liquidity.

The longer the demand for disambiguation goes on, without being satisfied by further recitals from policy makers of the standard mantras that can be characterized by such comments as "the fundamentals are sound" and "this is a liquidity issue rather than a solvency issue," the greater is the risk of systemic meltdown and a complete collapse in liquidity. Ironically the comment that "this is a liquidity issue not a solvency issue" is actually correct but not in the way the remark was intended. As seen at the height of the 2008 crisis market participants did not need to be reminded that there was "a liquidity issue." The scope of the crisis had moved far beyond any question marks concerning solvency of individual firms rather there was a pervasive fear that the money markets were dysfunctional and in danger of a meltdown. The inability to conduct almost any kind of interval financing and normal financial mediation threw into question the maturity transformation framework without which the banking and credit system would collapse.

In the extreme circumstances of 2008 where markets were not functioning and there were no bids from the private sector in most markets and only private sellers there was only one solution: the sometimes frantic requirement from the private sector to be sellers could only be matched by public sector bids (i.e. bailouts)

Systemic financial risk can be viewed, from the perspective of economic theory, as a "negative externality." A negative externality occurs when a transaction between two parties results in costs which accrue, in part, to one or more third parties, and most pertinently to society as a whole. In other words, the total cost of a decision by a firm is not borne by that firm, but rather in part by another party, and in the current context, inter-generational taxpayers.

Negative externalities are sometimes referred to as local or neighborhood costs – especially in cases where the externality is most impactful to those who are geographically proximate to the activity or transaction. The classic example of a negative externality is pollution, and public policy eventually took on board the fact that the costs of cleaning up the mess left by the polluters should be borne by those same polluters. As a society we have yet to take on board the fact that the costs of cleaning up the mess left by the financial crisis should be borne by those most responsible. This has nothing to do with attributing blame or "banker bashing," it is simply applying the symmetrical notion that there are consequences, intended and otherwise, to all human activity and the sanest way to ensure that people act with responsibility is to make each of us accountable for the consequences of our actions.

The existence of a negative externality, and its magnitude, may be known at the time or it may only become apparent after the fact. Surely one of the lessons that should be learned in the aftermath of the financial crisis of 2008 is that the negative externalities were entirely neglected and that their colossal magnitude was system threatening. Ironically, financial intermediary activities which increase the risk of financial distress, instability, and crisis may actually benefit a financial firm. As one rather perceptive commentator has observed "[t]he S&L Crisis of 1989 taught firms about the *taxpayer put* to protect firms from systemic risk but didn't teach the taxpayers anything." [3]

We should have learned that increased systemic risk is potentially costly to other firms, consumers, and the economy and financial markets at large. The growing acceptance of the external costs of a taxpayer funded safety net for the financial system were examined previously in Chapter 10 when the question was put by the editors at Bloomberg.com to Jamie Dimon in an article entitled "Dear Mr. Dimon, Is Your Bank Getting Corporate Welfare?" [4] To quote again just briefly from that article, the following is particularly relevant to the current discussion:

> JPMorgan receives a government subsidy worth about $14 billion a year, according to research published by the International Monetary Fund and our own analysis of bank balance sheets. The money helps the bank pay big salaries and bonuses. *More important, it distorts markets, fueling crises such as the recent subprime-lending disaster and the sovereign-debt debacle that is now threatening to destroy the euro and sink the global economy.*

The failure to have moved on a faster track to price in the negative externalities of systemic risk, four years after the events of the second half of 2008, is surely an example of extreme myopia or negligence on the part of policy makers and regulators. It has taken a long time but those industrial companies, at least those operating in the developed world, responsible for polluting the environment are now required to pay for their negative externalities. Should not the systemically important financial institutions (SIFIs), [5] also be required to recognize that the costs of bailouts (not even considering the lost GDP, the costs of welfare programs, and the human capital costs resulting from the economic fallout of the GFC), should be included as part of their cost of business?

The Financial Stability Board (FSB), which is associated with the Bank for International Settlements in Basel, has been established to coordinate at the international level the work of national financial authorities and international standard setting bodies and to develop and promote the implementation of effective regulatory, supervisory, and other financial sector policies. G20 leaders at recent meetings held requested from the Financial Stability Board a policy framework to address the systemic and moral hazard risks associated with SIFIs: [6] In the stated objectives of the FSB the following observations regarding its mandate are worth reciting:

> SIFIs are financial institutions whose distress or disorderly failure, because of their size, complexity and systemic interconnectedness, would cause significant disruption to the wider financial system and economic activity. To avoid this outcome, authorities have all too frequently had no choice but to forestall the failure of such institutions through public solvency support. As underscored by this crisis, this has deleterious consequences for private incentives and for public finances.

In its initial report the FSB states that

> [a]ddressing the "too-big-to-fail" problem requires a multipronged and integrated set of policies. Accordingly, the policy measures we have agreed comprise:
>
> iii) Requirements for banks determined to be globally systemically important to have additional loss absorption capacity tailored to the impact of their default, rising from 1% to 2.5% of risk-weighted assets (with an empty bucket of 3.5% to discourage further systemicness), to be met with common equity;
>
> iv) More intensive and effective supervision of all SIFIs, including through stronger supervisory mandates, resources and powers, and higher supervisory expectations for risk management functions, data aggregation capabilities, risk governance and internal controls.

The report also contains the statement that "[f]ull implementation is targeted for 2019."

On such a complacent timeline one has to hope that financial markets will cooperate until the systemic risk safety net has been properly installed.

16.1 SOME FINAL MUSINGS ON MARKETS AND MAYHEM

Wealth can expand and contract based upon human subjectivity ... there are no real world constraints on either process. The extremities or outliers of asset returns reflect the gestalt switches from mania to depression which are deeply ingrained in human consciousness as are other powerful drivers of binary behavior ... fear and greed. These ultimately provide the fuel for the bubble and bust dynamo emanating from the animal spirits which drives economic enterprise.

In principle there would not appear to be any constraints as to how far outliers can go, or how extreme financial mishaps may become. In slightly different terms, from an *a priori* perspective, there are no bounds as to how large a bubble can be blown up and how deep the subsequent collapse may go. Recognition of this deeply disturbing predicament which underlines the bubble/bust dialectic which is inherent in our *animal spirits* should temper all attempts to precisely quantify investment risk. In a worst case scenario, as dominoes cascade and the joint probability of defaults becomes nonlinear, the ultimate financial meltdown scenario of systemic collapse should not be underestimated.

One of the big differences between mainstream economic thinking and the more innovative approaches that were discussed in Chapter 10 is that the current orthodoxy relies a lot on exogenous causes to explain abnormal disequilibrating behavior. This indirectly has, as a consequence, the placing of the burden of accountability on wildcards, rogue events, and the *deus ex machina.* In turn this allows for victimhood and scapegoating. It also has, as a by-product, the convenience of allowing policy makers and economists to sidestep accountability by being able to "blame" adverse outcomes on external and unpredictable "shocks."

By seeing bubbles and busts as endogenous which is very much in alignment with the new consensus that is emerging and inspired by the writings of both Hyman Minsky and Keynes, the burden of accountability is placed squarely on the manner in which participants act within the financial/economic system itself. There is no room for victimhood or scapegoating and policy makers and economic principals should be held far more accountable for mishaps and failure to act when asset prices have detached from more sustainable levels.

Transferring miscalculations of risk made by the private sector banks to public balance sheets provides the only safety net from a complete collective "nervous breakdown." When critical minds demand disambiguation the only rescue that seems to have been devised by central bankers and regulators is to flood the financial system with liquidity or, to use a more modern metaphor, to build a "firewall." The critical problem is that whilst this liquidity is in the form of a debt, requiring repayment either within the time frame of the current generation, or more likely an inter-generational time frame, there has been no real resolution to the damage done by the original miscalculations. The only feasible solution is to recognize that the consequences of miscalculations made by private sector banks should result in their failure and a full blown participation by all stake holders in taking responsibility for their miscalculation.

As earlier discussions have revealed, the asymmetry of private gain and public pain is really symptomatic of a deeper asymmetry between the notion that equity holders are fully liable when things go wrong whereas creditors and owners of debt instruments are protected. Once there is a wider realization of the full implications of the manner in which rentiers are subsidized through the various safety nets provided at public expense there needs to a much greater readiness to write down the obligations incurred by all those engaged in enterprise. Only when such write downs become public policy will markets be able to clear properly, and only then will asset valuations return to a level at which they are affordable to most. Under the current misguided financial regime, just the converse is the case where they are becoming even less affordable to an increasingly impoverished household sector in the world's developed economies.

The misguided financial regime to which I just referred can be characterized in the following schematic:

- Safety nets for private banks, rentiers, and debt holders enable them to take risks without doing adequate due diligence.
- The true cost of this failure to accept consequences of their miscalculations of risk is externalized through the provision of safety nets, subsidies, and regulatory loopholes.
- Public balance sheets become inter-generational liabilities.
- A flawed set of concepts from macro-economic theory sees such risk miscalculations as the result of exogenous shocks.
- Being able to point to factors that are outside their models enables economists and policy makers to side step responsibility for what are, in most instances, endogenously created financial problems arising from the bubble/bust psychology which is implicit in our animal spirits.
- The exogenous shock model provides perfect alibis to economists, regulators, and bankers.
- While debt obligations remain "sticky" the consequences of the inevitable bursting of bubbles, which are a "fact" of economic life, will be borne disproportionately by those sectors of the economy which are most disadvantaged by the asymmetry of information.
- As the imbalances between the informed and uninformed sectors of the financial markets become even more exaggerated, the kinds of predator/prey dynamics that are embedded within markets, in which the absence of a level playing field deters new entrants to the uninformed tier of markets, will lead to extremely unstable oscillations and disruptions.
- At the extreme, a systemic liquidity breakdown will, to use a metaphor employed earlier in the first chapter, mean that, as with the sinking of the Titanic, even the first class passengers will go down with the ship.

Despite his thoroughgoing analytical tools, which have been embraced as cornerstones in outlines of his theory, Keynes often pointed to the visceral and non-rational elements in human behavior. There is a long philosophical tradition exemplified by David Hume which is essentially anti rationalist and I suspect that Keynes was much influenced by this. [7]

His use of the term "animal spirits" as the unpredictable variable which has to emerge at key inflection points in order to transition, for example, from a liquidity trap – or paradox of thrift – into a period of more sustained growth, is deliberately vague and mysterious as it should be. Two sections from Chapter 12, Section III, of the *General Theory of Employment* regarding the animal spirits seem especially appropriate at this point: [8]

> The outstanding fact is the extreme precariousness of the basis of knowledge on which our estimates of prospective yield have to be made. Our knowledge of the factors which will govern the yield of an investment some years hence is usually very slight and often negligible. If we speak frankly, we have to admit that our basis of knowledge for estimating the yield ten years hence of a railway, a copper mine, a textile factory, the goodwill of a patent medicine, an Atlantic liner, a building in the City of London amounts to little and sometimes to nothing . . .
>
> *Even apart from the instability due to speculation, there is the instability due to the characteristic of human nature that a large proportion of our positive activities depend on spontaneous optimism rather than on a mathematical expectation, whether moral or hedonistic or economic.* Most, probably, of our decisions to do something positive, the full consequences of which will be drawn out over many days to come, can only be taken as a result of animal spirits – of a spontaneous urge to action rather than inaction, and not as the outcome of a weighted average of quantitative benefits multiplied by quantitative probabilities. Enterprise only pretends to itself to be mainly actuated by the statements in its own prospectus, however candid and sincere. Only a little more than an expedition to the South Pole, is it based on an exact calculation of benefits to come. Thus if the animal spirits are dimmed and the spontaneous optimism falters, leaving us to depend on nothing but a mathematical expectation, enterprise will fade and die; – though fears of loss may have a basis no more reasonable than hopes of profit had before.
>
> It is safe to say that enterprise which depends on hopes stretching into the future benefits the community as a whole. But individual initiative will only be adequate when reasonable calculation is supplemented and supported by animal spirits, so that the thought of ultimate loss which often overtakes pioneers, as experience undoubtedly tells us and them, is put aside as a healthy man puts aside the expectation of death.
>
> We should not conclude from this that everything depends on waves of irrational psychology. On the contrary, the state of long-term expectation is often steady, and, even when it is not, the other factors exert their compensating effects. *We are merely reminding ourselves that human decisions affecting the future, whether personal or political or economic, cannot depend on strict mathematical expectation, since the basis for making such calculations does not exist; and that it is our innate urge to activity which makes the wheels go round, our rational selves choosing between the alternatives as best we are able, calculating where we can, but often falling back for our motive on whim or sentiment or chance.*

When reading these profound observations, which were written during the 1930's, one cannot help but feel that they resonate quite strongly with questions relating to our own era. When collateral values are depressed, and when there is a lack of willingness by risk averse investors to accept all but the safest forms of collateral, which are becoming increasingly scarce, no amount of liquidity is going to rejuvenate the animal spirits. These are the underlying conditions for a global depression.

If bubbles followed by bust are an inescapable fact of human nature, and with an economy so mired in debt that the bursting of the next bubble could lead to systemic meltdown, might it not be a good idea to re-examine the unquestioning acceptance of the notion that there should continue to be an asymmetry between equity which is treated rightly as risk capital, and the claims of debt holders which are wrongly considered as sacrosanct?

ENDNOTES

1. Statement by Ben S. Bernanke, Chairman Board of Governors of the Federal Reserve System, prepared for the Committee on Financial Services U.S. House of Representatives, February 10, 2010. The Federal Reserve notes the following:

   > Statement as prepared for delivery. The hearing was postponed due to inclement weather.

   Available online at http://www.federalreserve.gov/newsevents/testimony/bernanke20100210a.htm.

   Bernanke returned to the issue of how the Fed would exit from its super accommodative monetary policy in a speech given at the Economic Club of Indiana on October 1, 2012:

   > With monetary policy being so accommodative now, though, it is not unreasonable to ask whether we are sowing the seeds of future inflation. A related question I sometimes hear, which bears also on the relationship between monetary and fiscal policy, is this: By buying securities, are you "monetizing the debt" – printing money for the government to use – and will that inevitably lead to higher inflation? No, that's not what is happening, and that will not happen. Monetizing the debt means using money creation as a permanent source of financing for government spending. In contrast, we are acquiring Treasury securities on the open market and only on a temporary basis, with the goal of supporting the economic recovery through lower interest rates. At the appropriate time, the Federal Reserve will gradually sell these securities or let them mature, as needed, to return its balance sheet to a more normal size. Moreover, the way the Fed finances its securities purchases is by creating reserves in the banking system. Increased bank reserves held at the Fed don't necessarily translate into more money or cash in circulation, and, indeed, broad measures of the supply of money have not grown especially quickly, on balance, over the past few years.

   The full text of the speech can be found at http://www.federalreserve.gov/newsevents/speech/bernanke20121001a.htm.
2. Ben Bernanke gave a speech on October 15, 2010 in which he stated that "[t]he FOMC is prepared to provide additional accommodation if needed to support the economic recovery, and to return inflation, over time, to levels consistent with our mandate." *Monetary Policy Objectives and Tools in a Low-Inflation Environment* speech given at the Revisiting Monetary Policy in a Low-Inflation Environment Conference, Federal Reserve Bank of Boston, Boston, Massachusetts, http://www.federalreserve.gov/newsevents/speech/bernanke20101015a.htm.
3. The quotation that the "S&L Crisis of 1989 taught firms about the taxpayer put to protect from systemic risk but didn't teach the taxpayers anything" comes from a presentation by Edward Kane at the INET Conference in Cambridge 2010, http://www.youtube.com/watch?v=Mi38nQP7vfY.
4. Dear Mr. Dimon, Is Your Bank Getting Corporate Welfare? Bloomberg, June 18, 2012, http://www.bloomberg.com/news/2012-06-18/dear-mr-dimon-is-your-bank-getting-corporate-welfare-.html.
5. Financial Stability Board, *Policy Measures to Address Systemically Important Financial Institutions*, November 4, 2011. A list of those designated as SIFI's is as follows:

   Bank of America, Bank of China, Bank of New York Mellon, Banque Populaire CdE, Barclays, BNP Paribas, Citigroup, Commerzbank, Credit Suisse, Deutsche Bank, Dexia, Goldman Sachs, Group Crédit Agricole, HSBC, ING Bank, JP Morgan Chase, Lloyds Banking Group, Mitsubishi UFJ FG, Mizuho FG, Morgan Stanley, Nordea, Royal Bank of Scotland, Santander, Société Générale, State Street, Sumitomo Mitsui FG, UBS, Unicredit Group, Wells Fargo, http://www.financialstabilityboard.org/publications/r_111104bb.pdf.
6. See Financial Stability Board, *Policy Measures to Address Systemically Important Financial Institutions*, November 4, 2011.
7. The anti-rationalist stance in Hume's epistemology is best found in numerous sections of *A Treatise of Human Nature* (first published in 1739) where he examines causation and the manner whereby we

make generalizations about the natural world. Hume's treatment of the non-rational basis of inferences from induction has had a profound influence on philosophers and economists extending from his own day until the present.

Hume argued that we cannot rationally justify the claim that nature will continue to be regular or uniform. It is neither the result of demonstrative reasoning, i.e. it cannot be justified by logical deductions, nor can it be justified by a process of probabilistic reasoning. Hume argued that we cannot hold that nature will continue to exhibit regularity because it has been in the past, as it would be circular reasoning. In other words, he concluded, there is no rational basis for inductive inferences.

Hume's solution to this problem is to argue that, rather than reason, natural instinct explains the human ability to make inductive inferences.

8. John Maynard Keynes, *The General Theory of Employment, Interest and Money*, ch 12. The State of Long-Term Expectation. Available as an e-book at no charge.

Appendix

The following are the symbols and the names of the Exchange Traded Funds which are used in the correlation analysis and heat map outputs which are discussed in Chapter 9.

AGG	iShares Lehman Aggregate Bond ETF
BKF	iShares MSCI BRIC Index
DBA	PowerShares DB Agriculture
DBB	PowerShares DB Base Metals
DBC	PowerShares DB Commodity Idx Trking Fund
EEM	iShares MSCI Emerging Markets Index
EPP	iShares MSCI Pacific excl Japan
EWA	iShares MSCI Australia Index
EWG	iShares MSCI Germany Index
EWI	iShares MSCI Italy Index
EWJ	iShares MSCI-Japan
EWP	iShares MSCI Spain Index
EWU	iShares MSCI United Kingdom Index
EWZ	iShares MSCI Brazil Index
EZA	iShares MSCI South Africa Index
FEZ	DJ Euro STOXX 50 ETF
FXI	iShares FTSE-Xinhua China 25 Index
GLD	streetTRACKS Gold Trust
HYG	iShares High Yield Corporate Bond
IAI	iShares Dow Jones US Broker-Dealers
IEF	iShares Lehman 7-10 Year Treasury
IGE	iShares S and P GSSI Natural Resources Index Fund
IPE	SPDR Barclays Capital TIPS
IWM	iShares Tr Russell 2000 Indx
IYF	iShares Dow Jones US Financial Sector
IYH	iShares Dow Jones US Healthcare
IYR	iShares Dow Jones US Real Estate
IYT	iShares Dow Jones Transportation Average
JJC	iPath DJ-AIG Copper Total Return ETN

KBE	SPDR KBW Banks
LQD	iShares iBoxx Invest Grade Corp Bond
MBB	iShares Barclays MBS Bond
OIL	iPath S and P GSCI Crude Oil TR Index ETN
PCY	PowerShares Emerging Mkts Sovereign Debt
QQQ	NASDAQ 100 Trust Series I
RSX	Major Vectors Russia ETF
SHY	iShares Lehman 1-3 Year Treasury Bond
SLV	iShares Silver Trust
SPY	StandandPoors Dep Rcpt. Trust
TIP	iShares Lehman TIPS Bond
TLT	iShares Lehman 20+ Year Treas Bond
UUP	PowerShares DB US Dollar Index Bullish
XLE	SPDR Energy Sector
XLF	Financial Select Sector SPDR
XLI	Industrial Select Sector SPDR
XLU	Utilities Select Sector SPDR
XLV	Health Care Select Sector SPDR
XLY	Consumer Discretionary SPDR
XME	SPDR Metals and Mining ETF
XRT	SPDR Retail ETF

The following are some hints on the methods used to create the heat maps and also the stress regression analyses.

The average RSQ value is calculated as follows:

- Multiple correlation coefficients are calculated, using a 21-day window, on a trailing basis from the earliest available 21-day period all the way across the data until the most recent 21-day period.
- These R values are then squared and then averaged.

The whole period RSQ is simply the correlation coefficient for the entire set of data for the indicated period.

The beta values are determined in a similar fashion with regard to the separate time frames and the gradient of the linear equation from a regression is used as the beta value.

Shown below are three further outputs for the stress regression analysis. In the case of both sectors featured in Figure A.1 and Figure A.2 there are very striking increases in the degree of correlation for the outlier values only. The diversification values expected *under normal market conditions* will more or less be eradicated when markets are enduring critical episodes.

In the case of Figure A.3, which represents the outlier regression for SPY and GLD (see chart) there is absolutely no correlation for the outliers which is both a remarkable result and also a reflection that there is no tendency for gold to act in any fashion where the linear equation makes it possible to anticipate how the dependent variable, gold, will behave with respect to any movement of the independent variable, SPY.

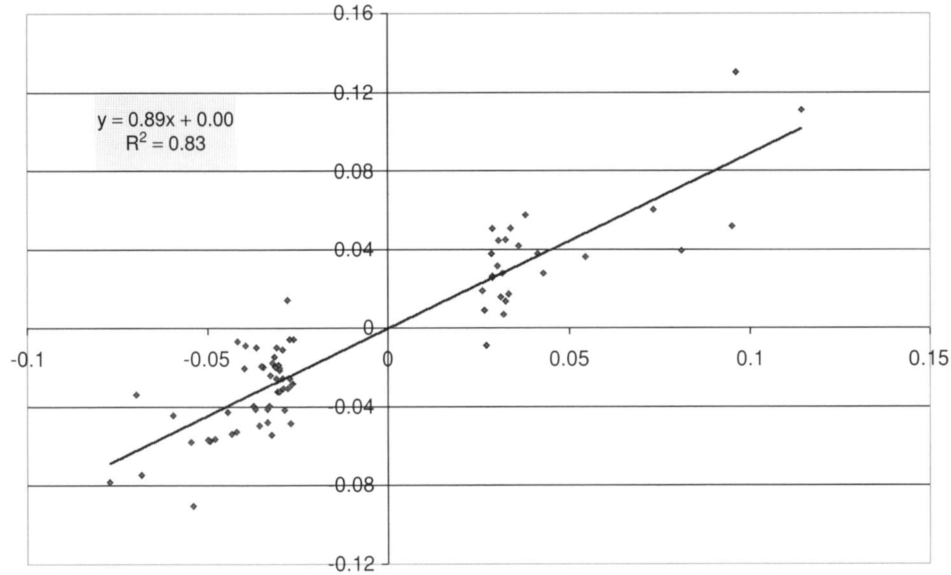

Figure A.1 Stress regression analysis for utilities and technology sectors (XLU and XLK) 2006–2012

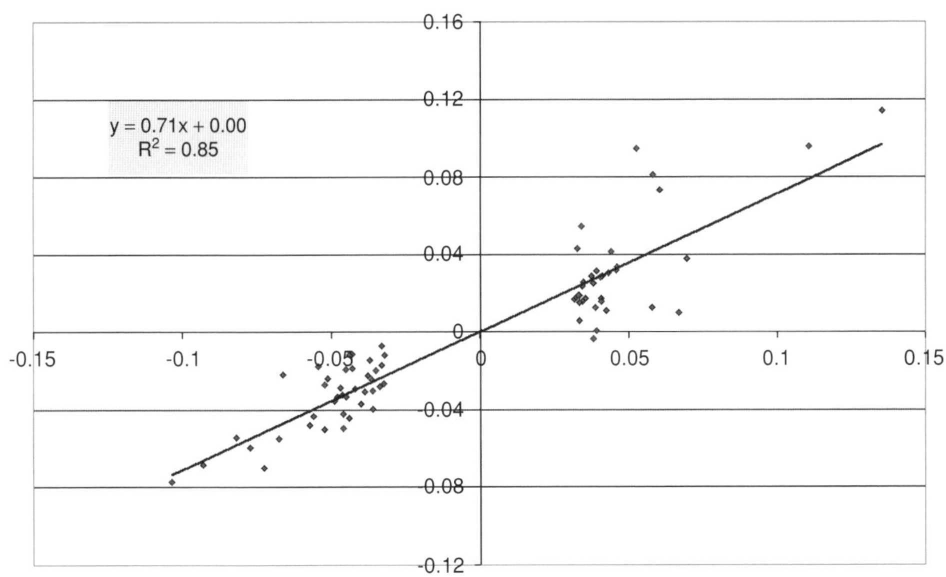

Figure A.2 Stress regression analysis for S&P 500 (SPY) and S&P Utilities Index (XLU) 2006–2012

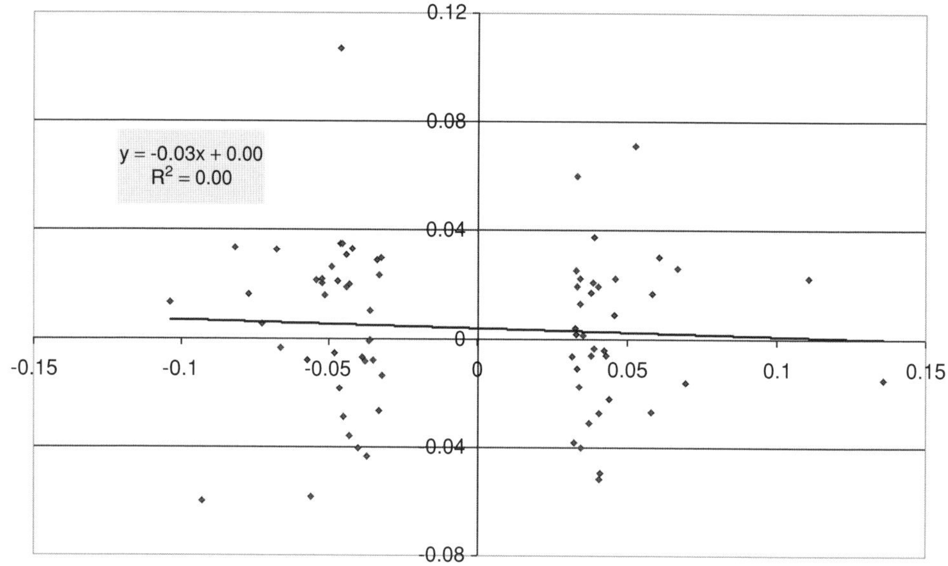

Figure A.3 Stress regression analysis for S&P 500 (SPY) and gold (GLD) 2006–2012

Independent Variable: XLU Dependent Variable: XLK
Period covered from 20060823 to 20120706

....

Independent Variable Performance 31.44%
Dependent Variable Performance 48.81%

....

Current Rolling Correlation 0.448966
Current Rolling RSQ 0.201570
RSQ from one week ago 0.352653

....

Current Rolling Beta 1.004446
Beta from one week ago 1.426383

****

OUTLIER CORRELATIONS, BETA AND RSQ VALUES

****

Outlier absolute change threshold: 2.59%
n Extreme Moves 75 percentage of data points 5.0%
Extreme Correlation Coefficient: 0.91
Correlation coefficient for whole period: 0.70

....

Extreme Beta: 0.89
Average Beta (based on rolling window period of size 21): 0.70
Beta for whole period: 0.83

....

Extreme RSQ: 0.83
Average RSQ (based on rolling window period of size 21): 0.38
RSQ for whole period: 0.49
Independent Variable: SPY Dependent Variable: XLU
Period covered from 20060823 to 20120706

....

Independent Variable Performance 17.79%
Dependent Variable Performance 31.44%

....

Current Rolling Correlation 0.580745
Current Rolling RSQ 0.337265
RSQ from one week ago 0.459577

....

Current Rolling Beta 0.292382
Beta from one week ago 0.305707

****

OUTLIER CORRELATIONS, BETA AND RSQ VALUES

****

Outlier absolute change threshold: 3.15%
n Extreme Moves 75 percentage of data points 5.0%
Extreme Correlation Coefficient: 0.92
Correlation coefficient for whole period: 0.78

....

Extreme Beta: 0.71
Average Beta (based on rolling window period of size 21): 0.61
Beta for whole period: 0.67

....

Extreme RSQ: 0.85
Average RSQ (based on rolling window period of size 21): 0.49
RSQ for whole period: 0.61
Independent Variable: SPY Dependent Variable: GLD
Period covered from 20060823 to 20120706

....

Independent Variable Performance 17.79%
Dependent Variable Performance 148.60%

....

Current Rolling Correlation 0.594848
Current Rolling RSQ 0.353845
RSQ from one week ago 0.002536

....

Current Rolling Beta 0.626042
Beta from one week ago 0.051636

****

OUTLIER CORRELATIONS, BETA AND RSQ VALUES

****

Outlier absolute change threshold: 3.15%
n Extreme Moves 75 percentage of data points 5.0%
Extreme Correlation Coefficient: –0.05
Correlation coefficient for whole period: 0.06

....

Extreme Beta: –0.03
Average Beta (based on rolling window period of size 21): 0.18
Beta for whole period: 0.05

....

Extreme RSQ: 0.00
Average RSQ (based on rolling window period of size 21): 0.16
RSQ for whole period: 0.00

Index

Compiled by INDEXING SPECIALISTS (UK) Ltd., Indexing House, 306A Portland Road, Hove, East Sussex, BN3 5LP, United Kingdom